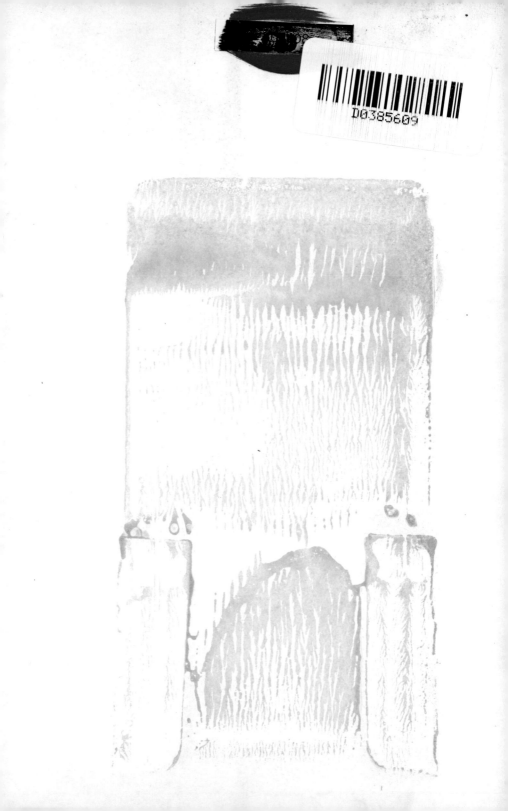

THE UNION OF BURMA

THE
UNION OF BURMA

A Study of
The First Years of Independence

BY

HUGH TINKER

Fourth Edition

Issued under the auspices of the
Royal Institute of International Affairs

OXFORD UNIVERSITY PRESS
LONDON NEW YORK TORONTO

1967

Oxford University Press, Ely House, London W.1

GLASGOW NEW YORK TORONTO MELBOURNE WELLINGTON
CAPE TOWN SALISBURY IBADAN NAIROBI LUSAKA ADDIS ABABA
BOMBAY CALCUTTA MADRAS KARACHI LAHORE DACCA
KUALA LUMPUR HONG KONG TOKYO

First edition 1957
Second edition 1959
Third edition 1961
Fourth edition 1967

Printed in Great Britain

CONTENTS

PREFACE

An endeavour is made in this study to present a survey of the wholeBurmese scene during the first eight or nine years after the attainment of independence in January 1948. Perhaps such a venture is over-ambitious; certainly it will not be possible to produce a definitive and objective review of this period for many years: the smoke of controversy and conflict lies thick upon the air. Yet in the absence of any detailed account of post-war Burma, the project seemed worth while. Burma has not, as yet, received the attention which certain other Asian countries (as, for instance, Japan or Indonesia) have been accorded by Western scholars. There are vast *lacunae*, such as an absence of even the most elementary information upon government and society. Burma has impinged on the Western mind in recent years only in a series of flashes: independence, the Communist rising, the Karen revolt, the Welfare State plan, the Chinese Nationalist invasion, the Sixth Buddhist Council. The present work attempts to illuminate the shadowy areas between these highlights, to present a coherent picture of Burma during the period of struggle and strain from 1948 to 1956. The picture is liable to be altered unexpectedly within the years that are to come: the reader is asked to remember, therefore, that this study was sketched out during 1955 and 1956, and represents a viewpoint arrived at in the months before Burma's second general election after independence.[1]

Although the author is a historian by trade, limitations of space have prevented any substantial historical introduction to contemporary activities. Fortunately, there is the masterly work of John L. Christian, published in the United States as *Modern Burma* (1942) and in India as *Burma and the Japanese Invader* (1945).

The present work, in some sort, sets out to provide a sequel to that of Christian. The criteria which the historian brings to his documents have been applied—or attempted—in this study. Sources have been verified, wherever possible, against an alternative authority; hypotheses have been adopted only when they appear to emerge from the evidence; when an alternative interpretation is possible, this has been indicated. The first class of material utilized was the printed reports and surveys issued by the Government of Burma. The second, newspapers, and I

---

[1] Following the government changes early in June 1956, certain minor textual alterations were necessitated: but no alteration to the general tenor of the work was attempted in the view that existing conclusions retained their validity.

must particularly mention my obligation to the editor of the *Nation*, who made available to me his excellent files of newspapers. The third source of information was opened up by meeting government officials. U Yaw, Director of Information, did his best to obtain interviews for me with the leading officials, and numbers of Secretaries to Government (certainly, the busiest men in Burma) gave me generously of their time. When travelling about up-country, many officials went out of their way to show me something of the situation in the districts. Finally, the greater part of my information was obtained through meeting the peoples of Burma. Almost without exception they were friendly and frank to an unknown foreigner: I trust that those Burmans who read this book will recognize a similar spirit of frankness and friendliness in my writing. While I have nowhere tried to gloss over the disagreeable aspects of Burma today, I hope that sufficient weight has been given to the many signs of promise. I have applied the same standard of judgement that I would employ in writing about my own country: this may be open to criticism as unrealistic, but I believe it to be less objectionable than consciously to adopt a double standard, one for the West and one for Asia. In ranging over a wide field the perpetration of a few errors is almost inevitable, and I was not always able to gain access to persons or institutions as I desired. I shall be grateful if any error of fact or of inference is brought to my notice.

This work was made possible, on the one hand by a commission from Chatham House, on the other by an invitation from the University of Rangoon to spend a year at the university as visiting Professor of History. At Chatham House, my particular thanks are due to Miss Margaret Cleeve, o.b.e., who gave me the kindly and practical assistance that she has extended to so many others. At Rangoon University, I must thank the Rector, Dr. Htin Aung, who provided accommodation for my family and helped me with many problems. My colleagues in the History Department did much to make me feel that I was among friends, and I experienced a most delightful response from my students. If any of them should open this book, I hope that they will recall some of our exchanges in the lecture room, when I tried to emphasize that the study of history is a process of considering evidence, drawing conclusions, arriving at a point of view: not of acquiescing in someone else's *ipse dixit*. The matters reviewed in my book will probably often lead them to arrive at conclusions different from my own. That will not matter at all, provided that they are led to think out the problems and answers afresh. Strenuous, unemotional thinking is earnestly needed in Burma in the years immediately ahead.

Other obligations must be briefly and inadequately acknowledged. In Burma, many put themselves out to offer kindness to myself and my family. Perhaps our warmest thanks are due to Dr. and Mrs. Philips Greene, Paul and Elaine Lewis of Pangwai, David and Margaret Morgan, Peter and Christine Neale, and the hospitable Toke Gales of Mandalay. Drafts of my manuscript have been read by Dr. Hla Pe, Mr. G. L. Merrells, and Professor B. R. Pearn, and I have profited greatly by their observations. Mr. H. F. Searle attempted to instil in me the rudiments of Burmese, and has allowed me to draw repeatedly upon his knowledge. Mr. F. S. V. Donnison (to whom I was a stranger) generously made available to me the results of his research upon British Military Government in the Far East. Mr. A. K. Robertson supplied me with factual information from Burma after my return to Britain. For all this assistance I am sincerely grateful, but nevertheless, for good or ill, this book remains 'all my own work'.

Or almost so: to one person I gladly ascribe a fuller share of responsibility. My wife accompanied me on almost all my travels, and through her training in Burmese classical dancing penetrated more deeply into the life of Burma than I did. My book owes much to her help.

In writing this study my guiding motive has been to assist in keeping open the bridge between Burma and Britain. Burma stands today at a challenging moment in her long history, when the attempt is being made to create a parliamentary democracy in the face of heavy pressures, known and unknown, internal and external. Although the principal inspiration for the leaders and thinkers of this new State will be their own national heritage, Burmese and Buddhist, the legacy of the British connexion in matters of government and political thought has a contribution to make in promoting stability and progress. Some Burman readers may allow, therefore, that a study of their country from a British or Commonwealth standpoint is not without value; but it is more to my purpose that British and other Western readers shall know something of this newly independent Asian country, and learn to realize that today, in Asia, new ideas and new movements are stirring; that today there is a new Asian leadership which is asserting its right to develop its own international viewpoint, without prior reference to either of the two great world power blocs.

February 1956

H. T.

NOTE TO SECOND EDITION

The text has been corrected and amended in accordance with information kindly supplied by Burmese and British correspondents. A few sections have been rewritten to take account of political developments during 1958.

November 1958   H. T.

NOTE TO THIRD EDITION

Since this work was last revised there have been further significant developments in Burma. These events are described in outline, but this book remains, substantially, 'a study of the first years of independence'. The reader who expects to obtain an account of Burma today from this Third Edition should be made aware that although there are references to the AFPFL in the present tense throughout the book, the League, as described herein, has now passed into history. In other major respects, the original analysis remains valid.

July 1960   H. T.

NOTE TO FOURTH EDITION

When General Ne Win seized power on 2 March 1962, setting up a Revolutionary Council and abolishing the 1947 constitution, the Burma of 'the first years of independence' described in these pages came to an end. In making a further revision of the text for a new reprint an attempt has been made to conclude the story of what we may now describe as the era of U Nu. This good man, despite his apparent failure at the end, strove more than almost any other statesman in South-East Asia to create a genuinely democratic community in his country. The military government which deposed him announced that it would restore peace and order to the countryside and introduce 'The Burmese Way to Socialism'. In 1966, both these objectives are very far from being realized. The present study does not purport to analyse the dilemmas of the last four years in any detail, but merely indicates in brief outline how General Ne Win has approached his objective.

October 1966   H.T.

ABBREVIATIONS

ABPO	All-Burma Peasants' Organization
AFO	Anti-Fascist Organization (later AFPFL)
AFPFL	Anti-Fascist People's Freedom League
BIA	Burma Independence Army
BNA	Burma National Army
BWB	*Burma Weekly Bulletin*
BWPP	Burma Workers' and Peasants' Party
CAS(B)	Civil Affairs Service (Burma)
FTO	Federated Trades Organization
GCBA	General Council of Burmese Associations
KMT	Chinese Nationalists (Kuomintang)
KNDO	Karen National Defence Organization
KTA	Knappen-Tippetts-Abbett Engineering Company
NUF	National United Front
PBF	Patriotic Burmese Forces
PVO	People's Volunteer Organization: later, People's Comrade Party: PCP
SAMB	State Agricultural Marketing Board
TUC(B)	Trades Union Congress (Burma)
UKL	Union Karen League
UKO	Union Karen Organization

GLOSSARY

(Unless otherwise indicated, all words are Burmese)

Abhidhamma, (Pali) metaphysics of Buddhism, one of the 'three baskets', see *Pitaka*.
Ahphwe, association.
Anyein pwè, variety show.
Aung, auspicious, victorious.
Ayaung-zon, 'multi-coloured', applied to the rebels with their different shades of ideology.
Bamā, Burman or Burmese. In this study, an attempt has been made to employ 'Burman' for all the indigenous peoples of Burma, and 'Burmese' for the majority community whose mother-tongue is Burmese. This follows the practice adopted in the Census of Burma, 1953, *et seq.*, but this practice cannot be regarded as definitive, and it is not claimed that complete consistency has been attained in this study. There is not, in fact, any agreed form for 'Burman' except the cumbersome form used in the constitution, 'Citizen of the Union of Burma'.

Basha, (Indian, Bengali? derivation) temporary hutment.
Bhikku, (Pali) Buddhist monk.
Bo, Captain in army, title often claimed by brigands.
Bogyoke, General, reserved in contemporary Burma for Aung San and Ne Win.
Chaung, river or stream.
Crore, (Indian) Rs.1,00,00,000; value, £750,000 or $2,100,000.
Dacoit, (Indian) armed robber, brigand.
Dah, long Burmese knife.
Damma, or *Dhamma*, (Pali) Buddhist law, teaching, hence *Dammayon*, prayer-hall.
Daw, courtesy title given to Burmese ladies (lit. 'auntie').
Daw, royal, state, sovereign.
Dobama, We Burmans, hence *Dobama Asi-ayon*, League of Burmans.
Duwa, (Kachin) chief.
Eingyi, jacket or blouse.
Galon, mythical bird, the 'Garuda'.
Gaung, lit. 'head', hence *zay-gaung*, bazaar headman, *ywa-gaung*, village headman, &c.
Hla, beautiful.
Kaing, tall river-grass, applied to riverine land.
Kaisha, (Japanese) company.
Kaungsi, council (one of the many words adapted from English into Burmese).
Kayaing, territorial area, district, formerly division.
Keibotai, (Japanese) civil defence organization.
Kempeitai (Japanese) secret police, Gestapo.
Kin, home-guard.
Ko, lit. 'elder brother', respectful term of address as between equals.
Konbaung, Burmese dynasty from Alaungpaya to Thibaw.
Kwet-thit, hutments, shanty town.
Kwin, circle, revenue unit, see p. 148 n. 2.
Kyaung, Buddhist monastery (properly, *phongyi-kyaung*), hence monastic school.
Kyat, Burmese coin, replaced rupee, 1952; value, 1s. 6d. or 21 U.S. cents.
Lakh, (Indian) Rs.1,00,000; value £7,500 or $21,000.
Lè, paddy field(s).
Longyi, skirt of cotton or silk worn by both sexes.
Lu, man, hence *ludu*, the people, (pol.) 'the masses'.
Ma, style applied to young woman (lit. 'sister').
Maha, (Pali) great, hence *Maha Avici*, great purgatory or hell.
Mahathera, great elder-monk, a senior rank in the monastic hierarchy.
Manao, (Kachin) annual feast of dancing, singing, drinking, eating, of ritual significance.
Maung, term applied to young man or inferior, lit. 'brother'.
Min, prince, hence *Thibaw Min*, Prince of Hsipaw, also used for officials.

Mujahid, (Arabic) one who fights in a holy war for Islam.

Myo, land or domain, hence, *myo-wun* (governor), *myo-ok* (township officer), *myo-thugyi* (circle headman).

Myochit, 'Lovers of the Land', party of U Saw.

Naingandaw Adipati, (Pali) Head of State, title assumed by Dr. Ba Maw, 1943–5.

Naingandaw Thamada, (Pali) President of the Union.

Nat, spirit or demon in Burmese mythology.

Ni, lit. 'red', Communist.

Paddy, (*padi*, Malay derivation) rice in the husk.

Pali, classical language of India, one of the Prakrits, the language of Theravada Buddhism.

Paya, respectful term, used to designate a ruler, a holy sage or a *stupa*, pagoda.

Phongyi or *pongyi*, lit. 'great glory', term commonly used for *bhikku* or Buddhist monk.

Pitaka, or *Tri-pitaka*, (Pali) lit. 'three baskets' of the Buddhist scriptures, the *Vinaya, Sutta, Abhidhamma*.

Pwè, festival, show, rejoicing.

Pya, small Burmese coin, 100 to the kyat (about 5 pyas would make 1*d*.).

Pyat-that, ceremonial multiple roofs, sign of status under the Burmese kings.

Pyidawtha, lit. 'royal (or sacred) pleasant-country', the new plan for Burma, comparable to 'the Welfare State'.

Rupee, Indian coin, in use in Burma up to 1952; value 1*s*. 6*d*.

Sangha, (Pali) the Buddhist order of monks, assembly of monks.

Sao, (Shan) title of respect assumed by members of the ruling clans in the Shan States.

Sasana, (Pali) religion, teaching, doctrine.

Sawbwa, Shan ruler.

Saya, teacher, term of respect for learned man, hence, *se-saya*, doctor, hence also *sayadaw*, senior monk or abbot.

Shwe, gold, golden.

Sinyetha, poor man; Dr. Ba Maw called his party *Sinyetha Wunthanu* (Association of Poor Men—Patriots: Proletarians?).

Sitwundan, lit. military-burden-carrier, territorial soldier.

Sutta, (Pali) the Sermon, Buddha's rules for the laity.

Tat, army or force.

Taung, hill, mountain.

Thakin, 'master', designation assumed by members of *Dobama Asiayon*.

Thamadi, village assessor of revenue demands (lit. 'reliable man').

Thathanabaing, (from Sasana) titular or nominal head of the Buddhist religion in the Theravada countries.

Theravada, (properly, Sthaviravadin), school of Buddhism followed in Burma, Siam, Cambodia, Laos, Ceylon.

Thugyi, lit. 'great man', headman of village or circle.

U, lit. 'uncle', respectful term of address to a gentleman.

Vinaya, (Pali) conduct, rules for the monastic order.

Viss, (Indian derivation), weight used in Southern India and Burma; in Burma a viss = 3 lb. 5½ oz.

Wundanhmu, lit. head-burden-carrier, government official, organizer.

Ye, water.

Yèbaw, 'comrade of boldness', honorific appropriated by former members of the BIA and others.

Yoma, range of hills.

Yon, shed or hall.

Ywa, village.

Zay or *Ze,* Bazaar (e.g. Theingyizay, the great bazaar of Rangoon).

Zedi, stupa or pagoda.

I

BRITISH RULE AND INDEPENDENCE

ON 1 January 1886 the independent kingdom of Ava was annexed to British Burma: its despotic monarch Thibaw had been deposed and exiled, and the absorption of Burma into the British-Indian Empire was completed. On 4 January 1948 Burma once again became an independent sovereign state: a parliamentary, democratic republic. The old Burma has bequeathed much to the new, but not in the sphere of government; the origins of the representative institutions of today must be sought in the British period.

Representative government had its beginnings in the municipal committees first set up in 1874; and yet until 1922 the régime was almost entirely official and autocratic.

In 1897 the executive head of the province (hitherto known as Chief Commissioner) became a Lieutenant-Governor, being provided with a Legislative Council which consisted entirely of officials and nominated non-officials. After the Morley-Minto Reforms of 1909, the legislative councils of the Indian provinces were expanded to include a sizeable elected element; but in Burma, although the Legislative Council was enlarged from nine to seventeen members, only one of these was elected— and he was chosen by the Burma Chamber of Commerce, an entirely European organization. In 1915 the legislature was further enlarged to a membership of thirty, but of this number only two were elected, the second elected member being chosen by the Rangoon Trades Association. The Council remained almost exclusively a vehicle for British official and mercantile opinion, while throughout the country districts the administration was directed by British officials who ruled their charges with a paternal authority.

The first embryonic expression of Burmese national feeling in a Western mould was the Young Men's Buddhist Association, founded in 1908 by a group of youthful Burmans, mainly students at Rangoon College. Amongst these young men were U May Oung, Sir Maung Gyee, U Ba Pe, U Ba Dun, and Dr. Ba Yin, all later prominent upon the political stage. The Association in its early days was concerned almost entirely with religion and social service, but during the First World War some of its leaders began to utilize its Burma-wide organization to stimulate an awakening of political awareness. During these war years the demand for political advancement in India was becoming ever more insistent and, in August 1917, evoked the famous declaration by the British Government promising 'responsible self-government' through 'the gradual development of self-governing institutions'. The Montagu–Chelmsford Committee appointed to devise means to implement this declaration did not visit Burma; their report stated that 'the desire for elective institutions has not developed in Burma'.[1] The province was excluded from their proposals. This casual relegation of Burma's case for future consideration, while India was awarded a substantial instalment of self-government, did more than anything else to arouse national pride and to direct this pride towards a demand for political freedom.

The Government of Burma thereupon formulated a scheme whereby Burmese opinion would receive some representation through a series of 'Boards' or committees of which non-official Burmans would be members, but which would be responsible to the Governor and not to the Legislative Council.[2] This proposal, it may be noted, was made against the advice of a majority of the British officials of the Burma Commission, who recommended that Burma should be brought into line with India. It proved quite unacceptable to Burmese public opinion which suddenly and unexpectedly crystallized in the 'December Boycott' of 1920. The new Rangoon University was in process of being planned; an educational expert from Madras drafted a constitution which would place the government of the new university largely under official control. The draft was rejected by Burmans associated with the new venture, and when the Government persisted in carrying it forward the national leaders called upon their countrymen to withdraw their sons and daughters from government schools and colleges throughout the land. This boycott was followed by the setting up of numbers of independent 'National Schools'. The boycott was by no means complete, but to the British rulers it was astonishing that Burmans could sustain a political organization with such a degree of success.[3] As a consequence of this and other political demonstrations (including the fight for a popular municipal council for Rangoon) it became apparent that Burma would have to be included in the new political

---

[1] *Joint Report on Indian Constitutional Reforms*, 1918, p. 162.
[2] A fuller account of this scheme is given in the *Report of the Indian Statutory Commission*, 1930, xi, 7.
[3] It may be worth recalling that Edwin Montagu, something of a Radical, had recorded in his diary his impression of the Burmese leaders who came to see him as 'nice simple-minded people with beautiful clothes. Complete loyalty; no sign of political unrest' (*An Indian Diary*, 1932, p. 86).

experiment of dyarchy; this had come into operation in the other provinces of India in 1920 or 1921; in Burma it was delayed until January 1923. The new constitution provided for a legislature of 103 members, 79 being elected and the remainder nominated; among the latter only 14 were to be officials. The executive government passed from the old Lieutenant-Governor to a Governor-in-Council; this Executive Council comprised (beside the Governor) two Members, one a British official and one a non-official Burman; two Burmese Ministers were responsible to the legislature for the 'transferred' side of government.[1] Of the 79 elected members 58 were returned by general (i.e. Burmese) constituencies; the remainder represented 'communal' seats (constituencies set aside for the Indians, Karens, Anglo-Indians, and Europeans) and certain special interests. Unless almost all the 58 Burmese seats were filled by one political party, it was therefore virtually impossible for a Burmese Minister to command a majority in the legislature without substantial backing from among the communal and nominated members. No doubt this arrangement was devised to secure adequate representation for the minorities and other special bodies of people, but its actual effect was to encourage these different groups within the legislature to exploit their votes for sectional ends. The constitution did little to promote the growth of a stable party system, nor did this come about.

The Young Men's Buddhist Association had been succeeded in the political field by the General Council of Burmese Associations or *Wunthanu*, whose principal leader was U Chit Hlaing. By the time of the first general election in 1922 the General Council had split into three main factions under rival leaders, while another section under the leadership of Ba Pe (the 'Twenty-one Party') had sheered off to contest the elections which the GCBA decided to boycott. The Twenty-one Party secured 28 of the 79 elected seats, while 13 of the remaining elected members combined with the 8 nominated non-officials under the leadership of (Sir) Maung Gyee, calling themselves the Progressives or 'Golden Valley Party'. These two groups were the only semi-organized elements in the legislature, the former in opposition, the latter giving general support to the Government. Some among the independent members accepted to some extent the leadership of Sir Joseph A. Maung Gyi, Minister, and Acting Governor of the province from 1930 to

---

[1] The transferred side, the 'nation-building' subjects, included education, local government, public works, the medical services, public health, veterinary services, the co-operative movement and the forests. For the distribution of these subjects in detail between the Ministers, see *Report of the Indian Statutory Commission*, xi, 38–52.

1931. It was during this time that there occurred the biggest demonstration of national feeling in these inter-war years: and it was by no means a political demonstration. The Saya San revolt of 1931 was a medieval outburst against the modern world, with Saya San the leader crowned as king with his five queens, his followers tattooed and provided with amulets to make them invincible and invulnerable as they swept forward to be mown down by machine-gun bullets. None of the political leaders were associated with the revolt, but afterwards some of the more extreme nationalists defended the *Galon* rebels (as they were popularly called) in court. Among those who made names for themselves in this way were U Saw and Dr. Ba Maw.

In 1930 was published the *Report of the Indian Statutory Commission* (usually known by the name of its chairman, Lord Simon). Amongst the many changes recommended was the separation of Burma from India.[1] This proposal aroused the suspicions of many politicians in Burma: was this another device to fob Burma off with a settlement inferior to that which would be accorded to India? This issue brought about a new alignment of parties, with all elements of the GCBA opposing separation: amongst the most compelling opponents was Dr. Ba Maw. A general election was held in 1932 to determine feeling in the country. The Anti-Separationists secured a majority, but the new Assembly spoke in muffled accents: Ba Maw joined the Separationists in a coalition in 1934, making another break in 1936 to form his own *Sinyetha Wunthanu* Party. The British Government decided to implement the policy of separation as recommended in the Simon Report. A new constitution, embodied in the Government of Burma Act, 1935, came into force on 1 April 1937: its main provisions were the termination of the century-old subordination to the Government of India[2] and the full introduction of responsible Cabinet government. The new constitution set up two chambers of Parliament, a Senate and a House of Representatives. Officials were entirely excluded from the new legislature. Half of the members of the Senate were to be nominated by the Governor, but the lower house was entirely elected under an

[1] *Report of the Indian Statutory Commission*, ii, 187–91.
[2] Although the control of the Government of India was entirely at an end, certain links remained. The Secretary of State for India was also Secretary of State for Burma, and the Burma Office remained housed in the India Office in Whitehall. Burma's currency was controlled by the Reserve Bank of India. The Indian tariffs remained in force, and might not be revised for three years. Burma acquired a national debt with India for past services and loans (mainly on account of the railways). Burma's defence arrangements remained closely linked with Army Headquarters, India.

extended franchise. Among the 132 members, 22 were elected by special 'communal' constituencies to represent the minority peoples (Karens, Indians, Anglo-Burmans); there were also 9 European members, largely representatives of commerce, whose influence was directed towards sectional ends, but the general territorial constituencies predominated. The government of 'Burma Proper' (a definition which excluded the hill areas) devolved upon a Cabinet led by a Premier and responsible to Parliament. This popular government now exercised control over the entire horizon of the national life, excepting only defence, foreign affairs, and monetary policy.[1] These subjects remained the direct responsibility of the Governor, who was appointed by the British Government. In addition, the 'excluded areas' (the Shan States, Karenni, the Salween District, and the remaining hill areas) were set aside from ministerial Burma and remained under separate forms of administration.

The first (and only) elections under the 1935 Act took place in December 1936. The outcome was a House of Representatives containing several political parties, as well as several groups based upon communal interests. The largest party was the United GCBA with forty-six members led by U Ba Pe, but he was unable to find sufficient adherents to command a majority. The first Prime Minister was Dr. Ba Maw, whose *Sinyetha Wunthanu* Party numbered only sixteen. But Dr. Ba Maw stood out as a commanding personality, a gifted orator, and a first-class political manager; he assembled together a motley band of allies and held office for two years. His *Sinyetha* (poor man's) policy achieved something in the sphere of land reform, but he lost much public following after the anti-Indian riots and student agitation of 1938. In February 1939 he was defeated, and a new ministry was formed out of Ba Pe's group and the new *Myochit* (Lovers of the Nation) Party led by the ambitious and thrusting U Saw. In September 1940, after a series of manœuvres U Saw captured the premiership, which he held until January 1942: after a visit to Britain and the United States to seek assurances of independence, he was detained in Uganda on grounds of contacts with the Japanese.[2] Sir Paw Tun then became the fourth Prime Minister within five years, remaining in office until the Japanese invasion.

[1] In India transfer of power at the centre under the 1935 Act never became effective as the Princes did not enter the proposed federal structure. Thus Burma was actually in advance of India in the range of subjects (such as the railways) which were handed over to ministerial control.

[2] U Saw is said to have purchased his paper, the *Sun*, with Japanese money. But equally, he is accused of taking money from British business firms.

Meanwhile the national leaders of the future were creating some clamour on the fringe of Burmese politics; their first platform was the Rangoon University Students' Union. In the autumn of 1935, when the annual election of a managing committee for the Students' Union was held, all the vacancies were captured by a group whose energies were focused upon a militant liberation of their country from foreign rule. The new President was Ko Nu:[1] born in 1907, the son of a merchant of Myaungmya in the Delta, as a lad he went to the Myoma National High School in Rangoon (the most famous of the national independent schools which were established after the 1920 boycott). He went on to Rangoon University, taking the B.A. degree in 1929; thereafter he worked as Superintendent of the National High School, Pantanaw, but he returned to the university later to study law. Thus he was considerably older than most of his *confrères*, of whom the most purposeful and stubborn was the new Students' Union Secretary, Aung San. Born in 1916 at Natmauk in Magwe District, near the sacred Mount Popa, his grandfather (some say great-uncle), a *myothugyi* (chief) under the old régime, was killed when leading a force against the British. Aung San, a moody, morose boy, grew up in the tradition of resistance; he came to the university in 1932. Other members of the committee or associates of the group included Kyaw Nyein, Kyaw Myint, Ba Swe, M. A. Raschid, Tun Win, and Thein Pe (later called *Tet pongyi*, from his book criticizing the monastic order). All these young men were, in the future, to become Cabinet Ministers.

The new committee at once commenced a campaign against the university authorities, who were not slow in answering the challenge. U Nu was suspended for a speech criticizing university government, and soon after Aung San was sent down for a libellous attack on a Burmese member of the university staff ('Hell-Hound at Large') published in *Oway*, the student journal of which Aung San was editor and Ba Swe was manager. The Union committee replied by convening a meeting of the whole undergraduate body in the Students' Union building and demanding that all should come out on strike. On 25 February 1936 over 700 obeyed the call, and the impending examinations had to be postponed. Finally, after several months and under pressure from Dr. Ba Maw and other Ministers, the university authorities readmitted the two leaders. From this time forth, the strike was the master-weapon of politicians in Burma.

---

[1] *Ko* means elder brother. He was later known as Thakin Nu, and since 1952 as U Nu.

When Aung San and Nu finally quitted the university, they became workers for the *Dobama Asi-ayon* (We Burmans Association), also known as the Thakins.[1] *Dobama Asi-ayon* had been founded by Thakin Ba Sein and Thakin Kodaw Hmaing about the year 1930 or 1931. It was a small group in terms of numbers (*Komin Kochin Ahphwe*, its parliamentary wing, had only three seats in the legislature), but it made a stir by the violence of its anti-British feeling and its revolutionary outlook. It contained a strong Communist element, whose leader was Thakin Than Tun. Born in 1913, in Toungoo District, he went to a village school and to the Teacher's Training College. He worked as a vernacular teacher, but he brought himself to the front by ability and drive. Thakin Nu now became Treasurer to this party ('a treasurer without treasure' he called himself) and spent much of his time in literary work; he founded the *Naga Ni* (Red Dragon) Book Club to foster leftist literature. Aung San became Secretary of *Dobama Asi-ayon*: at this time he was strongly drawn to Nazi concepts of power through force and uniformity; in 1939 the Thakins formed a private army, the *Bama Let Yon Tat*, usually known in English as the Steel Corps (other private armies were formed by U Saw, Ba Maw, and the Students' Union). During the 1930's the Japanese General Staff, as part of its preparations for conquest, introduced agents into Burma to gather information and to recruit allies: the Thakins as the most militant anti-British group were particularly singled out. Among the Japanese agents was a Colonel Minami (sometimes calling himself Colonel Suzuki), a staff officer whose previous career had been brilliant: in Burma he was 'disguised' as a correspondent of the Japanese daily paper *Yomiuri*. He appears to have established intimate relations with the younger Thakins, and early in 1939 he reached agreement with a section headed by Aung San for the dispatch to Japan of selected young Burmans for military training.

Meanwhile, after Dr. Ba Maw's downfall, his party linked up with the Thakins to form a new front called the 'Freedom Bloc'. It adopted a policy of combative opposition to Burma's participation in the war against Germany, which was carried into the bazaars and amongst the industrial workers. At the same time, in 1939, a group of young university Thakins headed by Ba Swe and Kyaw Nyein founded a secret organization called the Burma Revolutionary Party, which was to be the nucleus of the future Socialist Party.

---

[1] *Thakin* had become the respectful term of address to Europeans as *Sahib* was in India: *Dobama Asi-ayon* gave themselves this title to indicate that they were now the masters.

As the prestige of Aung San increased, he openly challenged Ba Sein for leadership of the Thakins, and in 1940 he attended the Ramgarh session of the Indian National Congress, being presented to Gandhi and to Nehru. At about the same time the Democratic Bloc launched a violent campaign against the Allied war effort, calling upon the oilfield workers to come out on strike. The Government responded by arresting Ba Maw, Ba Sein, Thakin Nu, and many others and detained them for sedition. A warrant went out for Aung San, but he contrived to evade arrest, and on 8 August he boarded a ship bound for China. From Canton he was taken to Tokyo where he spent some months at the War Office. In March 1941 he arrived back in Rangoon River in a Japanese ship. Secretly, he made contact with the Revolutionary Party, and a committee of five, including Kyaw Nyein and Ba Swe, recruited thirty volunteers for Japanese military training. They were mostly ex-students from among the Thakins and members of the Steel Corps: they were smuggled on board ship, and then to Japan. For about six months they underwent training, and were then sent to Siam to raise forces from amongst expatriate Burmans. By December 1941 this Burma Independence Army (BIA) numbered about 1,000 men. The original members met together in a house in Bangkok, pooled their blood in a silver bowl and, drinking therefrom, pledged themselves to win independence for Burma. Thus was born the comradeship of 'the Thirty', who have since become like heroes of legend in the mythology of modern Burma.[1] The Thirty assumed high-sounding titles: Aung San became Bo Teza (Fire General), Tun Shein became Bo Yan Naing (General Victory), Thakin Shu Maung became Bo Ne Win (Sun of Glory General), Hla Pe became Bo Let Ya (Right-Hand General), Aung Than became Bo Setkya (General of the Flying Weapon).[2] When the Japanese invasion was launched, the BIA entered Tenasserim in four columns. Recruits were enlisted as the advance drove on, and within a few months rose to a total of 30,000. Of these about 4,000 actually fought against the British forces, mainly in the Paungde–Shwedaung region where Bo Yan Naing is said to have particularly distinguished himself.

[1] Dr. Carleton C. Ames is at work on a detailed study of the Thirty Comrades. I am indebted to him for some of my information.

[2] The subsequent history of the Thirty forms a microcosm of modern Burma. Eight are now dead, mostly from violent causes; two have attained high command in the army; others have been Speaker of the Chamber of Deputies, Cabinet Ministers, and an ambassador. Two have left politics for big business; one is Ba Maw's lieutenant in legal opposition; three (perhaps more) are with the rebels. The remaining ten or so are mainly small-time political bosses or have faded into obscurity.

The two divisions of the [British] Burma Army, 1 Burma Division and 17 Indian Division, were steadily pushed ever northwards. That the long retreat did not become a rout was due in great part to the cool generalship of Lord Alexander and the sustained punching vigour of the 7th Armoured Brigade. By the end of May the Burma Army had staggered out into the Manipur hills; and there remained under British authority only the remote, seldom visited tribal areas around Fort White in the Chin hills and Fort Hertz in the extreme north. Amid the chaos of retreat, the erstwhile Olympian governors of the country were seen as human beings: some behaved nobly in the great Indian Civil Service tradition, some stumbled their way through unprecedented crises, a few did badly. The age of the enlightened despots was now over: British rule in India and Burma had relied not upon force but upon public confidence. In Burma the bluff was called, and that confidence was irrevocably broken.

As the smoke of battle rolled northward the BIA fell behind. Their activities were largely confined to Lower Burma, where internal security and the administration of the districts largely passed into their hands or into those of their political counterparts the Thakins. In Rangoon Thakin Tun Ok, who had gone to Japan in 1940 for special training, was installed as chief administrator at the head of the 'Burma *Baho* Government'.[1]

Among members of the BIA there were idlers, bullies, and actual bandits. Their overbearing conduct was felt everywhere, but most of all in the Karen areas. This is not the place to examine the long history of Burmese-Karen animosities; it will suffice to say that in 1942 the BIA regarded all Karens as British collaborators, as the enemy. In the mountains of Salween District the Karens, led by Hugh Seagrim of the Burma Rifles, kept resistance alive after the British retreat. The BIA arrived at Papun, district headquarters, and began to 'pacify' the surrounding country. One party was ambushed, whereupon, on 4 April, Bo Tun Hla, the BIA leader, shot seventeen law-abiding Karen elders out of hand.[2] In the Delta there was an even more horrible massacre. On arrival in Myaungmya the BIA placed all the Karens under open arrest, but did not actively molest them. A nearby Karen ex-army officer, San

---

[1] *Baho* means central: it is not clear from contemporary pronouncements whether the title of this Government had some political connotation. For details of administration, social life, politics, &c., 1942–5, see *Burma During the Japanese Occupation*, i, 1943, ii, 1944.

[2] See Burma, Frontier Areas Committee of Enquiry, *Report submitted to H.M.G. and to the Government of Burma* (Rangoon, 1947), Part II, p. 121, and Ian Morrison, *Grandfather Longlegs* (London, 1947), pp. 69–73.

Po Thin, impetuously decided to 'liberate' his fellows. Late in May he gathered a band together for an attack, and rashly sent a letter to the Myaungmya Karens telling them of his plan: this letter was intercepted by the BIA,[1] and in retaliation they slaughtered over 150 Karens, including a Cabinet Minister, Saw Pe Tha, as well as his English wife and children.

It may be noted that, in both the cases cited, it is possible for either side to accuse the other of starting the quarrel, and this recurs as a constant feature of the Burmese-Karen imbroglio. But few will deny that in 1942 the BIA were primarily responsible for opening again the ancient sore from which has flowed so much bitter blood between Karen and Burman: U Nu has frequently emphasized the BIA responsibility for this feud.[2]

On 5 June 1942, in an order signed by Aung San, the BIA was forbidden to interfere in politics or administration. But many units were uncontrollable, verging upon mutiny, and on 24 July the Japanese peremptorily disbanded the whole army. Aung San is reported to have collapsed, appalled at the destruction of the army he had created. He was removed to hospital, where he was nursed by his future wife.

Reform of the administration followed. Since the Thakins were almost entirely new to public affairs, the Japanese looked about for a more experienced political leader. On 1 August 1942 a Burma Executive Administration was set up, with Ba Maw at its head. His lieutenants were drawn from his own *Sinyetha* Party and from the Thakin leaders. Both parties were now merged in a *Maha Bama Asi-ayon*, Greater Burma front, and adopted the slogan *ta-thway, ta-than, ta-meint*—'one blood, one voice, one command'. An 'Independence Preparatory Committee' was formed to consider a draft constitution, and on 1 August 1943 Burma was declared an independent State, receiving recognition from all the Axis Powers. The Shan States and Karenni were incorporated within Burma, except for Kengtung and Mongpan which were ceded to Thailand. The head of the new State was, of course, Dr. Ba Maw, who assumed the title of *Naing gan daw Adipati* or generalissimo. Amongst his Cabinet of sixteen Ministers were Thakin Mya as Deputy Prime Minister, Thakin Aung San as Minister of Defence, Thakin Nu as Foreign Minister, U Ba Win as Minister for Home Affairs, Thein Maung as Finance Minister, and

---

[1] Morrison gives a full account of this episode (pp. 183–92) but he was misinformed as to the incident which precipitated the slaughter.

[2] Thus: 'During the war, some bad Burmans, with the Japanese behind them, took advantage of their position to harm the Karens. That was how the Karen-Burman conflict originated' (*Nation*, 6 January 1954).

Thakin Than Tun as Minister for Agriculture. The administration of the country was continued much as before the invasion, and a majority of the old Burmese officials were kept in their posts. The administration was flanked by a Burma Defence Army, whose formation commenced on 26 August 1942. Some recruits came from the defunct Burma Independence Army, and more from veterans of the Burma Rifles and Military Police: it was made a more disciplined body of men, its numbers being increased to some 5,000. On 16 September its title was changed to Burma National Army (BNA), but its role remained, very largely, that of internal security. Bo Ne Win was Chief of Staff with the rank of Colonel in the Japanese army. The force wore Japanese army uniforms and badges of rank. Aung San as Minister of Defence was awarded the rank of Major-General by the Japanese, together with the Order of the Rising Sun.

Aung San and Thakin Nu tried hard to win the confidence of the Karens by personal contacts and by associating them with the new régime: they at least realized that there could be no New Burma if the Karens continued to be treated as a servile, hostile people.[1] The Minister of Forests in Ba Maw's Cabinet was Hla Pe, a Taungthu (a community allied to the Karens); Sir San Crombie Po, the great Karen leader, was appointed a Privy Councillor, but took no part in the Government. Finally, proposals were made for the formation of a Karen battalion in the BNA: San Po Thin was the leading spirit in this enterprise. After the Myaungmya murders he had worked for a time in the cause of the British; arrested by the *Kempeitai*, the Japanese Gestapo, he purchased his release by betraying one of the Karen resistance heroes, Lester. Thereafter he managed to ingratiate himself with Aung San and the Thakins. Already San Po Thin was exhibiting that political equivocation which was to be such a disastrous asset to the Karen cause.

Meanwhile, the Governor of Burma had set up his 'camp' in the Himalayan hill-station, Simla. The Secretariat was reassembled, and in the absence of the great majority of erstwhile Ministers and M.P.s, two senior Ministers, Sir Paw Tun and Sir Htoon Aung Gyaw, were appointed Advisers to the Governor. A Reconstruction Department was created to prepare for the post-war period. Its planning was based largely upon the assumption that a period of reorganization and physical rehabilitation would precede any return to representative government. Some useful work was accomplished in planning for the rebuilding of Burma's economy, but the 'Simla

[1] Nu, *Burma Under the Japanese* (London, 1954), pp. 98–102.

Government' has been heavily criticized for its remoteness from reality, whereby there was a failure to grasp the significance of the contemporary political awakening in Burma and, indeed, throughout Asia. Certainly Simla, with its pines and twinkling lights and dispatch boxes, was a long way, physically and in spirit, from the bombed, choked alleys of Rangoon.

From 1 January 1944 the actual administration of liberated Burma was handed over to the Supreme Allied Commander, South East Asia, Admiral Mountbatten, for an undefined period of time.[1] A Civil Affairs Service (Burma), known as CAS(B), was constituted to provide a military administration. Certain officials of the Burma Government in Exile were seconded to CAS(B), but many of its officers lacked experience in administration and its numbers were quite inadequate for the tasks ahead. Moreover, although CAS(B), under the Supreme Allied Commander, was responsible for the immediate tasks which would confront it—restoration of law and order and rehabilitation of the economic life of Burma—it had no final authority in political matters. The 'Simla Government' remained *de jure* the Government of Burma, responsible for all decisions with long-term implications (the British Government being, of course, the arbiter of policy). In practice, it was quite impossible to separate the two spheres, and there were infinite possibilities for the Governor of Burma and the Supreme Allied Commander to pursue policies which might be antagonistic. A third complicating factor was the introduction into Burma of 'Force 136'. This organization to promote resistance movements in enemy-occupied countries was established at Kandy as an outlier of the Special Operations Executive under the Minister of Economic Warfare. It worked in consultation with the Supreme Allied Commander, but by no means under his direction: in the process of fostering underground activity in Burma, Force 136 appears to have been given quasi-political undertakings which were made without prior reference to either the Supreme Commander or the Governor of Burma or the head of CAS(B), the Chief Civil Affairs Officer.

The year 1944 saw a complete swing-round in the fortunes of war in Asia. In February the Japanese launched their abortive invasion of India, and in its repulse three crack Japanese divisions were annihilated. Then began the long, steady march forward of the British-Indian divisions of the Fourteenth Army. A year later, northern Burma was reoccupied, the China Road was reopened, and the Fourteenth Army was poised to cross the

---

[1] See *Report to the Combined Chiefs of Staff by the Supreme Allied Commander, South-East Asia, 1943–1945* (London, 1951), pp. 189 ff.

Irrawaddy as far down-river as Chauk. Plans went ahead for the recapture of Rangoon. These Allied successes gave a great fillip to the underground movement in Burma.

One group of the Communist Thakins opposed the Japanese right from the start. *Tet pongyi* Thein Pe and Tin Shwe managed to make their way to India in July 1942 and contacted the British authorities, professing utter disgust with the Japanese. These protestations were regarded somewhat coldly by the Government of Burma, as coming from members of a group notorious for violently anti-British views; but a warmer welcome was given them by Force 136. Thein Pe was employed largely on broadcast propaganda, but Tin Shwe twice returned to Burma and established contacts with Thakin Soe, a Communist Thakin, who had organized a resistance movement in the Delta with headquarters at Pyapon, and also with Than Tun.

Meanwhile relations between Aung San and the Japanese High Command were deteriorating, largely due to Aung San's determination to maintain the BNA as a separate force. Bo Let Ya, second in command of the BNA, and Bo Setkya, Vice Minister for Defence, were strongly suspected by the Japanese of 'treachery': as a precaution, they arranged for Bo Setkya to go to Japan as military attaché.[1] Aung San therefore made common cause with the other malcontents who now included all but Ba Maw's personal following. Some time late in 1944[2] a secret understanding was reached between the BNA and all the main political groups excepting the *Sinyetha* for co-operation against the Japanese. It is a mark of Aung San's influence over many of the Delta Karens that their central organization joined the confederacy, which took the name of the Anti-Fascist Organization (AFO).[3]

In mid-September 1944 Thein Pe prepared a lengthy statement which made many proposals for the future, including a request for recognition of the Thakins as a bona fide resistance organization. The Commander of Force 136 replied in a document, also of some length, which included these words: 'We take this opportunity of affording you our formal recognition as the Anti-Axis Association of Burma.' Whatever the value of this sweeping assurance for the political future, its immediate

[1] Ba Sein also went as Minister to Manchukuo as a form of punishment, but this was because he had fallen out with his fellow Thakins in 1943.

[2] August 1944 is the month usually quoted, but the sources are vague as to details.

[3] Other parties in the AFO included the Communist Party, the People's Revolutionary Party, *Maha Bama*, the Fabian Party, *Myo Chit*, the Shan Association, and the Youth League (established in June 1942 as the Burma branch of the East Asiatic Youth League). Some of these organizations cannot have joined as early as 1944.

effect was to lead Force 136 into sponsoring the AFO as a resistance movement in the Allied cause. During November 1944 Force 136 secretly dropped a Burmese wireless operator near Pegu. Through this man, contact was established with Than Tun, who transmitted a demand for 20,000 firearms and large sums in gold to build up a resistance movement. From January to March 1945 wireless operators were dropped down the whole length of Burma. Arms were also passed over to members of the AFO by Force 136. All this was done without the knowledge of either the Fourteenth Army or CAS(B). When, at last, as a result of protests by the Commander-in-Chief of the Land Forces and of the Chief Civil Affairs Officer, they were informed of these developments, they took strong exception to the haphazard distribution of arms to an unknown underground movement, and on 15 February the Commander-in-Chief, Lieut.-General Leese, ordered that all supplies should cease. The Commander of Force 136 protested to the Supreme Commander, Admiral Mountbatten, who on 24 February decided that the issue of arms should be continued. But for some weeks yet neither the AFO nor the BNA showed any inclination to reveal their hand to the British.

Meanwhile in the Karen hills another resistance movement was assuming massive proportions under the direct leadership of British officers of Force 136. From Karenni down through the Salween District, Karen guerrillas were enlisted to form four 'commands' or areas: the Karens under arms numbered (according to a careful recorder) 12,000 men.[1] Among those Karens who served who have since made their mark were Major Saw Butler, M.C., now Secretary to the Karen Ministry, Sao Wunnah, Minister for Karenni (now Kayah State) since 1948, and Mahn Win Maung, Cabinet Minister since 1947, who was parachuted in from India. From late February 1945 onwards this force mobilized for action.

On 20 March 1945, after cruel fighting, Mandalay fell to the 19th Indian 'Dagger' Division. About the same time Than Tun, ostensibly undertaking a Japanese war-propaganda tour, went into hiding near Toungoo. He was found by a British Force 136 officer, but declined suggestions of co-operation. Seven days after the fall of Mandalay the BNA at last decided to make a move. Units of the BNA marched out of Rangoon, to the music of Japanese military bands and to the cheering of the crowds, ostensibly to fight against the Allies. Instead, they vanished into the jungle, and Aung San issued the order 'We are now at war.' In subsequent attacks upon lines of communications the

---

[1] Morrison, *Grandfather Longlegs*, p. 161.

BNA and the AFO guerrillas together killed some 600 to 700 Japanese.[1]

On the same day that the BNA left Rangoon, 27 March, but in ignorance of this development, Admiral Mountbatten wired to the Chiefs of Staff proposing that he should support any AFO rising. On 30 March a guarded assent was returned by the Cabinet Committee to which the question had been referred. This communication observed that 'it should be made perfectly clear that these leaders must not consider their contribution of great importance, and that they must be reminded more clearly than you suggest, that as ex-collaborators with the Japanese they have a lot of lee-way to make up'. However, the future of Burma was not to be regulated thus in far-off London; it was to be decided in Kandy and Rangoon.

Meanwhile, there had begun what Field-Marshal Slim has called 'the fantastic race for Rangoon against the monsoon'. Toungoo was of key importance to both sides, but the Allied advance was slowed down by the desperate efforts of enemy suicide formations, while the Japanese 15th Division was ordered down to Toungoo from Loikaw. It was now that the Karen hill guerrillas went into action. They fastened on to the Japanese division like bulldogs, and virtually wiped it out, thus holding open the road to Toungoo for the arrival of the Fourteenth Army.[2] Other Japanese divisions retreating through the eastern hills were harried and pursued: altogether, the Karen guerrillas killed over 12,500 of the enemy.[3] Just before the Allies closed in on Rangoon, the Japanese pulled out, on 23 April. Until the city was occupied on 3 May, the only authority was that of the AFO, under the local leadership of Ba Swe, who had worked as chief of the Japanese *Keibotai* or civil defence organization. When the British arrived their prime efforts were directed to restoring the public services, moving in food-supplies, opening communications, creating law and order, and generally in bringing the city to life again. CAS(B) headquarters was marooned in Calcutta, and at this critical moment it was undergoing a change of direction, Major-General H. E. Rance taking over on 10 May. Rance did not arrive in Rangoon until 2 June, and meanwhile it was necessary to make contacts with Burman leaders, to establish some measure of confidence and stability in a city boiling with unrest.

[1] See *Report by the Supreme Allied Commander*, p. 145.
[2] ibid., p. 153.
[3] Morrison, *Grandfather Longlegs*, p. 164. At a conference at Kandy in September 1945 General Slim presented figures for the casualties inflicted by the Karens and the AFO and BNA which roughly corroborated the figures quoted above.

Early in April Admiral Mountbatten held a series of conferences at Kandy in which the Government of Burma (still located at Simla) was represented by Sir John Wise. Outlining his intentions towards the Anti-Fascist Organization and the Burma National Army, Mountbatten proposed to pursue 'Great Britain's traditional policy of leniency and conciliation.' The Burma Government, headed by Sir Reginald Dorman-Smith, took a different view of this matter, but Admiral Mountbatten made it clear that he reserved to himself 'all policy decisions to be taken in South-East Asia'.[1] On 15 May he proposed to the Chiefs of Staff that the BNA should be brought on to the strength of the British forces; the next day Aung San was brought before General Slim at Meiktila. Aung San demanded that his 'Provisional Government' should be treated as an ally, and that he should be recognized as an Allied Commander. These claims were rejected by General Slim, who pointed out that Aung San was, under British law, a traitor. On receipt of Slim's account of this meeting, Admiral Mountbatten asked Sir Reginald Dorman-Smith to agree to Aung San being informed that the AFO would be considered for inclusion in the Governor's Council when it was re-formed, but Dorman-Smith 'telegraphed that he could not for a moment contemplate giving an undertaking to consider this'.[2] On 21 and 22 May communications from the Chiefs of Staff emphasized the dangers of encouraging the BNA and approved plans for disbanding the force, but once again theirs was not the effective decision. On 30 May, at a meeting in Delhi presided over by Admiral Mountbatten, the BNA was accorded recognition as the 'Patriotic Burmese Forces' (PBF), and on 2 June the Supreme Commander issued a directive headed 'Policy Towards the Burmans'. Paragraph 4 reads: 'The guiding principle which I am determined shall be observed is that no person shall suffer on account of political opinions honestly held, whether now or in the past, even if these may have been anti-British.' This directive was issued before being approved by the British Government.[3]

When on 15 June a Victory Parade was held in Rangoon, the Resistance Flag of the AFO (a red flag with a white star) was flown alongside the Union Jack. The next day fifty prominent citizens were received in audience by Admiral Mountbatten; after this deputation had withdrawn Aung San

---

[1] *Report by the Supreme Allied Commander*, p. 200.
[2] ibid., p. 202.
[3] ibid., p. 230. Dr. Ba Maw, however, was held by the Americans in a Japanese jail as an alleged war criminal for about a year. Ba Sein was also interned for a period.

and Than Tun were given a separate, private interview. By thus setting his seal of approval on the AFO, Mountbatten was adopting a policy at variance with that of the British Government, and was overriding the advice of his own Civil Affairs officers who strongly urged that Aung San should be tried as a war criminal.[1] It was Admiral Mountbatten, in effect, who recognized the AFO as the genuine representatives of post-war popular opinion in Burma. As early as May 1945 the political future was decided virtually in favour of Aung San and the AFO.

The disbandment of the PBF, together with the registration of suitable men for the new regular army, was begun on 30 June. Almost within the first week difficulties were experienced. It soon became clear that Aung San was determined to prevent the splitting up of his BNA followers between army units whereby he would lose his main organized following. A series of meetings were held between Aung San and Admiral Mountbatten, perhaps the most important being that at Kandy on 6 September. U Tin Tut, the most senior Burmese member of the civil service, was deputed to assist Aung San in preparing his brief—perhaps in the hope that his moderate influence would prevail. But it was Aung San's influence that prevailed. These two strikingly dissimilar men were to work closely together in the next two years since Tin Tut was the one 'bureaucrat' whom Aung San trusted. The meeting was regarded on both sides as a success. By December 1945 about 4,700 former members of the PBF had registered for regular enlistment.[2] Some 3,500 did not volunteer, and these did not quietly return to civil life but within a few months had formed the nucleus of what was represented as an 'old comrades' association', *Pyithu Yebaw Ahphwe*, known in English as the People's Volunteer Organization (PVO). This was in fact a private army, with district formations throughout the country, all operating under a central headquarters controlled by Aung San, who turned down the offer of an appointment in the new regular army with the rank of Brigadier in order to take the lead in politics.

The Military Administration in Burma lasted until October 1945; it was carried on largely by the incorporation into CAS(B) of the old Burman officials, from clerks to Commissioners, who

---

[1] ibid., p. 201.
[2] It is impossible to estimate accurately the strength of the BNA or PBF. On p. 144 of the *Report by the Supreme Allied Commander*, the BNA is said to contain '5,000 armed men': on p. 202, referring to a date six weeks later, the *Report* speaks of 'something like 10,000 armed Burmese' in the BNA. Eventually, 8,300 members of the BNA passed through the demobilization centres by December 1945. Many of these were probably recruited into the PBF after hostilities were over.

had kept things going during the Japanese occupation. Although somewhat amateurish, the Military Government initiated certain lines of policy which were to become permanent features of post-war administration. A Supplies and Industries Department (later Department of Civil Supplies) was set up in March 1945 which, in view of the paralysis of private enterprise, was required to distribute food and a limited supply of consumer goods throughout the country. It included a projects section, whose task was to restore the main economic activities of Burma by organizing the big commercial firms into quasi-public corporations. The largest of these was the Rice Project.

On 17 May 1945 the British Government issued a statement of policy.[1] This amounted to a considerable setback in Burma's political development. The 1935 constitution would be in abeyance until December 1948: during the interim, the Governor would be responsible for the entire field of administration. He would shortly set up an Executive Council, 'at the outset a small and mainly official body', to be expanded later 'by the inclusion of non-official Burmese'. During this interim period a general election would be held, and the elected representatives would be invited to draw up a new constitution. Subsequently Burma was promised 'full self-government within the Commonwealth', but the Scheduled Areas (the Shan States and the other hill areas) would remain 'subject to a special régime under the Governor, until such time as the inhabitants signify their desire for some suitable form of association of their territories with Burma proper'. This could not be an attractive proposal to a people who had been independent—perhaps in more than name—and whose leaders had occupied high office and had treated with the other leaders of East Asia on a basis of equality.[2]

The reply of Aung San and his followers to this declaration came on 19 August at the Naythuyein mass meeting. The Anti-Fascist Organization was renamed the Anti-Fascist People's Freedom League (AFPFL), emphasizing that the goal of this alliance was not merely a Japanese defeat but also national independence.[3] Aung San called on all parties to support the AFPFL, and a demand was made, under the terms of the Atlantic Charter, for independence, the termination of

[1] Burma Office, *Statement of Policy . . . May 1945* (London, H.M.S.O., 1945).

[2] But compare the opinion of one of the best-informed foreign observers. J. L. Christian, in *Burma* (Bombay and London, 1945) foresaw the granting of Home Rule within six to ten years as 'a not unreasonable period' (p. 153).

[3] The new title in its Burmese version employed for 'freedom' the word *lut-lat-ye*, which is better translated 'independence'. At this period, the term 'Fascist' was used in all the Burmese newspapers to describe British officials rather than the Japanese secret police.

the military administration, the constitution of a popular government, the formation of a Cabinet, and the holding of elections based on universal suffrage.[1] In fact, the AFPFL enjoyed strong representation upon the Advisory Council which Major-General Rance had formed to keep in touch with his Military Government, but Aung San was determined to secure not representation but real power. On 1 September the secret Revolutionary Party became an open Socialist Party with Thakin Mya as President and Kyaw Nyein and Ba Swe as prominent leaders: there were seven founding members. The Socialists rapidly established themselves as an influential pressure group within the AFPFL, the source of its 'ideology'.

The dual pressure from the AFPFL and the Burma Government in Exile caused Admiral Mountbatten to agree to a resumption of civil government, and on 16 October 1945 Sir Reginald Dorman-Smith resumed charge after an absence of three and a half years.[2] It was already obvious that the time-table laid down in the May declaration would have to be speeded up. On 19 October the Governor met representatives of the AFPFL and other parties to discuss nominations to a new Executive Council. The League advanced a demand for eleven seats in a council of fifteen, with the right to put forward a panel of names for automatic acceptance, and demanding certain portfolios for their men; the Governor countered with an offer of seven seats in a council of eleven, stipulating that he would choose his AFPFL councillors on their merits. Since further negotiations also proved fruitless the new Council was formed without the AFPFL. It contained three former *Myochit* adherents, and was led by Sir Paw Tun, the former Prime Minister and war-time Adviser. Two dissident Thakins were later added to the Council: Tun Ok, and Ba Sein, who refounded *Dobama Asi-ayon* in 1946 on his release from internment.

Aung San's chief answer was the building up of the PVO as a weapon of force. Its numbers can only be guessed at,[3] but there was a PVO headquarters in every district and town. In addition, the Socialists built up the All-Burma Peasants' Organization (ABPO) and the Ministerial Services Union as a trade union of all clerks in government service. Indeed, the

---

[1] A narrative of this period is given in *Burma's Fight for Freedom*, issued by the new Burma Government in January 1948.

[2] The area east of the Salween remained under military government. CAS(B) was finally wound up on 31 March 1946.

[3] cf. F. C. Jones and others, *The Far East, 1942–46* (R.I.I.A., *Survey of International Affairs*, 1939–46), p. 286. The PVO strength is estimated at between 8,000 and 14,000.

AFPFL had its agents in all government departments and public services, and almost formed a parallel authority to the Government.

The position of the Communists was obscure; one group led by the intractable Thakin Soe refused to compromise in any way with the British; there must be a People's War against the Imperialists. The main body, led by Thakin Than Tun, hoped to bring about a Communist State by working from inside the AFPFL. The two groups split in March 1946, Thakin Soe leading his followers away to form a new Communist Party, commonly known as the 'Red Flags', while Than Tun's supporters were usually called 'White Flags'.

The only other active politician of importance was U Saw, who was released from detention in January 1946 and at once attempted to challenge Aung San's national leadership: soon there was bitter enmity between these two aggressive, ambitious men. U Saw called on the *Myochit* Ministers to resign from the Council, and all but one obeyed. He began to purchase arms and ammunition to build up his own private army, and he outbid the AFPFL in his demands upon the Government.

During Dorman-Smith's period of office the Government's attitude towards the AFPFL varied from proposals for all-out repression to plans for conciliation and co-operation.[1] In June 1946 Sir Reginald Dorman-Smith tendered his resignation for reasons of health. He was succeeded by Sir Henry Knight, the last of the long line of I.C.S. governors, but his was only a temporary appointment and on 31 August 1946 Sir Hubert Rance, the former CAS(B) chief, returned as civil Governor.

The political tempo was now becoming increasingly hectic. In July 1946 the Red Flags went 'underground' and began a campaign of violence against the Government. In the same month a four-man delegation representing the Karens went to London to put the case for Karen 'Home Rule'. During the first six months of 1946 the AFPFL pursued a policy of trying to overthrow the Government by a 'war of nerves': there were speeches, processions, quasi-military drilling by the PVO, raids on government installations, and, everywhere, rumour. The object was identical with that of the Indian Congress in its militant periods: to bring organized government to a standstill. This phase culminated in June, when a mass demonstration at Tantabin (a town to the north of Insein) clashed with the

---

[1] A vivid picture of these months of equivocation and uncertainty is given in M. Collis, *Last and First in Burma* (London, 1956). Proposals to arrest Aung San alternated with plans for bringing him into the Government, while Dorman-Smith also 'ran' Paw Tun and U Saw as challengers to the AFPFL.

police. There was firing, and four persons were killed. This produced an extremely explosive situation, but there was no mass rising of AFPFL supporters and the tension somewhat relaxed. It would appear that the driving spirit in the militant campaign had been Thakin Than Tun. The failure of the Tantabin demonstration served to discredit him, and from this time political leadership passed decisively into the hands of Aung San.

Six days after the arrival of Sir Hubert Rance, on 5 September, the police went on strike. They had considerable grievances with regard to pay. During the previous months, when they had been discharging their duties amid increasing difficulties and danger, there had been no response from the Finance Department of the Government to their application for increases in pay to meet the sharply rising cost of living. Union leaders within the police ranks brought the men out on strike, and Aung San stepped in to use this opportunity to obtain political power for the AFPFL and stake a bid for freedom for his country. Other public servants also stopped work: the posts and telegraphs, the clerks in government offices (organized in the Ministerial Services Union), and the staff of the railways. Many employees in foreign firms and in the oilfields also joined the strike, as did the students of the university and the schools. But it was the police strike which decided the issue: the Government had no alternative force upon which to fall back. There was but one battalion of British troops in the country, its thoughts concentrated upon demobilization; the Indian troops could not be employed in putting down a national movement, with a Congress Government newly in office at Delhi, while to bring the new Burma Army into the struggle would be to ignite strongly opposed loyalties.[1] Meanwhile the PVO were drilling in the streets, and dacoits were terrorizing the countryside in the name of patriotism. Sir Hubert Rance therefore sought to come to terms with Aung San. On 26 September a new Council was formed. Out of nine members, six were the candidates of the AFPFL, while another member was U Tin Tut. Aung San was virtually Prime Minister. The general strike was called off on 2 October.

Almost immediately Aung San found his leadership challenged from within the AFPFL. In appointing his ministerial team he chose one representative of the 'White Flag' Communists, *Tet pongyi* Thein Pe, who became Minister for Forests and Agriculture. Than Tun was passed over, and this rankled deeply, for he had been a close associate of Aung San:

[1] See below, pp. 320–2, regarding the tensions within the army.

the two men had married two sisters and they had, in the past,
figured as the joint leaders of the AFPFL, Aung San as the
military chief, Than Tun as political head. But Aung San was
not a man to brook rivals, as he had shown when he had thrust
aside Thakin Ba Sein from leadership of the Thakins. Than
Tun naturally felt jealous and resentful. He knew that the
Communist Party throughout the country districts was strong
and highly organized, close to the ear of the people; he knew
that the Socialist organization was still embryonic, and he
decided to make a determined bid for leadership; but he over-
played his hand. He demanded a larger representation in the
Cabinet for the Communists: Aung San refused. Thein Pe, the
Communist Minister, resigned after only two weeks in office,
and Than Tun declared another general strike, this time
against the AFPFL Government. Aung San wasted no words:
he expelled the Communists from the AFPFL and Than Tun
from the key post of Secretary-General without delay on
13 October. Than Tun was succeeded as Secretary-General by
Kyaw Nyein. Communists were then ousted from key positions
they had occupied in the trade unions and the workers' and
peasants' organizations. Than Tun was not entirely defeated,
for his followers remained secure in many positions and his
following in the rural areas remained dominant. For the time
being he withdrew into opposition, but he did not lead his
forces into militant, underground revolt like the Red Flags.
He believed that the British Government would resist the
AFPFL demand for independence, and he would then get his
opportunity. Once again he underestimated Aung San.

Cabinet office by itself did not satisfy Aung San; he presented
a demand for immediate independence, under the threat of an
AFPFL rebellion. On 20 December 1946 Mr. Attlee announced
a new policy for Burma in the House of Commons. A Burmese
delegation would be invited to London to discuss constitutional
advance towards a transfer of power. The Prime Minister
declared that it would be left to Burma to decide whether or not
to remain within the Commonwealth.[1] This invitation was
accepted by Aung San, but before his departure from Rangoon
he growled 'I hope for the best, but I am prepared for the
worst.' He went prepared as to encounter an enemy, but he
was met with all consideration as a friend. Perhaps it was from
this moment that his attitude to the British changed from one
of enmity towards co-operation.

Aung San was accompanied by Thakin Mya, Tin Tut,
Kyaw Nyein, U Saw, and Ba Sein; they arrived in London on

[1] H. C. Deb. vol. 431, col. 2342.

9 January 1947. With Tin Tut at his elbow, Aung San succeeded in securing everything he wanted from the British Government, and on 27 January a document known as the Attlee-Aung San Agreement was signed.[1] Its import was summarized by Aung San as 'full independence within one year'. It provided for elections within four months to set up a Constituent Assembly; the recognition of Aung San's Cabinet as an interim Government which was to enjoy the status of a Dominion Government; the nomination by Great Britain of Burma for membership of the United Nations and other international bodies, and 'the early unification of the Frontier Areas with the Government of Burma'. Annexed to the agreement was an assurance of a continuation of large-scale British loans to Burma, together with further grants and other assistance. However, this agreement, although it yielded so much while making no demands upon Burma in return, was repudiated by U Saw and Ba Sein: doubtless they hoped to represent Aung San as having 'sold out' to the British.

Aung San's return was a triumph, and efforts by the Communists to organize opposition to the agreement were largely unsuccessful. They concentrated on another campaign of strikes in the schools and university, lasting from January to March. The Red Flags intensified their sabotage activities, especially against the railways, and in January 1947 they were declared an 'unlawful association'. At the same time the Karen leaders became ever more restive, worried by the absence of any representative of the minorities on Aung San's mission, or any allusion to their aspirations in the agreement with the British Government. Saw Ba U Gyi, the leader of the Karen Central Organization, was a member of the Cabinet, as the KCO was a constituent organ of the AFPFL. On the advice of San Po Thin, as a token of Karen dissatisfaction, Ba U Gyi resigned from the Cabinet. San Po Thin promptly stepped into his place. There followed a breach in the Karen ranks: the majority, led by Ba U Gyi, formed the Karen National Union (KNU); even Hla Pe, the long-standing associate of Aung San, threw in his lot with the KNU. A smaller group founded the Karen Youth Organization (later called the Union Karen League); San Po Thin was President of this body, but the real leader was Mahn Ba Khaing, a forceful young man, similar to Aung San in personality. The KNU formulated a demand for a separate administration. This was no new claim: in his book *Burma and the Karens*, published in 1928, Sir San C. Po had pleaded for 'a country of their own where they may progress as

---

[1] Quoted in full in *Burma's Fight for Freedom*.

a race and find that contentment they seek. . . . Karen Country
—how inspiring it sounds!' (pp. v. and 81). The cantons of
Switzerland were looked to as a model. But whereas the British
Government felt compelled to accede to the demand of 80
million Muslims in India for Pakistan, it refused to listen to
the plea of 1½ million Karens.

A meeting of representatives of the hill peoples was convened
on 12 February at Panglong in the Southern Shan States.
Aung San, with Tin Tut and Bo Khin Maung Gale, represented
the AFPFL. The Shans were led by Sao Shwe Thaik, Sawbwa
of Yawnghwe, and the Sawbwa of Mongpawn. The most
prominent Kachin leader was the Sima Duwa, Sinwa Nawng
of Myitkyina, who had worked for the Japanese. The Chins
were represented by Vum Ko Hau, a former leader of the
Allied Chin levies. Aung San had determined to concentrate on
winning over the Kachins who, living on the China border and
contributing tough fighters to the new Burma Army, were in a
key position. He made a pact with the Sima Duwa whereby, in
return for the adherence of the Kachins to Burma, they should
receive a separate State comprising the Bhamo and Myitkyina
Districts, and including the low country with its Burmese
population. The Chins were also promised definite material
advantages, such as schools and roads, in return for their
adherence. The Shan Sawbwas received undertakings regarding their status and the constitution of a separate Shan State.
The Karens sent four observers to the conference, but 'they
were not consulted'.[1] After three days of discussion, and the
promise of these concrete concessions, Aung San returned from
Panglong with the agreement of the leaders of the hill peoples
(except the Karens) to enter into 'immediate co-operation' with
the interim Government. The Sawbwa of Mongpawn became
Counsellor for the Frontier Areas, and assumed the exercise of
that authority so long retained by the Governor himself. A
Supreme Council of the United Hill Peoples, a political coalition affiliated to the AFPFL, was established with Sao Shwe
Thaik as President.

The Panglong Agreement was registered, as it were, by the
Frontier Areas Committee, which conducted a whirlwind
inquiry during March and April 1947. The Chairman was
D. R. Rees-Williams, M.P., and the members were intended to
give equal representation to all sectors of public opinion in
Burma proper and the Frontier Areas. In fact the Committee
was packed with adherents of the AFPFL, the one outsider

---

[1] Burma, Frontier Areas Committee of Enquiry, *Report*, Part II, p. 124. See
p. 66 regarding Aung San's pact with the Kachins, and p. 78 regarding the Chins.

being Saw Sankey (late Captain with Force 136) elected from the Salween District and a member of the KNU. The Committee heard evidence from some representatives of the many tribal groups. The general sense of this evidence was for autonomy in internal administration and association with Burma, coupled with the right to secede from Burma if the association should prove burdensome. Many witnesses demonstrated clearly that they had no notion of the real purpose of the inquiry.[1] The Karens of the Salween District presented a demand for 'a separate administration from Burma proper, and under the direct control of the British Government as far as possible'.[2] The Shwegyin Karens asked to be joined to the Salween District. They recalled the many letters they had received from Field-Marshal Auchinleck and Admiral Mountbatten, praising their loyal services and promising a bright future: and now 'They feel very bitter to learn that the contents of the above letters are meaningless, and such other assurances are empty.'[3] Other Karens appeared to ask for the inclusion of the Salween District in Burma. It was all very confusing for the Chairman. The Committee then considered their report: it seems that at first the Chairman and the members were quite unable to agree upon the final proposals, but Tin Tut intervened and succeeded in devising an acceptable formula.[4] The principal contribution of the report was to lay down the procedure whereby the representatives of the frontier peoples were to be chosen to attend the Constituent Assembly; the Committee went on to recommend 'autonomous states' for the Shans and Kachins. Regarding the other peoples, it was non-committal: it anticipated the 'possible' incorporation of the Chin hills, and the 'probable' inclusion of the Salween District into Burma proper.

The Committee has often been criticized for the cavalier way in which it appeared to dispose of the future of the hill peoples, but in reality the whole issue had been prejudged under the Attlee-Aung San Agreement. The Committee's terms of reference were limited by this prior decision. Nevertheless, the hasty fashion in which its proceedings were concluded was certainly not encouraging to those of the hill peoples who needed reassurance on the intentions of the AFPFL leaders.

---

[1] cf. ibid., p. 37. Witness: 'The chieftain told me that he had received orders from Government to come and listen to what the Committee had to say. . . . I do not know anything [about the Committee]. . . . As for the future, we would like to remain as in the past, that is, independent of other people.'

[2] ibid., pp. 120–1.

[3] ibid., p. 176.

[4] U Nu, himself a member of the Committee, is the authority for this statement. See *Nation*, 20 September 1948.

Justice was not 'seen to be done'. In particular, the KNU leaders went away smarting from their brushes with the AFPFL Committee members, and bitter against the British who had used them and discarded them.

The next step was the convening of the Constituent Assembly. Elections were held in April 1947. There were 255 seats to be filled: 210 for Burma proper (of which, 24 were reserved for the Karens and 4 for the Anglo-Burmans) and 45 for the Frontier Areas.[1] The electorate cannot be said to have had a calm atmosphere in which to make its choice. In central Burma it was necessary to launch a military drive ('Operation Flush') of British, Indian, and Burman troops to clear the countryside of the Communist rebels, still euphemistically called 'dacoits', who had announced their intention of wrecking the elections by intimidation and the destruction of polling booths. Much of the polling was actually conducted under the protection of armed PVO guards. The Government information service was staffed by AFPFL supporters. The PVO marched the people to the polling booths. The count showed 248 members elected on the AFPFL ticket, predominantly as Socialists or as PVO members. Both the Karen National Union and the Communists boycotted elections which they knew they had no hope of winning, but seven individual Communists were returned.

As a prelude to the summoning of the Constituent Assembly the AFPFL held a General Convention at the Jubilee Hall, Rangoon. A fourteen-point resolution was placed before the meeting on 23 May. This was to provide the basis of the new constitution. The first point declared a resolve 'to proclaim Burma as an Independent Sovereign Republic', an independence which did not embrace Commonwealth membership, for the political horizon of the young AFPFL leaders had never lifted beyond their own hills; and if, perhaps, Aung San may have had glimpses of the potentialities of continued association with the British Empire during the few months after his London visit, it was necessary always to watch out for the Communists, ever ready to seize on any point to assert that the AFPFL leaders had 'sold out to the British', had secured only 'phony' independence.

The Constituent Assembly met on 9 June: a large number of the new members wore the quasi-military uniform of the PVO. There were five (later seven) women members. A late-comer was Thakin Nu. He had taken no active part in post-war politics, although he had continued to give strong support as Vice-President of the AFPFL. He did not offer himself as a

[1] Shan States, 26; Kachin Hills, 7; Chins, 8; Karenni, 2; Salween District, 2.

candidate at the general election, but the death of the member for Mergui led to an early by-election, and Aung San persuaded him to stand. On 11 June Thakin Nu was unanimously elected President of the Constituent Assembly. A Constitution Committee was appointed, consisting of seventy-five members, and a number of sub-committees were created to deal with specific subjects.[1] The Assembly then adjourned for a recess while experts worked upon draft sections.

Then came the event which, above all others, has made and marred modern Burma. At 10.40 a.m. on 19 July 1947 four youths dressed in army uniforms marched into the Secretariat carrying Sten and Tommy guns. They entered the Council Chamber where a Cabinet meeting was in progress. A systematic massacre of all present then took place. Those who perished were Aung San, Thakin Mya (Deputy Prime Minister), Ba Win (brother of Aung San), Mahn Ba Khaing, the Karen strong man, Ba Choe, the Sawbwa of Mongpawn, and A. Razak.[2] Three Ministers only survived the holocaust: Pyawbwe U Mya, Aung Zan Wai, and U Ba Gyan; but fortunately several others were saved through absence due to sickness or travel.

So died Aung San, the creator of Burma's independence. It is not easy for an Englishman to see the attainment of this young man free of all prejudice. His whole life (except, perhaps, during his last six months) was devoted to bitter and often unscrupulous opposition to Britain; his methods were often violent and sometimes cruel; he acted treacherously, first to the British and then to the Japanese; his concept of independence was narrowly nationalistic, and he failed to grasp the potentialities of the new multi-racial Commonwealth. But all this is, of course, completely irrelevant to the great mass of Burmans, whose admiration for Aung San is akin to worship. To them Aung San is the great patriot: his attitude to Britain and Japan, they believe, was determined solely by his passionate desire to see his own country free. Burmans are aware only of how Aung San first helped to obtain an independence under the Japanese that turned to ashes, and then, undaunted, fought for an independence from the British which was unequivocal and complete. No wonder he is called *Bogyoke*, the Great General, whose portrait is in every government office and in many Burmese homes.

From any standpoint his achievement is remarkable. It was not that the British Government opposed the demand for

[1] See *Burma's Fight for Freedom*, pp. 62–63 for details of procedure.
[2] The crime was carried out by henchmen of U Saw who hoped to step into the breach. U Saw and his accomplices were tried in Insein Jail, sentenced on 30 December 1947, and hanged on 8 May 1948.

independence: self-government was implicit in the British programme, at any rate from 1922 onwards. But this development was to be planned by Britain and was to proceed according to a British time-table. It was Aung San's achievement that he, the raw ex-student, dictated the terms of Burma's independence. The British Government at Westminster, Admiral Mountbatten, commander of massive armed forces, the British Government of Burma with its shrewd and experienced officers: Aung San outfaced them all. From varying points of view these Englishmen in positions of responsibility and power aspired to put their mark upon Burma's attainment of independence. But in the end Aung San towered above them all, and imposed his will upon the acts and scenes that led up to the final British withdrawal. Burmans have said that 'Everything Aung San touched turned to gold': perhaps this was most true in that, in the hour of his triumph, he was struck down, to become a martyr. Aung San has the glory of independence: he has no responsibility for the miseries of the civil war that followed. Many believe that this man of power could have moulded events after independence as he did before: this 'might have been' of history will long be debated in Burma.

Immediately after the assassinations the Governor called upon Thakin Nu to form a new Cabinet, and on 20 July a reconstructed Governor's Council was sworn in. Thakin Nu had no wish to step into the unique position which Aung San had made for himself, and extended an invitation to Than Tun and other Communist leaders (Ba Tin and Ba Thein Tin) to rejoin the AFPFL with representation in the Cabinet. This attempt foundered in Communist suspicion, and Than Tun's over-confident belief that he held the good cards and could ask his own terms.[1] On 1 August a reconstructed Cabinet was sworn in, with Thakin Nu as Premier, Bo Let Ya as Deputy Premier (with responsibility for defence), Tin Tut as Foreign Minister, Kyaw Nyein as Minister for Home Affairs and Justice, and nine other members. All except Tin Tut belonged to the AFPFL.

The Constituent Assembly met again on 29 July. U Nu's place as President was taken by Sao Shwe Thaik. A preliminary draft constitution was laid before the Assembly, and a clash of opinion developed, some wishing to accord greater powers to the Government.[2] The constitutional lawyers resisted this

---

[1] See Nu, in *New Times of Burma*, 27 November 1947.

[2] An appeal in January 1950 by Bo Yan Naing against his detention without trial as unconstitutional led to interesting discussions about the constitution, its making and meaning, especially between Acting Chief Justice E Maung and Attorney-General Chan Htoon. See *Nation*, 18, 19, and 20 January 1950.

move. An interim report was adopted on 1 August, and the Assembly was again prorogued. The third session began on 15 September, when for the first time, representatives of the Karenni Sawbwas attended: the three rulers had decided that they could not hope to attain independence outside Burma.[1] On 24 September Thakin Nu moved that the draft bill of the constitution be adopted. In his speech he averred that the new Burma

would be Leftist. And a Leftist country is one in which the people working together to the best of their power and ability strive to convert the natural resources and produce of the land . . . into consumer commodities to which everybody will be entitled, each according to his need . . . there will be no distinction between the employer class and the employed . . . no such thing as the governing class and the governed class.[2]

He went on, 'The ideology that Burma needs today is not Trotsky's "Immediate action regardless of the consequences", but Lenin's "Get strong first, everything else afterwards". The credo of our late lamented leader Bogyoke [Aung San] is the latter.'[3] He closed with a word of caution to the Communists: 'It will not do to place sole reliance on the Soviet Union', otherwise the whole speech was Marxist in tone. The same day, the constitution was formally adopted.

Chief credit for the drafting of the constitution has been ascribed by U Nu to Tin Tut.[4] Others who contributed greatly to its formulation were Sir Ba U, Justice E Maung, Justice Kyaw Myint (brother of Tin Tut), and Chan Htoon the Constitutional Adviser.[5] All these gentlemen had received their training in the Law Schools of Cambridge and the Inns of Court. The language of the constitution and some of its matter reflect this background.

U Chan Htoon has described the constitution as divided into 'high ideals' of social justice, and 'particular provisions' for particular aspects of government. It begins with a declaration of fundamental rights, a statement of the relations of the State to workers and peasants, and a directive laying down economic and social policies, all couched in 'Welfare State' terms. Then

[1] Unlike the Shan States, Karenni had never been annexed to form part of the British dominions, although the Karen Sawbwas had accepted British paramountcy. When British rule was withdrawn, Karenni would, technically, become sovereign.
[2] Nu, *Towards Peace and Democracy* (Rangoon, 1949), p. 2.
[3] ibid., p. 6.
[4] Nu's obituary tribute, *Nation*, 20 September 1948.
[5] Sir B. N. Rau, Constitutional Adviser to the Indian Constituent Assembly, also rendered assistance.

follow the 'particular provisions'. The President, *Naing gan daw Thamada*, is purely a ceremonial Head of State: his powers are circumscribed at every turn.[1] The legislature, as under the 1935 constitution, was bicameral. The upper house, the Chamber of Nationalities, is strongly weighted in favour of the minority peoples, the Burmese members being fewer in number than the remainder. The lower house, the Chamber of Deputies, is constituted on a basis of one member for each 100,000 of the population.[2] The constitution also provides for a Shan State, a Kachin State, and a Karenni State; the question of a Karen State was left open for decision by a referendum of the Karens.[3] Each State was to have a government responsible to a State Council. The constitution lays down a separate 'State Legislative List' which includes public order, communications, education, public health, and local government. The States have their own separate budgets and their own civil service.

The Constitutional Adviser, Chan Htoon, observed much later that 'our constitution, though in theory federal, is in practice unitary'. The structure of the Union, he said, is not like the United States, Switzerland, or even India: there are no separate State legislatures: the State Councils consist of assemblies of the *Union* M.P.s of the States. There are 'no organic independent legislatures' in his view: he likened the situation to that in the British House of Commons where, by convention, Scottish M.P.s only compose the committees which handle Scottish affairs.[4] The chapters setting up the States, together with the concession of a right of secession (under stringent safeguards), were inserted to assuage the doubts of the frontier leaders rather than to meet actual political or administrative requirements: a form of atonement for that age-old suspicion of the Burmese which the hill peoples could not at once discard. Chapter VIII, which establishes the judicial system, provides for a Supreme Court to be the final authority on any question of law and the arbitrator in disputes between the Union

[1] Possibly because Tin Tut had particularly studied the powers of the President of Eire, which are extremely limited. The Crown in Britain was certainly a model.

[2] Of the 250 seats in the Chamber of Deputies, 25 go to the Shan State, 7 to the Kachin State, 6 to the Chins, 2 to Karenni; 210 seats remain for Burma proper and 20 of these were reserved for the Karens. Of the 125 seats in the Chamber of Nationalities 25 go to the Shan State, 12 to the Kachin State, 8 to the Chin Special Division, 3 to Karenni, 24 to the Karens, and 53 to Burma proper. For the later modification of Karen representation, see p. 75.

[3] A demand by Arakanese Muslims for a separate unit of government.was rejected.

[4] *Nation*, 2 July 1952. This might seem to present a somewhat extreme interpretation of the constitution, but the Supreme Court, by its judgment, endorsed this view.

Government and a State government, or in inter-State disputes. Chapter XI provides that amendments to the constitution may be made by a two-thirds vote of both chambers of Parliament in joint sitting. Thus Parliament is sovereign: the function of the Supreme Court is limited to ensuring that the Government does not contravene the laws.[1] Altogether, the constitution runs to some sixty pages. By comparison with the American Declaration of Independence it is a long document: by comparison with its precursors, the Government of India Act and the Government of Burma Act of 1935, it is succinct and brief. Brief also was the time taken in its preparation: only fifteen weeks, including the adjournments; compared with the three years needed to create the Indian constitution and the nine years taken by Pakistan. Inevitably, the Burma constitution was not tested by lengthy examination in debate and committee and certain of its provisions were ratified without a clear understanding of their ultimate implications.[2] Nevertheless, its drafting within so short a time, whilst simultaneously a grave political catastrophe was faced and surmounted, was a notable triumph. And, in general, amid the trials of the succeeding years, the constitution has proved both tough and resilient.

Having designed the framework of a new State, there remained the need to obtain the assent of the British Government to the recognition of independence for Burma. This was embodied in a treaty signed in London on 17 October 1947 by Mr. Attlee for Great Britain and Thakin Nu for 'the Provisional Government of Burma'. Article I recognized 'the republic of the Union of Burma as a fully independent sovereign state'. Amongst the subjects dealt with in the remaining articles were a defence agreement and the cancellation of £15 million owed by Burma to Britain, together with other financial concessions. Under notes accompanying the treaty it was agreed that British interests in Burma might continue 'in the legitimate conduct of the businesses or professions in which they are now engaged', subject, however, to the possibility of 'expropriation

---

[1] The observations of Dr. E Maung as Acting Chief Justice nicely define the position: 'We feel that we cannot accept entirely the English mode of thought, nor entirely the American mode. There must be a middle way. In England there is no written constitution, and parliament is supreme. Here, parliament is not supreme. On the other hand, we would not go so far as to claim with the American judges, arbitrary powers, and to say that because we think that certain Acts of Parliament are unreasonable they must be contrary to the constitution. There are certain limits to our powers. We must act within the constitution' (*Nation*, 18 January 1950).

[2] Section 90, which lays down that Parliament is the sole maker of laws in the Union, has since been interpreted by the Attorney-General as meaning that all the by-laws made by the hundreds of local bodies from village councils upwards, must be laid before Parliament. If put into practice, such a procedure could effectively bring Parliament to a stop.

or acquisition . . . [with] equitable compensation'. Of these negotiations Thakin Nu said on his return

I want to make a public acknowledgment of the great wisdom and vision of the British Labour Government. No one can deny that the British Government are in a position to drive a hard bargain with us. Yet throughout the negotiations never had I met with any instance of hard-heartedness. From beginning to end, the British Government were at pains to win our goodwill rather than our treasure.[1]

The treaty was endorsed by the British Parliament in the Burma Independence Act (10 December 1947), which laid down the actual date of independence and withdrew British nationality from all but a specified few of the millions in Burma who had been subjects of the King-Emperor.[2]

On his return to Burma Thakin Nu once more tried to secure the co-operation of the Communists. On 8 November he made a public appeal to the opposition to

unite as one party making one common cause. Three parties should find it especially easy to unite under one common programme—the PVO, the Socialist and Communist parties. To my mind they resemble one another so closely already that but let them form a committee . . . and in a trice they would find themselves one and the same party.[3]

This generous gesture was not returned, for the parties named by Nu were divided not so much by principles as by personal rivalries and ambitions. The Communists launched a big propaganda campaign against the newly-signed treaty. Two features especially were attacked: the defence agreement[4] and the commercial provisions. These 'concessions', the Communists declared, had safeguarded British interests in Burma: the outcome was likened to the British relationship of surveillance with the Kingdom of Jordan: Thakin Nu had made the people of Burma the stooges of the British. In reply, the AFPFL announced on 17 November that efforts to bring the Communists back into the League would be discontinued. Another attempt at 'Leftist Unity' was the formation of the Marxist League on 24 November, to link up the Socialists and

---

[1] Nu, *Towards Peace and Democracy*, pp. 15–16.
[2] The text of the treaty and the Act is given in *Burma's Fight for Freedom*, pp. 101–4.
[3] Nu, *Towards Peace and Democracy*, p. 12.
[4] Concluded on 29 August 1947 between J. W. Freeman, M.P. and Bo Let Ya. It covered the gift of certain military equipment and naval craft to Burma, and provided for a British army, navy, and air force mission to be set up in Burma to assist with the training of the new defence forces. In return, the Burma Government agreed not to accept any other military mission from outside the Commonwealth.

the PVO. It was to be controlled by a Praesidium of ten: but this also came to nothing. The PVO, bereft of Aung San's leadership and deprived of their appointed role of 'Liberation Army', were increasingly restless and power-hungry.

The weeks passed until on 4 January at 4.20 a.m. the hour of independence arrived.[1] The Union Jack was lowered, the new Union flag took its place: it is similar to the AFPFL flag, a red standard with a dark-blue canton containing a large star and five small stars coloured white for the peoples of the Union.

The last British Governor, Sir Hubert Rance, departed, and the new President, Sao Shwe Thaik, Sawbwa of Yawnghwe, entered the neo-Jacobean portals of Government House. British troops marched away to the strains of 'Auld Lang Syne'. As in India and Pakistan, the departing British received many demonstrations of goodwill. It was difficult for the Burmans to realize that their erstwhile rulers actually were departing, as they had promised they would, without exacting anything in the nature of concessions and without a struggle.[2] Indeed, many nationalist politicians went on assuming the old attitudes towards 'imperialism' couched in the same violent language, and some continued with the worn-out technique of physical violence and negative opposition.

Meanwhile, crowds in villages and towns throughout the land joined in light-hearted, carefree rejoicings. Once again Burma was free: the 'Golden Land' of the olden times had come into its own again.

[1] Originally 6 January was to be Independence Day, but eventually the astrologers decided that 4 Janury was the most auspicious date.

[2] The introduction to the official record of the occasion, *Burma's Fight for Freedom*, states candidly 'The title of this publication is perhaps a little misleading. Freedom has been won without a fight, a fact which testifies to Britain's wisdom and Burma's unity.'

II

THE BACKGROUND OF CIVIL WAR
1948-60

FROM its very first weeks the new republic was confronted with challenges to its authority which rapidly developed into a civil war.[1] All economic and social progress had to be subordinated to the military struggle, certainly till 1952. And even at the time of writing trains and lorries are being sabotaged, cultivators intimidated, and rice-millers blackmailed by the insurgents, while a foreign enemy still harasses the Shan border. The advance of Burma to its chosen goal of a 'Welfare State' is still being retarded by the threat of the gun. To understand Burma today it is necessary to understand this background of civil war.

The year 1948 opened with two enemies already in the field, the Red Flag Communists and the *Mujahids*, bands of Muslim adventurers in the extreme north of Arakan, whose terrorist activities were already beyond government control, activities ostensibly devoted to the creation of a separate Muslim State. There was also the huge army of the PVO which, like the BIA its predecessor, used its powers to exact levies from the people and to make demands on public servants. The Government now asked the PVO to hand in its arms; the PVO refused; the order was postponed for a year. And the *Yebaws*, 'comrades of boldness', continued 'to live idly on what the villagers, no longer so willingly, provided'.[2] A more vigorous threat came from the White Flag Communists. Although outwardly accepting the new independence, they adopted a thesis formulated by H. N. Ghoshal (the party's principal authority on dogma) that the AFPFL had become the tools of the British imperialists, thereby making it necessary to overthrow the AFPFL and set up a genuine People's Government. This thesis was formally adopted by the Central Council of the Communists on 18 February 1948. A campaign to 'overthrow the Government by force' was at once launched, and the familiar weapon of strikes in key industries was invoked. Reluctantly, U Nu's Government decided to retaliate; definite information was received

[1] This description 'civil war' has been used by the Commander-in-Chief, Bo Ne Win (see *Nation*, 27 July 1952).
[2] J. S. Furnivall, 'Independence and After', *Pacific Affairs*, June 1949. Mr. Furnivall quotes a figure of 300,000 PVO's. This is much higher than any other estimate.

of an impending *coup d'état*, and orders were thereupon issued for the arrest of the Communist leaders on 25 March. This became known to the PVO who intervened, pressing the Government to come to terms with the Communists. They proposed that negotiations should begin again for the reunification of Red Flags, White Flags, PVO's, and Socialists, and that meanwhile the Government should refrain from taking any action. This was accepted, and the PVO attempted to secure a meeting of both sides to mediate. The Communists prevaricated and evaded the proposed meeting. On 27 March, celebrated as 'Resistance Day', U Nu made a further gesture of conciliation. In a public speech he promised that if unity was achieved he would resign from the Government and from the AFPFL. At the same moment, at a mass meeting in Bandoola Square at the centre of Rangoon, Than Tun was deriding the weakness of the AFPFL and PVO and calling for an armed rising. The Cabinet hesitated, then issued orders for the arrest of the Communists: when the police arrived at the Communist headquarters at 2 a.m. next day, Than Tun and his lieutenants had got clean away. They retired to Pyinmana and called out their active supporters in arms, some 25,000 in number.[1]

The Communist campaign developed mainly in Pegu District, and to a lesser extent in Myingyan, Bassein, and the Delta. Throughout April they seized police stations, occupied small towns and villages, looted rice, and sabotaged communications. But the Government struck back, and by May the rebellion was losing its momentum. Once again the PVO came forward: the blame for the revolt was placed on the Government for having tried to arrest the Communist leaders. The PVO offer of mediation was renewed, and a draft programme was presented as a basis for 'Leftist Unity'.

In reply, on 25 May, U Nu presented his own 'Leftist Unity' programme, echoing Aung San's fourteen-point resolution of twelve months before. The new 'points' aimed at the mobilization of the whole economic and social system by state action. The final point was 'to form a League for the propagation of Marxist doctrine, composed of Socialists, Communists, *Pyithu Yebaws* [PVO] and others who lean towards Marxism': when this was achieved the various existing parties would be disbanded. The two points which U Nu particularly emphasized were the nationalization of the land and the introduction of a system of democratic local administration.[2] This announcement

---

[1] Estimates of numbers vary. The front-line 'First Division' totalled some 13,000, the 'People's Militia' was considerably larger (see *Nation*, 25 October 1954).

[2] Full text given in Nu, *Towards Peace and Democracy*, pp. 92–97.

was headlined in the British and American Press as the signal for U Nu's accession to Communism, but to the majority of the PVO's it was not enough. During the following weeks a few of the *Yebaws* accepted U Nu's plan, some openly expressed their hostility to him. One such group was arrested on 24 June. Sections of the army began to side with the rebels; one battalion (6th Burma Rifles) stationed in Pegu District mutinied on 16 June and some of its members went over to the Communists. In July the tussle reached a climax. Within the Government the Socialists made a bid for power; U Nu resigned on the 16th, but the Socialists found themselves opposed by all the independents, the leaders of the frontier peoples, and the Karens; on the 26th U Nu agreed to stay on in office. Two days later the PVO began to 'go underground', probably 60 per cent. of them resorting to arms.[1] A police raid on the PVO headquarters in Pazundaung in east Rangoon failed to capture Bo Po Kun and the other leaders. Two weeks later two more ex-PBF battalions of the army mutinied. These were the 1st Burma Rifles, with headquarters at Thayetmyo, and the 3rd Burma Rifles stationed at Mingaladon. Both battalions were commanded by former members of the 'Thirty Comrades', who now decided to make a bid for political power. Demands were made for portfolios in the Cabinet, and when these were rejected the 1st Burma Rifles set out to capture Rangoon and take over the Government. They were halted at Kyungale, just north of Tharrawaddy, by loyal troops in an engagement on 9 August. The 3rd battalion, till then inactive, set out to link up with the shaken 1st battalion, but their convoy was attacked by Burma Air Force machines at Wanetchaung (10 August) and dispersed. The army mutineers abandoned any definite offensive plan, but seized Thayetmyo and Prome. Units of the Union Military Police (largely recruited from the PBF and PVO) also went underground, taking arms and cash to the value of 119 lakhs from government treasuries. Eighty-eight police stations were in rebel hands (out of a total of 311), trains and river steamers had almost ceased to run outside Rangoon, and martial law was in force in some districts. Rumour was rife: Indian troops were disembarking, the Fourteenth Army was on its way back. Certainly, the truth was no less fantastic.

At this crisis the Government had to lean heavily on the support of the minorities and especially upon the six battalions of Karen and Kachin Rifles. These were the troops which recaptured Prome, Thayetmyo, and the Pyinmana area for

---

[1] Nu, *Towards Peace and Democracy*, pp. 149–52.

the Government. Smith-Dun, the Karen Commander-in-Chief, was given overall command of the defence and police forces with the rank of Lieutenant-General, Bo Ne Win was placed in charge of the army as his deputy, and Major-General Tun Hla Oung (an ex-Sandhurst regular and prisoner of war under the Japanese) became Inspector-General of Police.[1]

There were disgruntled Karens who wished to take advantage of the Government's helplessness. A movement began in Papun to set up a Karen Government; a revolt broke out in Karenni, led by a pretender to the throne; Thaton and Moulmein were occupied at the end of August by Karen rebels, including Union Military Police mutineers. But all the Karen leaders, including Ba U Gyi, Saw Tha Din, and San Po Thin, worked for a peaceful settlement. Moulmein was handed back to the representatives of the Government, and dissident Karen Union Military Police were persuaded to return to duty by Brigadier Kya Doe. The Government, for its part, showed goodwill by appointing a Regional Autonomy Commission (9 September 1948) with the Chief Justice, Sir Ba U, as Chairman. Of the 28 members, 6 were Karens, 6 were Mons, 5 Arakanese, 7 Burmans, and 4 came from the other frontier peoples. Unlike the 1947 Committee, this body was genuinely representative of the minorities. The Commission was empowered to inquire into the question of autonomy for Karens, Mons, and Arakanese. In return, Saw Ba U Gyi pledged the loyalty of the Karen National Union to the Government. But much mutual suspicion remained. Even U Nu, the AFPFL leader most sympathetic to the Karen cause, stated 'I am cent per cent in disagreement with the present creation of separate states [for Mons, Karens, and Arakan]',[2] and many AFPFL and PVO leaders, lacking the goodwill of U Nu, nurtured pride and hate in their minds. Among the Karens there were feather-brained optimists who imagined that they could have complete independence—'like Laos', they said. British friends who had been ashamed at the abandonment of the Karens by the British Government encouraged them to believe that they would receive weapons and other aid from overseas. The activities of Lieut.-Colonel J. C. Tulloch, M.C., in Calcutta and Alexander Campbell of the *Daily Mail* in Rangoon (both formerly of Force 136) were discovered by the Burma Government, and Campbell was expelled from Burma.

At this moment one of the few influential Burmans, aloof

---

[1] *Nation*, 14 August 1948.
[2] *Towards Peace and Democracy*, p. 151.

from political and communal rivalries, was removed from the Government. U Tin Tut was assassinated on 18 September by the hirelings of a political opponent under circumstances which have never been satisfactorily explained.[1] For the second time death removed a keystone of the Union.

Meanwhile the insurrection of Communists, PVO's, and army mutineers was checked, and in many areas the rebels began to lose heart. In December the Communists in central Burma suffered a heavy defeat. Than Tun and Ghoshal were chased out of their stronghold, Pyinmana, and 3,000 of their fighters surrendered at Toungoo. These successes were gained by the 1st Karen Rifles and the 1st Kachins. Outstanding among the Kachins was their adjutant, Captain Naw Seng, of the war-time Kachin Levy, holder of the Burma Gallantry Medal with bar. His raids upon Communist villages were ruthlessly effective. A peace mission, headed by Sir U Thwin, made contact with the PVO and in October a declaration was signed by the members of the mission and three PVO leaders stating that understanding had been reached, and that the PVO would make 'unconditional surrender' to the Government. This declaration was repudiated by the Central Committee of the PVO, but nevertheless many of its adherents gave up fighting for the more congenial pastime of ravaging the countryside. The old BIA-Karen conflict was played upon, and in many areas the Government was powerless to intervene. Karen leaders meeting in conference at Bassein 'resolved that the KNU shall accept responsibility for safeguarding lives and property . . . in Karen majority areas'.[2] Late in 1948 Karen para-military formations were quietly being raised. Their name was the Karen National Defence Organization (KNDO), their commander Mahn Ba Zan, and their cap badge a bugle and cock.[3] Their strength only became clear when it was realized that the Twante canal, on the doorstep of Rangoon, had passed into their control. The extremists amongst the Karens now began to force the pace. It seems probable that Saw Sankey and Mahn Ba Zan tried to persuade the Kachins to enter into an alliance. The two Karens are said to have boasted that they could seize Rangoon within a week.[4] This was reported to U Nu, who passed orders to increase the security forces. By the end of 1948 over 100 territorial units (*Sitwundans*) were being

---

[1] Tin Tut resigned from the post of Foreign Minister on 16 August 1948 to take up the appointment of Inspector-General of the Auxiliary Forces with the rank of Brigadier.

[2] *Nation*, 22 December 1948.

[3] ibid., 10 December 1948.

[4] See Nu, *Towards Peace and Democracy*, pp. 212–13.

raised. Most of the recruits came from the adherents of the Socialists and the Yellow (pro-Government) PVO's. So there were thousands of trigger-happy Karen and Burmese amateur soldiers spoiling for a fight which was not long to be delayed.

It would be profitless to attempt to establish who offered the first, and most, provocation. The conflagration seems to have started on Christmas Eve 1948 when, in Palaw township of Mergui District, Burmese members of the Auxiliary Union Military Police entered churches in eight villages where Karen Christians were at worship and murdered more than eighty among them; these attacks were planned by the PVO in the knowledge that Karen Union Military Police had recently been withdrawn from the areas and disarmed.[1] A number of clashes between KNDO's and PVO's followed, the latter claiming to operate in the name of the Government. At this time the Socialists were negotiating with the army mutineers, the PVO, and the Communists, to obtain their co-operation against the KNDO.[2] In many areas government forces disarmed Karen village guards, and in the prevailing atmosphere of mounting hysteria the Karens believed that they were being deprived of their arms only so that they could not resist massacre. Their fears were fed by the bombardment of a village in Taikkyi township, some forty miles north of Rangoon, by auxiliary military police led by Bo Sein Hman, lately a PVO Cabinet Minister. Here 20 houses were destroyed and over 150 Karens killed, 30 being deliberately executed.[3] In reply the KNDO raided the armoury at Insein and the treasury at Maubin; in turn, the 4th Burma Rifles burnt the American Baptist Mission school at Maubin. All over the Delta the night sky turned red as villages burned. The Government looked on, seemingly helpless, in the face of these outbreaks, and tacitly accepted the claims of both the KNDO and the PVO to be working for the Government.[4]

At this moment of crisis the Government was facing financial collapse owing to the virtual cessation of land revenue collection, and the impossibility of exporting rice and timber with communications frozen. U Nu decided to impose salary cuts both upon the civil service and the Cabinet.[5] The All-Burma Ministerial Services Union promptly challenged the Cabinet's

[1] *Nation*, 6 January 1949.
[2] ibid., 27 December 1951.
[3] ibid., 16 January 1949.
[4] Nu, *Towards Peace and Democracy*, pp. 214–15.
[5] The cuts ranged from 50 per cent. for the Cabinet to 15–30 per cent. for officials and peons.

decision, while the Cabinet resigned on 21 January to permit U Nu to reduce its numbers.

Tempers grew ever more uncertain. The Rangoon Press was flogging up public opinion against the Karens by publishing the wildest stories about 'Karen provocation': only the *Nation* attempted to steer a non-partisan course. Amongst the AFPFL leaders only U Nu spoke in pacific tones, insisting that there was 'no Karen problem', only 'the problem of good citizens and bad citizens'.[1] For his pains, he was nicknamed 'Karen Nu'.[2] On their side, the Karen leaders still talked of co-operation, but in churches throughout the land Karen pastors, taking their text from Exodus—the lesson of Moses in Egypt—were preaching the lawfulness of leading their nation from out of the hands of the unbelievers. The climax came at the end of January. An attack was launched on Bassein town by the KNDO, and the government forces led by San Po Thin (now Brigadier and Special Commissioner for Bassein) were pinned down in one corner of the town. Two days later a battalion of the Burma Rifles drove the KNDO away. On 31 January a battle developed in Thamaing, a Rangoon suburb. It may have arisen out of the government order for the disarming of the Karens, it may have followed a KNDO bid to seize Rangoon. The situation was hopelessly confused; panic reigned in the city and the Government concentrated all available force against the Karens. The next day, 1 February, General Smith-Dun, the Karen Commander-in-Chief, was sent on indefinite leave (from which he was never recalled) and Ne Win took over the armed forces. In Ahlone the Karen quarter was set ablaze and fire-engines were prevented from reaching the area. As the Karens rushed in terror from their flaring homes they were shot down. At the same hour Karens raided Mingaladon Air Force Armoury, carrying off arms and ammunition. The KNDO was declared an unlawful association. The Mon National Defence Organization, the military wing of the Mon Freedom League (President, Nai Ba Lwin), was also declared illegal. The KNDO forces, which had for some days been concentrating near Insein, immediately seized this key town. The battle was joined.

As this news became known in the districts, it was the signal for every rowdy and fanatic to snatch up arms. Three Karen battalions, led by their officers, threw in their lot with their brothers,[3] and Karens all over the country responded to the cry 'Fight or perish'. Victory for the Karens could only come

---

[1] Speech of 1 February 1949, *Towards Peace and Democracy*, p. 167.
[2] Nu, *From Peace to Stability* (Rangoon, 1951), p. 70.
[3] 1st Karens at Toungoo, 2nd Karens at Prome, and 3rd Karens twenty miles south of Prome.

from a lightning seizure of Rangoon, but clearly they had prepared no co-ordinated plan of attack. Their scratch forces penetrated to within four miles of the city, but could not break through the line held by the Government's defenders—regulars, military police, auxiliaries (largely Gurkhas and Anglo-Burmans)—and their seeming allies, the PVO. Two of the rebel Karen battalions set out towards Rangoon, but they were held by government troops in Tharrawaddy District, and were strafed by the Burma Air Force. Within two weeks the Karens were driven back on to the defensive; they dug in, their foxholes about one mile in front of Insein. Of the Insein force, about 200 were army men, the remainder, about 800, were civilians.

Meanwhile the Government was undergoing attacks from its rear. The All-Burma Ministerial Services Union reacted to the January pay cut, without consideration of the enemy at the gate, by calling a strike of all government servants. On 7 February, all over Burma, the strikers came out: in most districts they were not joined by the police but the closing down of all government offices was the final blow in the collapse of the administration. There were mass demonstrations in the heart of Rangoon. The Executive Committee of the White PVO which, after the Karen revolt, had returned to some sort of alliance with the AFPFL, called for the overthrow of the Nu Government: to add point to their demands, the PVO began to drill with rifles in Bandoola Square The university students, almost as a matter of course, joined the strikers, and on the 16th the Railway Union declared a strike. Amid the confusion, U Nu and his supporters kept at their jobs. Parliament continued to meet, and indeed passed some highly important local government legislation. The people of the city continued to enjoy life: there were race meetings, cinemas, and for the more adventurous, special bus services to the Insein front where, for one rupee, you could take a pot-shot at the Karens: and all the while, in U Nu's words 'daylight dacoities were the order of the day, even in the heart of Rangoon'.[1]

If there was stalemate at Insein, there was activity in plenty elsewhere. In central Burma the rebel lead was taken by Captain Naw Seng, the terror of the Pyinmana Communists. That a Kachin should be harassing Burmese villages was repugnant to many influential people and, on the eve of the Karen revolt, Naw Seng seems to have been about to face a Court of Inquiry. He therefore came in with the Karens for mixed reasons, persuading numbers of the 1st Kachins to

[1] *Towards Peace and Democracy*, p. 201.

follow him. The obvious course would seem for the 1st Kachins and the 1st Karens to head south, to assault Rangoon; but instead, Naw Seng persuaded these troops to turn north.[1] With great speed a motorized column raced north, capturing in rapid succession Pyinmana, Yamethin, and Meiktila on 20 February, Kyaukse and the hill-station of Maymyo on the 21st. At Maymyo many Karen troops had been interned: many now joined the rebels, but some (including General Smith-Dun) steadfastly refused. Regrouping, the rebels went on to capture Myingyan, Myitnge, and, on 13 March, Mandalay—despite the arming of 3,000 PVO's for the defence of the city. The attitude of the PVO throughout this period was opportunist and equivocal. Because of their protests of loyalty they were armed and given administrative responsibility, but apart from venting their hate on unarmed Karen villagers they were valueless to the Government, and wherever opportunity arose they ejected the government officials and set up their own 'administration', as at Yenangyaung, Prome, Thayetmyo, Minbu, Magwe, Henzada, and Tharrawaddy.[2] Pegu was half ruled by the PVO and half occupied by government troops. The fog of war was made more obscure by the close Press censorship and the breakdown of all means of communication. At Pakokku the commanding officer of a Chin battalion, failing to receive orders and believing that all government had come to an end, evacuated the town (letting in the PVO) and marched his men back to the Chin hills.[3] The Communists were able also to exploit the collapse of authority to regain and enlarge their power: in Prome they ruled alongside the PVO; at Mandalay they took over the civil administration by agreement with the PVO's enemies, the Karens.

The Government scraped together companies of loyal troops, from Fourteenth Army scrap dumps they assembled one or two tanks, while R.A.F. other ranks from the British Military Mission manufactured crazy bombs which were dropped from trainer aircraft. With half a dozen Dakotas the Government were able to maintain some sort of liaison with the towns remaining in their control, while the Burma Air Force was

[1] At Thawatti in Yamethin District (the headquarters of the 1st Kachins at the time of the rising) the author was informed by local residents that Naw Seng's decision was made after a mysterious visit by an aeroplane from Siam. There does not appear to be any documentary evidence to confirm these assertions.

[2] U Win, as Special Commissioner in charge of Upper Burma, stated bluntly that the PVO were 'all enemies of the state . . . all they could be depended upon to do was to harass the army from the rear' (*Nation*, 7 September 1949). Five PVO leaders were sentenced to death (ibid., 2 November 1954) for high treason, as a result of their conduct in Minbu, Magwe, and Myingyan Districts.

[3] *Nation*, 26 May 1949.

able to machine-gun convoys and give warning of enemy troop concentrations.

Midway through March, U Nu flew to Upper Burma to tour round the districts to the west of the Irrawaddy still under government rule, and to discuss plans for the recapture of Mandalay. During his absence members of the Cabinet became despondent at the failure to check the Karens and at public criticisms of their failure. Four PVO and Socialist Ministers had already resigned; the remaining members of these groups wished to follow suit. A signal was dispatched to U Nu suggesting that the AFPFL should hand the Government over to the Communists. The Prime Minister at once flew back to Rangoon. He found that the Cabinet had approached Than Tun, offering to give way to him and stipulating only that U Nu should remain Prime Minister, and that they should be guaranteed freedom from trial before the Communist terrorist People's Courts. Once again the Communists over-estimated the strength of their position. A conference convened at Yenangyaung rejected these terms.[1] U Nu firmly repudiated any such capitulation. The Socialists and PVO's thereupon insisted on tendering their resignation (2 April), but U Nu announced that he would carry on.[2] He rebuilt his Cabinet with the co-operation of Independents, notably of the leaders of the minorities (of thirteen Cabinet Ministers, six were Burmese, six from the frontier peoples, and one Arakanese). Lieut.-General Ne Win became Deputy Prime Minister and Minister for Home Affairs and Defence. U E Maung, a Judge of the Supreme Court, became Foreign Minister and took charge of four other portfolios (Judicial, Rehabilitation, Public Health, and Local Government). U Tin, Finance Minister, assumed responsibility for two other ministries (Commerce and Supply, Industry and Mines).

At the same time the Government attempted to negotiate with the Karens: a Protection Committee had been formed, consisting of Burmans in whom the Karens would have confidence, such as Sir Ba U, Justice E Maung, and Professor Hla Bu (formerly Principal of Judson College), as well as Karens loyal to the Government, notably Mrs. Ba Maung Chain, daughter of Sir San C. Po, and the Revd. Francis Ahmya. Several missions to the Karen headquarters were made, mostly by Mrs. Ba Maung Chain, to urge Ba U Gyi and his colleagues to negotiate. They replied that they would meet the Government

---

[1] ibid., 14 January 1954.
[2] Sources for these events are: Nu, *From Peace to Stability*, pp. 202-3; *Nation*, 18 June 1954 (speech of Thakin Tin).

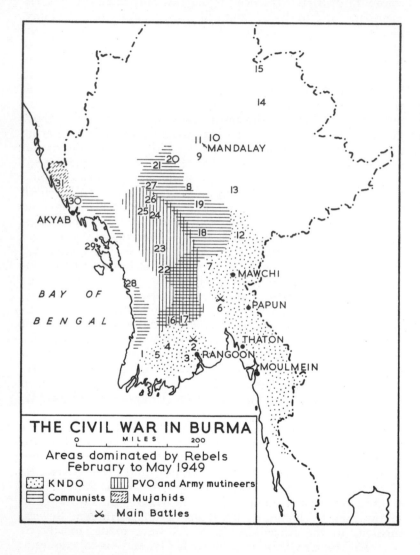

THE CIVIL WAR IN BURMA

0   MILES   200

Areas dominated by Rebels
February to May 1949

KNDO   PVO and Army mutineers
Communists   Mujahids
Main Battles

TOWNS CAPTURED BY THE REBELS IN 1949

(NOTE: Mawchi, Papun, and Thaton were already in KNDO hands.)

KNDO

1. Bassein (25–29 Jan. 1949).
2. Insein (31 Jan.–22 May 1949)
3. Twante (1 Jan.–13 June 1949).
4. Pantanaw (? Apr. 1949–10 Dec. 1950).
5. Einme (1 Feb. 1949–11 Nov. 1950).
6. Nyaunglebin (20 Apr. 1949–25 Feb. 1950).
7. Toungoo (25 Jan. 1949–19 Mar. 1950).
8. Meiktila (20 Feb.–23 Mar. 1949).
9. Kyaukse (with Communists, 21 Feb.–26 June 1949).
10. Maymyo (21 Feb.–17 Apr. 1949).
11. Mandalay (with Communists, 13 Mar.–24 Apr. 1949).
12. Loikaw (? Feb. 1949–12 Jan. 1950).
13. Taunggyi (13 Aug.–23 Nov. 1949).
14. Lashio (27 Aug. 1949).
15. Namkhan (31 Aug.–8 Sept. 1949).

Communists

16. Henzada (with PVO, Mar.–27 Aug. 1949).
17. Tharrawaddy (9 Apr.–27 Aug. 1949).
18. Pyinmana (20 Feb. 1949–29 Mar. 1950).
19. Yamethin (20 Feb.–? May 1949).
20. Myingyan (23 Feb.–10 July 1949).
21. Pakokku (Mar. 1949–29 Apr. 1950).

PVO and Army Mutineers

22. Prome (9 Aug.–9 Sept. 1948 and 1 Feb. 1949–19 May 1950).
23. Thayetmyo (8–30 Aug. 1948 and 17 Mar. 1949–5 Oct. 1950).
24. Magwe (25 Feb. 1949–8 Apr. 1950).
25. Minbu (25 Feb. 1949–15 Apr. 1950).
26. Yenangyaung (23 Feb.–10 June 1949).
27. Chauk (23 Feb.–? June 1949).
28. Sandoway (10 June 1949–27 Oct. 1950)
29. Kyaukpyu (10 June–15 July 1949).

Mujahids

30. Rathedaung (with Communists, 1 Jan.–4 Feb. 1950).
31. Buthidaung (1 Jan.–4 Feb. 1950).

only provided that the British Ambassador would guarantee the terms of the settlement. This being out of the question, a compromise was reached whereby all the Commonwealth ambassadors in Rangoon urged the Karens to negotiate under a guarantee of safe passage. For a week the guns were silent in front of Insein while the negotiations proceeded. A provisional surrender agreement was reached on 5 April. Saw Ba U Gyi intimated that he would have to obtain the assent of his comrades at the Karen 'capital', Toungoo, with whom he was in radio contact. The final signing of the agreement was arranged for the 8th. Saw Ba U Gyi did not appear until the evening; and then he brought fresh proposals. Two of the up-country leaders, Saw Aung Sein and Saw Hunter Thahmwe, had rejected the agreed terms and put forward conditions tantamount to an armistice between equal governments. These suggestions were, of course, unacceptable to the Government. Next day the fighting was renewed. Slowly the Karens were worn down. Naw Seng and the Karen rebels in Upper Burma now realized that their victories in the north had exerted no influence on the main issue. A column of some 2,000 men, led by Naw Seng, now set out for the south. Naw Seng reckoned to take Pegu on 26 April and Rangoon on 1 May. Pressing down through central Burma they were within 100 miles of Rangoon when they were opposed at Nyaunglebin by the crack 2nd battalion of the Burma Rifles, with Kachins, Gurkhas, and Burmese in its ranks. For three days the battle was fought out, and at last the 2nd battalion was forced to retire. But Naw Seng's troops were tired and their ammunition depleted after the struggle. Many returned to Toungoo.

With the last days of April went the last opportunities for the rebels to succeed. A great moral victory was the recapture of Mandalay on 24 April. Throughout the districts, men began to see that the Government was winning. On the 30th the strike of civil servants collapsed, and almost all crept back to their offices. Steadily, the Karens were driven out of their positions at Insein: the seminary, the railway workshops, the veterinary college were wrested from them, and on 22 May, after a siege of 112 days, the Karens retreated across the Hlaing River. Despite a colossal expenditure of ammunition, the destruction of men and materials was not very heavy.

Many of the KNDO (probably including Saw Ba U Gyi) judged that, as all hope of defeating the AFPFL Government had faded, they should make what terms they could. But the extremists, led by Hunter Thahmwe and Mahn Ba Zan, insisted on continuing the fight: all 'Karen country' was still firmly under their control, and with the mines of Mawchi and Tenasserim within their hands they had valuable sources of revenue for the purchase of arms and other materials. Among the other rebels there were similar divisions. At a conference held in Magwe in mid-May Bo Po Kun, the PVO leader, advocated coming to terms, but Thakin Than Tun insisted that they must fight on.[1]

The Government still had fresh blows to withstand. In June the 26th battalion, Union Military Police, mutinied in Arakan and two major towns, Kyaukpyu and Sandoway, were lost. With the *Mujahids* in the north and the Red Flags in the interior, government authority in Arakan was confined virtually to the port of Akyab. Throughout the monsoon months the Government slowly built up its forces and, one by one, towns were retaken: in June Kyaukse, Twante, Thaton, Yenangyaung, and Nyaungu; in July Myingyan and Tharrawaddy. August saw another bold thrust by Naw Seng. Striking up from Karenni, which was firmly in KNDO hands, the Karens occupied Taunggyi—probably with the connivance of dissatisfied Shan leaders. Naw Seng's plan must have been for a united rising of all the hill peoples: he pressed on to Lashio (27 August), but loyal Shan chiefs and army units were soon after him. He made a stand at Namkhan (31 August–8 September) and then hurried down towards Bhamo, where he hoped to rouse his fellow Kachins, especially the Nung tribe. He was stopped by another Kachin, Brigadier Louis Lazum Tang, and his forces were badly routed. Naw Seng retreated into the high hills of the Northern Shan States, and in the end crossed over into China where today he is reliably reported to be Colonel of a mixed, partly Kachin, battalion in Chinese service.

This was the last offensive in which the rebels made the running. By November 1949 initiative had passed to the government forces who re-took Taunggyi (23 November 1949) and the two main KNDO centres in the Delta, Yandoon and Danubyu. The war of spectacular gains and losses was now over; the next phase was the slow recapture of the district headquarters and other towns in rebel hands.

What were the numbers of the contestants in the field in 1949? A few months later U Nu estimated the rebel strength at 10,000 KNDO and 10,000 Communists. About half this number were deserters from the army, military police, and other services,[2] but despite this nucleus of trained men, the rebels

---

[1] *Nation*, 22 May 1949.

[2] See Nu in ibid., 22 May, 1950, and *From Peace to Stability*, p. 202. With characteristic sympathy, U Nu estimated the proportion of the Karen people who were pro-KNDO at 5 per cent.

were largely lacking in discipline and cohesion. The Government had at its disposal some six loyal regular battalions, about fifteen military police battalions[1] of lower quality, and thousands of hastily raised, undisciplined 'levies'. Numbers were on the rebels' side, but in arms and equipment the Government was superior. As to the costs of the rebellion, U Tin, in his budget speech in September 1949, revealed the losses up to then as 330 lakhs looted from treasuries, 1,978 lakhs' damage to Union property (including a bill for Burma Railways of 1,085 lakhs), and a loss on the land revenue not collected of 300 lakhs. U Nu later gave an estimate of the cost of material destruction during this period as 322 crores.[2]

The next year, 1950, was one of slow consolidation. The first big success was the capture of Toungoo (19 March), the capital of the rebel Karen State, 'Kawthulay'.[3] Thereby the Government gained control of almost all the important centres on the main Rangoon–Mandalay railway: but with the track largely torn up, bridges blown, and guerrillas active it was not possible to open up the line. Meanwhile, the alliance between Communists and PVO's broke down. The PVO drove the White Flags out of Thayetmyo town after heavy fighting, and clashes followed in their joint 'capital', Prome. This opened the way for a government offensive, and on 19 May Prome was retaken by the 2nd Chins. In May the Government issued a revised Amnesty Order, promising immunity to all insurgents who surrendered. As other district towns were recaptured U Nu was able to claim some success for his 'Peace Within One Year' campaign, and on 19 July 1950 the troublesome PVO was at last officially disbanded: hopes that the rebel PVO's would thereupon come in and surrender were not, however, realized. In August the KNDO received a heavy blow when Saw Ba U Gyi was surprised and killed in his jungle hide-out near Kawkareik (12 August). He was succeeded by Saw Hunter Thahmwe as Head of Kawthulay, and Colonel Min Maung as commander of the military forces. The year ended with the seizure of Einme, the last and strongest KNDO bastion in the Delta.

The year 1951 saw the slow process of attrition carried further. In the fight against the KNDO the two sides reached something like a stalemate. The main KNDO forces were driven back into the hills beyond the Salween into which the government forces could not, as yet, penetrate. South of

[1] Author's estimate from indirect evidence.
[2] About £248 million (see *From Peace to Stability*, p. 134). U Tin's budget speech is given in Dept. of Information, *Burma's Freedom, Second Anniversary*, pp. 98–106.
[3] Kawthulay—'Flowery Land'.

Taunggyi, Hla Pe and the Taungthu insurgents were invulnerable. The Delta Karens retreated into the foothills north of Bassein, and into dense jungle, swamps, and mangrove where strangers could not find them. The heart of Karen land across the Salween was still theirs, and morale remained high. Hopes were still fixed on the mirage of foreign aid, and their leaders were for ever planning the advance which they would make, as soon as they had the tanks and planes which would assuredly come—from somewhere. The Communists also put their faith in foreign aid to bring them victory. The Chinese Communists established themselves in neighbouring Yunnan late in 1949: surely they would assist their comrades in Burma? But in truth there is no real evidence of any such co-operation. During 1950, following the United Nations advance to the Yalu River and Chinese intervention in Korea, when a general war appeared possible, the Burma Communists concentrated their forces in Katha District, ready to link up with the Chinese army if it should take the ancient Bhamo invasion route into Burma.[1] But there is no evidence that any contact ensued. Next year, 1951, Than Tun planned to capture Mandalay by forces operating from the Shweli Valley in the Northern Shan States. But the army forestalled these plans by its own 'Operation Shweli' which broke the Communist formations, while a further column succeeded in breaking into Than Tun's stronghold, 'Sunflower Camp'. Thereafter, the 'People's Army' was never able to function as a military force, but broke up into bands of jungle guerrillas.

And so, by the end of 1951, the rebels no longer stood as alternatives to the AFPFL Government; some security returned to Burma.[2] But the government mastery was limited: outside the gates of the towns, its authority ceased at sunset.[3] There were vast areas of 'no man's land' through which the Government might send its armed convoys by day, while rebel agents collected 'supplies' and 'taxes' by night. However, the insurgents were now pinned down, and the Government could begin to plan for the future instead of improvising from day to day.

Led by U Nu, the Government now began to look beyond the bitterness of party and communal conflict to a new view of

[1] *Nation*, 25 June 1954.
[2] Martial law, imposed throughout wide areas, now began to end: on 19 February 1951 in Pegu and Insein Districts; on 1 June 1951 in Mandalay, Meiktila, Toungoo, and Prome Districts, the Kachin hills, Shweli (Northern Shan States).
[3] Kyaw Nyein, speaking as a Minister, averred that less than half Burma was under the control of the police (see *Nation*, 22 April 1951). A correspondent of *The Times* (13 March 1951) estimated that of the 311 police stations in Burma only 233 were in government hands.

society. The Prime Minister was moved to declare that 'the task of building up the stability of our country is an extremely difficult one'; men's minds had become set in a negative mould because 'so far, the course we have had to follow has been a course of destructive politics in order to destroy imperialist domination'.[1] The toll of destruction represented a formidable debit balance which the Government had first to wipe off, but fortunately the toll in lives had not been heavy.[2] In August the Government felt sufficiently sure of the security situation to summon a mass meeting at Rangoon to hear the new plans for a Welfare State. But within two months the Union was confronted with its gravest threat since 1949: the menace of the Chinese Nationalists[3] in Kengtung State. That the peril was not recognized earlier must be attributed to the remoteness of Kengtung from the life of the rest of the Union. Separated by the roaring Salween River and by high mountain ranges from the rest of the Shan States and Burma proper, it has a separate history with ties, political and economic, that run south to Siam rather than west to Burma.

After the collapse of the Chiang Kai-shek régime in Yunnan towards the end of 1949, a number of Nationalist troops straggled over into the Wa States and Kengtung. They were led by General Limi of the Eighth Army, General Liu Kuo Chwan of the Twenty-sixth Army, and Major-General Mah Chaw Yee of the 93rd Division. These troops were concentrated on the road leading down to Siam, with headquarters at Tachilek. At this stage the KMT behaved as an organized army on foreign soil: they kept to themselves, and did not molest the local population. Their strength was about 2,500. Units of the Burma Army[4] moved against them in July 1950 and took Tachilek. This success was earned at the expense of rebel revival in Burma proper; Pakokku, after three months in government hands, fell again to the Communists. The KMT regrouped at Monghsat and enlisted recruits from local Shans and tribesmen, bringing their numbers up to 4,000 by April 1951. Next month, General Limi launched an offensive into Yunnan. This was a failure, and within two weeks his forces were back on Burmese soil. In the autumn of 1951 a Chinese Colonel was arrested, under circumstances that are not altogether clear,[5] by Burmese security police near Kengtung town.

[1] *Nation*, 21 July 1951.
[2] Government casualties: 3,424 dead, including 1,352 army personnel (ibid., 16 September 1952).
[3] Invariably called the KMT in Burma.
[4] 1st and 3rd Kachins, and 4th Burma Regiment (Gurkhas).
[5] The allegation is made that he was held for ransom.

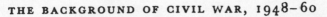

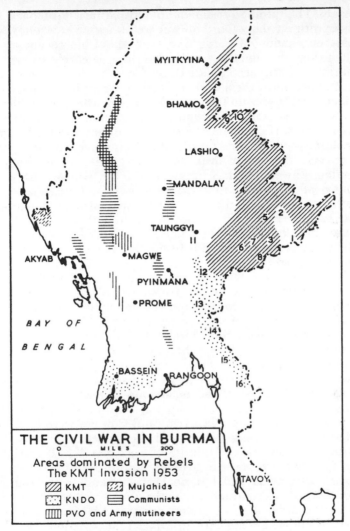

MYITKYINA

BHAMO

LASHIO

MANDALAY

TAUNGGYI

MAGWE

AKYAB

PYINMANA

PROME

BAY OF

BENGAL

BASSEIN

RANGOON

TAVOY

THE CIVIL WAR IN BURMA
0   MILES   200

Areas dominated by Rebels
The KMT Invasion 1953

KMT   Mujahids
KNDO   Communists
PVO and Army mutineers

THE KMT INVASION, 1953
Places mentioned in the text

1. Tachilek.
2. Kengtung town (threatened)
3. Monghsat
4. Monghsu
5. Mongpu-awn
6. Mongpan

7. Wan Hsa La
8. Monghan
9. Muse
10. Kyukhok
11. Yawnghwe
12. Loikaw

KNDO

13. Mawchi
14. Papun

15. Hlaingbwe
16. Kawkareik

The KMT's promptly issued an ultimatum: 'give back the officer within twenty-four hours or we attack'. There followed a panic evacuation of Kengtung, and the Chinese advanced. When they were only five miles from the defenceless town the young Sawbwa, accompanied by an American missionary, went out to meet them and, by sheer persuasion, managed to induce them to give up their attack. Two months later, sufficient Burma forces[1] had arrived to make possible a major attack, driving the KMT back into the border mountains. Once again the Burmese Communists profited by this diversion, being able to reassert their sway over 150 square miles of territory in Sagaing, Shwebo, and Kyaukse Districts.[2] During the early months of 1952 the army therefore switched its forces once again: only one battalion remained on guard in Kengtung. The greater part was employed in 'Operation Liberation' against the Communists; by May Than Tun's forces had taken a beating, several strongholds in the Pyinmana redoubt having been destroyed.[3]

During 1952 the KMT recruited and trained more troops, their numbers rising to 12,000 by the end of the year. Another attempt at a sortie into Yunnan in June was utterly defeated, and led to a change of temper among the KMT. From posing as a 'liberation army' on 'undemarcated territory' they now began to act as though they had acquired some legal right to occupy the borderland. They began to impose taxes on the local people and to impress them into service when required: in fact they reverted to the behaviour of the 'War Lords' of China in the 1920's. An air-strip was built at Monghsat, with regular services to Formosa. Arms and supplies were flown in, and there were strong rumours of the presence of American instructors. Towards the middle of 1952 the KMT extended their territory west of the Salween;[4] their forces also penetrated into the Myitkyina and Bhamo Districts, and to the south a loose alliance was contracted with the KNDO.[5] The scale of this threat, as previously suggested, only made its impact on Burmese understanding late in 1952. One reaction was that of the White Flag Communists who, in the wake of their recent defeats, launched a propaganda campaign for 'national unity'

[1] 1st and 3rd Kachins, 3rd Chins, 2nd Burma Regiment, 13th Battalion, Union Military Police.
[2] According to Bo Khin Maung Gale (see *Nation*, 27 March 1952).
[3] At this period Than Tun's forces totalled some 3,000. Their location: 1st Division, Myingyan District, 2nd Division, Monywa-Shwebo Districts, 3rd Division, Yamethin-Pyinmana, 4th Division, Shan States (see ibid., 8 May 1952).
[4] Martial law was declared in the Southern Shan States on 1 September 1952.
[5] An agreement was said to have been signed between General Limi and 'Brigadier' Saw Shwe in Bangkok in February 1952.

against the KMT. As a preliminary they rebuilt their association with the PVO and the Red Flags. The prospect of a *rap-
prochement* with the Communists was disagreeable to many
PVO's, but the 'old guard', such as Bo Po Kun, had lost
ground to a new group of 'Progressives'.[1] On 1 October a
Triple Alliance Pact was signed near Monywa, laying down
terms of co-operation and demarcating zones throughout
Burma wherein each group would have the power.[2] The
appeals issued by the Triple Alliance to the country made little
impression. The Alliance was in two minds whether to attempt
to attract, or to undermine the AFPFL.

Towards the end of 1952 the KMT carried out a definite plan
of attack. On 4 January 1953 their 1st Guerrilla Division
occupied Monghsu State, deposing the Sawbwa. On 8 February
a combined KMT and KNDO force attacked Loikaw, capital
of Kayah State, but failed to overrun the town. Three days
later they captured the capital of Mongpan State, and then
Kyukhok and Muse. Later in the month they appeared in
Yawnghwe State, within twenty miles of Taunggyi. This was
the limit of their advance. Early in March the Burma Army
swung into a counter-offensive. Three brigades were committed, under the command of Brigadier Douglas Blake.[3]
There was a speedy advance to the Salween River. After a
battle near Wan Hsa La, a ferry village, the bodies of three
white men were discovered; among their possessions were letters
with New York and Washington addresses. The KMT fought
back when pursued into Kengtung State, fiercely attempting
to recapture Mongpu-awn and Mongpan, garrisoned by
Union troops. Meanwhile, the focus of events shifted to the
United Nations General Assembly where, in April, a resolution
was adopted deploring the activities of the KMT and recommending negotiations for the withdrawal of the intruders.
Thereafter, a series of meetings took place at Bangkok from
which, after much Chinese prevarication, emerged an agreement for the evacuation of 2,000 troops (October 1953).
During the interim period contacts between both sides were
restricted to patrol brushes. The evacuation took place during
November and December, being carried out by General
Chennault's Air Transport Company. Into the stipulated 2,000
(actually 1,925), the Chinese introduced boys, Shans, and other
non-belligerents; the arms tendered for surrender were made

[1] The PVO have been called the 'Green Communists' by U Ba Swe.
[2] Eastern Command=White Flags (the Kachin and Shan States and central
Burma), Western Command=PVO (Chin hills, Arakan), Southern Command=
Red Flags (the Delta and Tenasserim).
[3] 4th, 6th, and 9th Light Infantry Brigades.

up of various museum pieces. The Burmese observers were left feeling thoroughly dissatisfied.

The year 1953 was not entirely dominated by the KMT problem. The Burma Army was now a much larger and more efficient force,[1] and could operate simultaneously against the internal enemies as well. It was a bad year for the KNDO. Several strongholds were captured. Action was particularly heavy along the 150 miles of mountain front: Hlaingbwe headquarters near Thaton fell in May, and on 22 November the Mawchi Mines were recovered by two brigades under the command of Brigadier Kyaw Zaw[2] after five years of occupation. This deprived the KNDO of one of their main sources of revenue: export of ore via Siam had been profitable in a period of high prices. Disheartened, many KNDO now began to surrender.[3] The Communists and PVO, too, were driven out of their strongholds, and even their top leaders had to keep on the run to avoid surprise and capture. In October 1953 the Burma Communist Party (White Flags) and the PVO were at last declared illegal by the Government. All the time the rebels' morale was falling, and their resemblance to bandits became more undeniable. To keep up their strength, they were reduced to shifts and manœuvres whose only plea was expediency. Thus the KNDO concluded an alliance with the KMT, although the outlook of most of their leaders (notably Mahn Ba Zan) had become soaked in Communist doctrine. The KNDO had an agreement with the White Flags for mutual co-operation and the demarcation of 'territory'. Finally, in January 1954, there was a split in the Papun Government, the leader, Saw Hunter Thahmwe (who now calls himself Saw Hunter Kawkasa—'ruler'), repudiated the unholy KMT alliance, and recent utterances have shown a desire to woo the favour of Communist Peking.[4] The Communist-PVO marriage of convenience was kept together only with difficulty, a proposal by Than Tun (October 1953) for a coalition with the AFPFL being defeated. In February 1954 the PVO and the *Mujahids* signed a 'non-aggression pact' to respect each other's territory, even though the *Mujahids* were persecuting and

---

[1] An informed estimate in the *Nation*, 16 April 1953, declared that in January 1952 the Burma Army comprised 9 battalions, expanded to 41 battalions in early 1953. The rebels' strength was estimated as 35,000 in January 1952, plus 7,000 KMT and 2,000 *Mujahids*. In early 1953 the numbers were: rebels, 9,000; KMT, 12,000; *Mujahids*, 300.

[2] 4th Light Infantry Brigade, Kalaw, and 2nd Light Infantry Brigade, Toungoo.

[3] Including Saw Michael, the defender of Sinywa.

[4] Major Saw Osborne and many of his '4th Kawthulay Brigade' (from Bassein District) surrendered in August 1954 in disgust with the Communist alliance.

mutilating any Burman who fell into their hands.[1] Finally, in May 1954, the Triple Alliance collapsed in a welter of mutual recrimination and personal abuse among the rebel leaders.

Early in 1954 the army mounted its largest offensive against the KMT, Operation Bayinnaung, led by Brigadier Kyaw Zaw. When the advance ceased, in April, Monghsat was taken (20 March), followed by Monghan (28 March), and the KMT forces were disorganized and decimated. Thereafter further KMT evacuations were arranged in Bangkok, including the withdrawal of those Chinese Nationalists fighting with the KNDO in Tenasserim.[2] Subsequent estimates put the KMT strength in Burma at about 6,000;[3] they were still capable of taking the field. Desperate efforts were made to storm Monghan (26–27 June) and Monghkak (28 June–9 July), but both ended in bloody KMT defeats.[4] There followed a further collapse in the morale and discipline of the KMT, but there are grounds for supposing that these troops received reinforcements from Formosa during 1954.[5] The Burma Army found it necessary to mount yet another offensive, Operation Yangyiaung, during April and May 1955; once again Brigadier Kyaw Zaw was in command, and his forces numbered almost the strength of a division. KMT losses were officially given as over 500,[6] but it may be doubted whether they were finally dispersed. They still appear to operate under central direction, although scattered along the Kengtung border. They control the local opium trade, manufacture counterfeit currency, and extort 'revenue' from the hill villages within their reach.

While Operation Bayinnaung was still in progress, a subsidiary attack was launched on the KNDO-KMT front in Tenasserim, Operation Sinbyushin (April 1954). This did not attain its ultimate objective, Papun, but many townships and villages were recovered, so that it became immediately possible to hand over powers in the area to the (legal) Karen State Government.

Next came the turn of the Communists: units of the 10th Brigade closed upon Than Tun's forces in Pakokku District.[7]

[1] *Nation*, 24 February 1954.
[2] Total KMT withdrawals numbered 5,328 troops and 1,142 dependants. Of the 1,600 KMT said to be in Tenasserim, some 1,100 were withdrawn.
[3] See 'Report to U.N. General Assembly of Three Nations Supervisory Committee, released 30 September 1954, and separate complaint to the General Assembly filed by Burma, dated 27 September 1954' (quoted *Nation*, 2 October 1954).
[4] The military administration in the Southern Shan States came to an end on 31 July 1954.
[5] cf. *Nation* 8 June 1955. It is suggested that 600 fresh trained troops were smuggled in.
[6] *BWB*, 2 June 1955.
[7] Operation Bandoola.

A column of the 1st Kachins almost succeeded in capturing Than Tun: his camp was seized, but he happened to be absent at that time. Other victories were registered in Katha, Toungoo, and Yamethin Districts. In the autumn the Communists tried to rally their followers with bold directives and the conscription of 'people's militia'; but the steady wearing-down process was not to be halted.

At the end of 1954 a local cancer of long growth, the *Mujahid* menace, was at last excised. Despite several assaults by government forces from 1950 onwards, the *Mujahids* maintained their reign of terror throughout Buthidaung, Maungdaw, and two-thirds of Rathedaung, causing an almost complete exodus of all non-Muslims and many Muslims. For some time there was a suspicion in Burma that there were elements in East Pakistan who were overtly assisting their *Mujahid* co-religionists. But in May 1954 their leader, Cassim, a fisherman, was arrested by the Pakistan authorities and lodged in Chittagong jail. In September 1954 a fast of Arakanese monks at the Sule Pagoda in Rangoon drew widespread attention to the continuance of the terror. An offensive[1] was begun in November, and the main *Mujahid* redoubts were stormed and the leading terrorists killed. The *Mujahid* menace was reduced to very minor proportions.

Early in 1955 the Burma Army launched a new offensive against the KNDO, following a revived sabotage campaign conducted by Bo Soe, the Commander of the '5th Kawthulay Brigade' (strength, 1,400 men) operating north of Thaton. In January 1955 the Rangoon–Moulmein railway was subjected to continual attack, trains being blown up and looted and passengers held for labour and ransom. On 21 January the 5th Light Infantry Brigade launched Operation Aung-theikdi (Final Victory). The KNDO fell back, deep into the jungle, surrendering their strongholds without contest. At length, pushing up an almost impassable hill track, the army penetrated to Papun, the Kawthulay capital, which was captured late in March after seven years in rebel hands.

Is this the end of the KNDO? It may well extinguish the last hopes of those idealists and hot-heads who believed they could secure a 'Karen Country' through force: it will not discourage those KNDO who, without any genuine enthusiasm for Karen nationhood, use the organization as a cover for their banditry and blackmail. Thus the most active leader, Bo Soe, is actually a Burmese Buddhist, and it is said that some half of his followers

[1] Operation Mote-thone (monsoon).

are also Burmese or Indian.[1] His men are heavily armed, unlike the KNDO's of the early days, and they live off 'territory', which is forced to yield a regular levy of blackmail. In addition, travellers and merchants have to pay 'tolls' and 'protection money', and any racket—such as opium smuggling—is given a trial if it seems profitable. This brand of KNDO guerrilla will contrive to hang on for years, slipping over the Siam border when an army or police raid threatens, obtaining recruits from among the growing hooligans of the next generation.[2] Among the Delta KNDO's there are still a few of the old faithful underground, but in general the story is again of banditry and the levying of 'taxes' on fisheries and paddy-fields. One of the areas of greatest strength is Tawgyidan, only twelve miles from Rangoon. It is an area of rubber plantations, which provide ideal cover for guerrillas—and a useful commodity, yielding revenue through black market sales.[3] In this area the KNDO share control with the Red Flags, and this appears to be a regular feature of the Delta today.[4]

There appears to be good reason to suppose that the surviving KNDO leaders have abandoned the somewhat conservative beliefs of their former leaders and are moving towards a Communist order. Thaton Hla Pe, former Cabinet Minister and Taungthu leader, is reported to have become a Communist Party member, and the KNDO leaders on the Salween and in the Delta are said to contemplate renaming their organization as the Kawthulay Revolutionary Council with their military units operating under the name of the Kawthulay People's Revolutionary Army.[5]

The other rebels did not suffer such a dramatic decline in their fortunes as that of the KMT and KNDO in 1954 and 1955, but their numbers dwindled even further. The PVO dispose of perhaps 200 'troops', with some village sympathizers in support. Their petty centres are in the west Chindwin valley and in Thayetmyo District. The White Flags are more numerous. Apart from a few last refugees in the Pyinmana hills, their

---

[1] *Nation*, 27 January 1955.

[2] The KNDO still has a high-sounding military organization: 'General' Min Maung is Commander-in-Chief, with a Delta and a Papun Command. The latter has two 'Divisions', comprising some four brigades: all except Bo Soe's 5th Brigade are of less than battalion strength (see ibid., 30 January 1955). The Delta KNDO's are even more depleted and appear to have almost abandoned regular military formations (see ibid., 19 September 1954). The '1st Delta Rifles' still controls the Danubyu area.

[3] *Nation*, 20, 21, and 22 January 1954 and 11 January 1955.

[4] Travelling in Maubin District, the author asked a friendly lawyer to describe the local insurgents. He said 'We have them all—Communists, PVO's and KNDO's. We cannot tell the difference: all are bandits.'

[5] *Nation*, 26 September 1954 and 14 December 1955.

guerrillas are scattered through the districts along the west bank of the Irrawaddy from Katha to Minbu.[1] Than Tun clings to a hide-out in the remote hill tracts west of the Chindwin. The Red Flags, least numerous of all the rebels, are not the least militant. In Akyab District a Red Flag leader, the 'Bomb Thrower', *Bonbauk* Tha Gyaw, conducts vendettas against his enemies; while U Sein Da, the 'King of Arakan', another Red Flag chief, attempts to unite the different rebel factions in a 'People's Liberation Army'.[2]

U Nu summarized his views of the situation in October 1954 in these terms: 'When insurrection becomes small enough, it is nothing more than dacoity.' Certainly the civil war, which at one time seemed likely to swallow Burma, is no longer a menace to the integrity of the State. Up to the end of 1954 the number of rebels giving themselves up to the government forces had reached 23,228.[3] Of this total some 4,500 were Communists. Some of these persons have subsequently gone underground again, finding it impossible to make a new start in everyday life: but these must be heavily outnumbered by those rebels who have quietly gone back to their villages without going through the formality of surrender.[4] Altogether, the number of guerrillas who are still fighting because of *genuine* political convictions cannot be more than a few hundred. But there are still thousands of 'insurgents' who are merely dacoits. Operating normally in bands of at most a dozen, they can at will make up a force of some hundreds, which will storm some unsuspecting market town and then dissolve and disappear. Their lack of beliefs or organization only makes them a greater danger.

How far has internal security returned to Burma? The rebels are unseen; the government guards are everywhere; and yet the atmosphere of uncertainty and impermanence is ubiquitous.[5] The town of Maubin in the Delta[6] may be cited as an example. Before the war, its population was 8,897. At the 1953 census the number recorded was 23,362, an increase of 160 per cent. Almost all these folk are refugees from the villages, living in temporary *basha* huts along the river bank, because they dare not return to their homes. Their fields are mostly

---

[1] *Nation*, 25 October 1954.
[2] ibid., 31 January 1955.
[3] *BWB*, 22 December 1954.
[4] The author met a number of young men in this category.
[5] The following notes represent nothing more than the author's personal impressions: he was able to travel widely around Burma without any restriction being placed on his movements by the authorities at any time. It is only fair to state that at no time was the author conscious of being in any worse danger than in a London street.
[6] Visited by the author in October 1954.

abandoned; they scratch a living by petty trading or occasional labour. Before the war, law and order was represented by a few dozen civil police. Today a battalion of the Chin Rifles is quartered in the spacious houses of the Deputy Commissioner and the District Judge (these officials now live in the town centre for safety); another battalion of the territorial force, the *Sitwundans*, occupy the old police lines; in addition, there are Peace Guerrillas and town guards. Communication with the outside world is made possible by a tall radio pylon. There is a curfew, and every person entering the town must (or should) report to the authorities for a security check. Outside the town gates is no man's land. There are Karen Peace Guerrillas— mainly ex-rebels—who are playing their own game. And there are other secret men whom the people half-dread and half-admire. They are not seen, but an occasional reminder is given of their presence by the looting of a rice godown, the shooting up of a police post, or an attempt to capture a river steamer.

Maubin may be somewhat less secure than other districts, but nowhere is there unchallenged peace. A scrutiny of elections for rural local authorities which began in May 1954 would illustrate this. Out of the thirty-three districts of Burma proper, it was possible to begin elections only in twelve, because of the widespread unrest. And no district was sufficiently settled to permit elections in every village, even with the assistance of army and police formations.[1] Only in three 'model' districts (Mandalay, Sagaing, and Shwebo) has it been possible to hand over the responsibility for law and order from the army to the Union Military Police and the civil police.[2] Much of the countryside, although under the civil administration, is parcelled out into units ruled by semi-independent leaders; a few miles ruled by the *Sitwundans*, the next circle under the Peace Guerrillas. This means that the villagers feed their guards and provide 'presents' to their captains when they sell the paddy.

Frequently the Government has been compelled to set a thief to catch a thief. Surrendered rebels must be given employment: after years of banditry they will not automatically find an orderly place within the social framework. A most imaginative effort was made to meet the problem with the creation of the Rehabilitation Brigade. The 1st Battalion was raised in April 1950, and its strength early in 1955 was over ten battalions. The training centre, Aung San Myo, near Rangoon, produces

---

[1] cf. Insein District: elections in 234 village tracts, 41 tracts in rebel hands. Kyaukse District: elections in 75 village tracts, 143 tracts in rebel hands.

[2] *Nation*, 26 November 1954. The 11th Infantry Brigade still remains in reserve at Mandalay.

some technicians and mechanics, but the majority of the brigade are employed as 'pioneers', a labour force available for major reconstruction jobs such as the rebuilding of Prome. Despite its rapid expansion, the Rehabilitation Brigade has been able to absorb less than half the surrendered rebels. Many of the remainder have been taken into the auxiliary military formations, and some into the army. These ex-rebels have undergone no change of heart: they became tired of life in the jungle, on the run, so they gave up, but their loyalties—particularly amongst the ex-Communists—are still partly with their former comrades.[1]

On 1 October 1955 the Government introduced the *Pyu Saw Hti* town and village defence scheme.[2] This organization soon became yet another instrument of political manipulation and extortion.

During 1958, the security situation became curiously distorted. On the one hand the 'underground' rebels suffered further setbacks and began to surrender (or, in the euphemistic language preferred, 'entered the light'). On the other hand the recognized political groups increasingly adopted para-military methods both in town and countryside. The most important rebel surrenders were those of U Sein Da, the Arakanese Communist, with 1,000 of his followers, and that of Thaton Hla Pe, 'king' of the Taungthu or Pa-O tribesmen, together with his adherents, virtually bringing the Pa-O revolt to an end. On 30 July the PVO (now People's Comrade Party) renounced the use of force, and on 15 August the party again acquired legal status. At the same time the split in the AFPFL was degenerating at the lower levels into an armed struggle, in which village political bosses increasingly exploited the Pyu Saw Hti. The PCP immediately returned to its old game of terrorizing the villagers. According to General Ne Win 'the situation was closely approaching that sad spectacle of 1948–49'.[3] Units of the UMP began to converge on Rangoon. There was a growing sense of apprehension, and many (including influential Colonels of the Staff) saw only one solution: a military take-over. On 26 October 1958 General Ne Win was asked by U Nu to take charge of the Government, and he assumed office, armed with drastic powers against subversion.

[1] One of the factors in the British success in creating peace in a hostile Upper Burma within five years (1886–90) was their employment of Indian troops and military police who were alien to the local population.

[2] Pyusawhti was, according to the Burmese chronicles, a warrior-prince who reigned from A.D. 167. It is hoped that the scheme will acquire an auspicious tone from association with his heroic name.

[3] Speech by General Ne Win to Parliament, 31 October 1958.

The army tackled the problem primarily as one of suppressing crime rather than of overcoming a politically-motivated insurrection. The public was required to hand in all illicit firearms, and within nine months over 14,000 rifles and other weapons were impounded. The powers of the village headman (who had been the butt of politicians) were restored. A system of informers ('People's Reporters') was developed. The Pyu Saw Hti were disbanded and formed into a Special Police Reserve under some measure of discipline. Trouble-making politicians were arrested: a total of 432, and 153 persons were banished to the Coco Islands. As a result of these measures, the incidence of crimes of violence was reduced to a level approaching that during the British period, while the rebels were harried and hunted down. From a figure of about 9,300, the insurgent forces fell to between 5,000 and 6,000. Official figures of rebel casualties between November 1958 and April 1960 were 2,278 killed, 2,351 wounded, 1,384 captured, and 4,022 surrendered.[1]

However, the period was not altogether one of pacification: a new revolt flared up in the Shan State. In April 1959, some 200 students in Kengtung State 'went underground'; they were persuaded to call off their protest by the personal intervention of the Kengtung Sawbwa. A more serious threat came in November, a revolt of UMP mutineers led by a Wa officer which was joined by several hundred tribesmen. The mutineers occupied Tang-yan, not far from Lashio, but were quickly ejected. Army communiqués discount the revolt as that of military racketeers, but there is some evidence that it forms a protest at the termination of Sawbwa rule in the state.[2]

When Ne Win seized power in March 1962, he proceeded to integrate the security services and posted military officers to the districts to build up 'grass roots' contacts with the rural people. However, the slender sense of confidence which U Nu had established with the border peoples disappeared under the military régime. The revolt in the Shan State grew to embrace many of the hill tribes. Elements among the Kachins resented the transfer of three villages to China and broke into revolt. Attempts to resettle some Kachins in new, planned villages were not welcomed. The Communists and the KNDO, pursued their endless campaign of sabotage and subversion. There were even accounts of a resistance movement organized by Bo Yan Naing and other former constitutional leaders. Early in 1966, General Ne Win admitted that the situation was worse than when he came to power in 1962.

[1] *BWB*, 2 June, 1960.
[2] See p. 163 n.1.

III

POLITICS, THE PRESS, AND PARLIAMENT

POLITICS in pre-war Burma were an affair of cliques and cabals, of alliances based on sectional interests and of management, bribery, and patronage. Then came the Japanese period, with new leaders and a new national coalition, the Anti-Fascist Organization. After independence several elements in the coalition completely abandoned constitutional methods but the parliamentary stage continued to be dominated by the AFPFL, regarding itself as a Freedom Movement, the embodiment of the national will, greater than any party. Because of the minuscule size of the parliamentary opposition group up to the 1956 general election, the AFPFL could ignore its opponents and could afford the luxury of internal arguments. Different groups claimed to represent the legitimate spirit of the 'Burmese Revolution'. For a number of years differences of policy and of personal ambition were kept within bounds, and a 'balance of power' was explicitly recognized. The 1956 election produced a larger and more vigorous opposition and accentuated the internal stresses within the AFPFL. Different forces began to manoeuvre for power and in 1958 the coalition split into two factions. One group, led by U Nu, supported by Thakin Tin and M. A. Raschid, called itself the 'Clean' AFPFL. The second, led by Ba Swe and Kyaw Nyein, called itself the 'Stable' AFPFL. There followed a period of intercine conflict, in which it seemed that Burma might at last develop a two-party system. However, the third general election, held in February 1960, resulted in an overwhelming victory for U Nu. Ba Swe and Kyaw Nyein failed to hold their own seats. In March 1960 the victorious party adopted the name of *Pyidaungsu Ahphwe-gyok* or Union League. The rump of the opposition was left with the now discredited title of AFPFL.

After the years of flux, 1956–60, political support seemed to polarize again behind a party symbolizing the national spirit. This phase proved to be temporary. General Ne Win proceeded to eliminate the open democratic political party from the scene. The search for Socialism through parliamentary techniques was replaced by the authoritarian Burmese Way to Socialism.

The Socialist Party, founded in September 1945, forms a 'party within a party'. It provides the political theory of the AFPFL Government. An outline of this ideology may be studied in a speech delivered by Ba Swe on 18 December 1951.[1]

Marxism is the guide to action in our revolutionary movement, in our establishment of a Socialist Burmese State for workers and peasants. . . . Our revolution is impossible without Marxism as our guide. We must understand this once and for all. [But] only a revolutionary movement which is entirely Burmese, conforming to Burmese methods and principles can achieve any measure of success. By this I do not mean to say that we must throw Russian or Chinese or any other country's methods to the winds. No doubt they are worth studying. . . . Marxist theory is not antagonistic to Buddhist philosophy. The two are, frankly speaking, not merely similar. In fact, they are the same in concept.

There are five fundamentals. They are (1) People's democracy, (2) People's economy, (3) People's education, (4) People's health, and (5) People's social security.

Politically we are independent, economically we are being dominated by Imperialist Capital. Economically we are in bondage.

When will our revolution be achieved? . . . No one is in a position to fix a definite date for the achievement. . . . [But] I can say for certain that we are achieving revolution, stage by stage.

Despite the insistence on Marxism as the basis of party planning, and the frequent citation of pronouncements by Marx, Lenin, and Engels in political speeches, a much closer parallel exists between the Burma Socialist Party and the British Labour Party. As the party which gave independence to Burma, Labour is held by the AFPFL, and the Socialists in particular, in a fraternal or avuncular esteem. The AFPFL programme has a close resemblance to British Labour policy, with nationalization as the foundation of party doctrine, subject to all sorts of modifications in practice, and with social welfare as the goal, rather than the downfall of the capitalist system.

One great difference between British and Burmese socialism, however, lies in the influence within the British party of the trade unions and their hard-headed working-class leaders. The Trades Union Congress (Burma) is little more than an appendage of the Socialist Party and the leaders are, almost without exception, bourgeois intellectuals. Not one Socialist leader comes from a family of 'workers' or 'peasants'.[2] All spring from families of merchants or officials in government service. Of the nine Socialist Party members of the Cabinet in 1955, all except one (Thakin Tin) were former undergraduates of Rangoon University. Some of the Socialists came to politics through

[1] Published by the Information Department, Rangoon, as *The Burmese Revolution*, 1952.

[2] Nu, 'Political leadership is the monopoly of the educated middle classes', *From Peace to Stability*, p. 39.

journalism, the law, teaching, or business: none worked their way up from the ranks of manual labour.

The structure of the Socialist Party remains amorphous and difficult to analyse. It has a central party executive, but no separate local organs in the districts.[1] Socialists continue to play their part in the AFPFL district activities although, from time to time, they have organized 'breakaway' AFPFL committees. Any estimate of Socialist Party membership must be guesswork: the numbers appear to be small,[2] but they form an *élite*, firmly established in positions of authority. The Trades Union Congress (Burma), the All-Burma Peasants' Organization, the Co-operative movement are all Socialist-dominated. The Auxiliary Union Military Police is virtually a Socialist 'private army'. Many leading officials and diplomatic representatives abroad and the chairmen of nationalized undertakings and public corporations are Socialist Party members. Its organization may be amorphous, but it is none the less powerful and able to impress others. During the first years after independence the party aspired to dominate the Government. Its attitude to all who were not in full agreement with its policy and methods was fiercely intolerant, and it built up many enemies, especially among the Press and among the frontier peoples. Consciousness of unpopularity was one of the main reasons for the Socialist resignations from the Cabinet in February and April 1949. U Nu was extremely anxious that the Socialists should not, like the Communists, renounce constitutional methods for force, and he kept the door wide open for renewed co-operation. Late in 1949 he offered portfolios to the party and, after some discussion, three Socialist nominees accepted office in January 1950.[3] For the time being the top leaders, Kyaw Nyein, Ba Swe, and Thakin Lwin, declined to enter the Cabinet.

At this period a crisis was boiling up within the party. An influential group was unwilling to agree to any compromise with capitalism and imperialism; more explicitly, it demanded the severing of the last economic and military ties with Britain and complete alignment with the Soviet bloc. Many verbal concessions were made to this group, but a breach became imminent when, on 1 May 1950, Thakin Lwin as President of the Trades Union Congress (Burma) announced the affiliation

[1] In January 1953 a Socialist conference at Rangoon attended by 125 delegates voted to establish a permanent organization (*Nation*, 16 January 1953).

[2] The *Nation* estimated (3 January 1951) that the Socialist numbers in previous years had totalled some 2,000, but after the split within the party (late 1950) membership was down to 200.

[3] U Win became Minister for Rehabilitation, Kyaw Myint Minister for Industries and Mines (this portfolio is almost a Socialist monopoly), and Bo Khin Maung Gale Minister for Forests and Agriculture.

of the TUC to the Communist World Federation of Trades Unions. After some months of hesitation, Thakin Lwin was expelled from the AFPFL (21 September 1950). His reply was to withdraw the TUC from the AFPFL (7 October). Two months later the Socialist Party was itself split in two. A manifesto signed by forty-three Socialist leaders denounced the Ba Swe–Kyaw Nyein group as 'deviationists' from the doctrine of Marx and Lenin. A new Burma Workers' and Peasants' Party was constituted; its chief support came from Thakin Lwin and his TUC, with Thakin Chit Maung bringing in a section of the Peasants' Organization. This mass defection gave a temporary knock-out to the Socialists, but the dissidents lacked the forcefulness of Ba Swe and Kyaw Nyein, who rapidly built up a new trade union organization and went out to bring the unions into its fold, also assisting the shaken ABPO to recover its hold in the countryside. Both Ba Swe and Kyaw Nyein took Cabinet office, and rapidly established a precedence second only to that of the Prime Minister.

The ancillary Socialist organs, the TUC(B) and the ABPO, merit further mention. Both are primarily political bodies[1] designed to mobilize the 'masses' into giving support to the party leaders.[2] Both bodies fell under Communist domination in the early post-war years and were 'purged' in 1948, when Than Tun went underground. In numbers the unions have increased from 25 in 1946 to 120, and in membership from 12,500 to (approximately) 50,000. This includes more than one-third of the numbers employed in industries.[3] Very few of the leaders of the TUC organization are drawn from the artisan classes. The President, Ba Swe, is a wealthy man by the modest standards of Burma, and his close relatives own big mining and other industrial interests; M. A. Raschid, the Vice-President, is an enterprising business man; Bo Setkya, Treasurer of the TUC and President of the Port Workers' Association, is a successful capitalist, proprietor of three factories. The May Day rallies of the TUC produce, every year, an effective demonstration of political mass power, and give Ba Swe a platform for an annual pronouncement on affairs, national and international. The ABPO fulfils a similar purpose

---

[1] Both march under party banners in which the hammer and sickle are displayed.

[2] A speech by Ba Swe on May Day, 1953, thus defined the role of the trade unions: 'Their principal duty is to give lessons in social revolution to workers.' This duty is later defined as 'To encourage the "camaraderie" feeling among the workers themselves, and to look after the interests of the workers as a class, and to support the activities of the AFPFL Government' (quoted in *Burma*, July 1953, pp. 8 and 9).

[3] Membership figures (1956) were given by Ba Swe, *BWB*, 2 February 1956.

in the countryside. Its President, Thakin Tin, is a member of the Central Executive of the Socialist Party; its Vice-President is Bo Khin Maung Gale, a prominent Cabinet Minister, and the Secretary-General is Thakin Kyaw Tun, Minister for Agriculture and Forests (1952–6): both are Socialists. The machinery of the ABPO is visible in party offices in market towns all over the country. There is a national party rally on 'Peasants' Day', 1 January, and an annual conference, usually held in May or June, attended by some 500 delegates. The organization has its own 'private army', the Peace Guerrillas, with units in every district. Nowadays its recruits are enlisted exclusively from ABPO supporters.[1] The organization has a monopoly of patronage in the countryside. The agricultural loans which have been dispensed so liberally during recent years (some 16 crores since 1948) are awarded by agents under ABPO influence. The land nationalization organizers and the Land Committees are almost all ABPO men. Conscious of their prestige in the countryside, ABPO leaders have challenged the power of the parent AFPFL in many cases.

Other bodies affiliated to the AFPFL are, in the main, non-Socialist, and largely represent different communal groups. There is the Burma Muslim Congress (founded 1945), whose President is the Minister for Judicial Affairs, Khin Maung Lat (Abdul Latif). It has twenty-two district branches. The Burma Muslims are a small but enterprising community: they take an important share in the administration, in business, and in the professions. The Kachin National Congress (President, Duwa Zau Lawn), the Union Karen League (President Mahn Win Maung), the Chin Congress,[2] and the United Hill People's Congress (President, the Sima Duwa) are similar bodies. During its early years the AFPFL included such diverse bodies as the All-Burma Fire Brigade, the St. John's Ambulance, the All-Burma Teachers' Organization, and the Youth League. Most of these non-political associations are no longer actively connected with the League. Among those still affiliated to the League are the All-Burma Women's Freedom League and the All-Burma Federation of Trade Organizations. The eclipse of the PVO parliamentary group has been almost complete; forty-four PVO representatives were elected to the Constituent Assembly; almost all of these joined the rebels, died, or withdrew from

---

[1] In earlier years the Peace Guerrillas were under the Socialist Party proper. U Win called them the 'walking stick' of the Socialists (*Nation*, 22 October 1949) and Kyaw Nyein said 'by and large they are Socialist adherents' (ibid., 22 April 1951). Their numbers were greatest in Lower Burma: 1,400 in Tharrawaddy District.

[2] Merged into the AFPFL, November 1954.

active politics. In the 1951 elections four former PVO adherents were returned and took their seats upon the opposition benches.

The League organization is strongly centralized. Its chief officers are: President, U Nu; Vice-President, Ba Swe; Secretary-General, Kyaw Nyein; and Treasurer, U Tin. A Central Executive Committee, meeting weekly or monthly, not only lays down policy and makes the final political decisions, but also exercises a firm control over the activities of all branches. For instance, the nominations to the Welfare Committees which administer the important *Pyidawtha* (Welfare State) schemes throughout the country are made by the Central AFPFL, right down to the township level. There are supposed to be AFPFL branches for each township and district, but many of them appear to be moribund. Others are split by rivalry into Socialist and non-Socialist factions.[1] The local organizations have little influence on party policy, but the local leaders are petty kings in their own districts. Where the local leader is the M.P., he is at least responsible in a general way to the electorate and to Parliament for his actions. But so many party bosses are merely former members of the BIA or PVO, contemporaries, and in some cases acquaintances of Aung San and the national leaders, but utterly deficient in ability and application. Jealous of the rise to power of better men, many find compensation in acting the tyrant in their own neighbourhood: in ordering around the Deputy Commissioner, in harassing their personal enemies, or in levying a quiet blackmail on all local economic and social activities.

It is not surprising that the central AFPFL ignores such supporters in formulating policy. The only role of the district organizations is to provide vocal evidence of the support of the *ludu*, the 'masses', for the AFPFL programme. District representatives are brought to Rangoon every year for Martyrs' Day[2] in July and National Day in November for mass rallies in the athletic stadium. The launching of the *Pyidawtha* plan in 1952 was similarly commemorated by a conference at the Rangoon Racecourse, attended by dozens of party chiefs from the districts. But although there is provision for a Supreme Council, to which each township may send two delegates for all-Burma meetings, there is in fact no organ, such as the annual conference of the British Labour Party, for expressing

---

[1] As at Myitkyina, where the two groups ended by opposing each other for the municipal elections. The Socialists had the support of the national party leaders, but the Independents had greater local standing. The dispute was settled only after a six months' quarrel, by the personal intervention of Kyaw Nyein as Secretary-General (see *Nation*, 22 May 1954 and 31 January 1955).

[2] The anniversary of the Cabinet assassinations.

the will of the party rank and file. This is not necessarily undemocratic in a country where a coherent public opinion has not yet been born. The Central Executive and the other leaders of the League are chosen by a process of inner selection rather than by any method of election. Party funds are largely augmented by the contributions of wealthy supporters, rice-millers, and other commercial magnates. There is a scale of party subscriptions, starting with K100 for Ministers and K20 for M.P.s, but these do not appear to be regularly collected.[1] There is an official party newspaper, the *Mandaing*.

The opposition parties were, until after the 1956 election, little more than coteries: the real opposition is, of course, the underground Communists.[2] The (legal) opposition is itself divided into groups to the right and the left of the Government. To the right, the most effective section is the Independent Arakanese Parliamentary Group, which is led by Ba Myaing and Kyaw Min, formerly an outstanding member of the Indian Civil Service and a Director of the *Nation* newspaper. This group owes its political birth to the widespread dissatisfaction in Arakan with the present régime. The Arakanese were amongst the first Burmans to realize the power of Western education, they were outstanding in Burmese banking and in the civil service; they produced some of the most able public men of the dyarchy days. To such as these, independence has brought few benefits; the Akyab rice trade has been disorganized under the present system of state buying; internal disorder has reigned unchecked with the *Mujahids* in the north and the Red Flags and Union Military Police mutineers elsewhere; and in the early days, AFPFL carpet-baggers were more blatantly overbearing in Arakan than anywhere else. Discontent has been translated into a political reaction: contesting a by-election in July 1950, Kyaw Min defeated the AFPFL candidate by 2,806 votes to 166. At the general election of 1951 every constitutency in Arakan save three rejected the AFPFL nominees for a local candidate. The seventeen Arakanese M.P.s thereupon associated themselves in the Independent Arakanese Parliamentary Group. Their opponents call them the 'millionaires' party'; their programme lays chief emphasis on good administration, sober finance, personal freedom, private enterprise—and a separate Arakan State within the

---

[1] *Nation*, 12 October 1954. The writer found the utmost difficulty in obtaining precise information about the structure and working of the AFPFL, even from senior members of long standing.

[2] Up to the time when the White Flags were, at last, declared an illegal body (October 1953). U Nu was for ever appealing to them to throw away their arms and accept the verdict of the polls.

Union. Other right-wing parties are the Patriotic Alliance, led by the veteran U Ba Pe, and Ba Sein's Burma Democratic Party. Ba Sein is firmly anti-Communist, looks to the monks for conservative support, and has an eye towards the United States.[1]

A newcomer to party politics, though a veteran of the political scene, is Dr. E Maung, who served as Foreign Minister in U Nu's 'emergency' Cabinet of 1949 and later acted as Chief Justice of the Union during the illness of Sir Ba U. At the time of the 1951 elections U E Maung, as a leading member of the Election Supervisory Commission, fell foul of the Socialists who complained that he was showing disfavour to the AFPFL;[2] E Maung replied with vigour, and thereafter he found himself 'dropped'.[3] At length he resigned from the Supreme Court and announced that he would form a 'Justice Party' which would be akin to the British Liberal Party, with 'Independent Administration of Justice' and 'Liberty of the People' as its party slogans.[4] The Justice Party may be expected to attract to its ranks disillusioned members of the AFPFL, as well as retired government servants and others to whom good administration and impartial justice are important. But U E Maung's comparison of his party with the British Liberals has proved all too apt in terms of election results.

One right-wing influence which has been mentioned in passing, but which, so far, has not played the part which its pre-war importance would suggest, is that of the monastic order in politics. In the 1930's no political mob was complete without its saffron-robed leader, and U Wisara, the monk who died on hunger strike, is venerated as a national hero.[5] Since independence, no section of the monks has taken any systematic part in politics, though individuals have intervened in certain cases of social-political significance. The only threat of large-scale monastic intervention arose in September 1954.

[1] In an interview with a *Nation* reporter (3 October 1954) Ba Sein gave a candid political testament which probably represents the attitude of other discarded pre-war politicians. He said 'Politics is a habit with me, and one that I can never get out of. It may not bring me money or power, but it is the only life I know and can be happy in.'

[2] cf. ibid., 5 June 1951 (complaint of Kyaw Nyein).

[3] When Sir Ba U was elected President, E Maung was passed over for the post of Chief Justice. In mid-1952 he failed to secure re-election as Vice-Chancellor of Rangoon University, thanks to the opposition of the Socialist electors (see ibid., 17 July 1952). His successor was a member of the High Court bench. He was then allotted the task of overseeing the reconstruction of the Shwemawdaw Pagoda, Pegu; when this work was completed, Justice E Maung was not invited to resume his place on the Supreme Court bench.

[4] See ibid., 19 August, 1 and 7 December 1954.

[5] At the same time, many thousands of monks steadfastly refused to interfere in politics, including all *sayadaws* and senior monks.

Certain *sayadaws* objected to Islamic teaching in state schools, under the provisions for religious teaching. They made representations to U Nu, who agreed that the teaching of Islam should cease; but being above any sort of discrimination, he insisted on the termination of Buddhist teaching also.[1] This aroused a storm of protest from the monks; there were great gatherings of angry monks, and for a few days there were rumours of U Nu's impending resignation. But the Prime Minister managed to smooth down the protests, and devised an acceptable solution, by his customary good sense and modest single-mindedness.[2]

So long as the Government is presided over by U Nu and others respected as men of piety, the monks are unlikely to subscribe to an opposition party with religion as its main plank. But if control over the AFPFL should pass to men who regard religion as secondary to other creeds, then a Buddhist party might well arise and form a very powerful rival to the AFPFL. In the absence of any such party, it is unlikely that any substantial opposition will develop to the right of the AFPFL; to catch the ear of the electorate it is needful to outbid the AFPFL, to shout noisier, bigger slogans. Only the left can offer such slogans.

To the left, there is Dr. Ba Maw, with the rump of his wartime *Mahabama* Party. He remains the most impressive orator and the most shrewd political operator in Burma; he is assisted by his son-in-law, Bo Yan Naing, who still retains something of his daring war-time reputation. Ba Maw stands as the advocate of a People's Democracy, but he gives an impression of realizing that, without a sudden turn of fortune's wheel, he cannot ever hope to enjoy again the delicious game of manufacturing a government.[3] The chief left-wing opposition group in Parliament is the Burma Workers' and Peasants' Party (BWPP), formed by the break-away of Thakin Lwin's supporters from the Socialists late in 1950. It was considerably strengthened by the slightly ambiguous adherence of Aung Than, elder brother of Aung San, after the 1951 elections. Aung Than left the Socialist Party in October 1949, announcing

---

[1] Statement of U Nu, *BWB*, 15 September 1954.

[2] A broadcast by U Nu of 25 September 1954 gives an interesting picture of the need for religious toleration in Burma, and the Prime Minister's own attitude. Full text in ibid., 29 September 1954.

[3] He told the *Nation*, 20 October 1954, 'We are prepared to take the long view. With all the cards in their hands, the AFPFL may stay in power for a long time, but the next generation will see drastic changes for the better. . . . After all, the AFPFL . . . is only a small pawn in the movement of history. We are living in the midst of an international revolution, and what happens in Burma internally will be largely conditioned by the inevitable developments of that revolution.'

that he disapproved of its increasing Marxist leanings.[1] He then led a 'neutralist' bloc of fifteen independents in Parliament. At the 1951 election he challenged the might of the AFPFL by standing against the Prime Minister in the Lanmadaw quarter of Rangoon which had been the constituency of his famous brother, and later of Mrs. Aung San (Daw Khin Kyi). Despite a fair measure of support, he was defeated. After the elections, with the Socialists back in power, he joined forces with the BWPP as head of the 'Democratic Rights Protection Committee'. The BWPP has an authoritarian character, although it claims to be the champion of democracy. It is ruled by a four-man 'politburo';[2] there is a wider based Central Executive Committee, but this cannot stand up to the politburo.[3] The party is said to receive directives from international Communist organizations in Russia and China.[4]

The pattern of politics was more sharply defined, and personal and sectional rivalries were crystallized into political manifestos, by the general elections of 1951. Under the constitution (Ch. XIV, sect. 233) elections were required to be held within eighteen months of independence. In fact, the prevailing insecurity compelled a postponement of three and a half years. Early in 1951 the Government set up a judicial Commission (Sir Ba U, Justice E Maung, Justice Tun Byu, and four others) to determine the prospects for the holding of free elections. It soon became obvious that the armed partisans of the Socialists and of the Communists would be able to overawe many sections of the country. At first it appeared that elections would be possible only in one-fifth of the constituencies,[5] but eventually a scheme was prepared for holding the elections in three instalments as security arrangements permitted. The first batch were to take place in June 1951, the second were fixed for August, and the final batch were to be completed in October 1951. Eventually 350 of the 375 constituencies (for both houses) were included within the scheme.

Electioneering began early in 1951. The AFPFL stood as the champions of independence, offering a 'welfare' programme for the future. Most of the opposition candidates attempted to outbid the AFPFL in the benefits they promised. Certain

[1] *Nation*, 4 October 1949.
[2] Thakin Lwin, Thakin Hla Kywe, Ba Nyein, and Maung Maung Kyaw.
[3] Originally the BWPP had ten representatives in Parliament; after the 1951 elections there were twelve BWPP members.
[4] *Nation*, 11 and 12 September 1954.
[5] ibid., 25 April 1951.

opposition groups attracted the support of dissatisfied sections of the monastic order. Only one party based its appeal on a moderate platform. U Chit Hlaing combined with Sir Paw Tun and U Ba Pe to launch the Union of Burma League which, somewhat hesitantly, advocated a return to the Commonwealth. The task of the AFPFL was rendered easier by the multiplicity of candidates coming forth. U Nu, contesting Lanmadaw, was opposed by nine other candidates;[1] nor was this unique. Also the hiatus between the various instalments of elections made it possible for the AFPFL to focus their organization upon different areas in turn—and gave certain defeated ministers a chance to make a second appeal to the electorate. With universal suffrage, tempered by gross omissions from the electoral rolls, about one and a half million citizens cast their votes out of a total electorate estimated at eight millions. About 60 per cent. of the votes cast were given to the AFPFL, who secured 85 per cent. of the seats (many seats were uncontested).[2]

How fair were the elections? There was inefficient supervision by those in charge of the polling booths, and some ballot boxes may have been tampered with. The armed forces were marched to the polls, and voted solidly for the Government. Out of the dozens of election appeals by candidates, not one was decided against an AFPFL candidate. Of the Rangoon seats Ba Swe remarked that they were 'pocket boroughs', because of the numbers of refugee voters in hutments controlled by the AFPFL.[3] All this may be recalled, and yet the results did represent the general will of the country: a vote of confidence in U Nu's administration.[4]

Among the frontier peoples politics have remained associated with personalities to an even greater extent than in Burma proper, and in many cases the political leaders are the traditional leaders of society. From the Shan States all the members of the Chamber of Nationalities are elected by the Sawbwas alone, and half the State Council consists of Sawbwas. In wide areas (as in Kengtung State) there were no electoral contests whatsoever. A popular 'anti-feudalist' movement appeared in the

---

[1] Result at Lanmadaw: U Nu, 5,166; Aung Than, People's Democratic Front, 2,824; Aw Myi Shu, Independent, 531; Ba Thaw, 294; Tun Nyan, BWPP, 165; E Maung, Independent, 164; Tun Sein, 80; Sein Tun, 67; U Myint, Burma Democratic Party, 38; Tilla Muhammad Khan, 11. U Nu secured an over-all majority.

[2] Some country districts showed minute polls. Cf. the Toungoo Karen Constituency: Hla Maung, 217; Johnson D. Po Min, 86; Saw Herbert Le, 73.

[3] *Nation*, 11 June 1951.

[4] The *Nation*, which has never given complaisant support to the Nu Government, concluded that there was 'no intimidation and no barefaced cheating' (13 June 1951).

south-western Shan States which was led by Tun Aye, M.P. from Namkhan: it is not clear how far it is spontaneous, how far dependent on outside influences. Shan politics have revolved round the issue of the limitation of the Sawbwas' autocratic rule. During 1955 rumours were circulated concerning an alleged movement among the Sawbwas for secession from the Union at the end of the initial ten-year period after 1947. Certain Sawbwas have, indeed, spoken in favour of secession, but there was no sign of any organized movement to this end before the 1956 elections.

In the Kachin State the rivalries between the Duwas, the chiefs, and attempts by commoners to overturn the rule of the Duwas, have formed the main themes. The Sima Duwa, Sinwa Nawng, associated with the AFPFL from its beginnings, predominates in the huge Myitkyina District of the north. But in Bhamo District, which contains some Kachins more in contact with education and the ways of the West, the prevailing influence is that of Duwa Zau Lawn (Finance Minister in the Kachin State, 1948–51), and he has received the greater part of Kachin support. Apart from their keen personal rivalry, the two men stand for different ideas. The Sima Duwa, a Buddhist who worked with the Japanese during the war years, is a somewhat eccentric Socialist. Zau Lawn is a Christian: he led Kachin levies in the Allied cause, and he is a moderate. At the 1951 elections each Duwa received the support of seven Kachin M.P.s:[1] the balance was held by the five Burmese AFPFL M.P.s from Kachin State constituencies, who were instructed to support the Sima Duwa. Encouraged by his victory, the Sima Duwa became more ambitious; in April 1953 he launched a new party, the 'People's Economic and Cultural Development Organization', with the main object of industrializing Kachin-land. He was joined by some Communists, PVO's, and others opposed to the AFPFL. In consequence the AFPFL group were instructed to withdraw their support from the Sima Duwa—who thereupon offered to resign from the People's Economic and Cultural Development Organization. For some time he successfully avoided summoning the State Council, which he knew would pass a vote of 'no confidence', but eventually he was compelled to resign, uttering the whimsical comment 'Only now I understand what politics is.'[2]

---

[1] The Sima Duwa persuaded one, Labang Grawng, to stand against Zau Lawn but the man's mother thought this unseemly and made him stand down (*Nation*, 4 July 1951).

[2] ibid., 22 May 1953. State Councils normally meet biennially, immediately before the meeting of the Union Parliament. The Shan Council holds one meeting per annum at Taunggyi; otherwise all the councils meet in Rangoon.

Duwa Zau Lawn succeeded as Head of the State, forming a Kachin National Congress–AFPFL coalition.[1]

Chin political divisions have arisen largely from personal cleavages.[2] The Minister in power from 1948 to 1951 packed the services and offices of the Division with his own relatives, and he was defeated at the general election on a wave of resentment, led by Za Hre Lian, a young and capable former army officer and Deputy Commissioner. The United Chin Freedom League of Vamthu Maung disappeared: the new leader of the Chin Hills Congress utilized his energies in bringing social benefits to his people rather than in creating political excitement.

In tiny Karenni there is as yet no awareness of politics, but the remaining Karens have produced a multiplicity of parties. During the immediate post-war years the Karen cause suffered through the lack of an adequate successor to Sir San C. Po. Saw Ba U Gyi and San Po Thin, the main rivals in Karen politics, both lacked responsibility and stability, and both underwent a collapse of political judgement.[3] After the political suicide of the KNDO, three main parties emerged: the Union Karen League (UKL), President Mahn Win Maung and Vice-President Aung Pa, the allies of the AFPFL; second, the Union Karen Organization (UKO) led by Dr. Hla Tun, which is also pro-AFPFL but draws its strength from inside the Salween area, and which has certain Socialist affiliations; third, the Karen Congress (formed April 1951), representing those sections of the Karen National Union which did not go underground or later broke with the KNDO. Its leaders are Saya Ba Than, Saw Po Thein, and Saw Norton Bwa, a Mon adopted into a Karen family.

During 1951 a conflict developed in the Karen Affairs Council[4] between the Congress and the UKL. The Government and the UKL promoted legislation to create a Karen

---

[1] Other parties in the state are the Kachin Youth League (semi-moribund), the Pawnggyawng Progressive Youth Organization, led by Duwa Zau Rip (Finance Minister for the Kachin State during the Sima Duwa's régime), and the Pawnggyawng Animist Youth Organization, led by Bawk Naw. Both the latter profess Marxist-Socialism, but the PPYO is allegedly Christian and 'feudalist', the PAYO is non-Christian and 'anti-feudalist' (ibid., 12 November 1954).

[2] The first Chin leader, Vum Ko Hau, left politics for a career in the Foreign Office.

[3] San Po Thin ceased to be Special Commissioner, Bassein, in January 1949. He was arrested in May 1949 on suspicion of attempting to form a private army. Released, he joined Ba Sein's Democratic Party in January 1951. He was arrested while electioneering in Bassein District in April 1951. Released, he attempted to join forces with the KNDO, who repulsed all overtures. He is now alleged to be living near the Siam border as an agent for the KMT.

[4] Formed in 1948 under sect. 181 of the constitution in anticipation of the creation of a Karen State.

State which was to consist of the Salween District and such adjacent areas as might vote for inclusion, on a referendum to be held when peace returned.[1] A certain price was demanded for this concession: the number of Karen M.P.s in the Chamber of Nationalities was reduced from twenty-four to fifteen and in the Chamber of Deputies from twenty to seven; the separate Karen institutions in Burma proper were gradually abolished.[2] The prospect of uniting Karenni with the Karen State which had been written into the constitution (sect. 150) had to be renounced for ever, and Mongpai (a small state, 90 per cent. Padaungs, closely linked with the Karens), which was to have received the choice of accession to Karenni, continued to be incorporated in the Shan State. Karenni was now renamed the Kayah State.[3]

As the 1951 elections loomed near, the Union Karen League was uneasy about the difficulties of its position: it was bound to be associated with all the repression and bitterness of the Karen defeat, and the grudging recognition of Karen autonomy. Accordingly Mrs. Ba Maung Chain, who had played a major part in various peace moves and in measures for settling Karen refugees, was invited to join the League and to become Karen Minister in the post-election Cabinet. Mrs. Ba Maung Chain must have realized that she was being used as a stalking-horse but, believing that she might do some good for the Karens, she agreed to stand, was elected on the UKL ticket, and was appointed first Minister for the Karen State. The strength of the parties in the Karen State Council was as follows: UKL 21 seats, UKO 9 seats, Karen Congress 7 seats. It soon became apparent that the different groups were out to play the party game, despite (or perhaps because of) the feeble resources of the new state. Mrs. Ba Maung Chain was able to do something for the hundreds of Karen soldiers eating their hearts out in 'rest' camps: some were brought to trial, others were discharged from the service. And she was able to persuade many of the younger Karens that their community would be better served if they learnt trades and professions rather than by adhering to their vow not to cut their hair until the Burmese had been defeated. But she was no politician and, finding she was the centre of various party manœuvres, she resigned (against the

[1] At present the Karen State (population *c*. 400,000) includes about 25 per cent. of the Karens of Burma.

[2] *Nation*, 29 June and 6 October 1951.

[3] A racial distinction as between the Karens and the Red Karens or Kayahs has now been invented. One leading Burman remarked to the author: 'It has been left to the Burmese to carry out the policy which they always attributed to the British: divide and rule.'

wishes of the Prime Minister and the President) just one year after taking office. She was succeeded by the UKL Vice-President, Aung Pa. As the structure of the state was built up, it became apparent that the UKL was packing its own supporters into the administration. The UKO, whose guerrillas were partly responsible for the maintenance of security, became restive, and a compromise was negotiated, whereby the UKO should receive a share of political power, including the reversion of the leadership of the state to the UKO chief, Dr. Hla Tun. After much delay, this pact was implemented at the end of May 1955: Saw Hla Tun became Minister for the Karen State, and the former Minister, Aung Pa, took over the portfolio of Health in the central Government.

The relationship of state governments with the Union Government appears to be that of dutiful adolescents to a severe parent. As long as the children behave in a way which the father approves, they are permitted a reasonable degree of freedom. But immediately they assert an independence which is contrary to the parental wishes, they are reminded sharply of their dependence. Although the constitution permits (Ch. X) under formidable safeguards a right of secession from the Union, it is doubtful if this right would be permitted to be exercised. With regard to the Karens, there is no doubt: the legislation under which the Karen State came into being (Constitution Amendment Act, 1951) included a section 181 (10), which definitely denied any right of secession to the new state.[1] An attempt will be made in Chapter VI to indicate how government policy aims at emphasizing the unity of Burma through an extension of Buddhism, the Burmese language, Burmese dress, and other cultural models amongst the frontier peoples. It is noticeable that, when a choice is possible, U Nu and his Burmese colleagues choose those frontier leaders for office who identify themselves most closely with their Burmese cousins. A high favourite is the Sima Duwa (specially brought back into the Cabinet in May 1955 by creation of the new office of Minister for National Solidarity). He is one of the few Kachin Buddhists (he was educated in a monastery), he is married to a Burmese lady, and he has adopted a Burmese name (Kyaw U). The Karen leaders Mahn Win Maung and Aung Pa, who were both Christians, have renounced Christianity for Buddhism. Both are Burmese-speaking Karens (Aung Pa cannot speak any Karen language). Sao Hkun Hkio, Head of the Shan State, is ruler of that Shan principality which is

---

[1] The Kachin State was excluded from the right of seccession under section 178 of the constitution.

nearest to Burma proper and, indeed, during periods of its history, has been governed as part of a Burmese *myo*, district. The avowed aim of the AFPFL Government is the integration of all the peoples of Burma into a unified whole, and this is much to be desired and encouraged. But it is not pleasant to see Burmese public men behaving towards their frontier colleagues like a 'master race', insisting that the only true Burman is a Burmese Buddhist. Both President Ba U and U Nu are entirely free of racial prejudice. To the Prime Minister a Karen Christian or a Kachin Animist is, in every way, a full citizen of the Union. But this liberal attitude is by no means general.

With AFPFL domination beyond challenge, and with only the most limited previous training in Western democratic institutions, there might appear to be serious obstacles to the development of a democratic political life. But Burma today is a democracy, beyond question. In part this may be ascribed to the social structure. The poverty of the poor is not heart-breaking; the wealth of the rich is not ostentatious and oppressive. It is perfectly possible for any Burman of ability to move easily through the social scale in Burma (whereas in India or Japan it would be impossible): neither speech nor clothes nor physical features stamp a man with a fixed place in society. Burma must be the least caste-conscious country in the East.[1] Then, Burmans are great individualists and great critics:[2] they have a wry sense of humour and of the ridiculous: Ba Maw's war-time attempts to create an aura of splendour around his position only provoked the Burmese to mirth. The Press reflects these characteristics: it is highly critical and not over-impressed with self-importance. And the proportion of the population which is literate and able to buy a newspaper is high.[3]

It must be acknowledged that there are also forces in Burma working against democracy. There are the insurgents whose dogma is imposed by an intellectual *élite*, enforced by the gun and the *dah*. And there are leaders within the AFPFL to whom any criticism of their programme is criminal obstruction. Pride and ignorance sometimes rule in high places. It would be a wise man who could foretell today which path Burma will finally follow, democracy or authoritarianism.

In these circumstances the Press has a heavy responsibility

---

[1] This does not mean that there are no class distinctions. In particular, the members of the families of the old officials of Mindon and Thibaw are very particular about matters of family and status and etiquette.

[2] During his travels, the writer was continually approached by complete strangers who would launch into violent criticism of the Government and all its works.

[3] The 1931 census showed the percentage of literacy as 50 per cent. among men and 14 per cent. among women. After the wasted years of war and insurrection, the percentage today may perhaps be lower.

as the guardian of liberty. At times it has been in danger of losing its freedom, and if today it is unmuzzled, that is partly because the Government is conscious of the constitution's expressed declaration of 'the right of the citizens to express freely their convictions and opinions', slightly self-conscious in its frequent adumbrations of democracy, and also conscious of its now unchallengeable authority throughout Burma.

A thick blanket of censorship on the publication of news in connexion with the rebellion was, not unnaturally, enforced during the bad months of 1948 and 1949. Drastic measures were taken against publishing news or opinions not approved by the Government: in June 1949 the offices of four papers were raided and the contents confiscated.[1] In November 1949 two more dailies were penalized: having been required to deposit sureties for good behaviour, these were now forfeited.[2] One of these papers, the *Sun* (*Thooryah*), which was owned by the widow of U Saw, ran into so many difficulties that it was compelled to cease publication on 15 November: so ended the oldest Burmese-language newspaper, founded in 1911. Thereafter the grip of the Government was relaxed but its power was still available in reserve. In July 1953 a monk was wounded resisting police attempts to dismantle one of the Rangoon shanty colonies: the *Ludu* of Mandalay reported that the monk was dead, whereupon the editor was arrested and the paper was closed down.[3] In August 1954 an attempt was made to enforce drastic limitations on the Press. On 21 August a government bill was introduced which had the purpose of making criticism ('defamatory allegations or charges') concerning public servants, including Ministers as well as officials, into a cognizable criminal offence. Any person accused of 'defamation' of a public servant would be liable to arrest without warrant. The overwhelming government majority pushed the bill through the Chamber of Deputies: Independent Arakanese Parliamentary Group and BWPP opposition members spoke vigorously against the bill and staged a walk-out of the entire opposition. The Press discussed the proposal with indignation: the Burma Journalists' Association organized a united protest. One week later, the offending measure was dropped, the Government deciding that it could not ignore the voice of the Press and the public.

Newspapers are also liable to pressure of a more irregular kind: it has become an unpleasant political habit to break up the offices of any paper whose criticisms are unwelcome. In March 1948 three newspapers were broken up for criticizing

---

[1] *Nation*, 21 June 1949.   [2] ibid., 3 November 1949.   [3] ibid., 12 August 1953.

the AFPFL: these attacks incurred the immediate castigation of U Nu as President of the AFPFL.[1] Two and a half years later one of these papers, the *Oway*, was again smashed up, this time by monks who objected to the paper's attitude to the *sasana*. But, in general, there is freedom of speech in Burma.[2]

All the most important papers are published in Rangoon: indeed, it would be impossible to gather the news or carry out the distribution of a paper with national pretensions from anywhere else. The Press is divided into groups by language: Burmese, English, Chinese, and Indian-language newspapers; and into at least three groups by political affiliation: with the Government, or to its right or left. Some of the most influential papers are in the English-language group. The oldest[3] is the *New Times of Burma*, which began publication as the *Liberator* under the aegis of the CAS(B) Information Department; it was then taken over by the civil Government's Public Relations Department and renamed. In May 1946 it was acquired by U Tin Tut (during his tenure of ministerial office) who had the ambition of giving the paper the authority and prestige within Burma of *The Times* of Printing House Square. Under Tin Tut's vigorous direction, the paper attained a circulation of 8,000 per day, and a high reputation; since his death its direction has been disputed between his widow and his son-in-law, and the circulation has dropped to some 4,500 copies; but the *New Times* still retains its distinctive gravity and solid caution. Unfortunately its technical production is somewhat inferior. The *Nation*[4] first came out in July 1948: if the *New Times* wishes to emulate *The Times*, the *Nation* has taken as its model a judicious combination of the *Daily Telegraph* and the *Express*. It aims at liveliness, and has consistently adopted an independent (though positive) line of policy. Under the audacious editorial direction of Law Yone, with the backing of the formidable Kyaw Min, it probably carries greater weight than any other Burmese journal. And yet the editors would be the first to admit that far too many of its pages consist of unattractive advertisements and chunks of syndicated news off the tape.

---

[1] Nu, *Towards Peace and Democracy*, p. 46.

[2] A strange example of how that freedom might be interpreted was shown when Justice E Maung announced the formation of his new party, and delivered himself of pungent criticisms of the Government. The Minister of Information was interviewed by a *Nation* reporter two days later, following up a rumour that E Maung would be impeached. Tun Win replied that 'the collective view of the government would be against impeachment', but, he stated, 'I personally would like to see appropriate action taken. . . . Such a step would give an impetus to the democratic process' (*Nation*, 21 August 1954).

[3] The old *Rangoon Gazette*, founded in 1861, has not resumed publication since 1942.

[4] Perhaps the title is designed to evoke the prestige of the British *New Statesman and Nation*, as well as that of the Calcutta *Statesman*.

Till 1955 the *Nation* was pegged to a circulation of 10,000 per day, the full capacity of its printing machines; but thereafter new plant capable of printing 25,000 copies was due to be installed. Of the other English-language newspapers the *Burman* claims a daily sale of 12,900, but a large part of this is actually made up of competition vouchers: its sale of actual newspapers is limited to 2,000 or 3,000. This group is completed by the *Union Gazette* and the *Star of Burma*.

Amongst the Burmese-language papers, undeviating support for the Government is provided by *Mandaing*[1] (the official organ of the AFPFL), the *Tribune*, and the *New Light of Burma* (founded in 1914, and long managed by U Tin, the Cabinet Minister). To the right of the Government are *Bamakhit* 'Burmese Era' (once official mouthpiece of the Japanese-sponsored régime), *Hanthawaddy* (first founded as a printing press in 1881), and *Htoon* daily, founded and edited by Tun Pe, former Minister of Information. The editor of *Hanthawaddy* is reputed to be a close friend of the Prime Minister, but that does not prevent the paper from attacking the Government with gusto. The Burmese-language papers with the highest circulation are *Hanthawaddy* and the *New Light*, which sell about 15,000 copies every day, covering most of Lower Burma as well as the railway towns of Upper Burma. *Mandaing* has a circulation of about 3,000.[2] There are five other Burmese-language papers.[3] Of the five Chinese papers probably the most influential is the Communist *Freedom Daily*.[4] There are seven papers catering for Indians and Pakistanis: surprisingly, a larger number than before the war.[5]

As in pre-war days, newspaper owners and editors have played their part as leaders of post-war politics. Beside U Tin and Kyaw Min, there is Tun Pe, editor of *Htoon*, formerly editor of *Bamakhit* and of *Hanthawaddy*, who served as Cabinet Minister from 1948 to 1953; Tun Win, former editor of *Mandaing* and a Minister from 1952; Mahn Win Maung, Cabinet Minister since 1948 and one-time editor of *Taing Yintha* journal.

In sum, the Press fulfils many of the functions of an opposition and of a lobby 'pressure group'. It possesses at least as much freedom and as much consciousness of its public responsibility

---

[1] Literally, 'The Gong Post', or 'King Post'. Something fixed, central, reliable.
[2] Circulation figures are a closely guarded secret: the figures quoted were supplied by 'a highly reliable source', but not one that is infallible.
[3] *Economic Daily, Oway, Progress, Rangoon, Tainglonekyaw.*
[4] The others are *China Commercial Times, New China Pao, New Rangoon Evening Post,* and *Zin Min Pao.*
[5] *Andra Mitra, Bala Burma, Daur-I-Jadeed, Nootan Burma, Prachi Prakash, Rasika Ranjani,* and *San Thi.*

as any other national Press in Asia. But the last word rests with the Government.

The responsibility of Government is centred upon the Prime Minister and Cabinet: the constitution squarely states (Ch. VII, sect. 115) 'The Government shall be collectively responsible to the Chamber of Deputies', and the Lower House is, in the British tradition, the council of the nation.[1] Under the constitution (Ch. V, sect. 56) the Prime Minister is appointed by the President 'on the nomination of the Chamber of Deputies'; other members of the Government are appointed 'on the nomination of the Prime Minister'. To retain office the Prime Minister must retain the support of a majority in the Chamber of Deputies (Ch. VII, sect. 119). The Prime Minister may demand the resignation of any member of the Government 'for reasons which to him seem sufficient'. Thus the Prime Minister is the keystone of the Union.[2]

U Nu, as unchallenged leader of the nation, had to submit only to a formal ratification of his premiership by Parliament. U Nu also named his successor, Ba Swe, with the authority of a large AFPFL parliamentary majority to support his nomination; thus a convention for the selection of a Premier has not so far been elaborated. In the matter of U Nu's choice of Ministers certain trends appeared. The Socialist Party, with its special status, has received special treatment. The party has been invited to select its candidates for certain stipulated portfolios, and the nominees were almost automatically acceptable to the Premier. On the two occasions when the Prime Minister wished to dismiss Socialist Ministers because of corruption, he had to ask the Executive of the Socialist Party to make the dismissals.[3] Over the remaining members of his Cabinet U Nu exerted his authority more sternly. When the 1951 elections resulted, in the Kachin State, in a stalemate

[1] The Chamber of Deputies meets, as did the Constituent Assembly, in the building of the former legislature, within the Secretariat; the Chamber of Nationalities sits, as does the Supreme Court, in the building of the New Law Courts, Strand Road.

[2] The first two Presidents of the Union have not been ex-politicians; they are men who have had no desire to enlarge their role, and who have made no attempt to direct the activities of the Government. The President has, therefore, only appeared as ceremonial Head of State. It is just possible that he might, under different circumstances, assume a more active lead. Can the President, under the constitution, take over power? If no candidate for the premiership could obtain a majority from the Chamber of Deputies, then Parliament would automatically be dissolved. A new Parliament need not be summoned to meet for four months. The President has power to promulgate Ordinances 'with the same form and effect as an Act of Parliament', when Parliament is not in session, though these must be laid before Parliament within forty-five days. Perhaps a dictatorship might be evolved out of these possibilities, but the contingency seems very remote.

[3] However, U Nu has stated that when the corrupt activities of Ko Ko Gyi, Socialist Minister of Commerce, were discovered, he gave the Socialists four hours in which to force him out of the Cabinet (*Nation*, 18 August 1952).

between the Sima Duwa and Duwa Zau Lawn, U Nu kept his friend the Sima Duwa in office by placing behind him the votes of the Burmese AFPFL M.P.s from within the Kachin State; when the Sima Duwa embarked upon political adventures which were disapproved by the AFPFL high command, the support of the Burmese M.P.s was withdrawn and he was compelled to resign. When, in the Chin hills, the people demonstrated their disgust at the management of Vamthu Maung by endorsing the leadership of his opponent, Za Hre Lian; despite an overwhelming vote in his favour by the Chin Council of M.P.s, U Nu refused to accept him as Minister on grounds of his youth (he was 29: at the same age Aung San was principal Minister). U Nu named an older man, Shein Htang, and, despite a boycott by the Chins, installed him in office. Za Hre Lian agreed to serve as Parliamentary Secretary, and two years later he was accepted by U Nu as Minister.[1] It has been asserted[2] that in 1948 U Nu reversed the decision of the Shan M.P.s to elect Tun Myint as Head of the Shan State in favour of Sao Hkun Hkio. It is certain that M. A. Raschid, the energetic Minister for Housing (1952), and for Trade Development (1954), has been sustained in office almost entirely through the Prime Minister's steady support. U Nu had to resist pressure from influential quarters against his appointment, on the grounds of his Indian blood, but he refused to budge.[3]

In his dealings with his colleagues U Nu has also shown certain divergences, some ministries being left almost entirely alone (especially the Ministry of Industries, under Kyaw Nyein), others being subject to almost daily supervision by the Prime Minister—such as the Ministries of Education, Religious Affairs and Union Culture, and Information. Tun Pe (Minister for Information, and later for Union Culture) when he resigned revealed that one of his major reasons was the transaction by the Prime Minister of the business of the Ministry of Information without his knowledge as Minister.[4] Numbers in the Cabinet, apart from the 'emergency' period of 1949–50, have always been somewhere around twenty. There was, until after

---

[1] *Nation*, 13 October 1954.
[2] By Tun Aye, M.P. (see ibid., 3 September 1953).
[3] cf. his rejection of the Resolution of the Burmese Chamber of Commerce of November 1954 presented by Henzada U Mya, former AFPFL Minister.
[4] *Nation*, 14 July 1953. U Tun Pe, previously a newspaper editor, is a moderate man and his remarks deserve attention. He alleged that the Socialists have a working arrangement with U Nu whereby they have a clear field with land nationalization, the co-operatives, the trade unions, labour, commerce, and foreign affairs (this last item is most debatable). In return they do not interfere with the Prime Minister's activities in the ministries of Finance, Education, Culture and Communications. Some such 'arrangement' is generally accepted in Rangoon as a fact.

the 1956 election, a core of some ten Ministers who had held office continuously ever since 1950, a few having served throughout since 1947. Some Ministers have been dismissed for incompetence or dishonesty, and new men have come forward, but the general character of the Cabinet has remained remarkably constant. Most of the Ministers have been former undergraduate acquaintances of U Nu, or worked with him in the Japanese time; almost all are men in their forties.[1] Those who have gone are mainly the failures but certainly exceptions must be made for able Ministers who went because they would not toe the party line. A convention of Cabinet responsibility seems to be firmly established: whatever their private disagreements, in all their official utterances Ministers speak in unison. It is not easy to decide whether the meetings of the Cabinet are formal, or actually determine the business of the Government. Probably the meetings of the Executive Committee of the AFPFL are the place where all the political decisions are made.[2] Also, the Economic and Social Planning Board is, in effect, a sub-committee of the Cabinet: its members were (in 1954 and 1955) U Nu, Kyaw Nyein, Ba Swe, U Win, and U Tin, with U Thant as Secretary. This body makes the executive decisions throughout the whole range of national planning and development. All important tenders are referred to this Board and the allocation of the national income which it approves virtually decides the shape of budget expenditure; decisions made by the Board are not reviewed by the whole Cabinet. Then the Prime Minister has his own 'secretariat'—Prome Court—and he keeps a wide range of activities under his own, extra-Cabinet, control. The Bureau of Special Investigation, Burma's F.B.I., is directly responsible to the Prime Minister. U Nu also maintained a special watch over the Agricultural and Rural Development Corporation, the Burma Translation Society, and Rangoon University, of which he is Chancellor.

Decisions of policy affecting the different ministries are made by the Ministers themselves at meetings of the Cabinet: the senior civil servants have hardly any responsibility in matters of importance. Many Ministers carry their control over detail to extremes. There may be a few instances where the Minister is particularly easy-going and leaves affairs to his officials, but they are very few.

How far is the Government held to its constitutional obligation of responsibility to the Chamber of Deputies? The

---

[1] U Shein Htang at 60 is the doyen; U Tin is 58.
[2] As, for instance, the decision to proceed against U Ba Pe for treason (see *Nation*, 24 October 1954).

Government's overwhelming majority gives it the power to make Parliament its instrument: yet it should be recognized that U Nu and his colleagues have given much thought to building up the dignity and authority of the House. Nevertheless, it has not so far developed into the political forum of the nation.

Parliament normally holds two sessions per annum, one lasting from August to September, when the budget is introduced, and one from February to March. Before each session the AFPFL members meet in conference under the designation of the 'All-Member Parliamentary Committee of the AFPFL', and they are informed of the Government's forthcoming legislative programme. Following the 1951 elections, on the eve of the new Parliament, the AFPFL choice for the President, the Speakers of both Houses, and the Chief Justice of the Union was ratified by this preliminary meeting. Parliament was merely asked to rubber-stamp the AFPFL decision.[1] The budget and the government bills are thereafter passed through Parliament with only a very occasional attempt at modification from the Government back benches.[2] The opposition's ability to criticize measures, apart from its numerical weakness, is restricted by the fact that the draft bills are frequently only available to members on the same day that they are passed through the House, and also by the almost invariable exclusion of any opposition representation from the all-important committees of the House.[3]

And yet, because Burma is a democratic country, because the Government cannot steam-roller its programme through against the weight of public feeling, the opposition (if it will) can sometimes play a useful part as a watch-dog of civil liberties. A good example was that of the Defamation Bill, to which allusion has already been made. Despite its ability to steam-roller the bill through Parliament, the Government could not ignore the storm of protest from the Press and the public. Eventually, the offending measure was dropped, following representations by AFPFL M.P.s themselves to the Executive Committee.[4] When the bill was presented to the Upper House, the Government joined with the opposition in voting to delete the sections relating to defamation.[5]

---

[1] *Nation*, 3 March 1952.
[2] Thus, the Democratization of Local Government Bill, one of the most far-reaching measures drafted since independence, was given two readings in one morning.
[3] cf. letter from Kyaw Min, M.P., *Nation*, 4 September 1954.
[4] ibid., 29 August 1954.
[5] ibid., 21 September 1954.

The sittings of the House are conducted with a regard for decorum and the rules of procedure which echoes, in many respects, the mother Parliament at Westminster. The Burmese are not great devotees of ceremony; almost every occasion is reduced to informality by the refusal of the ordinary spectators to take the affair very seriously.[1] Also, their extreme individualism makes any display of authority almost an incitement to defiance. The early sessions of Parliament were conducted in a casual, almost slovenly manner, with members dropping in, often dressed in old and easy clothes. But Burma had a rigid etiquette at the old court of Ava, and something of the old ceremonial, combined with a growing acquaintance with the customs of the legislatures of the Commonwealth and the United States, has had its influence on the development of the dignified side of Parliament. The change has been gradual, but may be said to have crystallized with the 1952 sessions.

M.P.s now appear in full Burmese national dress with *gaung baung* and *eingyi*. The Shans wear their baggy trousers, *baungbi;* one solitary Muslim M.P. appears in Indian *achkin*; a very few members wear European suits. The women members (one in each House, 1951–6) wear the old-fashioned hair-style, *sadon*. The day begins with the assembly of the M.P.s. The legislative building was originally constructed for a House of 100 members; in order to provide seating for the 250 of today it has been necessary to modify the original 'Westminster' seating arrangements. The Speaker's chair faces the assembly, with the clerks' table below. To the right of the Speaker is the Government front bench, and behind additional benches for the parliamentary secretaries. To the left are the opposition benches. But the great mass of the M.P.s, the rank and file AFPFL supporters, sit in close rows facing the Speaker's chair. As the members stand, waiting, the Speaker's procession passes the saluting police inspectors in the lobbies [2] and enters the Chamber. First comes the Serjeant at Arms, Bearer of the Mace, *Kyaing Daw Gaing Ayashi*,[3] then Mr. Speaker followed by the clerks. Before seating himself the Speaker bows to the assembly, who bow in return. A striking feature of Parliament is the unquestioning deference shown to the Chair. The day begins with question time. This is a distinctly stilted performance and

---

[1] It has often been remarked that the Hindu *Ramayana*, an awesome tragedy of the gods, has been transformed in the Burmese drama into a comedy about human beings.

[2] Ever since the 1947 assassinations Parliament has met behind armed guards. Most Ministers live in a special compound, surrounded by barbed wire and sentries.

[3] As in Britain, he is a senior retired service officer.

does not really have the effect of keeping Ministers and government departments on their toes. The debates which follow, upon the budget or upon the Government's proposed legislation (private bills hardly ever appear before the House), vary tremendously in quality. There are many speakers who stand up, stolidly read a set speech, and sit down, without any effect being perceptible upon themselves or their listeners. There are others who have acquired an intimate, House of Commons manner, and whose discourse is built up out of the feeling of the House. The technique of interruption by question is successfully employed by a few parliamentarians. All proceedings are in Burmese,[1] but bills (particularly in respect of amending legislation) are still sometimes published in English.

The general impression given by Parliament in session is of a responsible body of middle-aged men, mostly drawn from the ranks of the professions (especially law) or retired public servants and, apart from the national political figures, mostly elected because of some local connexion. The salaries of M.P.s are modest,[2] and although their parliamentary duties do not fill the year, most are full-time politicians. In pre-war Burma the great majority of politicians were notoriously corrupt: how far has this bad practice lasted up to the present day? All Ministers and M.P.s certainly enjoy many advantages from their position: trips abroad, especially to America, and constant travel facilities and entertainment at home. Many politicians, in addition, receive much profitable attention from salesmen and industrialists, foreign and native, who desire a share of the extensive orders placed by the Government. And some quite bluntly sell their favours for cash. Clearly it is not easy to assess to what extent this represents the lack of a tradition of clean public service—which may arise in time—and to what extent the deliberate malversation of unworthy men. U Nu is in no doubt of the answer: his constant theme is the need to eliminate corruption.[3] In October 1951 he revealed that since 1948, 464

---

[1] The use of English was allowed in the first Parliament, but a motion by the veteran Chit Hlaing to permit its continued use, soon after the second Parliament met, was defeated (*Nation*, 20 September 1952). The present Speaker has only a few words of English.

[2] Speaker, K3,500 per month; Deputy Speaker, K750; Prime Minister, K2,300 plus K1,000 allowance, house, and car; Cabinet Ministers, K1,700 plus house (or K250 allowance) and car; the Foreign Minister receives an additional allowance of K1,000; Parliamentary Secretaries K1,000, M.P.s K300 plus certain travelling concessions.

[3] 'I have to admit with shame that I am painfully aware of the prevalence of corruption, like mushrooms, around politicians, government servants and business men. But although we may know these things, we cannot take action when actual proof is lacking. . . . We can but look on with folded hands. . . . Unless the guilty persons overcome their greed, the Union of Burma will go to rack and ruin' (*Nation*, 27 March 1951).

cases of corruption had been unearthed, their estimated cost to the country being 130 lakhs.[1] To meet this problem, the Special Bureau of Investigation was set up directly under the Prime Minister, with extensive powers of search; its inquiries range over the whole field of public service, the nationalized industries, and political activities throughout the Union. Two special judges were deputed to try corruption cases. The Bureau of Investigation has certainly exposed many cases of fraud, but it is open to question whether its investigations amongst politicians, especially those in high places, have been pressed with the same ruthlessness as among officials. Beginning towards the end of 1954 U Nu intensified his condemnation of the 'vipers within the midst of the AFPFL. . . . Idlers, self-seekers, opportunists, power maniacs.'[2] In May 1955 an all-Burma AFPFL Preliminary Conference was convened. This heard some trenchant criticism of AFPFL members and methods from the Prime Minister and other leaders. A purge of undesirable elements was mooted, and a committee appointed to 'screen' politicians and civil servants.

Can the League be purified, without being split apart? Self-seekers cling like leeches to the AFPFL because no other party can promise power. Is there any possibility that the domination of one party may gradually give way to a party system in which governments will be answerable to the verdict of the electorate? As yet there is no sign of any such development.

A rehearsal for the 1956 general election was provided by the Rangoon municipal election of 23 February 1955. The Government treated the election as a test of the solidarity of its support. The opposition managed to agree to sink their differences; to make their challenge effective, they united under the banner of the Patriotic Alliance. All the leading personalities, including Ba Pe, Aung Than, Thakin Lwin, and Bo Yan Naing, offered themselves for election.[3] Dr. Ba Maw did not contest a seat, but he was very much the master-organizer of the opposition. He announced, as a platform, a 'people's democracy', stressing that the election was one aspect of the 'people's revolution which is changing the world'. An ambitious thirteen-point programme for a new city (including a new municipal Act) followed.[4]

[1] 'I am not an alarmist, but look where you will, government circles, political circles or business circles, I see people out for gain, devoid of all scruples, as if they were possessed by the demon of greed. . . . If we let them, they will go on scrambling for their filthy lucre till they bring down our country about our heads in ruins' (ibid., 5 October 1951).
[2] ibid., 27 November 1954.
[3] Only Ba Sein refused to co-operate with any organization that included the Communists.
[4] *Nation*, 25 January 1955.

In reply the AFPFL put their election campaign into the charge of Ba Swe, and some of its best orators were mobilized for the fight. In an eve-of-election speech, Kyaw Nyein issued a threat: 'If the opposition should come into power in the Corporation, then its policy and programme would certainly not be in line with the Government, and the Government would not be willing to give financial assistance to an organization which would not be in unison with it.'[1] The AFPFL showed an impressive range of party organization. The opposition relied on flogging up mass emotion at rowdy meetings: the AFPFL deployed teams of organizers throughout the city, right down to the level of a door-to-door canvass. And everywhere there were great red banners stretched right across the streets proclaiming 'The people of this quarter will vote for the AFPFL candidate'. When the day came, like every other Burmese event, the first impression was of an enormous *pwè* or festival. There were brightly coloured *mandats* (booths) for the ward organizers, jeeps and buses swathed in slogans and candidates' portraits, street bands playing frenetic tunes, loudspeakers blaring 'the AFPFL is winning everywhere'. Behind all this there was organization: an AFPFL 'operations centre', and canvassers ready to mind the baby or watch the cooking-pot while the housewife voted.

The result, as everyone anticipated, was a landslide for the AFPFL who won 33 out of the 35 seats (at the previous election it had been 34 out of 35). About 54 per cent. of the electorate voted, and of these 67·5 per cent. voted for the AFPFL, 29 per cent. for the united opposition, and 3·5 per cent. for Independents. One united opposition candidate was successful, and one Independent, to whom no one had paid any attention: he had been standing, unsuccessfully, at every election for years.

Once again, the election appeared to be properly conducted, except for the fantastic inefficiency with which the electoral rolls were prepared: of the Rangoon population of 737,000, only 200,000 were registered as electors.[2]

One particular feature of the 1955 Rangoon election threw a ray of light upon the pattern of contemporary politics in Burma. The one poster which the AFPFL chose to paste up everywhere around Rangoon was a portrait of a determined-looking young man in Japanese army uniform: Aung San. Out of the thirty-five united opposition candidates, the only

---

[1] *Nation*, 21 February 1955.

[2] On the morrow of the election, the writer talked to a prominent newspaper editor, who was disgusted because his entire household was excluded from the register. He was somewhat mollified when a visitor informed him that the Minister of Information himself had been disfranchised.

one to achieve election was that man's brother, Aung Than. The legend of Aung San and the 'Struggle for Independence' still looms large in Burmese politics. It may be many years before it is replaced by a new mystique.

The ruling AFPFL coalition awaited the 1956 election with a confidence that was dangerously akin to complacency. Their major preoccupation was the struggle for power within the League, between the rival leaders and between the constituent organizations, with the ABPO staking an aggressive claim to the vote of the cultivator and the Socialists attempting to re-establish their ascendancy in the management of the League. The opposition appeared to be impotent in the face of the over-whelming advantages of the AFPFL in the form of a well-developed electoral machine, as well as control over state services and funds. However, there was much public discontent, mainly passive but by no means dumb, which the opposition might be able to exploit. The prosperity which had followed the world boom in rice prices, and the much-publicized benefits of the *Pyidawtha* programme were concentrated very largely in Rangoon, and perhaps the other centres of the rice trade. The impact of the financial crisis of 1955 which set prices of consumer goods spinning upwards, while the rice trade stagnated, was a universal experience. And while the Government, with some justification, claimed that the rebels were everywhere defeated, normal life had not come back to the countryside. Unrest and insecurity continued, while communications and public services remained vestigial. All this fermented a discontent which was accentuated by the individualism and *insouciance* of great num-bers of Burmans who, almost instinctively it seems, feel a compulsion to criticize and oppose established authority. Many groups in the opposition, including the BWPP and other leftist organizations, combined to set up a National United Front. Many moderates saw this Front as the only effective means of opposing the AFPFL, and Dr. E Maung was included among them. To the right there was the Burma Nationalist Bloc and the Independent Arakanese Parliamentary Group, now renamed the Arakan National United Organization. Altogether, the 220 AFPFL nominees found themselves con-fronted on polling day by about 300 other candidates; a majority of the latter were identified with the 27 opposition parties, but many moderates and conservatives stood as Independents.

Elections took place simultaneously on 27 April, but con-tinuing insecurity prevented them being held in 10 constituencies. As results were declared in the urban areas, the anticipated AFPFL landslide appeared to be rumbling to total victory. All 9 Rangoon seats were retained by the League, who secured two-thirds of the total vote: U Nu's majority was 15,000 and those of Ba Swe and Kyaw Nyein were similarly massive. But U Tin in a contest against Aung Than secured only 19,082 votes, whilst Aung Than mustered 16,700 for the opposition, although the full weight of the AFPFL juggernaut was specially mobilized in this constituency. As the up-country returns began to come in, it became apparent that the hold of the AFPFL over the rural areas was far from complete. Many seats confidently regarded as safe by the Government were lost, particularly in middle Burma. Here, where the Communists have never lost the 'grass roots' loyalty of the people, the National United Front secured notable successes. Final figures indicated that the AFPFL had won 145 seats, while other parties associated with it obtained 28 seats.[1] The National United Front won 47 seats, and other opposition parties gained 7 seats.[2] There were 13 Independent M.P.s to complete a total Chamber of Deputies of 240, with 10 seats to be decided when security should permit. These figures represented a comfortable majority for the AFPFL, but the actual voting figures showed a considerably higher proportion of support for the opposition: about two-fifths of the electorate actually voted: of these, 48 per cent voted for the AFPFL and 30 per cent for the NUF.

As a result of the elections the opposition was considerably reinforced and invigorated. Dr. E Maung emerged as its outstanding figure, although his personal following was small. The AFPFL sought to explain their misfortunes by asserting that the opposition had utilized threats and violence to intimidate the electorate, and hinting at political intervention by foreign embassies. More solid reasons for their reverses were provided by their own record: the failure of the Government to ameliorate the disordered conditions in the countryside, and the corruption, self-seeking, and indifference to public feeling which had characterized so many of the lesser leaders of the AFPFL.

On 5 June 1956 U Nu announced that he would relinquish the premiership for one year in order to undertake the reorganization of the AFPFL and the elimination of corrupt

---

[1] *AFPFL allies*: United Hill Peoples' Congress, 14, People's Economic and Cultural Development Organization (Kachin, Sima Duwa), 4, All-Shan States Organization, 5, Kayah State, 2, Shan State Peasants' Organization, 1, Kachin National Congress (Kachin, Duwa Zau Lawn), 2. The adherence of some of these allies, e.g. PECDO and SSPO, cannot be regarded as unqualified.

[2] *Combined Opposition, NUF allies*, Arakan National United Organization, 5, Burma Nationalist Bloc, 1, Union National Pa-o Organization (Taungthu), 1.

elements. During this period U Ba Swe became Prime Minister with three Deputy Premiers: Kyaw Nyein (Minister for National Economy) and Thakin Tin (Minister for Social Services)—Ba Swe's rivals in the leadership of the Socialist Party—along with Sao Hkun Hkio as Foreign Minister. Despite Nu's withdrawal from formal leadership, he remained closely associated with government policy, particularly in the realm of foreign affairs. He resumed the premiership in June 1957.

Towards the end of that year the rivalries within the Cabinet and the party became acute. For some time the demarcation of boundaries of power between the 'Swe–Nyein' group and Nu's associates had ceased to satisfy the Socialist Party, whose programme of industrialization and nationalization had been practically suspended in consequence of the continuing balance-of-payments difficulties. In these circumstances, U Nu's continuing religious and cultural undertakings were resented. A disturbing factor was the growing power of the mass political organizations, whereby certain leaders were acquiring an importance based upon numbers rather than personal stature. Ba Swe's Trades Union Congress was probably the most powerful, but it was rivalled by the All Burma Peasants' Organization of Thakin Tin and Thakin Kyaw Tun, as well as the Federation of Trade Organizations. These buttresses of power were balanced, to some extent, by U Nu's influence over religious, cultural, and educational bodies, but one outstanding politician, Kyaw Nyein, was unable to marshal a similar following. As the principal intellectual of the Socialist Party, and a senior minister, Kyaw Nyein was particularly dissatisfied with the new trends.

With the Socialist leaders divided and restless, U Nu chose to toss an intellectual bombshell into their midst. On 29 January 1958 the Third All-Burma Congress of the AFPFL was opened. To an audience numbering over 100,000, Nu delivered a four-hour speech defining the ideology of the AFPFL. In the course of a detailed analysis of Marxism, he exploded the theory of Dialectical Materialism in the light of Buddhist belief. He concluded, 'the AFPFL rejects Marxism as a guiding philosophy or as the ideology of the AFPFL'. He went on to describe his own idea of a Welfare State, and to appeal for higher moral standards within the party. His supporters praised the speech as a contribution to national unity, but the Swe–Nyein group accepted it as a direct challenge to its Marxist Socialist philosophy.

Subsequently, relations between the two groups deteriorated rapidly and on 4 June 1958 fifteen ministers and twenty-two Parliamentary Secretaries resigned from the Government.

Ba Swe and Kyaw Nyein took with them almost all the former 1936 Student Committee, the originators of the AFPFL, only M. A. Raschid continued to support U Nu. Thakin Tin and Thakin Kyaw Tun also remained. Nu had now to confront the well-organized Socialist parliamentary faction. He was reinforced by elements of the opposition, and strengthened his Government by the addition of a number of Frontier leaders to his Cabinet, together with Kyaw Min of the Arakanese group as Finance Minister. Faced with a Socialist motion of no confidence, he secured a majority of seven. Nu was joined by Dr. E Maung, Bo Hmu Aung, and others, but his parliamentary position remained unsure. To break the deadlock, Nu announced that a fresh election would be held in November, but he became alarmed at the threat to freedom of electoral choice which the increasing number of 'private armies' appeared to forbode. On 28 October parliament was assembled and Nu announced that he was handing over the premiership to General Ne Win, as head of a non-party Government. The general initially took office for six months, but his tenure was extended to April 1960 by a constitutional amendment approved by a joint session of Parliament, with 304 members assenting and 29 dissenting. Meanwhile, the 'Clean' and 'Stable' groups were mobilizing their forces. The former relied almost entirely on the personal prestige of U Nu, who toured the country, promising to make Buddhism the state religion and offering to consider the creation of new Mon and Arakanese states. The Swe–Nyein group had a much better party organization, but no clearly defined programme.

The election took place in February 1960, and the magnitude of Nu's victory came as a surprise, even to his supporters. In the Chamber of Deputies (250 seats) the 'Clean' party won 156 seats and their Frontier allies won 10. The 'Stable' group won 34 seats, and their Frontier allies 4. The Arakan Organization won 6 seats, and other independents 16: 24 seats could not be contested. In the Chamber of Nationalities (125 seats) the 'Clean' party won 48 seats, and the 'Stable' 27; there were 50 independents. During the last two years of parliamentary government, political debate took place mainly within the *Pyidaungsu* Party. A cleavage developed between the Old Guard and the younger politicians. Once again, U Nu reacted to the divisions in his Party by resigning from the office of president (in January 1962) in order to promote reform from outside. Soon afterwards, General Ne Win stepped in to send all the politicians packing.

IV

TOWARDS A WELFARE STATE

SINCE their earliest days AFPFL leaders have linked the idea of political independence with that of economic advance: the 'Naythuyein Declaration' of August 1945, which brought the AFPFL into being, contained economic objectives.[1] On 6 June 1947 Aung San convened a meeting of politicians and senior officials at 'Sorrento Villa'. The general purpose was to bring to an end the 'colonial economy', based on the export of raw materials, and to create a new Socialist system with the accent on nationalization and industrialization. In particular, a steel mill and a textile factory were planned. Owing to Aung San's sudden death, the conference 'did not come to any final conclusion'.[2]

Economic and social welfare were prominent themes in the new constitution.[3] Chapter II, which lays down certain Fundamental Rights, has a section (23) concerning economic rights, mainly devoted to circumscribing these 'rights' by prohibiting trusts, syndicates, and cartels and by establishing the State's right to nationalize 'branches of the national economy or single enterprises'. Chapter III lays down the 'Relations of the State to Peasants and Workers', beginning with the statement (sect. 30) that 'The State is the ultimate owner of all lands', and going on to lay down the State's power to nationalize land for 'collective or co-operative farming or [for] agricultural tenants'. Workers are promised state assistance in promoting trade unions, housing schemes, and social insurance. Chapter IV enumerates 'Directive Principles of State Policy', which is in effect a welfare programme directed to securing (i) the right to work, (ii) the right to maintenance in old age and during sickness, (iii) the right to rest and leisure, and (iv) the right to education. The chapter ends with the pronouncement (sect. 44): 'The State shall direct its policy towards operation of all public utility undertakings . . . [and] exploitation of all natural resources in the Union by itself or local bodies or by people's

---

[1] Some of these appear strange to the outsider, e.g. 'Everybody should have the right to obtain free supply of timber and bamboo for the construction of one's own dwelling house': this demand arises from the British state conservation of timber, an outstanding grievance to the Burmans.

[2] Speech of Kyaw Myint in Ministry of Information, *The Pyidawtha Conference* (Rangoon, 1952), p. 36.

[3] *The Constitution of the Union of Burma* (Rangoon, 1947).

co-operative organizations.' Finally, Chapter XIII, headed 'General Provisions', lays down special provisions for private enterprises working public utility services (sect. 218): only concerns with at least 60 per cent. share-capital owned by the Union, or by Union citizens, will be authorized to operate public utility services. Furthermore, 'timber and mineral lands, forests, water, fisheries, minerals, coal, petroleum and other mineral oils, all sources of potential energy and all other natural resources shall be exploited and developed by the Union'; 'specific exceptions' might be made to this rule, and private enterprises (with 60 per cent. Burman participation) might be admitted to these fields only by special Act of Parliament.[1]

The advent of independence put the responsibilities of government into the hands of a Cabinet which, with one or two exceptions, lacked any practical experience of administration. Firmly believing that the wealth of Burma had in the past been drained away by the British, they were convinced that a new era of unprecedented prosperity awaited them.[2] U Nu in his early speeches was careful to stress that state Socialism might be attained by two alternative approaches: the British, democratic, evolutionary method, and the Soviet technique of violent revolution: from the very beginning he advocated 'the circle of democracy'.[3]

A Ministry of National Planning was set up on the eve of independence, and an outline Two-Year Economic Development Plan was announced on 1 April 1948. An Economic Council was established, whose main function was to advise on the suitability of the various commercial activities for state or municipal control or for continuance under private ownership. Shortly after, measures were announced for the nationalization of those activities which were particularly associated with foreign domination. On 20 April 1948 the Inland Water Transport Nationalization Act passed through Parliament: this measure was more radical in name than in effect. Since CAS(B)

---

[1] These conditions are subject to amendment 'when the public interest so requires' and under this clause Joint Undertakings in which foreigners hold over 40 per cent. of the shares have been upheld as valid by the Supreme Court (10 February 1953).

[2] Speech by U Nu, National Day, 8 November 1947; 'We must show ourselves equal to the rich natural resources of our country. For our masses to come up to standards of living befitting the natural wealth of our country we must all work to the limit from this day and hour. If we all resolve to do so, with one mind, I shall predict that within five years at the longest, this country of Burma, bountifully provided by nature . . . will see once again such a golden age as Pagan, in the days when Shin Izza Gawna was exercising the magic of his alchemy' (*Towards Peace and Democracy*, p. 19).

[3] cf. broadcast, 'I Choose Democracy', 3 April 1948, quoted in ibid., see especially pp. 60–64.

days an Inland Water Transport Board had controlled the whole of Burma's river shipping. The Inland Water Transport Board operated in three sections: an Irrawaddy Section, a Lighterage Section, and an Arakan Section, using British companies as its agents. The Arracan Flotilla Company was permitted to carry on in Arakan waters, but the great Irrawaddy Flotilla Company, whose ships had carried the army which occupied Thibaw's Mandalay, was taken over on 1 June 1948. The Government set up a Nationalization Commission to determine the question of compensation; its award, announced in January 1950, gave the Irrawaddy Flotilla Company 41·22 lakhs or £309,000 as against the Company's claim of £1,452,000. The measurement adopted—original value, minus depreciation—did not perhaps recommend itself to the dispossessed management: to Burmese nationalists, conscious of the fat profits of former years, it erred in generosity.[1]

On 1 June 1948 the timber concessions of the Bombay Burmah Trading Corporation, Foucar's, MacGregor's, and the other foreign firms were taken over by the Union, together with certain of their sawmills and timber-yards, and passed to a State Timber Extraction Organization under the State Timber Board.[2] And so time gave its answer to the events of 1885; the conquest and occupation of Upper Burma by the British, following the dispute between Thibaw and the Bombay Burmah Trading Corporation concerning the felling and export of teak.

The third, and potentially most far-reaching, nationalization measure was the Land Nationalization Act, passed on 11 October 1948. The declared purpose of the Act was 'to put an end to landlordism and to usher in an era whose ultimate objective is collective farming'.[3] This Act was not, in fact, put into operation, except on a limited scale in Syriam township. The motive behind the measure was very clear: it was the reclamation of

---

[1] The principles which have guided Burma's judges in awarding compensation are set out in some detail in the award made following the later nationalization of the Arracan Flotilla Company. The presiding judge observed: 'We come to the most difficult part of the enquiry, viz. the fixation of the equitable compensation for the assets taken from the Company. Once again, we repeat that in arriving at this compensation we are not bound to follow any legal principles, and are to be guided solely by the rules for natural justice. Clearly, a government cannot be treated on the same lines as a willing buyer who is out to make profits, nor can it be expected to pay market value for the assets taken over. Hence, in the absence of special circumstances, the most that a Company whose assets have been nationalized can expect is depreciated first costs of those assets' (full report of award quoted *Nation*, 4 January 1955).

[2] In the British period teak forests were partially worked direct by the Government, yielding a sizeable revenue.

[3] Ministry of Agriculture and Forests, *The Land Nationalization Act, together with speeches by Thakin Tin and Thakin Nu* (Rangoon, 1948).

the 3 million acres which had passed from the cultivators to the big landlords, of whom the great majority were Indian Chettyars, a caste of financiers from Madras.[1] For the cycle of events from 1937 to 1948, reviewed in the first chapter, had a dual significance. Most obvious was the act of shaking off the ties which bound Burma to Britain; but of equal, or perhaps greater, importance was the disentangling of the bonds which joined Burma with India. The elimination of Indian participation from the administration, the army, the worlds of commerce, agriculture, and labour was nothing less than a second revolution.

As the whirlwind of civil war blew ever more gustily, the programme of nationalization had to give way to the country's immediate needs: to achieve solvency and to maintain national integrity. The Finance Minister's 1949 budget speech revealed a deficit during the previous year of 744 lakhs (or £5,720,000), largely owing to the almost complete drying up of the land revenue.[2] It became necessary to transfer the funds accumulated for development purposes to the revenue account. Requests were made to Britain for a further loan to cover the deficit. Britain took counsel with other Commonwealth countries, and a joint offer of a loan of £6 million was eventually agreed, but not until June 1950.

Under these circumstances the Cabinet (no longer predominantly Socialist in membership) made drastic modifications in its planning. On 14 June 1949 U Nu made a statement of policy concerning the role of foreign capital. He declared: 'Since we do not possess either the capital or the technical resources necessary for industrialization, we must enlist the help of foreign capital and technicians.' He cited the example of Soviet Russia as a country developed through foreign aid. But he did not announce any measures to attract the desired foreign capital (a desideratum of 200 crores, $600 million or £150 million, was mentioned) and no assurances on nationalization were offered.[3] Three months later the Foreign Minister, U E Maung, visited Britain and the United States, partly with the purpose of attracting foreign investors. He quoted a pronouncement by the Planning Board that 'nationalization would need to be deferred until the country was in a position to

---

[1] Even U Nu, the pattern of Buddhist tolerance, permits himself to dislike the Chettyars. Cf. his remarks at the 1952 Pyidawtha Conference concerning 'the Chettyar with the bloated abdomen named Allagappa'.

[2] Full text of Finance Minister's budget speech given in Dept. of Information, *Burma's Freedom, the Second Anniversary* (Rangoon, 1950), pp. 98–112.

[3] 'Foreign Capital in Burma', statement on government policy laid before Parliament by Thakin Nu, quoted in ibid., pp. 70–73.

pay for the businesses taken over'.[1] A more trenchant exposé of the country's critical situation was made in a report of the Economic Council[2] published on 28 September 1949. The existing state of affairs was described as 'very dangerous and almost desperate. . . . Production is less than half the pre-war level, and the surplus available for export . . . is only about one-fifth.' The remedies proposed were firstly, austerity, a drastic scaling down of imports; secondly, the encouragement of Burmese cottage industries; and finally, the development of large-scale enterprises through foreign capital. Amongst the terms that should be offered to foreign enterprise would be guarantees of exemption from nationalization for a stipulated period.[3]

It cannot be said that these policy statements had any great effect upon the attitude of foreign capital to investment in Burma: it was not interested. As a result of the insurrection, almost all existing industrial installations in the country closed down. The railways were virtually at a standstill and river traffic was dead. The Burmah Oil Company had been endeavouring to restore its pre-war plant and pipeline ever since 1945. Expenditure was endless, and the Company applied to the Burma Government for a financial guarantee. This was refused, but the British Government came to the rescue. By late 1949 £8 million had been spent on rehabilitation with hardly any sign of the oil beginning to flow. In January 1950 the British Government withdrew its guarantees. The BOC suspended working. Early 1950 was the lowest point in Burma's economic misfortunes.

Early in 1950 the United States regarded Burma as finished: in February George McGhee, Assistant Secretary of State, characterized the country as 'unstable', and President Truman's roving ambassador, Philip Jessup, called the situation 'well-nigh hopeless', observing that 'fighting is continuous'.[4] U Nu was reported to be asking Jessup for $50 million aid from the United States;[5] in April the Griffin Mission visited Burma, in order to investigate conditions, and to determine whether Point Four Aid might be granted. The Mission appeared to be adversely impressed,[6] but six months later, in September, an

[1] There was also some discussion with the Irrawaddy Flotilla Company regarding the resumption of conftrol by the company, but no agreement could be reached (see *Nation*, 8 September 1949).

[2] Members: J. S. Furnivall, Planning Adviser, Professor Hla Myint, Bo Khin Maung Gale, and Ba Nyein.

[3] Quoted *in extenso* in *Burma's Freedom, the Second Anniversary*, pp. 113–18.

[4] *Nation*, 19 February 1950 and *Daily Telegraph*, 25 March 1950.

[5] *Nation*, 5 May 1950.

[6] Mr. Griffin, when asked whether a necessary condition for the sanctioning of aid would be the adoption by Burma of an anti-Communist attitude, tartly replied 'Our government will be satisfied if you can drive all over Rangoon and not see a single road-block' (ibid., 4 April 1950).

Economic Aid Agreement was negotiated in Rangoon,[1] under which aid to the value of $8–10 million was to be made available in the year 1950–1.

This aid was in contrast to the British loans of previous years.[2] It had been left to Burma to spend the British loans and grants as she thought fit, subject only to agreement on the dates when the monies should be released for use. American aid was administered by an elaborate Technical and Economic Mission which numbered sixty members at its peak, and the shape that assistance might take was largely in American hands. A proportion of the aid was in the form of 'services': that is to say, of American experts and advisers on loan to Burma. The erection of this elaborate machinery meant that the impact of American assistance took a lengthy period to develop and reinforce Burma's economy. The Union of Burma was also required to pay into a Special Account, sums in kyats equivalent to the dollar value of the commodities and services furnished by the United States. This 'counterpart fund', as it is usually known, was utilized to pay the expenses of the American mission in Burma, but a substantial balance accumulated for other purposes.

The Government was now able to lift its eyes from the task of propping up the administration, and to think about the future. Hope was in the air again.

U Nu has described[3] how he read a report in an English newspaper that the Persian Government had employed a foreign firm to compile a survey and a report upon the economic resources of Persia. He called in U Hla Maung, Secretary for National Planning, and instructed him to find a suitable firm to undertake a similar task in Burma.

Two or three firms were considered, and the final choice rested on Knappen-Tippetts-Abbett Engineering Company of New York (invariably known in Burma as KTA). This organization enlisted the services of Pierce Management Inc. (mining specialists) and Robert R. Nathan Associates Inc., a group of economists.[4] Robert Nathan, Professor Everett E. Hagan, and

---

[1] Text and correspondence given in Dept. of Information, *Burma, the Third Anniversary* (Rangoon, 1951), pp. 89–95.

[2] This question is very complex, but it would appear that British loans to Burma, 1945–8, totalled some £75 million. £48·5 million was written off, £1·1 million was repaid, and the remainder, £25·4 million, has since been virtually wiped out. U.S. aid to Burma, 1951–5, totalled $18·95 million, as compared with $653·59 million to Indo-China, $67·16 million to the Philippines, and $21·34 million to Siam: all exclusive of defence aid. (American aid: source: FOA, *Operations Report*, May 1955.)

[3] *Forward with the People* (Rangoon, 1955), p. 107.

[4] The contract with these firms expired in August 1953, when a new contract was entered into and financed by the Government of Burma. The group was thenceforward known as Knappen-Tippetts-Abbett-McCarthy Engineers.

others of his associates had been lieutenants in the 1930's of President Roosevelt and his 'New Deal' administration, some having worked in the Tennessee Valley Authority. Thus, although the Burmese Socialists had gone to the stronghold of individual effort for their mentors, they had nevertheless succeeded in finding men who were in sympathy with their ideals. The KTA heads arrived in Rangoon in September 1951, and soon a resident staff of 150 were at work, with Colonel Homer B. Pettit as General Manager. The costs of this enterprise were charged to American aid funds.[1]

The principal KTA assignment was the preparation of an 'Economic and Engineering Survey' of Burma. A beginning had already been made by a group of Oxford economists who visited Burma in March–April 1951 under United Nations auspices. Working from official records they produced estimates of the country's gross national income for 1938–9 and for the years subsequent to 1946. Their statistics showed that the national income, reduced to 1951 terms, had fallen from K330 per head in 1939 to K182 in 1951: within twelve years, following the war and independence, the income of the people of Burma had been halved.[2] The Oxford economists went on to make certain recommendations for future lines of development,[3] but it was left to KTA, using these estimates, to build up a planning programme for the rehabilitation of the whole economy.

The year 1951 was also election year, and the AFPFL put before the country the outlines of a welfare programme. From 1 April 1951 education throughout the land, from primary school to university, became free for all.[4] Early in the year another welfare agency, the National Housing Board, was started. On 30 August U Tin presented a 'welfare budget'; he dismissed all its predecessors' as 'police budgets'. Now, he claimed, the insurrection was 'no longer news', and the rebels were disorganized; the new estimates were prepared 'with the objects, primarily, of developing and improving education, health and moral character and strengthening of our economy and national solidarity'.[5] There were great increases in expenditure on development, the defence services, and social welfare. Out of a total of 9,192 lakhs, there was provision for 3,768

[1] Since American aid ended, the Burma Government has paid the bill. Dollar costs of the KTA Survey approached $2 million, besides extensive costs in kyats.
[2] See Ministry of Information, *Pyidawtha Conference*, pp. 36–37.
[3] cf. Miss Peter Ady, *Some Notes on Burma's Post War Economic Potentials*, unpublished.
[4] Except for the Faculty of Law at the university where fees continued: residential students are, of course, required to pay boarding fees.
[5] *Burma, the Fourth Anniversary* (Rangoon, 1952), pp. 1 ff.

lakhs on capital account; the budget anticipated a deficit of 1,736 lakhs or £13,400,000, but experience was to show that a programme of capital investment could not be achieved merely by making budget provisions: the actual build-up was slower to develop.

GOVERNMENT INCOME AND EXPENDITURE
1949–54

(million kyats)

EXPENDITURE	*1949–50*	*1950–1*	*1951–2*	*1952–3*	*1953–4*	*1954–5*
Civil Administration	148·6	146·0	170·4	187·6	193·7(?)	226·5(?)
Defence	120·4	139·0	213·8	317·0	390·0	400(?)
Social Welfare	26·6	50·3	110·0	132·9	210·0	250(?)
Development	100·1	87·9	150(?)	181·3	395·6(?)	500(?)
Other	40·8	49·6	237·4	302·9	308·0	147·5(?)
Total	436·5	472·8	881·6	1,121·7	1,497·3	1,524·0
INCOME						
SAMB (profit)	169·7	178·6	217·7	250·6	300(?)	300(?)
Customs	112·3	171·5	193·1	190·1	228	216·9
Income tax	48·7	44·6	44·5	51·2	62(?)	86
Other taxes	71·3	70·6	67·0	94·5	242·7	262·3
Total	458·6	561·1	633·5	713·5	832·7	865·2
Capital receipts	147·9	119·6	247·2	293·8	261·2	282·7
Total receipts	606·5	680·7	880·7	1,007·3	1,093·9	1,147·9

(NOTE: The above table is based largely upon the *Economic Surveys* issued annually by the Government and the budget statements of the Finance Minister, but no claim of finality as regards detail is made. There are so many discrepancies between 'estimates', 'actuals', and 'revised actuals' that any reconciliation on the basis of published data is impossible; but general trends emerge clearly enough.)

The budget for 1951–2 did represent the beginning of a new phase of expanding government expenditure. This expansion was considerably assisted by adventitious outside circumstances: the outbreak of the Korean War, world rearmament, and the United States' rush to stockpile essential commodities, led to a phenomenal rise in the price of raw materials in which Burma's rice had a share. The world price of rice rose from £40 per ton in mid-1950 to £60 at the end of 1951, touching £80 in 1952. Burma's foreign-exchange reserves, which stood at 56 crores in December 1949 and 60 crores in December 1950, rose to 80 crores in the next twelve months and to 100 crores by December 1952. It was against this background of apparent buoyancy and prosperity that KTA presented its *Preliminary Report* in May 1952.

Its central theme was the expansion of the national economy through a seven-year programme which would restore and improve upon the pre-war standard of living. Income per head should be raised from the K182 of 1951 to K340. This would necessitate an increase of 78 per cent. upon 1951 production, or an increase of 40 per cent. *per capita* over pre-war production, leading to a gross production of 700 crores by 1959. A national capital investment of 750 crores (£562 million) would be required; it was proposed to assign 65 crores to 'social capital', 300 crores in planned productive projects, and 295 crores in unplanned productive projects. A number of specific schemes in various fields (mining, power, industry, communications) were proposed for early development at a cost of some 108 crores. Except in the case of about half a dozen schemes, these plans were admittedly based on the sketchiest information (KTA men viewed one mine from an aeroplane) and were not supported by field surveys or detailed costing. The Government accepted this plan 'in principle' and decided to allot 110 crores for development purposes over the following two or three years.

The year 1952 gave the country an opportunity to judge the first two big development works: the new aerodrome at Mingaladon, the airport for Rangoon, and the new government cotton-spinning and weaving factory at Thamaing, a Rangoon suburb. Perhaps not surprisingly these two undertakings exhibited in acute form the problems likely to arise in a country which, attempting to take a short-cut from colonial status to full autonomy, discards overnight all the administrators and technicians of the old régime and pushes up new state enterprises regardless of a total lack of experience and expertise.

The Mingaladon airfield, largely rendered useless in the war, was hastily rebuilt by the R.A.F. in May 1945 with perforated steel plates: it was calculated to have a 'life' of three years. In February 1948 the Director of Civil Aviation put up proposals to the Ministry of Transport for new runways. The papers came back in October 1949 with two sentences inscribed: the Public Works Department could not undertake the work. Meanwhile, the Director called in a Danish firm to carry out a survey: this went to the Ministry of Transport, the Ministry of National Planning, the Ministry of Finance, on to the Economic Council, and finally reached the Cabinet, which sanctioned construction at a cost of 27 lakhs. The matter was handed over to a Cabinet sub-committee, which decided to call for tenders on a 'cost-plus' basis[1] and, ignoring other competitors, an agreement was concluded with the Danish firm on 11 October 1950. An American Supervising Engineer was appointed to watch the Government's interests. The firm went straight ahead, seventy Danes were taken on the pay-roll, with lavish transport and accommodation facilities; no plans had been drawn up, no proper accounts were maintained, 50 per cent. errors in some works were reported. The Government thereupon appointed KTA as advisers in their interests; KTA were required to approve all purchases of equipment and machinery, but this precaution did not, in practice, ensure a check on expenditure. Eventually, the American Supervising Engineer became worried by the manner in which costs were mounting and defects multiplying: in October 1951 he resigned, and thereby public attention was drawn to the state of affairs at Mingaladon.[2] A secret inquiry was then made by U Win, Minister for National Planning, and was followed by a public inquiry presided over by a High Court judge. Hearings began in January 1952. The committee's findings were published in July 1952.[3] These stated that expenditure to date had reached 505 lakhs; the committee found that there had been excessive expenditure by the Danish construction firm and slack supervision on the part of the Supervisory Committee. Finally, the contractors returned 8 lakhs on account of a building which had completely collapsed, but the total loss to the State remained colossal. Final figures of costs have never been fully revealed, but they must have topped 6 crores, or £4 million, as against the original 27 lakhs (£200,000).

[1] The contractor receives as his profit a figure calculated as a percentage on the eventual costs of the work.

[2] *Nation*, 26 October 1951.

[3] Published in ibid., 15 July 1952. The above account is drawn entirely from these findings and from the evidence of witnesses. See reports in ibid., especially 19 and 23 February and 2 April 1952.

The story of the spinning and weaving factory was somewhat less spectacular. Negotiations first began in December 1947 for the purchase of textile machinery in the United States and Japan. An American manager and assistant were hired at large salaries, and the factory was completed in November 1949, but eighteen months went by before it was officially opened (17 May 1951). Part of the delay was due to the need to recruit Japanese overseers; part to the discovery that the machinery was quite unsuitable for the use of Burma cotton so that it was necessary to import cotton from the United States and elsewhere. During its early years the mill worked at 25–33 per cent. capacity. In 1952 a Committee of Inquiry was appointed, with Justice E Maung at its head; it recommended that no further expenditure should be incurred without parliamentary sanction. No proper accounts have been published to show the costs involved in erecting the factory and in its subsequent operations, but it is possible to penetrate the veil of silence to some extent. U Nu has stated that the cost of building the factory was 'approximately' K2·40 crores (about £2 million);[1] a question in Parliament revealed that during 1953–4 operating costs were over K70 lakhs and earnings K57 lakhs.[2] The quality of yarn produced has been limited to counts of 10 and 12: much below those in normal commercial use.[3] Output of cloth has been particularly low, and has been restricted to the production of 'greys' or unbleached material. The KTA *Report* departed from its usual tone of optimism when describing the textile mill: 'top-heavy labour costs and lowered efficiency and standards' were the first of a long list of defects which it enumerated.[4] Allusions to the textile mill in recent government publications are very rare:[5] it does not appear that its lessons have exercised any great influence in government circles.

Following the presentation of the KTA *Preliminary Report* the Government stepped up their planning activities. On 'Martyrs' Day' in July 1952 (a favourite occasion for announcing major government policy decisions) U Nu delivered a speech which has probably been quoted subsequently more than any other of his utterances. In reply to those who tried to make capital from the Government's acceptance of aid from Britain and the

[1] Nu, *Speech to Old Myoma Association*, 23 November 1951.

[2] *Nation*, 13 September 1955. In January 1953 the Mill Workers' Union alleged that losses of 30 lakhs had already been incurred (ibid., 27 March 1953).

[3] Producing a sack-like texture: most textiles have counts from 30 to 70.

[4] Knappen-Tippetts-Abbett-McCarthy Engineers, *Comprehensive Report on Economic and Engineering Survey of Burma, for Ministry of National Planning*, 1953, iii, 1684.

[5] Ministry of Finance, *Economic Survey of Burma* (Rangoon, 1954), p. 25, provides a solitary reference.

United States, he made a public appeal to China and Russia to offer aid to Burma (his appeal was not acknowledged by those countries). He recalled the slogans of the past, Aung San's call for 'Independence Within One Year', and his own promise of 'Peace Within One Year', and he announced a new slogan: 'Towards a Welfare State'. He looked forward to the time when every family in Burma would possess a house, a car, and an income of 800–1,000 kyats per month: 'your country is rich enough to provide these amenities', he asserted.[1] Next month, a mass rally was convened at the Rangoon Racecourse; the delegates numbered 1,000, and included M.P.s, officials from Commissioners down to Sub-Divisional Officers, and supporters of the AFPFL and its constituent organizations. For a fortnight (4–17 August) the conference listened to statements of the Government's plans.[2] After each resolution had been introduced by a Minister, it was 'supported' by delegates from the states and districts represented. There was no discussion or criticism of the subject-matter by the delegates: their role was simply to set the seal of approval on decisions already made.

This meeting has subsequently been called the 'Pyidawtha Conference'. *Pyidawtha* (literally, 'sacred-pleasant-country') has been equated with 'Welfare State', but it has also a more specific application as 'local self-help' or 'community co-operation'.[3] The intention is that, while the big development schemes are carried out by government agencies, smaller improvements will be effected by local effort, drawing upon the Buddhist belief in the acquisition of merit through acts of charity and public benefit, to encourage the voluntary contributions of labour, materials, and money towards community development projects.

Without any doubt, this aspect of Pyidawtha did make an appeal to the Buddhist traditions; there was much excitement, songs were composed and sung, meetings were held and promises of support were offered with enthusiasm.[4] A good deal

---

[1] *Nation*, 21 July 1952.

[2] Conference Agenda: 4 August, Prime Minister's opening speech, 'Towards a Welfare State'; 7 August, Bo Min Gaung, 'Plan for the Devolution of Powers'; 8 August, Ba Swe, 'Democratization of Local Administration'; 9 August, Bo Khin Maung Gale, 'Agricultural and Rural Development Five-Year Plan'; 11 August, Kyaw Myint, 'Target for Economic Development'; 12 August, Thakin Tin, 'Land Nationalization Plans'; 13 August, Ba Saw, 'Development Plan for the Under-developed Areas'; 14 August, M. A. Raschid, 'Housing Plan'; 15 August, Mahn Win Maung, 'Transport and Communications'; 16 August, Than Aung, 'Education Plan'; 17 August, Khin Maung Lat, 'Medical and Public Health Plans'.

[3] The word has been grossly overworked in recent years, being applied to almost any activity in Burma. In Sule Pagoda Road, Rangoon, there is a 'Pyidawtha Taxi Stand'; but its drivers are as imbued with the profit motive of individual capitalism as any others.

[4] cf. Nu, *Forward with the People*, pp. 16–19.

of this excitement has been translated into activity: the Finance
Minister announced in August 1953 that, whereas the Government had contributed only 110 lakhs to the development funds
of the township welfare committees, public contributions 'in
cash or in kind' totalled some 200 lakhs. Wells, roads, schools,
reading-rooms have been among the amenities most widely
created.[1]

To implement their larger schemes, the Government introduced certain structural changes late in 1952. Three new
Development Corporations were established, the Agriculture
and Rural Development Corporation (Chairman, U Nu), the
Industrial Development Corporation (Chairman, Kyaw Nyein),
and the Mineral Resources Development Corporation (Chairman, U Tin): a fourth corporation to take over transport was
mooted but has not been created. The intention in forming
these bodies was to speed up the processes of development.
The Secretariat, always cautious and slow-moving, had in
recent years slowed down almost to a dead stop. Whereas the
various state boards had been subject to considerable departmental control, the corporations were to be endowed with wider
freedom of responsibility. In a preliminary announcement, the
then Minister for Industry and Mines (Kyaw Myint) announced
'These corporations will be set up on business principles and
will operate on business lines. . . . They shall be free from
departmental rules and restrictions which are now an effective
barrier to carry out any work of development.'[2] Unfortunately,
the executive members of the corporations were, in every case,
the same overworked Ministers, senior civil servants, and chief
technicians who headed the departments in the Secretariat,
so that the dynamic approach which was required has not, so
far, developed. The over-all planning authority was also
reorganized. Previously proposals had first been reviewed by
the National Planning Board, and then submitted to the
Economic Council of eight members (Kyaw Myint as Chairman and J. S. Furnivall as Planning Adviser): but even this
body had no real executive authority; it acted as a sieve, proposals were scrutinized and passed to the Cabinet for action.
Frequently, the Cabinet would refer a big scheme to a sub-
committee, and in the case of the Mingaladon Airport, day-by-
day supervision was entrusted to a Construction Committee
consisting of the Minister of Transport and senior officials.
The disastrous waste under these arrangements (revealed by

[1] A quantitative estimate of this Pyidawtha programme could only be produced
after a most detailed inquiry: the present tendency to call all routine P.W.D. work
'Pyidawtha' is confusing to everybody.
[2] Ministry of Information, *Pyidawtha Conference*, p. 41.

the Inquiry Committee) was still fresh in the public mind when a more watertight structure was created. From 1 October 1953 the National Planning Board and the Economic Council were replaced by an Economic and Social Board, with the Prime Minister as Chairman, to take the major decisions on the process of development. A Social Planning Commission and an Economic Planning Commission, of eight members each, were also established to 'initiate, stimulate, and co-ordinate' planning activities by government departments, corporate bodies, or individuals. A Social and Economic Advisory Council composed of the representatives of different bodies completed the structure.

In 1952 expenditure on 'nation-building' activities further increased; nevertheless, in February 1953, U Nu found it necessary to observe: 'Up till now, this programme [of development and social welfare] has hardly gathered momentum, owing principally to lack of skilled personnel, capital equipment and other internal difficulties.'[1]

Early in 1953 the pattern of Burma's development programme was once again modified. On 17 March the Government suddenly notified the United States Government that the aid programme would be brought to an end on 30 June 1953. This abrupt decision was almost certainly the result of the KMT crisis [2] and the suspicion that America was furnishing aid to the KMT. The aid programme was arrested at a stage where it had still to assume any definite form. A quantity of equipment, much of it for schools and hospitals, had been supplied but few Burmans had been trained in its handling. A number of advisers had arrived, but had still to learn their way around Burma. The Burmese decision may have been influenced by a suspicion that some of these advisers were not of the highest calibre. American aid did yield two tangible assets: the KTA survey and report, and the programme of rehabilitation in the Rangoon dockyards, which made a definite contribution towards getting trade moving once again. In other respects the piecemeal supply of miscellaneous goods and services, although quantitatively not insignificant, contributed very little towards Burma's development.

In the changed circumstances, to find the necessary technicians and equipment Burma needed, a series of purchasing missions, headed by Cabinet Ministers, were dispatched overseas. One party, headed by Bo Min Gaung, Minister of

---

[1] *BWB*, 25 February 1953.
[2] See above, pp. 52 and 53.

Supplies, travelled round the world.[1] During its tour it placed orders for £3 million in Britain, £1,250,000 in Europe, $750,000 in the United States, and £1,750,000 in Japan. Almost simultaneously, a 'Planning Projects Implementation Mission' was dispatched to Europe from July to November 1953.[2] This was charged with negotiating contracts for five specific projects; the major part of their orders were placed in Britain.

While American advice had been largely sought in the worlds of engineering and economics, Burma looked mainly to the United Nations for assistance with social and health problems. About one year after her admission to the United Nations (on 19 April 1948) Burma had secured membership in certain United Nations agencies, including FAO, WHO, the ILO, UNICEF, and UNESCO. United Nations activities in Burma commenced soon after, and a national commission for UNESCO was formed in November 1949, but partly owing to the revolts, partly to a certain hesitation on the part of the Burma Government, these preliminaries yielded little. In 1951 a UNICEF mission began work in Burma[3] under the able leadership of John Barnabas of India. Its principal task was the distribution of powdered milk, but assistance was also given in the setting up of maternity and child-welfare centres. WHO started operating in 1951, its activities including an antimalarial campaign and work for the prevention and cure of tuberculosis.[4] An overseas training programme for Burma nationals in medical and public health techniques was also instituted.

In 1952 the Burma Government decided to approach the United Nations with a request that a mission, similar to KTA, might be sent to undertake a parallel assignment in the field of social welfare. Application was made for suitable experts to undertake a survey of social service facilities, resources, and problems in Burma; they were required to draft a plan for social services, to provide for their administration and development, and to indicate which tasks should receive priority.

A mission of six members arrived in October 1952; there were representatives of WHO, UNESCO, ILO, and the United Nations Technical Assistance Administration; it was led by Dr. J. F. Bulsara of India. The Social Planning Commission,[5]

---

[1] Europe, the United States, the Far East, April–July 1953.
[2] Members: U Tin Pe, Secretary, Ministry of National Planning, G. S. Dillon, Secretary, Ministry of Social Services, and J. S. Furnivall.
[3] An agreement was negotiated with UNICEF on 22 April 1950.
[4] These problems had, of course, been tackled in pre-war days, but the major part of the equipment and clinics was destroyed or lost in the Japanese period.
[5] See the previous page.

with Daw Khin Kyi as Chairman, was set up at this time to co-operate with the mission. A preliminary draft was presented to the Burma Government in July 1953, after nine months of inquiry.[1] The recommendations of the mission were forwarded to the United Nations headquarters for scrutiny and the preparation of a final report. The impact of the findings of the mission does not seem to have been very incisive: a review in a government publication[2] noted

It is not possible for any small group of men, however expert they may be, to study and assess the needs of a people alien to themselves within a very limited period of time. Perforce, the Mission has had to confine itself to broad issues, giving details only in isolated cases for future guidance. . . .The surface has been scratched, it remains to dig deep.

The review ends: 'A few community centres, a Citizens' Referral [sic] Bureau, and perhaps a Child Guidance Clinic may be about all the visible results within the next one or two years.'

Meanwhile, in August 1953, KTA submitted their *Comprehensive Report*, a blueprint for Burma's future. The work is divided into three bulky volumes comprising over 2,000 pages. The first volume ranges over the financial resources of Burma, the structure of government, the capabilities of Burma's brainpower and labour, land and agriculture. The other two volumes handle transport and communications, and minerals. This report made a slight readjustment of the preliminary forecast for completion of the programme: the terminal date was postponed from 1959 to 1960. Otherwise the purpose of the report was to elaborate the first generalized recommendations. Probably the most interesting feature was a suggestion for the development of heavy industry in three major concentrations: around Akyab, at Myingyan, and in Greater Rangoon. A 'Master Plan' was laid down for development in three stages, forming, broadly, three Five-Year Plans. The effect would be to make Burma self-sufficient in a wide range of basic products: paper, salt, cement, gunny bags, chemicals, low grade steel, &c.

The ambitious K750 crores investment programme was confirmed: KTA believed that rice exports would continue to provide Burma with a handsome foreign-exchange surplus: 'it is hardly conceivable that Burma will not have adequate foreign exchange to finance the full development programme which has been recommended. She should proceed . . . with no hesitation whatsoever on this score.'[3] It was explicitly stated[4]

[1] See remarks of Dr. Bulsara, *BWB*, 8 and 15 July 1953.
[2] Dept. of Information, *Burma, the Sixth Anniversary* (Rangoon, 1954), pp. 51, 55.
[3] *Comprehensive Report*, i. 107–8.   [4] ibid., p. 102.

that the whole KTA plan was based on the assumption that the export price of rice would not fall below £55 per ton or, at the very lowest, £50 per ton. KTA were not very lucky in their economic forecasting: this assumption had ceased to be valid even before the report was published.

Another assumption, not stated quite so explicitly, was the belief that Burmans and Americans would react in identical ways to identical sets of economic conditions. The report affirmed

The best industrial machines will be outmoded in twenty years; the best present strains of seed and the best agricultural methods will gradually be replaced by better ones. [Burma] must adopt practices and attitudes and methods of training which will induce her producers to be for ever dissatisfied with 'the best' and to seek continuing improvements in materials, methods and products.

There is no known limit to possible improvements in materials, methods and products. . . . Burma must become a progressive nation, so that her people not only live better in 1960, but look forward to continued improvement without limit.[1]

A beneficent circle is envisaged: the increased employment of more Burmans in new enterprises at higher rates of pay will both increase national productivity and increase demand, and so stimulate a better standard of living. Difficulties in the way are brushed aside: if Burma lacks managers and technicians, then these can be 'hired', brought in from abroad, while Burmans are trained to fill their posts.[2]

All this is in striking contrast to the traditional British policy of non-interference as regards the social habits and customs of the peoples of India and Burma. In principle, the British have been content to introduce the rule of law, institutions of representative government, and a system of higher education to provide officials for the administration. In practice, they have found themselves going a good deal further, with the provision of railways, medical services, and much of the machinery of modern Western society. But there has never been a deliberate attempt to rebuild the economic and social framework.[3]

---

[1] ibid., pp. 66–67.

[2] 'An otherwise advantageous new industry, or use of new methods in an old industry, may suffer a temporary disadvantage in Burma because skilled and technical labour of the types required are not available. In general, this factor should not be given great weight, since labour can be trained. . . . If an industry once established will be advantageous, temporary inefficiency while the necessary skills are being acquired . . . is a price worth paying' (ibid., p. 72).

[3] Even the colossal achievement in northern India of bringing some 25 million acres of semi-desert into fruitful cultivation by vast schemes of irrigation was largely carried through by indigenous means. There were a few British engineers and settlement officers, but the science of canal engineering grew entirely out of experience gained in India. The great mass of labour, materials, and skills were Indian. In the new Canal Colonies no attempt was made to create a social system different from that of the parent peasant villages.

Perhaps the British are to blame because they did not make more efforts to change India and Burma into something like the West: but at any rate, they did not do so. The American engineers, social scientists, and college professors who have come to Asia in sudden crowds in the last few years have blown in like a keen, fresh, bracing wind, seeking to stir up the ancient world of Asia, to raise the dust which has lain for centuries. They bring the belief that 'know-how' and will-power and enthusiasm can do for Asia what they have done for the United States. Some Americans, going outside their own country for the first time, have perhaps been too cock-sure of the rightness of all that is American, too anxious to sell their way of life to Asians, and too apt to become impatient and disillusioned when the Asian recipient of their attentions has shown himself indifferent to these new ways, or has proved unskilled in their handling. But it is not for an Englishman to pass judgement on an attitude that is so dissimilar to his own. The short-term effects of American attempts at social change have not been impressive; but their intervention in Asia (outside the Far East) is not yet ten years old. Their long-term influence may be much greater than that of Europe in Asia.

The KTA report, handed over with due ceremony by Colonel Homer B. Pettit to the Minister for National Planning, U Win, on 25 August 1953, was never applied in the manner its authors intended, being hampered by all kinds of obstacles. The rebellion, which limited the comprehensive development of Burma's economy; the sluggish system of administration, which continued to hamper the actual work of development; the influence of politicians, which injected adventitious influences cutting across the schemes of the planners; the difficulties of Burma's economy in the world market—high costs and high prices, when outside prices were falling or customers were finding alternative sources of supply: all these exerted their adverse influences on KTA planning and precluded any properly co-ordinated programme. It has since become plain that both the idea of a Five-Year Plan and the goal of a 750 crores investment programme have been abandoned as unrealistic. Even had all the circumstances been favourable, however, it seems most unlikely that the plan would have come anywhere near fulfilment.

A critical review of planning in Burma in general, and KTA methods in particular, was conducted by a four-man mission from the World Bank,[1] headed by Mr. Demuth of India, which visited Burma in March and April 1953. Their report begins

---

[1] International Bank for Reconstruction and Development (IBRD), *The Economy of Burma*, November 1953 (mimeo.).

with a trenchant general comment on planning assumptions in Burma:

The principal limitation of the planning activity so far, appears to be a preoccupation with the engineering and financial aspects of individual projects without adequate consideration for Burma's limited administrative, managerial and technical capacities. Personnel limitations make it improbable that Burma can undertake any large number of new development projects within a short period. . . . In much of the planning activity, the availability of effective programme administration and efficient management of individual operations appears to have been assumed rather than established.

The review of industry included a critical appraisal of the progress of the textile mill,[1] an exposé of the functioning of the Development Corporations,[2] and an examination of the whole KTA concept of new industrial complexes:

A considerable part of the KTA project rests on assumed relationships among projects which may or may not materialize. For instance, the soundness of a project for establishing mineral processing facilities and a number of related installations at Myingyan will depend, among other things, on the technical and economic feasibility of developing the Kalewa coal deposits and on the size and nature of zinc deposits at Taunggyi which are not entirely certain. A market for a proposed hydro-electric power project at Saingdin depends on the establishment of the pulp and paper mill which is being considered for the same region, and on the type of heat generator to be used at the mill. . . . Justification of portions of the transport programme rests on execution of other projects which may or may not materialize.

In addition to these technical uncertainties, much of the project planning has concentrated on engineering and financial aspects of individual projects, without adequate consideration of the heavy personnel demands which execution of a large proportion of the project proposals would require. To a large extent the planning activity so far seems to have assumed the availability of effective programme administration and efficient management of individual

---

[1] 'The record of the mill has been generally unsatisfactory and large financial losses have been incurred. The intention to use only locally produced raw cotton has not proved technically feasible. . . . Costs have been high and productive efficiency low, in spite of the modern equipment installed. Labour relations are . . . most difficult . . . because of workers' resistance to the efforts of management to improve output, and the abetment of their resistance by political groups acting through rival labour organizations within the mill' (ibid., p. 21).

[2] 'In practice, the objective of autonomy, specialization and independent responsibility remain largely unrealized simply because the corporations are staffed by the same senior government officials who carry the major responsibilities in the related ministries. This is but one example of the multiple responsibilities of a very limited number of individuals in the whole field of public administration' (ibid., p. 42).

operations. Such an assumption does not appear realistic in Burma's circumstances. Experienced indigenous management . . . is almost completely lacking.[1]

The report ended with the proposal (p. 47) that the Managing Agency system should be substituted for the hiring of individuals: management of new enterprises should be entrusted to foreign firms with previous experience in Burma able to command a fund of managerial and technical personnel with knowledge of local conditions.[2]

Such an analysis, couched in the pragmatic, unemotional language of banking and capitalist economics, naturally seemed a little unsympathetic to the Government of Burma, and they took no action on its proposals.

The termination of American aid in March 1953 came at a time when the social-welfare building programme was getting under way, while 'productive' development was about to pass from the relatively simple and inexpensive phase of paper planning into the more expensive and arduous period of construction. Burma was well provided with foreign-exchange reserves,[3] and there seemed no reason why monetary shortages should restrict expansion.

The planning of the AFPFL Government rested on two major bases: Socialism, the promotion of state enterprises and social welfare; and nationalism, the eradication of British and Indian control over the economy, and the stimulation of Burmese commercial enterprise. Of the original members of the Nu Government, Bo Let Ya, formerly Deputy Prime Minister, and Henzada U Mya, formerly Vice-Chairman of the National Planning Board, had abandoned politics for big business. Other leading politicians are considerably interested in trade and industry through their wives and relations. Among the planning assumptions of both the KTA reports was the view that private enterprise must be responsible for some 240 of the 750 crores of the projected capital investment programme.

The Government's proposals for encouraging this sector of the economy were presented by U Nu on 1 December 1953 at the 'National Day' mass rally.[4] He first reaffirmed the 'ultimate objectives' as a democratic Socialist state, but disavowed any

---

[1] *The Economy of Burma*, p. 46.

[2] The Managing Agency system has been widely developed in India from the mid-nineteenth century onwards, especially in the textile and plantation industries. The foundation of modern Indian industrialization, it has been a target for the criticism of Indian writers. See Vera Anstey, *The Economic Development of India* (London, 1929), especially pp. 113–15 and 501–5.

[3] Reserves attained a post-war peak in June 1953 at K126·9 crores (or £97 million).

[4] 'Our Goal and Our Interim Programme', see *Forward with the People*, pp. 74–83.

implication that this would entail Communism or 'state capitalism'; he defined the goal as 'full political rights, economic security, and a high standard of living with spiritual uplift and morality'. He confessed that 'not much success' had attended the Government's hopes for the development of national participation in trade and industry. He cited a lack of financial resources and lack of experience as among the chief reasons for failure. He directed the Economic and Social Board to make recommendations to rectify these shortcomings. He propounded two general principles: commerce and industry must serve the people, and not vice versa, and 'ultimately all trade and industry must be organized into public corporations and co-operatives controlled and managed by the representatives of the workers and consumers'.

U Nu concluded by detailing the types of enterprise to which 'aid and assistance shall be given', in order of priority: state enterprises, joint ventures between government and private concerns, co-operative societies, limited companies owned by nationals, limited companies in which nationals owned 60 per cent. of the shares, private companies. Two aspects of this list might be considered significant: the high priority given to joint ventures (which in practice would always have to be negotiated with foreigners), and the complete absence of any degree of consideration for purely foreign firms. Clearly, government policy would be unfavourable to the characteristic British import-export firm, and to the ubiquitous Indian merchant.

The Economic and Social Board duly considered the Prime Minister's statement and submitted a number of recommendations; these included the encouragement of Burmese concerns making direct contact with foreign manufacturers, the setting up of a Polytechnic to teach business methods, the making available of loans at low interest, and the revision of the licence lists of imports to favour nationals.[1]

One aspect of this revised policy was the introduction of a system of state banking. Up to 1952 Burma's currency and credit was controlled through the Burma Currency Board in London.[2] Of the five members of the Board, one was nominated by the Governor of the Bank of England, and Burmese money had the full backing of sterling. From 1 July 1952 the function of currency issue passed to a new Union Bank of Burma (Chairman, Kyaw Nyein). This bank is not linked to sterling and is freed from the restrictions on monetary expansion which

[1] See 'Our Goal and Our Interim Programme', version issued by Economic and Social Board, 27 November 1953.
[2] See Tun Wai, *Burma's Currency and Credit* (Calcutta, 1953), pp. 157-9.

limited the Currency Board.[1] In February 1953, as forecast in the Pyidawtha Conference, a State Agricultural Bank Act was passed, and banks were subsequently introduced in a few selected districts.[2] Then on 1 June 1954 a State Commercial Bank was incorporated, with capital entirely contributed by the Government, opening for business on 11 August 1954: paradoxically, almost all its transactions in its early days have been with state institutions as it lacks the facilities of the exchange banks.

A more positive aspect of the interim programme was the expansion of the organization of joint ventures. The first joint venture was negotiated on 16 October 1951 with the Burma Corporation, the company controlling the great Bawdwin-Namtu Mines (whose products include silver, lead, zinc, copper, and gold). The Burma Government agreed to take up 50 per cent. of the shares in a new company, Burma Corporation (1951) Ltd. The share value was calculated on a valuation of the company's assets: a figure of K3,30,00,000 was agreed for the Government's half-share. Half this sum was paid in cash, the remainder was to be subscribed in ten annual instalments. The Government acquired the right to appoint three of the board of directors of six: the former Australian Managing Director continued as Chairman of the new venture. A feature of this new arrangement was an undertaking by the company to give young Burmans technical and managerial training with a view to eventually taking key positions in the company.

Government participation was also achieved in the oil industry. Since the war the old oil companies had been operating as a combination, Associated Oil Companies, in which the Burmah Oil Company owned 76·8 per cent. of the assets, the Indo-Burma Petroleum Company owned 17 per cent., and the British Burmah Petroleum Company owned 6·2 per cent. Almost from the date of independence negotiations were conducted with the Government towards some form of partnership, and finally an agreement was signed on 12 January 1954.[3] A new organization, Burma Oil Company (1954), was launched, taking full legal shape in October 1954. A new share-capital

---

[1] *Burma's Currency and Credit*, pp. 209–10. The new coinage replaced rupees (with 16 annas to the rupee) by kyats, with 100 pyas to the kyat. The old silver coinage was replaced by new cupra-nickel '*chinthé*' coins. The old 'King George' coinage was withdrawn from circulation, but is still to be found in use among the hill peoples: 1 King George silver rupee has an unofficial exchange value of 2 paper kyats.

[2] See Chapter IX for details.

[3] In the first instance the Burma Government attempted to obtain a loan from Britain to finance its purchase of shares from the Company. Meeting with no success, there was a delay before the necessary funds were made available (see Nu, *From Peace to Stability*, p. 193).

of K19,50,00,000 or £15 million was issued to the three oil companies. The Burma Government then acquired a one-third interest from the companies (value K6,50,00,000), making an immediate cash payment of K3,30,00,000 or £2½ million, and agreeing to pay the remainder by instalments. Two of the five directors of the new concern were to be appointed by the Government, and a programme of accelerated Burmanization was agreed upon.[1] Negotiations were also set on foot towards establishing joint ventures with the Directors of the Mawchi Mines and with the Anglo-Burma Tin Mines at Tavoy. The Union Government stated in November 1954 that it would not enter into a joint venture at Mawchi until the mines had been rehabilitated and production resumed. The Company there-upon raised an additional capital of £450,000, and pressed ahead with the work of restoration. The years 1953 and 1954 also saw further instalments of nationalization. It will be recalled that the Arracan Flotilla Company escaped nationali-zation in 1948. In March 1950 an Inland Waterways Inquiry Commission was set up, and reported in favour of the nationalization of the Arracan Flotilla Company (March 1951). The Government did not act upon that recommenda-tion, and instead began to consider an alternative proposal to operate the Arakan waterways on a joint venture basis with the Arracan Flotilla Company.[2] However, this scheme came to nothing, and after delays attendant on the internal state of the country, the Arracan Flotilla Company was taken over on 1 October 1953, and became the Arakan Division of the Inland Water Transport Board.[3]

On the same date the Rangoon Electric Tramway and Supply Company, the undertaking which distributed power throughout the Rangoon area, was nationalized. This was the fulfilment of the electricity nationalization programme, whereby all undertakings, whether owned by municipal bodies or by private contractors, were taken over by a national Electricity Supply Board. About the same time, the Sooratee Burra Bazaar, the main shopping market in Rangoon, was nationalized and its Burmese name, *Theingyizay*,[4] was generally adopted.

[1] The new concern controlled the pumping and processing of the oil. Marketing continued to be carried out by a British commercial venture, the Burma Trading Company.

[2] J. S. Furnivall, in a note of dissent from the conclusions of Inland Waterways Inquiry Commission, urged the advisability of such an arrangement.

[3] The Company claimed K28,36,000 as compensation, the Commission awarded K9,99,976, less amounts already received from the British and Burma Govern-ments; the final award was K5,67,063.

[4] The owners of the bazaar (mostly Indians) claimed 192 lakhs for their rights: 18 lakhs was awarded.

Further nationalization took place in 1954. The Burma Cement Company, whose plant is at Thayetmyo, had been considered in the same category as the Burmah Oil Company for operation as a joint venture:[1] however, the Government reversed its decisions and nationalized the Cement Company on 1 October 1954. On the same date the Dyer Meakin Brewery at Mandalay was taken over by the State, while a bill to nationalize the Indian-owned Zeyawaddy Sugar Factory passed through Parliament in October 1954. The Yatanabon Wolfram Mine at Namyenin in Mergui District was nationalized in 1955.

The principles which qualify an industry for nationalization, for conversion into a joint venture, or for continuation as a business concern are not clearly defined. Why should a brewery or a sugar works or a bazaar be selected for state operation, while the oilfields remain under foreign management, and other important 'natural resources' (such as the rubber plantations), although scheduled under the constitution, have been left entirely in the hands of foreign commerce?

Perhaps a partial clue may be gained from the very blunt remarks made by U Nu at the opening of the 1952 Pyidawtha Conference. He observed that the oil installations and the Namtu-Bawdwin mines

suffered terrific damage during the Second World War. For the rehabilitation of these enterprises we need much essential machinery and equipment which we ourselves cannot procure. Neither have we sufficiency of funds to purchase such machinery and equipment. Again, even if we possessed the necessary funds, it is impossible to purchase and procure whatever you require easily under present-day conditions. . . . The operation of such enterprises also needs high technical ability which at present we do not adequately possess. . . . These enterprises are by nature very complex. . . . Those who will manage and control [them] must possess first-rate administrative ability plus a great degree of astuteness. We have none with such qualities. . . . Burma is not the only producer. . . . These products are abundantly found in many other parts of the world. Consequently these products have to be sold in open competition in the world markets. . . . It means that you must maintain for such purpose an organization with established reputation in the international market.[2]

With regard to joint ventures, U Nu observed on the same occasion, 'as soon as we have rehabilitated these enterprises and acquired all necessary knowledge and ability to manage and operate them, we shall nationalize these enterprises'.[3]

[1] cf. Nu, *Towards a Welfare State* (Rangoon, 1952), pp. 19 and 21.
[2] ibid., pp. 21-22.
[3] ibid., p. 22.

Against this approach, it is difficult to see how the joint venture idea will achieve any dynamic success. The British managers and technicians must remember that, although labour conditions (housing, hours of work, pay, medical facilities) in the oilfields are distinctly superior even to those in government service, many of the present Cabinet Ministers served their political apprenticeship in stirring up unrest among the oil-workers. They see that the Burma Government regards the existing arrangement only as a *pis aller*; they will not be encouraged to pump in capital, when India and Pakistan offer more favourable conditions and prospects. On their side, the Burmese politicians still appear to regard the joint ventures as not 'ours', but 'theirs'; the contribution of the government representative is often confined to continuous pressure for Burmanization at any cost.

However, as nationalization is extended, it becomes obvious that it is creating more problems than it is solving, and it may be that the emotion and prejudice which have hitherto clouded the issue may decrease in force. Speaking on 30 September 1954, in a debate on the joint oil venture in the Chamber of Deputies, Ba Swe strongly defended the arrangement: he emphasized that, if the State had decided to handle the oil industry alone, it would take from fifty to a hundred years to reach the Government's goal. The joint oil venture was a short cut to this objective. Lenin himself had seen the uses of foreign capital and had put his views into print. He concluded: 'Our goal is a Socialist State, and we are convinced that this measure adopted by us . . . is a step towards that.'

On the same day that it carried a report of this speech (1 October 1954) the *Nation* carried a wise leader on the subject, remarking

The bringing in of foreign capital in the form of joint ventures is one of the most practical and useful approaches to the problems of an under-developed country such as our own. The foreign partners in the joint venture provide the capital, the technological skill and managerial experience which Burma lacks, and which are essential for the launching of an industrial enterprise. Furthermore, they bring to the project the approach of sound commercial practice, as opposed to the bureaucratic attitudes of mind of the Government participators.

Then again, the foreign partners in a joint venture have an incentive which is not provided in any other form of technical assistance, namely, they work directly for themselves. It stands to reason therefore, that they will provide the best technicians they can find . . . the more efficient and prosperous [the venture] becomes, the more profits they are likely to reap.

Another satisfactory point about joint ventures is that their terms are specific and the position of the parties is clear. . . . This is no donor-recipient relationship, but a down-to-earth, practical arrangement of mutual convenience.

During the second half of 1955 there were indications that the Government had revised its policy on nationalization: on 9 June a statement was issued declaring that all new enterprises would receive a guarantee against nationalization 'for an agreed period which will normally be not less than ten years'. It was added that this guarantee might be extended to existing enterprises, 'in case of extension or modernization'. Other incentives to investment in Burma were promised, and a list of industries particularly essential to the country's economy was appended.[1] On 16 August the Government announced its decision not to nationalize the rubber plantations during the next thirty years. It remains most doubtful, however, whether these guarantees will stimulate any significant flow of new private investment. The Government may be compelled to 'prime the pump' by putting its own capital into joint ventures with foreign firms. It may be recalled how the Gezira Cotton Scheme, a partnership between the Sudan Government and a British-owned syndicate, has been the foundation of the modern Sudan, creating the very conditions for economic autonomy and national independence:[2] if a more modest role awaits joint ventures in Burma, they could, nevertheless, play a significant part in future development.

The welfare programme began to swing from planning towards actual building during 1954. The most ambitious group of projects was that under the direction of the Special Projects Implementation Board. This was yet another planning body, set up in December 1953, consisting of seven members with U Win as Chairman. This board is charged with supervising the erection of six major projects: a pharmaceutical factory, a new engineering college and technical institute, a polytechnic and high school, and research and training institutes in the fields of agriculture, forestry, and veterinary science. Bold and attractive building schemes are being designed and constructed by British firms of architects and building contractors. The contracts are being executed on a basis whereby a fixed commission is received, based on the estimated costs of construction, but not increased if costs should rise. Other new major constructional work begun in 1954 included a new radio station, the Union hospital, a market centre for Rangoon, an agricultural station, new hostels, lecture blocks, and laboratories

---

[1] Full text in *BWB*, 23 June 1955.
[2] cf. A. Gaitskell, 'The Sudan Gezira Scheme', *African Affairs*, October 1952.

for the University of Rangoon, and a new medical college and hospital at Mandalay, as well as housing schemes and government offices.

A major part of this activity was carried through by Chinese and Indian contractors: some large-scale works were allotted to a Singapore firm. The investment figure for 1953–4 was estimated at 91 crores (or £68 million); it was hoped to raise this to 130 crores for 1954–5 and, of this sum, 79 crores would be public investment with 51 crores as the estimate for the private sector.[1] The Finance Minister estimated that this programme could be carried through by drawing upon reserves accumulated in previous years. In September U Tin himself led a highly important purchasing mission to tour Japan, the United States, and Europe: it returned to Rangoon on 15 November, having set up a 'purchase point' in London. K10 crores of equipment—telephone and radio, railway stock, ships, power plant—were among the principal items in this 'shopping list', a 'considerable portion' of the orders being placed in the United Kingdom.[2] However, as 1954 came to an end, it became clear that Burma's reserves were being swallowed more rapidly than had been envisaged and were not being replenished. Under these circumstances, the successful negotiation of a peace treaty with Japan, involving substantial sums in reparations, was heralded as a notable contribution to the economy. Japan agreed to supply Burma with 'the services of Japanese people and the products of Japan' to the value of $200 million, and in addition to invest $50 million in Burma in the form of joint ventures, these payments and investments to be spread over a ten-year period.[3] This treaty promises to initiate another phase in Burma's welfare and industrial development: Japan and Burma have very real complementary interests. Burma is finding difficulty in securing markets for her rice—and Japan desperately needs to replace the lost paddy-fields of Korea and Manchuria. Japan is having to look around for export markets for her goods and services to maintain an ever-expanding population—Burma wishes to avail herself of these goods and services. The peace treaty may well be a decisive turning-point in Burma's economic evolution; the annual Japanese contribution as it becomes effective will represent one-quarter to one-third of the public capital formation of Burma for a period of ten years; it is possible that Burma's trade, hitherto thickly woven into the sterling area,

[1] See budget speech, *BWB*, 25 August 1954.
[2] *Nation*, 4 December 1954.
[3] Full text of treaty and reparations agreement in *BWB*, 17 November 1954.

will have assumed a very different pattern at the decade's end. But the Japanese agreement was of long-term rather than immediate significance.

As expenditure mounted without apparently producing results, doubts as to the efficacy of the existing state development structure became more vocal. On 28 September 1954 an Inquiry Commission was set up with U Nu as Chairman and a High Court Judge as Deputy Chairman, to investigate the various state enterprises, boards, and corporations, with the purpose of examining their administration, financial methods, and general efficiency: losses in the railways, the Inland Water Transport Board, and the textile factory totalled 2 crores in 1953–4. Immediately after the announcement of the formation of this commission, news became public of a grave scandal in the State Agricultural Marketing Board (SAMB),[1] and the Government decided to set up a special Inquiry Commission, presided over by the Premier's Parliamentary Secretary, Captain Mang Tung Nang, to review the whole working of the Board, and to decide whether changes in the world rice situation necessitated a new policy.

A striking comment on the progress of welfare development was delivered by U Nu on 28 November 1954. He announced that the Rehabilitation Corps would be greatly expanded and entrusted with the bulk of the Government's construction programme, giving as his reason the wastage and leakages under existing conditions. He remarked that construction expenditure was running at 10 crores annually, but out of this some 6 crores was going to waste, consumed in bribes, excess profits, barren projects, and other non-productive expenses: only 4 crores out of the 10 was actually producing buildings and plant.[2]

The opening months of 1955 began another phase in the development programme. It had become clear that the fall in the balance of payments was accelerating the country towards a crisis. Foreign-exchange reserves, which stood at K126·87 crores in June 1953 and K96·81 crores in January 1954, fell to K53·32 crores in January 1955, reaching the lowest point, K36·6 crores, in August 1955. Much of the Government's reserves was ear-marked for specific purposes (such as the steel mill which was, early in 1955, beginning to be more than just a blueprint), so that it became necessary to scrutinize and pare down the plans for the future. At a Press conference held on 31 January U Nu revealed that the Finance Minister had

[1] *Nation*, 2 October 1954.
[2] Speech to All-Burma Fire Services' Association (see *Nation*, 29 November 1954).

recently placed an embargo on certain KTA projects, and that the Government's planning advisers, J. S. Furnivall and Dr. Hla Myint, had 'counselled against embarking upon too ambitious a programme', a view which the Cabinet perforce accepted.[1]

During the early months of 1955 the plans for future development were reviewed at a series of conferences of heads of departments at the Premier's residence, and almost all schemes not actually started, or for which agreements had not yet been signed, were quietly shelved, temporarily or permanently. On 19 July, 'Martyrs' Day', Kyaw Nyein announced drastic cuts in expenditure: the current year's welfare programme was to be spread over three years, imports were to be cut, and attempts made to substitute home products for imports. A few weeks later, addressing the Colombo Plan Consultative Committee at Singapore, Kyaw Nyein gave a fairly detailed account of the progress of the KTA Plan: he indicated that investment from 1951 to 1955 had totalled K233 crores (almost £180 million), which represented 31 per cent. of the projected investment programme, supposed to be completed by 1959–60. This was a satisfactory achievement, but unfortunately the fall in rice prices necessitated a period of retrenchment. Kyaw Nyein revealed that, unless substantial foreign aid was forthcoming, it would be necessary to postpone the date for completion of the KTA programme until about 1968.[2] Meanwhile, new planning bodies were brought into being to meet the requirements of retrenchment. A Development Projects Coordination Board, presided over by Ba Swe, was given authority to examine development and rehabilitation schemes being undertaken by the various ministries, deciding which should be continued without urgency, which expedited, and which deferred. A Foreign Exchange Control Authority was established under the Economic and Social Board to screen the commitments of the Government, with a view to reducing inessential expenditure. No contract involving payments in foreign currency could be entered into by government departments without prior reference to this Control Authority.

What is the possibility of obtaining foreign aid? Burma has Japanese reparations to lean upon, but Japan has made it clear that assistance will not be automatic; it will depend upon the prevailing state of her own economy. Burma may find herself being utilized as a safety valve for Japanese industrial prosperity. Another approach was made (late in 1954) to the

---

[1] *Nation*, 1 February 1955.
[2] *BWB*, 3 November 1955.

United States for financial assistance. Burma does not want to repeat the former experience of administered aid, and a proposal was made whereby her surplus of half a million tons of rice would be bought by the United States for distribution to needy countries.[1] The first American reaction to these proposals was unfavourable. Burma also applied for a loan from the World Bank, and officials of the Bank spent a week in Burma, late in 1954, making a brief survey of the prevailing situation. Two loans were eventually granted to Burma in May 1956. It is understood that sanction was delayed until the Burma Government had agreed to revise its development programme, concentrating upon essential projects for the rehabilitation of the national economy. One loan of $14 million was made to the Commissioners for the Port of Rangoon for the reconstruction of cargo berths and storage facilities, &c. The second loan of $5,350,000 was to be applied to the rehabilitation of the railways.

On 20 September 1955 the Finance Minister announced that India had accepted 'in principle' the grant of a loan of Rs.20 crores to Burma, to bear interest at 4 per cent., half to be made available as cash and half as a credit for the purchase of goods in India. This agreement required to be negotiated in detail during 1956. The foreign aid which remains at Burma's disposal is of a modest nature. Colombo Plan assistance provides a useful adjunct to development. Burma adhered to the Colombo Plan at the beginning of 1952, but no particular interest was taken in its potentialities until 1954, when Burma began to call upon the Colombo Plan organization for assistance. The greatest emphasis had been laid on the training of Burmans in Commonwealth countries; 110 Burmans had proceeded on overseas courses by mid-1955. Most of these trainees have been workers in education, health, medicine and social service; some are training for industry and banking. Up to mid-1955 Burma received equipment and materials worth about K18 lakhs, while aid to the value of K20 lakhs was due for early delivery. Australia has contributed more than half of this aid, beginning with a K16 lakhs' consignment of trucks and road-making equipment, as well as livestock for breeding purposes worth over K2½ lakhs (69 of the trainee-Burmans went to Australia in 1954–5). New Zealand assisted Burma with approximately K13 lakhs towards the erection of a fertilizer plant; Britain's contribution (1954–5) amounted to K2 lakhs, most of this being applied to a building research institute. Seven Commonwealth consultants and educationalists took up

[1] An agreement to purchase 100,000 tons of rice was reported in March 1956.

posts in Burma by 1955, coming from Britain, New Zealand, and Canada. Israel and Yugoslavia have also been approached for assistance in various aspects of planning and development, but clearly there are narrow limits to the range of their aid.[1]

United Nations agencies continue their work: by 1954 seven organizations were in the field. The Technical Assistance Administration was giving assistance with statistics, town planning, co-operation, building, cottage industries, trade promotion, and medical social work, while Dr. Bulsara returned to Burma on 4 March 1954 to act as Social Welfare Adviser in the planning of integrated social service administration. The ILO had experts working on social security, labour statistics, and co-operation. FAO was concerned with forestry, farm machinery, agricultural statistics, sericulture, and veterinary work. WHO assisted in malaria control, preventive and training work in tubercular diseases, VD clinics, and child and maternity welfare, in which UNICEF also played a part. The International Civil Aviation Organization also awarded overseas scholar-ships.[2] But even when all this assistance is considered in aggregate, Burma will still find it wellnigh impossible to mount a programme on the KTA scale.

Some generalizations on the first steps 'towards the Welfare State' may be useful. It must be obvious at once that, on a short view, the defects of the Welfare State in Burma stand forth clearly: the benefits, although perhaps considerable, are less obvious and indeed may not emerge for a full generation. Experience in Britain has, to some extent, been parallel: the achievement of full employment and social security has in con-siderable measure brought an end to any acknowledgment of individual responsibility and self-support, while a concept of corporate social responsibility has not yet been realized. At times we can see little but greed, sloth, and indifference in our new society, and yet, as the impulse of the new world of equal opportunity stirs amongst our children, new attitudes, new ideals may already be emerging unawares. Perhaps the present era in Burma may in the same way prove to be a time of fruitful gestation.

One aspect of the Welfare State which is by no means peculiar to Burma is the 'world owes me a living' attitude which one meets so often in young Burmans (and some not so young). It is part of the *credo* of every politician that Britain utilized Burma as a source of raw materials and as a market

---

[1] *BWB*, 10 February 1955. In March 1956 Israel agreed to supply technical and managerial staff for joint ventures.

[2] Reviews of U.N. activities are contained in ibid., 7 July and 27 October 1955.

for British manufactures, thus keeping 'our people as serfs, all our workers and peasants in sub-human standards'.[1] As Britain made vast profits out of Burma (so the myth goes) in the past, so it is as nothing less than a right that Burma has received loans from Britain and treated them as outright grants. American aid also was received without sense of obligation, and it is assumed that the World Bank will hasten to provide funds as required. The equipment and experts which come to Burma are not regarded particularly highly: they are used casually, with no sense of urgency. Many of the younger men who have been promoted to positions of responsibility apply this 'world owes me a living' attitude not only to their country but to themselves: in the expanding Welfare State they have stepped into big jobs without any great effort on their part; they feel no great compulsion to justify their stewardship.

The foreign experts, on their side, have not always set themselves to work for Burma as they might for their own country. The contrast between the foreigners who come to Burma today under United Nations and other international bodies and the former British officers of the old Burma Commission is striking. The District Officers, Police, Forest Officers, and the others of the old days gave their lives, and often their hearts, to Burma: they knew that for thirty or forty years Burma was their home; they learnt her languages, lived among her peoples and, in most cases, identified themselves with her aspirations. The foreign expert of today flies back to Europe or America each year for his leave; he may spend only a few months in the country; at the very longest he will stay for three or four years. He is an expert in his own technical field: but he knows nothing of Burma. And in the vast majority of cases the expert is an adviser, a planner, only. If he is a transport expert, he may prepare a blueprint for a system of trunk roads: but he will not spend weary months in camp, surveying, taking levels, driving the road on, worrying about materials, equipment, and labour. He will not have the headache of stretching a departmental budget allocation to keep up maintenance, to cope with rising costs, to foresee a sudden economy cut. And so he is tempted to produce a fine plan that looks bold, comprehensive, progressive—and not to worry about possible snags and obstacles. To this writer, the crux of Burma's planning failures lies here. During the last eight years a procession of experts have spent a month or two in Rangoon's Strand Hotel, have duly produced surveys and proposals, and have passed on, never having caused a ripple in the life of Burma. Time and again

[1] Ministry of Information, *Pyidawtha Conference*, p. 31.

heads of departments have had to reconcile the blueprints presented by foreign advisers to their Ministers with the meagre realities of their actual resources in men and materials. And these foreign experts have not been cheap. Even in the case of United Nations personnel Burma pays half the cost of their salaries, and salaries are high: a United Nations nurse receives K2,800 per month, or more than the Prime Minister.[1] The top KTA experts receive salaries that are ten times as great as those of the Cabinet Ministers (three times greater than that of the former British Governor). It is a matter seriously open to question whether, if Burma had not had the services of any of the foreign experts engaged under the various 'aid' programmes, conditions would have differed to any material extent from those actually obtaining.

One aspect of development activity which strikes an observer only after travelling about the country is the extent to which energies have been concentrated near Rangoon. Nine-tenths of the development works of the last eight years can be seen in a forty-minute drive, going no more than ten miles from the city, in the triangle formed by the Hlaing River and the Pegu River. Heavy and light industries, the institutions of higher education and technical training, social service ventures, veterinary and agricultural stations, housing estates, the radio station, almost all can be viewed on a trip down Rangoon's Prome Road. The chief reasons for this concentration are, of course, security and transport problems. Only within the Rangoon area can internal security be guaranteed: United Nations organizations (still largely tied to the capital) have frequently asked for their activities to be extended to outlying country districts, only to be informed that Government could not guarantee adequate security precautions. In the matter of transport, freight charges on a ton of equipment from Liverpool to Rangoon are still lower than from Rangoon to Mandalay. The inadequate state of both rail and river transport puts a definite limit to the possibilities of erecting factories up-country, with all the problems of handling equipment, raw materials, and manufactures that would ensue. And so development is concentrated around the capital, leading to shortages of labour, high wages and high costs, inflation, accommodation problems, congestion and strain on public services, while elsewhere in Burma there is unemployment and stagnation.

Burma's attempt to find a short-cut to Socialism and

[1] In 1955 there were fifty-six foreign U.N. experts at work in Burma, some employed in distinctly narrow fields: e.g. experts to advise on an Industrial Manpower Survey and on labour statistics—when so many practical problems of labour organization remain totally unexplored.

industrialization, to compel wishes to become reality, may have been responsible for the development of the phenomenon of planning for planning's sake. One detects the feeling that if they do not possess a steel mill or an institute of technology, then a plan will be the next best thing. A peculiar sanctity seems to attach to reports, statistics, and, above all, to diagrams and scale models which give the desired future an illusion of immediacy. The impression is gained that planning is becoming not a prelude to, but a substitute for, actual constructional effort. Nowhere else can there be such elaborate pyramids of boards, committees, commissions, projects, conferences, seminars, inquiries. When extra-national organizations are concerned the hierarchy becomes even more involved: the creation of a few dozen modest maternity and child health centres has entailed administrative activity on the part of the Ministry of Health, WHO, UNICEF, the former Technical Co-operation Administration, the National Health Council, and many other bodies. And very often planning administration remains the administration of planning. The most acute example met by the writer emerged from a conversation with a disheartened Scandinavian United Nations expert who was engaged in producing elaborate schemes of town planning for Rangoon which, he was aware, would not—and could not—be put into practice.

This divorce of planning from reality becomes apparent when one examines the manner in which the Government's programme has been applied by the different departments. In theory, planning lays stress on 'simultaneous and co-ordinated development';[1] time and again emphasis has been laid on the comprehensive character of the programme, of the integration of the parts with the whole. In practice, the different ministries have shown themselves very jealous of their particular sphere of activity. Each ministry has regarded the increase or decrease of its budget appropriation as a prestige matter, and co-operation between ministries has often been slender. For instance, the Government has been committed, since 1948, to a policy of decentralization (it was prominent among U Nu's fourteen points of 1948 and at the Pyidawtha Conference) and legislation has been passed to create a system of local authorities: and yet the other ministries have been strengthening their control over such services as health and education, so that, in fact the tendency has been towards centralization. In another field we see the Mass Education Council receiving the most lavish grants in aid, while another (and perhaps more valuable)

[1] Economic and Social Board, *Pyidawtha, the New Burma* (Rangoon, [1954]).

extra-mural organization, the University for Adult Education, is starved of money. While the planners have been busy in their paper world, government servants in the districts have been making do with makeshift or out-worn rules.

Burma has now, willy-nilly, come to the end of the first phase of her welfare and development activity. The 200-crore programme which was made possible by the Korean War rice boom has now been liquidated. This first phase cannot be said to have made any radical impact on the country: as a result, Burma has a number of impressive new buildings, a good deal of useful equipment (and some not so useful) and a large number of persons trained and equipped to various degrees of competence in various skills, most of which can be put into use. But the investment of so many crores has not achieved anything absolute: the money has been scattered in such a wide variety of ways that it has nowhere been of decisive worth. Ceylon during recent years has utilized certain of her resources to reclaim large areas of barren land to agricultural use, thereby helping to meet a definite national need by increasing the production of rice, and at the same time raising the standard of living of the new settlers; a definite lift has been given to the nation's economy. Burma might have worked to a comparable plan: might perhaps have overhauled the whole machinery of rice production, storage, transport, shipment, and marketing: in that way she could have regained her pre-war position as the world's foremost rice exporter. Or she might have gone all-out to diversify her agriculture, to become less dependent on the price movements of one crop. In the end, the pattern of Burma's economy is the same today, in 1956, as it was five years ago: a pale imitation of the same economy fifteen years ago.

And yet there is no need to linger, mourning lost opportunities and wasted assets, providing that the lessons which are writ large in this first experiment in development and welfare are truly learned. A detailed economic history of Burma has yet to be written, but the evidence of Burma's past which is visible to every traveller shows that through the ages the economic structure has been remarkably buoyant and resilient. The kings of Burma built great cities—only to abandon them; they waged long wars of attrition with Siam; they poured out their treasure upon pagodas and monasteries. All this did not exhaust Burma: the villagers and their rice-fields have supported these vast expenditures of men, materials, and money, and have added to them their own works of merit. Burma is a land where nature is very bountiful: the natural resources which have helped to thread the countryside, forest, river, fen and mountain with myriads of pagodas, snow-white and silver and gold, can be turned to making schools, hospitals, and—if they really are needed—factories.

By 1958 it had become apparent that many of the short-comings of hasty, over-ambitious development had been realized by thoughtful Burmans. U Nu frequently laid emphasis in public pronouncements upon the mistake his Government had committed in attempting to embark on a programme of industrialization and economic experiment instead of first concentrating on the defeat of the rebels and the restoration of order and good government. Whether justly or not, the KTA group was often cast in the role of scapegoat by Burmese intellectuals and politicians and blamed for the disappointment of hopes so optimistically voiced in earlier years. Soon after General Ne Win came to power, the activities of the remaining members of the KTA group, those of Robert R. Nathan Associates, the economic consultants, were brought to a close. The General called upon a retired mining engineer who had spent his working life in Burma to return as economic adviser.

One of the main developments of the late 1950s was the entry of the armed forces into the economic sphere. They set up undertakings under military management in wide areas of production, transportation, and distribution. These were jealously watched during U Nu's last two years in office, and a supposed factor in the second military intervention was a suspicion that these undertakings might be threatened.

After the 1962 coup, the General ordered investigations into the actual effect of foreign technical and financial aid in Burma. The evidence which was disclosed seemed to confirm the view that this had been largely non-productive, while proving expensive to the country. All remaining organizations providing assistance, such as the Ford Foundation, were required to terminate their activities. Subsequently, any foreign experts required to work on government projects were drawn, as far as possible, from non-aligned countries like Yugoslavia. The whole fabric of economic life was drawn into the net of government control, and the foreigners were eliminated from their last niches in trade and industry.

A new economic philosophy was promulgated. Burma, the leaders declared, would set its own standards, ignoring the world outside. These postulated the equality and the advancement of the peasant and worker. The goal was a sufficiency of food, goods, and opportunities for the mass: not refinements for the élite few. Turning their backs upon the symbols of the affluent West, the Burmese were to learn to be content with what they have.

V

THE CHANGING STRUCTURE OF
GOVERNMENT AND ADMINISTRATION

MUCH has changed, yet much remains the same in the administration, as in many other aspects of life in Burma during the first post-war decade. The framework of the old 'colonial' administration still stands, the old rules and manuals are still followed and observed, officials from the former régime still provide the backbone of the Government: and yet the meaning, the spirit has gone out of it all. The talk is all of a new, democratic system which is to grow up from the grass-roots: but by the middle-1950's the new democratic administration was still largely a dream. There was a time of twilight, with little to show what new forms of government will finally emerge in the future.

The old order has not passed away: but this is not due to acquiescence in existing institutions by the new rulers. When the AFPFL leaders took over charge of their country they ardently desired to create a new world, in government as in social welfare, but in this sphere also they found themselves unable to carry through their plans. When U Nu presented his fourteen-point programme in May 1948 he laid great emphasis on the need for administrative reform: 'the machinery of bureaucratic administration must be transformed into the machinery of democratic administration . . . authoritarian rule must end'.[1] At the same time, in April 1948, a Committee of nine members for the Reorganization of Administration was set up, with U Lun Baw, Chairman of the Public Services Commission, as its Chairman, to 'prepare a plan for administration . . . [for] the new democratic Burma' and 'to make proposals for the reorganization of the existing system'. An interim report was submitted in August 1948, its principal recommendation being the introduction of a new structure of local authorities: a Local Government Bill was drafted and submitted to Parliament in February 1949. A final report was published in December 1951, with a wide range of detailed proposals in the fields of administration and social services.

Decentralization and local government formed the subject-matter of the first two resolutions at the 1952 Pyidawtha Conference: it was stated that 'the red tape system which

[1] *Towards Peace and Democracy*, p. 95.

existed during the time of the British administration and which was designed to delay matters' would be replaced by 'democratic machinery',[1] which was described in some detail by Ba Swe in moving the resolution for the democratization of local administration.[2] This restatement of policy was followed by revisory local government legislation and, in the sphere of central government, by investigations under United Nations auspices. G. T. Jackson of the Civil Service Commission of Canada worked upon Secretariat problems from November 1952 to April 1953, presenting a report[3] which analysed existing defects and made recommendations for improvement in office procedure. F. J. Tickner, a specialist in organization and methods at the British Treasury, followed up with suggestions for training courses in administration for junior officials.[4] But still, in 1956, both in central and local government the old 'bureaucratic' system continues, interlarded with political influences which have stultified most of the merits of the past order, without producing any genuine injection of democracy.

In pre-war days the country was divided into administrative districts ruled by Deputy Commissioners, these being grouped into divisions under Commissioners.[5] The greater part of the country was governed according to a uniform legal system and revenue code, but the Frontier Areas, and of course the Shan States, were set apart, a system of indirect rule being applied; the frontier peoples' chiefs and rulers were loosely supervised by officers of the Burma Frontier Service.[6] The whole system was kept closely under the Secretariat in Rangoon.[7] This consisted of ten departments: a home department which was in charge of general administration, and others having various specialist functions.

One major difference which Burma's 1947 constitution appeared to introduce was the setting up of constituent 'state' governments: but to repeat an authoritative legal dictum, 'the constitution, though in theory federal, is in practice unitary'.

---

[1] Ministry of Information, *Pyidawtha Conference*, pp. 5 and 6.
[2] ibid., pp. 12–21.
[3] Ministry of Home Affairs, *Report of a Survey of Public Administration in Burma* (Jackson Report) (Rangoon, 1954—confidential).
[4] U.N., Technical Assistance Administration, *Report on Public Administration in Burma*, by F. J. Tickner, prepared March–April 1954 (mimeo.).
[5] There were thirty-nine districts, grouped in seven divisions, as well as the Federated Shan States under a Commissioner.
[6] The term 'indirect rule', first applied in Nigeria, was never used.
[7] The Secretariat is, literally, the group of neo-Jacobean buildings round a quadrangle facing Sparks Street, Rangoon: it may be equated in administrative jargon with 'Whitehall'. Originally, the Lieutenant-Governor carried on the whole business of government with one Secretary, but gradually different Secretaries became responsible for different departments.

The state ministries are all accommodated, cheek by jowl, in the central Secretariat, which remains the hub of Government throughout Burma. The 10 departments of pre-war days have expanded into 25 ministries, responsible for over 40 government departments, as well as the various boards and corporations. With three exceptions, these ministries are all squeezed into the old Secretariat buildings. The creation of ministries has been somewhat haphazard: new ones have been formed *ad hoc* as the growth in the scope of government activities has necessitated, but other ministries which have outlived their original purpose have not, at the same time, been abolished. As an example, an attempt was made to combine all the social services under one ministry; this proved increasingly unwieldy, and in 1952 education became a separate ministry. In the following year (September 1953) a separate Ministry of Health and Local Government was created, leaving a truncated Ministry of Social Welfare. Then local government was separated from public health, being absorbed into the new Ministry for the Democratization of Local Administration. Finally, in 1956, a new 'super-ministry' for social services was evolved to oversee all these ministries. All this time separate ministries for Relief and Resettlement, and for Rehabilitation have existed; having been called into being in the dark days of 1948 and 1949, they have long failed to have any justification in the petty extent of their responsibilities.

It has been a common matter for Cabinet Ministers to hold more than one portfolio: the considerations which govern the combinations of portfolios are personal and political rather than related to administrative convenience. There was in 1955 a Minister for Defence and Mines, for National Planning and Religious Affairs, and for Judicial Affairs and Health. Some Ministers have monumental responsibilities: Kyaw Nyein has been simultaneously Minister for Industries, Co-operatives, and Commodity Distribution, as well as acting periodically as Foreign Minister; by contrast, Shein Htang is responsible only for the minute Ministry for Rehabilitation.

The organization of ministries might be illustrated by two examples:

MINISTRY OF AGRICULTURE AND FORESTS

Dept. of Agriculture and Fisheries	Dept. of Forests	Irrigation Dept.	Salt Revenue Collector	Veterinary Dept.	Agricultural Development Corporation

MINISTRY OF TRANSPORT AND COMMUNICATIONS

Civil Aviation Dept.	Marine Dept.	Meteoro- logical Dept.	Dept. of Posts	Dept. of Tele- communi- cations	Road Transport Dept.
Board of Management, Port of Rangoon	Extra- Municipal Tramways		Union of Burma Airways	Union of Burma Railways Board	Union of Burma Shipping Board

There are many areas where responsibilities clash or overlap. To cite examples from the above ministries, the Ministry of Transport has a Road Transport Department: but the upkeep of the roads is primarily the responsibility of the Ministry of Public Works. The Ministry of Agriculture is answerable for the State Land Committee, the Ministry of Land Nationaliza- tion for the State Colonies Department, yet the functions of the two departments coincide. In some cases these discrepancies have been tidied up: for example, until November 1954, for no valid reason, the SAMB formed an appendage of the Ministry of Commerce, while the State Timber Board (an organization with parallel functions) was controlled by the Ministry of Agriculture. Subsequently, both boards have been brought under the newly designated Ministry of Trade Development. The senior permanent official at the head of each of the various ministries is known as a Secretary to Government; these gentlemen, some twenty-five in number, are the keystones of the whole country; they keep the system working. The head of the Ministry of Home Affairs is Chief Secretary. Questions of policy, the drafting of legislation, the putting up of major problems, are in the hands of Additional Secretaries, Deputy Secretaries, and Assistant Secretaries: these are all 'administrative' officials. The various departments subordinate to a ministry are headed by 'technical' officials. There is frequently a division of responsibility: the KTA report observed that 'in some instances nobody seems to be clearly in charge of anything'.[1]

The Administration Reorganization Committee in its 1951 report diagnosed (p. 9) the prevailing inefficiency in the Secretariat as due to, first, centralization, with frequent transfers as a natural sequel; second, internal friction within the departments (by which was meant lack of discipline and order, and political unrest); and third, departmentalism. These evils have been exacerbated rather than ameliorated during

[1] KTA, *Comprehensive Report*, i., 206.

the succeeding years. While government policy has been announced as decentralization, departmental practice has further tightened the grip of centralization. Before 1942 the whole range of primary education, as well as a few institutions of middle and high school standard, came under the control of local authorities; today only Rangoon Municipality still functions as an education authority, otherwise education is entirely controlled by the Ministry. Hospitals and dispensaries were also run by local bodies until 1953 when they were taken over by the Ministry. Similar centralization has taken place with regard to vaccination, the upkeep of district roads, veterinary services, and electricity supplies. Besides the stripping of the municipalities and the old district councils of their responsibilities, the powers of the district officials have been greatly circumscribed. Centralization has increased in other ways: whereas in pre-war days the senior civil servants were able to talk on equal terms with their Ministers, few officials nowadays are prepared to adopt an independent attitude: decisions are now taken by an even more restricted circle at an even higher level and, as the KTA report complained, when Ministers are on tour up-country or abroad on a mission (which they very frequently are) then 'work on important matters often comes to a standstill. The Secretary is hesitant to make decisions except on relatively minor matters, and business is delayed.'[1] The extent of such delays was examined by the Canadian United Nations expert: he concluded that matters referred to the Ministry of Finance by other ministries are subject to a delay of six months; matters put up from the districts which require Finance sanction undergo, on the average, a delay of three years before receipt of an answer.[2] The other aspect of centralization specially mentioned by the Reorganization Committee—unduly frequent transfers—has also not improved: the Jackson Report (p. 15) mentions cases of officials being moved around after four months. The responsibility of making postings rests entirely, nowadays, with the Premier and the Ministers, so that no local adjustments are possible,[3] and an officer may be posted from Tenasserim to the Upper Chindwin and down to Arakan within a single year.

[1] ibid., p. 207.
[2] Jackson Report, p. 31. There were, of course, serious delays under British rule, especially in the days before dyarchy. Examples are cited in the author's *Foundations of Local Self-Government in India, Pakistan and Burma* (London, 1954), especially pp. 69, 99, 299. But during dyarchy and after (1923–47) policy decisions were speeded up, though British civil servants and Burmese politicians were not always pulling in the same direction.
[3] In pre-war days, the Commissioner had power to make transfers within his division.

The second major defect noted by the Reorganization Committee, internal friction, or lack of discipline, must strike every visitor to departments of government today. The passages of the Secretariat are taken up by slovenly youths, lounging and smoking, who are in fact the peons, the office messengers.[1] Inside the offices there is an atmosphere of casual chaos: 'files piled everywhere, on the floor, on tables, or on shelves, sometimes gathering dust over a period of years'.[2] At any given time about half of the clerks will be sitting with their feet on their desks, smoking, reading the newspaper, chatting to friends who have dropped in. Office hours are nominally from 9.30 a.m. to 4.30 p.m., with a greater number of public holidays than in any other country in the world (over twenty days in the year). But even this not over-strenuous schedule is hardly anywhere maintained: many senior officials set a poor example by arriving in the office after 11 a.m.[3] The casual, amateurish atmosphere in the government offices may largely be attributed to the appointment of large numbers of political nominees. With an entirely inadequate cadre of responsible officials, some attempt at compensation has been made by the lavish recruitment of untrained clerks. These clerks are appointed almost always because of some political or personal association with someone in power; their posts are temporary, and prospects of promotion are negligible: there is little incentive to do more than laze away the day, secure from dismissal, but debarred from advancement.

The third factor raised by the Committee—departmentalism—is of course an occupational disease of bureaucracy, which only forceful restraint from above will abate. The legacy of British-Indian office procedure was leisurely, of the eighteenth century in its elaborate ritual. First there was the putting up of cases by a clerk to the office superintendent, with copies of all previous references in correspondence flagged, and with other relating files neatly tied up with pink tape. Then the case would go up through the hierarchy, from Superintendent to Assistant Secretary, on to the Secretary, and at each stage a minute expressing assent or dissent would be added, until at length the Minister would scribble 'approved' upon the jumble of curling papers and pins and red and blue markers. This

[1] The 1951 report of the Reorganization Committee remarked pertinently, 'Formerly the Indian *chaprassi* lent dignity to the office and money to the clerks. The Burman lads who have replaced them have little dignity and no money. Only too often they have bad manners' (p. 86).

[2] Jackson Report, p. 31.

[3] In fairness, it must be mentioned that most of the Secretaries themselves carry on concentrated work for long hours.

system was an anachronism already under the old 'law and order' administration; it was not efficient even when upheld by experienced, conscientious Indian clerks. In the conditions of today it has produced deadlock: and yet the proliferation of departmental regulations and rules of procedure is growing. Probably, in this manufacture of delaying devices, the Secretariat must give best (or worst) to certain other departments, notably the Immigration Department, the Post Office, and the Customs and Excise: but the whole government machine is under its sway. The increase in the numbers of central government departments from ten to over forty has clearly led to further possibilities of departmentalism, of conflicts between the various branches of the Government. To meet this difficulty the technique of the inter-departmental committee has been widely employed—and has perhaps defeated its object by absorbing a large proportion of the working time of the key officials.[1]

Departmentalism spreads its coils out into the districts. The principle of British district administration (which was, however, vastly modified in earlier decades of the twentieth century) was of a single key official who would supervise all the activities of Government throughout his district. Today a District Officer possesses only the shadow of his former authority. The various ministries have their offices throughout the countryside. In every district there are representatives of no less than eighteen central departments; some of these officials were familiar in pre-war days (as, for instance, the Deputy Inspector of Schools), but the majority are new officials with nebulous responsibilities: District Relief Officers, Public Relations Officers, Religious Affairs Officers, and the like. The District Officer is not even kept informed of many of their activities: if he wishes to approach the District Forest Officer, he has to correspond through the Minister of Forests, and similarly with the District Medical Officer.[2] In other cases his authority is limited to taking the chair at committees: one District Officer told the writer that he was Chairman of twenty administrative committees, and this is understood to be quite usual. One of the most important of these is the District Welfare or Pyidawtha Committee, which has some twenty to thirty members, the great majority officials, with three or four representatives of the AFPFL.

In pre-war days the District Officer had two main duties: maintenance of law and order, and the collection of the land

---

[1] U Kyin, when Secretary for Finance and Revenue, was a member of twenty-seven boards and committees.

[2] See *Speech by Thakin Tin to M.P.s on Democratization of Local Government*, 10 March 1954, p. 10.

revenue. The first task of the District Officer, that of maintaining law and order, has largely passed into the hands of the army,
the military police, and other, irregular, forces. The District
Officer still has a certain responsibility in the organization of
the town and village guards,[1] but he has only the most vague
standing with the main security forces.[2]

In regard to the revenue collection, the District Officer's
work has also largely disappeared. Since 1948 the collection
of land revenue (for which the whole hierarchy of district
officials—village headman, *myook*, Sub-Divisional Officer,
District Officer, and Commissioner—was primarily created)
is no longer the basic function of the administration. During
the upheavals of 1948–9 the district administration ceased, for
a period, to exist at all. Treasuries were looted, officials had to
flee, offices were destroyed. The land revenue was collected
only in the small pockets where the Government remained
master. When the first emergency was over the Government
decided to 'write off' the uncollected land revenues for all the
post-war years, up to and including 1948–9.[3] It has never
thereafter been possible to return to the old world where the
peasant knew he must pay his revenue without question or face
legal proceedings. The 'writing off' of land revenue continued:
by 1950, 4·56 crores (equivalent to the total land revenue for
three years) had been cancelled.[4] The peasant had now
discovered what can be done if one has influence with the local
political bosses of the AFPFL or ABPO. In a special conference
convened by the Prime Minister in November 1954 it was
revealed that, by comparison with the figures for 1938–9, only
9 per cent. of the dues were collected in 1948–9 and, despite
the return of more peaceful conditions, the proportion was
only 32 per cent. in 1952–3.[5] Land revenue has completely

---

[1] Known as *kins*, the chief of the village watch is called *kin hmu*.

[2] It has been a frequent experience for district officials to be evicted from
their bungalows and offices by army units requiring accommodation for
themselves.

[3] Finance Minister's budget speech, 1951, quoted in Dept. of Information,
Burma, the Fourth Anniversary, see especially p. 6.

[4] See speech by U Nu at Conference on Land Revenue and Agricultural Loans,
BWB, 10 November 1954.

[5] ibid. An analysis by divisions shows the following collections, calculated as
percentages of the 1938–9 total.

	1948–9	1949–50	1950–1	1951–2	1952–3
Arakan	7	9	13	11	10
Pegu	7	11	43	50	48
Irrawaddy	5	6	11	19	31
Tenasserim	57	59	63	61	52
Magwe	0·02	1	1	0·9	10
Mandalay	9	20	22	17	14
Sagaing	9	42	37	25	9

lost its old status as the backbone of the national revenues: in 1938–9 it formed 33 per cent. of the total revenue: in 1952–3 it had shrunk to 2·3 per cent. of the total.[1]

While land-revenue collection has collapsed the field records of agricultural holdings have crumbled into shreds. The work known in the past as 'land settlement' (a field survey of agricultural holdings, their evaluation, and the determination of revenue obligations) has, by reason of the insurrections, virtually come to an end. During the troubled years 1948–9 most district offices were burned, the old land registers were destroyed, and with them the exact knowledge of all agricultural rights which was one of the chief features of British district administration. In 27 of the 33 districts the new settlements are due (in most cases, long overdue) for revision; the records of holdings and the tax obligations of the peasants should be calculated anew;[2] the cultivators are paying (or refusing to pay) revenue on assessments made over thirty years ago. So-called 'experimental revision settlement operations' are being conducted, in order to train a few field workers in the technique of settlement work, but regular surveying is still out of the question 'on account of unsettled local conditions'.[3] Attempts are being made to reconstruct the old records, but much data has been lost for ever. Nowadays land-revenue demands are frequently based on a rough 'lump sum' assessment which, lacking the scientific accuracy of the old methods, affords the peasant another reason for resisting payment. Altogether the District Officer's former importance as arbiter and guardian in the life of the countryside has almost vanished.

Today the giants in the district are the political bosses. In the early days of independence this power was wielded openly, unconcealed. In Arakan three districts were handed over to party politicians as Deputy Commissioners: *Myochit* Kyaw U, appointed to Akyab District, was not even a matriculate; he was subsequently arrested for rice smuggling.[4] This political administration lasted some two years and contributed largely to the loathing for the AFPFL out of which emerged the Independent Arakanese Parliamentary Group and the demand

---

[1] Total revenue, 1938–9=16·43 crores, land revenue=5·42 crores; 1952–3, total =80·9 crores, land revenue=1·9 crores. Revised estimates for 1953–4 would make the proportions roughly the same: total=93·3 crores, land revenue=2·3 crores (Ministry of Finance, *Economic Survey of Burma*, 1954, p. 33).

[2] Dept. of Information, *Burma, the Sixth Anniversary*, pp. 15 and 16.

[3] Dept. of Information, *Burma, the Seventh Anniversary*, pp. 20–21.

[4] *Nation*, 26 January 1952.

for a separate Arakanese State.[1] Elsewhere political control
was not so blatant, but politicians were appointed as 'Special
Commissioners'—in effect, as commissars—with supervisory
powers over the 'career' officials. San Po Thin acted as Special
Commissioner for Bassein; others similarly employed were
Bo Hmu Aung and Ba Swe. At the height of the insurrection
U Win was appointed Special Commissioner at Mandalay,
being virtually Governor of Upper Burma, as he held charge
of fourteen districts during the days when control from Rangoon
could not be effective. Direct supervision by politicians over
the administration lapsed around 1950, but the exercise of
power without responsibility has continued, adding to the
further decline in the authority of the District Officer. He is
now liable to be summoned, day or night, to the house of
Bo Maung Gyi or Thakin Maung Lat or Yebaw Maung Gale,
and told to suppress this case or prepare an adverse report on
that official. All but the most unsophisticated Burmans are
aware that real power rests with the political bosses.[2] If a
Deputy Commissioner should attempt to stand up against
political influences, even though he is acting in the public
interest, he can expect no support from those above him.
Instead, somebody will pour poison into the ear of the Minister,
and a transfer to a jungle district wracked by malaria is the
probable sequel.[3] The great majority of District Officers will
therefore accommodate the local bosses whenever they can.
The position at the present time is probably at its worst. In
pre-war days members of the Indian Civil Service (the top-
ranking officials) were normally given charge of a district after
seven to ten years' service; members of the provincial civil
service would have to wait twenty years or more for their
district. Today all former Burmese members of the Indian
Civil Service or the pre-war Burma Civil Service are employed
in senior posts in the Secretariat, as Commissioners of divisions,
in management of government corporations, or as the representatives of Burma overseas. The great majority of the present-
day Deputy Commissioners have been promoted from the

[1] The politicians were eventually ordered to resign, after a personal visit by
U Nu.

[2] When the author asked a particularly candid and straightforward official
whether the corruption revealed by the *Report of the Bribery and Corruption Committee*
(Rangoon, 1941) still prevailed, he replied that among the majority of officials,
bribery was distinctly less common. Somewhat wryly, he added: 'It is not much
use bribing an official, he has no power nowadays: the people who get the bribes
are the politicians.'

[3] The official called as witness above, in the same conversation, related that when
he refused to kow-tow to a *yebaw*, a local tyrant, he received no official backing
whatever. Therefore, he added, 95 per cent of the officials will capitulate to political
pressure.

subordinate civil service,[1] or may even have been head clerks or employees in the Civil Supplies Department. Most of them are now in sight of their pension; they have no ambition to rise any higher, but a great fear of being relegated to their former grades. And so they play for safety: they are content to keep up the appearances of administration, to send in their returns to Government, and to keep their service records unblemished. It will be greatly to the advantage of the Union when this generation of District Officers depart on pension. A few of the post-independence entry have been appointed to the charge of districts (the average period of service for the new officials of the Burma Civil Service before receiving their district is five years) but, for reasons that will be discussed in detail, the calibre of the new officials is not so high that they may be expected to overhaul the rusty district administration, when their time comes.

Above the Deputy Commissioner, there remains the Commissioner at the headquarters of the division.[2] The powers of a Commissioner have always been somewhat undefined; unkind British officers used to call him a 'post office'; much of his time was occupied by hearing appeals in revenue cases, and he had a responsibility for the supervision of local authorities. Nowadays, with the land records in chaos, the work arising from land rights and revenue obligations is no more. With the old structure of local authorities in abeyance, this work also has ceased. And yet the present Government has thought the post of Commissioner sufficiently important still to appoint some of the most able of its trained administrators to the charge of divisions during recent years. A great number of quasi-political, quasi-administrative duties have appeared (such as the divisional Pyidawtha work) which require a strong personality to impose some control over the activities of leaders— political, religious, or communal—who have set themselves up as the representatives of 'the masses'.

The structure of the judiciary is still set in the pattern existing

---

[1] By a lucky chance, of these ex-*myooks*, those who were recruited in the 1930's are of a high standard. The 1930's, the period when Rangoon University began to produce graduates in large numbers, was also a period of slump and unemployment. Some graduates, who would normally have competed only for the I.C.S. or B.C.S., were forced by the prevailing economic difficulties to enter the subordinate civil service: their quality is distinctly better than the post-war entry to the higher civil service.

[2] There are seven divisions, as in pre-war days: Mandalay, Sagaing, and Magwe Divisions in Upper Burma, and Pegu, Irrawaddy, Arakan, and Tenasserim Divisions in Lower Burma. There is also the Chin Special Division. Altogether there are thirty-three districts in Burma proper, as compared with the pre-war thirty-nine. Two districts form the Kachin State, two the Chin Special Division. The Salween District and five other townships form the Karen State.

during the British time, with the addition of a Supreme Court
at the summit.[1] In the districts there are Magistrates' Courts
to try criminal cases where the maximum sentence is two
years (Special Magistrates may award seven years) and a
District Court, with jurisdiction in civil cases. There are Sessions
Courts to hear serious criminal charges and to hear appeals
from the magistrates' courts. The High Court exercises ordinary
original jurisdiction for the City of Rangoon, and also acts as
an appeal court, both in criminal and civil cases, for the whole
Union. All capital sentences require the confirmation of the
High Court. The Supreme Court is the final court of appeal.[2]

Before making comments on the judiciary it is, perhaps,
pertinent to recall that the *New Times of Burma* was prosecuted
and fined for an article entitled 'Is the Judiciary Independent'?[3]
Certainly, the tradition that the courts must not be influenced
by political or personal considerations is one British concept in
which most educated Burmans, including the best practitioners
at the Bar, would concur without reservation: but it is a tradition that is in danger. While the higher courts—particularly
the Supreme Court under the presidency of Justice E Maung—
have continued on many occasions to give evidence of their
independence and impartiality, the conduct of the lower courts
has been less impressive. Concepts of justice are changing: a
quotation from a letter to the Press, written by a Public
Prosecutor, provides an illustration. He criticizes a previous
leading article:

As regards your remark about 'a peculiar misapprehension [of the
AFPFL Government] that justice is a thing which can be dispensed
or withheld at will', I must remind you that the State . . . has the
prerogative of mercy and can either pardon an offender or prosecute
him in accordance with the interests of the State. 'Justice' in its
abstract sense is unobtainable. The interests of the State transcend
Law.[4]

If 'the State' should be equated with 'the Government' and the

---

[1] cf. 'The Legal System of the Union of Burma', *Burma, the Fourth Anniversary*,
p. 21, and 'Trial of Criminal Cases', *Burma, the Seventh Anniversary*, pp. 147–9.

[2] Its position was indicated in a judgment on an application for leave to appeal
(which was dismissed) in the Hla Maung defamation case. It was observed that
'This court is no ordinary court of criminal appeal, and ordinarily no such leave
[to appeal] would be granted unless it can be shown that grave and substantial
injustice has been done [or unless there are] exceptional or special circumstances
which would warrant our interference' (*Nation*, 21 September 1954).

[3] ibid., 25 March 1954.

[4] ibid., 12 December 1954, letter from U Hpay Latt, Public Prosecutor, Toungoo.
The occasion for these remarks was the Government's decision to prosecute U Ba Pe
and his associates in 1954 for offences alleged to have taken place at the beginning
of 1949. The charges were dropped, and Ba Pe released in October 1958.

Government with the political preponderance of one party, this doctrine could lead to a collapse of present ideals of impartial justice. Justice E Maung has voiced such fears from the Bench, remarking 'As judges our duty is not to help the Government. Why do the judges concerned go out of their way to try and find excuses for their [the Government's] decisions, as it were?'[1] Later, in retirement, U E Maung expressed himself with even greater force:

The party in power [he said] would use all means to serve the ends of political expediency. It was up to the judiciary to check these actions, justly and fearlessly. The present judiciary was incapable of doing this because it was too weak and too terrified of possible reaction from the executive. This was the main reason why he had decided to leave the judicial service . . . because he felt that he could not conscientiously discharge his duties under the prevailing conditions.[2]

U E Maung is famous for his boldness of speech, but he is a man whose whole career has trained him in the necessity of weighing words before using them.

Some of the actions of Deputy Commissioners, in their magisterial capacity, have come in for severe criticism from the appeal courts. In Arakan a District Superintendent of Police, R. D. Kirkham, an officer with many years of service and decorations for good conduct, was arrested by one of the political officials: the Supreme Court found that his arrest had been entirely without cause.[3] Other persons arrested have not had the means to secure speedy redress, as did Mr. Kirkham: in 1951 the Supreme Court had occasion to release numbers of persons who had been confined in jail for years: one district magistrate made arrests 'with a rubber stamp', only bothering to look for evidence against his prisoners when the Karen leaders appealed to the Supreme Court.[4] Another (the Deputy Commissioner of Tavoy) was rebuked by the court because he had 'violated the law of the country',[5] and in a third case the District Commissioner of Shwebo was censured and ordered to release persons held without trial since December 1947.[6]

The use of the Public Order (Preservation) Act to incarcerate political suspects without trial presents one of the most

---

[1] *Nation*, 20 January 1950. A passage in the hearing of the appeal of Bo Yan Naing, previously mentioned on p. 28 n. 2, as having considerable constitutional and legal interest.
[2] Transcript of an interview, ibid., 19 August 1954.
[3] ibid., 1 June 1949.
[4] ibid., 13 July 1951.
[5] ibid.
[6] ibid., 25 October 1951.

debatable aspects of Burmese justice today.[1] An attempt was made by the opposition in Parliament to secure the repeal of the Act in October 1953; it was then stated that 287 persons were detained under the Act, with no prospect of trial.[2] One year later a petition was addressed to the Minister for Judicial Affairs from 500 inmates of Rangoon Central Jail, all being *détenus* or 'under trial', who stated that the minimum period any signatory had been in jail was six months and the maximum two years: all without any sentence having been passed.[3] Probably the most appalling example of 'the law's delays' is that of six Karen army officers who were involved in the capture of Maymyo by the KNDO in February 1949, being arrested two months later. After being held in captivity for six years, their court-martial proceedings still had not been brought to completion.[4] They are stated to have grown white-haired and bent with worry during the weary years of waiting. It is impossible to believe that all is well with a juridical system in which such delays and irregularities are an everyday feature.

In part the present-day shortcomings of the administration and the judiciary are attributable to the uncertainties of the future and unsatisfactory conditions of government service. The civil service is faced with a complete transformation of its activities when the Government's plans for democratic local administration come to fruition. Hitherto it has proved impossible to implement the reforms, and administration of the districts, towns, and villages remains in a condition of suspended animation.

Municipal committees were first established in the 1870's; an abortive attempt was made to set up rural representative bodies in the 1880's; only in 1923 was there a renewed attempt to establish a system of rural local government consisting of district councils, circle boards, and village councils charged with responsibilities for primary education, the roads, public health, and other social services. This attempt to create a demand for local government in Burma enjoyed only very

---

[1] For instance, Saw Benson, alleged to be a KNDO sympathizer, was detained for over four years under the Public Order (Preservation) Act (*Nation*, 27 August 1952).

[2] ibid., 1 October 1953.

[3] Reference to the *Prison Administration Report*, 1951, reveals a high proportion of prisoners detained without trial and sentence. Thus:

	Jail population	Convicted persons	Détenus	'Under Trial'*
1.1.50	11,435	5,254	4,459	1,722
1.1.51	9,546	5,502	2,389	1,654
1.1.52	9,216	5,893	1,637	1,685

* i.e. not yet brought to trial.

[4] *Nation*, 9 February 1955. These cases were still not settled one year later.

limited success.[1] All these institutions were, of course, obliterated during the Japanese occupation, and they were not revived after the return of the Burma Government from Simla. The powers of the district councils were henceforth exercised by the District Officers, and there were long delays before the municipalities began to resume some of their old functions. The Nu Government was not anxious to reconstitute these authorities, in view of the plans for a comprehensive reform of local government: but the delays in the launching of the new system have been so protracted that it is to the older type of local bodies that one must look for evidence of local democracy in action.

Rangoon Municipality was reconstituted in 1949. Previously the municipal machine had been managed by an administrator: this gentleman now appointed himself to the post of Municipal Commissioner and resisted all subsequent attempts to dislodge him. Elections were held in February 1949, when the authority of the AFPFL Government was at its lowest: a small Independent majority was thereupon returned, and the next three years saw constant conflict between Independents and AFPFL nominees. Early in 1951 an Inquiry Commission[2] was appointed to examine the Corporation's activities. Their report (published 1 August 1951) disclosed every sort of irregularity.[3] The Municipal Commissioner and the heads of all but three departments were castigated. Undue influence by Councillors had led to losses of revenue and to 'moral degeneration' among employees, expenditure was rising far above income and debts had mounted to 3·39 crores.

In the election of February 1952 the AFPFL, whose forces had been strengthened and augmented from the central organization, secured an overwhelming victory. The AFPFL Mayor elected in early 1954 gave out as his slogan 'Towards a Socialist City', but evidence of this new orientation was somewhat hard to find amid the shanty quarters and the piles of refuse. In January 1955 Ba Swe summed up the city as 'one big stench'.[4] In truth, the whole municipal machine has collapsed in the face of mounting difficulties; the Rangoon population has expanded from the 400,415 of 1931 and the 500,800 of 1941 to 737,079 in 1952; the extra numbers are

[1] See the author's *Foundations of Local Self-Government*, pp. 214–44.
[2] Its members were a judge, two retired I.C.S. officers, and a former municipal commissioner.
[3] The All-Burma Trades Federation, an organization of the AFPFL, collected Rs.60 protection money from all street stalls in the city, who, in return were given immunity from prosecution for 'encroachment'.
[4] Adding, a little disingenuously, that 'there had been some improvement' during the AFPFL years (*Nation*, 24 January 1955).

almost all 'squatters', living in *basha* huts, some in the heart of the city, others spilling out over all the open ground around. None of these thousands pay one kyat in municipal taxes, although they have created countless complicated needs in the fields of civic services. Of the pre-war dwellings listed for house taxes the great majority are subject to rent controls, so that it is impossible to raise their assessments (or so the argument runs). Altogether, the Corporation has to provide services for a population that has grown by 50 per cent., at a time when costs have risen by over 100 per cent., on an income that (without subventions from Government) is appreciably the same as before the war. In addition the pre-war staff, the men with experience, who were largely Indians, have been replaced by new men, Burmans, most of whom owe their jobs to nepotism. So that to sheer incapacity is added inefficiency, besides the problems raised by war and insurrection. Any proposals for reform must be radical to master all these problems.[1]

The other municipalities, some sixty in number, with their functions pared down to little more than the management of the municipal bazaar, have not had to face such pressing problems, and have not been the centre of so much controversy. As in the British days, these municipalities have been constituted by election: Bhamo alone has continued to have the District Magistrate as Chairman. Almost everywhere there have been tussles between supporters of the AFPFL and their adversaries; elections in eight leading towns in 1951 produced AFPFL control in five towns and Independent régimes elsewhere: in most instances these results are reflections of the power and prestige of local personalities rather than of movements of public opinion. Some municipalities have been suspended, or superseded for inefficiency or corruption: as in pre-war years, Mandalay has headed the list.[2]

Meanwhile, plans have been slowly maturing for a new and more far-reaching system of local government, which will embody a vision of society in which the charitable feelings of the Burmese (for which the distinctive word *ahlu* is used) will be yoked to civic services in a more comprehensive manner than is possible under the Pyidawtha programme. It will be recalled that the first Local Government Act was passed in 1949, but the rebellion prevented its being introduced anywhere. The Government took advantage of the delay to introduce

[1] On 1 December 1958, Colonel Tun Shein took charge of the Municipal Corporation. Vigorous measures were taken to make the city clean and orderly. Markets were regulated, street traders were removed and the streets were cleaned.

[2] In March 1951 the Chairman and seven members of Mandalay Municipality were jailed for embezzlement (*Nation*, 10 March 1951).

further legislation in 1953 to make its arrangements more watertight. Sanction now exists for a hierarchy of local bodies, building up to the district council as the major authority: to these councils will be transferred (if the scheme materializes) a large proportion of the present functions of the central Government.

The structure begins with the village council, *kye ywa kaungsi*, which may have jurisdiction over several hamlets or one large village: there will be from 5 to 7 members, who must be residents in the locality,[1] aged at least 18 years, of either sex. Their period of office is 5 years. The Chairman will be elected for 1 year from among their number. Voting at the village elections will be compulsory (actually attendance at the voting-booth is compulsory), the penalty for non-attendance being a fine up to a maximum of K10.[2]

Provision is made for the inclusion of urban communities within the scheme. This appears to be a most imaginative innovation: in the past the existence of large numbers of small municipalities established in petty market towns has been a distinct weakness. The urban bodies will consist of ward committees and a town committee. The ward committee, *yatkwet* or *ayat kaungsi*, will have 3–5 members, directly elected as for the village councils. Each ward will send 1–3 representatives to the town committee, *myoma kaungsi*. Next comes the township council, *myonè kaungsi*, which is composed of two classes of members, rural and urban. Each town will contribute 5–10 members, depending on its size, and each village tract will send one member: all these members will be chosen by the subordinate village or town councils. As in every township there are some 50–100 village tracts, and no more than two towns, there will be a clear predominance of the rural members, and this is deliberately contrived.[3] The total membership of each township council will vary between 60 and 100.

Finally, each township will contribute 4–8 representatives to the district council, *kayaing kaungsi*. Where there are large towns, such as Akyab or Pegu, these will by-pass the township council and contribute members direct to the district council. When the scheme is fully functioning all the municipalities will be absorbed into the district councils, with the exception

---

[1] There is no residence qualification for members of the Union Parliament.

[2] Proposals have been made to introduce compulsory voting at parliamentary elections, but at present it is optional.

[3] This is a rough generalization: actually the number of village tracts ranges from 16 in Maliwun Township (Mergui) to 135 in Wakema Township (Myaung-mya). In one township only are there more than two towns (i.e. urban areas of 5,000 population)—this is in Insein, where there are 6 towns and 110 village tracts.

of Rangoon and Mandalay, which will have a separate status.[1] It is contemplated that, under certain circumstances, the voters of an area will have the right to recall their member: if a member of a village council is elected to the township council, and then to the district council, the village electorate by withdrawing their mandate will exclude him from all three authorities.[2]

The village council is intended to form the basic unit. Each council will employ a full-time Village Executive Officer (paid approximately K100 per month) selected not so much for formal qualifications as for local knowledge and standing. In the first stage of the scheme the village council will enjoy only the limited administrative and judicial powers at present allotted to the village headman, but in due course it is intended that the council will co-ordinate almost all the activities of the village. It will serve as a village court (three council members will form a quorum) with powers in civil suits up to a value of K500, and in criminal cases it will have the powers of a third-class magistrate. The intention is that the village court will be the authority in all issues of purely local significance: cases which involve the outside world must be tried in the regular courts. Village watch and ward will also be controlled by the council. The transfer of responsibilities for primary education and health matters is also probable; it is hoped that eventually the village council will be associated with every aspect of the village economy, so that the present constant necessity to refer petty matters to departments in the Secretariat will be terminated.

The other main working authority will be the district council. At present no particular powers have been allotted, but under Section 19 of the 1953 Act it is open to the President to transfer responsibility for education, public health, agriculture, and the civil police—all at present central subjects—to the district councils. It is envisaged that these councils will function as miniature parliaments: they will meet to choose a 'Prime Minister', and he will then appoint his 'Cabinet'. Different 'Ministers' will exercise control over different departments. For instance, a 'Minister for Home Affairs' will be in charge of the police, the fire service, and the auxiliary defence services.[3] The council as such will, like Parliament, only meet annually

---

[1] Although no provision has been made for their separate treatment, it may not be simple to include Moulmein (pop. 102,777), Bassein (pop. 77,905), and Henzada (pop. 61,972) within the district council framework.

[2] The right of recall is contemplated also for Union M.P.s, but so far no legislation has been promoted.

[3] See *Speech by Thakin Tin to M.P.s on Democratization of Local Government*, 10 March 1954, p. 9.

or biennially to consider general matters of policy.[1] It seems certain that the district council Prime Minister, and probably his Cabinet also, will necessarily become full-time politicians *cum* administrators. Can Burma find the large numbers of public men in her thirty-three districts equipped to take on this task, in addition to the 375 members of Parliament and the men who will direct the government corporations and boards and departments? It seems most unlikely, and the pace at which the local-government policy is being implemented seems to prove that the Government is doubtful of the outcome also.

If these district 'Ministers' do eventually assume their promised powers, the roles of the District Officers and the officials of the central Government in the districts will need to be redefined. It is envisaged that the District Officer will surrender his judicial powers to an official who will thereafter be District Magistrate *per se*, with no administrative responsibilities.[2] The District Officer will become chief Executive Officer to the district council. Other senior officials, such as the Superintendent of Police and the District Executive Engineer, will similarly become the servants of the council.[3] But although these officials will be in the service of the council, they will be appointed (and presumably paid) by the central Government, and they will continue to be answerable to their various departments in the Secretariat. It is not impossible that a local authority may adopt a policy at variance with the policy of the department or the Government.[4] The Executive Officer and the departmental heads would then be placed in an impossible position, under fire from two directions. The likely result would be attempts to please both sides, confusion, and the bringing of all activity to a standstill.[5] The

[1] This represents a complete departure from English local government, which is the original model for the Burmese system. English county councils and rural district councils meet once every month, and the committees, composed of members responsible for the different departments, meet more frequently still. In English local government the elected representative plays his part in actual administration as well as in policy-making. But English counties are reasonably compact, and communications are good. Burmese districts are large, and communications, especially in the rainy season, are often non-existent. The new proposals may well suit Burma best.

[2] Similarly the Sub-Divisional Officers and Township Officers will become magistrates alone.

[3] It has not been decided whether these senior officials will be members of the district council; a probable compromise will be to permit these heads of departments to attend meetings where their department's affairs are to be debated, to offer advice, but not to vote.

[4] In this connexion the statement by Kyaw Nyein, previously quoted (above, p. 88) should be recalled.

[5] A comparable position developed in United Provinces, India, in the 1920's when education inspectors were required to serve two masters, the Education Department, and the District Board: the result was a stalemate. See the author's *Foundations of Local Self-Government*, p. 255.

Commissioners are totally excluded from any association with the new scheme of democratic local administration. If and when the new scheme is in full operation there would appear to be an overwhelming case for the abolition of the office of Commissioner.

Another difficulty which has to be resolved is the question of finance. At present the district councils are virtually moneyless: during the year 1954–5, for example, no funds whatsoever were allotted for the maintenance of district roads (which have almost disintegrated, following thirteen years of complete neglect). The launching of the new district councils will only become possible if the Government is able to provide large subventions from the central revenues; in the present straitened circumstances this could only be done by cutting down on those Pyidawtha activities which are really only of propaganda value, such as the work of the Mass Education Council and the Environmental Sanitation Board. One source of revenue which, it is hoped, may become available to the district councils in 1956 is the land revenue. This once all-important tax is now so precarious that the Government has decided to abolish the existing revenue structure and hand over the proceeds of the tax for local use. Assessment, it has been announced,[1] will in future be made by the district council (and when a district council does not exist, by the district tenancy committee or district land committee) for each *kwin*[2] or revenue unit. The Settlement Department will fix the maximum rate at which land revenue may be levied; it will be for the council to decide whether to levy up to the maximum, according to the needs of the district. Within each *kwin*, individual assessments will be made by 'a mass meeting of the peasants concerned'.[3] Where village councils are functioning, they will collect the revenue. Every year the Union Government will make allocations of the total revenue to the districts; the district councils will apportion their quota to the townships and the villages (where district councils have not been created, the District Pyidawtha Committee will exercise this function). The intention of this reform is, of course, to provide some local incentive for the better collection of the revenue. It is desirable that those district councils which are the most conscientious shall receive

[1] At the Conference on Land Revenue and Agricultural Loans, November 1954.
[2] *Kwin*, literally, a 'circle' or circuit of land, a survey unit introduced during the British period to correspond with the village lands, being about 700 acres. Nowadays, Lower Burma villages may contain two or more *kwins*; some Upper Burma village lands are less than a *kwin*.
[3] This sounds a haphazard method of assessing tax responsibilities, but there is a strong Burmese tradition of assessment by the village elders; this was the custom with the *thathameda* tax of the old kings.

a reward in the shape of handsome allocations. For the village councils, a proportion of their income is expected to accrue from the fines imposed by the village court. It is envisaged that the court shall have the power to exact a fine in terms of labour service, and in this manner the moneyless village ne'er-do-wells will not escape penalties. It is also probable that tax obligations will be permitted to be commuted by labour service.

The first local elections took place, at village and ward level, during May and June 1954 in Kyaukse, Meiktila, and Insein. As in the parliamentary elections, there were the wide divergences that might be expected in a country emerging from the Middle Ages. In places there was a plethora of candidates; elsewhere there were not sufficient candidates to necessitate elections. The AFPFL and the ABPO dominated the scene (in many places the AFPFL was actually opposed by its constituent peasants' organization). Some communal candidates (Karens in particular) stood as 'Independents', and there were many genuine Independents, often retired government servants. Elections were subsequently held in nine more districts in late 1954 and early 1955.[1] Despite attempts by the Communists to wreck these elections (notably in Pegu and Shwebo Districts), 85 per cent. of the electorate recorded their vote:[2] a figure which would be excellent in an English local election and which affords some vindication for compulsory voting. The necessary steps were taken to select members for township and district councils, but the actual transfer of power to local bodies did not follow automatically. This transfer is contingent on the assent of the Ministry for the Democratization of Local Administration and of other ministries. The former is, naturally, desirous that the new scheme shall be launched under favourable circumstances: if the new experiment is a failure, then public disillusionment and revulsion may cause a setback to democratic institutions for a generation; there must also be at least a minimum of security, an absence of large-scale rebel activity, to make for success. The other ministries, for their part, are by no means anxious to yield the powers they have wielded from the centre. It was necessary for the Minister, Thakin Tin, to plead with each department in turn for consideration of what was declared to be government policy over six years before. It may be that the existing hiatus will continue for a decade until all thirty-three districts have been fitted into the new structure. Meanwhile, a start has been made. In

[1] These were: Hanthawaddy, Pegu, Toungoo, Tharrawaddy, Prome, Henzada, Pyapon, Shwebo, and Myingyan.

[2] By comparison, 54 per cent. voted at the Rangoon Municipal Election, 1955, when voting was not compulsory.

Insein, Kyaukse, and Meiktila Districts the new councils for
the district, the township, the town, and the village were all
set in motion in April 1955. They began work with distinctly
limited authority: district councils received the powers of the
pre-war district councils under an Act of 1921, together with
those of the district Pyidawtha committees; township councils
were similarly enfranchised; town councils received the powers
of the old municipalities and the village councils those of the
village headmen. In addition, village councils were to act as
village courts. In areas where these new bodies began work,
the Commissioner and the Deputy Commissioner were completely eliminated from local administration.[1]

Inaugurating the Insein District Council, U Nu was at pains
to emphasize the challenge offered by the new experiment.
'Power corrupts', the Prime Minister reminded his listeners:

> I regret to say that quite a number of these [Tenancy] committees
> are more concerned with their own welfare than that of the people
> . . . there are many other organizations and individuals in the Union
> which are equally crooked. It is time to put a stop to such disgraceful
> practices. . . . It will be a national calamity if it [the new scheme]
> fails ignominiously due to the inefficiency of the people, the
> dishonesty of the people, the lack of courage of the people. . . . If it
> fails, then the people of the Union . . . will be floating in the world's
> spit, as our saying goes.[2]

U Nu's warning has been ignored in some areas where rival
political bosses of the AFPFL and the ABPO have used the
new councils to promote their own ends, while the underground
Communists have attempted to sabotage their development,
not scrupling to stoop to murder in order to damage the efforts of
council members and officials. However, the new scheme has been
deemed sufficiently successful to warrant its extension to other
areas. In January and February 1956 power was transferred to
the councils of Tharrawaddy, Prome, and Henzada Districts.

In the greater part of Burma, however, the sinister rule of
the district bosses continues, neither bureaucracy nor democracy.
And in the atmosphere of uncertainty, the civil service becomes
ever more discouraged. The decline of the civil service presents
one of the most disquieting features of the present day. The
British bequeathed plenty of problems to their successors, the
present Government, but they also bequeathed one asset of
great value: a professional, non-political, administrative civil
service, with a tradition, a sense of duty, a reputation among

---

[1] Details of the powers assigned to the new bodies in accordance with former
legislation may be found in the author's *Foundations of Local Self-Government*,
pp. 114–15 and 228–43.

[2] *Democratization of Local Administration*, 9 April 1955.

the people (as regards the higher ranks) and an *esprit de corps*. In the neighbouring countries of India and Pakistan this asset, the civil service, has enabled the new Governments to overcome the immediate crisis of partition and the mass migrations, and to tackle the longer battle between a rising population and a barely balanced economy. Despite the abrupt transfer of power in the sub-continent, taking Indian politicians and British officials alike by surprise, there has been a wide degree of continuity between the old and the new: and the civil service has forged the links in this continuity. Of course, neither India nor Pakistan were subjected to the scourge of invasion and the devastation of war (except for their most easterly districts), nor have they undergone (except on the most minor scale) the even greater disruption of civil war; nevertheless, the comparison is not entirely inappropriate.

On the eve of the Japanese invasion, in the higher ranks of the administrative services the proportion of Burmans was about 70 per cent.; the subordinate civil service was, of course, entirely Burman.[1] British officers predominated in the senior ranks, but among the younger men there was a high proportion of Burmans, carefully selected for their qualities of intellect and character. Of the thirty-nine District Officers in 1941 only fourteen were British. In other departments—police, medical, education, forests, and agricultural services—there were wide variations in the proportions of Burmans employed. The Forest Service and the Civil Police were almost all Burmans, except for a few Europeans in some of the senior posts; the Agricultural Service, too, was largely Burman; but in most other departments there was a high proportion of Indians—many of them domiciled in Burma for one or two generations. The Indian middle class was many years ahead of the Burmese in recognizing that the acquiring of a university degree or of technical training was the key to the door of advancement in government service.[2] Hence, a large proportion of the medical department, teachers in high schools and the university, and employees in the post office were Indians.[3] At the time of the Japanese invasion all the British and Indian officials who could make the journey

---

[1] In 1940, in Class I Civil Service, out of a total strength of 162 officers Burmans numbered 62, Anglo-Burmans 3, Indians 2, and British 95; in Class II, out of a total strength of 221 officers, 207 were Burmans and 14 Anglo-Burmans; in the Subordinate Civil Service there were 425 Burmans and 4 Anglo-Burmans.

[2] As late as 1937, out of the 138 students graduating that year from Rangoon University only 60 were Burmans; of the 128 licentiates from the Medical School only 39 were Burmans, and of the 20 who passed from the Government Technical Institute Insein, only 4 were Burmans (*Pyidawtha Conference*, p. 96).

[3] The Military Police battalions were largely Indian; treatment of the Military Police is reserved for Chapter XI.

evacuated to India. A majority of the Burmese officials stayed at their posts and continued to work under the Japanese régime. To many there came unexpected opportunities for promotion to the highest posts; while young university graduates—some with good qualifications—were recruited into the junior ranks of the services.[1] The British Military Government took over the officials of the Ba Maw Government (after certain screening operations) to staff its temporary administration.

On its return from Simla, among the many problems facing the Burma Government was the reconstruction of the civil services. For three and a half years there had been no recruitment of new officials, and now many senior officers were overdue for retirement, while others had died or disappeared. The superior civil services were brought up to strength by the recruitment of probationers from among British and Burman officers of the armed forces, from 1945 onwards. However, it rapidly became plain that the plans prepared at Simla for a period of administrative and economic reconstruction to precede further political advance were being extinguished by the AFPFL pressure for immediate independence. By the end of 1946 there could be no expectation of further British participation in the Government of Burma. Early in 1947 many British officials were sent on leave, whence they never returned: by mid-1947 the majority of 'superior' civil service posts were filled by Burmans. Only in the Frontier Areas were British officers working in any numbers.

The Burmese decision to dismiss all British officials immediately, like the decision to quit the Commonwealth, was at variance with the policy of India and Pakistan, where British officials were retained if there were no suitable nationals to fill specific appointments (as, for example, that of India's representative at Lhasa). These British officials have been gradually retired as nationals have come forward with the experience to take charge: but still, at the time of writing, there are at least two British District Officers in India and several more in Pakistan, with other Englishmen in advisory posts. But Burma, in her determination to achieve 'real' independence, discharged all her foreign officials. British officers were relatively few, but large numbers of Indians in the services were removed to make way for Burmans. Certain

---

[1] The *Report by the Supreme Allied Commander*, in reviewing civil affairs, remarks that the officials working under Japanese rule had been first distrusted as British sympathizers, and then despised by other Burmans as collaborators, concluding, 'As a result, many of them being irrevocably compromised, had become demoralized and corrupt' (p. 190). This is too sweeping: the officials were neither more nor less 'compromised' and 'demoralized' than the politicians and others who experienced Japanese Co-prosperity.

selected Indians and Anglo-Burmans, who were prepared explicitly to renounce their Indian or British nationality and to adopt Burmese citizenship, were permitted to continue in their posts. These mass dismissals of Indians and Anglo-Burmans caused something near chaos in certain departments, notably the Posts and Telegraphs.

Having made a clearance of the foreigners, the new Burmese Ministers remained highly suspicious of all officials of Burmese race associated with the previous régime: it was made very plain that, unless they were prepared to adopt the AFPFL policy as their own, they too would be sent packing. This attitude was voiced by U Nu (himself not an extreme exponent of this view) in a speech made on 29 September 1949 to Secretariat officials. He first observed that the civil service during the British period was an 'instrument in suppression of all nationalist movements'. He contrasted the old days when 'the bureaucracy was the Government itself, the last word in every government measure lying with the official opinion'— and the position under independence when 'direction in governmental administration should come from the chosen leaders of the people who compose the Government'. He bluntly laid it down 'that those who would not fall in line with the new order of things had better quit'. U Nu reminded his audience: 'You are a body of servants whose work is liable to be brought at any moment under the master's eye.' He dwelt at length on complaints of 'a certain sense of frustration with its attendant evils of lack of initiative and drive'. He reiterated that officials certainly could not themselves originate policy: this was the responsibility of the Ministers (if officials did not realize this fundamental change, they had become 'misfits'), but he went on to rebuke them for 'receding into the background, content that all the initiative, not only in policy matters but also in all other matters, should come from the Minister. This is the worst stage of degeneration that members of the civil service . . . can reach.'

U Nu proceeded to chide the officials for their 'caution or timidity' when faced with public opinion; he accused them of 'an *esprit de corps* which, in the extreme instance of the highest civil service, has fostered a system which developed a very close and jealously guarded doctrine of vested interests'. He concluded by warning officials against becoming a party civil service and by commending them to the path of duty.[1]

[1] 'The Role of Government Servants', *From Peace to Stability*, pp. 27–36. The speech should be read in full. The writer has utilized excerpts to show the particular attitude of the AFPFL leaders in 1949, but there is much good sense in U Nu's words.

Whatever may have been U Nu's intentions in addressing the officials, their reaction was to leave initiative to the politicians. Some of the more single-minded officers found that they could not reconcile the traditions they had learned to accept with the new requirements of expediency, and there were several resignations of those in high places. Another discouraging factor was the imposition of pay cuts in 1949 when the financial situation of the Government was desperate. At the time U Nu assured the civil service that 'if we could afford, we would pay [higher salaries] but the fact is that we simply cannot do so'.[1] In the following years, Burma accumulated large overseas balances, while the cost of living advanced to figures three or four times higher than pre-war.[2] But the salaries of the senior officials have remained pegged, well below those of before the war. A High Court Judge receives K2,500, as against Rs.4,000 before; the Chief Secretary draws K1,800, compared with K3,000 in pre-war days; Deputy Commissioners are paid K800 (plus K200 allowances), whereas the scale of their predecessors ranged from Rs.1,000 to Rs.2,250. Lower down the official hierarchy the difference between before and after independence narrows, and a junior official of today receives roughly the same as his pre-war counterpart. At the very bottom, a peon is paid K82–97 (including cost-of-living allowance) compared with Rs.14–20 in the old days.[3] Judged by abstract canons of equity, there is much to be said for lowering the pay of the highest ranks and raising that of the lowly.[4] But senior civil servants with large bungalows to maintain, cars to run, and sons to educate cannot be expected suddenly to throw overboard a standard of living which forms,

[1] *Towards Peace and Democracy*, p. 176.

[2] There has been no satisfactory measurement of the cost of living in Burma in recent years. There are official figures, and these show 1949 as the high-point: thereafter costs are supposed to have fallen. But official publications all ignore the rising costs of imported articles, rents of upper-class houses also have soared.

[3] The following are representative posts throughout the public services: Chief Justice of the Union, K3,500; Supreme Court Judge, K3,000; Chief Justice, K3,000; Puisne Judges, K2,500; Attorney-General, K2,500 plus right of private practice (worth K2,000); Auditor-General, Chief Secretary, Financial Commissioner, K1,800; Secretary to Government, Divisional Commissioner, Departmental Heads of Police, Posts, Telegraphs, Public Instruction, and Accountant-General, K1,600; Deputy Secretary, Deputy Commissioner, District and Sessions Judge, K1,000; District Superintendent of Police, Superintending Engineer, K1,300; Sub-Divisional Officer, Treasury Officer, Assistant Engineer, K350; Sub-Inspector of Police, Settlement Inspector, K185; Head Constable, Assistant (untrained) Teacher, K97.

[4] The 1951 *Report of the Administration Reorganization Committee*, while approving this process in general terms suggested 'that better work could be obtained from a smaller and better qualified staff which would justify higher rates of pay' (p. 7). This goes straight to the root: but is such a remedy possible, either in political terms, or in terms of trained personnel available?

in effect, part of their administrative superiority. They are likely to turn to other, better-paid walks of life; they may even be tempted to augment their insufficient resources by irregular means. Officials in charge of national boards and corporations and other authorities spending large sums on capital purchases might be particularly tempted to accept 'commissions' and otherwise augment their salaries. Because it became clear that some were yielding to this temptation the Bureau of Special Investigation under U Nu was brought into being. There has been a long procession from the government offices to the jail, including a Commissioner of Police for Rangoon, the Chairman of the Inland Water Transport Board, the Commissioner of Commercial Taxes, and many others. The number of those detected but not prosecuted may well be higher. But in addition to exposing palpable scandals, the Bureau of Special Investigation has also spent much energy in ferreting out errors of form and procedure. Officials have been arrested and held responsible for the irregularities of subordinates. Overworked men who, under pressure, have certified accounts or sanctioned expenditure without a proper check have found themselves in trouble. And if an official is associated with a venture that is a failure, he will be lucky if he is not caught out in the search for scapegoats.

All these elements—the snatching away by the politicians of the reins of power, the diminution of salaries, fear of being faulted by the Bureau of Special Investigation, uncertainty concerning the future—combine to lower the morale of the old civil servants and to discourage the new entry. Several former Indian Civil Service officers have retired prematurely, despite the financial loss,[1] and are practising as barristers. Those that remain are working under great strain. Among the middle ranks of former junior members of the Burma Civil Service Class II, now promoted to senior posts in the administration and the nationalized concerns, there is much less unrest. Their conditions of pay are at least as advantageous as they would have been in former days when they would have to await their turn behind the ranks of the Class I officers. These are the men who will 'carry' the Government for the next twenty years, and fortunately for Burma they are up to the task. There has been an extensive expansion of the whole civil service; its numbers

[1] At the time of the transfer of power officials, both British and Burman, in the 'Imperial' or 'Secretary of State's Services' became entitled to compensation. The terms awarded to Burmans were, by arrangement with the British Government, less advantageous than those given to their British colleagues because it was assumed that the Burmans would receive further well-paid employment in Burma after independence.

are now over three times greater than before independence, totalling some 125,000 members. This huge increase has entailed the large-scale promotion of head clerks to gazetted (or 'officer') rank, and the recruitment of many 'political' civil servants. Among these stopgap officials there are not many men of character and ability.

Regular recruitment to the administrative service continues to be free, very largely, from political influences. There is a Public Services Commission presided over by U Lun Baw, himself an ex-politician but fully cognisant of the prime need to rebuild a non-political tradition of service. Recruitment is at two levels, there being a senior and junior branch or class. The Burma Judicial Service maintains a certain standard of entry. Candidates for the Junior Branch are required to be graduates or higher grade pleaders; they are obliged to take a 'simple examination in law' to qualify for selection. For the Burma Civil Service (the administrative service) there is no entrance examination. The Senior Branch (pay scale, K350–700) is recruited half by direct entry of university graduates, half by selection from among the *myooks*, who are given five years' seniority.[1] Recruits to the Junior Branch are, in general, drawn from among young men of intermediate standard; their starting pay is K200. The candidates for the Senior Branch are, in general, drawn from the less promising arts graduates of the university, most of whom have unsuccessfully attempted to enter some other career first. There are, of course, exceptions, lads of promise, but neither the pay, prospects, nor prestige of the civil service today are such as to appeal to men of ambition.[2]

Before 1931 the fledgling administrator began his career in a training school at Meiktila (it was then closed down as an economy measure). In subsequent years beginners were placed under the wing of a particularly experienced District Officer and were systematically trained in the different branches of district work: the treasury, settlement, the magistrate's court. Nowadays the young Senior Branch Officer begins as an Assistant Township Officer, and after a year or two is promoted to Township Officer. Absorbed in the petty detail of an isolated township he is unlikely to acquire a broad

---

[1] During the year 1954–5 there were 24 direct appointments and 24 promotions of *myooks*.

[2] What particularly impressed the writer was, that of all the senior officials he questioned (and they included men of the rank of Ambassador and High Court Judge), not one intended to enter his son for the civil service. And yet in the past there has been a strong family tradition of government service, extending often to three or more generations.

understanding of the problems of administration, to be conscious of the *camaraderie* of a great service. There is a clear need for a less casual introduction to a career in the public service.[1]

What is there today to stimulate the civil servant to render loyal, creative, honest service? Only patriotism and self-respect remain. It is somewhat remarkable that there *are* officials who continue to give faithful service. Those among Burma's politicians who are also statesmen are beginning to realize that they have come near to spoiling their country's finest human asset. U Nu in a recent appeal to senior officials told them

> As politicians are leaders in political fields, you are also leaders in administrative fields. You have a great part to play in our stupendous work of building a new nation. Politicians will rise and fall on the wish of the people, but you stay on for ever. . . . As leaders . . . discharge your duties with courage and determination. . . . Politicians should co-operate whole-heartedly with the Government servants in this joint endeavour.[2]

So far other Cabinet Ministers have confined themselves to urging officials 'to work efficiently and courageously as front-line leaders of the country'.[3] Problems of service conditions, of the responsibility of politicians to abstain from meddling in executive decisions, of the need to attract a proportion of the best youth of the country into administration, have not yet been squarely faced.

One aspect of present-day Government remains to be considered: the new state governments, which are responsible for administration throughout almost half the area of Burma (albeit mostly mountain and jungle) and for about one-fifth of the population. The constitution lays down a wide range of subjects that are to be the states' responsibility: only foreign affairs, defence, major lines of communication, lawmaking (in general), and the national taxes are reserved to the Union Government.[4] The states are allotted the land revenue, excise duties, and other taxes to finance their activities but, in

---

[1] A draft outline of a training scheme was sketched out by F. J. Tickner. Plans are being furthered by U Lun Baw and an official committee.

[2] *BWB*, 10 November 1954.

[3] Speech of Ba Swe (ibid., 10 November 1954). A few months earlier the same Minister said publicly 'We shall have to eliminate the bureaucratic who are the sons-in-law of the feudalists' (ibid., 5 May 1954).

[4] The constitution makes the states responsible for police, prisons, justice (under the High Court), education, public health (including hospitals), agriculture, fisheries, land and colonization, markets, water-supplies and irrigation. Land nationalization and local government would be state subjects.

practice, the states depend on large subventions from the Union Government.[1]

The state ministries work in Rangoon. Departments of the Shan Government are located at Taunggyi, and some offices of the Karen Government are (or were) located at Moulmein, but the other state departments remain in Rangoon. There are series of departments, having parallel functions to those of the Union Government.[2] It is not always clear whether these are the product of administrative necessity or of state *amour propre*. It is certain that where a subject is also the concern of the Union Government, the interpolation of another tier in the administrative structure introduces further impediments.

Problems of administration in the states are affected by their history. With regard to the Chins, Kachins, and Karens, there is a necessity to build up a 'state' government *ab initio*: during the British period, these 'excluded areas' were districts where the normal rules and regulations were modified and simplified to suit the frontier peoples. By contrast, in the Shan and Kayah States there is no background of regular British administration or of dependence on Rangoon, there is instead a strong tradition of local freedom and local rule, but in the Marxist jargon popular in Burma today it is 'feudalist' rule.

The Special Division of the Chins has been formed by a readjustment of former administrative boundaries out of which two new districts have been created. It is under the direction of a Commissioner (hitherto Burmese) over whom the Minister for Chin Affairs has not entirely precise powers. The Chins are still largely administered under the simple provisions of the Chin Hills Regulation of 1896.[3] Elected circle and village councils have been set up since independence.

The Kachin State (*Jinghpaw Mungdan*) also consists of two districts, but there is no Commissioner. The mountain tracts

[1] The states would insist that these are not subventions, but their rightful share of customs duties and the profits on state trading.

States' Budgets 1948–53	1948–9	1949–50	1950–1 (million kyats)	1951–2	1952–3
Contributions from Central Government	15	15	18	19	23
Other income	1	2	2	4	6
Total income	16	17	20	23	29
Current expenditure	6	14	13	16	19
Capital expenditure	2	3	3	3	13

[2] For instance, the Shan Government has a Ministry of Information, Ministry of Education, Ministry of Health, Ministry of Works, Ministry of Agriculture and Forests, and Ministry of Finance and Revenue. The Chin Affairs Ministry is composed of departments for General Administration, Education, Co-operatives, Public Relations, Medical and Public Health, Public Works, Veterinary, Judicial, Posts, Telecommunications.

[3] The Chin Hills were not formally declared to be part of Burma until 1895.

continue under the customary law of the tribes and the rule of the Duwas (chiefs), as provided in the Kachin Hill Tribes Regulation of 1895. The lowlands are administered under the same provisions as in Burma proper.

The Karen State was established by law in 1952, but it was not until 1 June 1954 that three of its constituent townships[1] were handed over to the control of the Karen State Government. On 1 July 1955 two more townships passed from military to state rule,[2] and only the Salween District—which is, of course, the heart of the state—is left under Military Government. All the constituent states are deficit areas, but the Karen State is virtually without any resources save for the central contributions. Administration is headed by a Special Commissioner, Thra Donation, who is a political leader turned official. Indeed, the whole government of the state is a patchwork of the 'territories' of political bosses. The Karen State Ministry in Rangoon can, under these circumstances, only plan for the future.

The Chin Division and the Kachin State are underdeveloped areas, but on the credit side they can boast the highest degree of internal security in the Union, and they have energetic, plain, clear-thinking young leaders to guide them in the future. They have no special administrative problems, except those general to Burma proper, and the complications of political influence and departmentalism are not so acute as in the more 'advanced' districts of Burma.[3] The Karen State has the gigantic task of reconstructing an area backward under British rule, and now exhausted and devastated.

The Shan and Kayah States face an entirely different situation: an integrated social structure exists, but it is built up round a system which appears to be an anachronism to the leaders of the new democratic republic of Burma. And so an attempt is being made to substitute an entirely new system of government which, if it should be carried through, will certainly produce far-reaching effects upon a social order which has remained stable for many hundreds of years.

The impact of British rule upon the Shans was probably less significant than upon any of the remaining peoples of Burma. Since 1922 the Shan States have been grouped in a federation, with a Federal Council of chiefs and certain federal services: public works, medical, forests, education, and agricultural services. These were supported by contributions from the

[1] Hlaingbwe, Pa-an, Thandaung.
[2] Kawkareik and Kya-In townships.
[3] This generalization ignores a host of sociological problems, and would shock an anthropologist: but this is a chapter on administration.

Sawbwas equivalent to 25 per cent. of their revenues: a token contribution was made to the revenues of the Government of Burma, and a (larger) contribution was made by the Burma Government to the federal funds. British control over the thirty-two states was slight; there were two Superintendents, for the Northern and Southern Shan States, the southern Superintendent ranking after 1922 as Commissioner of the Federation. There were a number of Assistant Superintendents, but only in the case of a minority (as at Kengtung, 1935-47) was a British official directly concerned with administration. The Sawbwas ruled their little kingdom like medieval rulers, with powers of life and death.[1]

After independence the new Shan State came into being. The Shan Government is administered by a Cabinet of six. Two members are Sawbwas, the Head of State, Sao Hkun Hkio of Mongmit, and Sao Htun E, Sawbwa of Hsamonghkam; two are retired Burmese Indian Civil Service officers[2] and two are M.P.s, one a Shan, Yee Tip, and one a Kachin, Zaw La.[3] The old Burma Frontier Service having been abolished, a new Shan State Civil Service was set up in 1948: several of the Sawbwas and aristocratic hereditary officials have entered the service of the State Government. The old Superintendents were renamed Residents (about 1945);[4] and in 1950 a new administrative unit was created, the Eastern Shan States, formed out of Kengtung and the Wa States. The KMT invasion and disruption of communications necessitated the creation of yet another unit, the North-Eastern Special District. For about two years the Southern Shan States lived under martial law, while in the north the Sawbwa of Hsenwi, the Resident at Lashio, was given the powers of a Special Commissioner.

There has been steadily growing pressure to abolish the age-old rule of the Sawbwas and bring the Shan country into line with Burma proper. The chiefs had originally accepted the idea

---

[1] Among the Shan chiefs there are great distinctions of rank and precedence. First comes Kengtung, the only ruler with the right to actually sit upon his throne (none of the others dared so to challenge the Burmese kings). Other leading states are Yawnghwe, Mongnai, Hsipaw, and Mongmit. The rulers of these five states were entitled to salutes of nine guns. Altogether, seventeen rulers enjoyed the title of Sawbwa. Eleven were *myosas*, hereditary governors, and four were known as *Ngwegunhmus*, 'superintendents of the silver revenues'.

[2] Under the constitution it is not necessary for state ministers to be members of the Union Parliament or the State Council.

[3] It has become an unwritten convention to include one Kachin Minister in the Shan Cabinet to keep good relations with this somewhat favoured group. Kachins form about 5 per cent. of the population of the Shan States. Shans number some 45 per cent., Burmese 1 per cent., Karens 18 per cent., Chinese 5 per cent.; hill tribes, Was, Lahus, Palaungs, Akhas, &c. make up the remainder.

[4] As British representatives in the Indian Princely States were entitled: the Shan States, being British (not protected) territory did not know the term.

of union with Burma with varying degrees of enthusiasm and reluctance; but all had insisted on internal autonomy as the condition of adherence to the Union. By 1950 the Union Government, by no means satisfied with the attitude of certain chiefs during the KNDO occupation of Taunggyi, was prepared to make the grip of the central Government more effective: first, the Sawbwas were invited to make proposals for their own liquidation. In December 1950 the Sawbwas evolved a formula: they agreed to renounce their judicial powers, but proposed to retain their administrative and legislative rights. On 18 August 1951 they announced their willingness to hand over their administrative powers also. They asked for an Inquiry Commission to be set up to examine the existing situation and to make proposals for the future. The commission was established and reported next year, recommending, with one dissentient, a continuation of the existing régime. This only seemed to arouse the 'anti-feudalists' to greater fury. It is not clear how far this anti-Sawbwa movement is spontaneous, how far manufactured from outside. Shan popular politicians, like nationalists under colonial rule, really have no option but to be in opposition: there is nothing else to do. The truth seems to be that there is discontent in those of the southern states where the chiefs are absentees. But in the Northern and Eastern Shan States the rulers are popular with their subjects, with whom they still have a paternal, benevolent-despot relationship.[1] But whatever the truth, the 'anti-feudalists' became more noisy in their attacks until finally the Sawbwas deemed it politic to make a further gesture of conciliation. On 25 October 1952 the Sawbwas' Association formally intimated their assent to the termination of their existing administrative powers, upon certain stipulated terms. At the same time a joint statement by Sao Hkun Hkio and U Ba Swe was issued, announcing the formation of a Shan political united front on AFPFL lines.

At this stage the Union Government appears to have decided to consider the position in relation to the treatment accorded to the Princely States of India, which had been summarily liquidated by Sardar Patel. In December 1952 a Shan State Reforms Fact-Finding Delegation, headed by Justice Myint Thein, was dispatched on a month's tour of India.[2] Further development was more or less at a standstill during the military régime (September 1952–July 1954). In August 1954 a powerful

---

[1] This is probably generally true only of their kin, the Shans, not of the hill folk. But in Kengtung, the young Sawbwa is much loved by the hill tribes also.

[2] *BWB*, 28 January 1953.

group among the Sawbwas challenged the policy of capitulation; they intimated that they would oppose any attempt to introduce Socialist ideology into the Shan State under the Sao Hkun Hkio–Ba Swe agreement. So urgent was the situation that Sao Hkun Hkio, who as Foreign Minister was abroad, had to be recalled to stem the revolt.[1] A counter 'anti-feudalist' agitation, centred on Kalaw, was whipped up, with a demand for the merging of the Shan State under the central Government. On 20 October six representatives of the Sawbwas met five representatives of the Government to discuss their future.[2] The chief demands made by the Sawbwas were: compensation for relinquishment of administrative powers and revenues of $6\frac{1}{2}$ crores; retention of their titles, which should devolve upon their descendants; retention of their seats in the House of Nationalities, which should also pass to their descendants; retention of their family estates; and opportunities for advancement in the service of the state.[3] Subsequent negotiations took place in December 1954, but no statement was issued[4] and no decision was reached. In October 1955 one Shan Minister (Sao Htun E) gave his opinion that, despite orders from U Nu to hasten matters on, no agreement would be completed before the 1956 general elections.[5] It is apparent that the Union Government is handling this matter with considerable patience and restraint: at the same time one may question whether there really is any demand for ballot-box democracy in these remote hills and valleys.

The first steps have already been taken towards the administrative overhaul of the Shan State. The long-term intention is to group the states into five districts, with administrative subdivisions similar to those of the plains districts of Burma. Two districts have already been formed, with headquarters at Taunggyi and Loilem. Kengtung will constitute another district and the Northern Shan States will be divided into two, with headquarters at Lashio and Hsipaw. In the Loilem and Taunggyi Districts the officials of the State Government are installed as supervisors, but they are unable to take any active part in the actual administration. The Sawbwas continue to rule through their traditional officials, to collect the revenues,

---

[1] *Nation*, 12 September 1954.
[2] For the Shans, the rulers of Kengtung, Yawnghwe, Hsenwi, Tawnpeng, Samhka, and Kehsi-Mansam; for the Union Government, Ba Swe, Kyaw Nyein, Bo Khin Maung Gale, Justice Myint Thein, and U Win Pe.
[3] *Nation*, 21 October 1954.
[4] It is understood that one of the proposals of the Union Government which is not acceptable to the Sawbwas is that they must undertake to reside outside their own states.
[5] *Nation*, 12 October 1955.

to maintain their own police forces, and even to administer justice (nominally renounced in 1950). Tradition and custom still reign, and Rangoon is very far away.[1]

Karenni, the Kayah State, although the one corner of Burma which was not formally annexed by the British, has bowed to the dictates of the central Government with more alacrity than the Shan States. In great part this is because many of the traditional leaders, such as the Sawbwa of Kantarawaddy and his heir and the Sawbwa of Bawlake, were associated with the KNDO, and have departed into banishment. The present Head of State, Sao Wunna, another son of the Sawbwa of Kantarawaddy, is half-Shan in blood. The Kayah State is also being brought into line with the district administration of Burma proper: a Deputy Commissioner has been appointed at Loikaw. For many administrative purposes (as, for instance, in the control of education) the Kayah State is an appendage of the Shan State.

The process of adapting the 'feudal' frontier areas to democratic government thus entails a transition period of 'bureaucratic' rule on the British model. This, no doubt, is logical if it is deemed necessary to bring these areas into line with the rest of Burma. But when the traditional, hereditary system of authority has been destroyed, it will not be easy to substitute a new official administration. For example, in the whole of the Shan State there is one pre-war gazetted officer;[2] the remainder are either post-war appointees or promoted clerks. The problem will not be solved by a snap solution, by an attempt to introduce Burmese officials, or to hand Government over to carpet-bag politicians. If the new régime is to be successful, it must incorporate the best in the old order. For instance, no one else is half so well qualified to tackle the job of District Officer, Kengtung, as the energetic, Australian-educated, down-to-earth young Sawbwa.

But all change is still in the womb of the future. At the present moment administration in the states, as in Burma proper, is in a time of twilight. Whether at the level of the township, the district, the state, or the central Government, the

---

[1] On 21 April 1959 the Sawbwas in a body signed an agreement whereby they surrendered all their rights to the Union Government, including the right to fill the 25 Shan seats in the Chamber of Nationalities. In return, they retain the title of *saopha*, they keep their personal estates and palaces, and receive compensation amounting to K 2½ crores. Kengtung Sawbwa receives the largest award: K½ crore. The Sawbwas were now free to stand for election to both houses of parliament, and after the 1960 election they again filled all the 25 seats in the Chamber of Nationalities: evidently, their day is far from done.

[2] The Resident, Eastern Shan States, U Nyo.

old order survives, yet in form only: the old spirit is dead. At the time of the 1962 coup, the superior Courts were abolished and a simplified juridical structure substituted, with a former journalist and publicist, Dr. Maung Maung, as the new Chief Justice. Most of the senior officials closely indentified with U Nu's policies were retired, or moved to posts of relative obscurity. A number of suspect former administrators were arrested over the years. The only civil servant to remain in a position of trust was U Thi Han who was made Foreign Minister (the only civilian in Ne Win's Cabinet). In the ministries and in the districts, military officers were placed in the key positions. Aware that he is not trusted or accorded complete responsibility, the civil servant or the judicial officer in Burma under the military carries out his duties as a mechanical ritual whose significance has ceased to have any genuine meaning.

VI

CULTURE AND RELIGION

U NDER the armed might of the British, our country remained
secure and stable. When this armed protection was withdrawn, our country tottered and threatened to collapse. In
the reconstruction of the tottering edifice of our Union into a structure as strong as a granite pillar, the important materials are the
qualities of education, health, economy, national solidarity, and in the
same way, the quality of devotion to one's own religion. . . . I want to
impress upon you that religious influence has contributed very remarkably to the strengthening of the once shaky foundation of the
Union. . . . We must strive for national solidarity. This solidarity is
not a gift of independence. We must exert all our mental, social
and physical qualities to bring the indigenous races together.

These were two of the themes U Nu chose to dwell upon in
his opening speech at the 1952 Pyidawtha Conference:[1] the
paramount need for unity and the importance of religion in
its attainment. The essential cultural unity of Burma is one
of the principal themes of leaders in many walks of life in
Burma today,[2] and—as the quotation above may indicate—
although it is realized by the more clear-sighted that independence did not, of itself, bring Burma nearer to nationhood, it
did create the opportunity for fostering the spirit of national
unity. Amongst the most powerful forces in the creation of
nationhood are a common religion and a common language.
In Burma today there is tremendous emphasis upon both these
forces, as well as upon unity in historical tradition; in dress, in
the arts, in education, and in all tangible aspects of national
culture.

Many writers have enlarged upon the consequences of the
British failure to maintain the special relationship of the
Buddhist hierarchy in Burma with the State:[3] the moral
degeneration of small sections of the monastic order and
monastic intervention in politics must largely be ascribed to
the uncompromisingly secular attitude of the British administration. Nevertheless all influential sections of the Buddhist

---

[1] *Towards a Welfare State*, pp. 11 and 24.
[2] For a good example, see U Nu's speech at the Mon Cultural Conference,
January 1954, included in *Forward with the People*, pp. 113–20.
[3] That shrewd old soldier Lord Roberts was one of the first to appreciate this
necessity (see *Forty-one Years in India*, 1897). For the views of a modern authority,
see G. E. Harvey, *British Rule in Burma* (London, Faber, 1946), pp. 25–29.

order set their faces absolutely against any intervention in politics. From early in the twentieth century a considerable religious revival was noticeable. One example was the Young Men's Buddhist Association which, under the leadership of U May Oung, continued with religious work even after some of its members became absorbed in politics. Another development was associated with U Kanti, the hermit of Mandalay Hill. The religious revival may be said first to have stressed the social-obligation side of Buddhism, charity and the giving of alms. During this phase many institutions were founded and endowed. Then, as the prosperity of the 1920's was succeeded by the depression of the 1930's, the emphasis was placed more upon the moral aspect of Buddhism, the observance of the precepts and conformity with the rules of conduct. As will be seen, this in turn has been followed by a third phase during the independence period in which supreme emphasis is placed upon meditation and the collation of the sacred texts. Many would say that in this return to meditation, Burmese Buddhism may attain a new and higher plane.

In the preparations for independence and in the first years thereafter, while the Socialists were in the ascendant and while the hand of negotiation was still held out to the Communists, religion was given much less emphasis than Marxism.[1] Aung San, whatever his personal views (he married a Christian lady), did not introduce religion into politics, although he frequently recalled the historic past of Burma in his speeches. U Nu, by contrast, has always made religion the basis of his personal approach to politics: on the eve of independence he publicly announced 'I have just returned from my religious observance at the Myathabeik Pagoda Hill. I made a solemn prayer while I was there that if by any chance I misuse my powers as Premier for my personal gain in any respect, may I go headfirst to the lowest hell of Maha Avice [sic].'[2] Gradually U Nu saw the need for religion not only in his personal attitude but in the entire political life of the country. In February 1950 he affirmed that 'religion is the last hope of this world which is ridden with insurrection, acts of lawlessness and oppression. By "religion" ... I have in mind all the religions professed by various peoples of the world.'[3] About this time, while Burma was still rent by civil war and had reached the lowest point in economic collapse, great public rejoicing was aroused by the arrival of sacred

---

[1] In moving the adoption of the constitution, and in setting out his programme of May 1948, U Nu did not make one reference to religion.

[2] *Towards Peace and Democracy*, p. 16. *Maha Avici* is one of the eight purgatories. cf. G. P. Malasekera, *Dictionary of Pali Proper Names*, 1937.

[3] Speech delivered to the Y.M.C.A. (see *From Peace to Stability*, p. 72).

Buddhist relics from Ceylon (February 1950) and India (June 1950). These were received with great ceremony by the President, Sao Shwe Thaik, and the Prime Minister, after they had been borne in state through the streets of Rangoon. U Nu was warm in his thanks to Ceylon and India for 'their genuine friendship [in] sending these Sacred Relics to us and allowing us to worship in Burma for a long time, at this hour of trial'. He went on, 'It is our firm belief that the Sacred Relics would shed rays of Light and Love, Peace and Plenty, all over the country. The noble presence of the Sacred Relics would certainly mark a turning-point in that they are bound to bring to us days of peace and bliss.'[1]

In 1950 a Ministry of Religious Affairs was established to strengthen the ties between the State and Buddhist doctrine, the *sasana* (U Win served as Minister until November 1955). The *Vinnicchaya Htana* Act of 1949 established a hierarchy of ecclesiastical councils or courts, from the township through the district up to a Supreme Court (*Nainggandaw Vinnicchaya Htana*). These courts have exclusive jurisdiction in ecclesiastical matters, such as disputes involving monks (other than criminal cases) or between monasteries, or in matters of *wuttagan* or monastic lands.[2] The judges (*Vinayadhara Mahatheras*) are monks learned in the law, appointed strictly by seniority. The presiding judge of the supreme monastic court is regarded as *Thathanabaing* or 'moderator' of the *sasana* throughout Burma.[3]

It may be recalled that government proposals to create a similar supervisory structure for the *sasana* in 1928 had to be dropped after extensive agitation and opposition. The cry then was that the Government was 'tampering' with religion; in 1949 there were no such protests, a tribute to public confidence in the Buddhist integrity of the Nu Government. Nevertheless, the new authority was not recognized by two of the sects that go to make up the Buddhist church in Burma: the *Shwegyin*[4] and *Dwara* monks refused to acknowledge the jurisdiction of the courts; the main *Thuddama* sect has, in general, accepted the rulings of the courts. Nevertheless, there has been some murmuring at their operation: judges elected upon a basis of seniority have not (according to the critics) always been fully conversant with the law. Representations have been made to

[1] Speech, 'Holy Blessings', *From Peace to Stability*, pp. 77–78.
[2] The Supreme Court of the Union has power to hear appeals from the *Nainggandaw Vinnicchaya Htana* on points of law, but it exercises this power with circumspection. cf. *Nation*, 10 August 1954.
[3] The last true *Thathanabaing*, whose jurisdiction did not extend beyond Upper Burma, died in the 1930's.
[4] *Shwegyin* might be defined as the 'Puritan' branch of Buddhism. Its internal discipline is said to be very strict. *Dwara* and *Kam* are two very minor sects.

the Government by certain of the *sangha*, but no action has followed.[1]

Two further religious measures were passed through Parliament in 1950: the Pali University or *Dhammacariya* Act, and the *Buddha Sasana* Organization Act. The first act is intended to re-establish monastic scholarship. During the British period the Education Department had organized annual *Pitaka* examinations in Pali for monastic candidates: it is now intended to place these examinations on a more regular basis. Certain monks will be recognized as 'lecturers' and others will be encouraged to pursue higher studies, being assisted by state grants. An annual *Dhammacariya* examination is held under government auspices, and normally some 200 monks pass. The *Patamabyan* (sometimes loosely termed 'ordination' examination) is also held under government auspices, and there is a final *Tipitaka Dara* examination, in which only two or three monks are successful every year, these few being honoured by a ceremony at the President's house.[2]

While the relations of the State and the *sangha* have to a large extent been redefined in recent years, problems of monastic discipline remain unsolved. U Nu has observed 'Everybody who puts on a yellow robe is not a *phongyi*. . . . If [he] indulges in all sorts of evil deeds, like having an affair with a woman, gambling, and drinking, then . . . he is just a rogue in a yellow robe.'[3] Apart from the very few who are flagrantly immoral, like U Nu's 'rogue in a yellow robe', there are others to whom the monastery is merely a cover for an idle life; these may be seen in dozens at the cinema, smoking cigars and flaunting wrist-watches and other gadgets. When youth is the reason for this shallow attitude it may well be excusable: but a mature monk leading a life of indolence interspersed by flaccid pleasure is an unpleasing spectacle.[4] Altogether there are said to be 800,000 monks in Burma, equivalent to one adult male in ten.[5] Among such a multitude there are bound to be some back-sliders. At a ceremony to mark the reorganization

---

[1] *Nation*, 11 August 1954.

[2] A very few laymen and nuns also pass the *Dhammacariya* examination. At 'undergraduate' level there is the annual *Mingala Sutta* scripture examination organized by the Young Men's Buddhist Association, which several thousand youths and girls take each year.

[3] *Forward with the People*, p. 62.

[4] The writer is aware that the Church in England has its quota of vacant and venal minds.

[5] This figure was quoted in a government statement in Parliament (see *Nation*, 5 March 1954). It is far higher than pre-war estimates, among which the figure of 120,000 is given by J. L. Christian. The Social Planning Commission has produced an estimate (1953) of 100,000 (see Dept. of Information, *Burma, the Sixth Anniversary*, p. 53). This is probably a distinct under-estimate.

of the *Patamabyan* examination under the Ministry for Religion, the President, Sao Shwe Thaik, condemned the presence of undesirables in the order.[1] U Win promised the support of the Government for any action which the *sayadaws* may take against these 'parasites of the *sasana*',[2] but no effective proposals to restore strict discipline followed. Proposals that the Government should prepare registers of bona fide ordained monks and issue them with some means of identification were not put into effect. Many monks, even if ejected from their monasteries, could still enjoy an itinerant life, supported by the alms of the credulous and the ignorant.[3]

However, despite occasional blemishes the *sangha* continues to give meaning and inspiration to the people. Every Burmese boy continues to follow the tradition of spending a fortnight or a month as a novice, compelled to turn his mind to the traditional teachings. Everywhere the monks are the mentors of the people, counselling right living and right thinking; in a world which is no longer a familiar place of customs and long-acknowledged authority but a vortex of strident shouts and slogans, the monks offer repose and confidence.

The *Buddha Sasana* Organization Act of 1950 set out, in the words of the Minister of Religion, 'to organize the Promoters of the Faith into some kind of Parliament of *sasana*. All religious measures will be undertaken by the Union Parliament through the good offices of this Parliament of *sasana*.'[4] Introducing the bill in Parliament, U Nu defined the aims of the new organization as 'to propagate the *dhamma* [teaching] in foreign lands . . . and . . . to lay solid and lasting foundations of Buddhism in this land'. Amplifying his second point, the Prime Minister remarked 'Most of us are simply content with paying visits to the pagodas, telling beads or reciting prayers without actually practising what Lord Buddha wanted us to practise.' The act would strengthen true religion. As regards missionary activity, U Nu hastened to emphasize that 'It is far from our intention to disparage in any way other religions like Mohammedanism, Hinduism, Christianity or spirit worship. We have been prompted by the sole consideration to combat effectively antireligious forces which are rearing their ugly heads everywhere.'

[1] *Nation*, 6 June 1950.
[2] ibid., 20 May 1954.
[3] It is essential to an understanding of discipline within the monastic order to realize that there is no Buddhist 'church' or church organization as such. Each monastery is autonomous: the abbot of the monastery is responsible for the discipline of his own monks: nobody else is responsible, and the abbot is not accountable to any higher authority. This rule is age-old.
[4] Speech by U Win at the inaugural meeting of the *Sasana* Organization, 26 August 1951. See Dept. of Information *Burma, the Fourth Anniversary*, pp. 22–24.

He made it clear that Communism was foremost in his mind,
'It will be our duty to retort in no uncertain terms that the
wisdom or knowledge that might be attributed to Karl Marx
is less than one-tenth of a particle of dust that lies at the feet
of our great Lord Buddha.'[1]

Under the Act, the Organization is governed by a Union
Sasana Council, consisting of nineteen members, the Minister
for Religious Affairs, nine laymen nominated by the President,
and nine *sayadaws* nominated by the *sangha*. The Chairman of
the Council is Sir U Thwin, a trustee of the Shwe Dagon
Pagoda. The Vice-Chairman is Chief Justice Thein Maung
(also a trustee of the Shwe Dagon), Justice Chan Htoon is
Honorary Secretary. The actual administrative work, therefore, appears to be in the hands of laymen, and the chief
business of the organization is to guide the laity in all matters
of religion.

The principal activities of the Council have been the encouragement of missionary work, the restoration of ruined pagodas,
the fostering of Pali literature, the foundation of meditation
centres, and the study of the Scriptures, culminating, of course,
in the preparations for the Sixth Buddhist Council.

While missionary activity is carried on in foreign lands,[2] by
far the biggest effort is within Burma, in missions to the non-
Buddhist hill peoples. The work is partly undertaken by
preaching missions: venerable *sayadaws* and others less eminent
tour the frontier areas, bringing the message of the Lord
Buddha (there is one distinct society, the Frontier Buddhist
Mission). Another important method of linking the more
remote areas with central Buddhism is attained by the planting
of saplings, shoots taken from the sacred *bo* tree under which
Gautama attained enlightenment. Parties of hill folk, Kachins,
Chins, and others, are brought on visits to the sacred places
of Buddhism, Mandalay, Sagaing, Pagan. And, of course,
monasteries are endowed in the hills to become permanent
centres of enlightenment. Particular attention has been paid
to the Karen State: this is the only state government to have
a separate Ministry of Religious Affairs, established in January
1953.[3] A big attempt is being made to identify the remote hill
Karens with the religious festivals and practices of Burmese
Buddhism. A decided increase in the numbers of Buddhists
among the hill peoples may be expected within a decade or two.

[1] *From Peace to Stability*, pp. 106–9.
[2] There is a Burmese monastery in Colombo and a mission is preparing to work
in Germany, among other activities.
[3] Some three-quarters of the Karens are Buddhists, the remainder are mainly
Christian: but the Ministry is concerned only to propagate Buddhism.

Even when Buddhism is not explicitly accepted by people of other creeds and races, its spreading influence is manifested indirectly. For instance, Buddhism abhors the taking of life and, with its ancient Hindu associations, particularly objects to the killing of cows for meat. Within recent years a vegetarian movement has gained ground among leading exponents of Buddhism in which U Nu is particularly prominent. The Prime Minister has disavowed any intention by those in power to prohibit the killing of animals for food,[1] nevertheless, this practice is definitely becoming increasingly restricted. This is partly because of government controls: slaughter-houses are under public supervision, and during religious festivals they are completely closed.[2] In Lower Burma the sale of beef has ceased entirely, owing to restrictions. Apart from direct government control, a good deal of influence and suggestion has been at work. There are religions in which animal sacrifice has a ritual significance: these practices have been diminished, and may eventually be abolished, in deference to Buddhist susceptibilities. Each year, the number of animals sacrificed at the Muslim festival of *Id-ul-Zuha* is progressively decreased: in 1953 there was a cut of 50 per cent.[3] At the great Kachin national *Manao*, held every January at Myitkyina, buffalo sacrifices (which many would say formed an integral part of the ceremonies) have been stopped since 1951. Chan Htoon, the Secretary of the *Sasana* Council, has stated that

The practice is now definitely discontinued in the Kachin State. But there are certain other tracts in the hilly areas where animal sacrifice on festive occasions still prevails. There, also, efforts are still being made by our leaders to bring an end to this practice, and I can assure you that it will not be long before it is totally stopped in all parts of the country.[4]

In the work of strengthening Buddhism among its existing adherents, great importance is attached to the restoration of pagodas ruined by time, nature, or man. Clearly this has a high symbolic significance; the visible renascence of the former splendour of the faith and of the nation. Recent years have witnessed the rebuilding of the Botataung Pagoda in central Rangoon (destroyed by war-time bombing) and the Shwemawdaw Pagoda, Pegu (wrecked by earthquake). The hoisting of the *hti*, the ornamental 'umbrella', to the topmost summit of

[1] e.g. Nu, *Forward with the People*, pp. 42–44.
[2] As, for example, from 15–18 May 1954, during the opening days of the Sixth Buddhist Council.
[3] See *Forward with the People*, p. 43, and *Nation*, 21 August 1953.
[4] *BWB*, 14 October 1953.

these pagodas, the Botataung in December 1953, and the Shwemawdaw in April 1954, were the occasions for rejoicing among the thousands of pilgrims who participated in the hoisting ceremony. Those present included the President and the Prime Minister.[1] The second occasion was marked by a reduction of one month in the sentences of all in prison throughout the land.

The Shwesandaw Pagoda at Toungoo is also being reconstructed by national efforts, the Ananda at Pagan is being regilded under the Prime Minister's direction, and the Kyauktawgyi at Amarapura is almost restored to its former magnificence.[2] The plan to reafforest sacred Mount Popa may be regarded as a tribute to the *Mahagiri Nat*, the guardian spirit, to Burmese literature and legend, or as a practical rehabilitation project.[3] The work of the Archaeological Department at Pagan and elsewhere continues, on a scale somewhat diminished from pre-war days: awareness of the wonder of Pagan is always found in any Burman with any pretension to culture, and a surprising number have made the far from simple journey to this, the greatest of their nation's monuments.

To return to the work of the *Sasana* Council: the practice of periodical retirement for meditation is being fostered by the opening of meditation centres such as the *Sasana Yeiktha* retreat in Hermitage Road at the Council's headquarters. But the principal activity has been the work of purifying the Buddhist Scriptures. To this end, a *Pitaka* Bill was promoted in Parliament in March 1954 to 'take action against owners of Pitaka presses who have the bad habit of printing the Scriptures with a lot of mistakes'.[4] This was followed by a greater venture, the summoning of the Sixth Great Buddhist Council.

The idea may be said to have first taken shape when, on 1 October 1951, the Union Parliament passed a resolution that 'this Parliament declares its firm belief that it is necessary to devise and undertake such measures . . . as would . . . help man to overcome Greed (Lobha), Hatred (Dosa) and Delusion (Moha) which are at the root of all the violence, destruction and conflagration consuming the world'.[5] To this end a sum of 1 crore was appropriated. The greatest blessing stems from a

---

[1] *BWB*, 13 January, 21 and 28 April 1954.

[2] A melancholy omission from these restorations is the *Shwesandaw Kyaung* at Mandalay, the only surviving example of the woodcarver's art, so characteristic of Mindon's palace city. Unprotected, it is unlikely to survive for many more years the assaults of the termites and the monsoon rains.

[3] *BWB*, 17 February 1955.

[4] Nu, *Forward with the People*, p. 157.

[5] Quoted in 'The Sixth Great Buddhist Council', *Burma, the Sixth Anniversary*, p. 1.

Great Council, *sangayana*, for the clarification and codification of Buddhist teaching. Such a council, to be truly oecumenical, must include at any rate the representatives of all the *Theravada* countries: Burma, Siam, Cambodia, Laos, and Ceylon.[1]

The timing of the Sixth Council is of great significance. The Council deliberated for two years, closing on *Vesakha*, full moon day of *Kason*, May 1956, which marks the 2,500th anniversary of the Buddha's decease, the *Maha Parinibbana*, 'final blowing out'.[2] This (according to one section of Buddhist thought) will bring to an end the present era. Teaching and tradition appear to offer no clear indication of what is to follow, but U Nu has stated the 'firm belief' of Burmese Buddhists that the anniversary year 'is to be the most auspicious since the spread of the Lord Buddha's teachings began'.[3] Many Burmans believe that the Lord Buddha charged Sakya (or Sakka) to assume sovereignty over the world on the 2,500th anniversary of his decease: Sakya was empowered to reward the virtuous and punish the wicked. This belief has influenced many towards supporting the present Buddhist revival, and towards contributing to preparations for the Council.

Preparations for the Council were organized on two planes: the practical problems connected with inviting and accommodating the delegates were handled by the *Buddha Sasana* Council, with the close co-operation of the Government; questions of procedure and the programme of the Council were the functions of the *sangha*. The choice of a site for the meeting was attended by some of the mystery and mysticism which is traditional in Burma.[4] The central *Kaba Aye Zedi*,

[1] The tradition of the Buddhist Councils relates that the First Council was held at Magadha in Rajagaha, soon after Lord Buddha's death. The Second Council met at Vesali, about 376 B.C. (traditional date 443 B.C.) and here a schism developed between the orthodox *theravadi*, 'believers in the teaching of the elders', and the *mahasanghika*, 'members of the great community'. The Third Council was held under the patronage of Asoka, greatest of all Buddhist rulers, at Pataliputta about 240 B.C. (traditional date 308) and led to the establishment of the *theravada* as orthodox: it also heralded the development of Buddhism as an international religion. The Fourth Council, according to the *theravada*, was held in Ceylon about 29–13 B.C., when the texts were committed to writing. According to the *mahayana*, their Fourth (and last) Council was summoned by Kanishka, *c.* A.D. 100, at Jalandhara, Kashmir. The Fifth (*theravada*) Council was held under the patronage of Mindon at Mandalay in 1871: it was attended by only a few foreign monks and was not at the time regarded as oecumenical. A further codification of the Scriptures led to their inscription upon 729 marble slabs, still to be seen in the Kuthodaw or Lokamarazein Pagoda, Mandalay.

[2] The traditional date is 544 B.C. Western scholars assign the Buddha's death to about 483 B.C. cf. A. L. Basham, *The Wonder That Was India* (London, 1954), p. 257.

[3] *Nation*, 1 December 1952. U Nu was speaking during his pilgrimage to Sanchi in India.

[4] The full story is related in an article by U Ohn Ghine (David Maurice) in *BWB*, 18 November 1953.

World Peace Pagoda, which was planned before the concept of the Council took final shape, was located, according to certain omens, three miles north of the Shwe Dagon near Yegu village on a hillock named Siri Mangala or 'Glorious Bright Omen'. The foundation-stone was laid in 1950 and the pagoda was completed in March 1952. Then all around buildings began to arise, the most remarkable being the *Maha Pasana Guha*, the Great Cave, a vast assembly hall capable of seating some 10,000, being built inside an enormous rockery, designed to recall the First Council's meeting-place in Satta Panni cave.

This work provided a remarkable demonstration of the power of religion in modern Burma: led by the Prime Minister, thousands gave their labour and their money towards the acquisition of merit by participating in the raising of the Cave. The Central AFPFL gave over 2 lakhs for the six great concrete columns which support the roof of the hall; constituency organizations of the AFPFL brought along parties of workers who gave their labours; in similar fashion the staff of various government departments volunteered their labour. By May 1954 the concourse of buildings was complete: their total cost was some 3 crores, or £2,250,000.[1]

Preparations for the Council were assisted by an advisory committee of senior monks or *mahatheras*, which included representatives from Ceylon, Siam, Cambodia, and Laos. Preliminary work towards the editing of the texts from the various extant versions was also begun by scholars of different nations.[2]

Finally, on 17 May 1954, at exactly twelve minutes thirty seconds after noon, there commenced the striking of brass gongs and of drums and the blowing of conch shells: the Council had begun. To commemorate the occasion the Government released all prisoners serving sentences of three months or less, granted a remission of three months to all others, and reprieved all under sentence of death (transportation for life being substituted). As President of the Council, *Sangha Nayaka*, the eighty-year-old Nyaungyan Sayadaw of Mogaung Monastery, seated himself in complete silence upon the dais (*therasana*). After the dignified ceremonies were completed,[3] the business of reviewing the Scriptures commenced. The 2,500 learned monks who were the delegates were divided into groups of 500 each, and the first session of 500 spent from May to July 1954 in

---

[1] *Nation*, 11 May 1954.

[2] A detailed account of the procedure is given in 'Printing and Publication of Pali Scriptures', a broadcast by U Nu (see *Forward with the People*, pp. 150–5).

[3] A full account of these opening ceremonies is given in *BWB*, 19 and 26 May 1954.

chanting 2,310 pages of the *Tipitaka*. Other sessions have followed: the third session (presided over by leading monks of Cambodia and Laos) was marked by the attendance of delegates from China. The leader, the Venerable Shirob Jaitso, declared that 'the forms of Buddhism in China and Burma were like two branches of one Bo tree'.[1]

Another event of international significance was the third conference of the World Fellowship of Buddhists, a predominantly lay organization with wide affiliations throughout the world. Some 230 delegates and 350 observers attended, representing 30 countries. They convened in the Great Cave in December 1954; in his presidential speech Dr. G. P. Malasekera of Ceylon extolled U Nu, declaring that he was 'unique amongst the world's statesmen by his unparalleled piety and the embodiment of the ideal of *Rajarsi*, the ruler who is also a sage'. He had brought about a great renascence of Buddhism in the country.[2] After meeting and meditating at Yegu the delegates visited sacred places at Mandalay and elsewhere.

After the Great Council dispersed, the Yegu campus became the home of an International Institute for Advanced Buddhistic Studies. Its purpose is to foster the cultural and spiritual ties of South East Asia and to promote the study of comparative religion.[3]

Burma is thus in many ways becoming the acknowledged centre of the Buddhist world: it is attracting pilgrims both from the *mahayana* countries and from the *theravada*. In May 1955 twelve Japanese monks and one nun, all *mahayanists*, came to study in Burma, and in August of the same year the monks were re-ordained as *theravada* novices. All this took place with the co-operation of the Japan Buddhist Federation. During his visit to Japan in July 1955 U Nu spoke at the Soojiji Temple, Tsurumi, and strongly advocated the need for a single Buddhist school or faith, urging that this only was the way to Nirvana.[4] Religious missions have also been exchanged between Burma and China: in October a mission headed by Chief Justice Thein Maung returned with the Sacred Tooth of the Buddha, a gift from China to Burma. Such intercourse across Asia among Buddhist pilgrims has not been seen since ancient times, and Burma is the centre of this movement. Moreover, the intellectual attraction of the Buddhist philosophy, its core of tolerance and non-violence, its absence of obligatory ritual and of social taboos make a considerable appeal to other

[1] ibid., 5 May 1955.
[2] *Nation*, 4 December 1954 and *BWB*, 8 December 1954.
[3] Financial and other assistance is being given by the Ford Foundation.
[4] *BWB*, 4 August 1955.

Asians who have shaken free from the ties of more demanding religions in India, China, and Japan. Pandit Nehru is one who is clearly influenced by a philosophical interpretation of Buddhism. Burma's leadership in this new intellectual Buddhism may be a potent factor in the political thought of Asia in years to come.

Among other government measures to promote Buddhism have been the elaboration of titles for religious leaders. To the existing title *Agga Maha Pandita*, instituted during the British period, was added an even more lofty title, *Abhi Dhaja Maha Rattha Guru*, which is reserved for the most venerable *sayadaws*.[1] Other orders were created for exceptionally meritorious laymen. These titles are awarded by the President: for, it is often emphasized, there is once again in Burma the Faithful Ruler, Promoter of the Faith, Protector of the *dhamma* and the *sangha*.

Buddhism is invoked as a means of moral regeneration among those in prison. Monks attend regularly to teach the Scriptures: prisoners are encouraged to sit for the scripture examinations, held twice each year: those who are successful earn remissions from their sentences, up to a maximum of three months.[2] Buddhism is invoked as a means towards better standards in public administration. Most public offices have a *dammayon* or prayer hall, large or small, where officials and clerks will retire for prayer, often led by the head of the department. At the commencement of the legal terms, the Chief Justice and the Judges of the Supreme and High Courts repair to the Shwe Dagon and take the five precepts, renewing their pledge to carry out their duties faithfully.

It is impossible for an outsider to assess the total effect of this religious revival, but it can be asserted with confidence that the climate of opinion now regards religious observance as an essential duty. As in early-Victorian England, open disregard of religion stamps the Burman with a position in society as a man apart. Neither the Deputy Commissioner nor his clerk would pass a pagoda in their town without stopping to make obeisance at the shrine. The worst accusation that can be levelled at the Communists is their open contempt for religion: U Nu in accusing Than Tun of being a man capable of despoiling the Shwe Dagon was employing the vilest epithet

---

[1] The first three *sayadaws* to receive this highest honour were Payagyi Sayadaw, aged 86 of Henzada, Sankin Sayadaw, aged 83 of Sagaing Hills, and Nyaungyan Sayadaw of Mandalay (*BWB*, 22 July 1953).

[2] A former Cabinet Minister, and a former Commissioner of the Rangoon Police, both sentenced to twelve months imprisonment, were actually released after four months under these provisions (see *Nation*, 28 November 1954).

in his vocabulary. The Marxists within the Government, whatever their private views, are careful to subscribe publicly to the
idea that dialectical materialism and Nirvana are quite compatible.[1] But only the most cynical would wish to disparage
the beliefs of the present-day generation, or to discount the
force of Buddhism in Burma today. Its serene insistence on
the transient and illusory importance of all mundane affairs
has assisted Burmans to view, with an equanimity quite beyond
a Westerner, the total collapse of authority, the breakdown
of the motive force of the economic and social system during the
past years of civil war. Those of the nation's leaders who are
the most enlightened Buddhists, men with unlined brows, calm
eyes, and humorous mouths, have been enabled to pick their
way through a jungle of insoluble problems and threats of
disaster with minds unclouded by doubt and despondency. In
the person of U Nu, Buddhism has utterly confounded the
dictum that power corrupts. As a hasty, hot-tempered young
man, full of prejudices and dogmatic assertions, he was plunged
into supreme responsibility, supreme power; and amidst
unceasing trials and upheavals he has emerged a selfless being,
completely relaxed, without tension, inspired by vision and
compassion; and his driving-force is a Buddhism which
permeates his every thought and action.

Second only to Buddhism as a unifying factor is the development of Burmese as the national language. The constitution
states (sect. 216) that 'the official language of the Union shall
be Burmese, provided that the use of the English language
may be permitted'. The first two copies of the constitution, as
signed by the President of the Constituent Assembly, were
written in both languages, and both were to be regarded as
equally valid. In this manner, both languages continued for
some time to be used as was convenient: but it was ever the
intention of the Government to establish Burmese in general
use. Whereas the two languages were heard in the first Parliament, the use of English was definitely prohibited in the
second Parliament. A directive was issued in 1948 laying down
Burmese as the language for all state correspondence; this was
permitted to lapse, but four years later the order was renewed
in more minatory tones: from 1 April 1952 Burmese became
obligatory in all state business. Its introduction in the states

---

[1] 'Marxist theory is not antagonistic to Buddhist philosophy. The two are, frankly
speaking, not merely similar: in fact they are the same in concept. But if we want to
have the two distinguished, one from the other, we can safely assume that Marxist
theory occupies the lower plane, while Buddhist philosophy occupies the higher'
(Ba Swe, *The Burmese Revolution*, Rangoon, 1952, p. 7). In the same speech Ba Swe
also makes an interesting differentiation between Marxism and Communism.

was somewhat more gradual: Burmese was quite unfamiliar to many of the officials and clerks in the Shan State and elsewhere, but its use is now spread wide. The effect of the change-over from English to Burmese was described to the author by one official with a striking turn of metaphor as 'like trying to drive a high-power car with all the brakes full on'. Whereas colloquial Burmese is a racy, pithy tongue, literary Burmese is involute and elaborate; it has hardly any punctuation; it possesses a vocabulary which, while rich and graphic in some directions (as, for instance, in the description of family relationships), is singularly rudimentary in the phraseology of politics and administration. One word will have to cover a wide range of categories or of ideas, while in many cases there is no term available so that cumbrous portmanteau words have to be invented.[1] As a result, a message which could be conveyed in ten lines in English has to take up a whole page: time is consumed in rendering and unravelling correspondence, and the meaning conveyed is not always clear. It is no secret that the Prime Minister, U Nu, himself an accomplished Burmese scholar, occasionally has to call in an official who has submitted a report in flowery Burmese to request him to append an English translation.

All this is related not to denigrate the Burmese language, or to criticize its employment on the nation's business, but to explain the complications which have attended the switch-over from English. In time written Burmese will probably evolve a more flexible syntax as it becomes adjusted to modern needs, and in time an administrative jargon generally understood among the *cognoscenti* will replace the strange parody of eighteenth-century English which was the lingua franca of British-Indian administration. But for a decade or so government and administration in Burma will be presented with one more obstacle to surmount.[2]

Burmese has also become the language in use throughout the educational system. In the case of the Shans, Karens, and other peoples who speak a different language, the mother tongue may be used up to the third standard, but thereafter all teaching is in Burmese. From the fifth standard English is

---

[1] e.g. *lut-lat-yé*, 'free-empty-business'=independence; *pyé-daung-soo*, 'country-establishment-collection'=Union [of Burma].

[2] In case a verdict from a Burman on this point might carry more weight, the opinion of a senior retired Burmese member of the I.C.S. is appended. In a foreword to *Local Government* by Myo Sin (a book whose value was recognized [1954] by the award of a government prize), Sein Nyo Tun writes: 'In spite of the wishful claims that have been made on behalf of the Burmese language its adaptation to scientific [meaning systematic] usage (with its rigid definitions and exact terminology) can only come with time.'

introduced as a separate subject, but the normal teaching language remains Burmese, right up through the high school.[1] From 1955 the matriculation examination (the door through which all with even the most modest ambitions must pass) will be conducted entirely in Burmese. At the university, courses up to the intermediate examination are available either in Burmese or English (the great majority of the students follow the Burmese lectures). Thereafter teaching up to B.A. level is conducted in English, but the declared aim of the Government is to adopt Burmese as the teaching language up to and beyond the B.A. as soon as textbooks are available in the vernacular. The first date laid down for abolishing university teaching through English has passed by, but the pressure to change over to Burmese may be expected eventually to become irresistible. Indeed, it is only logical when the entire school system has adopted Burmese that the university should follow, for the great mass of the undergraduates have not even the most elementary acquaintance with English as a medium of speech.

It is perhaps noteworthy that the languages of the Shans, the Karens, the Kachins, the Chins, and the other frontier peoples have no place in the studies of Rangoon University: they are not even included among the university's research activities. Only the classical languages, Pali and Old Mon, are studied alongside Burmese. The inference is obvious: these languages have no place in the future of the nation. This policy of deliberately replacing the lesser languages by Burmese may be somewhat arbitrary, and will certainly accentuate the difficulties of the frontier races in finding equality with their Burmese cousins: but it is certainly the right policy for the long haul. There is no place for parochialism and clannishness in Burma today, and nothing will create a true sense of solidarity so surely as the acceptance of a common language.

One great bar to the employment of Burmese as a means of disseminating knowledge is the lack of suitable works in the language. To overcome this barrier the Burma Translation Society was established, largely through the personal efforts of U Nu, who is Chairman of its Council of Management. The society was founded in 1947: it has a triple function, first, to arrange for the translation of foreign works into Burmese; secondly, to foster the growth of Burmese literature and culture;

---

[1] This places a strain on the children of the frontier peoples beyond that imposed on Burmese children: the frontier youngsters have to acquire two additional languages and to obtain their schooling through a foreign language. But this strain is, of course, not much greater than that imposed in pre-war days on Burmese youngsters taught exclusively in English.

and thirdly, in U Nu's phrase, as a 'means of transforming our Mr. Zeros into intelligent and well-informed citizens'.[1] In a survey of the society's achievements, delivered on the occasion of the opening of new premises in April 1955, the Prime Minister observed that

the Society had published over 200 books on the accumulated knowledge of the other countries of the world as well as of Burma. There were books on agriculture, industry, health and vocational subjects. The range of publications had been widely spread to meet the needs of the masses, the children, the students in the Primary, Middle and Secondary Schools and in the University, and of the teachers.[2]

The total number of copies issued by the end of 1954 was 5,472,000. Texts for use in the university have been produced by the different university departments: at this level the difficulty of adapting Burmese to the requirements of technical and special vocabularies has been very great, and a special committee has been set up under the society's auspices, to consider and approve new terminology for the language. The chief production of the Society has been the *Encyclopedia Birmanica*, which is being printed in Britain: the first volume arrived in Rangoon in February 1955. The Society was equipped with printing and binding machinery as one of the last items of American aid: the Monotype machines, which are the first adaptations of the Monotype process to the Burmese script, were manufactured in Great Britain.[3]

Other government institutions have been established to encourage the flowering of the arts, under the direction of a Ministry of Union Culture set up in March 1952.[4] There is a State Orchestra (composed of traditional Burmese instruments), State Schools of Music and Drama, and a School of Fine Arts: these schools began teaching in Rangoon in July 1952 and in Mandalay twelve months later. These institutions train young state scholars in traditional Burmese instruments, classical Burmese dancing, and the graphic arts. A national library, museum, and art gallery was constituted in June 1952 in the old Jubilee Hall, absorbing the contents of the Bernard Free Library and other collections presented by former British officials: there are now some 20,000 volumes.[5] There is a

---

[1] *From Peace to Stability*, p. 143.
[2] *BWB*, 12 May 1955.
[3] ibid., 2 June 1954.
[4] The first minister was Tun Pe, previously Minister of Information. He was succeeded by U Win, also Minister for Religious Affairs. In November 1955 he was succeeded by Than Aung, Minister of Education, the two ministries being merged.
[5] 'Reviving Burma's Cultural Heritage', *Burma, the Seventh Anniversary*, pp. 108–13.

Department of Ancient Literature and Culture which has collected 134 ancient manuscripts and is preparing a bibliography of Burmese printed books. A government venture of a somewhat different order is the setting up of a Historical Commission, presided over by U Kaung, and subsequently by Dr. Htin Aung. The commission will supervise the production of a four- or five-volume history of Burma, whose main purpose will be to illustrate the 'essential unity' of the peoples of Burma.

But government encouragement of a national culture, even on such an all-embracing scale, cannot actually create a living culture. Can one observe any significant development in the brief period since independence?

It is almost axiomatic among Burmese writers that foreign conquest killed the living cultural tradition of old Burma.[1] To what extent has independence produced a renascence of the arts? The answer is not, so far, easy to determine. The arts seldom flourish in a period of social disintegration such as the recent period of invasion and civil war. The wealthy patrons of former days, the landlords and rice merchants, are now less wealthy: the village patrons, prosperous cultivators, are today hard-pressed. Patronage in the new age must come largely from the State, or from that section of the urban middle class which has a monopoly of wealth today—government contractors, the new business barons, certain politicians; and their taste is often for the more vulgar products of America and Europe. And so today the woodcarver who can create a screen which is a pageant of moving figures, the silk weaver who devotes a month to the weaving of a *paso* or a *htamein* with the *acheik* ('dog tooth') wavy pattern, is no longer much in demand. The traditional skills are being forgotten, and the younger craftsmen are driven to lesser work. The Burmese orchestra, with its repertoire of music recorded only in the ear of the musician, has turned (in part at least) for inspiration to the music of the West,[2] often to its trashier Tin Pan Alley products. The traditional dance-drama of Burma, the *pyazat*, is kept going almost solely through the efforts of the Translation Society, with performers from the state schools and the State Orchestra. The most common form of entertainment is the *anyein*, a variety show with singing, dancing, and clowning, which was brought to a high technical point by the master,

[1] cf. Dr. Htin Aung, *Burmese Drama*, 1937. One leading scholar, Dr. Hla Pe, has argued that the prosperity brought to British Burma in the 1860's and 1870's was responsible, not for a decline but for a blossoming of Burmese art and literature (see the Introduction to his translation of *Konmara Pya Zat*, vol. i, 1952).

[2] The Burmese National Anthem is said to be derived from an English hymn tune.

Po Sein, but which is somewhat tawdry and hackneyed in the form in which it is duplicated in the wayside theatres throughout the land today. Towards the development of a new serious dramatic form perhaps the most significant contributions have been made by U Nu, whose best-known plays are *Yet Set-Pa-Be Kwè* (translated 'Oh How Cruel') and *Ludu Aung Than* (literally, 'Victorious Voice of the People' but usually called 'The People Win Through'). Both these plays have a rustic village background, but the first is a picture of the national struggle in colonial days against landlords, money-lenders, and the alien Government; the second is a drama of the civil war, of a young man's conversion to Communism, his disillusionment, and the vindication of democracy.

The novel has, as yet, barely won a place as an established literary form in Burma. A translation of *Robinson Crusoe* appeared in 1902, and was followed in 1904 by an adaptation of *The Count of Monte Cristo* by James Hla Gyaw under the title of *Maung Yin Maung Ma Mè Ma*. The story was translated to a Burmese setting, and the writing shows considerable creative power. Many original novels have followed, and a high place is generally assigned to *Sabèbin* and *Shwepyizo* by U Lat. Since independence novels have poured off the printing presses in a flood and, according to U Nu, 'the Burmese novel is now exerting a profound influence on our daily life, as poems and poetic literature did during the days of the Burmese kings'.[1] To encourage new novels the Burma Translation Society instituted an annual award, the *Sapebeikman* prize of K1,000 for the best novel. For 1948 *Mo Auk Mye Byin* (The Earth Under the Sky) by Min Aung received the prize for a portrait of up-country village life. The Society found itself unable to make another award until 1950, when the winner was 'Tet Toe' (U On Pe) with *Min Hmu Dan* (The Civil Servant). During the following three years only one further prize was awarded, although every year some forty or fifty novels are submitted for consideration. In 1952 the award went to *Tat-Htè-Ga Myat Ko Ko* (Noble Brother from the Army) by Tha Dhu. Speaking in December 1954 U Nu remarked that 'the authors seem to have written with the notion that in this world there is nothing of consequence except love and love-making; in short, love makes the world go round. They have altogether ignored nature, life, and character.'[2] One must honour the firmness and frankness of the Burma Translation Society in setting a definite standard of judgement, and adhering to that standard

---

[1] 'Encouraging Burmese Literature', *Towards Peace and Democracy*, pp. 216–19.
[2] *Nation*, 23 December 1954.

even when the world does not appreciate their judgement. There are in Burma such groups of 'professionals' who refuse to lower their standards to the amateur, however powerful the pleading of expediency: such men are the pride and hope of their country.

An honest Burman might admit that, as in Britain and America, the older cultural tradition of creation and participation has given way to the passive synthetic 'culture' of the cinema. Rangoon has a desperate housing shortage, but from the bombed, crumbling heart of the city there are rising not houses but cinemas. On Bogyoke Road (late Montgomery Street) one can see five cinemas in concrete contiguity, and they are shooting up everywhere. Almost no little market town is so remote or old-fashioned but it has its cinema, run from some rickety, salvaged Fourteenth Army power plant. The most widely advertised films are Indian or American, although Chinese films are now making an appeal. There is a Burmese film industry[1] and there are Burmese film stars, but the industry has not progressed far either in technical competence or in its scripts and stories.[2] Foreign films are restricted largely to the bigger towns (Rangoon must have a large proportion, perhaps 50 out of a total of 150, of all the cinemas in Burma) but the Government has thought it desirable to introduce a quota system to encourage the indigenous film industry.[3]

In turning from the cinema, a last general comment might be recorded: that in borrowing from the West, Burma seems to have drawn most heavily on what is least worth while. The dim tranquillity and mystery of the innermost shrine of an ancient pagoda will be made garish and cheap by the glare of neon lighting; the pleasant burbling of a rustic *ozi* orchestra will be outrageously distorted by microphone and amplifier out of a Broadway night-club. Some moralist of the far future can decide who is to blame for these unhappy incongruities.

One aspect of Burma's culture where the West has gained no entry is that of dress. Burma more than any country in Asia today clings to the national costume both for men and women, for villagers and for Cabinet Ministers. The last few years have witnessed an even sharper emphasis on the national dress. Elderly judges who have been accustomed to formal European clothes since they ate their dinners in the Inns of

---

[1] The chief companies are British Burma Film Company, Aungzeya Film Company, and A1 Film Company.

[2] The reason advanced to the author was that there are no critical reviews of films in the Press, and there is no incentive to attempt to make good films because the cinema proprietors book every film for a standard period, and because the public will go anyway: these arguments do not appear entirely convincing.

[3] See editorial comment in *Nation*, 4 September 1954.

Court forty years ago have now reverted to the dress of their grandfathers. Youthful engineers, newly graduated from the University of California, regretfully pack away their T-Shirts and jeans when they return to the Rangoon office. As for the women, there are probably not half a dozen Burmese ladies who have adopted Western dress, although nylon has been adopted happily as the only possible material for their dainty blouses (*eingyis*), despite the stern condemnation of the more puritanical among the monks. Burmese dress is also being adopted among the frontier peoples in place of their own traditional costume. So far this movement has only gained ground among politicians and officials, but the hundreds of tribal visitors from the frontier regions who are brought to Rangoon for the Union Day celebrations are all sent home with gifts of Burmese clothes. The increasing intercourse between the frontier peoples and Burma proper will, almost certainly, end in the adoption of Burmese dress among all but the most remote tribal folk.

In the process of cultural assimilation some members of two minority groups have experienced particular difficulty in readjustment: the Christians and the Anglo-Burmans.

Christians in other Asian countries newly emancipated from colonial rule have encountered great difficulties in the immediate post-independence period. Willy-nilly, they have become identified with the foreign colonial régime, and they are forced to 'work their passage', to prove themselves worthy, before they are accepted as equal citizens with those of other faiths. In Burma, their position was made more hazardous by the KNDO rebellion in which Christians were prominent leaders, although proportionately they may not have been more numerous than those of other religions. For a time the Christians found themselves regarded almost as aliens, particularly those of the largest community, the Baptists.[1] Early in 1949 Bishop George West gave a clear call to the Anglican Burmans to be loyal to the Government, and the Roman Catholic Bishop gave a similar pledge,[2] but no such voice was heard from among the Baptists.[3] And so for several years these folk were suspect, and

---

[1] At the time of the 1931 census, Christians in Burma numbered 331,106. Of these Baptists contributed 212,990, Roman Catholics 89,678, Anglicans 22,853, Methodists 1,952, and others 3,603.

[2] Statement of U Nu, *BWB*, 29 September 1954.

[3] In October 1954 the Burma Baptists were able to point out to U Nu, when he visited their Convention, that any such pastoral leadership was impossible in a community which holds tenaciously to the conviction that there is a direct link between God and each church community—and indeed, between God and each believer—so that no man may stand in spiritual authority over any other. U Nu was much struck by the force of this argument.

there was even considerable pressure upon Christian Burmans
in leading positions to renounce their 'alien' faith and return
to Buddhism. The numbers in the community remained
stationary, or may even have declined. The leaders of the
Baptist community met this crisis with quiet wisdom. The
foreign missionaries (all members of the American Baptist
Foreign Mission Society) who in days gone by had shepherded
their flocks with the masterful fervour of the old Prophets of
Judea now elected to become self-effacing, humble helpers of
the Burma Christians: one might almost say that the American
missionaries have, by choice, become the clerks, drivers, and
mechanics of their Church. They have withdrawn their
counsels from all the governing bodies and committees of the
Church: at the annual All-Burma Convention the whole
proceedings are in the hands of indigenous leaders. This
withdrawal of foreign control and emphasis upon the all-Burma
character of the Baptist Church does seem to have allayed the
suspicions of many who had labelled the Baptists the 'stooges
of foreign imperialism'.

It does appear, therefore, that the period of spiritual exile
for the Christians is coming to an end. U Nu plays a large
and generous part in emphasizing Christian participation in
the national life of Burma. Addressing the 1954 Baptist Convention, the Premier spoke to his audience 'as leaders of the
Christian community and as leaders of the Union'. He declared
that he would 'entrust' them with an assignment: to practise
forbearance, taught both by Lord Buddha and by Jesus Christ,
and to work for 'religious harmony' and for 'the increasing
stability of the Union'.[1]

Will the character of the Christian Church be influenced by
the present-day emphasis upon all things Burmese? Many of
the senior leaders of the Christian community are conservative
in their outlook and would resist proposals for change: but
among the younger leaders there are those who wish to move
towards a more characteristically Burmese expression of their
worship. Western hymns might be replaced by Burmese
chants and the order of service might be radically modified.
There might even be some study of Buddhist literature and
ceremonies for inspiration in constructing a truly Burmese
Christianity.

Another community at the cross-roads are the Anglo-
Burmans, who are facing a much more clear-cut dilemma.
This community never numbered more than a few thousands,
but its contribution to Burma's national development and

[1] *BWB*, 20 October 1954.

security has been memorable in the past and is still considerable in the present. Unlike the Anglo-Indians, they have not through the passage of time (and possibly, the influence of caste) settled down as an indigenous community: almost all the Anglo-Burmans of today can claim a British grandparent, many a British parent; so that the ties with 'home' are still real. The community has, by tradition, looked to government service for employment: the police, the railways, the customs, and the telegraph departments have, in particular, found a recruiting ground among the Anglo-Burmans. During the Second World War, when so many loyalties went into the melting-pot, the Anglo-Burmans stood firmly alongside their British brothers; very many made the hideous trek out to India; a high proportion of the men served in the armed forces, and the nursing service of the Fourteenth Army included large numbers of Anglo-Burman Sisters. After the liberation, most of the community were re-absorbed into government employment.

Then came the shock of Burma's departure from the British Commonwealth. Many rapidly decided that they could not fit into this new Burma and emigrated. In particular, the most enterprising of the younger generation left the country, the young men to enlist in the R.A.F., the girls to become stenotypists in London. Those who were in government service found themselves (not unnaturally) required to adopt Burmese citizenship: some hoped, quietly, to maintain a dual nationality, to keep their British passports[1] while accepting Burmese citizenship in Burma. An act introduced in the Burma Parliament in March 1954 tightened up the regulations: Anglo-Burmans were required to make a definite declaration of Burmese citizenship and to renounce their British nationality before 1 April 1955, or to forfeit their posts in the services and to become subject to the restrictions regulating aliens. A further problem was the announcement of the Government's intention to require all candidates for matriculation to take the whole examination in Burmese. While many Anglo-Burmans (but by no means all) are fluent in spoken Burmese, few have any acquaintance with the literary language, and the new

[1] Under the Independence Act passed by the British Parliament, the first schedule permitted persons to retain their British nationality if the father or the paternal grandfather was born *outside* Burma, in the United Kingdom or the British Empire, or had acquired British nationality by naturalization. This provision could exclude an Anglo-Burman whose grandparents were pure British who was born in Burma of 'service' parents. Also many of those who evacuated to India in 1942 lost all their documents, all proof of British ancestry. At first many were unable to substantiate their claims, but later British government departments interpreted the regulations in a more liberal spirit, and most applicants with a bona fide claim have received a square deal.

ruling would virtually compel the children of the community to merge their cultural identity into that of the nation at large. The need to come to a decision on these two matters has brought the community to a show-down: many have made the difficult decision to leave their jobs and their dwellings and make the long voyage to the land they have never seen but have always known as Home.

But there are others who have decided to stay, and most of these (if they have children) are learning to regard themselves as Burmans. Many have adopted Burmese dress, some have assumed Burmese names, and most are teaching their children to regard Burmese as their mother tongue.[1] The future of this group may be brighter than that of their cousins in India and Pakistan. Those Anglo-Burmans who have taken pains to show themselves patriotic Burmans have been treated on their merits, and some hold important posts in the services. The Minister for Education (1952–6), U Than Aung (A. Rivers), is perhaps the most highly-placed Anglo-Burman. He is President of the Anglo-Burmese Association. At one stage three of the seven divisional Commissioners were Anglo-Burmans; for some years, one held the premier post in Burma's Foreign Service as Ambassador at Washington, and another was Inspector-General of Police. An Anglo-Burman is at the head of the Burma Air Force; several hold senior appointments in the army as brigade and battalion Commanders. Contrary to what Rudyard Kipling and some other English writers have implied, mixed marriages in India and Burma have as often brought out the best qualities of both races, as they have the worst. Many Anglo-Burmans are tough and not afraid of responsibility, while they often inherit the Burmese good humour and lack of tension. They will be an asset to Burma or Britain or Australia or wherever they make their final home.

The remaining minority groups may be expected to be assimilated gradually into the Burmese social structure without undue strain. An example was provided by the Burma Muslim Dissolution of Marriages Act. This measure, which was approved by the Burma Muslim Congress without undue difficulty, became law in March 1953. It gave Muslim women equal rights to those of Buddhists: that is, equal opportunity to divorce their husbands, and a right to a return of their marriage

---

[1] Before the war there were some 25,000 Anglo-Burmans (for census purposes they were listed with the Europeans to form a total of 30,851). About 10,000 may have since emigrated, most to Britain or Australia. Some 3,000 still remained in Burma at the end of 1954, registered as British subjects. About 10,000 have accepted Burmese citizenship. Exact figures for this latter group are not obtainable as they are classified with the main Burmese group for census purposes.

portion on dissolution of the marriage.[1] This measure occasioned loud protests in some other Muslim countries where the wife has no redress against the arbitrary decision of a husband to carry through a divorce, with or without cause. But the Burmese Muslim woman goes forth unveiled and emancipated; if married, she is the sole wife of her husband, with the same status as her Buddhist sister.

Finally, Burma has a share in the common problem of South East Asia, the problem of the 'plural society', with foreign Asians entrenched in key positions in the country's economic system.

The Indians have fallen right away from the pre-war position when they dominated trade and commerce and were found throughout the middle ranks of all government departments. The 1931 census recorded over 1 million Indians in Burma; 1942 saw them on the road as refugees in numbers that have never been accurately computed. Perhaps half a million set out, but thousands never completed the nightmare journey over the mountains to India.[2] After 1945 many returned, but since independence there have been rigid restrictions upon the number permitted to enter, and a tiresome system of registration and stay-permits for those who do gain entry.[3] Almost entirely excluded from the public services, dispossessed of their lands, discriminated against in commerce, Indians and Pakistanis still find it profitable to come to Burma. About half the dock labour, and most of the remaining coolie labour in Rangoon are Indians (Ooriyahs and Tamils), as are large numbers of medical and professional men.[4] Up-country, Gujarati merchants are still to be found, even in remote towns and villages. One may guess that Indians will form an element in the economy of Burma for many years to come, but although Indians first came to 'the Land of Gold' long before the Burmese themselves, they will never be accepted as native citizens of the country. They are *kalas*, despised foreigners; nevertheless, they are tolerated as necessary cogs in the social machine.

If the fortunes of the Indians are on the wane, those of the Chinese are rising. There has never been a 'Chinese Problem'

[1] In fact, divorce is said to be very infrequent in Burma throughout society.
[2] The author saw hundreds dead and dying on the Tamu–Manipur road, May–June 1942.
[3] The official immigration figures show 226,743 Indians and 96,000 Pakistanis as resident aliens in Burma: unofficial but authoritative estimates put their combined numbers at 800,000. There is a fair amount of illegal entry.
[4] Before the war Indians formed over half of the Rangoon population (1931: 212,929 out of 400,415). The 1953 census listed 140,346 Indians and Pakistanis out of a total of 737,079.

in Burma,[1] and there is not one today. Those Chinese who have been domiciled in Burma for two or more generations become entirely assimilated into the general population and regard Burma as their homeland.[2] Today the numbers of Chinese in the country are rising rapidly: before the war the total was 193,594; the immigration figures show a present-day total of 157,000, but this is definitely far short of the actual total which must number about 350,000.[3] Whereas there were 30,626 Chinese in Rangoon in pre-war days, 70,366 were enumerated at the 1953 census. The all-Burma figures must bear some relation to this increase of 133 per cent. Almost all the Chinese are engaged in commerce or the professions. Few are poor, and some are very rich.[4] Unlike the Government of India, which makes no attempt to foster the activities of its nationals in Burma, the Chinese Republic maintains a close watch over all who originally came from the Middle Kingdom. There are Chinese schools, Chinese trade unions, Chinese trade associations, and there is an unseen but highly efficient system of registration and supervision over every kind of activity in which they are concerned. The prestige of the new China is kept before these overseas Chinese constantly. During January and February 1955 a most impressive Chinese cultural mission came to Burma, comprising sixty-seven members and led by Cheng Chen-to, a notable scholar in the field of literary history and Vice-Minister for Cultural Affairs. The mission gave a season of Chinese opera, dancing, and orchestral music at Rangoon which was almost overwhelming in its splendour of colour, richness of sound, gaiety, beauty, superb artistry, and professional verve. Every night, an audience of 2,000 or more watched these dazzling performances: and 95 per cent. of the audience was composed of Chinese residents of Rangoon, made proud almost to the point of arrogance by this Chinese cavalcade, discreetly presented to combine qualities both proletarian and classical—but always Chinese.

And yet, the two items—and the only two—which stirred this crowded Chinese audience to rise to their feet, cheering and clapping and demanding an encore, were a rather feeble Burmese dance and a Burmese song, which the troupe had learned as a compliment to their hosts. There might be more

[1] Except, presumably, in A.D. 1287 when Chinese armies destroyed the Pagan kingdom.
[2] The most sincerely and actively patriotic Burman known to the author is a young army officer whose grandparents were Chinese.
[3] Victor Purcell in *The Chinese in Southeast Asia* (London, Oxford University Press for R.I.I.A., 1951) gives an estimate of 300,000. The author was assured by an independent and authoritative source that this represents the minimum figure.
[4] The largest garage organization and car mart in Rangoon is Chinese-owned.

than one explanation of this intriguing incident: but there are other signs also that seem to indicate that the Chinese in Burma, despite the powerful attractions of the new China, are still content to be absorbed into the very agreeable (and for them, profitable) system into which members of their community have fitted for generations.

The Chinese community survived the military takeover. The once-dominant Indian community was a special target for liquidation. The Indians were driven out of their shops and petty factories. They were still driven out, even if they fulfilled an irreplaceable role, as in the medical profession. Even when their contribution had been honoured, as in the case of Dr. Suvi, the eminent botanist, they were required to depart. By the mid-1960s the Indians were little more than a memory in Burma.

Buddhism went through a cycle of elevation and depression during the 1960s. A main plank in U Nu's election programme of 1960 was to acknowledge Buddhism as the state religion. In August 1961, after much preliminary consideration, a Bill was introduced to amend the constitution to make Buddhism the state religion. The Bill was criticized by those who said that it ran counter to the constitution by discriminating against other religions (these opponents came mainly from the religious minorities), while the Buddhist activists declared that the measure did not go far enough in making Burma officially a Buddhist country. The Bill was passed by a large majority in Parliament, after the Government had taken the precaution of surrounding the building by troops to give protection against militant demonstrations by the activist monks.

When Ne Win came to power again he reversed Nu's policy of emphasizing the bond uniting religion, government, and people. Emphasis was given to Marxism as the ideology of the revolutionary régime, and action was taken to register and regulate the monks. Monastic discontent mounted, until early in 1965 the Mandalay monks came out in open defiance of the Government. Numerous arrests were made and the agitation subsided. However, by arousing the hostility of the unruly element among the younger monks, Ne Win has (like the British in the 1920s) set in motion a wave of unrest which may prove irrepressible. The absence of organizational structure in the Burmese Buddhist 'church' means that it is not possible to isolate and suppress the leadership. The *sangha* remains the voice that cannot be silenced in Burma.

VII

EDUCATION AND THE SOCIAL SERVICES

BURMA'S educational and social services were among the
sectors of the national life most damaged by the war
and the insurrection. In administration, political activity,
and religious and cultural experience, there was some continuity during the Japanese occupation, and it was possible
after the liberation to build upon existing foundations, however
mutilated; but in education and the social services there was
an almost complete breakdown which the subsequent upheavals of the post-independence years have only intensified.
Today there is a nation-wide effort to repair the almost total
losses of the ten years of destruction and to initiate a new era.
But the break in continuity imposed by these lost years may
well never be repaired: earnest leadership may succeed in
overcoming the physical destruction, and may at length even
create the numbers of trained personnel that are required for
the new Welfare State: but it is more questionable whether
professional and academic standards and traditions, barely
established in the years of British rule, will ever return.

Present-day Burmese critics frequently insist that the structure of education built up in the British period was planned
only 'to produce salaried servants in their imperialistic
machine':[1] and it is certainly true that the most able alumni
of the high schools and the university aspired to the prestige
and authority of the civil service. Critics further emphasize the
'tendency to stress the distinction between the privileged few
and the mass of the people':[2] some 2 per cent. of the population
attained high standards of education, while the great majority
attended an ordinary village school and afterwards many of
them lapsed into illiteracy.[3] There were further shortcomings
arising out of Burma's relatively late introduction to Western
thought and the fact of its absorption into the British-Indian
Empire, so that Indians elbowed Burmans aside in the schools
and in the scholastic and technical services. It would be

---

[1] U Nu, *Convocation Address at Rangoon University*, 22 December 1951.
[2] Ministry of Information, *Education in Burma before Independence and after Independence* (Rangoon, 1953).
[3] Yet J. S. Furnivall in *Colonial Policy and Practice* (London, 1948), says that
the British Government 'favoured the spread of primary instruction; Burmans set
more store on higher instruction' (p. 202).

possible to explain and defend the manner in which the educational system of British Burma was evolved, but it would not be especially fruitful; particularly as the leaders of Burma today (to their great credit) do not spend over-much time in dwelling upon the mistakes of yesterday, but concentrate on the hopes of tomorrow.

The pre-war system was 'compartmental', both vertically and horizontally. There were divisions according to age: there were primary schools (for ages 6–10), middle schools (ages 10–14 or 15), and high schools (ages 13–16). But there were also divisions according to the language used in teaching: vernacular schools, where all the teaching was in Burmese or some other national language; Anglo-vernacular schools, where English was taught as a second language and was used, with Burmese, as a teaching language; and finally, English schools, where this language was the medium of all instruction.[1] The great majority of the schools were vernacular schools, and critics have argued that this was 'blind alley' education, because the only government employment open to 'vernacular hands' was that of village schoolmaster, vaccinator, or settlement surveyor. However, this is to overlook the system of 'bridge' scholarships, whereby promising pupils were assisted to cross over into the Anglo-vernacular stream. Critics have complained that such scholarships were few, but it may well be that in the 1920's and 1930's almost no intelligent youth failed to receive his chance in education.[2] Supervision of the schools was in the hands of a wide range of authorities. Primary education was largely controlled by the headmasters of private schools who, if their standards were acceptable, were 'recognized' by local authorities and awarded grants-in-aid: there were a few hundred monastic schools which agreed to conform to the syllabus of the Education Department and thereby qualified for aid. Middle schools were also mainly private institutions under departmental supervision qualifying for grants. Of the high schools about half (54) were established and controlled by Christian missionaries, and the remainder were government institutions (33) or 'national schools' (23) which had come into being in the wake of the upsurge of national feeling in the 1920's.[3]

---

[1] All primary schools (4,519 in 1938) were vernacular schools. Of the middle and high schools, 27 were English schools, 287 were Anglo-vernacular, and 963 were vernacular schools. Details are given in Ministry of Home Affairs, *Final Report of the Administration Reorganization Committee*, 1951, pp. 57–58.

[2] The Burmese tradition of charity also helped: poor boys were often assisted by benevolent headmen, landlords, or merchants.

[3] Total numbers: government schools 45, missionary schools 107, board schools 142, 'recognized' private and national schools 5,546.

From 1920 the goal of the most able youngsters was Rangoon University. The University, founded in a decade of considerable prosperity for Burma, was, at the time of its inception, probably unsurpassed throughout Asia in its buildings and in its potentialities. Profiting from the manifold mistakes made in setting up Calcutta University upon the model of the old London University when it was an examining authority only, the new institution went back to the fountain-head of Oxford and Cambridge. There were two colleges; University College,[1] the largest unit, contained some 800 students by the 1930's; Judson College[2] did not exceed 300 in numbers, mainly Christians and mainly Karens. The constitution of the new university was 'federal', and new colleges were later incorporated.[3] The university was residential: both teachers and students lived together in a 400-acre campus set amid rural woods and lakes. If numbers were small,[4] standards were high. There was considerable intercourse between teachers and students, with opportunities to enter the atmosphere of learning, where student thought was stimulated by men who included scholars of international standing, such as H. Stanley Jevons, Gordon H. Luce, D. G. E. Hall, and J. R. Andrus.

It is true that the cream of the men who graduated in the 1920's and 1930's went into government service: not only into the administration but also into the education, public health, archaeological, forest, and other services. Such a concentration on government service is open to criticism: it was partly responsible for some over-emphasis on the arts side of the university, because this gave advantages when taking the civil service examinations. But the truth is that in an underdeveloped country such as Burma no other outlet is so promising to the young man with a Western education. Trade, in its traditional patterns, has nothing to offer; there are the starveling ranks of journalism, the dull days of the schoolmaster, the Bar with its tantalizing prizes and its queues of briefless advocates, the ever-swelling army of politicians; but these things could not compare to the interest and prestige of life in government service. Perhaps it was just as well: today it is those graduates of the 1920's and 1930's who elected to become officials who form

[1] Successor to the old Government College, established 1885, and affiliated to Calcutta University.

[2] Formerly the American Baptist Mission Intermediate College. The new college remained under A.B.M. control, with a largely American staff.

[3] The Burmah Oil Company Engineering College (so called because endowed by the B.O.C.) was a department of University College; the Medical College and the Teachers' Training College were separate institutions. At Mandalay there was an Agricultural College and an Intermediate College.

[4] Some 500 in the beginning, rising to 2,000 in the 1930's.

the principal supports of the Union during these critical first years of independence.

During the 1930's, the decade of depression and international turmoil, omens were not wanting to point towards the problems which were to trouble the future: ministerial pressure upon university direction, political strikes and constant agitation among the students, expansion of student numbers, and pressure for the lowering of academic standards. Awareness that all was not well in Burma's educational system led to the setting up of the Campbell Committee in 1934. Its report,[1] published in 1936, condemned the prevailing reliance upon private schools and also the different 'avenues' of education: it recommended a single type of school for all children up to the age of fifteen, and thereafter a division into vocational and handicrafts schools for the generality, with pre-university schools for the few, where there would be a strong emphasis upon English. In all the lower schools English would be taught as a second language from the fourth standard, and Burmese would also be introduced into all non-Burmese schools. These proposals were accepted by the Government and began to be applied when the Japanese invasion brought all education to complete collapse.

After an interval the Japanese made some pretence of furbishing up an education system. A few schools were re-opened (with Japanese as a second language) and the façade of a university was erected for a brief while. The whole system of local authorities having collapsed, there were no aided primary schools, but the majority of the old monastic schools somehow kept in being.

The British Military Government reinstated the outlines of a schools system, based upon plans prepared by the Burma Government in Exile, based in turn upon the Campbell proposals. The new pattern was of state primary schools and of 'post-primary' schools (equivalent to high schools), where English and Burmese were both employed as teaching languages. During the first five months after liberation 2,060 primary schools and 42 post-primary schools were opened. With the return of the civil Government orders were passed to more than double the numbers of schools,[2] and the proposals of the Campbell Report for the institution of pre-university schools were implemented: during 1945–6 five such schools were

---

[1] *Report of the Vernacular and Vocational Educational Reorganization Committee*, 1936.
[2] Sanctioned numbers in October 1945 were: primary schools 4,500 and post-primary schools 125. Actual numbers achieved in 1946 were 2,718 and 42 respectively.

established.[1] But while it was possible to issue instructions and provide the necessary funds, the physical task of rebuilding post-war education was formidable. High school and university buildings were extensively requisitioned for military use,[2] and many had to open in makeshift premises; books and equipment were in short supply; teachers had been dispersed, many had taken up alternative employment; and, worst of all, the youth of the country had drifted for three and a half years and had long discarded the virtues of diligence and discipline. Almost as their doors were opened the schools were drawn into the prevailing political maelstrom; strikes and protest marches filled the children's time. The Education Department struggled wearily to plan for the unknown future. In 1946 an Educational Policy Inquiry Committee was formed, and a report covering most aspects of education was submitted at the end of that year. In the political confusion which then prevailed no action was taken at ministerial level, but finally, in 1948, after independence, the recommendations of the Committee were embodied in a Statement of Policy. Then came the insurrections, and the report was not adopted until 1 June 1950.

The new scheme made several changes: the post-primary schools were abolished, and there was a return to the old hierarchy of primary, middle, and high schools (the post-primary school had never been liked, because the public would not believe that schools with that name could be equal to high schools). Now the primary schools would teach up to the fourth standard (ages 6–10), the middle schools up to standard seven (ages 10–13), and the high schools up to standard nine (13–16). All schools financed by public money would be run directly by the State, and all teaching in the state schools was to be in Burmese. English was introduced as a compulsory subject in all schools from standard five (the lowest class in the middle school). At the same time education became entirely free to all, except for the purchase of textbooks.

While a policy was slowly being established, the actual expansion of schools was impeded by every kind of difficulty. There was the physical disruption of the civil war. Something like three-quarters of the school buildings were destroyed or looted by the insurgents. Throughout the countryside the task of departmental inspection and supervision became utterly

[1] This experiment, launched under the worst possible difficulties, was considered to absorb an undue proportion of trained staff. The schools were abolished in April 1947. See Dept. of Public Instruction, *Report on Public Instruction in Burma*, 1946–7, pp. 7–10.

[2] The formal surrender of the Japanese forces in Burma was enacted in front of Convocation Hall at Rangoon University.

impossible and the rural schools largely ceased to function. Official figures show a sad decline in the numbers of schools. Among post-primary or high schools, the figure of 120 established on the eve of independence fell to 97 in 1949, and did not overtake the 1947–8 figures for four years, until 1952–3. In the case of primary schools the collapse was worse: in 1948 the number was 4,328: they fell to 2,186 in 1949 and did not attain the previous level until 1952–3.[1] Such figures for pupils as have been published tell of a similar fall: in 1946–7 there were 438,000 pupils in state primary schools; the following year must have shown an increase to somewhere near half a million on the eve of independence; the year 1948–9 witnessed a decline to 382,000, and not until March 1953 were the pre-independence figures overtaken.[2] The actual collapse in education was in all probability much worse than the official figures indicate. A child who was five years old in 1942 would probably have received only three years' schooling (1945–8) by the time he had reached fifteen years of age in 1952. Besides the hiatus imposed by the civil war, there were other legacies from independence: in the high schools there was an exodus of the long-service Indian teachers, and they were in many cases impossible to replace. There were few suitable Burmans to take over the teaching of English, for instance, which was supposed to be compulsory from the fifth standard.

Rehabilitation of education began to make way from 1952, and was given a fillip by the Pyidawtha Conference, at which the 1950 scheme was restated and was given popular form in a five-point plan.[3] The chief proposals of this new plan were concerned to diversify and broaden the school curriculum so as to free it from the narrow 'academic' course of the past, and to make school something of a training ground for a career in life. But once again, the best of plans had to be adapted to the realities of contemporary Burma. No programme could even begin before the teachers had been found and the schools built. The building programme has concentrated upon high and middle schools; in some instances 'Pyidawtha' efforts have

---

[1] See *Education in Burma* (Rangoon, 1953), pp. 5–7.

[2] Ministry of Home Affairs, *Report on Public Instruction in Burma*, 1946–7, and *Final Report of the Administration Reorganization Committee*, p. 59; *BWB*, 9 September 1953.

[3] (1) To ensure that every citizen of the Union shall have a basic foundation in the three R's; (2) to train an adequate number of technicians and technologists for the rehabilitation and further development of the Union; (3) to train and equip young men and women so that they can shoulder their responsibilities as citizens of the Union; (4) to eradicate illiteracy and imbue all citizens of the Union with the 'five Strengths' (*Bala-Nga-Dan*); and (5) to perpetuate the principles and practice of democracy throughout the Union.

contributed towards their completion. Primary schools continue to be housed in the precincts of monasteries or in the homes of village headmasters. The new plan envisaged the opening of 1,000 new primary schools every year. To assist towards the provision of teachers emergency two months' training courses were improvised at the headquarters of the inspectors of schools, and some 3,000 'emergency' teachers were rushed out to the schools. There followed a rapid increase in the numbers of pupils, and numbers may be expected to mount steadily for several years to come.

SCHOOLS AND TEACHERS

	State schools				Recognized schools			
	High	Middle	Primary	Teachers (total)	High	Middle	Primary	Teachers
1952	108	72	3,335	9,318	10	5	7	200
1953	148	227	5,507	16,652	9	6	21	227
1954	202	347	8,888	21,679	?	?	?	?
1955	220	405	8,951	27,997	?	?	?	?

PUPILS

	State			Recognized		
	High	Middle	Primary	High	Middle	Primary
1952	10,670	35,103	392,398	1,595	1,404	3,975
1953	16,628	54,960	633,707	948	1,914	2,361
1954	23,169	80,426	771,525	?	?	?
1955	42,600	103,600	1,096,000	?	?	?

(SOURCE: *BWB*, 9 September 1953 and 17 November 1955 and information from Ministry of Education.)

By 1954 the education programme was beginning to issue out of the emergency phase. In the field of primary education the goal of the Government is the establishment of a school in every village tract: there are some 30,000 village tracts in Burma, and so far almost 9,000 primary schools have been opened. Many of these are old private 'aided' schools which have been absorbed into the new system. The majority of these village schools are entirely operated by a headmaster or headmistress (about 60 per cent. of primary school teachers nowadays are women) but others have two to three teachers in the school. The old problem of 'stagnation', of pupils drifting on for several years in the bottom class, has probably become less acute; but 'wastage', the withdrawal of youngsters from school before they have achieved real literacy, remains a serious difficulty and can only be solved by compulsory education. This in turn raises greater problems, for it would not be possible to make attendance at school compulsory until there are sufficient places for all children of school age: which at present, manifestly, there are not.[1]

The primary teacher is himself required to have studied up to the seventh standard, but shortages of qualified applicants has often necessitated the acceptance of people whose own school days ended in the fifth or sixth grade.[2] The pay is modest, although much better than before the war.[3] In former days there was a two-year training course for all entrants; this has now been reduced to one year, but up to date the majority of entrants have been put through only the two-months' 'emergency' courses. From October 1953 to May 1955 7,498 teachers underwent the emergency courses and only about 1,500 took the one-year courses at the regular training colleges at Kanbe (Rangoon), Mandalay, Meiktila, Moulmein, Bassein, and Kyaukpyu.[4] In addition, those of the 'old hands' who never received proper training are to be given 'in service' training, or refresher courses, as opportunity permits; it is also planned that the emergency teachers will be recalled for further training when they have completed two years' service. In May 1955 it was possible to suspend the two-months' emergency courses: by then, over 10,000 student-teachers had undertaken these courses.

The young teacher spends three or four years working as an assistant and then takes over his own village school as headmaster. The problem of keeping the teacher in the village, always a difficulty in former days, is now most acute. The ambitious young teacher frets at the monotony and isolation, at the lack of congenial company and the complete absence of the amusement for which he acquired such a taste at his training college, the cinema. Today there is the added risk of being a particular target for the attention of the rebels, as the representative in the village of the Government. And other departments can offer posts with better pay and prospects. Too

---

[1] A 'pilot' scheme for compulsory primary education, was introduced in four areas in the environs of Rangoon (Thamaing, Kanbe, Kamayut, and Thamainggon) in 1948; since 1953 there has been a similar scheme in Syriam town. Compulsion is applied to both boys and girls from 6 to 11. The public response is said to be favourable, and it has not been necessary to apply sanctions to recalcitrant parents.

[2] Nu, *Forward with the People*, p. 59.

[3] Assistant teacher, K70–110 p.m. plus K42 cost-of-living allowance. Headmaster K90–130 p.m. Equal pay for women.

[4] A full account of life at these colleges is contained in an illustrated booklet, *How a Teacher is Trained*, sent out by the Education Department, 1955.

often only the dullards remain as village teachers: the keen youth has only the inherent idealism of his vocation to hold him.

One of the failures of the British effort in rural education was the inability to yoke the monastic schools to the government system: for more than half a century the effort was made, but finally collapsed in the early 1920's.[1] The present Government has renewed the effort to find a place for the monastic schools in the national system, but there is always the difficulty that few monastic *sayas* will consent to the large-scale modification of the traditional studies which is necessary to accommodate the monastic curriculum to the Education Department's requirements. The present policy is to provide material aid, textbooks, equipment, &c., and in some cases to arrange for lay teachers to teach subjects not dealt with by the monks. In such institutions (at present very few) it will be possible for promising pupils to take the fourth standard examination, and thereafter transfer to a state middle school.[2]

The Government's aim in respect of the middle schools is to provide a school in every community of any size; already there are middle schools at most township headquarters; gradually they will extend to every market centre of 2,000 or 3,000 souls. Middle schools cannot, of course, be accommodated in private houses or monasteries, and there is at present an acute shortage of proper buildings; only about one-quarter are in reasonable accommodation, the remainder are in *basha* huts or other temporary quarters. But after independence 67 new secondary schools were built by mid-1955, with 45 others under construction. There is something of a staff shortage: many of those employed at present are unqualified, and it has become necessary to relax standards: the normal minimum qualification for a teacher has been a pass in matriculation, but this is now often an ideal only, especially in the backward areas (teachers do not seem to be very mobile, they like to work near their homes). About 400 new entrants were undergoing training at Kanbe and Mandalay during 1954–5. The syllabus at the middle school consists of Burmese, English, mathematics (all compulsory), and history, geography, civics, nature study, general science, and agriculture, some or all of which may be included. It is planned to modify the syllabus to suit the student's background: there will be 'rural bias' schools where animal husbandry, agricultural methods, and botany will be

---

[1] See the author's *Foundations of Local Self-Government*, pp. 253–4 and 260–1.
[2] Much of the above material on primary schools was provided by U Ba Kyaw, Secretary to the Ministry of Education. There is little in print on the subject.

given emphasis, while in certain city schools there will be classes in commercial subjects such as book-keeping.[1] From 1954 a seventh standard examination ('middle school pass') has been instituted; this will be a necessary prerequisite for all matriculation candidates.

There are high schools already in many townships: the government building programme accorded them a high priority. The problem of staffing these schools is the most acute of all. All high-school teachers used to be graduates, but nowadays a pass in the Intermediate is the most that can be expected. One considerable difficulty in attracting applicants is the somewhat unfavourable pay-scale[2] which has less to offer than elsewhere in government service for similar qualifications. The training of a high-school teacher was formerly carried out in the Faculty of Education of Rangoon University: this is still the pattern, but other centres now cater for high-school trainees. The high-school syllabus is, of course, geared to the requirements of matriculation, but there are plans to give some choice to the students. At Pyinmana an agricultural high school was started in 1953, and twenty-four urban high schools run courses in industrial arts and commercial subjects. Five schools include a 'pre-medical' course, and it was planned to open a technical high school in Rangoon in 1955. There are also arrangements for a division into a 'modern' and an 'academic' side in the large high schools.

These achievements represent a notable attempt to accelerate the educational advance of the nation. But there have been difficulties; some unavoidable, some unnecessary barriers to advancement. The shortage of teachers must continue for many years, especially in the higher classes.[3] There is an almost complete absence of qualified science teachers, so that even in the latest high schools in Rangoon scientific equipment (much supplied from American aid or Colombo Plan sources) can be seen lying around, often not even assembled, waiting for years to be put to proper use. Inevitably there has been a fall in scholastic levels, and there is pressure all round to capitulate to this situation and to lower examination standards. All this is in large measure unavoidable, but development is further impeded by the cross-currents of politics. There are two 'unions' which claim the adherence of school-children; the All-Burma Students' Union, which supports the AFPFL, and

---

[1] There are also domestic science and home nursing courses for girls in selected schools.

[2] Teachers, K200–300 p.m., headmasters, K330–450.

[3] One of the teacher's grievances is that almost all are employed on a 'temporary' basis and have no permanent tenure or pension rights.

the All-Burma Federation of Students Union, which is controlled by the 'Progressives', the allies of the Communists. These unions have their branches throughout the high schools and even in the middle schools, and there are constant tussles in which the teaching staff have to face the demands of their pupils—and may well be called to account by M.P.s and politicians from above: perhaps urged to expel certain pupils and accept others as candidates.[1]

The whole educational structure below university level is organized and controlled by the Department of Education. Under the Director there are Inspectors in charge of each division (called an Education Circle in the department), and then there are District Education Officers for each district. The inspectorate is recruited from among existing teachers and also direct from outside.[2] The whole system is official in composition, except that Rangoon Municipality still has the powers of a local education authority in respect of primary education and employs its own inspectorate. Elsewhere there are 'school managing committees' which include representatives of the public and have some influence in the running of the school, although all questions of finance, staffing, curriculum, school buildings, &c., are the sole concern of the department.

Outside the state system there remain a few private schools which must be registered and are liable to inspection. The missionaries still play an important role in education in the Frontier Areas, where state schools are only now being established, and they still operate excellent high schools which play a key part in educating the leaders of tomorrow: their standard of teaching and of school discipline compares very favourably with the state schools. Probably the most outstanding are three in Rangoon: the Methodist English High School, St. Paul's High School (Roman Catholic), and St. John's Diocesan Boys' School (Anglican). There is keen competition among the Burmese middle classes to enter their children into these institutions although their fees are not low. At Taunggyi the former School for the Sons of Shan Chiefs has been restarted with the support of the Sawbwas on the lines of an English public school with an English headmaster provided by the British Council: it is now named Kanbawza College. This

---

[1] cf. Allegations of All-Burma Federation of Students Union, *Nation*, 8 October 1954.

[2] The lowest rank, that of Deputy Inspector, ranks with a senior teacher as a member of the Junior Branch of the education service. The District Education Officers rank with certain selected headmasters and belong to the Senior Branch of the service, drawing salaries from K350–700 p.m. The Divisional Inspectors form a 'selection grade' and rank with university lecturers.

social experiment, which could provide a most useful element in Burmese education, may not be able to adapt itself to the changing requirements of the government system. Finally, amongst the private schools there are a number of so-called 'matric schools', cramming establishments, which operate solely to push their charges through matriculation. That they do not lack for pupils is some comment on the state schools.

Matriculation is, of course, the climax of the whole education system: this is the doorway through which all aspirants to the university must pass. The numbers of those sitting for the examination have risen rapidly since the war and the proportion passing has fallen steeply, from 46 per cent. in 1946 to under 12 per cent. in 1955.[1]

The present standard set is certainly not unreasonable: a pass is awarded to all who attain 30 per cent. in each subject. The results have afforded a somewhat dramatic illustration of the superior standards in the missionary schools, whose candidates have consistently topped the list.[2] The authorities have not accepted this situation as satisfactory and have introduced two new measures. From 1955 all candidates for matriculation must have passed the middle school (seventh standard) examination, followed by two years' further study (previously any youngster aged fifteen years had been eligible to sit). The second measure is the termination of the provision whereby answers may be submitted in the English language: from 1955 all candidates must answer in Burmese (except, of course, for the compulsory English paper). Nobody expects this measure to improve the results from the state schools, but it will certainly adversely affect the results of the foreign mission schools. Hitherto they have utilized English in large measure as a teaching language, and have employed staffs who have included a proportion of qualified Europeans, Americans, and Indians. It will now be necessary to reorganize from the bottom: textbooks, teaching methods, staff—all will be subject to change. This measure will almost certainly spell the end of the English-language school in Burma: and perhaps also the end of that proficiency

[1]	Year	No. of candidates	No. passing	Percentage of passes
	1946	1,167	538	46
	1947	3,896	1,214	31
	1948	3,926	867	22
	1949	3,610	801	22
	1950	5,119	994	19
	1951	8,804	1,700	19
	1952	13,045	1,938	15
	1955	24,384	2,874	11

(SOURCE: *Nation*, 31 July 1952 and 23 September 1955.)
[2] ibid., 28 November 1952.

in a world language which has been such a useful tool to the Burmese leaders in these early years.

Most students enter the university at sixteen or seventeen, taking four or five years to obtain their degree. Numbers have multiplied in a sensational manner, especially since 1951, when free tuition (except in the faculty of law) was introduced. When the university reopened after the war in temporary premises some 600 old students returned. Within fifteen months the total had passed 2,000; the figures thereafter remained fairly constant until 1951, when they began to soar until in 1955 some 10,000 students were registered at the university.[1]

This increase has entailed a reorganization of the country's university structure. As a temporary measure after the war the university was placed under an 'administrator', Dr. Htin Aung, until a new framework should be created.

The Judson College buildings were released by the military in June 1947, and the American Baptist Mission began negotiations to reopen their college, actually assembling a new lecturing staff. However, it gradually became obvious that the Government was strongly opposed to the idea of a separate Christian college.[2] First, Judson College was done away with as a separate teaching institution, and then the American Baptist Mission was compelled to relinquish control over the various Judson hostels. Judson Church was left under Baptist control, and a university chaplain is appointed by the Mission. The church remains the centre of Christian undergraduate life, filled to capacity every Sunday.[3] The Mission planned to build a new Judson College at Moulmein, with emphasis upon science, sociology, and business administration. This project secured Cabinet approval, new buildings were erected, and an opening date, 1 July 1952, was announced. But at the last minute the Cabinet reversed its earlier decision, and the newly completed buildings were taken over by the State.

[1] Total student numbers: 1946–7, 2,127; 1947–8, 2,762; 1948–9, 3,043; 1949–50, 2,797; 1950–1, 3,620; 1951–2, 4,171; 1952–3, 5,346; 1953–4, 6,936; 1954–5, 10,000 (*BWB*, 25 November 1953 and University Registrar).
[2] The prevailing attitude is well exemplified in the following quotation from an official publication, *Burma and the Insurrections* (Rangoon, 1949), pp. 39–40: 'KNDO leaders are generally men trained in the Judson College of the Rangoon University. Their entire cultural life in the University has been punctiliously segregated from the rest of the Burmans by the missionary authorities of Judson College with the result that when out of College they find themselves out of place and difficult to fit in the general society. . . . This mental atmosphere . . . created a rabid desire for a separate State of their own.'
[3] Gradually, Christian work is rebuilding a place in the university. The foundation-stone was laid on 16 October 1954 of a new Student Christian Centre by the Prime Minister as Chancellor of the University. This centre will, in U Nu's words, 'regardless of race or religion . . . assist students of different backgrounds to meet together . . . to create better understanding' (*Nation*, 17 October 1954).

The new constitution of Rangoon University[1] which came into force in 1949 provided for a unitary organization, controlled by a University Council. This was drawn from among representatives of the teaching staff, of the Students' Union, the graduates, and certain civic organizations. There were also certain political nominees: altogether the Council numbered about thirty. This body is the executive organ of the university, but major decisions have to be ratified by the Senate, a much larger body. The executive head of the university is the Rector, a permanent academic official; from 1949–58 this post was held by Dr. Htin Aung. The university authorities are most insistent that there should be independent control over the university, and this is certainly true in the making of appointments and in most routine affairs. Nevertheless it would be unrealistic to omit notice of the close interest taken in everything by U Nu as Chancellor, and to observe that university development is entirely dependent on government money, now that fees have been abolished and now that the very considerable munificence previously shown by the British, Indian, and Chinese commercial magnates of Rangoon has almost entirely evaporated. Thanks to the large and increasing assistance afforded by the Government,[2] university facilities have been widely extended. The building programme on the central Inya university estate includes several new hostels and accommodation for staff, a new Engineering College, a new School of Social Studies, and a rebuilt Educational Faculty building. In order to meet the tremendous influx of students a policy has been adopted of decentralizing university teaching. Mandalay has been raised to the status of a degree college (it now has about 1,000 students), and four new intermediate colleges have been opened. In June 1953 the college prepared by the American Baptist Mission at Moulmein opened as an Intermediate College and its numbers soon rose to over 500. In 1954 three new Intermediate Colleges were opened: in Rangoon one college commenced at Yankinmyo in June 1954 with 1,429 students, and a second was opened at Hteedan in October with 980 students. The Kyaukpyu Intermediate College for Arakan began work in July 1954 with 62 students. A branch Medical College was opened at Mandalay in June 1954. In 1955 yet another Intermediate College was established at Magwe, beginning in July with 70 students.

[1] See *University of Rangoon (Amendments) Act*, 1949, and the *Repealing Act* of 1949.
[2] Grants: 1947–8, 14.25 lakhs; 1948–9, 13.86 lakhs; 1949–50, 16.90 lakhs; 1950–1, 41 lakhs; 1951–2, 61 lakhs; 1952–3, 99.65 lakhs; 1953–4, 103.48 lakhs; 1954–5, 145 lakhs. From 1951–2 the above includes non-recurring capital grants (e.g. 1954–5 recurring=70 lakhs, non-recurring = 75 lakhs).

This mass expansion has taken place, it would seem, without sufficient consideration by the authorities of its implications. The university was founded at a time when, in Britain, a university education was regarded as the privilege of an *élite*. The privileged few obtained entry either by intellectual ability or wealth. In the years since 1945 this concept has been stretched and transformed; British universities now admit all who have given evidence of ability to derive profit from higher education; but the ideal still remains (and is still applied at Oxford and Cambridge): a university is a place where knowledge is related to life, and men strive to attain the highest in both spheres. At Rangoon University in the 1920's the students were an *élite* (about half of them were holders of scholarships) and the British idea of a university was accepted. The ideal still stood during the 1930's, when standards were coming under political pressure. But since independence the declared goal is the admission of as many students as can be accepted. Without any explicit change of policy the whole concept of a university has altered: it is now, for all practical purposes, the employment exchange of the Welfare State, a pool from which may be scooped the hundreds of executive and technical personnel to operate an industrialized, socialist society. Numbers are first priority: standards have to adjust themselves to this priority. The change is most noticeable at intermediate level where the bulk of the students are found. According to U Nu, speaking as Chancellor, over 80 per cent. of freshmen register for one of the science courses, but after one or two months drift away to an arts course because they find that they cannot keep up with the demands of science.[1] Indeed, many students drift from subject to subject, year after year, never managing to pass the intermediate examination, whatever combination they attempt. Candidates can choose to sit for this examination in English or Burmese; the great majority choose the latter, not because their written Burmese is fluent, but because their knowledge of English is negligible. The Burmese-language lectures are therefore packed out and lecturers are compelled to deliver their discourse at dictation speed, frequently being required by students to repeat a passage not understood. As there are virtually no textbooks of the required standard available in Burmese, students rely entirely on their lecture notes. Students are required to submit essays, but because of their inordinate numbers these are read by 'tutors' who are young graduates. There is therefore no direct contact between students and staff. A large proportion of the students fail their

[1] Convocation speech (*BWB*, 29 December 1954).

intermediate examinations every year and remain to clog the lower classes, hampering the efforts of their more able brethren. Those who succeed in passing the intermediate almost *en masse* enter for a pass degree. There is no incentive to obtain anything better than a bare pass, for this is the highest qualification demanded for the government appointments to which the successful graduate still aspires: there is no point in trying for honours when this will carry no greater weight (the politician who makes the appointment will himself have no more than a pass degree).

The pass degree entails taking papers in three main subjects: English, Burmese, and History are a favourite combination. The B.A. standard at Rangoon is now no great test for any youngster of moderate intelligence, but there is a high proportion of failures. Among the causes that may be mentioned are the lack of contacts with teachers, failure to read, accommodation difficulties, and student politics. Even among students in the final year of their B.A. or B.Sc. course, it still remains true that the lecturer or professor is only a figure on a platform dimly heard: few faculties have active societies or other means whereby students and staff can mingle. The gulf between staff and student is fixed, as between 'we' and 'they'. The decline in reading might be anticipated when all the textbooks are in English, and this has ceased to be a second language as it was to pre-war students. But matters are made worse by the appalling library facilities at the university: deliberately wrecked by the Japanese, the library has never been reorganized. Thousands of volumes have been added since the war (many given by British and American universities), but the task of arranging and cataloguing the books seems to have been insuperable. The library remains a muddle, and it is therefore deserted by students and staff. Probably the only books which undergraduates ever read are one or two unpleasing little 'cramming' guides to passing examinations. The accommodation problems are partly inevitable because of the mass expansion. About half the students now live out with relatives and friends. Those who live in hostels are crowded together (although since 1953 the physical overcrowding has greatly abated) and there is no hostel discipline. With blaring gramophones and raucous laughter all around the conscientious student finds it hard enough to concentrate; the idler finds every encouragement for his idleness.[1]

[1] These remarks do not apply to the women's hostels: some women come to the university to have a good time, but most come to work. About one-third of the students are women.

Finally, there is the bogey of political licence to inflame and disorganize the lives of the students. Over all the activities of the post-war student population has loomed the shadow of Aung San and defiance of the university authorities, strike and boycott. University strikes have occurred with depressing regularity in 1946, 1947, 1949, and 1953. The ostensible motives have changed, but the underlying reason remains the same: a weariness with hard work, dislike of any restriction on personal liberty, and contempt for authority. The post-independence scene has been dominated by a struggle between the AFPFL or Socialist-sponsored Democratic Students' Organization and the 'Progressive Student Force' with strong Communist affiliations. The Democratic Students' Organization was brought into being after 1949, when student leaders came out in support of the Ministerial Services Union[1] and were promptly committed to prison. Thereafter, with government backing, the Socialist spokesmen managed to gain control of the Rangoon University Students' Union, and rapidly took to themselves that careless abuse of power which has often characterized the AFPFL bosses in the districts. The opposition elements—previously disorganized in their various support of Than Tun's White Flags, the Red Flags, and the BWPP— joined together in 1951 as the Progressive Student Force. Their first attempt (in 1951) to contest the annual elections for the offices of President and committee of the Union was unsuccessful, but in 1952, receiving support from various 'independents' who were disgusted with the Democratic Students' Organization régime, they captured the committee. Most observers are agreed that their year of office formed an agreeable contrast, in concern for student activities and in efficiency, with the record of the Democratic Students' Organization. It looked most probable that at the following elections their hold on the Union would be further strengthened. But the backers of the Democratic Students' Organization took alarm and influence was brought to bear upon the results. On election day, in August 1953, some eighty cars appeared with workers in the Socialist cause; there were widespread accounts of impersonation and the bringing in of outsiders to vote. As a result, when counting began, it was soon clear that the Democratic Students' Organization would secure a victory. Enraged, the Communists proceeded to break up the ballot boxes, scattering the voting-papers, and demanding a new election.[2] But the university authorities did not accede to this demand:

[1] See above, p. 41.
[2] *Nation*, 29 August 1953.

Democratic Students' Organization candidates were declared elected to the presidency and the other Union posts. The Communists launched a protest campaign. The Rector called together the students and administered a warning: he declared that the name of 'university student' had become 'a badge of shame', and he gave warning that the university would be closed if hooliganism continued.[1] But the Communists discovered an excellent basis for further agitation in a decision, announced at this very moment, to curtail the annual October university vacation from the customary month to fourteen days. In protest, the Communists launched a boycott of all classes: students remained in their hostels while lecturers addressed empty class-rooms. The Government decided to break the boycott by force: encounters between police and students followed, culminating in a pitched battle in front of Ava Hall in which a thousand students fought it out against tear-gas, fire-hydrants, and (according to eye-witnesses) bullets.[2] The students were beaten, and the university was occupied by a battalion of Union Military Police. Sympathetic strikes were launched at Mandalay and Moulmein colleges, and thousands of pupils from thirty schools demonstrated in the streets of Rangoon, but eventually these demonstrations petered out. Retaliatory measures were taken: over 50 students were expelled from Rangoon and 25 from Mandalay; many were taken into custody, and eighteen months later 19 students were still detained in prison.[3] This 'October Revolution' had the effect of disgusting most sensible students with militant politics. Next year when election time came near neither the Socialists nor the Communists were ready to come forward under their own banners. The former took shelter behind a non-political 'Neutral Front', while the Communists sponsored a 'United Front' which also included non-political student leaders. In the autumn of 1954 the university authorities took thorough precautions against disorder or improper electoral practices. There were no disturbances,[4] but the Communist-sponsored 'United Front' secured over 70 per cent. of the vote. At Mandalay and Moulmein where the Socialist Democratic Students' Organization stood under their true colours they were also decisively defeated by Progressives and Independents.[5] In 1955, despite

[1] *Nation*, 5 September 1953.
[2] ibid., 4 October 1953.
[3] ibid., 18 February 1955.
[4] A feature of the student elections is the extensive coverage given by all the national papers, week after week, to the state of university politics. The interest which, in Britain or the United States, would be reserved for a national election is focused upon activities on the campus.
[5] *Nation*, 17 September and 3 October 1954.

the break-away of the Vice-President of Rangoon University Students' Union, the Communist 'United Front' again scored a decisive victory at Rangoon, securing over 60 per cent. of the student vote. At Mandalay and elsewhere they were also successful. It is not simple to interpret these results. Among factors which are certainly influential is the 'agin the government' attitude fostered in the struggle against the colonial Power, which has become ingrained among students; a revulsion from the casual monopoly of power claimed by the protégés of the AFPFL; and the disgust of the students at their inadequate facilities, especially in the newly opened colleges, caused by the Government's policy of break-neck expansion (by a curious paradox, the only reason why the majority of these same students have ever come near a university). Finally, student election results may perhaps be interpreted in part as representing the repudiation of politics by that minority of students who desire to do some work at the university: for only 60 per cent. proceeded to vote at the 1954 and 1955 elections. But it is impossible to deny the attractions of Communism, or Marxism, for the younger generation in Burma, the leaders of tomorrow.

Recognizing that the cancer of political unrest is gnawing at the heart of university life, U Nu has frequently urged the students to leave politics to the politicians, saying 'Our Union underwent a complete transformation at [independence]. . . . Every one of us need not take up politics . . . as before. . . . The duty of the students is to try to become educated.'[1] But the students do not heed U Nu's admonitions: his own student example is more powerful. In consequence, in his Convocation speech of December 1953 Chancellor Nu was forced to observe that 'although the University has an increased student population of over seven thousand students, in quality and calibre there has been a great fall. This deterioration has caused all the citizens of our Union, who have been expecting great things from University students, enormous regret.'[2] Attempts by the university authorities to tighten up discipline continually run up against the political tradition. In 1954 the University Council proposed to introduce regulations whereby those students who had failed in their final examinations for three years running (popularly known as 'the 3 F's') should not be permitted to occupy urgently needed hostel accommodation but must make their own boarding arrangements. This modest proposal was loudly opposed by the Students'

[1] Convocation speech, *From Peace to Stability*, pp. 186–7.
[2] *Forward with the People*, p. 98.

Union as an act of tyranny: the university authorities eventually introduced the measure, whose unpopularity was almost certainly a factor in the Communist success at the 1955 student elections.

The only students who are pursuing studies which have something of a university flavour are the candidates for the Master's degree, a minute fraction of the whole.[1] Attempts are being made to maintain the old standard at this level. Higher studies are catered for by selecting large numbers of graduates for courses overseas. With hardly any exceptions, these students are sent to countries where English is the (or a) teaching language: the United Kingdom, the United States, Australia, New Zealand, India, and Israel (a handful only to these last two countries).[2] These studies are financed by a wide range of scholarship schemes organized by the United Nations, the American Fulbright programme, the British Council, and the Colombo Plan. But the majority go as 'state scholars' under Burma Government auspices. The greatest number are sent to the United Kingdom, and a large proportion of the remainder to the United States.[3]

The pull of the United States may be expected to increase over the coming years. To an increasing extent Burmese students are finding difficulty, both by reason of linguistic and academic shortcomings, in adjusting themselves to the standards of British universities. Some American institutions have adopted a double standard, with only nominal requirements for Asian students, and it is much easier to secure a place in American universities where scholarships are offered on a much more lavish scale than in Britain. Whereas at present the great majority of the leaders of educational life in Burma have British degrees and diplomas, within a few years the majority will be men and women with American Master's and Doctor's degrees. It will be surprising if this reorientation does not have a considerable influence on university methods and courses in Burma, which at present are still largely modelled upon those at London University, the undergraduate's studies culminating in a marathon ten-day examination. Should the 'America-returned' scholars come to form a dominant majority in the university, there will probably be pressure to base the students'

[1] Of some 2,000 students reading history in 1954–5, less than 40 were working for their Master's degree. The old B.A. Honours degree has lapsed as its requirements were similar to M.A. Part I.

[2] A few students have gone to Yugoslavia and several Yugoslav students have come to Burma: but this exchange is more of a political gesture than a practical contribution to education.

[3] In 1954 there were about 160 State Scholars in the United Kingdom and 140 in the United States.

results upon a system of 'credits' designed to reflect his work, term by term, with only a modest test of factual data at the end of the course. Few would pretend that the existing system is ideally suited to present-day requirements, but any such departure is likely to lead to a further softening of the standards.

Expansion among university staff has by no means kept pace with expansion of students, mainly because there are no trained reserves upon which the university can draw: even in obtaining a supply of able young graduates, the university has to compete against other bodies which can offer conditions equally attractive for the present, much more attractive for the future. The university teacher has to face a life of routine lecturing to mass audiences, and the drudgery of marking thousands of papers for university examinations and for the matriculation examination which will absorb almost his entire long vacation. There are, in most fields of study, no opportunities for specialized research, and even the task of keeping abreast of his subject in learned journals and other publications is not possible for many. The numbers of senior posts are exceedingly limited, and the staff of the associated colleges at Mandalay, Moulmein, and Kyaukpyu have no hope of rising out of the lecturer grade,[1] so that appointment to either of these institutions is regarded as equivalent to professional extinction.

Shortages among staff have been partially met by the employment of lecturers from India; these, however, are but stop-gap appointments, and the temporary Indian lecturers cannot be expected to make a significant contribution to university life. With existing staff immersed in routine teaching, and likely to become further submerged as student numbers continue to rise, the future for the leadership of academic life in Burma is somewhat obscure.

Every aspect of university work seems to call for examination by a responsible commission who should inquire into the consequences of the uncontrolled expansion of the last years and should determine a definite programme for the future.[2] At present the university is expected to assume responsibility for every sort of training venture. The civil servants, the managers of the public utilities and nationalized industries, medical and public health personnel, engineers, lawyers,

---

[1] Proposals to make Mandalay a separate university were approved by the Rangoon University Senate in February 1955, and came into effect in 1958. U Ko Ko Lai became first Vice Chancellor. Among other benefits, the lecturers at Mandalay will be able to look forward to better professional prospects.

[2] Early in 1958 an Education Commission was appointed, with U Nu as Chairman. It held a number of sittings, recorded evidence, and consulted the inevitable foreign experts, but came to no agreed conclusions.

agricultural experts: the future practitioners in these and many other callings and professions are sought from the university exclusively. During 1955 plans were drafted for the promotion of an institute of business administration—an excellent proposal, but without any doubt this will end up as yet another department of the university. In theory the university remains the apex of intellectual efforts in Burma; in fact it has flung its doors open to a crowd of low-grade trainees who block the path of the really talented youth of the country and waste the time and energy of Burma's leading scholars. The pressure upon the university reflects the prestige of a degree as a symbol of status and a passport to superior employment. Other avenues of technical and professional training remained undeveloped.

Thus whereas in 1955 there were 700 university students at the Engineering College, there were only 367 trainees (half of them being in their first year) at the Government Technical Institute at Insein, where technological training is given at the level of the foreman or skilled mechanic. In almost every other country the proportion of persons being trained in 'top' and 'middle-grade' skills is reversed.

The university entered a new phase, late in 1958, with the return of Dr. Hla Myint from Oxford to take over the post of Rector. He promptly introduced a series of radical reforms. The inflation of student numbers was halted and reversed by raising the standard of the Matriculation Examination (drastically limiting the numbers qualifying), by reintroducing tuition fees, and by excluding from the university all students who failed twice in their final examinations. Student discipline was considerably improved, and agitators were banished. Emphasis was placed upon honours courses. The esoteric departments which had proliferated in recent years were reduced or wound up.

Dr. Hla Myint was unable to withstand pressure to relax standards after the return of the Nu Government and he felt compelled to resign. When General Ne Win seized power in 1962 the students resisted the direct supervision over their activities instituted by the military. In July 1962 there were protest demonstrations at Rangoon University, with violent consequences. The army moved into the university campus, and at least 15 students were killed by firing. The university was closed, and the Students' Union (centre of political agitation since the mid-1930s) was demolished by army engineers. Subsequently, under the military régime, politics was channelled into a university institute for Marxist study.

In the field of social services, the Welfare State in Burma

covers a much more narrowly restricted range of activity than in Britain although, in the very long run, Burma would wish to evolve a comparable system of social security. Up till the middle 1950's practical development in the field of social services and social security has been confined largely to the rehabilitation of the pre-war medical and public health services.

In former days medical relief was largely a public service.[1] The Christian missions operated a number of well-equipped hospitals, particularly among the frontier peoples; there was also the Hindu Ramakrishna Mission Hospital in Rangoon. In the large towns there were doctors in private practice,[2] catering almost exclusively for the middle classes: but throughout the greater part of the country private medical care was represented by the *se saya*, the indigenous allopathic practitioner, and the *let thé*, the indigenous midwife with her traditional birth practices. Modern medicine was therefore largely made available only through the hospitals and dispensaries organized by the Medical Department and administered by local authorities under a system of grants-in-aid. By 1939 there were 315 public hospitals with 9,364 beds; the larger institutions were concentrated in the main towns, but there were also rural hospitals in every township. More than 3 million patients were treated annually, and all medical services were free, except that private wards could only be secured by payment (as under the British National Health Service). In public health or preventive work, activity was concentrated on fighting malaria and smallpox and on the enforcement of hygiene regulations throughout the towns and villages. The Harcourt Butler Institute of Public Health, established in 1926, served as the centre for training and research; a Malaria Bureau was opened in 1927, and a Vaccine Depot at Meiktila supplied several varieties of serum throughout Burma. Public health work was largely concentrated in the towns;[3] health supervision at the port of Rangoon was well developed, as was necessary in order to control the immigrant coolie traffic.[4] Other public health work was not notably effective; a façade of cleanliness, hygiene, and building regulation existed, but behind the clean main streets of Rangoon lay a labyrinth of

[1] Writing in the pre-war period, J. L. Christian observed 'Socialized medicine is long past the experimental stage in Burma' (*Burma and the Japanese Invader*, p. 155).

[2] More than one-third of the medical practitioners in Burma were resident in Rangoon. Of the total, almost two-thirds were Indians (see Ministry of Home Affairs, *Final Report of the Administration Reorganization Committee*, p. 52).

[3] Of the 59 municipalities 22 employed Health Officers; of the 28 district councils only 4 had Health Officers.

[4] In the peak year, 1925, there were 330,212 immigrants and 301,846 emigrants.

squalid alleys and foetid tenements.[1] Maternity and child welfare was the one sphere in which there were a number of voluntary organizations at work: as a result infant mortality figures in the city declined from 32·8 per cent. in 1922 to 24·8 per cent. in 1937. But, as such figures indicate, health improvement in Burma was far from satisfactory, and the incidence of malaria, tuberculosis, venereal diseases, and cholera was very heavy. In numbers the medical and health services were far from adequate: there were some 570 doctors in the hospitals and dispensaries and some 80 doctors working as health officers. A high proportion of these were non-Burman—mainly Indian, with some Chinese—as few Burmans were ready to take the long and arduous medical course at Rangoon University. The shortage of nurses was even more acute: these were drawn almost entirely from the Christian community, being Karens or Anglo-Burmans. But an even greater bar to improvement in public health was the state of public opinion. Buddhism with its emphasis upon the sanctity of life would abhor the destruction of pariah dogs, rats, flies, or mosquitoes. Town-planning and the regulation of building was regarded as yet another harassment of officialdom which must be circumvented by a judiciously placed bribe. By the 1930's the people of Burma had come to accept Western curative medicine, but preventive health measures were outside their understanding.

The pre-war health services, inadequate as they were, collapsed completely during the Japanese régime. A major factor was the flight of large numbers of Indian health personnel, from doctors to sweepers, towards India. Rangoon became a vast slum, following the breakdown of the public services and the influx of thousands of refugees who erected *basha* huts in the main streets and in all open spaces. Everywhere malnutrition was widespread, malaria was rampant, not one vaccination was carried out after 1941, and there were several smallpox epidemics.[2] The British Military Administration was able to restore the framework of a health service: by the end of 1945, 225 hospitals with 8,400 beds had been reopened, and 8 Malaria Control Units were working in the worst-affected malarial areas. Gradually doctors, nurses, and other health personnel came back to work again, but much that had been destroyed could not be replaced: for instance, the Vaccine Depot at Meiktila was razed to the ground and supplies must be imported from Bengal and Bombay.

The work of rehabilitation was soon complicated, as in all

---

[1] See the author's *Foundations of Local Self-Government*, pp. 299–306.
[2] See *Report by the Supreme Allied Commander*, pp. 194–5.

other fields, by the problems of independence and insurrection. With independence, the services of large numbers of trained foreign medical and other health personnel were terminated; with the civil war almost all medical and health services came to an abrupt halt: at least half of the district and township hospitals were totally destroyed by the rebels. It was not until 1951 that the Government could begin to rebuild the shattered system.

Attention was first devoted to the provision of doctors: in 1951, as against a pre-war cadre of 650, there were only 400 doctors in the employ of the State.[1] In former years the Medical College of the university produced twenty or thirty new doctors every year, but the out-turn in the immediate post-war years was very low.[2] Also the government Medical School, whose four-year courses produced large numbers of licensed medical practitioners, was closed down in deference to the views of the Burma Medical Association. To meet this acute and continuing shortage of doctors the Medical College could only promise forty medical graduates per annum.[3] Government proposals to cut down the medical course from seven to five years met with a blunt rejection from the medical profession;[4] it was eventually decided to reduce the course to six years, providing that physics, chemistry, and biology were introduced into the high schools.[5] It was also decided to set up a second medical school, attached to Mandalay College: this institution has now been built and is ready to receive students (1955). But these remedies still leave vast gaps in the medical services;[6] as a temporary expedient 300 doctors were recruited from India and Pakistan on contracts lasting three to five years. These young men were promptly posted to the most remote and unpopular stations in the Union, and it has been made clear to them that they will be dismissed immediately Burma nationals are available to take their place. Not surprisingly, therefore, there has been a good deal of discontent among these reinforcements.

[1] Dept. of Information, *Burma, the Fourth Anniversary*, p. 25: text of a report from the Government of Burma to UNICEF, Asian Region, quoted in full, pp. 25–35— an excellent statement of the health problem in 1951.
[2] Numbers of M.B. and B.S. graduates: 1947, 7; 1948, 4; 1949, 25; 1950, 19; 1951, 26.
[3] The Director of Medical Services thereupon observed that, on these terms, Burma would have to wait 300 years before an adequate supply of doctors would be available (Ministry of Home Affairs, *Final Report of the Administration Reorganization Committee*, p. 53).
[4] Nu, *Forward with the People*, p. 60.   [5] ibid., p. 122.
[6] New doctors: 1952, 29; 1953, 40; 1954, 50; 1955, 75 (estimate). The examiners, senior Burmese doctors, set a high standard and fail a very large proportion of the candidates.

A second expedient was the training of 'health assistants' to work in the rural areas, taking on the more elementary duties of doctors. These assistants are recruited from among matriculates and undergo a two-year training course at the Health Assistants' School, Rangoon. The first batch of 108, recruited in October 1951, was ready for service at the end of 1953. The intention is to train 800 health assistants within six years. In order to provide an incentive to these new assistants to stay in the countryside they are receiving a rate of pay (K200–300 per month) which, for their modest attainments, is high (it is the pay of the old Sub-Assistant Surgeons who were qualified doctors). Much is expected of these health assistants: it remains to be seen whether their qualifications will enable them to accomplish much more than the public health inspectors of the past.

The pre-war shortage of nurses has become even more acute: whereas the names of 1,051 nurses and 1,628 midwives remained on the register, it was announced in 1952 that there were only 400 nurses and 200 registered midwives in service (many left the country before and after independence).[1] Training of nurses is largely carried out at the Rangoon General Hospital, where they undergo a three-year course: by mid-1954 over 100 new nurses had been taken on to the register, with some 280 undergoing training.[2] The other personnel necessary for the health service are also being trained under considerable difficulties: specialist training is obtained overseas, largely under United Nations auspices. In order to meet a total lack of dentists, five are being recruited from India and thirty from Japan, under contract.

The Government's broader plans are framed in relation to the two aspects of medicine, preventive and curative. Preventive work is being developed by the creation of special organizations to combat the main diseases afflicting the nation. Malaria is the first enemy, and it has been estimated that over one-half of the population is afflicted by the disease. The technique of special malaria control units, which was inherited from the British Military Administration, has been brought into operation in the worst malarial areas. The most spectacular progress was achieved in the Lashio area: a malaria team provided by WHO began work in 1951, spraying houses and huts with

---

[1] Ministry of Information, *Pyidawtha Conference*, p. 113. An excellent statement of Burma's health resources, requirements and plans is contained in the Medical and Public Health Plans and the supporting speech of the Minister. pp. 102–14.

[2] U Nu has observed that 'the nursing profession is not looked upon with favour by the Burmese public' (*BWB*, 21 April 1954).

DDT throughout 350 villages over an area of 800 square miles: as a result the disease has been almost entirely eliminated.[1] Two teams were also provided under the American aid programme, together with one operated by the Burma Government. These have now been replaced by permanent malaria control units under the Health Department: 37 units were functioning in 1955, when almost $5\frac{1}{2}$ million people had received protection from malaria. Probably the next important danger is venereal disease. An official report declared that 'not less than 25 per cent. of the residents of big towns such as Rangoon, Mandalay, and Bassein have contracted one form or another of venereal disease',[2] and its incidence is acute everywhere. Clinics have now been reopened to assess the extent of the disease in Rangoon and other towns, while eight V.D. teams have been formed under WHO direction, one for each administrative division. So far the numbers undergoing treatment have been relatively few.[3] A third menace comes from tuberculosis: it is estimated that there are probably 300,000 T.B. cases throughout the country. A T.B. clinic has been opened in Rangoon, and another is projected for Mandalay. Ten BCG vaccination teams are working, testing and vaccinating the country people. Leprosy is another disease that has been accorded special attention: there are said to be 100,000 lepers in Burma. Fourteen anti-leprosy clinics have been opened and some 15,000 lepers are receiving treatment.[4]

The last major preventive activity is the maternity and child-welfare campaign. Infant mortality figures have risen since the war (in so far as the present incomplete statistics provide a basis for comparison) and the proportion of infants dying at birth or within twelve months thereafter now approaches one in three.[5] It has not, so far, been practicable to introduce any very adequate measures to relieve this appalling situation. The Rangoon Dufferin Hospital has long provided the main facilities; there is a state welfare centre in Rangoon containing ante- and post-natal clinics and a seventy-bed lying-in ward, and there is a maternity ward at the General Hospital; 250 maternity and child health centres (all in urban

[1] 'World Health and Burma', ibid., 29 April 1954.
[2] Dept. of Information, *Burma, the Fourth Anniversary*, p. 31.
[3] Dept. of Information, *Burma, the Seventh Anniversary*, p. 48.
[4] One of the many informal ties which still link Burma with the Commonwealth is the continued inclusion of Burma within the orbit of the British Empire Leprosy Relief Association.
[5] Pre-war infant mortality was about 18 per cent. Urban figures were almost twice as high as the rural figures: it is possible that the present rate does not fully take into account the lower rural ratio.

areas) have been started throughout the country, most of which are staffed by a lady health visitor and two midwives. Many of these centres have developed out of voluntary welfare work, of which the National Council of Women in Burma is the most prominent example. In addition, UNICEF is supplying expectant and nursing mothers with powdered milk and vitamin tablets. But it cannot be pretended that these measures meet a fraction of the nation's needs.

On the curative side the Government's programme provides for a system of hospitals and dispensaries organized on a national basis. Between April and October 1953 the 150 hospitals managed by local authorities were placed under state control: the administration of the local authorities, never wholly satisfactory, had collapsed after independence with the drying up of their funds. In 1953 there was an administrative re-organization at the centre whereby the health services, pre-viously under three departments, were brought under one Director of Health Services. He is assisted by two Assistants, responsible respectively for Upper and Lower Burma, and by a number of deputy directors who are each in charge of a different service: administration, hospitals and dispensaries, leprosy, tuberculosis, nursing, school and maternity services, laboratories, and public health. The new arrangement provides for a hierarchy of hospitals, largely based upon the existing system but commencing at a lower level.

It is planned to open new rural health centres, with one for every fifteen village tracts, making a total of some 700 in all. The staff will consist of a health assistant, a lady health visitor, a vaccinator, and five midwives. These centres 'will treat simple listed diseases . . . their main duties will be to promote health societies, maternity and child welfare societies, conduct health education and introduce measures for environmental sanitation'.[1] By 1955 centres had been opened in 257 localities and health teams were formed, consisting of (at least) one health assistant, one vaccinator, and one midwife (there is a great shortage of lady health visitors). At the next level most of the former township and district hospitals have been reopened; in 1955 these numbered 43 district hospitals and 225 township hospitals and dispensaries. Many have to be housed in tem-porary *basha* accommodation, but a building programme of 90 new hospitals is envisaged; by 1955 only 3 new hospitals had been actually completed, with 9 under construction. Above the district hospitals it is hoped to create six regional hospitals[2]

---

[1] Ministry of Information, *Pyidawtha Conference*, p. 112.
[2] At Moulmein, Bassein, Akyab or Kyaukpyu, Myitkyina, Taunggyi, and Magwe.

which will receive the services of specialists and will possess a wider range of equipment: this scheme has not yet been launched. Finally, there will be two key hospitals at Rangoon and Mandalay. In April 1954 the President laid the foundation-stone of the Union Central Hospital at Rangoon, which it is hoped to complete by 1958 at an estimated cost of K4 crores or £3 million.

In the formation of a national health service certain further small but useful measures have been initiated. A schools health service was started in Rangoon in 1953, and has since been extended to Mandalay, Moulmein, and Bassein. There are five mobile health units and one mobile dental unit; children are examined[1] and passed on to the maternity and child health clinics for treatment. A pilot health insurance scheme has begun in the Polyclinics Scheme whereby, in return for a monthly subscription (ranging from 25 pyas to K5 according to the subscriber's income) a family becomes entitled to full medical care: two polyclinics were established in Rangoon in 1953 and are said to have proved popular. In 1953 a health scheme was introduced for all government servants, whereby medical treatment is made available to themselves and their families.[2] Social insurance, in the wide sense now operative in Great Britain, is foreshadowed in a few measures. All mothers giving birth to triplets are given monetary grants. Under the Leave and Holiday Act of 1951 workers in factories are entitled to a total of thirty days' leave and thirty days' sick leave with pay every year: it is not clear whether these lavish provisions are actually enforced. Legislation was introduced in Parliament in September 1954 to provide for free medical service and sickness benefits, maternity benefits, and payments in the event of death at work for workers in factories. Contributions will be payable both by workers earning over K48 per month (virtually everybody) and by employers. The scheme was due to come into force in Rangoon on 1 January 1956, and would eventually be extended to other areas. At the time of this announcement it was declared that no scheme of unemployment pay or of old-age pensions could be entertained for the present.[3] At Burma's present stage of development it would indeed hardly be possible to carry matters further.

It should be remarked that in Burma it is less necessary for the State to assume responsibility for those unable to fend for themselves because of the Burmese tradition of family

---

[1] Up to August 1954 120,000 children had undergone examination: 60 per cent. were found to be suffering from physical defects.

[2] *BWB*, 15 September 1953.

[3] ibid.

responsibility. The Burmese family is not so tightly knit as, for instance, the Hindu joint family, but nevertheless any person who is in distress can look with confidence to some relation for support. This support may be offered without undue tenderness; the cousin or niece who is the family drudge is a feature of many Burmese households; but at its least charitable, the Burmese system does ensure a home and food for almost all in want. There are some exceptions—orphan children torn from their villages by the civil war, lost to their relatives, wanderers in the streets of the big towns; but these are exceptions: in general, the only really distressing beggars and vagrants are Indians.

In order to meet the large demands for drugs and serums which mass health campaigns entail, a large pharmaceutical plant is in process of erection. This is an all-British project: the chemists, manufacturers, engineers, and architects who are combining to launch the new industry are all British firms. Work began in April 1954, and a small plant capable of producing several basic chemicals should begin production in 1956; the main plant is to be ready in 1957 or 1958.

In the sector of public health concerned with sanitation and public hygiene the former inadequate services have become markedly less adequate. Only a few major municipalities, such as Rangoon, Mandalay, and Bassein, employ assistant health officers (i.e. sanitary inspectors), there are no medical officers of health available, and if there were, the municipalities could not afford to employ them. Municipal services such as refuse collection, street cleaning, and supervision of the sale of foodstuffs have almost entirely collapsed, and every town provides examples of encroachments on to public spaces and the defiance of building by-laws. Rangoon has, until recently, formed the most conspicuous example of the decay of the corporate spirit, but in 1954 and 1955 some attempts were made to limit the worst *basha* encampments in the main streets and parks. It is still true to say that public opinion is hostile to Western concepts of public health (the destruction of disease-spreading creatures is still not acceptable), and without a transformation of the prevailing Burmese attitudes any advance on the preventive side of public health can only be carried through by massive government action, which is quite impracticable under present circumstances.

The last social-service function with which the State is concerned is that of housing. This work is in the hands of the National Housing and Town and Country Development Board, which has taken over the housing responsibilities of the Public Works Department. A number of housing schemes have been set on foot, notably the building of six-story flats on 51st Street, Rangoon, and the construction of Yankinmyo as a new suburb of Rangoon, with other housing schemes in the environs of the capital. These schemes are designed first to house government servants, and secondly to relieve some of the squatter colonies around the city: by mid-1955 about 2,000 housing units had been constructed. Problems which have exercised the planners have been the absence of a sewage system, except in central Rangoon, the out-of-date character of the city's building regulations, and the high cost of labour around Rangoon where demand exceeds supply. As a result new buildings have been erected at inordinate cost, and it will be impossible to charge rents which bear any relation to costs to the sort of tenant for which they were designed. Plans for low-cost housing, employing timber and local materials, have been mooted; hitherto the bulk of the works constructed by the Housing Board have been designed in steel and concrete, materials which are costly and alien to the traditional Burmese building skills.[1]

It is apparent that the social-service programme falls even farther short of Burma's ideal requirements than the education programme, though many critics assert that in both cases Burma is trying to carry through undertakings beyond her capacity. It appears to the writer that the principal failing of social planning in Burma lies in the introduction of all sorts of luxuries and accessories into the structure before the foundations of basic social services have been firmly laid. There is the importation of elaborate audio-visual equipment for teaching when children lack elementary textbooks and writing materials; the holding of elaborate conferences and seminars on the technique of social welfare when destitute orphans are roaming the Rangoon streets. The desire that Burma shall appear a modern, progressive state to visiting politicians and United Nations officials all too often predominates over practical requirements.

But even this desire is not merely symptomatic of the pride of the new nationalism; it is also based on the genuine desires of Burma's statesmen, technical experts, and officials that their country shall enter a new and better era. This is the great hope for Burma: that cynical exploitation in the name of the people

---

[1] For a fuller account, see Ministry of Finance, *Economic Survey of Burma*, 1954, pp. 65–66, and Dept. of Information, *Burma, the Seventh Anniversary*, pp. 92–94.

for private or class ends prevalent in other Asian countries is almost wholly absent from the leaders of Burma. And the bulk of the people do believe that the social-service planning, inchoate though it may be, is directed to their welfare, to a better future for Burma.

As in other spheres, social service policy was given an almost complete change of direction by the Ne Win régime. All foreign participation in medical and health work was stopped, and the Christian missionary hospitals were taken over by the State: even though there were few Burmese doctors to staff them. Great emphasis was placed upon the goal of social policy as service for the common people. Led by the Colonels, military personnel, civil servants, students, and other privileged groups went into the countryside to labour in the fields and upon road-building and other public works. A university college for the workers was opened to give a second chance to those denied higher education in youth. All these activities were symbolic gestures rather than constructive measures to mobilize the nation. But even as symbols they had some value in bringing together different levels of society in common experience: even if this common experience is, in the expressive phrase of Clifford Geertz, 'shared poverty'.

VIII

THE LAND:
AGRICULTURE AND FORESTS

RICE, timber, oil, and minerals: these were the foundations of the prosperity of Burma during the period of
British rule. Today only rice remains as the basis of
Burma's export trade and of her internal economy. There is
the rueful paradox that whereas the policy of the Government
in these first years of independence has been directed to diversi-
fying the range of agricultural products and to modernizing
methods of production by plans for socializing peasant society,
the actual condition of agriculture in Burma has dwindled
towards a primitive economy not far advanced beyond subsistence level, relying almost entirely upon the raising of
paddy.

The growth of the rice industry is, in essence, the story of
modern Burma: most of the achievements as well as the
problems of the last hundred years are bound up with this
phenomenon. Originally the centre of rice production was in
Upper Burma, especially in the irrigated Kyaukse, Shwebo,
and Mandalay Districts, but the modern rice industry is based
upon the clearance of the Delta jungles during the last century,
during which period the area under paddy in Lower Burma
has increased tenfold.[1] In the 1920's there were $19\frac{1}{2}$ million
acres under cultivation in Burma; of this total, over 11 million
acres were situated in Lower Burma, with 10 million acres
devoted to paddy. Over 8 million acres were cultivated in
Upper Burma, but only about $2\frac{1}{2}$ million were paddy lands.
In Upper Burma the traditional pattern of rural society has
continued relatively stable, with small holdings mainly in the
hands of owner-cultivators and an economy which still rests
upon a 'subsistence' basis. In Lower Burma society has undergone many stresses. The rapid creation of wealth where none
existed before naturally brought many benefits: the cultivator
of the Delta in the late nineteenth and early twentieth centuries
enjoyed a standard of living unequalled elsewhere among the

[1] 1855, 993,000 acres; 1875, 2,379,000 acres; 1895, 5,007,000 acres; 1915,
8,285,000 acres; 1930, 9,911,000 acres. For detailed figures see *Burma Handbook*,
1944, p. 23.

peasants of Asia.[1] But if the first fruits of contact with world capitalism were well-built houses, fine clothes, jewellery, and other modest luxuries, the final harvest was less agreeable. *Laissez-faire* wrought an industrial revolution in Britain: it wrought an agricultural revolution in Lower Burma. The land was cleared and planted by pioneers from Upper Burma, employing traditional techniques, but the new factor, the introduction of Burma's rice in the world market, was brought about by Indian traders and British shippers: they created the whole machinery of marketing and transport. Gradually control over the greater part of the agricultural machine passed into Indian hands: the Burmese cultivator lived increasingly on the future, borrowing on the strength of next year's harvest. And gradually the land passed to non-cultivators, many of them Indians but many belonging to the small Burmese middle class; rents rose and the position of the actual tiller of the soil became ever more precarious. Responsible British officials could see that a peasant-proprietor community was being transformed into an absentee-landlord society, but although many remedies were proposed, no effective action was taken.[2] The whole edifice collapsed in the world slump of 1930, when the market price of paddy fell from Rs.200 to Rs.50 per hundred baskets: the peasant-cultivators failed to pay their debts and the money-lenders foreclosed.[3] As a result in Lower Burma almost 48 per cent. of the farm land passed into the hands of absentee landlords: of this alienated land some two-thirds was now owned by the Chettyar caste of money-lenders from Madras. The Chettyars (who have some 1,600 firms in Burma) have been accused of adopting the most villainous practices in order to enslave the Burmese peasant: in fact the majority of Chettyars are honest business men,[4] thriving, certainly, on the prosperity

[1] J. S. Furnivall in *An Introduction to the Political Economy of Burma* (Rangoon, 1931) states: 'The demand for paddy after the opening of the Suez Canal and its rise in price brought the Delta cultivator more money than he knew how to spend' (p. 148). Mr. Furnivall develops the idea that in the Delta agriculture has the characteristics of industry and capitalism.

[2] This subject is examined at length by B. O. Binns, *Agricultural Economy in Burma* (Simla, 1943), Furnivall, *Colonial Policy and Practice*, and Harvey, *British Rule in Burma*.

[3] The sudden nature of this transfer of land is not always emphasized by writers. In 1926, out of a total cultivated area of 18,271,000 acres, only 3,471,000 were held by non-agriculturalists. In 1935 the total area under cultivation was 19,430,000 acres. The acreage in the possession of non-agriculturalists was now almost double, i.e. 6,138,000. See U Nu's speech to Parliament, 11 October 1948 (printed with the *Land Nationalization Act*, 1948).

[4] cf. Mr. Harvey's view: 'he was the most moderate of money-lenders indeed he was honesty itself' (*British Rule in Burma*, p. 55). The vicious money-lenders were found amongst certain Chinese and Burmese who led their victims to drink or opium and deliberately ruined them.

of Burma's agriculture, but actually averse to becoming proprietors of land, which was not to them a satisfactory asset—not easily to be realized and transferred. However, the Chettyars now found themselves involved in the *laissez-faire* agricultural revolution as involuntarily as the Burmese cultivators.

The various aspects of the agrarian problem, together with attempted remedies, may be analysed briefly under three heads: alienation of lands, high rents, and indebtedness. The growth of an alien landlord class arose partly from the purchase of land as an investment by middle-class Burmans of the official and business classes, but also through the surrender of lands for debt. By the 1930's in the Delta area there were numerous landholdings of 300–400 acres;[1] in Upper Burma holdings remained small and were distributed, very largely, among the actual cultivators whose average holding was from five to ten acres.[2] There was a long history of abortive effort by British officials to halt the process of alienation, but there was little legislation until the 1930's. In particular, Dr. Ba Maw's ministry attempted to produce a remedy in a Tenancy Act (1938) which was devised to fix fair rents. Its purpose was largely frustrated by the faulty drafting of the bill and a lack of trained staff to enforce the provisions. A second measure, the Land Purchase Act of 1941, empowered the compulsory purchase of land for distribution to landless cultivators; it barely became effective before Burma was invaded.[3]

The root cause of land alienation, indebtedness, was also tackled ineffectively by the authorities. The impact of a money economy upon the Burmese cultivator was not gradual but sudden, and the peasant never grasped that a certain reserve of money was a necessary adjunct to the growing of cash crops. Any extra funds were spent on domestic necessities or luxuries, jewellery or more land: there was never a surplus to pay the land revenue, to finance the next crop, or to meet unforeseen troubles. The invariable remedy was that of borrowing: by the 1920's and 1930's between three-quarters and nine-tenths of the agricultural population were in debt, and their total debt

---

[1] Of the lands held by landlords of the 'non-agriculturalist' category 40 per cent. was in the possession of big landlords, some 6,000 in all, who formed only 4 per cent. of the total of owners. See U Nu's speech of 11 October 1948 on the Land Nationalization Bill.

[2] In 1939 in Lower Burma 59 per cent. of the land was let to tenant-cultivators and 48 per cent. was owned by non-agriculturalists; in Upper Burma the percentage for these two categories were 32 (tenancy) and 14 (non-agricultural landlords) (KTA, *Comprehensive Report*, i. 381).

[3] Other measures were the Land Alienation Act (1939), and the Tenancy Ordinances of 1940 and 1941.

amounted to between 50 and 60 crores.[1] Rates of interest were huge (*sabape*, or loans to be repaid out of next season's crop, averaged 250 per cent. per annum). Amongst the money-lenders the Chettyars' rates were, by comparison, the most reasonable and their terms the most regular.[2] The principal remedy evolved by the British Government was the provision of alternative credit through co-operative societies at a rate of interest of 15 per cent. per annum. Beginning in 1905 the number of societies rose to over 4,000 within twenty years with a membership of 90,000. And yet the movement not only failed to solve the problem of debt but by the late 1920's became almost discredited, largely because of the failure of borrowers to repay their loans.[3] During the 1930's co-operative societies were reconstructed, and their numbers revived from only 300 to 1,500 in 1940, with a membership of 30,000.

A problem associated with indebtedness was the growth of rack-renting. Much of the land in Lower Burma was hired out to the highest bidder with no proper security of tenure.[4] The major clearance of the Delta was completed by the second decade of the twentieth century: thereafter considerable competition for land developed in which Indians, with their more humble living standards, were keen contestants. Rents rose to figures representing from 25 to 60 per cent. of the value of the crop, and when interest on loans was also deducted the tenant was reduced almost to the status of a serf. The sudden accentuation of all these problems as a result of the 1930 world slump led to widespread unrest among the agricultural population,[5] but towards the end of the decade prices were rising once again and production was expanding.[6] So much has been written concerning the woes of the Burma cultivator that it may be useful to indicate that this is not a complete picture. A Burmese

---

[1] Estimate made by the Burma Provincial Banking Enquiry Committee, *Report* (Rangoon, 1930). Only about one-third of cultivators were estimated to have accumulated debts beyond their capacity to repay.

[2] Advances on security of land were at 9–15 per cent. (see Tun Wai, *Burma's Currency and Credit*, p. 53).

[3] See Furnivall, *Colonial Policy and Practice*, p. 114. £400,000 or Rs.52 lakhs was overdue out of a total of £450,000 borrowed by 1935.

[4] U Nu's speech of 11 October 1948 quotes examples from Settlement Reports, e.g. Yamethin District, 46 per cent. of tenants were on one-year tenancies (*Report*, 1925–7), Insein, 47 per cent. held one-year tenancies (1933–5), Toungoo, 55 per cent. held one-year tenancies (1910–13).

[5] KTA, *Comprehensive Report*, i. 331. Many observers believed that Saya San's rebellion was in part an expression of agricultural distress.

[6] Paddy prices at harvest time received by the cultivator in the late 1930's were from Rs.100–130 per hundred baskets. The KTA report (i. 358) quotes prices up to Rs.262 per hundred. Christian (*Burma and the Japanese Invader*, p. 109) quotes prices up to Rs.275 per hundred; but the cultivator did not get the benefit of these high prices because of his need to sell immediately after harvest.

official, writing in a Burmese government publication (1953), has this to say of those pre-war days:

> The Burman was not as much worse off as might be imagined, because the fact that the country has an abundance of primary foodstuffs, house-building materials and an equable climate served to make up for his deficiencies in other respects. So all went well with him in the happy years before World War II. . . . Then came World War II to upset his self-satisfaction.[1]

The Japanese occupation did indeed upset everything. Burma was cut off completely from its normal export markets and even internal trade was almost entirely disrupted by the fighting and by the transport breakdown; prices fell to figures lower than in the worst days of 1930 and 1931; in 1941 the Ba Maw Government therefore issued a Tenancy Ordinance reducing agricultural rents by 50 per cent. But this could not check the decline in production and by 1945 the acreage sown was little more than half of that before the Japanese invasion; total production was less than 40 per cent. of pre-war. In 1944 Thakin Than Tun, as Minister for Lands and Agriculture in the Ba Maw Government, announced a scheme for the distribution of the lands of *émigré* landlords to the cultivators. This undoubtedly contributed towards the growing conviction of the peasants that the land belonged to them, not to the landlord or to the Government.

The first measure directed towards the restoration of Burma's agriculture, after the liberation, was the British Military Administration's Rice Project which by the end of 1945 was handling the marketing of a quarter of a million tons of rice.

Area under Paddy (000 acres)

1938–9	1945–6	1946–7	1947–8	1948–9
12,816	6,983	8,242	9,597	10,128

Percentage of Pre-War Cultivation

100	54	64	75	79

Production (000 tons)

8,050	2,822	3,968	5,535	5,264

Paddy yields per acre (nos. of baskets)

30.58	20	23.43	28.09	25.30

During the next three years, the total area under paddy rose once more to over 10 million acres. The yield per acre also

[1] *Burma*, July 1953, p. 15.

worked up towards the pre-war level. This recovery was assisted by a policy of awarding 'bounties' to farmers for every acre brought back into production. But the most significant development of the early post-war years was the fading out of the alien landlord. The Japanese invasion brought an end to almost all the obligations of the tenant-cultivator; rents and debts could be forgotten. A large proportion of the Chettyar landlords fled to India and many Burmese landlords lay low, making no attempt to press their claims. In the political turmoil which followed the British return the peasants found themselves being urged not to pay their dues as a patriotic duty. When the AFPFL came into power, it proceeded to pass a number of measures in 1947 which had the effect of legalizing this new situation: the sitting tenants were given fixity of tenure, rents were pegged at pre-war levels, and agricultural debts were put into cold storage.[1] The immediate effect of these measures upon the landlords is not quite clear; there were transfers of land on a large scale between 1945 and 1947, and many Indian landlords undoubtedly cut their losses, took whatever money they could realize, and went back to India.[2] However, disposal was not simple: there were no sales to the tenant-cultivators who had already obtained all they wanted under the new legislation, and after independence most of the Chettyars were left holding their now worthless title-deeds.[3]

With independence, the AFPFL Government was resolved to carry through an even more radical settlement of the land problem: nothing less than the nationalization of all agricultural lands and the imposition of a '100 per cent. revolutionary' system of collective farming.[4] The early months of 1948 found the AFPFL Government locked in a struggle with their erstwhile comrades, the Communists. The Communists had an almost complete monopoly of peasant support through their superior rural organization, and they placed land nationalization at the front of their programme; in the areas which came under their control they at once began to put through *ad hoc* schemes of land redistribution. The AFPFL in answering the Communist challenge therefore made haste to produce their

[1] The new laws were the Tenancy Standard Rent Act, Disposal of Tenancies Act, and Burma Agriculturalists Relief Act. Under this last act all debts incurred before 1 October 1946 were cancelled outright. For debts incurred after this date, only the principal need be repaid (see Nu, *Forward with the People*, pp. 21–23).

[2] 187,829 acres, 10 per cent. of the total farmland, exchanged hands from 1945 to 1947 (see speech by Thakin Tin, 11 October 1948, printed with the *Land Nationalization Act*, 1948).

[3] See the *Hindu* (Madras) 28 February and 20 March 1954. Chettyar holdings are variously estimated at 2 and 3 million acres.

[4] Words used by Thakin Tin in introducing the Land Nationalization Act, 1949.

own land nationalization programme, and this, together with democratic local administration, appeared in the forefront of U Nu's policy statement of May 1948.[1]

A measure was therefore rushed through Parliament on 11 October 1948 (only two Karen M.P.s opposed its passage) and became the Land Nationalization Act, 1948. Introducing the bill the Minister for Agriculture, Thakin Tin, observed that its 'main provision is to resume all lands held by non-agriculturalists. As regards agriculturalists, they will be allowed to retain up to the extent of fifty acres. . . . *Dhani* land, garden land, rubber estate and religious land will not be resumed.'[2] No definite date for bringing this measure into force was laid down in the act: in fact it was tried out only in one township (Syriam) of Hanthawaddy District, where the experiment was an almost total failure. Mr. Furnivall, always a friendly commentator, attributed this failure to 'favouritism', 'mistakes', 'bribery';[3] the whole scheme was ruined by the incompetence and corruption of the politicians and officials who perverted it for their own ends.

Meanwhile the onslaught of the civil war paralysed the whole machinery of agricultural production and marketing; the area under cultivation once again contracted and did not attain the previous level until 1953. Among the causes of this decline the actual fighting was not significant: more important was the continuing insecurity, the absence of law and order. Many farmers were forced to abandon their former routine of living in field huts to cultivate their more distant holdings; when the harvest was gathered they found themselves often compelled to pay tribute to the rebels and to the more doubtful allies of the Government; and frequently, in the more inaccessible areas, the paddy piled up for months on end, before the ruptured communications system could cope with its disposal.

In consequence the standard of living of the cultivators almost everywhere stagnated and declined. Figures have been produced to show that Burma (with 85 per cent. of its population dependent on agriculture) has a lower standard of living than India or Pakistan.[4] This appears to be debatable; Burmans

---

[1] *Towards Peace and Democracy*, pp. 94–95.

[2] *Dhani*, *Nipa fruticans*, a species of palm whose leaf is employed for roof-thatching. Land belonging to religious institutions, *wuttagan*, or land whose income is applied to religious purposes is specifically exempt.

[3] See *Pacific Affairs*, June 1949.

[4] Annual income per head: Japan, £50; Ceylon, £42; Siam, £29; Pakistan, £23; India, £18; Burma, £13. These figures are quoted in the draft version of *Pyidawtha, the New Burma*, produced by the Economic and Social Board. They have been omitted from the final published version. In 1951 the Oxford economists calculated that the annual income per head in Burma was £14.

must surely still enjoy a better diet than their neighbours
westwards; but the distinct contrast between the condition of
the Burmese and the Indian cultivator, remarked upon by so
many observers in pre-war days, is no longer of much account.[1]
Certain factors today are more favourable to the Burmese
cultivator: the burden of high rents and crippling debts has
been wiped out, and land revenue has virtually ceased to be
levied. But on the other hand, while the population has been
rising, agricultural production, both in aggregate and *per
capita*, has markedly declined. Government policy has concentrated upon the buying of the paddy crop under a state organization, the State Agricultural Marketing Board, and has
imposed a standard price, K285 per 100 baskets,[2] which has
not varied despite the tremendous rise in the world price of
rice and substantial increases in prices of consumer products,
especially all imported goods.

Certain reforms have been introduced by the AFPFL
Government to stimulate agriculture, but many foreign
observers have criticized these as inadequate:[3] certainly,
agriculture, the mainstay of the nation's economy, has received
least attention from the planners and politicians.

For the first three years after independence the Government
was fully occupied in fighting the civil war; one measure was
worked out, the Tenancy Standard Rent Act of 1950, which
laid down that the maximum rent must not exceed twice the
land revenue: as the majority of tenants had long ceased to
pay any rent, the chief importance of the Act was as a declaration of policy. In July 1951 Government summoned a National
Convention on Co-operation. The Prime Minister presented
a co-operative plan to the conference[4] which put forward a
series of broad proposals, including a marketing co-operative
in each village, consumers' co-operatives in every town,
industrial co-operatives, and a nation-wide organization to
supervise their progress, with District Co-operative Unions and
a National Co-operative Council. It was also announced that
the SAMB and the Civil Supplies Department would be
gradually handed over to co-operative control.

---

[1] Tun Wai considers that agricultural incomes 'are probably about the same as
pre-war' (*Journal of the Burma Research Society*, December 1954, part 1). The World
Bank observed that 'the margin of net profit to the cultivator is small or negligible'
(*Economy of Burma*, p. 12). Government rice prices are 'well below parity with prices
of other goods'.

[2] A 'basket' contains 46–50 lb. of paddy. The peasant's price approximates to
£10 per ton. Official calculations rate Burma's prices and wage-rates at four times
pre-war figures.

[3] cf. F. N. Trager, *Towards a Welfare State* (1954), p. 16.

[4] Nu, *From Peace to Stability*, pp. 160–79.

This massive plan was not fully carried through as announced, but there was considerable development in the co-operative movement. Agricultural co-operatives, which numbered 1,982 in 1948, were expanded to 4,428 by January 1955.[1] Forty District Unions had also been formed by 1955, mainly with the purpose of marketing paddy under the central working of the Union of Burma Co-operative Wholesale Society. The volume of paddy handled by the Union Society totalled 150,000 tons in 1952–3, but thereafter production and marketing difficulties restricted its operations.

The original purpose of the co-operatives was the financing of agricultural loans: this has continued to be a prominent function of the movement, and the former defect of failures in repayment has been perpetuated.[2] The AFPFL Government did not consider that the co-operative movement offered sufficient credit facilities to the cultivators (the pre-war system of credit whereby loans to the extent of Rs.20 crores were drawn by agriculturalists from Chettyar and other money-lenders has, of course, completely collapsed). Direct government loans were instituted under the Agriculturalists' Loan Act (1947): this scheme was largely administered by village Land and Tenancy Committees formed almost exclusively of ABPO members, and loans were awarded with a lavish hand —to ABPO supporters, it is alleged.[3] The sums distributed rose rapidly from about 3 crores per annum in the years 1945–7 to almost double in 1952–3.[4] Before independence about 70 per cent. of these loans were being repaid, but thereafter persons who were able to extract loans for political or other reasons saw no reason to bother about repayment.[5] To meet the mounting tide of debt the Government first decided to wipe out uncollectable arrears; in the 1952 budget all arrears from before 1949 were cancelled, a total of 7½ lakhs being wiped off on this

[1] cf. Ministry of Finance, *Economic Survey of Burma*, 1954, p. 81. The gross total number of co-operatives in 1954 was 5,903. (cf. Dept. of Information, *Burma, the Seventh Anniversary*, p. 44) but the *Economic Survey* makes it clear that some registered co-operatives were in fact moribund.

[2] Loans to the extent of K2,29,96,000 were issued in the years 1945–52 (including loans to non-agricultural co-operatives) and the sum of K1,54,27,000 was recovered, a figure which includes some repayments of pre-war loans; 35 per cent. of the advances were not repaid (see Ministry of Finance, *Economic Survey of Burma*, 1954, p. 81).

[3] *Nation*, 11 August 1954.

[4] Figures extracted from *BWB*, 15 September 1955, quoting 1955 *Economic Survey*: 1946–7, K3,37,41,000; 1948–9, K9,573,000; 1952–3, K5,62,72,000.

[5] U Nu has declared that many loans were actually granted to non-agriculturalists as political subsidies. Many peasants declared that they would pay up only when others did: many believed (and believe) that when the Government come to accept that they cannot realize their debts, they will cancel all outstandings (see Nu's speech to ABPO annual conference, *BWB*, 23 June 1954).

occasion. U Tin hoped that this 'would enable the cultivators to start life, as it were, afresh'[1]—but in fact this gesture only seems to have encouraged the defaulters. In mid-1954 the over-due debts had risen to over 7 crores, i.e. almost half the total advances made as 'direct' loans.[2] This unhealthy situation has caused increasing concern to the Government and particularly to U Nu. He devoted the major portion of his address to the 1954 ABPO conference to this theme, concluding 'Frankly speaking, if the situation does not improve, things cannot go on at this rate for long. It will be the painful duty of the Union Government to put a stop to the whole process.'[3] A further conference was convened five months later (November 1954) to hammer home the vital importance of this problem to ABPO leaders. Apart from exhortation, the Government hopes to regularize agricultural credit by the creation of an agricultural bank. Proposals for such a bank were put forward in 1948 by a committee presided over by J. S. Furnivall, but the bank was not finally established until June 1953.[4] The head office is located at Rangoon; it started with branches in Mandalay, Pegu, Insein, and Henzada Districts. The branch banks deal with their clients through intermediary village banks and co-operatives.[5] The proportion of loans which was repaid as they fell due was encouragingly high.[6] With this promising beginning, the bank's activities were extended to five additional districts for the 1954–5 season. In the first case cultivators are permitted to borrow up to K20 per acre, but during the 1954–5 season, in the four original districts this has been raised to K35 per acre. The rate of interest is 12 per cent. per annum. For the season 1954–5 the percentage of repayments has fallen ominously to 62.[7] Now that the harsh process of foreclosure and dispossession for debt no longer operates, the Burmese cultivator has little incentive to learn the basic lessons of the mechanism of credit. Meanwhile, as compared to pre-war commercial credit facilities, the present-day state credit

---

[1] Dept. of Information, *Burma, the Fourth Anniversary*, p. 6.

[2] Up to 1954 K16,07,88,677 had been issued in direct loans since 1947, and only K8,78,69,636 had been recovered (see Ministry of Finance, *Economic Survey*, 1954, p. 78).

[3] *BWB*, 23 June 1954. The total of loans issued has fallen considerably from the peak figures of 1952–3, but it would hardly be politic to cancel the loans entirely in the months before a general election (due April 1956).

[4] State Agricultural Bank Act of February 1953.

[5] First year, 50 village banks, 214 co-operatives.

[6] An account of the State Agricultural Bank included in Dept. of Information, *Burma, the Seventh Anniversary* quotes (p. 33) a repayment rate of 97·4 per cent. Later figures (*Economic Survey*, 1955) indicate that final repayments 1953–4 were equal to 79 per cent. of the advances.

[7] *Economic Survey*, 1955, reproduced in *BWB*, 15 September 1955.

structure remains restricted in scope, thus affecting the possibility of restoring pre-war production.

Another measure introduced by the British Military Administration and continued by the AFPFL Government was the payment of a subsidy of K10 for each acre brought back under paddy cultivation. The first goal was the reclamation of the millions of acres which had gone out of production during the Japanese occupation—and later during the civil war. In 1950 the paddy acreage was some 72 per cent. of the pre-war figures; by 1954 about 81 per cent. of the pre-war acreage had been reclaimed. Of the abandoned lands, which amount to 2½ million acres, 70 per cent. lie under wild grass, and the remainder is 'infested with scrub trees and bushes'.[1] The paddy acreage subsidy payments have totalled K245 lakhs, which may be held to have assisted in rehabilitating almost half a million acres.[2] By mid-1954, with the termination of the international rice boom, the Government reversed its policy and withdrew the subsidy, clearly believing that the paddy acreage should now be consolidated rather than expanded.[3]

While encouragement of paddy production was the first priority of the Government during the period of post-war rice shortage, its long-term policy has looked towards a more diversified system of agriculture. The first important planning statement was produced at the 1952 Pyidawtha Conference, which sketched out a 'Five-Year Agricultural and Rural Development Plan', providing for a number of 'commodity projects'.[4] The over-all purpose of this programme was to make Burma self-sufficient in the production of foodstuffs and to make a substantial contribution towards the production of raw materials which would supply projected industries, notably cotton and jute. Once again, the first task was to restore pre-war levels and to rehabilitate abandoned land; in some instances the aim was to cultivate a better quality strain, and in particular to introduce the culture of long-staple cotton. The major sections of this programme (which ought to reach fruition by 1958) were a proposed increase in the area under paddy by 3 million acres, an increase for groundnuts of 700,000 acres, and in new cultivation the growing of 150,000 acres of jute and 200,000 acres of long-staple cotton.

To implement these plans an Agricultural and Rural

[1] IBRD, *The Economy of Burma*, p. 12.
[2] See Nu, *BWB*, 10 November 1954.
[3] Dept. of Information, *Burma, the Seventh Anniversary*, p. 29.
[4] There were separate projects for rice, groundnuts, cotton, pulses and beans, soya beans, sugar-cane, onions, spices, wheat and barley, jute, maize, tobacco, tea, coffee, coconut, vegetables, livestock, dairy products, fish.

Development Corporation came into being in October 1952, with U Nu as Chairman. The policy of the corporation has largely concentrated on the award of acreage subsidies (as, for example, K15 per acre for new groundnut land, K50 per acre for jute) and the provision of improved seed to the cultivator. The first three years after the Five-Year Plan was inaugurated do not provide much evidence as to the future course of development. Expenditure was much below budget estimates: K7 million in the first year, K20 million in 1953–4, and K15 million in 1954–5. Agricultural production reached a post-war peak in 1952–3, and declined in the following two years, partly because of unfavourable climatic conditions, partly because of the slackening in world demand for Burma's products. Production of crops other than paddy has been

AGRICULTURAL PRODUCTION, PAST AND FUTURE
(000 tons and acres)

	1938–9		1952–3		1953–4		Plans, 1959–60	
	ACRES	TONS	ACRES	TONS	ACRES	TONS	ACRES	TONS
Paddy	12,816	8,050	10,331	5,740	10,398	5,527	13,300	9,000
Sesamum	1,401	53	1,328	54	1,352	44	1,500	55
Ground-nuts	808	180	744	176	821	191	1,500	326
Pulses	1,329	198	1,050	181	1,108	187	1,600	280
Cotton	453	18.8	294	24	304	22	500	32
Sugar-cane	64	520	65	384	70	400	90	730

(SOURCES: *Economic Survey*, 1954, pp. 11 and 12; *Pyidawtha Conference*, p. 28.)

restored more fully to pre-war output, and in a few cases has actually outstripped the former level. But the 1952 plan for a diversified agriculture cannot yet be said to have got under way: rice still accounts for 63 per cent. of the sown acreage of Burma (67 per cent. pre-war) and is not only the sole profitable export crop but also the one crop which the great majority of the cultivators know how to grow.

The KTA report did not produce any co-ordinated plan for agriculture, although it presented a useful survey of several outstanding problems and made certain specific proposals, in particular with regard to irrigation. However, agricultural policy has been restated in *Pyidawtha, the New Burma, Report . . . on our Long-term Programme for Economic and Social Development*, published in 1954 by the Economic and Social Board. This formulated a general target of production increases of 77 per cent. over 1951-2 levels by 1960. This would raise production to approximately 33 per cent. above pre-war levels, a not over-ambitious target (especially as the country's population will at the same time have risen by some 25 per cent. since 1940)—yet by 1955 agricultural production was still only some 80 per cent. of the pre-war figures.

The chief measures to implement this plan are

the return of all previously cultivated land to active production . . . an increase in per acre yield through improved farm practices . . . large-scale irrigation projects, introduction of new crops and new plant varieties, improved marketing and storage facilities, expansion of farm facilities, expansion of government research into agricultural problems, expansion of educational and advisory services.[1]

Certain aspects of this programme have already been touched upon: most of its proposals are only now being brought to the first stage of practical exploration.

Large-scale irrigation, which received most attention in the KTA report, had by 1956 made no progress. Irrigation canals have existed in the central districts of the dry zone (where the rainfall is an uncertain 20-40 inches per year) for centuries, and during the British period the area under irrigation (mainly in the Mandalay and Sagaing Divisions) was increased to over $1\frac{1}{2}$ million acres (1939). During the years of civil war some 106,000 acres have had to be abandoned.[2] The Irrigation Department possesses a cadre of trained Burmese engineers, but as yet their work has been confined to routine 'special repairs and minor works', a few petty improvements.[3] Draft schemes have been put on paper for a number of massive new projects which would open up about 2 million acres to cultivation.[4] Preliminary surveys have been initiated, but against the background of the present phase of consolidation rather than expansion actual construction is unlikely to follow for several years.

The introduction of improved strains of seed is being under-taken in a series of 'pilot' ventures such as a cotton-seed farm at Meiktila, nurseries for seed coconuts, an onion-seed farm in Kyaukse District, and the production of Virginian tobacco in

---

[1] Economic and Social Board, *Pyidawtha, the New Burma*, p. 30.
[2] KTA, *Comprehensive Report*, i. 403.
[3] Phrase used in *Economic Survey* of 1955, reproduced in *BWB*, 22 September 1955.
[4] The Mu River Project, Yamethin District Project, Kandaw Village Project, and Loikaw Area Project are the most important (see Economic and Social Board, *Pyidawtha, the New Burma*, pp. 39-41).

Mandalay District.[1] The translation of these activities into better production figures is, however, dependent on outside factors such as prices, marketing organization, and availability of consumer commodities for the rural population.

Among the new ventures 10,000 acres were planted under jute in the year 1954–5 as a first step towards producing the raw material for the proposed gunny factory.[2] The acreage under long-staple cotton was expanded to about 50,000 acres in the same season, producing 13,000 bales of cotton for the government textile mill. The other projects should begin to show results within a few years. At present, these new ventures are necessarily supported by government subsidies, technical services, and other assistance: it will not become apparent for some time whether these crops can be produced in competition with other world producers.

Government research and advisory activities are at present extremely limited—in the first place, by the small numbers in the agricultural and veterinary services.[3] During 1954 a ten-fold expansion of the Agricultural Department over the following five years was sanctioned by Government, but it may not be simple to obtain the necessary recruits. Considerable difficulty is being experienced in enrolling students for the Agricultural College at Mandalay, and the numbers studying agriculture represent about 2 per cent. of the total student population.[4] In addition, youngsters passing out of the high schools are now offered a two-year course at Pyinmana Agricultural Institute: the first batch of fifty began training in July 1954. The eight farm-schools in the Union provide ten-month courses for promising peasant lads: formerly about 150 passed through these schools each year, but in 1954 the numbers were stepped up to 400. On completion of training a proportion are taken into the Agricultural Department as Field Men: the remainder return to their villages and, it is hoped, will act as village leaders.

As has been mentioned, the Department is responsible for a number of research and demonstration centres. There are eight central farms, at Hmawbi (concerned primarily with rice culture), Mudon, Myaungmya, Akyab, Mandalay, and

---

[1] *Burma*, April 1955, pp. 5–7.
[2] See below, p. 306.
[3] The 1951 Administration Reorganization Report listed (p. 40) 32 Senior Branch officers, 100 Junior Branch officers, and 137 Field Men. The World Bank in its report of November 1953 stated that there were only fifty agricultural officers in Burma: this discrepancy may be due to transfers to the Agricultural Development Corporation and to non-agricultural departments (including the Foreign Office) where pay and prospects are better.
[4] Ministry of Finance, *Economic Survey of Burma*, 1954, pp. 77 and 86.

elsewhere.[1] The most important centre is at Pyinmana; this was established by the American Baptist Mission and provided a training and research centre before the war. After independence this establishment was taken over by the Government and is now operated in association with the Ford Foundation, who provide a nucleus of American agricultural experts. These are experts of a sort that Burma can use in plenty: men who are ready to get their hands dirty, and who demonstrate to young Burmans that advanced theoretical knowledge is quite compatible with manual toil. Pyinmana has been particularly associated with experiments in mechanized farming. While the role of the tractor can be over-stated—it has acquired a tremendous symbolism to the disciples of both the Russian and the American ways of life—it could be useful in Burma both in agriculture and forestry, in which the pre-war animal 'labour force' has been greatly depleted. There are some twenty tractors at Pyinmana, and a tractor expert has been hired from Israel: during 1955 1,000 acres of land for groundnuts was prepared by tractor and some machines have been hired out on contract to farmers, with successful results. A new Agricultural Research and Training Institute is at present being built at Gyogon, near Rangoon, to replace the former research establishment destroyed during the war. There will be eight 'divisions', dealing with different subjects: three Dutch experts have been engaged to lead the new venture which is expected to begin work in 1956.[2]

The functions of the Veterinary Department include the treatment of animal diseases, training, and the promotion of improved breeding. Activities at present are largely concentrated at the Veterinary College and Research Laboratory at Insein. The numbers in the veterinary service are even more inadequate than in the agricultural service, and those under training numbered less than seventy in 1955.[3] The Department has the important task of reinforcing the cattle production of Burma: during the war years the numbers of plough cattle declined by one-quarter, largely due to seizure by the Japanese army and to unchecked epidemics. Subsequently, attempts have been made to replace losses by importing cattle (as from Australia and Pakistan) and by improved breeding; numbers have risen to more than 90 per cent. of pre-war.[4] Experiments have also been conducted in modern dairy farming.

[1] In pre-war days there were 14 experimental farms and 5 seed farms.
[2] Dept. of Information, *Burma, the Seventh Anniversary*, pp. 97–98.
[3] *Burma*, July 1953, pp. 56–59; 'Veterinary Services in Burma', *Burma, the Seventh Anniversary*, pp. 39–40.
[4] Ministry of Finance, *Economic Survey of Burma*, 1954, p. 13.

All these activities indicate the intentions of the Government to stimulate agricultural production, but by far the most widely publicized activity has been the revival of the policy of land nationalization. The AFPFL hold upon the allegiance of the people has always been most slender in the countryside, where the underground Communists have continued to exercise a strange compulsion on the loyalties of the peasants: at the same time the cultivator has become uneasily aware that the rice he is compelled to sell to the Government for about £10 per ton has been exported by the Government for £50–60 per ton. He thinks that he is being exploited to bolster up the country's finances and he is dissatisfied, despite the virtual cessation of liability for rent and land revenue and the receipts of bounties in the shape of unrequited loans and acreage subsidies (when they have not gone astray to political hench-men).[1] In order to secure the support of the cultivator, there-fore, the Government has given wide publicity to the nationalization of the land and its allocation to the tillers of the soil.

Following the failure of the 1948 Act the Government moved most cautiously in formulating further legislation. One feature of the 1948 Act was the omission of any definite basis for compensation for land forcibly expropriated;[2] the frank inten-tion of the Government was to award only 'nominal' compen-sation. This aroused immense indignation amongst the dis-possessed landlords and particularly amongst the Chettyars, who called upon the Government of India to intervene on their behalf. In June 1950 a delegation headed by the Indian Ambassador to Burma, Dr. M. A. Rauf,[3] conducted con-versations with the Government of Burma. As a result an undertaking was given to lay down a definite scale of com-pensation.

A new bill was passed through Parliament in September 1953;[4] it was also designed to introduce a greater measure of popular supervision over the actual process of distribution, in order to mitigate the corruption and political domination which has permeated the activities under the 1948 Act.

The 1953 Act authorizes the President to order the resump-tion of all lands (including waste-land) except such as may

---

[1] Rents are said to amount to only one-sixth or one-seventh of the pre-war figure (KTA, *Comprehensive Report*, i. 155).

[2] See Land Nationalization Act, 1948, sect. 7 and Schedule II.

[3] A brother of M. A. Raschid, Minister in the Government of Burma.

[4] The main provisions of this bill were drafted considerably earlier, and the Government began to put them into force in June 1953, in anticipation of the bill's being carried through Parliament unaltered: an interesting sidelight on the relation of Parliament to Government in Burma today.

qualify for exemption. Among those to whom exemption is granted are 'agriculturalist families'[1] and to any 'non-agriculturalist family' whose head undertakes to reside permanently on his land and work it himself,[2] and to all land dedicated to religious purposes.[3] The 1948 Act imposed a limit of 50 acres as to the amount of paddy-land which an 'agriculturalist' family might claim for exemption: this restriction is varied under the 1953 Act: an additional $12\frac{1}{2}$ acres is admissible for every member of the family over a total of four adults.[4] Land which is resumed is to be distributed to 'agriculturalist families' who are citizens of the Union, and who must undertake to join whatever agricultural organization may be formed (i.e. mutual-aid teams, or farmers' co-operatives, of which more later). The new 'allottees' shall be endowed with certain rights in their newly acquired land, including the right to sell the land,[5] to exchange it for any other agricultural land, to bequeath it freely, or to split it into sub-divisions. The work of redistribution is entrusted to a hierarchy of land committees. There are a Central Land Committee and District Committees, who are all nominated bodies charged with supervising the election and working of Village Land Committees, who are to carry out the actual redistribution process. Provision is made for appeal against the decisions of the village committees.[6] Chapter XVIII lays down the principle that compensation shall be paid in accordance with a definite schedule; the first 100 acres of a holding are to be paid for at a rate equivalent to twelve times the land revenue; the scale of payment falls until the rate for acreage above 1,200 is a flat rate equal to the land revenue.[7] The manner in which compensation shall be

[1] Ch. III defines an 'agriculturalist' as one who is engaged in cultivation, or who supervises the actual cultivation of the land, which must form his principal means of subsistence; one member of such a family must have been in possession of the land from 4 January 1948, the land must have been worked since that date, and a majority of members of the family must be citizens of the Union.

[2] This concession is a departure from the 1948 Act which excluded all non-agriculturalists. Such families are limited to a maximum holding of 20 acres of paddy-land. The residence qualification, even, may be waived—providing that the non-agriculturalist works the land. See Ch. III, sect. 6, clause (e).

[3] Ch. III, sect. 7, sub-sect. 3, permits a member of a religious order to hold land providing that the income is used for religious purposes.

[4] A father with three sons and two daughters, all over 18, would be entitled to retain 75 acres. A married agriculturalist son living separately would be regarded as a separate family, entitled to a full 50 acres.

[5] The Act lays down that land must be sold to the agricultural organization to which the family belongs: this proviso appears to be modified in practice.

[6] 1953 Land Nationalization Act, Chs. VIII and XIV.

[7] According to the graduated scale, the owner receives the benefit of the higher rates upon part of his acreage: thus for a holding of 500 acres the owner will receive compensation at rates varying from twelve to eight times the land revenue, making an average payment of ten times the land revenue on the total acreage. Some 95 per cent. of landowners in Burma hold 500 acres or less.

awarded is not defined in the Act, but is to be worked out in rules to be framed later. Finally, the 1953 Act repeals the 1948 Act, and cancels all awards made under this Act in Syriam township.

The 1953 Act is much more carefully worked out than its predecessor and is more detailed in its provisions (in its English version, it runs to 54 sections and 43 pages, as compared with the 20 sections and 9 pages of the earlier Act) but, nevertheless, it leaves as much undecided as it purports to decide. For example, it begins with the statement that 'it shall apply to the whole Union of Burma', whereas the constitution explicitly excluded all matters appertaining to land and agriculture from the Union legislative list, and specifically included these subjects in the states' legislative lists (Union constitution, 3rd schedule). As a result, the states have refused to entertain any schemes for land nationalization within their areas.

The declared aim of the Government was to nationalize some 10 million acres, and yet another 'plan' was announced for the establishment of a New Order for peasants, to be spread over the decade 1953–63. Thakin Tin, Minister for Land Nationalization, delivering his presidential address to the ABPO in June 1953 outlined the measures which would be taken to implement this plan.[1]

Thakin Tin explained that it would first be necessary to train organizers to supervise the scheme, and then would follow the election of the land committees which, he promised, would be 'neither AFPFL nor ABPO, but . . . elected by the peasants themselves'. Distribution would, roughly, result in each family receiving a holding sufficient to be worked by one yoke of oxen (normally about 10 acres); these farming families would then join together in mutual-aid teams consisting of five families who would 'co-operate in cultivation . . . manure lands by modern methods, and borrow loans and market their produce collectively'. The redistribution of the 10 million acres would be completed by the end of 1955.[2] As experience of co-operative methods was gained, so every four teams would be grouped together in Agricultural Producers' Co-operatives: during the years 1956–62, he declared, the 200,000 mutual-aid teams would have become 50,000 co-operatives, when 'the system of agriculture will change from present obsolete methods to fully mechanized agriculture'. But even this will be a transitional phase: from 1954–5 (according to Thakin Tin)

---

[1] See *Seventh Annual Conference of the All-Burma Peasants' Organization*, published by the Ministry of Land Nationalization, 1954.

[2] *Seventh Annual Conference of the ABPO*, p. 16.

producers' co-operatives would be grouped into collective farms of 800–1,000 acres: a complete revolution in Burmese agriculture would be accomplished.[1]

As with most plans, the first years of the programme have not yielded the expected dividends. By the end of 1954 the area distributed amounted to 142,737 acres, and by late 1955, when according to plan nationalization should be almost complete, a total of 604,435 acres had been nationalized—about 6 per cent. of the target figure.

Problems which have retarded the implementation of the programme include, as always, insecurity: an inability to carry out elections or redistribution because of rebel activities, lack of trained personnel, and the unreliability of political elements who use nationalization for their own ends. The first schemes carried through in 1954 applied to eight townships, in which certain areas (normally selected because of favourable security conditions rather than in relation to economic needs) were designated for nationalization. In these 167 village tracts, 142,737 acres were nationalized and 125,495 acres were exempted: thus 47 per cent. of the areas was unaffected by the new reform. An official account of these developments stated that 'more than 16,000 landless tenants and some agricultural labourers have been raised to the status of landowning agriculturalists'.[2] The Ministry has laid down a certain 'order of priority' in which allocation of land shall be made: first priority goes to working tenant-farmers and small landowners with less than 10 acres; the second group are 'other landlords', i.e. those whose holdings are less than the optimum for which they would be entitled to claim exemption;[3] then come the landless farm labourers, and finally any other village residents (such as weavers or other artisans).

In order to discover how these arrangements fall out in practice, a more detailed study of the process of redistribution in Amarapura township might be helpful.[4] The order for nationalization was given on 6 June 1953. Out of the 95 villages in the township, 24 were selected for nationalization during 1954 (the 24 nearest to Mandalay and therefore most securely under government control). Twenty-eight more were scheduled for nationalization in 1955. In November 1953 it was

[1] Thakin Tin planned the establishment of 8 collective farms by the end of 1954 and of 66 such farms between 1956–62.
[2] Dept. of Information, *Burma, the Seventh Anniversary*, p. 19.
[3] e.g. the owner of 45 acres who has four grown-up sons might expect to receive up to 17½ acres in addition. See above p. 239 and n. 4.
[4] The writer was afforded facilities to examine this undertaking with the local land settlement officials.

announced that nomination for candidates for election to the village committees (each with a membership of seven) would be accepted: in the event, no elections were held as nowhere did the number of candidates exceed the vacancies: everywhere the local leaders of the AFPFL and the ABPO were accepted as the natural committee members. These new members were given fifteen days' training at Amarapura.[1] The first task was to prepare lists of all cultivators, the second to consider applications for exemption; this occupied from December 1953 to March 1954. In all, 1,516 cultivators were granted exemption in respect of 9,418 acres: in every case these holdings were much below the 50 acres permitted to be retained; 353 acres were recognized as the property of religious persons or institutions, 54 in number.

Then came the work of nationalization. In practice, this was very largely a matter of readjusting the holdings of the sitting tenants. An 'economic holding', which in theory is the basis of redistribution, was calculated as being from 10 to 18 acres in Mandalay District: the actual units allotted were all very much smaller.

As the first priority, 6,818 acres were apportioned among 1,036 families, i.e. tenants and small cultivators possessing less than one-fifth of a 'yoke' of land (about 2 acres). Then 795 acres were distributed to 259 landowners with holdings of up to 10 acres. Finally, 4 field-labourers were allotted 25 acres, and 96 villagers who were not agriculturalists were given 303 acres; 2 co-operatives were confirmed in their holdings of 78 acres. Out of a total acreage of 17,780 acres, 7,941 acres (or 44 per cent.) were affected; but in great part this was merely a matter of confirming the sitting tenants in their existing possessions. The pattern of agricultural life remained almost entirely undisturbed: the minute area transferred to labourers and non-agriculturalists (less than 2 per cent. of the land under review) is only sufficient to give these few folk allotments with which they might supplement their ordinary daily labours.[2]

The new scheme does not appear to have caused much excitement among the twenty-four villages affected: there have been about 200 appeals, mainly from two particular villages, and these appear to be occasioned by the failure of the local government information service to acquaint the villagers

---

[1] A cadre of *wundanhmus*, or organizers, have been trained at Toungoo to supervise the work of the village committees.

[2] Whereas the average award to tenants and small land-holders is about 7 acres, the labourers and non-agriculturalists receive an average of 3 acres, quite insufficient to provide them with a living.

with the implications of the new scheme. By early 1955 no mutual-aid teams had been formed or were even being planned in Amarapura township; farming went on in its age-old ways.

A similar pattern emerges elsewhere. Pyinmana township in Yamethin District was the largest area brought within the scheme in 1954: 70,479 acres were under review. Of these, 48,888 acres owned by 7,129 cultivators were exempted from nationalization. Thus 70 per cent. of the area was exempted: in two village tracts all the land was exempted. Of the 21,591 acres nominally redistributed, 1,800 acres were left in the hands of the sitting tenants, 2,698 were added to the holdings of small landowners, and only 884 acres were transferred to new owners, i.e. 330 labourers who each received a small-holding of 2·7 acres.[1] At Pyinmana mutual-aid teams were formed in June 1954, but they did not introduce co-operative methods of farming.

During 1955 the pace of nationalization has been stepped up and almost half a million acres has been 'nationalized'. The target figure for resumption has been scaled down from 10 million to 6 million acres,[2] and the date for completion is revised to 1956. One of the largest schemes of 1955 was in Hlegu township of Insein District where 45,000 acres were reapportioned among 3,000 cultivators (the larger size of individual holdings, compared with the Upper Burma districts, may be noted). Altogether, by late 1955 distribution schemes had been carried out in 678 village tracts situated in 33 townships scattered through 28 of the 33 districts of Burma proper. It seems unlikely that the full 6 million acres will be brought into the scheme within the target period, despite a big effort to press through as much as possible before April 1956, when the national elections were held. If the suggestion that nationalization is being used to fortify the political position of the AFPFL and the ABPO seems unworthy, attention should be paid to the manner in which the presentation of certificates is stage-managed. In every township affected a massive ceremony is organized under ABPO auspices, and in almost each case a Cabinet Minister presides, often with other Ministers present; their speeches are afforded wide publicity through government propaganda organs, and in all possible ways the contrast between the good works of the AFPFL

---

[1] *BWB*, 16 June 1954. Of the redistributed land 15,000 acres had previously belonged to three once-powerful landlords.

[2] Out of a total of 6,226,150 acres, 5,470,253 are paddy-land, 662,717 are *ya* (upland), 83,700 are *kaing* (island or inundated land), and 9,480 are sugar-cane.

Government and the barren promises of the Communists is emphasized.[1]

What exactly is the status of the cultivator after nationalization? Is he now a landed proprietor, or does he hold the land on trust from the State? The 1953 Act gives no clear indication.[2] In Burmese he is termed *Mye ya shi thaw taungthu le tha ma*, which merely indicates that he is the cultivator of the soil. The constitution declares that 'The state is the ultimate owner of all lands': but the rights of the new 'allottees' are almost as extensive as acknowledged landlords elsewhere. The 'allottee' can sell, divide up, or transfer his land as he pleases; the only restriction which appears to obtain in practice is that land received under nationalization can only be sold to one who undertakes to reside within the village, responsible himself for working the land. This provision will tend to keep land within the existing village community. Altogether it becomes clear that land nationalization carried through on the present model will not 'revolutionize' agricultural society, as its protagonists have so often and so loudly proclaimed. It is true that when landlordism is abolished there is much greater security of tenure, and the industrious peasant is given a useful incentive to farm his land better and to make improvements, secure in the knowledge that he cannot be evicted; but the feckless land-holder will be given security to ruin that land and persist in his folly.[3] Either way, nationalization will not transform Burmese agriculture as collectivization did in Russia.

Two features of the new venture remain to be recorded. First, the new rights which the cultivator acquires are little more than the receipt of a piece of paper, a land certificate. Land nationalization is supposed to be accompanied by a new survey of the actual ground which will determine the new boundaries of the holdings and provide legal evidence as to ownership. In the case of Amarapura township positively, and in the case of all other areas probably, the entire scheme has been worked out on the basis of dusty old settlement surveys, thirty or more years out of date. Unlike the settlements carried

[1] Thus Thakin Chit Maung, Minister of Information, at Yegyi, Bassein District: 'The AFPFL Government is distributing land free in order to free the peasants from the bondage of absentee landlordism. What the recalcitrant oppositionists and the multi-coloured insurgents could not do, the AFPFL Government had accomplished. . . . It was therefore imperative for the peasants to unitedly co-operate with the government' (*BWB*, 2 June 1955).

[2] The English translation of the Act made by the Ministry (which is specifically not authoritative) refers only to 'agriculturalists'.

[3] The Government does contemplate taking sanctions against those 'allottees' who fail to repay loans or omit to pay their land revenue. One result of nationalization will be that a defaulting tenant will not in future be able to shelter behind a landlord's inability to pay revenue: the allottee will himself be the landlord.

out during the British period, the latest operation is merely an office transaction, the tracing of lines upon out-of-date maps: there is no physical verification of the boundary marks and the rights of the cultivators by walking over the actual fields with measuring rod and chain. After another decade, when land has been sold and divided and disputes arise, such matters will have to be settled by rough and ready justice; there will be no reliable records to which the dispute can be referred.

Secondly, although the Land Nationalization Act lays down a scale of compensation for dispossessed owners, no word is said about payment by the new legatees: in fact the land is received free of any obligation and the State assumes the entire responsibility for payment of compensation. This would appear to place a heavy burden upon the tax-payer, but upon inquiry it becomes evident that the Government is making no provision whatever for the payment of compensation. No consideration has been given to the form it shall take—whether in cash or government bonds—no budget provision is ever mentioned, and in none of the many financial forecasts for the development of the nation's economy does land compensation ever feature as an item in the balance sheet. A silent decision seems to have been taken at some stage: to expropriate the land without payment;[1] after all, the case is different from that of industry, where the Government still wishes to attract foreign capital to Burma.

The Government does not regard nationalization as the last word in agricultural reform. Once again there is a buyer's market for rice, and the poor quality of Burma's produce within recent years has been losing her customers. Part of the solution lies in better marketing methods, but production also needs to be improved. The Government has now begun to institute measures to improve standards. A short-term scheme is the raising of high-quality paddy on government farms. In 1954 15,500 acres were planted with high-grade seedlings by peasants who were given unprecedented incentives, including loans at the rate of K50 per acre to a total of K7 lakhs. This paddy was distributed as seed during the 1955 planting season and served for the planting of 140,000 acres; it is hoped to use this in turn to provide seed for planting 1 million acres in 1956, and so on to 9 million acres of high-grade paddy in 1960.[2] Another innovation is the institution of prizes for the best crop

[1] The Union constitution lays down (sect. 23). 'Private property may be . . . expropriated . . . in accordance with law which shall prescribe in which cases and to what extent the owner shall be compensated.'

[2] *BWB*, 29 September 1954 and 9 June 1955.

yields, on a district and a national basis: almost 7 lakhs were allotted for prizes in 1954.[1] Finally, the Government decided that the existing organization of the Agricultural and Rural Development Corporation and SAMB was not sufficiently comprehensive and co-ordinated. Many plans and programmes had been promulgated, and some were mutually inconsistent, even irreconcilable. On 23 November 1954 a new superorganization was established, the Land and Agricultural Planning Commission: this incorporates divers bodies, governmental and political,[2] but its 'teeth' will be provided by an executive committee headed by the Financial Commissioner, U Ba Htay.[3] The first task is the preparation of a comprehensive agricultural plan for the whole Union. Inevitably, foreign experts are being brought in to assist: two from Israel, and two provided by the ILO arrived in mid-1955.[4]

In pre-war days Burma was noted almost as much for its teak as for its rice: it was the world's leading exporter of both commodities. If Burma has kept something of its old importance as a rice-growing country, timber has dropped low down the list of the country's products. In 1940 there were about 34,800 square miles of 'reserved' forest and about 139,000 square miles of unclassed forest. In the latter areas the population was free to cut timber, but from the reserved forests timber was extracted only under licence or lease. Strict control was maintained to conserve the forests and to check the extraction of immature trees.[5] The export of teak and other hardwoods was largely in the hands of five large British companies; the Forest Department also directly participated in timber extraction, being responsible for about 20 per cent. of the total brought to Rangoon in the 1920's. Departmental activity was later restricted to permit Burmans to compete with the big firms.[6] The largest Burmese (actually Indo-Burmese) concern was U Ba Oh & Sons.

During the war years all organized forestry ceased completely. Perhaps most important, the great labour force of trained elephants, numbering over 6,500, was scattered and many were lost; when their numbers were reckoned up at the

[1] *BWB*, 17 November 1954.
[2] The first general meeting of the Commission, held on 7 May 1955, was attended by, among others, the Minister for Industries, members of the Social Planning Commission, high officials and AFPFL and ABPO representatives from all over the Union (ibid., 19 May 1955).
[3] ibid., 2 June 1955.
[4] The agricultural plan was due to be completed by 31 March 1956.
[5] A teak tree with a circumference of seven feet round the trunk takes over 160 years to grow.
[6] *Report of the Indian Statutory Commission*, xi, 55.

war's end only 3,000 could be traced.[1] At the same time the reserved forests were indiscriminately plundered, much damage being caused by the Japanese army;[2] some 260,000 acres of forest land were devastated. Much of the Forestry Department's plant and buildings were also wrecked.[3]

After the liberation the big timber firms were formed into a teak consortium, and a partnership was established between the firms and the Government. This was managed by a Timber Project Board, with equal representation for the Government and the companies. With the advent of independence the AFPFL Government declared its intention of nationalizing one-third of the teak concessions, and from 1 June 1948 the teak forests in the Pegu Yomas were taken over by the Government. However, as internal security collapsed, the teak firms found themselves unable to work their concessions, and later in the same year they voluntarily surrendered all their rights in return for an immediate consignment of timber. The State Timber Board became responsible for working the reserved forests of the whole country.[4] The State Timber Board took over the activities of the Timber Project Board and became responsible for extraction, milling, and marketing, including export sales. The Forest Department (much depleted by the dismissal of its foreign officers) is responsible for the general supervision of the forests and for research.

The effect of the insurrection was to bring the industry once again to a halt. In the production of teak there are a number

TEAK PRODUCTION
(tons)

Output		Exports	
1941–8	249,872	1947	51,994
1948–9	214,210	1948	76,280
1949–50	30,881	1949	34,302
1950–1	127,595	1950	12,474
1951–2	128,000	1951	45,983
1952–3	132,673	1952	29,943
1953–4	115,000	1953	25,710
1954–5	133,000	1954	20,582

NOTE: Average output 1935–9, 475,600 tons; average exports, 274,000 tons.

(SOURCES: Burma Chamber of Commerce, *Review for 1954*; *Economic Survey, 1954*; *The Times*, 23 November 1955.)

---

[1] KTA, *Comprehensive Report*, iii. 1947.

[2] 'The Japanese army . . . cut down our most valuable teak trees for air-raid shelter props, &c.' (Nu in *BWB*, 14 July 1954).

[3] *Burma*, April 1953, p. 71.

[4] See Dept. of Information, *Burma, the Fourth Anniversary*, pp. 36–38, for a fuller history.

of interrelated processes. First, the trees must be girdled and left to stand for three years, otherwise the wood will be too heavy to float in water. Then, having been felled, they must be hauled to a local river, whence they will be floated to the Chindwin, Salween, or Irrawaddy, where they will be lashed together to form great barges and floated down to the sawmills. Clearly interruptions at any one stage of the process can bring about cumulative delays later on. Thus girdling was neglected for several years after independence, and when after 1951 it became possible to resume large-scale felling, the inadequate girdling of previous years soon hampered expansion.[1] Floating the logs down from Upper Burma to Rangoon is an operation taking many months, or even years; as a result, the sawmills at Rangoon continued to work at low pressure up to 1954. Late in 1955, as the security situation improved, it became possible to reopen the Sittang River (previously dominated by the KNDO) to timber traffic. Under the protection of the army, nearly 6,000 logs were floated down-river from Toungoo. This was not completed without counter-attacks by the rebels. Even after these operations, by far the greatest proportion of the extracted logs remained up-country, unshifted.[2] It seems unlikely that timber will ever again hold the key place in the economy which it occupied in former times.

The Forest Department, which at one time was second to none, has considerably diminished in stature. Its senior members are still men of high calibre, but they are frustrated by lack of constructive work, and several seniors have transferred to other departments; the total number is now considerably less than pre-war.[3] The present responsibilities of the Department are not precisely clear: 'conservation', the control and replenishing of the forests, seems to be largely at an end. The present-day emphasis is on 'natural' rather than 'artificial' regeneration.[4] A recent visitor quotes a forest officer as declaring that 'the Government had abandoned the reafforestation plan in favour of encouraging natural growth'.[5] The very limited opportunity which the present writer had of judging the position is in line with this observation: the forest reserves, seemingly, are becoming choked with a secondary growth,

[1] Ministry of Finance, *Economic Survey*, 1954, pp. 14–16.
[2] *The Times*, 23 November 1955; the *Nation*, 3 December 1955, reported 30,000 tons of seasoned teak in central Yamethin District awaiting transportation.
[3] In pre-war days there were about 230 senior staff (conservators, &c.); now there are 134.
[4] cf. 'The Forest Department', *Burma*, April 1953, p. 73.
[5] Ethel Mannin, *Land of the Crested Lion*, p. 105.

there is no thinning or clearing of the forests, the old trees crash down and ruin the young saplings: it forms a melancholy scene. But natural growth in Burma is so luxuriant and the forests are so widespread that the unregulated jungle may well suffice to meet the present reduced needs of the industry.[1] As regards the working of the forests, the elephant force has been further reduced in the years of civil war and is now said to number 1,200.[2] The remedy is sought in increased mechanization. In former days experiments in mechanization were not a success, but recent rapid strides in forestry technique in America and elsewhere may show a new way. Since March 1955 direct extraction by tractor and haulage by truck has been employed in an experiment which, it is said, 'has obviously not been operating long enough to permit reaching any conclusions'.[3]

Recent forestry policy in Burma has largely been formulated under the auspices of the FAO. Emphasis has been switched from the production of teak for export to the exploitation of 'jungle wood' for home consumption and the erection of 'fabricating units' for the manufacture of doors, windows, &c., on mass-production lines. The possibility of utilizing the 'waste' from the sawmills—calculated to represent 60 per cent. of the timber extracted from the forests—in new processes, such as the manufacture of 'chipboard', is also being explored by FAO consultants. All these ventures still remain at the planning stage.

During 1954 reafforestation was viewed by the Government from a different aspect—that of soil conservation. In a speech on 27 June to celebrate World Festival of Trees Day, U Nu gave a warning of the dangers of erosion and climatic deterioration which might follow from the indiscriminate cutting of trees. He declared that every year 200,000 acres of trees are destroyed in the hill tracts in order to make possible the system of shifting cultivation. He observed that 'our reserved forests are being exploited without any thought of the future'. As an immediate remedy 300,000 seedlings would be planted to celebrate the World Festival, and provision would be made for the establishment of nurseries of seedlings throughout the Union.[4] In addition, there are to be more concentrated projects,

---

[1] An official statement expresses the hope that a production of 500,000 tons of teak and 900,000 tons of other hardwoods will be achieved by 1960 (Economic and Social Board, *Pyidawtha, the New Burma*, p. 51). This appears to be straining optimism too far.
[2] ibid., p. 51.
[3] Ministry of Finance, *Economic Survey*, 1955, quoted in *BWB*, 22 September 1955.
[4] *BWB*, 14 July 1954.

in particular a scheme to reafforest 200,000 acres in three districts in the central dry semi-desert zone—Magwe, Myingyan, and Meiktila.[1] It is notable that these and other reafforestation projects are to be administered not by the Forest Department, but by the Agricultural and Rural Development Corporation. The danger of soil erosion may appear remote, in view of Burma's miles of evergreen forest, but the dead city of Pagan, brooding in a desert which was once a garden, affords a grim warning of what might come to pass.

Thus, in agriculture and in forestry Burma is confronted with both short- and long-term problems whose solution would tax the ingenuity of any government. But Burma has much on which to build: a climate perfectly adapted to monsoon agriculture and land in abundance for the population.[2] Burma's fields and forests will yield in plenty: if trade can be encouraged and order maintained (no small caveat) the people can, as in past generations, look with trust to their land to fulfil their every need.

[1] *BWB*, 6 October 1954.
[2] In Burma there are 2 acres of cultivable land for every member of the population. Comparable figures per head for neighbouring lands are, India 1·1 acres; Pakistan 1 acre; Ceylon 0·8 acre; Japan 0·2 acre.

IX

TRADE

FOR Burma, with a large surplus of certain commodities and an almost equally large deficit in other requirements, foreign trade is of vital importance. In the 'colonial' period Burma's commerce was integrated with that of Britain and India; this triangle has remained the basis of trade into the 1950's, but there are indications that new patterns will evolve in response to independent Burma's experiments in trade, diplomacy, and national finance.

The growth in the volume of Burma's trade during the British period was spectacular, and was much more rapid than that of India during the same years. Between 1868 and 1926 Burma's exports were expanded twentyfold; whereas in the same years India's exports underwent a fivefold increase only.[1] Except at rare intervals, Burma always enjoyed a favourable balance of trade: the annual surplus of foreign exchange was largely absorbed by the profits of British, Indian, and Chinese capital, by 'invisible' items such as insurance and shipping costs, and by the claims of the Government of India, Burma's 'overlord' until 1937, for 'services rendered': some positive (such as the provision of credit for railway construction), some a little nebulous (such as the defence of the Afghan frontier). Burma's trade ties became increasingly involved with India: at the time of political separation, India was taking three-fifths of her neighbour's exports and supplying over one-half of her imports.[2] Indeed, the economies of the two nations were strikingly complementary: India needed Burma's rice, timber, and oil products; Burma wanted India's coal, textiles, iron, and steel.

Burma's overseas trade was conducted almost entirely with the sterling area; the only important outside countries with whom there were dealings were (in order of importance) Japan, Germany, the Netherlands, and Belgium. All the non-sterling countries accounted for less than 10 per cent. of Burma's trade.[3]

[1] Burma's exports increased from 3·22 crores in 1868–9 to 65·47 crores in 1926–7, thereafter falling away (1939–40, 54·75 crores). Imports for the same period were 1868–9 2·75 crores, 1926–7, 38·65 crores, 1939–40 25·22 crores. cf. India, 1868–9, exports 55·8 crores, imports 31·7 crores; 1926–7 exports 301 crores, imports 231 crores.

[2] Furnivall, *Colonial Policy and Practice*, p. 182.

[3] Figures for the years 1935–40 are quoted in great detail in *Burma Handbook*, 1944, pp. 31–39.

The only countries with whom Burma had an unfavourable balance of trade were Japan and the United States.[1] Roughly half the exports were made up of rice; about one-quarter were the products of the oil refineries; minerals accounted for 12–14 per cent. and timber for approximately 7 per cent. of the total exports in terms of money value.

Burma led the world in the rice trade: nearly 54 per cent. of the net rice exports of Asia (not counting trade between Formosa and Korea with Japan as external trade) came from Burma. The flow of rice from Burma to India represented on the one hand 90 per cent. of India's rice imports, on the other 50–75 per cent. of Burma's exports; about three-quarters of India's intake was processed rice, the remainder being paddy. Ceylon and Malaya were also regular customers taking some 25 per cent. of Burma's exports.[2] A specialized market for high-quality rice lay in Western Europe: Germany was the biggest buyer, utilizing rice in the production of alcohol and in industry, and the Netherlands was another big importer. In the United Kingdom the imperial preferential tariff of 1*d*. per pound acted in Burma's favour. Other important markets were the West Indies and Mauritius. Burma catered for each of these customers with special types of rice, varying not only in size, quality, and colour, but also in the techniques of preparation for sale.[3]

Burma's second most important series of exports, oil products, was largely absorbed by India. The petrol and kerosene oil on sale throughout South and East India were largely supplied by Burma oil companies. Paraffin wax and candles were also exported to a wide range of countries, Britain being by far the largest customer for the paraffin wax. Burma was the world's leading exporter of teak; some two-thirds to three-quarters of Burma's surplus timber was sent to India, with Britain as the only other major consumer. Indeed, the only class of exports in which India did not largely figure was that of minerals: India took almost all the tin, and a little lead and silver; everything else—wolfram, copper, zinc, and most of the lead—was exported to Europe and Japan.

The handling of this export business was largely conducted by a small number of powerful British companies of long standing. The only competition came from a Scandinavian and a Dutch firm, and relatively unimportant Indian, Chinese,

---

[1] Burma imported lubricating oils from the United States and from 1937 began to buy several hundreds of cars and other vehicles.

[2] Siam and Indo-China found their main customer in China.

[3] Dept. of Information, *Burma, the Third Anniversary*, pp. 49–56.

and Japanese merchants. Burmans only participated in the process as middlemen in the rice and timber trade.[1]

The return which Burma received for her exports was composed largely of consumer goods. Textiles and clothing accounted for almost one-third of the total, with foodstuffs making up about one-quarter. Paper, fuel (mainly coal), metallic manufactures (hardware, iron and steel, &c.), and machinery formed the other major items. About 55 per cent. of these imports came from India, some 18 per cent. from the United Kingdom, and about 8 per cent. from Japan. This import trade was conducted largely by the same big Rangoon firms which controlled the export business, with the addition of some smaller European agencies whose range might include whisky, surgical instruments, and motor-cycles. Few of these importers were in a position to offer technical advice or, in the case of machinery or equipment, maintenance services and supplies of spare parts. Their only positive contribution to the distributive process was their specialized knowledge of conditions in the Burma trade.

The internal commerce of Burma reflected situations previously noticed in administration and external trade: others had forestalled the Burmans in many positions. A small sector of the retail trade, what might be described as the 'luxury' trade, was controlled by British department stores, such as Rowe's, with a large establishment in Rangoon and branches in the chief towns. But the major portion of the retail trade in textiles and 'stores'—household goods of foreign origin—was in the hands of Indian merchants, many of them Gujaratis or Khojas. Certain special lines (such as the car trade) were largely manipulated by the Chinese. Burmese commercial enterprise was almost entirely confined to petty trading, especially to the sale of fresh foodstuffs, cheroots, local jewellery, and hand-woven textiles. In all but the most remote villages there was a demand for imported goods: Japanese umbrellas, Indian cottons and hurricane-lamps, British bicycles; so that every large village had its Indian or Chinese store. A large proportion of the purely Burmese commerce was carried on in markets, large and small, where almost all the stall-holders would be women, Burmese women having an excellent business sense.

The Japanese invasion utterly disrupted almost every section of trade, internal and external. India and all the Western markets were now cut off completely. Previously only 10–15 per cent. of Burma's trade had flowed towards the Far East,

[1] Furnivall, *Political Economy of Burma*, p. 158.

and the Japanese 'Co-Prosperity Sphere' showed itself quite unable to absorb the surplus stocks which now lay unmoved. Siam, Indo-China, and to some extent Malaya and Indonesia were all able to adapt their trade patterns into the Japanese hegemony. Burma, right at the end of the line, could not: seaborne trade was precarious, and the Burma–Siam Railway, when it was at last completed, was almost entirely utilized for military traffic. In consequence Burma's foreign trade fell to something like 5 per cent. of the pre-war level.[1] The only important 'export' after the occupation was the seizure and transhipment by the Japanese of quantities of loot: vehicles, machinery, scientific instruments, and scrap metal, including all the metal statues.[2] Imports were limited to a little sugar from Java, some textiles from Malaya, cigarettes from Siam and Japan. The internal trade promptly reflected the collapse of foreign trade: there was a slump in paddy and other primary products, and the prices of consumer goods jumped to twenty or thirty times the normal. The breakdown of communications splintered the national economy into fragments: while rice was rotting, unsaleable, at Bassein, there was an acute shortage in the Upper Burma districts. The only healthy development in this period was the revival of handicrafts and cottage industries to replace the usual imports of factory products.

Another feature was the change in the management of business and trade. All the British and many of the Indian and Chinese leaders of big business left Burma. The role of the British was taken over by Japanese industrial combines: in banking the Yokohoma Specie Bank and the Southern Development Bank took over from the predominantly British 'exchange' banks. In trade and industrial development, where firms like Steel Brothers and the Bombay-Burmah Company had been supreme, Mitsui Bussan Kaisha, Mitsubishi Shoji Kaisha, and some fifty other firms now reigned. But in the retail and distributive trades Burmese mercantile associations under Japanese supervision played a much larger part in affairs than in pre-war days.

In 1945, as the Japanese régime crumbled, this façade of commercial activity collapsed. The country had been flooded by Japanese currency notes, the so-called 'banana currency',

---

[1] This statement is derived from the admirable short summary of economic conditions under the Japanese prepared by Dr. J. R. Andrus. See Burma Intelligence Bureau, *Burma during the Japanese Occupation*, ii, 173.

[2] The Burmese say that the statue of Sir Arthur Phayre 'refused to leave Burma': it was dropped in the mud of Rangoon River, and was later restored to its old site. The kindly inhabitants of Moulmein bought back their statue of Queen Victoria from the Japanese, and returned it to its plinth, where it still stands.

which had all along steadily lost its value and now became almost worthless.

The country to which the British returned was virtually bankrupt, and was only kept solvent through the following two years by assistance from the British Treasury. Nevertheless, as lines of communication were restored, the docks repaired, and the paddy-fields planted, the national economy came back to life with surprising rapidity. Recovery was, of course, greatly aided by the demand created through the world shortage of foodstuffs, especially the hunger throughout the rice-consuming countries of Asia. The returning British Government introduced into the economy, both internal and external, a considerable degree of state control and even state trading. Prior to the actual return two 'procurement' missions had been set up, one at London and one in India, to obtain supplies of food, clothing, and capital goods for liberated Burma. Distribution of these essential supplies inside Burma was entrusted to a Civil Supplies Board, partly non-official in membership, with a Commissioner as chairman and chief executive. The Board had to put into effect a rationing system in Rangoon and an allocation system in the districts. This organization came in for much criticism, and an Inquiry Committee, appointed in 1946, recommended its abolition. In May 1947 its assets and functions were transferred to a (temporary) Civil Supplies Department, but meanwhile political control had passed to the AFPFL with its Socialist programme, and an AFPFL committee, headed by U Ba Win (elder brother of Aung San), recommended that the Civil Supplies organization should not be wound up, but rather that its functions should be expanded. In particular two objectives were suggested, the introduction of a 'most rigid form of rationing, something on the lines of the British system' and secondly, the promotion of consumers' and wholesalers' co-operatives. As a result, consumers' co-operatives ('concos') were set up in every township to distribute bulk imports. The major items of export were also dealt with by semi-state organizations, the Rice Project, and the Timber Project Board (the oilfields were still ineffective after war-time destruction; the mines were also barely in production).

In 1946 the whole process of rice marketing was handed over to the SAMB. The post-war world rice situation was perilous: whereas pre-war world exports averaged 8·6 million tons, in 1946 the world exports were only 2·2 million tons. While South East Asia had been paralysed under the Japanese grip, new producers had been expanding their output in the Americas, the United States and Brazil being the principal producers, with Ecuador, Mexico, and Chile assuming increasing importance. An emergency world allocation system was worked out under the International Emergency Food Control Organization. Thereby Burma's rice was largely directed to its old markets, India and Ceylon, but with increased exports to the Far East.

RICE: WORLD ALLOCATION, JANUARY 1946–DECEMBER 1949

	Quantity (million tons)	Proportion of world total (per cent.)
Burma	3·79	30·4
Siam	3·32	26·6
Indo-China	0·64	5·1
Australia	0·07	0·5
Egypt	0·98	7·8
U.S.A.	1·87	15
Brazil	0·83	6·6
Others	0·72	5·7
Outside allocation scheme	0·32	2·3

Apportionment of Burma's share, Jan. 1946–Dec. 1949
(per cent.)

United Kingdom	2
Malaya	17
Indonesia	7
China	6
Japan, Korea, Ryukyus	2
India/Pakistan	42
Ceylon	19
Others	5

(SOURCE: *Burma, the Third Anniversary*, p. 53.)

Burma's traditional customers, India and Ceylon, now drew considerably more than half of their requirements from new suppliers, Egypt, Brazil, and Siam among them.

Selling arrangements for Burma in these early years were handled by the British Ministry of Food. Picking up slowly, Burma's rice exports reached their peak in 1947–8:[1] this was only one-third of the volume of pre-war figures, but with the new high prices, relative to world prices of other food-grains, the pre-war exports were rapidly overtaken in value. At first imports were in excess of exports as attempts were made to repair the war-time damage to the nation's equipment, but by 1947 a balance had been reached and Burma entered independence with the customary favourable balance of payments restored.

[1] 1945 100,300 tons, 1946 431,000 tons, 1947–8 1,251,000 tons. This total was not equalled again until 1953–4.

	1945–6	*1946–7* (crores)	*1947–8*
Imports	19·4	47·3	59·6
Exports	6·7	47·9	75·7

A dangerous feature of these early post-war years was the flight of foreign capital from Burma. During 1946–7 30 crores was transferred out of the country, very largely to India: in the following year the total rose to 39 crores. Thereafter a rigid system of exchange control was enforced, and during 1948–9 these transfers declined to just over 3 crores.[1]

With the coming of independence the relations between the foreign business community and the new AFPFL Government were not cordial, and the suspicions of the foreign merchants were intensified by the hasty introduction of nationalization measures and by numerous Marxist out-pourings: the reasonable assurances of the Prime Minister did not succeed in allaying these suspicions.[2] A certain amount of foreign investment had come into the country during the years 1945–8, but this now dried up completely. At the same time the onset of civil war interrupted production and disrupted communications. During 1948 300,000 tons of rice were reported to be lying in up-country godowns which could not be moved.[3] The effect upon trade was widespread: not until 1951 were the 1947 export figures overtaken, and further recovery thereafter was languid. The seizure of the oilfields and of all the mineral areas in Karenni and Tenasserim by the rebels killed any hope for the early revival of these industries, while the ferrying of logs down to Rangoon and Moulmein also completely ceased. The revolt had the effect of wrecking the government distribution organizations: out of 42 Civil Supplies establishments in the districts only 16 survived. Stores were pilfered and damaged; everywhere prices soared, reaching the highest levels in July–August 1949.

Even at its lowest point, the Nu Government managed to keep some sort of authority in the rice ports and somehow trade went on. It would have been possible for the rebels, especially the KNDO, to prevent supplies of rice entering the ports, thereby making exports impossible and driving the Government into bankruptcy. But the rebels, divided in their counsels, never made the attempt: they calculated that they were drawing revenue from these same rice supplies, and they too

[1] Tun Wai, in *Journal of the Burma Research Society*, December 1954.
[2] Nu, *Towards Peace and Democracy*, pp. 164–6.
[3] *Nation*, 14 January 1949.

depended on this revenue to support their own 'governments'. And so the Nu Government survived.

The SAMB was broadly responsible for internal purchases and external sales, but in 1948 84 per cent. of the paddy crop was bought by private traders and only 16 per cent. by the Board; about 40 per cent. was sold overseas by direct government deals.[1] During 1949, as prices began to rise rapidly, the procedure of selling through the agency of the British Ministry of Food was abandoned. This procedure had ensured ready cash for Burma (the Government received credit for 90 per cent. of the price as soon as a consignment was aboard ship at Rangoon) but had pegged the price at £38 per ton. For a while British buying was transferred to Siam, a departure which was much resented in Burma.[2]

World demand for rice was stimulated by the outbreak of the Korean War in June 1950, leading to a rush by the United States and other countries to stockpile raw materials, thereby driving prices skywards. Even though rice was not among the commodities directly affected it was much in demand, world supplies still being inadequate. Before 1940 rice was slightly cheaper than wheat, bulk for bulk, a ratio of 90 : 100 or 100 : 100 being normal. But in the post-war years the ratio has become wheat 100: rice 300. Even so, a complete 'sellers' market' prevailed, the deficit nations competing avidly for any available supplies. A contemporary Burma Government analysis of the situation included this candid comment: 'During this post-war period of acute shortage the deficit countries are in such dire need of supplies that any rice, so long as it is adjudged fit for human consumption, will sell easily. This encourages the tendency to lower the quality of the rice delivered.'[3] The only exceptions were the nations of Western Europe, who remained particular about quality, and they tended to draw their purchases from Brazil or Italy, whose rice was even more costly but still retained its quality.

During these years the SAMB extended its grip upon the trade; during 1950 20 per cent. of the crop was permitted to be exported by private traders, but thereafter all (or almost all) passed through government hands. Internal buying was also taken out of private hands: 98 per cent. of rice purchases in 1952 were undertaken by government agency, much being handled by the co-operatives.[4] This entailed a rapid expansion of the state marketing agencies (the SAMB employs a total of

[1] Burma Chamber of Commerce, *Annual Review* (see *Nation*, 26 February 1949).
[2] *Nation*, 25 December 1950.
[3] Dept. of Information, *Burma, the Third Anniversary*, p. 54.
[4] *Union Bank of Burma Bulletin*, 4th Quarter, 1953.

1,300 persons) and neither men nor methods were scrutinized particularly closely: the SAMB was making handsome profits, presenting the Finance Minister with his largest source of revenue, and there seemed to be every cause for satisfaction. The volume of rice exports remained almost constant over the years 1948–53, but the value in the same years was doubled.[1]

One important new feature of these years was the introduction of reciprocal trade agreements between Burma and the more important consumers of her rice. The first was an agreement with India, negotiated between May and September 1951; this fell into two parts, the first providing for an immediate exchange of commodities (240,000 tons of Burma rice against gunny bags, groundnut oil, cotton yarn, and galvanized sheets) and the second for further exchanges over a four-year period.[2]

The pattern of imports was also undergoing change. The Imports Control Act of 1947 had regulated the flow of goods by a system of licences. Thereby quotas were laid down for different classes of commodities, and the import of certain luxuries was entirely prohibited: orders from abroad could be placed only if a licence had been obtained from the Ministry of Commerce. As part of its policy of 'nationalization' (in the sense of reducing foreign control over the economy) the AFPFL Government laid down an allocation of 60 per cent. of the licences to nationals and 40 per cent. to foreign firms. This innovation was of doubtful value; dozens of mushroom Burmese import firms sprang up, without capital, without the slightest experience of trade, their only asset some obscure connexion with an influential politician or official. When such concerns received their licences they promptly peddled them around amongst the foreign firms, so that most commodities continued to be imported and sold by the foreigners, with the new Burmese 'importers' drawing commission on the transaction but playing no useful part whatever in the economic process. U Nu gave his opinion that '98 per cent. of the indigenous business men were dependent . . . upon the big British, Indian, and Chinese business men',[3] and the KTA consultants, who certainly were not predisposed to look with favour upon British and Indian interests, presented a lengthy indictment of the functioning of the licence system in their 1953 report, commenting upon

[1] Rice exports:

	1948–9	1949–50	1950–1	1951–2	1952–3	1953–4
Volume (000 tons)	1,194	1,129	1,367	1,161	1,200	1,300
Value (K million)	595	576	758	809	1,019	810

[2] Full text in Dept. of Information, *Burma, the Fourth Anniversary*, pp. 39 and 40.
[3] *Towards a Welfare State*, p. 19.

The granting of licences without investigation to wholly unqualified persons, provided only that they were Burmese nationals . . . the open sale of these licences to foreign trading firms, the accompanying favouritism and sometimes corruption, the maintenance of exorbitant profit margins on scarce commodities—these things are commonly acknowledged.[1]

Licensing was somewhat relaxed in 1950 and 1951 when certain classes of imports (such as cotton piece-goods) were placed under Open General Licence, which meant, virtually, that they could be imported without licence. This resulted in a rapid increase in the volume of imports, assisted by a much more liberal issue of licences in respect of the restricted items, especially in the next year (1952).

VALUE OF IMPORTS (in crores)

	Open General Licence	Licence	Total
1950	14·6	30·36	44·96
1951	32·84	21·01	53·85
1952	41·34	24·24	65·58

(SOURCE: *Burma*, April 1953, p. 29.)

The majority of these imports were obtained from the sterling area, with which Burma's trade ties remained strong: up to 1953 over 60 per cent. of Burma's trade was conducted with the sterling area.

	1948	1949	1950
	(per cent.)		
Exports to sterling area	86·5	79·7	60·9
Imports from sterling area	81	76·3	73·5

(SOURCE: *Union Bank of Burma Bulletin*, 4th Quarter, 1953.)

This alignment was soon to be challenged. An early warning came in the case of textiles. Britain had been first in the post-war field, and from 1948 to 1951 the bulk of Burma's supplies were British goods. Japan, however, was feeling the way back into this former market, and after 1951 Japanese cottons—at distinctly lower prices—largely displaced the British. Over-all, however, the pre-war trade configuration continued, with India as the most important source of supply and Britain as a strong second source.

Burma's commercial network retained many of its former features, but British business activities were now confined almost entirely to Rangoon. The big British banks have not

[1] KTA, *Comprehensive Report*, i, 178.

opened their former branches at Mandalay or the ports, the big retail firms have closed down their up-country branches, the import-export houses have ceased to participate in productive enterprises within the country. The Civil Supplies Board has only eighteen district branches: the blow inflicted by rebel attack upon the organization in 1948 is still felt. The Indian business community still continues to provide the commercial backbone of the country; the ornate houses of the Chettyars stand empty, often half-destroyed, but Gujarati traders are found in many country towns: their absence may be taken as an indication of acute agricultural depression in a district. Well-stocked Chinese shops are also to be seen in many of the towns. But altogether in these years when the fires of revolt have been stamped out, yet still smoulder on, the volume of internal trade has remained very weak: of 1952 an official review recorded 'business continues slow, unemployment hangs on, consumer demand stays weak, inventories remain high':[1] such a verdict remains valid for the years that followed.

While the AFPFL Government devoted incessant attention to problems of industrialization, and produced some measures for the support of agriculture, the subject of trade—the lifeblood of Burma—was largely overlooked. The foreign merchant was regarded not as fulfilling a vital economic function, but as a leech, living upon the labour and natural resources of the country. At the 1952 Pyidawtha Conference practically the only reference to trade was a pronouncement by U Nu which well illustrates the general attitude of Burmese leaders that the foreign traders serve no useful function. Describing the pre-war economy, he observed,

Although the annual profits from the rice trading ran into crores, it was not a difficult undertaking. To be precise, all the activities related to the rice trade, from ploughing the swampy paddy lands with oxen, to final loading of rice in hessian bags aboard the outgoing ships, were carried out by Burmese themselves. The British merely poured [*sic*] through accounts books beneath the ceiling fans in their offices. Besides, the rice trade was not subject to any severe international competition. . . . Hence, inasmuch as the rice trade fetched fabulous profits it was not difficult to handle. . . . Like the rice trade, the timber industry was easily manageable by ourselves. The entire operations . . . were done by our own nationals. . . . Like rice, too, the timber market was not very competitive and the buyers vied with each other to buy our teak.[2]

The only other allusion to trade at this conference was in

[1] *Union Bank of Burma Bulletin*, 4th Quarter, 1953.
[2] *Towards a Welfare State*, pp. 6 and 7.

connexion with the announcement of the KTA industrial programme which would entail an expenditure of K250 crores in foreign currency. 'It should not be difficult to meet this requirement fully from domestic resources', the Minister for Industry and Mines declared, and passed on to deal with more important matters.[1]

One year later the Government came out with a definite pronouncement on trade policy. U Nu declared that up to that time 'not much success had been achieved' by Burmese traders and would-be industrialists, despite such measures of support as the reservation of 60 per cent. of import licences to nationals. The Government anticipated that 'our people will soon degenerate into agents and stooges of foreign commercial interests'. U Nu therefore announced that in future licences to import restricted commodities would be issued almost without stint—to those Burmese enterprises which could establish direct contacts with foreign manufacturers, to whom loans at low cost would be available from the Government. This programme[2] represented a direct effort to squeeze out foreign companies and to stimulate Burmese enterprise, but the immediate effects were insubstantial.

During 1953, almost imperceptibly, Burma's position in world trade slid into a less favourable balance. 'One sign of the changes to come emerged in Japan's attitude to Burma's rice. During 1952 heavy buying by Japan was one of the main factors in driving prices up to the limit in November 1952. Yet by late 1953 Japan was already demanding certain guarantees before concluding further purchases.[3] It was still far from clear to expert observers that the boom had attained the highest point of the curve. In this year prices up to £90 per ton were obtained for best quality rice, as Burma's transactions were on a government-to-government basis, with prices agreed for a stipulated period, the highest prices were missed: but the SAMB was receiving £60–£70 per ton in the middle of the year. The harvest of 1952–3 was the best following the war, and exports were a record: in June 1953 the reserves of foreign exchange attained a peak figure of K126·9 crores or £97 million. Nevertheless, large stocks of rice could not be shipped owing to delays at the Rangoon docks. Moreover, all over the world harvests were good in 1952–3, and for the first time in ten years

---

[1] Ministry of Information, *Pyidawtha Conference*, p. 41.
[2] 'Our Goal and our Interim Programme', address at National Day Mass Rally by U Nu, 1 December 1953. Published, together with report of Economic and Social Board, under first title (Government Publications, 1953).
[3] It is relevant to interject that some of the rice consigned from Burma to Japan in 1953 was adjudged unfit for human consumption.

supply was equal to effective demand. By the end of 1953 prices were beginning to weaken.

At first the Government discounted the possibility of excessive stocks, as first reports indicated that the 1953–4 harvest would be small. A considerable portion of the previous crop was still lying in warehouses unsold, but this was not regarded as a danger. Overtures from foreign countries for sales at reduced prices were viewed without interest. Finally, in December Burma concluded an agreement with Japan—and accepted definite cuts in prices: shipments during 1954 were to be made at £50 per ton and thereafter at reduced rates. Meanwhile the new harvest was being reaped, with warehouses still full of the previous paddy crop: some 900,000 tons lay unsold in government stocks. During December the SAMB suspended all purchases, and prices in the rural markets slumped in response: at Tharrawaddy only K180 per 100 baskets was offered (about 60 per cent. of the official rate).[1]

Even during the opening months of 1954 the Government was reluctant to accept the idea of a worldwide fall in rice prices; they continued to make plans in the belief that there was a temporary glut only, which consumers were attempting to exploit to force down prices artificially. They were influenced by the advice of their American consultants who continued to assure them that rice would find its level at £55 or at the least £50 per ton.[2]

At last the Government took alarm: the stocks in the godowns were deteriorating, and buyers were still holding off. Almost desperate, Burma turned to her oldest customer, India. A series of discussions followed in Delhi; bargaining was stiff; Burma wanted £50 per ton, India was prepared to pay only £30; neither side was disposed to give way. Finally, an agreement was signed by U Win and M. A. Raschid for Burma which accepted the specified price of £50 per ton during 1954, £48 for 1955, and £46 for 1956—but subject to the stipulation that £15 per ton should be set aside in partial repayment of Burma's post-separation debt to India. The total delivery was 900,000 tons (equivalent to the whole of Burma's accumulated surplus), which might be spread over three years at the above-quoted rates, or might be supplied entire during 1954 at a price equivalent to the three-year average (i.e. £48 per ton).[3]

[1] *Nation*, 24 December 1953.
[2] And yet in 1948 U Nu had forecast with astonishing accuracy that the rice boom would have a duration of five years (see *Towards Peace and Democracy*, p. 83).
[3] Full text in *BWB*, 21 April 1954. Burma's debt to India amounted to 20 crores: approximately 15·6 crores would be repaid under the above arrangements. The remainder was to be waived and regarded as Indian Colombo Plan aid to Burma.

For several years India had been taking a decreasing share of Burma's rice: the new deal brought India back as the leading customer.

RICE SALES, 1949–54
(per cent.)

	1949	1950	1951	1952	1953	1954
India	31	30	24	28	15	39
Ceylon	21	25	29	17·5	14·5	15
Malaya	11·5	8	4·5	9	13	2
Indonesia	11	15	16	14	19	10
Japan	4	6	14	11	19	22
United Kingdom	6	3	—	6	5·5	5
Others	15·5	13	12·5	14·5	14	7

(SOURCES: *Union Bank of Burma Bulletin; Annual Review* of Burma Chamber of Commerce. Figures for 1950 are approximate.)

Efforts were made to actually move the 900,000 tons before December 1954; this was not achieved, but the total transaction was completed by May 1955. Considerable delays occurred because the SAMB attempted to include old and unfit rice in their consignments (the agreement stipulated that supplies should come from the 1953 or later harvests). As a result the Indian agents scrutinized the loading minutely, and endless disputes arose as to the fitness of individual consignments. Burma also had the agreement with Japan for the sale of 300,000 tons of rice, and Ceylon was prepared to take from 200,000 to 600,000 tons, so the situation in 1954 was more reassuring: but from all across the world came reports of the falling away of demand, and Burma's customers did not always show themselves eager to take up their quotas.[1] Burma was by no means the only country in South East Asia to encounter difficulties. The struggle in Indo-China had largely eliminated that country as an exporter, but Siam had her export problems—she too attempted to stand against the fall in world prices, and in 1954 her exports dropped by over one-third. Burma once again emerged as the world's leading exporter: the biggest importer was Japan.

The gathering unease in the rice-growing lands of South East Asia was given expression when, in November 1954, an international rice conference was held under the auspices of the FAO at Rangoon, with delegates from sixteen countries. In his opening address Kyaw Nyein advocated a policy of restriction in place of the efforts in expansion of the past years.

[1] After the early complaints from Japan, the SAMB was careful to ship only fresh, good quality rice to the Japanese.

He declared that 'the exporting countries were faced with a situation in which not all the exportable surplus of rice could be marketed. It appeared that production had exceeded the demand and the question was whether a halt should be called to efforts in increasing rice production.' Carrying the argument further, Mr. Raschid said he 'would like to suggest that it seemed timely that an international body like the FAO should use its influence so that countries which had not been exporting their rice formerly should not enter or enlarge the business of rice exports.'[1] A different feature of the problem was presented by India and Indonesia, former large-scale importers, who declared that they would shortly attain self-sufficiency in food grains. Both Burma and Ceylon expressed concern over the United States surplus disposal programme, fearing the 'dumping' of rice in Asian consumer countries,[2] thereby further depressing world prices. The United States delegate gave certain assurances designed to allay these fears. The conference ended by adopting a series of twelve resolutions which attempted to co-ordinate the differing viewpoints of the delegates: steps should be taken to expand rice consumption, prices should be reduced, quality should be improved, restrictions on consumption should be relaxed. But no agreed plan on a definite over-all rice policy was achieved.

Burma's concern to ensure that new rice producers should not enter the export trade, and in particular that the United States should not dispose of farm surpluses at cut rates, was given simultaneous expression at a General Agreement on Tariff and Trade conference at Geneva: 'Trade and not aid should be the basis on which future relations of the countries are founded', declared Burma's delegate, U Aung Soe.[3] As 1954 came to a close, Burma found itself carrying over 700,000 tons of rice, with prospects of increased competition at falling prices.

Compared with rice, the other former export lines were all unimportant, contributing altogether only about one-quarter of Burma's overseas earnings:

VALUE OF EXPORTS, 1949-54
(in crores)

	1948-9	1949-50	1950-1	1951-2	1952-3	1953-4	1954-5
Rice	59·5	57·6	75·8	80·9	101·9	81	80
All other exports	13·2	8·1	21·7	28·4	27·6	32	35

[1] *BWB*, 17 November 1954. A full report on the conference was carried in this number and that of 24 November 1954.

[2] India, Pakistan, Japan, the Philippines, and Yugoslavia are among countries which have received gifts of food from America.

[3] *Nation*, 12 November 1954.

Oil products, the second largest category of exports in pre-war days, have contributed nothing towards post-war exports: indeed, Burma has throughout been compelled to import a considerable proportion (about two-thirds) of her own needs from the Persian Gulf. Mineral ores have fallen right away from their former importance; thanks to the fabulous rises in prices in the post-war world, their monetary value has still been appreciable although their physical quantity has been minute, representing at the highest 18 per cent. of the former tonnage, and at the lowest (1949) only 2·5 per cent. For several years the mines remained in rebel hands, and a certain amount of clandestine export into Siam went on, providing the KNDO with one of its principal sources of revenue. Even after the rebels were expelled there was little improvement: the British and Australian managers were not permitted to return to their mines in the Tenasserim area but had to accept such consignments as were sent down to the coast. Undoubtedly a large proportion of the output of these mines continues to vanish illicitly over the Siam border. Timber exports, after a fairly satisfactory recovery in the brief years before independence, formed only from 2 to 5 per cent. of post-independence exports. From 1 October 1953 the State Timber Board became the sole exporter of teak, though others engaged in the trade were given up to 31 March 1954 to clear outstanding contracts. The new arrangements did not lead to any early increase in sales: as in pre-war days, India has remained the principal customer, with Britain as the only other important buyer. Teak has remained the chief export line, with some other hardwoods, such as gurjan and pyinkadoe, of secondary importance.

TIMBER SHIPMENTS, 1948–54
(tons)

	Teak		Other Hardwoods	
	To United Kingdom	To India, &c.	To United Kingdom	To India, &c.
1948	16,713	59,567	14,807	8,400
1949	6,927	27,375	1,659	1,400
1950	2,308	10,166	3,100	843
1951	4,215	41,768	17,916	2,574
1952	5,164	24,779	16,433	2,328
1953	7,479	18,231	11,988	760
1954	5,395	15,187	3,615	1,842

(SOURCE: *Annual Review*, Burma Chamber of Commerce, 1955.)

The ending of the rice boom was also a time when the development programme was beginning to make its impact upon import figures: actually the effect was less important than in the case of the relaxation of controls in 1950: the rise in imports was less steep from 1952 to 1954 than in the two preceding years,[1] but whereas 85 per cent. of imports in 1950–1 were consumer goods, in 1953–4 the proportion was 75 per cent. with 25 per cent. in capital goods. Licensing continued to impede the even flow of certain imports: no licences would be issued for several months, and then, unexpectedly, a large quota would be sanctioned. For months the bazaars would be empty of particular goods, with supplies available only at black-market prices: then suddenly the shops would be flooded with arrivals and a glut would result. This method of regulating trade had the most adverse effect upon the small shopkeepers— precisely the men the Government was supposed to wish to encourage.[2]

One important decision of policy was the abolition of the preferential tariff, the 'Ottawa Agreement', which operated in favour of the Commonwealth countries. This came to an end from 1 October 1953 (the new customs tariff introduced increases of 30–200 per cent.). This change did not have any great effect upon British goods which on the whole were not competitive in price but made their appeal to the 'quality' buyer: but imports from India and Pakistan were badly affected. In the case of textiles India was displaced from the position of chief purveyor of piece-goods to the advantage of Japan: India now dropped into third place in textiles, with the United Kingdom in second place. Owing perhaps to increased purchases of capital goods, the United Kingdom became Burma's main source of imports for the year 1954, supplying 25 per cent. by value. Japan came second, supplying 22 per cent. as compared with only 18 per cent. in the previous year. India, which in 1953 had been the principal supplier, furnishing 26 per cent. of Burma's imports, now dropped into third place with only 18 per cent. of the total.[3]

Japan's newly commanding position was reinforced by the conclusion of a reparations agreement in November 1954. Among the countries of South East Asia Burma was the first to come to terms with the former invader; a considerably lower scale of compensation was accepted than the other countries (in particular, the Philippines and Indonesia) were demanding, in the hope that aid would be secured at a moment when it was particularly needed. Japan agreed to supply reparations

[1] Imports: 1949–50, 43·2 crores; 1950–1, 67·3; 1951–2, 81·9; 1952–3, 89·5; 1953–4, 98·7.
[2] See *Annual Review*, Burma Chamber of Commerce (*Nation*, 26 February 1955)
[3] Figures drawn from *Union Bank of Burma Bulletin*, 4th Quarter, 1954.

in the form of 'services of Japanese people and the products of Japan' to an annual value of $20 million;[1] Japan also agreed to invest each year sums equal to $5 million[2] in 'joint enterprises' to be contracted 'between the Government or people of the Union of Burma and Japanese people'. Both forms of investment were to be effective for a ten-year period.[3] This contribution when in full operation will represent an annual investment equal to one-quarter to one-third of the annual capital investment of the Burma Government, and it seems possible that this will effect a definite orientation of Burma's trade into Japan's orbit. Announcements from Tokyo rapidly made it plain that the new arrangement was regarded in Japan not as an act of conciliation by a defeated nation but as a business deal planned to support the Japanese economy. It was stated that Japan would adopt a 'sliding system' of payments whereby reparations would be utilized as a sort of safety valve for the Japanese economy.[4] During the first two years after the signing of the agreement almost the whole of the reparations were absorbed by the Balu Chaung hydroelectric scheme, which is being undertaken by a Japanese firm. Although this project promises great benefits, the cost of its erection only adds to Burma's difficulties: of the total cost of K17 crores, over K5 crores must be found from Burma's own funds.[5] Any hope that Japanese reparations would provide a solution to Burma's balance-of-payments problem was therefore disappointed.

At the end of 1954 the balance between exports and imports was definitely tilting in the latter direction. By now the development programme was passing from the planning stage into the building stage: from 1953 to 1955 some 59 crores was spent overseas for capital purchases, while the 83 crores spent on development within Burma had its effect in a higher demand for consumer goods. All this time Burma was actually increasing the volume of exports, but as the terms of trade moved against her their value declined. During 1952–3 Burma shipped 1,200,000 tons of rice, which earned 102 crores; next year exports were larger by 100,000 tons, but receipts were smaller by 21 crores. During the same two years earnings of foreign exchange (on account of all exports) dropped from 135 crores

---

[1] Equivalent to K9·5 crores, 7,200 million yen, or £7 million.
[2] Equivalent to K2·4 crores or 1,800 million yen or £1¾ million.
[3] Full text of treaty and reparations agreement in *BWB*, 17 November 1954.
[4] *Nation*, 10 November 1954, reporting *Yomiuiri*, quoting Japanese Finance Ministry.
[5] *The Times* for 28 December 1955 reported that Japan agreed to pay 5,650 million yen in goods and services up to March 1956, Balu Chaung being the major project listed.

to 113 crores in 1953–4: foreign payments increased from
110 crores in 1952–3 to 156 crores in the following year.[1] This
new situation clearly demanded a radical review of government
policy.

During the five years 1948 to 1953, whilst a 'sellers' market'
prevailed, the SAMB had merely to sort out the application
forms of foreign governments and furnish a quantity of low-
grade rice from out of its general pool. In 1954 it became
necessary first to go out and find customers, and secondly to
cater for their particular requirements as regards quality. The
former mechanism of private merchandising, the operation of
the law of supply and demand, had met these requirements,
but the AFPFL Government showed no inclination to return
to a system of private trading in which the foreigners would
be in effective control. Instead the machinery of state trading
was overhauled and even further elaborated.

The Ministry of Commerce was reconstituted as the Ministry
of Trade Development from 3 November 1954, with control
over the SAMB, the State Timber Board, and the merchandising department of the Mineral Resources Development
Corporation (formerly, these establishments were each under
the control of different ministries and departments). M. A.
Raschid, himself an acute man of business and affairs, who
had shown his abilities in a series of difficult assignments,
became the first Minister of Trade Development.[2]

During the years when any rice could find a sale the SAMB
had not been subjected to particularly close government
supervision. Late in 1954 the Board's activities were examined
more closely. A special Inquiry Commission was set up to
examine the malpractices which had seeped into the SAMB's
operations, of which a glimpse was provided by Mr. Raschid
when he remarked soon after taking up his new appointment:
'I know that there is a lot of stealing in mills. SAMB inspectors
are bribed, with the result that standards are not maintained.'[3]
Late in November a government news release revealed that
$1\frac{1}{2}$ crores could not be accounted for in the Board's books,
while 200,000 tons of rice could not be traced in the warehouses.[4]
But probably such major scandals are less detrimental than the
cumulative effect of petty irregularities throughout the whole

[1] Speech on the financial position by U Nu, *BWB*, 6 October 1955.
[2] The post of Minister of Commerce had not proved particularly auspicious: three
politicians had found political extinction in it, one being jailed and another saved
from arrest for embezzlement only by timely flight.
[3] *Nation*, 23 November 1954. A year later Raschid stated that 'Very few of our
staff have had any real training for the work they are doing' (*BWB*, 1 December
1955).
[4] *Nation*, 23 November 1954 and 22 May 1955.

range of the Board's working. From the point when grain is purchased from the cultivator to that of shipment aboard a foreign vessel there are innumerable irregular 'commissions' and 'considerations' which pass from hand to hand.[1] In addition, there is widespread inefficiency: when SAMB agents purchase grain from the cultivator it is often discovered that there is no money in the local government treasury to cover their purchases, and the peasant is compelled to wait several months for his money. He therefore often prefers to sell to a middleman at a lower rate, if he thereby can obtain spot cash.[2] In the past storage accommodation has been quite inadequate and frequently bags have been stacked in the open, sometimes even through the monsoon. Overseas demand, or the capacity of the ports to load the rice, has frequently been over-estimated; paddy has been prematurely milled into rice, and then perforce has lain deteriorating for months before clearance. Finally, the book-keeping side has often been faulty: delays in presenting accounts to Burma's customers have often cost the country appreciable sums.[3]

These and other problems faced the new Minister for Trade Development, but even more pressing was the need to obtain overseas customers. With the normal channels seemingly reluctant to take rice on normal commercial terms, Burma was forced to enter into barter deals. On the same day that the new ministry came into being a contract was signed in Peking whereby China would purchase 150,000 tons of rice at the rate of £40 per ton; 20 per cent. of the payment was promised in sterling, 60 per cent. would be 'adjusted' against the purchase of Chinese products, and 20 per cent. would be paid for in goods of Russian or East European origin.[4] This agreement, although acclaimed by the Burma Government as an act of friendship, took many months to become effective. During the following spring Burmese trade delegations journeyed around Russia, East Germany, and elsewhere signing contracts to follow up the Chinese deal: all this did not solve the pressing problems which overshadowed the passing of 1954. Overseas balances had fallen from the high point of K126·9 crores to 54 crores; stocks of 700,000 tons of rice, including 200,000 tons from the 1952–3 harvest and earlier

---

[1] At least one foreign shipping company has a regular tariff of payments, from the night-watchman upwards, which are regularly disbursed after each shipment is loaded: without such payments, they say, business would be made impossible.
[2] *Nation*, 10 February 1955.
[3] Early in 1955 three U.N. experts were engaged to overhaul the entire SAMB organization (ibid., 22 May 1955).
[4] *BWB*, 1 December 1954.

(by now unsaleable for human consumption) were lying un-
disposed in the SAMB godowns; this was the core of the
problem.

The protection which long-term agreements were designed
to provide against changes in world conditions was also found
to be far from complete. Ceylon had negotiated a four-years'
agreement, commencing in January 1954, agreeing to pay
£50 per ton during 1954 and £48 during 1955 for annual
shipments of 200,000 tons. During 1954 only half the agreed
quota was actually shipped owing to the usual difficulties at
the ports. In November 1954 the Ceylon Government asked
for a substantial reduction in the 1955 price. For some months
the Burma Government rejected any reduction, until Ceylon
intimated that she would be unable to take delivery of the
agreed 200,000 tons for 1955. After further bargaining, the
Burma Government finally agreed to an amended price of
£42 per ton.[1]

Meanwhile Burmese government missions were seeking
buyers in the Far East, especially in Hong Kong and Singapore.
On 23 February Mr. Raschid announced a new rice export
policy, which involved the scheme for growing improved
strains of paddy,[2] a more efficient purchase system, better
storage, and improved milling. In addition, private traders
were to be permitted to export rice to countries where no
government-to-government contracts were in operation, at
prices to be regulated by the SAMB.[3]

However, the balance-of-payments situation was now
worsening so rapidly that measures to stimulate trade could
not suffice: it was essential to check the melting away of overseas balances by pruning all unnecessary imports. During
February 1955 a series of conferences were held between the
Prime Minister and Ministers and principal officials of the
main spending departments to co-ordinate the cutting back
of the development programme. The savings which were
effected represented 2·19 crores from current expenditure and
8·10 crores from capital expenditure: altogether this amounted
to a reduction of over 10 per cent. in government spending
for the year 1954–5.[4]

During the early months of 1955 these difficulties were
freely discussed in Rangoon society. Sections of the business
world interpreted the omens as foreshadowing a complete
bankruptcy of the Burma Government. Rumour whispered

[1] *Nation*, 13 February 1955.
[2] See above, p. 245.
[3] 'Burma's New Rice Export Policy', *Burma*, April 1955, p. 1.
[4] Details announced in budget speech for 1955 (see *BWB*, 8 September 1955).

that the kyat (whose value in the free markets of Asia was much depreciated) would soon be devalued. On 7 March the Government announced that importers holding licences might enter into orders for only 50 per cent. of the value of their licences, up to 30 September. This measure induced a wave of speculative commercial activity, including massive orders for all commodities not restricted by licence. The Government's hand was forced, and on 10 March all imports under Open General Licence were completely suspended.[1]

With trade virtually at a standstill, the Government hastily reviewed the economic outlook. Occasion was taken to reinforce the Government's plans for discouraging foreign business houses and assisting Burmese traders. After the introduction of Open General Licence conditions in 1950 and 1951, Burmans had found it exceedingly hard to compete with the established foreign firms. A return to licensing, with its automatic reservation of 60 per cent. of imports for Burmese firms, automatically worked in their favour. When on 21 March the 50 per cent. cut in licences was cancelled, Open General Licences were only restored for thirty-five selected commodities. The quota of licences allocated to Burmese firms was increased to considerably more than 60 per cent. of the total. The proportion now varied from 89 per cent. (fountain-pens) and 88 per cent. (textiles) to a minimum of 65 per cent. for books and periodicals. Altogether Burmese firms now received at least three-quarters of the import licences. This did not mean that three-quarters of the import trade was now in Burmese hands: a large proportion of the licence-holders either sold their licences direct to foreign importers or sold their allocation of goods 'forward' to foreign traders before arrival. As a result the public had to provide profits for two sets of middlemen. As part of its revised policy the Government also increased the share of the Civil Supplies Department in the import trade to about 30 per cent. of the total, including all imports of cotton yarn (the Department already handled the entire import of sugar and tinned milk).[2]

The first noticeable effect of the restrictions was a rapid rise in prices; amid a general upward movement, the biggest increases were recorded by Indian piece-goods, which were selling at K36·60 per 40 yards before the restrictions and which rose to K68 per 40 yards by the end of May, and by coconut oil, which rose from K3·5 per viss before the restrictions to

[1] See address by M. A. Raschid to Union of Burma Chamber of Commerce (*BWB* 28 April 1955).
[2] See speech by M. A. Raschid to annual meeting of Union of Burma Chamber of Commerce, 22 February 1956. The Minister took the opportunity to criticize severely the activities of bogus Burmese business ventures.

K8·75 by the end of June.[1] The March measures had very little effect in damping down the inflow of goods, and foreign currency was consumed as rapidly as ever. Foreign reserves, which had strengthened from 54 crores to 61 crores between January and March, fell to 51 crores by June. Preliminary figures showed that the 1954–5 income from rice would again decline, despite considerable increases in the volume of exports:[2] clearly, really drastic remedies were necessary, and the decision was taken to slash the country's development programme for the following year, 1955–6, from 80 crores to less than 56 crores.[3] The worsening balance-of-payments position was at last steadied: foreign reserves were down to less than 37 crores in the first week of August 1955, but a month later these reserves had risen to K42·44 crores and the worst of the crisis was over.

Meanwhile trade missions were touring the continents of the world in order to discover outlets for Burma's rice. The new policy, as enunciated by M. A. Raschid, spelt the final departure from *laissez-faire* trading conditions. He declared:

The pattern of our export trade is changing. Some of our old customers have reduced their purchases of rice, while we have secured some new ones. . . . With the change of our market for our products a change in the trading pattern of our country will also come about. We shall be buying more and more from countries which buy from us. In this connection, I would like to make particular mention of the trading arrangements that have been arrived at with the People's Republic of China, the Democratic Republic of [East] Germany, Yugoslavia, Czechoslovakia and Hungary. . . . A great deal of stress is laid in this country on trade marks and trade names. . . . If our export trade makes it necessary that we should buy from these new countries, then our customers and traders will have to get used to new trade names and new trade marks.[4]

The year 1955 saw the initialing of an unprecedented number of reciprocal trade deals, many on a simple barter basis. A series of deals were signed in Eastern Europe by a mission headed by Thakin Tin, involving in all the sale of 200,000 tons of rice.[5] An eight-man mission to Peking, led by Bo Min Gaung,

[1] *Union Bank of Burma Monthly Review*, April–July 1955.
[2] In 1954–5, 1,600,000 tons of rice were exported, including about 500,000 tons to 'new customers' (China, Eastern Europe, &c.), a considerable increase on previous years, but receipts were only 80 crores, and this included 'credit' for barter transactions.
[3] Speech by U Nu to a gathering of business men (*BWB*, 6 October 1955).
[4] ibid., 28 April 1955.
[5] Czechoslovakia is to receive £3 million worth of rice in exchange for industrial and engineering goods; East Germany is buying 50,000 tons, as well as £3 million worth for three years in exchange for machine tools, &c.; Hungary is buying 20,000 tons; and Poland made an offer for 20,000 tons, 50 per cent. to be paid for immediately, the remainder over a ten-year period.

concluded an agreement whereby China was to buy 150,000 tons of rice at £40 per ton (the standard rate in these deals) in exchange for a wide range of supplies (cotton yarn, newsprint, glass, blankets, tiles, &c.). A straight barter deal with the Philippines provided for the exchange of 20,000 tons of rice against an even tonnage of sugar. A similar deal with Indonesia was planned: 50,000–100,000 tons of rice were to be exchanged for sugar, copra, coffee, pepper, and rubber, which Burma will, presumably, exchange with someone else for something else. Yugoslavia accepted 50,000 tons of rice annually for five years against consumer and capital goods and technical services. Russia agreed to buy 150,000–200,000 tons in return for Soviet equipment, machinery, and other goods. Japan also entered into a contract for 220,000 tons of paddy from the 1955 crop.

If all these agreements were carried through Burma's market for over half of the 1955 crop was assured. These new arrangements seemed to portend a complete break-away from traditional patterns of trade, but until the new agreements have been in operation for a substantial period, it will be impossible to assess the extent of the change. Burma's technical, social, and economic habits have been formed in combination with patterns developed in British and Indian industry and commerce: to take simple examples, measurements of weight and length are standardized on British-Indian tables. One might elaborate examples across a wide field of technical experience. Almost all Burma's existing stock of equipment, transport, and machinery is adjusted to British standards. It may by no means be convenient to confront the technical expertise of Burma with a miscellaneous assortment of Chinese, Russian, Yugoslav, and Czech formulae.[1]

Any attempt to interpret the changing economic situation in Burma in terms of consistent policy is, indeed, bound to fail. Although the AFPFL Government has a concrete programme of socialization and self-sufficiency always in view, modifications—even reversals—of policy occur without warning. Despite the suggestions of placing restrictions upon the world rice trade made in November 1954[2] and the attempts to maintain scarcity prices into a period of competition, a year or so later the Burma Government appeared to have adopted

---

[1] Burma's first experience of trading with the Communist bloc was not auspicious. Early in 1956 large shipments of cement arrived in Rangoon from East European countries. Being unable to dispose of such quantities, Burma attempted to sell the surplus to India: only to discover that India had bought cement from the same Communist sources at two-thirds of the price paid by Burma.

[2] See above, pp. 264–5.

an entirely new policy of expanding output and competitive prices. A rice export target of 2 million tons was laid down for 1955–6, and early in 1956 government representatives were indicating that a selling price of £36 or £37 per ton would now be accepted. A sign that Burma had not completely abandoned her former trade ties was shown with the announcement in September 1955 of an Indian Government Loan to Burma of 20 crores or £15 million, most of which will be spent on the purchase of Indian products. U Nu utilized the occasion of the loan to emphasize the paramount importance to Burma of the 'substantial help' rendered by India to Burma at crucial moments since independence, and to underline the permanent nature of the two countries' associations.[1] But the position at the end of 1955 remained quite fluid. The logic of international economics would seem to draw Burma into the same kind of relationship with Japan as was formerly established with India. Since the loss of her overseas empire, particularly Manchuria and Formosa, Japan has been cut off from sources of essential foodstuffs and raw materials, and at the same time has been excluded from her main export markets in China. Japan finds it even more necessary not only to export her manufactures, but also her peoples. But many of the other Asian countries are attempting to fortify their own industries and are averse to letting Japan in. Burma, with her acute need for foreign technicians and her incapacity for many years to fulfil her own needs for consumer goods, is one of the few countries anxious to absorb Japan's goods and services; at the same time Burma is ready to export all the rice that can be shipped to feed Japan's expanding millions. But the two countries are not, in fact, so nearly complementary as were pre-war Burma and India. Japan needs to import, as well as foodstuffs, large quantities of raw cotton, iron, coal, and other raw materials. These are available in China, and perhaps a 'triangle of trade' might be developed in which Burma would procure some of the required products from China for re-export to Japan. Such an idea was certainly tentatively formulated when the Bo Min Gaung mission visited Japan in January 1955.[2]

Among the changes which are almost certainly coming will be the pulling down of British business from its privileged redoubts in the import-export trade of Burma. As an exporting nation Britain must expect the same powerful challenge from Germany, Italy, Japan, and the East European States which is being met throughout the world. As an example, one of the

[1] *BWB*, 29 September 1955.
[2] *Nation*, 27 January 1955.

most successful post-war British exports has been the Land
Rover all-purpose light truck; this is met everywhere in Burma,
pounding over rough tracks and standing up sturdily to hard
driving, foul weather, and complete lack of maintenance. But
in 1954 a Japanese 'Land Rover' appeared, professedly the
same—or better; whatever its merits, it was certainly cheaper.
This type of challenge will be encountered throughout every
branch of British exports: familiarity and a reputation for
quality will impel Burmans to choose British products at
competitive prices, but there will not be an automatic inclination towards British products as there was in the past (especially
in the purchasing of government departments).

But the more particular challenge to British interests is
directed at the import-export houses and the big 'exchange'
banks whose impressive porticoes have so long dominated
Rangoon's Merchant Street and Phayre Street. Allusion has
been made to certain aspects of the Government's intentions
towards commerce. In addition, during 1954 a series of measures
to restrict foreign activities was formulated. Transfers of money
from Burma to other countries were even more closely regulated
(partly, it should be related, because of the uncovering of
fraudulent transfers), and foreign business men wishing to take
money from the country on retirement had to undergo search-
ing inquiries. The Burma Companies (Amendment) Act
placed foreign concerns on a different footing from those of
nationals: the foreigners were required to furnish detailed
information about their trading activities, showing costs and
profits at different stages of their various transactions. The
Registration (Importers and Exporters) Order stipulated that
no firm shall be registered (without which, no licence may be
granted) unless 50 per cent. of the staff receiving over K500
per month and 75 per cent. receiving less than K500 are citizens
of the Union. These provisions were to come into force on
31 May 1956. Under these regulations the nationalization of
business activity is brought appreciably nearer. Some of the
more long-sighted of the British firms, in anticipation of future
developments, have selected the most promising young
Burmans for higher training in banking, insurance, &c., in
the United Kingdom. It has been common experience that
when these Burmans return from their training they are at
once attracted away from the British company to take a senior
post in a Burma Government organization in the same field
of activity.

Most of the resident British business community see in all
these moves evidence of their early liquidation: responsible

business leaders are heard to say that there are ten or five or three years only of commercial activity left to hope for. Many of the smaller British concerns are selling out to indigenous interests while their agencies still possess a fair market value.

Trade, like everything else in Burma, came under the severe scrutiny of the military regime. 'Economic insurgents' or black marketeers were dealt with ruthlessly. A widespread reduction in prices followed (not perhaps as spectacular as the army claimed) and in addition, the military went into business. Defence Services Institutes were established for retail distribution and also for trade: their enterprises came to include a shipping line and a bank. All firms in the export business were inspected and over 1,400 spurious operators (mainly Burmans) were deprived of their licences. Greater vigour was given to the state export agencies. Both rice and timber exports improved, and there was an assuring increase in the foreign exchange reserves. After the collapse of the reserves in 1954–5 they had failed to rise appreciably, and in January 1959 stood at K65·5 crores. By October they rose to K78·5 crores, but with a return to less rigid restrictions on the import of consumer goods they fell to K70·9 crores in February 1960. Subsequently they remained firm.

The movement of international trade, distorted by the barter agreements, largely returned to traditional patterns. During 1959, Burma's principal customers were, in order, Indonesia (taking 18·5 per cent of exports), India (16·1 per cent), Ceylon (12·9 per cent), Britain (8·4 per cent), Pakistan (6·4 per cent) and Japan (3·9 per cent). Burma's main suppliers were Japan (20·3 per cent), Britain (17·8 per cent), India (10·8 per cent) China (9·7 per cent) and the United States (3·7 per cent). The outlook for British companies trading in Burma darkened further, as measures were intensified to improve the position of indigenous export firms and to impose restrictions upon the foreigners.

Between 1962 and 1965, all foreign participation in the trade of Burma was finally liquidated. The entire import-export trade became a Government monopoly. The balance of payments depended (as during the 1950s) upon the export of rice for between 70 to 80 per cent of all foreign exchange earnings. With prices averaging £37 per ton, and output relatively static, Burma was able to maintain an export surplus only by severe limitations upon imports.

X

COMMUNICATIONS, INDUSTRY, AND LABOUR

GEOGRAPHY has moulded historical evolution in Burma, perhaps to an even greater degree than in most countries; and the past, present, and future development of communications and industry can only be understood by constant reference to geographical factors. Burma has one magnificent artery, the Irrawaddy, which provides over 900 miles of navigable waterway from Bhamo to the sea; the Chindwin tributary gives another 400 miles of navigable waters, while in the Delta the 'fingers' of the Irrawaddy stretch out in a system of riverine highways and byways. The other rivers do not offer the passage which a map would suggest: less than 100 miles of river from Moulmein northwards up the Salween is navigable. All the rivers flow from north to south: from east to west the going is all 'against the grain' of the country and travel is difficult. As a traveller approaches any one of the frontiers high mountains, jungle-covered, rise against the sky. Points of entry are few, and the passes through which entry or exit must be made wind through remote, dangerous, hill country, where the traveller moves only by permission of the tribal folk whose domain this is, or was. Entry into Burma by land being so very difficult, there remains the sea—and the air.

The sea coast of Burma is girdled by clusters of islands for long stretches, where currents are treacherous and shallows and hidden reefs abound. Harbours and other anchorage for sea-going vessels are limited: Rangoon is the natural focus for the nation's trade. It has a deep river which may be navigated by ships drawing 30 feet of water and of up to 15,000 tons burthen. Its river is not actually a tributary of the Irrawaddy, but access to the great river has always been simple, and since the digging of the Twante Canal[1] large river ships have been able to voyage from Rangoon through the Delta waterways and up the Irrawaddy. Communications with Pegu and the Sittang Valley, and with Moulmein and the Salween, are also without serious obstacles.

---

[1] The Twante Canal was first dug in 1883, widened in 1913, and widened again in 1933-5 to permit the passage of the big mail steamers.

The basic pattern of Burma's economic development has stemmed, first from the Irrawaddy River as the axis of the old Burmese kingdom, and secondly from the rise of Rangoon as a great port and the opening up of the Delta rice granary; thirdly, the railways have enlarged the radius of the economy. At each stage, geography has determined development, and the first attempts at industrialization were related to the same factors: industries were largely centred on Rangoon, or on major rail or river lines of communication.

As a result of the Japanese occupation and the insurrection, the economic system ceased to function for over a decade; such advantages as nature had given to Burma were sterilized by the devastation of war and the anarchy of civil war; for a time communication was only possible by means of those instruments of modern technology which can ignore geography, the radio and aeroplane, while all that remained of industrial activity was concentrated at Rangoon, the only place accessible to the outside world. The KTA plan, which sought to bend Burma's economy into a new form in which industry would be of first importance, also sought to impose a new design, a new assessment of the physical configuration of the country: but the actual industrialization measures which were started in the following years have almost all been concentrated in Rangoon, and until the continuing effects of the war and rebellion upon the transport services can be overcome, a new phase of more widespread industrialization cannot even begin.

The system of communications which had been built up by 1940 was, within the terms dictated by geography, designed largely for the exploitation of Burma's export commodities, and to a very minor degree for reasons of security and defence. The main railroads, from Rangoon to Prome and from Rangoon to Toungoo and on to Mandalay, ran through important rice-producing districts; a private line ran out to the great Bawdwin mines in the Northern Shan States. The main line north to Mandalay crossed the Irrawaddy at Sagaing and curved far north to Myitkyina; in part this northern section was designed for strategic purposes, but it carried its share of traffic. Altogether it is estimated that the 2,060 miles of the Burma Railways carried about 4 million tons of freight and 20 million passengers every year. The railways were constructed by the State; they were leased to a private company for operation during the period 1896–1929, and thereafter returned to state management. The capital for their construction was derived from loans by the Government of India: this formed the bulk of the national debt with India, assumed in 1937. Railway building was not cheap, largely because of the many thousands of bridges necessitated by rivers, *nullahs*, and mountains. Among the most spectacular feats of engineering were the sixteen-span Ava Bridge, 4,000 feet in length, across the Irrawaddy, completed in January 1934 at a cost of Rs.1·43 crores (over £1 million), and the Gokteik Viaduct (opened 1913) on the Lashio line, which carries 2,260 feet of track across a gorge where tumbles a stream 870 feet below.

The backbone of the railway staff was provided by Anglo-Burmans and Anglo-Indians who served as drivers, guards, and senior station staff. A large proportion of the remaining employees were Indians. By 1940 the railways had reached something like maximum limits in terms of economic operation. There were obvious blanks on the railroad map: not one yard of track in Arakan, only 150 miles of line in the districts to the west of the Irrawaddy below Sagaing, and, most remarkable, not one single rail link between Burma and her neighbours, India and Siam. But any attempt to fill in these blanks would have necessitated heavy expenditure—the physical obstacles were overpowering—and would have been of marginal utility.

Where the railway was lacking, its place was partially taken by water transport. The two great companies, the Irrawaddy Flotilla Company and the Arracan Flotilla Company, between them had services over some 2,550 miles of waterways. Their craft included long-distance express steamers and smaller local steamers, both screw-ships and stern-wheelers; often with 'flats' filled with cargo and passengers lashed alongside the powered vessels on many routes. The bigger ships had British (usually Scots) captains, engineers, and chief officers; the smaller craft were controlled by Indians and a few Burmans. The bulk of the crews were made up of Chittagonians, many of whom had sailed the ocean routes of the world. The two big companies carried about 1¼ million tons of freight and 8 million passengers every year. Perhaps the most vital sector of their business was the portage of rice and paddy from the Delta towns to Rangoon. But of even greater importance were the hundreds of small vessels with sails and sweeps, slowly, majestically gliding, their holds piled with paddy for the rice-mills. In this trade, the Burmese had no competition: its total volume may have been not far short of the tonnage carried by rail. The provision of river 'maintenance' services, including buoying the sandbanks in the shallow Irrawaddy, revising charts, providing pilots, and keeping up the landing stages was all undertaken by the Irrawaddy Flotilla Company, although the Government operated a number of dredgers.

COMMUNICATIONS, INDUSTRY, AND LABOUR 281

Until the 1920's Burma very largely made do with the same old roads as had existed for centuries: tracks that were dust-clouds in the dry weather and bogs in the monsoon. In the 1920's the main trunk roads were metalled and bridged up to a reasonable standard.[1] In 1940 there were 6,800 miles of surfaced road, 5,600 miles of dry-weather road, 4,700 miles of cart tracks, and 8,300 miles of mule tracks. Arakan was almost entirely cut off from the main Burma road system, except for the little-used, hazardous Taungup Pass. Burma was backward in its roads even by comparison with India: once again part of the reason was the high cost of road construction and maintenance (almost twice as high in Burma as in India). Until the 1920's the only vehicles upon the roads were the high-prowed bullock carts; then, within a few years, the roads were invaded by cars, lorries, and garishly painted buses which lurched up the side-roads through ruts and pot-holes to the remotest villages. This revolution in transport brought rapid changes into the social and economic life of the countryside.

If Burma had no railway communications with the outside world, its external road links were exiguous. There were no overland connexions with India whatever; Kengtung was linked with Chiengmai by a road over which the bulk of the imports into the trans-Salween states were carried. There were ancient trade routes from Bhamo and Myitkyina through into Yunnan; these were little used. But one transfrontier route became briefly world-famous: the 'Burma Road' from Lashio railhead to Muse on the border and on to Kunming. This road was made passable to motor transport in 1938 by the efforts of thousands of Chinese coolies. For three years the Burma Road shuddered with the passage of several thousand trucks carrying war-supplies to China. Contemporary Burmese political leaders regarded operations on this road with the very reverse of enthusiasm.[2] The desire to keep the doors of Burma shut against foreign intruders who may prove troublesome and overbearing is one of the oldest themes in Burmese history.

To a remarkable degree roads, railways, and river traffic all converge on Rangoon. There are certain regions, each of which has its own local centre: Arakan looking to Akyab, a small area west of the Irrawaddy converging towards Bassein; the lower Salween and Moulmein; the long coastline of Tenasserim with Mergui and Tavoy. But altogether these minor ports only accounted for 15 per cent. of the oversea commerce of the country; 85 per cent. of foreign trade and almost all migration

---

[1] *The Burma Handbook*, 1944, pp. 52–70, lists all main roads.
[2] Christian, *Burma and the Japanese Invader*, pp. 224–36.

was channelled through Rangoon. The port facilities consisted of about 15 miles of anchorage in the river, with some 4 miles of dockland. There were 10 deep-water berths for liners, 17 jetties, and about 40 pontoons. There were dockyards capable of taking vessels up to 1,200 tons for repairs, but their facilities were intended for inland and coastal shipping. In the years before 1942 Rangoon was receiving over 500 ships every year; these discharged about 1½ million tons and loaded 3½ million tons of cargo, a trade with an annual value of 60–70 crores.[1] Measured by the value of the trade handled, the remaining ports would be placed in the following order of importance after Rangoon: Bassein, Akyab, Moulmein (each handling trade worth 2 or 3 crores every year), Tavoy, and Mergui.

Industrial development was concerned almost entirely with the extraction and processing of Burma's natural products. Of the 1,007 factories registered under the Factories Act, 70 per cent. comprised rice-mills and sawmills. The biggest single employer was the Burmah Oil Company, followed by the leading mining companies.

The rice-mills fell into two main classes: the big mills at the ports, owned by European firms, and much smaller mills at rural centres, almost all on river banks, owned by Asians. Out of a total of 692 mills in 1939, 27 were owned by Europeans, 164 by Chinese, 190 by Indians, and 311 by Burmans.[2] Over 80 per cent. of the mills employed less than 100 workers. The machinery and methods used were often extremely crude.

The petroleum industry has ancient origins: for centuries the hereditary *twin-zas*, 'well eaters', of Yenangyaung brought up the 'earth oil' which was sold, mainly, as weather-proofing for houses. The Burmah Oil Company was first organized in 1886, but its large-scale operations date from the beginning of the present century when American drillers introduced modern techniques. The company (which controlled about five-sixths of Burma's oil production) pumped the crude oil from the field through a 350-mile pipeline to Syriam, opposite Rangoon, where the oil was refined prior to internal use or export. By 1942 Yenangyaung was largely worked out and was taking second place to the nearby field at Chauk; other important subsidiary fields were Lanywa and Yenangyat in nearby Pakokku District. Total output in the 1930's amounted to

---

[1] Before separation Rangoon ranked after Bombay, Calcutta, and Karachi, but before Madras.
[2] Furnivall, *Colonial Policy and Practice*. p. 189.

250–80 million gallons per annum.[1] The Burmah Oil Company was notable not only for technical achievements in oil production, but also for an enlightened policy in labour relations as regards housing, hospital care, and other welfare services. This did not prevent its being the main target of Burmese politicians who saw the company as the outstanding example of 'economic imperialism'. The first exercise in mass political agitation conducted by the Thakins was a campaign in the oilfields in 1938, culminating in a general strike: Aung San was the chief organizer of the movement.

The next most important industrial enterprises were the Bawdwin mines near Lashio, and the Mawchi mines in Karenni. The former, situated about eighty miles from the Chinese border, is another ancient industry, worked since the sixteenth century by the Chinese who are said to have employed 10,000 workers. The Chinese concentrated on silver mining, transport difficulties preventing them from exploiting the lead deposits. Since the (British) Burma Corporation took over the site, early in the twentieth century, it has been served by a branch line whose working provided one-twelfth of the revenues of the Burma Railways. The products of the Bawdwin mines were valued at over £2 million annually. Mawchi was the greatest tungsten mine in the world. Its annual production had a value of over £720,000.[2] Employees at these mines included local people, Indians, Chinese, and Gurkhas; almost no Burmans were employed. The total output of tin and tungsten from the remaining mines located in Tenasserim was rather greater than that of Mawchi. Chinese formed an important group in the working population: a few mines were Chinese-owned.

There was also a small amount of industrial activity designed to cater for Burma's own requirements. Textile weaving was very largely a cottage industry, but Steel Brothers opened a spinning and ginning mill at Myingyan with over 1,200 employees and a production of 3½ million lb. of yarn, mainly coarse quality (1938–9 figures). Just north of Insein an Indian firm opened a knitting factory, the Violin Hosiery Works, producing under-jackets (bodices). There were three sugar

[1] Production in 1940 (the last pre-occupation year for which complete records exist) was as follows:

	No. of producing wells	Gallons per day
Yenangyaung	2,580	295,307
Chauk	670	377,703
Lanywa	100	63,315
Yenangyat	240	12,679

[2] *Burma Handbook*, 1944, p. 27 gives detailed figures for Bawdwin and Mawchi.

refineries, the largest being the Indian-owned Zeyawaddy Sugar Factory, a modern concern with 800 workers; a British-owned factory at Sahmaw in Myitkyina District employed 500 workers. Steel Brothers operated the Burma Cement Company whose plant at Thayetmyo, utilizing local limestone, supplied 93 per cent. of Burma's cement requirements as well as exporting to Malaya. Steel's also invested in a rubber-processing plant. Other factories produced matches, soap, umbrellas, rope, tin trunks, aluminium pressed ware ('tiffin carriers' and *dekchis*), and miscellaneous household goods. Whereas the large-scale establishments were British-owned, the smaller works requiring less elaborate machinery and technical supervision were controlled by Indian and Chinese capitalists. Burmans participated little outside the rice-mills and sawmills.[1] Burmans had a monopoly of the traditional industries: boatbuilding, and the manufacture of cheroots, lacquer ware, furniture, &c.

During the 1920's and 1930's middle-class Burmans made a considerable issue of their weak position in the country's economy. Mr. Furnivall's *Introduction to the Political Economy of Burma* probably played a large part in stimulating public feeling. During the 1920's, following nationalist demands in the legislature, government assistance was afforded to the Burma Spinning and Weaving Company, an enterprise under purely Burmese direction although employing Indian labour: the Burmese directors eventually called upon the Government to take over their property, and a resolution to that effect was carried through the legislature: this experiment involved the Government in a loss of more than Rs.5 lakhs.[2] In general, government assistance was devoted to the encouragement of cottage industries: the Department of Industries, created in 1921, concentrated on pottery, lacquer, and weaving. The department operated the Technical Institute at Insein and the Saunders Weaving Institute, Amarapura. As an industrial employer the State's principal establishments were the railway workshops at Insein, Myitnge, and Kanbalu.

Such was the slender industrial framework erected during ninety years of *laissez-faire* British rule. Why was industrialization carried no further? In part the reason was a shortage of raw materials. There were coal deposits near Akyab, in the Mergui area, in Shwebo District not far from the Irrawaddy,

---

[1] Of industrial establishments owned by Burmans, 89 per cent. were rice or timber mills. Figures compiled in 1927 showed ownership of industrial establishments distributed as follows: Burmans, 309, Indians, 128, others, 290. (see *Report of the Committee on Technical and Vocational Education*, 1927).

[2] A full account of this episode is given in *Report of the Indian Statutory Commission*, xi. 132.

near Kalewa on the Chindwin, and elsewhere. But apart from the Mergui seams the quality was so wretched that, with cheap Indian coal available, its sale was not a commercial proposition. Iron ore was found only in minute quantities. Cotton and rubber were of little importance; jute there was none. But all these shortages have also been experienced by Japan: there were more solid reasons. Perhaps most important was the absence of a pool of suitable labour. Right up to the 1920's it was necessary to look to India to supplement an inadequate labour force for the needs of agriculture. Burmans, by temperament individualists, averse to any form of discipline, lovers of gaiety and variety, did not take easily to the dull routine of the factory. Moreover wages were high in Burma compared with India, China, or Japan. Technical experience had almost all to be imported, capital for industrial development had to be sought from the foreigners: Burmans with capital to spare would invest in land, or in the age-old pursuit of merit, in the raising of a pagoda. And so Burma remained almost entirely a land without factories; and all but a handful of advanced nationalist intellectuals were glad that it was so.

As a consequence of the Japanese invasion at least half of Burma's capital of modern communications and industry was destroyed. The first Japanese blows were heavy raids on the Rangoon riverside. As the Japanese advanced, a 'scorched-earth' policy was put into effect: the cranes on Rangoon's wharves were destroyed, bridges on the railway were destroyed, two spans of the mighty Ava Bridge were destroyed, about 220 of the 350 railway engines were put out of action, at least half of the 600 craft of the Irrawaddy Flotilla Company were sunk, the Syriam Oil Refinery, the pipeline, and the plant at Yenangyaung were almost entirely destroyed. Allied air attacks added to the destruction: time and again the Rangoon waterfront was pounded, while marshalling yards at Rangoon, Insein, Myitnge, and elsewhere were bombed, leaving twisted tracks and the skeletons of locomotives. Much of Burma's industrial capacity not directly related to purposes of war was also involved: amongst the losses were the Sahmaw sugar factory, Steel's Myingyan cotton-mill, and the Swedish match factory at Mandalay.

The Japanese attempted to repair only such undertakings as would contribute to their war effort. Strenuous endeavours were made, despite repeated Allied bombing, to bring Yenangyaung back into production. The Bawdwin mines were handed over to the Mitsui Company and Mawchi to Kobayashi Mining Company, and ore was worked for transhipment to

Japan. Other factories (such as the Zeyawaddy Sugar Factory) were placed in charge of Japanese companies. Perhaps the biggest operation was the removal of the rails from one line of the double railroad track from Rangoon to Toungoo and their utilization in the building of the infamous 'death railway' over the Three Pagodas Pass to connect with the Siam–Malaya railway system. The line was completed in November 1943 by the forced labour of many British, Australian, and Dutch prisoners of war, as well of the conscripted Burmese 'Sweat Army'. Another work carried through by the Japanese, employing forced labour, was the road over the An Pass in the central Arakan Yomas. Other undertakings which were not required by the Japanese for their own purposes were allowed to fall into ruin. When the retreat began their demoralization was too great to allow of much systematic demolition, but attempts were made to put as many essential works and services out of action as possible: for instance, the lofty Gokteik viaduct was badly damaged by retreating Japanese.

When the British Military Administration arrived, one of its main tasks was the rapid rehabilitation of ports and communications. At Rangoon the entire dock area was a ruin; cranes, pontoons, and bridges were dumped in the river, sunken steamers and other wreckage blocked access to the moorings, mines were laid in the river approaches. But the probability of such a situation was appreciated beforehand, and improvised schemes of clearance and repair were rapidly brought into operation. A channel up the river was swept clear of mines, military pontoons were towed in, and two and a half miles of Nissen hutting was erected to replace the bombed storage sheds. The KTA report describes how the port was 'in operating condition in a remarkably short time'; by 1947 about 40 per cent. of the pre-war tonnage was being handled.[1] The essentials of the rail services were equally rapidly restored. In 1945 a survey known as the Edwards Evaluation Report stated that the Burma Railways 'had ceased to exist as a transportation system': it was calculated that 48 per cent. of its assets had been destroyed.[2] Nevertheless, within two years 1,800 miles (as against 2,060 pre-war) were open to normal traffic, most of the wrecked locomotives and carriages had been replaced by rolling-stock from the Indian Railways, and by 1946–7 the railways were actually operating again at a profit.

River transport was first undertaken by Inland Water

---

[1] KTA, *Comprehensive Report*, ii. 646.
[2] ibid., p. 585.

Transport Operating Companies, formed by the British Military Administration largely out of the evacuated employees of the Irrawaddy Flotilla Company. Emergency craft, built in India, Canada, and the United States, were utilized, together with salvaged vessels of the company. This organization was the chief means of carrying rice supplies from the Delta to Upper Burma, then on the verge of famine. On 28 January 1946 the Irrawaddy Flotilla Company signed an agreement to take over its old functions under the control of a state Inland Water Transport Board. A new fleet was delivered between 1946 and 1948, largely from British yards, and pre-war services were restored.

In the industrial sphere out of the 1,007 establishments registered under the Factories Act before 1942, only 355 were registered in 1946: progress towards industrial recovery was slower, and by the beginning of 1948 only 155 additional factories had been added to the list. A major factor was the reluctance of foreign, particularly Indian, capital to invest in the new, unknown Burma.[1]

At the time of independence the process of rehabilitation came to a complete halt as civil war flared across the country. The efforts during the period of the return of British rule were very largely negatived, especially as regards the railways, which were a particular target for the attacks of the rebels. For over two years no trains ran farther than ten miles outside Rangoon; about twelve miles of track north of Pyinmana were taken up, and here the main line from Rangoon to Mandalay and Myitkyina completely ceased to exist. Between Rangoon and Mandalay every station except that at Pegu was burned down, almost every bridge was dynamited, the signalling system was wrecked beyond repair, hundreds of railway quarters were burnt and the staff was compelled to take shelter in wagons and sidings. Not until February 1950 was it possible to run a test train from Rangoon to Pegu. Not until November 1951 was it possible to close the gap between Pyinmana and Tatkon and begin running skeleton services between Rangoon and Upper Burma.

River transport was also severely affected by the insurrection; the Twante Canal, Rangoon's link with the Irrawaddy, was seized by the KNDO, while the Irrawaddy traffic was paralysed by the Communists and the PVO; 24 powered craft and 37 flats were captured or sunk by the rebels. For several months river traffic was confined to the immediate Rangoon area, except for occasional organized convoys which ventured forth

[1] Ministry of Information, *Factories in Burma* (Rangoon, 1949).

under close escort by Burma Navy vessels. However, it was possible to restore the river services more quickly than the railways. The Twante Canal was opened to traffic on 18 June 1949, and from 11 February 1950 the Delta service was resumed; on 16 June 1950 the main service from Rangoon to Mandalay came back into operation. Ships were armoured with bullet-proof sheets and military guards were provided; night sailings were completely abandoned. Under these restrictions, and subject to occasional interference (such as firing from rebel villages, or sometimes the seizure of craft by rebels disguised as passengers, usually as monks), the service was maintained. From 1949 to 1951 the ships of the Inland Water Transport Board carried more freight than the railways: thereafter, although remaining well below the pre-war figures, carriage by rail came back into the lead.

PASSENGER AND FREIGHT TRAFFIC

	FREIGHT (*million ton miles*)		PASSENGERS (*thousands*)	
	Railways	River Services (*estimated*)	Railways	River Services
1940–1	708	150	19,800	8,000
1946–7	319	52	18,200	1,000
1947–8	383	62	10,200	900
1948–9	100	25	4,600	400
1949–50	57	66	6,500	1,500
1950–1	123	134	9,700	2,500
1951–2	180	130	11,700	3,100
1952–3	260	124	15,300	3,200

(SOURCE: Ministry of Finance, *Economic Survey of Burma*, 1954.)

During the crisis months of 1948 and 1949 the keeping open of communications was possible, very largely, because of the newly-formed Union of Burma Airways. Air services after the liberation were undertaken by the R.A.F. who rebuilt Mingaladon airfield and established airstrips at several points up-country. During 1946 a private company, Burma National Airways, was given a contract for the management of all internal airways, but this company was unable to maintain proper services and its monopoly was terminated in August 1947. A state-operated service was substituted under the Nationalization of Air Transport Order, 1948. The Union of Burma Airways Board was constituted on 23 March 1948, and flying began in September and October 1948 with a fleet of six de Havilland Doves. The flying and maintenance personnel (and in the early days, the management also) were Britons, Australians, and South Africans. Soon after operations began ground communications were paralysed by the KNDO revolts. All government authority in the interior must have been abandoned, had it not been for the few airplanes which kept open communications and flew essential supplies to the small pockets of government-held territory. To augment the services, Catalina and Dakota aircraft were leased on charter, up to 25 being on hire throughout 1949 and 1950. The increase in traffic was striking; during the first four months of service a monthly average of 4,000 passengers and 820,000 lb. of freight was carried; one year later, three times as many passengers and about six times as much freight was being handled.[1] The routes flown totalled 3,000 miles and extended to Kengtung, Myitkyina, and other hitherto remote places. During 1950, as ground communications recovered, the volume of traffic was reduced, being stabilized at a monthly average of about 9,000 passengers and $3\frac{1}{2}$ million lb. of freight. At the end of 1950 Union of Burma Airways acquired seven Dakotas of its own, and the employment of chartered planes (an expensive device) was largely discontinued. In April 1950 the organization of the airway was considerably expanded and elaborated.[2] The staff now numbered some 500, of whom the technical side were all non-nationals, except for 3 Burmese co-pilots and the Technical Manager. On 3 November 1950 the first external service was inaugurated, from Rangoon to Bangkok.

The violence which followed independence had the effect of bringing industrial activity in Burma almost completely to a halt. The oilfields, sabotaged in 1942 by the British, had been dynamited in 1945 by the departing Japanese. During the years of exile the Burmah Oil Company had prepared for the rehabilitation of the industry, new equipment had been accumulated in Britain, and a resumption of production was planned on a basis of 540,000 tons per annum: this would be little more than half the pre-war figure but would more than meet Burma's needs and would prolong the period of working of the existing fields. During the period 1946–8 the company expended some £8 million on the oilfields and the pipeline, but all progress was halted by the insurrection. The PVO occupied the Yenangyaung area, which was looted and

---

[1] Dept. of Information, *Burma, the Fourth Anniversary*, p. 62, gives full figures, September 1948 to September 1949.
[2] ibid., p. 62 for full details.

wasted, and the British staff were withdrawn to Chauk, where the PVO 'Government' exacted payment of oil royalties and excise from the company. The company kept production going to a very limited extent at Chauk, but elsewhere in Burma all activity came to a halt. Eventually, in July 1950, the company was compelled to abandon its rehabilitation plan, and notice was given to 5,000 employees that, as there was no prospect of resumption of work, their employment would cease. The Burma Government thereupon ordered that the case must be referred to arbitration: this meant that the company was forced to retain all its labour force until a decision was eventually reached in January 1952, whereupon all but essential employees were discharged after receiving a further three months' wages.

Similarly the mines of Bawdwin, Mawchi, and Tenasserim were seized by rebels and the European staff were hastily evacuated. From 1949 to 1951 industry was all but dead: in any event, before production could be restored the country's battered communications must be brought back to something like normal.

Impetus towards this end was provided by the offer of American aid in 1951. Independence had coincided with a complete cessation of repair work upon the Rangoon docks; for more than three years the temporary post-war repairs sufficed to permit the handling of the much-reduced traffic which, during 1948, fell from 40 per cent. (1947) to about 25 per cent. of the pre-war norm. After the signing of the Economic Aid Agreement with the United States in September 1951, funds again became available for further rehabilitation. A Five-Year Plan was drawn up, designed to restore the port to its previous capacity to handle 5 million tons of freight per annum. Among results seen in 1952 were 2 transit sheds as big as football fields, and 16 pontoons, including a 500-foot pontoon large enough to accommodate the biggest ships calling at the port. Unfortunately the programme was strangled by the Burma Government's termination of American aid in March 1953.[1] However, the Government carried on with its own plan for recovery: references to port reconstruction in the discussions on transport at the 1952 Pyidawtha Conference were exceedingly brief, but thereafter proposals were published for an expenditure of K13 crores (£10 million) during the quinquennium 1954–9. By 1955 7 berths were again in working order out of the original total of 10. This was generally adequate, for although the volume of trade increased it remained only 45 per cent. of the pre-war total at the end of 1954.

<hr />

[1] See above, p. 106 and n. 2.

RANGOON PORT: VOLUME OF TRADE
(*ooo tons*)

	1940–1	1947–8	1948–9	1949–50
Exports	3,552·2	1,214·1	969·9	857·3
Imports	1,394·1	823·6	513·3	532·3
Total	4,946·3	2,037·7	1,483·2	1,389·6

	1950–1	1952	1953	1954
Exports	1,260·8	1,223·2	1,182·6	1,328·4
Imports	650·8	775·3	989·8	1,150·6
Total	1,911·6	1,998·5	2,172·4	2,479·0

(Figures up to 1950–1 relate to the financial year: thereafter to the calendar year.)

(Sources: Ministry of Information, *Rangoon: a Pocket Guide*, 1954 and reports of Burma Chamber of Commerce.)

Apart from the years 1946–8, Rangoon port suffered a complete eclipse during the decade 1942–52, and three years later there could be no surety that it would ever regain its former importance. As in other departments, the Port Commission has suffered from the discharge of all non-nationals, leaving uncomfortable gaps in technical knowledge and experience. One shortcoming of present-day management is the inadequate training and dredging of the river: like the Irrawaddy, the Rangoon River is liquid mud, and its channels require constant surveying and dredging. Within recent years some of the largest ships in regular service to Rangoon have been compelled to weigh anchor without full holds in order to make passage down-river. It would be a grim paradox if plans for developing the facilities of the port (for which a World Bank loan of $14 million was granted in May 1956, and for which British consultants have been engaged) should be brought to fruition only for the Port Commissioners to find that the big ships that have plied to Rangoon can no longer enter the river.

Among the minor ports by far the worst damaged was Akyab. When the British returned over thirty wrecks were sunk in Cherogeah Creek, all port installations without exception were destroyed, and only one building remained undamaged in the town and port. Slowly the wrecks were removed and the harbour dredged; by 1952 shipping was able again to call at the port. But complete rehabilitation was not possible; by 1955 the volume of trade was calculated at 50 per cent. of pre-war, but shippers complained of serious congestion and delays in loading. Moulmein experienced heavy air attacks, but the town was damaged more than the port which was almost completely repaired by 1955. Bassein underwent very little war damage, and its importance increased in the post-war years, its share in Burma's foreign trade amounting to 10 per cent. Mergui and Tavoy were not adversely affected by reason of war, but in common with Moulmein their coastal trade was severely limited by the proximity of the rebels, who have cut these ports off from most of their former hinterland. Government reconstruction proposals do not include anything more than routine improvements for any of these minor ports, except for Akyab.[1]

A new government venture which has entailed a heavy capital outlay has been the provision of a national merchant marine. The Union of Burma Shipping Board was created in June 1952. Its functions were to institute coastal services which had formerly been provided by British-Indian steamship companies, but which were no longer adequate. The Board purchased for £160,000 a British-built steamer which had seen considerable service, S.S. *Bali*, which was renamed *Pyidawtha*. After conversion for the Burma coastal trade, it arrived in Rangoon in January 1953. The Master, Chief Officer, and two Engineers were British, but the remaining officers and crew were Burmans. The *Pyidawtha* worked on the Arakan run for two years but was sunk off Kyaukpyu on 8 May 1955, largely because buoys marked upon the charts had been removed from their positions. Two new cargo ships were built for the Board at Hamburg at a cost of £1,300,000 and entered service in 1954; the *Aungmyitta* (arrived July) and *Aungthitsa* (arrived October). The ships' officers were Germans, the crew mainly Burmans. The two vessels, with a gross tonnage of over 5,600 tons, are designed for the rice and coal trade between India and Burma. Two other ships were built upon the Clyde at a cost of £785;000: *Pyidawaye* and *Pyidawnyunt*; they entered service during 1955. Smaller in size, they were designed for the coastal trade, with cabin accommodation for 33 passengers and deck accommodation for about 400.[2] These ships have taken over the Arakan run—now extended to Chittagong, while the terminal port for the Tenasserim run is Penang.[3]

---

[1] Economic and Social Board, *Pyidawtha, the New Burma*, pp. 61–2.
[2] *BWB*, 20 October 1954 and 15 September 1955.
[3] The *Matang*, for long an institution on the Tenasserim coast, is still running.

The river fleet is in need of modernization and expansion. About 500 craft were inherited from the Irrawaddy Flotilla Company, including 58 passenger ships and 140 cargo boats. Capital outlay during the years 1952–5 amounted to K50 million.[1] The building programme entails the addition of 50 large 'H'-class vessels to the fleet: the engines are to be manufactured in the United Kingdom and the hulls in Japan. The final task of fitting out these craft is to be undertaken in the Dallah Dockyard. Thirty-six of these 'H'-class boats had arrived by August 1955. In addition, a tanker fleet and several hundred miscellaneous craft are to be acquired. All this is planned as the first big instalment of a ten-year programme to be completed in the early 1960's.

Until this new fleet comes into being the river services must remain somewhat inadequate. Probably the biggest contrast with pre-war days is to be found in the express services; there are no vessels to compare with the *Siam* and the *Java* which were over 325 feet long; the largest ships are those of the 'M'-class (*Mindon* and *Mandalay*) only 200 feet long. None of the long-distance services run to the old schedules. Part of the problem lies in navigational difficulties: there is no systematic overhaul of the river buoys and charts and, most important, there is constant shoaling which is not arrested by dredging or river training. In part the shoaling is the result of sunken craft which create new mud-banks—there is a particularly bad section between Sagaing and Myingyan where there are some forty sunken wrecks. In consequence there is only one-way traffic in several sections of the Irrawaddy, while it is quite common for vessels to stick fast on mud-banks, or even to run ashore.

It is difficult to avoid the conclusion that precipitate nationalization of the service is the origin of many difficulties. The former British ship's officers have, of course, all gone. This is quaintly symbolized in the present command situation on the big express steamers, where there is no captain. A *serang* is in charge of the bridge and engine room, a mate is in charge of the deck and cargo, a steward is in charge of the cabins and the catering. They pursue their separate functions without any particular consultation, so that it is possible for a ship to be too overloaded to negotiate a particular stretch of river. Now that the British captains have departed it is the Pakistani *serangs* who hold things together, pulling other vessels off sand-banks, piecing together intelligence about the river's changing course:

[1] Outlay: 1952–3 11·2 crores, 1953–4 6·9 crores, 1954–5 32·3 crores, plus 3·5 crores for Arakan.

but they too are living under the shadow of early dismissal. Soon there will be inexperienced Burmans on every bridge and, no matter how many new ships are commissioned, the service will suffer further hazards. Inexperience is seen also in the shore organization of the Inland Water Transport Board. Freight is often delayed because of slow clearance of consignment notes in the office, unnecessary difficulties are created (for instance, it is not permitted to book through goods from Rangoon to Bhamo: they must be off-loaded at Mandalay and handed in afresh for further shipment), and there is the proliferation of petty regulations which is endemic in Burma today. However, as with most institutions in independent Burma, there is almost never a complete breakdown: somehow, the service is maintained.

Railway rehabilitation also proceeds slowly. In 1951 the structure of the railway board was reorganized and placed under a full-time Chairman. At about the same time that the main line came back to life with the closing of the Pyinmana breach (November 1951), the first major work of repairing war-damage was also brought to completion: the Gokteik viaduct was reopened to trains in August 1951. The work of repair began in October 1947 under the direction of Mr. W. J. Stone, with Bombay *khalasis*[1] providing the skilled labour. At one stage the surrounding country was infested by Communist insurgents who pestered the camp, but the party kept at work, not knowing what the future would yield, until the job was done.

At the 1952 Pyidawtha Conference a re-equipment programme was announced to provide 1,400 goods wagons and 170 passenger coaches. During the following three years this programme was largely implemented: capital expenditure rose from K2·5 crores in 1951–2 to K2·83 crores in the following year and rose steeply to K7·92 in 1953–4. Thereafter capital development was slowed down and the estimates for 1954–5 amounted to K5·91 crores. Much of the new rolling-stock was acquired from Japan, first-class carriages were bought from Germany, and special goods trucks from Holland. As a consequence of the civil war the total length of railroad in operation was reduced from 1,800 miles (in 1947) to 1,500 miles in 1951, when the line was brought back into service after two years of almost complete immobility. It was possible to restore an additional 150 miles of track by 1955, but some 400 miles of the pre-war system have either been abandoned or await repair in the unspecified future. Furthermore, the second line of track from Rangoon to Toungoo has not been replaced,

---

[1] *Khalasi*, a caste of tent-pitchers often employed as sailors and riggers. See *Hobson-Jobson*, 'Classy'.

although the necessary embankments exist and there is not an inordinate number of bridges on this route. The link with Siam, built under the Japanese, has been completely obliterated. Most of the actively-used permanent way is badly in need of relaying: apart from short sections renewed between Rangoon and Toungoo, all the rails have been worked far beyond their normal term of service.

During 1954 two major reconstruction works were completed. A new central station at Rangoon was opened in June 1954: work had started in 1946, and the whole scheme was completed at a cost of 48 lakhs (£370,000).[1] In October 1954 the Ava Bridge was reopened to rail traffic, and with it the direct rail link between Rangoon and Myitkyina. Reconstruction work had been commenced by departmental engineers in 1946, with a British firm acting as consultants. Orders for steel were placed in the United Kingdom in 1948, but the steel work did not reach Rangoon until September 1953. Once construction work could begin it was pressed on with speed, and the gaps in the bridge were closed in May 1954. The final date of completion was three months ahead of schedule. Reconstruction cost K58 lakhs (over £400,000)—about two-fifths the cost of the original bridge.[2]

Despite these improvements, the operation of the railways is still on a makeshift, 'emergency' basis. Every mile of line beyond the Rangoon suburbs is liable to insurgent attack. The rebels appear to have evolved a policy which is designed to cause the maximum disturbance without all-out effort on their part. They are accustomed to concentrate their activities upon one particular stretch of line: late in 1954 the chosen sector was the Pegu–Moulmein line, and in particular Thaton and its surroundings. The chosen sector is kept constantly under attack, until traffic entirely breaks down. The Government is then compelled to move large numbers of security forces to the danger area, and when troops, police, and home guards are deployed in encampments along the line, the rebels transfer their attentions elsewhere—usually with spectacular effects.

The legacy of eight years of such activities can be viewed on any main line: almost every hundred yards there will be a clutter of twisted goods waggons and perhaps a locomotive, lying with wheels uppermost as if upset by some careless giant. Almost every bridge, large or small, is propped up by emergency supports, baulks, and scantlings of timber. Not infrequently

[1] *BWB*, 9 June 1954. U Nu, when performing the opening ceremony, deplored the ornamentation of the station with *pyathats*, the ceremonial roofs which the old Burmese sumptuary laws reserved for royalty and religious institutions.

[2] A full account of the bridge and the repair work is in ibid., 3 November 1954.

the track makes a diversion to bypass a dynamited culvert and a chaos of wreckage not yet cleared. The isolated rural stations are surrounded by blockhouses and dense thorn hedges; many burnt-out minor halts have not been reinstated, and a name-board askew, almost illegible, is practically the only evidence that here was once a station. Train-running has to be adapted to these circumstances; from dusk to dawn no trains may run; every morning each section of the line is 'opened' by a pilot armoured train, pushing empty trucks ahead which, it is hoped, will detonate any new-laid mines. All the principal trains are furnished with armed escorts, and travellers accept the possibility of an 'incident' with complete sang-froid. The journey from Rangoon to Mandalay which was made in 14 hours up to 1942, now takes 36 hours (if the train arrives on time, which is no certain matter). The journey from Sagaing to Myitkyina also takes 2 days instead of the former 12 hours. These are the speeds achieved by the 'express' trains, but most local services are supplied by 'mixed' trains, goods and passenger combined; these mixed trains make so many halts for loading and unloading of freight that they could be out-paced by any cart drawn by a reasonably active pair of bullocks. As the trains rumble along, they are forced to slow down to a crawl to negotiate every half-dynamited propped-up bridge: the old mechanical signalling system having been completely destroyed, new electric signalling equipment has been installed at the main stations, Rangoon, Pegu, and Pyinmana, but at all the small stations and at all track junctions signalling is reduced to the manual operation of the points by a man with a red flag. Inability to restore the double track from Rangoon to Toungoo (beyond which lines branch out in several directions) means that all traffic on the nation's busiest line has to be operated on a shuttle system, with trains halting at every intermediate station until the line ahead is clear. When it is recalled that there is no mechanical communication between stations (apart from radio links between the biggest towns), then the congestion and delay may be envisaged.

Under such conditions there can be no return to pre-war levels for freight traffic, although passenger figures may be equalled (persons journeying at the expense of the State must form a sizeable minority of the travelling public). One effect of this situation is that Burma cannot hope for many years to be again a single economic unit: the national economy remains fragmented. Thus at the beginning of 1955, failure of the rains had produced in Yamethin District a crop failure of the dimen-sions of a famine, yet a few miles down the main line at Toungoo there were godowns bulging with grain which could not be moved, either up the line to Yamethin or down to Rangoon port.

Such criticisms of the state of the Burma Railways do not, however, constitute criticism of the railways staff. All grades have shown very real loyalty to the old-established tradition of the railways to 'keep the wagons moving'. Anglo-Indians and Anglo-Burmans have continued to provide an important stiffening in the middle grades of the services, but within a few years this element will have largely disappeared, and it is unlikely that sufficient new men of the right quality will have been trained to take their place. There are defects in the railway service as in the other public services; corruption is alleged, and at the Pyidawtha Conference of 1952 the Minister of Transport singled out 'dishonesty on the part of the railway employees' as a major reason for the service operating at a loss; he also spoke of 'bribery' and 'illegal gratification' in connexion with the employees of the Inland Water Transport Board.[1] A somewhat spectacular demonstration of such evils was given in 1953 with the arrest of the Chairman of the Board and the Chairman of the Railway Board on account of the alleged sale of Inland Water Transport craft for their own profit.[2] But it would be unfair to assume that delinquencies among the rank and file of the railways go further than the acceptance of 'tips' by certain persons to facilitate and expedite the normally somewhat laborious working of the railway services.

Burma's highways have received next to no attention since 1942. The blowing up of road bridges and culverts is routine activity for the rebels, who also make a particular target of any technicians or labourers of the Public Works Department attempting to carry out road maintenance. The department was clearly unable, with its limited resources in men and equipment, to fulfil all the State's demands in respect of roads and buildings, their erection and upkeep. It therefore was reorganized: the National Housing Board took over all Public Works Department work on buildings and a redesignated Highways Department became solely responsible for the roads. Its first major accomplishment was the building of the new Taungup Road across the Arakan Yomas. This undertaking, started in 1954, was completed by April 1955. For the first time heavy earth-moving machinery and road-building equipment were employed in Burma; manual labour was provided almost entirely by units of the Rehabilitation Brigade.

The Government has long discussed the desirability of

---

[1] Ministry of Information, *Pyidawtha Conference*, p. 78.
[2] *Nation*, 27 June and 6 October 1953.

placing road transport under state or co-operative ownership but, up to 1955, motor transport has remained largely in private hands. Of Burma's motor vehicles 45 per cent. are said to be registered in Rangoon (which contains about 9.5 per cent. of the population).[1] Most of vehicles in use in 1955 are survivors from the motor transport of the Fourteenth Army: in particular jeeps, put together from army scrapheaps, form 45 per cent. of the total number of registered vehicles. Almost 50 per cent. of the motor vehicles are trucks, mainly old Indian Army 3-tonners: almost every one of Rangoon's buses consists of an aged military chassis with a highly-painted local-made body superimposed. Public road transport in Rangoon is provided by 'unions' consisting of small capitalists, some owner-drivers, others owners of a dozen racketty buses. In 1955 the various bus unions were absorbed by an organization described as a 'Workers' Co-operative', but it appeared that early changes in methods of operation were unlikely. A few modern buses, made in Japan, have appeared on the Insein route; others are promised for the future.

Among the imports of new cars the products of the British 'Big Four' motor manufacturers form a large majority: however, their predominance is now challenged by Fiats and Volkswagons. In former days large, high-slung cars were popular for Burma's primitive country roads: nowadays hardly anybody dares to take a car beyond the environs of Rangoon and emphasis is all upon the small, economical car. Big American limousines are now available only to American temporary residents and to the highest-ranking politicians: imports amount only to about a score a year. The contribution which motor vehicles make to the carriage of people and goods in Burma is certainly important over short and medium distances: the overloaded jeep is one of the main supporters of the country's economy. Nevertheless, in all probability the bullock and the buffalo still pull a greater load across the land of Burma than does the internal combustion engine.

The regular means of long-distance travel for politicians, officials, traders, professional people—and a surprising number of folk in apparently modest circumstances—is the Union of Burma Airways which spans the whole length and breadth of the Union. From Rangoon to Mandalay there are passenger flights three times in the week and freight services every day; to more remote termini (such as Kengtung and Myitkyina) there are twice-weekly services. The airways depend almost entirely upon that most sturdy old workhorse of the air, the

---

[1] KTA, *Comprehensive Report*, ii. 932.

Dakota. The safety record is good, with only three fatal accidents in the first eight years of operating: only two planes have been lost in the air, despite appalling flying conditions during the monsoon months, when flights have to be maintained from primitive airfields with practically no ground-to-air navigational aid whatsoever. In addition there are hazards unknown to most airlines: one such occurred in June 1954 when, in mid-flight from Rangoon to Akyab, a plane carrying bullion was 'kidnapped' by KNDO gunmen, forced to land on a beach near Bassein, and relieved of its treasure before being permitted to fly on to Akyab.

Union of Burma Airways underwent a considerable crisis in July 1954 when a dispute arose with the non-national (mainly British) pilots and maintenance staff. The outcome was the discharge of all those associated with the dispute in August 1954. Apart from three or four foreign pilots who had been out of the country during the quarrel, the Airways was now dependent on three Burman pilots who kept the services going, somehow, during the monsoon months until a further six Burmese pilots could be promoted to take charge of aircraft. The departure of the foreigners created more of a problem upon the maintenance side: the resources of the Burmese staff were unequal to the new situation and, by mid-1955, all but four of the Union of Burma Airways air fleet were grounded. In November 1955 the Airways decided to recognize the existing shortcomings and advertised for British senior engineers and a chief inspector to take over charge of the maintenance work. A contract has been placed with Vickers-Armstrong for the supply of three Viscounts, and with these planes it is hoped to extend the external services to Ceylon, Malaya, Indochina, the Philippines, and Japan.

The development of industries has necessarily been limited by inadequate transport. The KTA report laid considerable emphasis upon the building up of new industrial complexes at Myingyan and around Akyab. Two years after the presentation of the final report nothing has occurred to suggest that these two massive proposals have been carried as far as even the earliest phase of actual planning. Indeed, one major component of the Akyab scheme, the proposed jute mill, was transferred from Akyab to Rangoon when the time came to start building in 1955.[1] An indication of the impact of transport difficulties upon up-country manufacturers was provided when the new

---

[1] The first (mimeographed) version of the Economic and Social Board's *Pyidawtha, the New Burma*, pp. 72–73, may be compared with p. 102 of the published version. The jute plant appears at Akyab in the first version and at Rangoon in the second.

Chauk refinery was opened: the Chairman of the Burmah Oil Company made it clear that the cost of transporting one ton of oil from Chauk to Rangoon was then five times greater than the cost of transporting the same quantity from the Persian Gulf to Rangoon.[1] In considering the feasibility of exploiting the Kalewa coalfield, the KTA consultants calculated that Kalewa coal could be put on sale in Rangoon only at a rate of K13 per ton or more above the price at which Indian coal sells there.[2] Until the capacity of the roads, railways, and rivers to handle large quantities of freight expeditiously has been demonstrated, the expansion of industries up-country cannot be postulated on an economic basis.

A publication by the Census Office[3] in 1954 showed that the 1947 figures of 473 industrial establishments employing 46,480 workers had, over the course of seven years, increased to 1,982 establishments and 90,887 workers.[4] Of this total, about 24 per cent. of the industrial establishments are located in Rangoon and its environs. Other towns with some industries attached are (in order of importance) Mandalay, Moulmein, Mudon (15 miles from Moulmein), Bassein, Myingyan, Pegu, Akyab, and Prome. Most of these establishments are weaving sheds, potteries, garages, and other such petty concerns; 479 establishments are controlled by companies or partnerships, 368 being Burmese-owned and 101 foreign-owned. The remainder (1,503) have one owner apiece who is usually the working overseer.[5] The pre-war pattern of industry still prevails, with rice-mills as the largest single element.[6]

The oil industry is described in a recent government publication[7] as being in 1954 'semi-prostrate': nevertheless the position is vastly better than during the black days of the civil war. Production has steadily climbed, set back from time to time by labour disputes; whereas the 1949 output was equal to 3 per cent. of pre-war production, output in 1955 was nearly 20 per cent. of pre-war. An important advance was the opening

---

[1] *Nation*, 7 January 1954.

[2] KTA, *Comprehensive Report*, iii. 1518.

[3] Industry Release no. 5, October 1954.

[4] The figures given by the Census Department may be compared with those of the Labour Directorate (quoted in *Pyidawtha, the New Burma*, pp. 83–84) issued in 1951 showing a total of 1,359 industrial establishments and 43,000 workers. Clearly, different definitions of what constitutes an 'industrial establishment' have been employed.

[5] Of these 'single-owner' establishments Burmans own 1,316, Chinese own 46, Indians 43, and Pakistanis 15.

[6] The census says 390 mills employing 32,025 persons; the Labour Directorate says 882 mills. Probably the census enumerators have omitted the rural mills as their activities have been confined to the main towns.

[7] *Pyidawtha, the New Burma*, p. 81.

CRUDE OIL PRODUCTION
(tons)

1939	1,080,000
1947	11,000
1948	44,500
1949	33,700
1950	64,200
1951	96,300
1952	95,300
1953	121,200
1954	145,400
1955	153,200

of the new refinery at Chauk in January 1954. This new installation, assembled largely from equipment salvaged or manufactured in the Burmah Oil Company's own workshops, was stated to have a capacity of 100,000 gallons of crude oil per day. The Chauk field will continue to work at low pressure until refinery and transport facilities have been sufficiently expanded to permit increased production. The Yenangyaung field offers few attractions for a resumption of working: it is still a lawless area and anyhow its drillings are old and largely exhausted. Yenangyaung is therefore given over to the activities of small-scale operators, many of them former employees of Burmah Oil Company, who produce bootleg 'petrol' which is much used by the jeep drivers of central Burma, often with unexpected results. The company's plans go no further than envisaging the organization of these small operators into gangs under contractors who could deliver crude oil to the company on the forshore for later refining.

The products of Chauk have been distributed during the years since independence almost entirely in Upper Burma, but plans are being developed for marketing in Lower Burma again. The first need is to reduce the transport costs involved in shipping oil down to Syriam to a level which will compete with freighter costs in bringing oil from the Persian Gulf. The Inland Water Transport Board have acquired (1955–6) a tanker fleet which will be able to give an economic service.[1] The next requirement is to restore the Syriam refineries. Reconstruction work began in 1954, with January 1957 as target date for completion, at a cost estimated at £500,000.

---

[1] The new 'tankers' will consist of 6 tugs, each tug will push 6 oil flats, each flat will have a capacity of 500 tons. This new method of locomotion with what are virtually articulated tankers is said to be much cheaper than older means of river haulage.

Syriam will then have a daily capacity of about 150,000 gallons and total oil productive capacity in Burma will rise to about 340,000 tons per annum. Thereafter Burma will be self-sufficient once again for all petroleum products except aviation spirit, and will be able to export small quantities of petrol and wax products. A further important development in the oil industry is the acceleration of Burmanization throughout the upper grades of the managerial and technical staff. Large numbers of young graduates and others are being sent to Britain for further training and are being employed in responsible positions. Within a decade the numbers of senior British employees will probably be reduced to a handful. A possible new opening for the industry is envisaged in plans for prospecting for potential oil deposits in the Delta (a few trial drillings were made in 1938, with only modest results); a substantial oil strike would open up a much brighter future for Burma, as present known oil reserves are calculated to provide yields only for some twenty-five years more.

Of the other major enterprises the Bawdwin mines resumed working late in 1952; production was worked up to 8,500 tons of lead and zinc ore per day by 1955. Plans were prepared for a new smelting works which would permit a considerable increase in processing; but action was deferred due to lack of proven reserves of ore. The immediate surroundings of Mawchi mine were freed from the grip of the insurgents late in 1953, but eighteen months later the road from Mawchi to Toungoo was still subject to constant attack. Work at Mawchi has therefore been confined largely to 'care and maintenance', but the mining company has raised a sum of £450,000 for re-equipment to enable production to commence whenever the security position permits. The mines in Tenasserim continued to be dominated by the insurgents well into 1955: several British concerns have sold their interests to Burmese capitalists, and a certain improvement in security conditions has sometimes followed such transactions. The great majority of the Tenasserim mines lie semi-derelict, plant is deteriorating, not

| | 1953 | 1954 |
	(tons)	
Wolfram concentrates	1,580	1,283
Tin concentrates	597	776
Mixed concentrates	381	—
	2,558	2,059

(SOURCE: *Annual Reports*, Burma Chamber of Commerce.)

even inspected for seven years, and output remains pitifully small. One Mergui mine (the Yatanabon Mine) has been nationalized, but until a thirty-three mile approach road has been built production cannot be large.

The Thayetmyo cement factory did not begin operations after the war until 1951; it closed down from July to October 1952 for lack of orders; another closure (July–October 1953) was due to a major overhaul of the plant. Output has remained well below rated capacity (60,000 tons), being 35,961 tons in 1951–2, 44,582 tons the following year, and 44,727 tons during 1953–4 up to nationalization.

Thus the output of the industrial undertakings established before the war remains only a tithe of former achievements. Private enterprise has made no significant new contribution to post-war industrial development. The blunt truth is that, in face of internal unrest, unpredictable import and export restrictions, transport limitations, the threat of nationalization, and the uncertainty of the country's political future, British and Indian enterprise, which in the past provided the bulk of capital investment, no longer intends to tie up money in what are now speculative ventures. A big concern like Steel Brothers, which in the past has contributed in no small measure to developing the wealth of Burma, has now perforce to act almost entirely as an importer and shipping agency; its activities in the field of productive enterprise have been largely transferred to Africa. The foreign industrial investment which takes place today is of marginal importance, such as the new Chinese-owned biscuit factory at Kamayut.

New industrial development must now be instituted by the Government, for wealthy Burmans have not yet become accustomed to investing capital in long-term economic development. Houses erected for letting to wealthy foreigners, new cinemas, garages, and motor firms: these are among the investments most favoured by present-day Burmans with surplus capital. And so, partly from necessity, but more because of ideological belief, the AFPFL Government has placed state industrialization at the forefront of its programme. The one major undertaking which has actually been functioning for several years is the government textile mill, whose early misadventures were related on p. 103. By 1955 there was no published evidence to suggest that this factory was working more profitably. The government industrial venture of which most has been heard is the projected steel-rolling mill. The first tentative suggestion of this mill has been attributed to a former Professor of Engineering at Rangoon University who put the idea before Aung San in 1947. In 1949 an American firm made a survey of Burma's resources of scrap-iron and made a recommendation for a large-scale plant, based on very optimistic estimates of the scrap position. A further study was made in 1952 under the auspices of ECAFE, and two Indian experts (Mr. Subramanian and Mr. Powala of Tata Iron and Steel Company) reported in favour of a small plant. A United Nations survey of the scrap position was also made, and it was calculated that 175,000 tons of scrap existed in Burma (mainly war wreckage, bridges, locomotives, tanks, airfield strips). Tenders were then invited (in 1952) from Germany, Britain, Switzerland, Japan, and other countries. A contract was finally signed in May 1954 with Demag Aktiengesellschaft. This provided for an all-electrically operated plant capable of producing 20,000 tons of steel per annum in the form of 4,000 tons of re-rolled steel and 16,000 tons of corrugated sheets, drums, bars, nails, and barbed-wire. The cost of this undertaking is estimated at K6 crores or £4½ million. The plant will be built in the suburbs of Rangoon between Kamayut and Thamaing beside the Hlaing River. The KTA report ventured to criticize this choice of site, which is covered by marshy paddy-fields, liable to annual flooding.[1] As plans progressed (the target opening-date for the factory being April 1956), doubts were exprsesed as to the actual extent of Burma's store of scrap-metal; it appeared likely that suitable scrap for about five years only (some 100,000 tons at most) was available. Other estimates have placed the total at figures as low as 25,000 tons: it is not easy, even for experts, to calculate what will be usable: much of the metal which lies strewn in the former pathways of war is toughened armour, useless for the projected plant, or has been rusted by ten monsoons or more into uselessness. To discover alternative supplies of metal, prospecting was undertaken for deposits of iron and promising reports were received from Tavoy and Taunggyi.[2] Construction of the factory has somewhat lagged behind schedule: it is hoped that it will be possible to begin the output of structural steel and wire products in November 1956, but the main production effort will have to await the installation of an open-hearth furnace, plans for which are still to be completed.[3]

An enterprise which has advanced somewhat more rapidly is the Kalewa coalfield. Although the Kalewa seams had not been highly rated in pre-war years, the AFPFL Government

---

[1] KTA, *Comprehensive Report*, iii. 1881.
[2] Other deposits of zinc, manganese, and copper have been discovered in the Chin hills and the Shan hills.
[3] *Nation*, 30 January 1956.

decided in its earliest days to exploit the coalfield. A reconnaissance was made in 1948 by Dr. Ba Thi (later Director of
the Burma Geological Department) who found thirty seams
about 4½ miles west of Kalewa. Nothing further was done
because of the rebellions. In November 1951 an investigation
at Kalewa was made by a geologist of the KTA group, and the
KTA final report gave a guarded recommendation in favour
of exploitation. The potential yield was estimated at 750,000
tons per annum; the best mine would be exhausted in 17 years,
the second site in 34 years; it would take 4 years to get the
area ready for working. KTA reported adversely on the quality
of the coal, finding that its friability 'precludes its satisfactory
use as a hand-fired fuel for most industrial purposes',[1] but that
it might be used in furnaces or in briquette form on the railways.
The Government continued to give a high place to this project:
prospecting and drilling were carried out, and by 1955 a small
drift-mine, intended mainly for training purposes, was yielding
20–30 tons a day. The coal has been successfully used in
boilers with mechanical stokers and, mixed with Indian coal,
the best screened Kalewa coal has proved usable on the railway.
A proposal has been drafted (mainly by a United Nations
mining consultant) for two collieries to work the main seam;
they are expected each to produce 500 tons a day of run-of-
mine coal, giving a total of 300,000 tons per annum—enough
to supply the railways, river steamers, and electric power
stations. The cost of the plant and accommodation at Kalewa
is estimated at K2 crores (£1½ million) spread over three or
four years.

Certain problems have not yet been squarely faced. First,
where will Burma obtain the thousand miners and skilled
technicians that will be needed? Kalewa is regarded as a place
of exile by most Burmans, and coal-mining is unlikely to
recommend itself as an attractive occupation. Pioneer work
has been done by local people, mainly Chins, but it may be
necessary to import Indian or Japanese labour and technicians
fully to implement the scheme. Secondly, it will be necessary
to transport the coal down the Chindwin, which is almost
unnavigable in the dry season; its depth is only two or three
feet, and there are shifting sandbanks; very special craft will
be required to meet these difficulties. Unless the Myingyan
industrial scheme is suddenly given a high priority, the coal
will have to find its main market in the Rangoon area: nothing
has occurred to change the KTA verdict that this will be
anything but a commercial proposition. The first consignment

[1] KTA, *Comprehensive Report*, iii. 1503.

of Kalewa coal arrived in Rangoon on 29 January 1956. It consisted of thirty wagons of coal-dust for use by the Electricity Supply Board. It was then announced by Ba Swe that, currently, production was running at 50 tons a day which, it was hoped, might be raised to 1,000 tons daily by 1957, after the installation of new machinery to be carried out by a British (Welsh) firm of engineers.

Construction of a state jute factory commenced in April 1955, and was completed (ahead of schedule) in January 1956 by a British firm from Belfast. Production was due to begin in April 1956, reaching the full annual capacity of 24 million gunny bags in the following December: sufficient to fulfil all Burma's needs. To maintain this production a supply of 15 million viss of raw jute will be necessary, and initially substantial imports of raw jute will have to be drawn from India. Four state tile factories, producing Japanese-type roofing-tiles, were scheduled to begin work in February 1956. Two new sugar-mills have been built: one at Namti in Myitkyina District was supplied with machinery from Holland, and was due to begin crushing sugar-cane in May 1956. The second factory at Pyinmana, built by Hitachi of Japan, was to begin operations in March 1956. The over-all cost of this series of factories is expected to be in the region of K18 crores (about £14 million).

Without publicity, a small government sugar factory began working at Bhamo in January 1955. This modest plant was equipped almost entirely with machinery fabricated in government workshops (almost no foreign spending was involved) and was assembled entirely under the supervision of a Burma Indian manager. Not one single highly-paid foreign expert was concerned. Many would think that it is by such unassuming but practical ventures that Burma's industrial revolution might find its way most successfully, and with the minimum of heartbreaking failure, through the first experimental phase.

Perhaps the most vital item in the Government's industrial policy is the hydro-electric programme. The various municipal electricity undertakings which have been nationalized were all (with the exception of the Rangoon service) small and out of date, most consumed coal in their generating plant, a few used oil fuel.[1] The Electricity Board's first necessity was to modernize these local undertakings, and new diesel generators have been installed in thirty towns. The Board's long-term plans are designed to create a national grid system with power

---

[1] The Electricity Board claims to be the only department which has paid compensation to expropriated concerns promptly and in full.

supplied by hydro-electric stations. The Pegu Project was the first scheme upon which planning commenced: it was hoped to harness the Pegu River forty miles upstream from the town, thereby producing a total of 15,000 kilowatts of power for distribution in Rangoon and Henzada: but this project was overshadowed by another scheme. This second scheme, the Balu Chaung Project (sometimes called the Lawpita Project), was originally classified only among 'other possible power developments under consideration for later development',[1] but late in 1954 it was suddenly given the highest priority. This followed the signing of the Japanese reparations agreement, when the decision was taken (whether under Japanese or Burmese advice is not clear) to make the Balu Chaung Project the first major reparations undertaking: the cost is estimated at K17 crores (over £12 million) out of which the Japanese will contribute nearly K12 crores, and this will absorb seven-eighths of the reparations funds for the first two years. The contract has been awarded to Nippon Koei Kabushiki Kaisha. The power station is to be sited in the Kayah State by the Lawpita waterfall upon the Balu Chaung (river), a fast-flowing tributary of the Salween. When completed, this station will generate 84,000 kilowatts of electricity, and supplies will be carried to Rangoon by way of Toungoo and Pegu, and to Mandalay via Taunggyi, Meiktila, and Myingyan. The plant should be ready to begin operating by August 1957. It is expected to revolutionize the power resources of Burma, providing a tremendous boost to industrialization by the provision of cheap power: in Rangoon the proposed rate should be 12 pyas a unit (about 2d.), less than half the existing rate. Final success will depend not so much on the ability of the contractors to produce cheap electricity at Balu Chaung, as on their ability to extend this power over the 300 miles to Rangoon without incurring undue intermediate costs.

The speed with which these designs for development can be given practical shape will depend largely on the outcome of Burma's trade negotiations, and whether Burma's new customers can provide the necessary technicians and equipment. Already Yugoslav and Czech engineers have been seen in Burma. The whole position with regard to industrialization should be considerably clearer in 1965 than it was in 1955.

Organized labour as a factor of importance in industries and the public services is a very recent phenomenon, dating almost entirely from the post-war years. A 'Trade Union Act' has

[1] Economic and Social Board, *Pyidawtha, the New Burma*, mimeographed version, p. 61.

been in force since 1926, but in pre-war days very few labour associations registered under the Act. The first body to be recognized by an employer for negotiating purposes was the Burmah Oil Company Refineries Workers' Union, Syriam, organized by M. A. Raschid. In the first post-war years the trade unions were regarded, both by the Communists and the Socialists, as key organs in their struggle for power within the AFPFL. The Socialists have succeeded in ousting their rivals from the open leadership of the movement, but many with Communist leanings remained entrenched in the offices and branches of the unions. A feature of unionism in Burma is the large part which personal leadership plays in bodies in which, as yet, no closely-knit organization has been built up. Nothing has developed in Burma like the monolithic unions of Britain or America, able to claim membership throughout an entire industry and across the whole country. The chief large-scale unions are the Burma Railway Workers' Union and the All-Burma Petroleum Workers' Union, formed in July 1954: membership of these unions is, at most, 5,000 apiece. The former union underwent a split in 1954; a break-away organization, the Burma Railways Workers' United Front, was formed and succeeded in registering 4,000 members within a few months, many from among the ranks of its rival (railway employees number less than 20,000 in all). Bo Min Gaung, a leading Socialist Minister who is also prominent within the TUC(B), presided over a conference aimed at uniting the two rival unions; but six months later the two bodies were still in active rivalry. Such splintering is a common tendency, although not always on such a large scale: most unions are petty bodies, often limited to the workers in a single privately-owned factory or a single government establishment. It is not uncommon for two or more unions to be found within the same establishment.[1] Figures for the trade union movement are by no means complete because not all the unions are registered with the Directorate of Labour, but the incomplete figures serve to indicate the narrow field of the trade unions in Burma. Continuous

TRADE UNIONS, 1946–52

	1946	1947	1948	1949	1950	1951	1952
Unions	25	54	92	115	122	140	146
Membership	12,588	29,618	26,971	30,597	31,974	34,217	32,775

(SOURCE: Union Bank of Burma, *Quarterly Bulletin of Statistics*.)

[1] Dept. of Information, *Burma, the Seventh Anniversary*, 'The Labour Directorate in 1954', p. 159.

unemployment, bad conditions in the smaller workshops and factories, the absence of a regular wage structure: all these are features of industry and labour in Burma in the 1950's.

One major development in the sphere of labour has been the termination in the Rangoon Docks of the employment of casual labour, and the registration and regular payment of dockers under a Dock Labour Board. This scheme (which affects about 1,300 workers) came into force in February 1952.[1] The scheme has brought considerable benefits to the dock labour force, but there have been many complaints from shippers of delays, thefts, and a failure to enforce discipline by the Dock Labour Board. Many of these shortcomings, it is hoped, will be ameliorated as experience is gained. For the purpose of this study, a point of interest is the extremely small part played by the port workers' unions in this major development: it was confined, virtually, to explaining the new scheme to their members as a *fait accompli*.

The role of the trade unions has as yet not become properly defined: first utilized as a weapon in the national struggle against colonialism, they were then involved—again as a political weapon to demonstrate mass political power by processions and mob pressure—in the Communists' struggle to overturn the AFPFL Government. They have remained primarily a political movement, and the AFPFL Government has attempted to utilize the unions as a lever to fortify government and political policy, somewhat as Soviet trade unions are utilized. It was noticeable that, at the Asian Trades Union Seminar held in Rangoon in May 1955, a Burmese representative felt it desirable to state that 'the TUC(B) had in view the decentralization of powers so as to allow the basic trade unions affiliated to it to function on their own, independent of control from headquarters'.[2] Such a concept of the relations of unions with their national congress would make no sense in Britain or the United States where the process of evolution has begun with the foundation of local unions, followed by their gradual affiliation within a national organization. Every year in his May Day speech to the assembled ranks of the TUC(B), Ba Swe surveys the whole field of national and international politics; he barely devotes a moment to specifically trade union matters—wages, conditions of employment, and the like. During his 1955 speech practically his only reference to the trade unions was a denunciation of slackness among workers. He stated

[1] 'Dock Labour', *Burma*, July 1953, pp. 60–62.
[2] *BWB*, 19 May 1955.

We have enacted laws for our workers, so that their rights are not lower than those in the most progressive countries in the world. But performance of their duties has been found to be very unsatisfactory. The workers are not yet quite dutiful. In offices, too, instead of doing the work assigned to them diligently, they are simply wasting the time. It is said that it sometimes takes one whole week for a case to be shifted from one table to another. . . . There are many workers too who waste time.[1]

He went on to recommend that the unions should introduce Stakhanovite incentives. All this indicates the prevailing concept of the unions as an adjunct to the leadership of the Government. But it should not be overlooked that individual trade union leaders often have very different objectives, looking more towards winning political power for themselves, through the manipulation of followers who are largely ignorant and credulous.

Like so many aspects of Burma in the first decade after independence, the condition of urban labour and industry is in a state of flux, of transition. The economic structure built up during the British period stands derelict, half destroyed; and as yet only the bare scaffolding—in many directions only a half-drawn blueprint—can be discerned to indicate the possible lines of the future economic order.

The great question which Burma, as well as other newly emancipated Asian states, seeks to solve is whether a short cut can be found towards greater industrial self-sufficiency. Some may say that there cannot be a short cut towards the acquisition of industrial capital and technical mastery, that the process of training managers, engineers, and experts of all kinds must necessarily be slow, and any attempt at acceleration by means of bringing in foreign experts who are ignorant of the special requirements of Burma will only cause harm. Others point to Russia as a country that has successfully made a short cut to industrial power through the employment of foreign technicians and the enforcement of over-all planning regardless of the human consequences. Some are convinced that technology can solve any problem—as has been done in America. But may it not be possible that there is a Burmese solution to this great question?

Past experience seems to indicate that the Burmese temperament is less adaptable to the demands of large-scale industry and mass production than, say, the Indian or Japanese temperament. On the other hand many Burmans are first-class craftsmen, capable of improvising technical processes or

[1] *BWB*, 5 May 1955.

equipment out of paltry materials; and in the type of business which is based on everyday personal contacts, such as trading in the market place, Burmans are equal to other comers. It seems possible that Burma could create her own industrial revolution, based upon cottage industries or small rural factories where all the processes are completed under the supervision of one master. The coming into operation of the Balu Chaung Project could make such a rural industrial network possible if ample cheap electric power becomes available. Such a small-scale industrial revolution might do much for Burma to relieve unemployment and to supply many articles at present imported: why, to take random examples, should Burma import toys from Japan and sports goods from Pakistan, when local skill and resources could turn out products their equal or their superior?

The thinking of the revolutionary government proved to be somewhat on these lines, though cramped by a rigid, doctrinaire approach. A programme of import substitution, based upon local manufactures of somewhat crude level of finish, made it possible to dispense with a wide range of imported goods. Despite unfavourable conditions there was a considerable growth in small-scale entrepreneurial activity in the late 1950s and early 1960s. But the determination of the military to follow the Burmese Way to Socialism cut all this short. Even such time-honoured enterprises as the small oil wells of the Yenangyaung area, operated by the *twin-za* or owner-producer, were expropriated. The last foreign firms to be taken over were the Burma Corporation and its mines, and a Unilever factory making soap products. These concerns, previously run as joint enterprises, were wholly nationalized in January 1965. Lack of success in nationalized industry was countered by increasing still further the extent of centralized government control.

XI

DEFENCE

URING the first critical years of independence the army
has played a larger part than any other section of the
community in saving Burma from disintegration: and
yet during the same period large sections of the army did their
utmost to rush the country to destruction. The process whereby
the Burma Army first became a major factor in politics and
political leadership, and then was directed towards a non-
political role, subordinate to the civil Government, is one of
great interest yet, despite the vital part of the armed forces in
national development, their contribution still remains to be
objectively assessed. Since 1958, interest has focused upon the
role of 'the colonels' in their Cromwellian work of reform. The
emergence of a national army as a broad-based, cohesive,
professional force has still not been given adequate attention.

Burmans take pride in the military traditions of the past.
Under the kings the basis of society was not so much the
village in which a man lived as the regiment to which he
belonged; up to quite recent years villages in Upper Burma
have been known as *myin*, cavalry, or *thenat*, musketeer, villages,
and older people still recall seeing the tattoo marks which
indicated a man's regiment. The armies which marched with
Alaungpaya, Bodawpaya, and other kings in the bloody wars
against Siam were composed, as to their *corps d'élite*, of the men
of Shwebo, Madaya (Mandalay), and Kyaukse Districts; but
with them marched regiments of Mons, Shans, Kachins, and
Manipuri horse. Of all the Burmese generals the best-remem-
bered is Bandula, conqueror of Manipur and Assam, who was
killed by a British shell at Danubyu. Since independence the
former Fytche Square in the heart of Rangoon has been
renamed Bandoola Square, and it is a representation of the
'Bandoola Helmet' which all ranks of the modern Burma Army
wear upon their sleeves. And yet the origins of the modern
army must be sought in the disciplined troops which the British
raised rather than in the picturesque, bold, but disorderly
armies of the kings.

Forces were raised by the British in Burma immediately
after the first territories were annexed. The Arracan Light
Infantry was formed in 1824; its ranks were first filled by
Arakanese, and to them were added Chins and Manipuris.

A Talaing Corps was also formed, for which Mons and Malays were recruited. These units were 'local corps', of which there were many in the armies of the old East India Company, formed for local defence rather than general service. The organization, drill, and uniform of the Burma battalions were similar to those of the Indian regiments, and the officers were seconded from the Bengal and Madras armies. The Arracan Light Infantry fought well during the Second Anglo-Burmese War, at the capture of Rangoon and after, but the unit's days were numbered, owing entirely to policy laid down in Army Headquarters, India. After the Indian Mutiny, when the Indian Army was reorganized under the Crown, most of the 'local' corps were disbanded, the Burma troops with them, many being absorbed into the police.

During the Third Anglo-Burmese War Karen units were raised for active service, largely owing to the advocacy of civil officers who knew the Karens and of the American missionaries, one or two of whom themselves girded on the sword of Gideon. The pacification of Upper Burma proceeded slowly. Thibaw's army had melted into the jungle, and almost the entire Madras Army was employed in pursuing the 'Bos', captains of the jungle. To relieve the Madras Army several battalions were raised for local service, three as Burma Infantry, regiments of the regular army, the rest as Burma Military Police. Despite their 'Burma' designation, recruits for these new formations were drawn almost entirely from the martial races of Punjab. The intention, when the military police were first raised, was to recruit half the force from amongst the peoples of Burma.[1] But those Burmans who offered themselves for enrolment were not of high standard: presumably young Burmans of the best stamp were unwilling to serve those who had but now arrived as conquerors. The British officers from Indian regiments who were employed in raising the new force followed the easiest line and drew their recruits from the races which were familiar to them. One Karen Military Police Battalion was constituted, but after a few years the Karens were allocated among the Indian battalions: this followed the prevailing practice in the Indian Army of making up units by 'class companies', meaning that a battalion of Punjab Infantry might be composed of 1 company of Sikhs, 1 of Dogras, and 2 of Punjabi Mussulmans (these classes were all enlisted in the 'Burma' battalions). In part this system was designed to cater for religious prejudices and customs, in part to discourage intriguing amongst men of one caste by the stimulus of inter-company rivalry. The system

[1] Sir C. Crosthwaite, *The Pacification of Burma* (London, 1912), p. 16.

has been condemned as another manifestation of a 'divide and rule' policy: in fact the regimental comradeship which often developed between men of different races was all too seldom echoed in the communal atmosphere of the villages and towns from which they had come. Gradually the hill peoples of Burma were recruited into the military police, particularly Kachins from Bhamo District. The only regular army unit recruiting Burmans was a field company of Sappers and Miners (Engineers) formed in 1887: its composition was almost completely Burmese, many being former soldiers of Thibaw.

During the First World War, when the Indian Army was greatly expanded, four battalions of Burma Rifles were formed for general service. Officers came from the Indian Army and the Burma Commission, non-commissioned officers were drawn from the military police, and recruits were mostly straight from the villages. The battalions were constituted on the standard 'class company' basis. Karens provided the largest element; Burmese, Arakanese, Kachins, Chins, Shans, and Gurkhas were also enlisted. Motor Transport Companies and Labour Corps were formed. The infantry served in the Middle East, and Sappers and Miners came under fire. Considering the difficulties of service in lands alien to the troops—Mesopotamia, Egypt, and Palestine—the Burma units acquitted themselves well.

After the war, when there was a drastic reduction in the armed forces, the number of battalions of Burma Rifles was reduced to three and Burmese recruitment was completely terminated in 1925.[1] The standard composition of a battalion of Burma Rifles was 2 companies of Karens, 1 of Kachins, and 1 of Chins. In 1927 the senior Burmese unit, the Sappers and Miners, was disbanded. Thereafter the only opportunity open to Burmese for military service was with the military police. Originally organized on a basis of one military police battalion to every district, improvements in internal security had led to the force being cut by half: in 1918 there were 13 battalions, and these were then reduced to 10. Personnel were partly Indians and Gurkhas, together with Burmese, Karens, Kachins, and Chins.

In 1937, following separation from India, the Burma Rifles ceased to be numbered as the 20th regiment of the Indian Army; nevertheless, many characteristic features of the Indian Army were preserved. Two leading writers on Burmese history, men with distinctly different points of view, G. E. Harvey and

---

[1] Reasons given for discontinuance of Burmese recruitment are stated in *Report of the Indian Statutory Commission*, xi, 23.

J. S. Furnivall, are both agreed in condemning wholeheartedly the effects of Indian Army policy upon the Burmese military tradition.[1] Their arguments have much substance: the Indian Army had its eyes fixed on the North-West Frontier, the Afghan border, and the Russians beyond. In this view the Punjab was 'the Sword Arm of India', and beside Punjabis only Gurkhas, Rajputs, and a few selected Pathans were thought to be fit for the work on the Frontier. The national development of Burma was of interest only to officers actually serving in Burma. But whatever one's opinion of the influence of the Indian Army, the pattern it had set could not rapidly be altered. And so units continued to be formed on a class basis, and the military tradition was of close identification of the soldier with his tribe or community rather than with the nation at large. Although parade-ground discipline was strict, off parade the relations between officers and men were much more intimate, candid, and personal—even paternal—than in other armies. British officers were few in number, the backbone of the service was provided by 'Viceroy's Commissioned Officers',[2] Jemadars and Subadars, for whom there is no parallel in other armies. These officers were selected from the ranks; they were usually men of mature years, but sometimes a young man would be directly commissioned because of his superior education or perhaps his hereditary status as son of a chief or headman; all belonged to the same community or tribe as their men. They commanded platoons and often companies and the most outstanding G.C.O. acted as 'Woordy Major', the Commanding Officer's right hand man. These indigenous officers commanded great prestige and confidence among their own folk, as well as the respect of the British officers: they contributed greatly to the salty, intimate relationship which existed between all ranks.

After separation from India the number of Burma Rifles battalions was raised to four, while ancillary services were also formed: a Burma Army Service Corps, Signals, medical and ordnance services, &c. Once again Burmese were recruited, but they were at a certain disadvantage; the other races, by reason of seniority, were in much greater numbers in the higher ranks; this was not agreeable to Burmese feelings.[3] The military police battalions were reorganized into two

---

[1] Harvey, *British Rule in Burma*, pp. 41–42 and Furnivall, *Colonial Policy and Practice*, pp. 178–84.

[2] Known after separation from India as 'Governor's Commissioned Officers', G.C.O.s.

[3] The most senior officer to hold the King's Commission was Burmese, Captain (later Major General) Tun Hla Oung, son of the former Minister, U May Oung.

bodies. In Burma proper there remained three battalions of military police, the 1st and 2nd Rangoon Battalions and the Mandalay Battalion. The remaining six battalions were organized as a Frontier Force for watch and ward in the border hills.[1]

In 1939 the defence forces consisted of some 12,000 in the Frontier Force and Military Police, and some 5,000 regular troops: the four battalions of Burma Rifles and two battalions of British infantry. One British and one Burma battalion were stationed at Mingaladon, one Burma battalion was at Mandalay, and the remaining battalions (one British, two Burma) were quartered at Maymyo. The vast majority of the inhabitants of Burma never saw a soldier throughout their lives, and only occasionally a military policeman on treasury guard or on riot duty.

After the outbreak of war with Germany in 1939 there was some expansion of the armed forces. As regards the Burma Rifles, a 5th and 6th Battalion were raised by 'milking' the regular battalions, and each contained one Burmese company; a 7th Battalion was made up of drafts from the Military Police, mostly Gurkhas and Indians; the 8th Battalion, Sikhs and Punjabi Mussulmans, was similarly formed from the Frontier Force; the 9th was a reinforcement battalion and the 10th the training centre. Four more battalions were formed from 1939 to 1941: the 11th and 12th Battalions were composed of Burmese and Karens, some joining as Territorials[2] The 13th and 14th Battalions were entirely recruited from the Shans. The majority of officers were Britishers in civil or commercial employment in the country, but after 1940 the proportion of Burmans greatly increased: the new Shan battalions were officered largely by the Sawbwas and Shan gentry.

Burma also raised new services. In June 1940 the Burma Royal Naval Volunteer Reserve came into being. Unlike the Burma Army, its parent service was British not Indian; thus enlistment was on an individual, not a 'class', basis; a man was considered on his mental and physical merits, not according to some communal classification. The Burma Navy therefore soon contained representatives of almost all the communities of Burma, but as a higher standard of education was required than in the army, the urban communities (as, for instance, the

---

[1] Their distribution was as follows: Southern Shan States, Northern Shan States, Chin hills, Myitkyina, Bhamo, and Reserve battalions.

[2] There were two volunteer forces, the Burma Auxiliary Force, largely composed of Anglo-Burmans and Europeans with some urban Burmans; and the Territorial Force, completely Burman, which included the Rangoon University Training Corps.

Anglo-Burmans or Sino-Burmans) were more heavily represented. Two senior officers were provided by the Royal Navy,
but the junior officers included a high proportion of Burmans;
soon after its formation, the 29 officers included 9 Burmans,
Sub-Lieutenant Than Pe being the first Burman officer. The
new navy was equipped with a scratch collection of small
vessels, tugs, launches, and motor-boats. By 1942 there were
about 50 officers and 600 naval ratings.

The formation of an air-training unit was also sanctioned in
1940, but it was unable to make much progress for lack of
equipment. A few young Burmans managed to join the R.A.F.
as flying officers.[1]

During 1940 and 1941 there were increasing indications that
Japan was preparing for a campaign of expansion to the south.
But, except for brief periods, the Government of India had
always regarded the lands to its east as an area from which no
major danger need be anticipated, and from 1939 onwards the
main weight of the Indian war effort was directed towards
North Africa. The defence of Burma (as of Malaya) was
entrusted more to bluff than to arms. The raw Burma infantry
battalions were organized in the 1st Burma Division during
July 1941: this comprised 1st Burma Brigade Group (Shan
States), 2nd Burma Brigade Group (Tenasserim), and 13th
Indian Infantry Brigade Group (Shan States).[2] The strength
of this division was only about 8,000, little more than half
that of a standard British division. During December 1941
and January 1942 the 17th Indian Division was formed (or,
rather, re-formed) in Burma out of Indian and British troops
as they arrived. All these forces were seriously under-equipped,
particularly as regards artillery and automatic weapons. Other
reinforcements included the 7th British Armoured Brigade
from North Africa and 50,000 Chinese 'troops' (many being
unarmed boys).

The defending army was quite unequal to its burden; there
could be no question of defending the whole of the long,
winding, barely accessible frontier from attack; Burma Command had to make an intelligent guess as to where the Japanese
would attack, and dispose the troops accordingly. As it happened, they guessed wrong.

The Burma Army could hardly have received its baptism of

---

[1] Air defence in Burma was confined to No. 67 Fighter Squadron, R.A.F. and the
American Volunteer Group.

[2] Initially, 1 Burma Brigade was composed of the King's Own Yorkshire Light
Infantry, and 1st and 5th Burma Rifles; 2 Burma Brigade contained the 2nd, 4th,
6th, and 8th Burma Rifles. There were many transfers of units after the fighting had
begun.

fire under worse conditions: semi-trained, under-strength, incompletely equipped, fighting in a cause for which few were wholeheartedly enthusiastic against some of the best divisions of a ruthless foe riding high on the wave of victory. Some of the raw Burma battalions broke at their first engagement; others held together until after the fall of Rangoon.[1] By the time the Allied forces were retreating towards the Indian border most of the newly-raised units had been reduced to their British officers and their Indian clerks. One battalion remained a fighting unit to the last—the 2nd Burma Rifles, whose feats included a march of over 200 miles through hostile, roadless country in 14 days; its strength when it finally halted at Kanglatongbi in Manipur was between 400 and 500.[2] Altogether, about 800–1,000 survivors of 'Burcorps' arrived at journey's end.[3] They were given the option of returning to their homes, taking their discharge, together with their pay, a rifle, and rations, or of staying on with the army. To their immense honour, about 500 men volunteered to stay on: the majority of them were Delta Karens, whose families were even then in mortal danger from BIA tyranny; others were hill Karens, Kachins, and Chins. There were also a few Burmese officers and other ranks. The infantry soldiers were formed up in the 2nd battalion; B.A.S.C. and other personnel were formed into small separate units.

The 2nd battalion was trained in a reconnaissance role, and was taken by Wingate for his Chindits. They accompanied the first 1943 raid into Burma, and earned much praise for the manner in which they acted as the eyes and ears of the columns. For their conduct during this operation 11 officers and 21 other ranks were awarded decorations, while 27 were mentioned in

---

[1] An objective record of the performance of the Burma battalions is contained in the *Official History of the Indian Armed Forces in the Second World War, 1939–45* published by the Combined Inter-Services Historical Section (India and Pakistan), *The Retreat from Burma, 1941–42*, edited by Bisheshwar Prasad [1955]. Among the battalions engaged in the Tenasserim fighting five are stated to have been 'totally valueless' (p. 158). By 23 February 1942 three battalions (3rd, 4th, and 8th) were amalgamated to form one weak company, following desertions (p. 185). At the same time the Army Commander ordered the release of all Burma Riflemen considered unreliable and the disbandment of some battalions (p. 225); it is then stated that 'the Shans of the 13th and 14th Battalions proved most unreliable, deserting in large numbers and often taking with them arms and ammunition. On one occasion officers went with the deserters. These Battalions, however, were never actively engaged.'

[2] Two companies of Karens from the 1st Burma Rifles were sent to strengthen the Karen levies in the Salween District: these 'fought most gallantly' against very superior Japanese forces advancing on Mawchi (*Retreat from Burma*, pp. 226 and 361–3).

[3] This total does not include the Indian Army battalions or the Indian members of the Frontier Force who 'in the day when heaven was falling', naturally made for their own homeland.

dispatches. For the second and much more ambitious Chindit operation it was decided to expand the Burma Rifles reconnaissance platoons from 10 to 48: practical recognition of their worth. New recruits were trained, mainly Chins and Kachins, and Burma's soldiers played a full part in the 1944 operations, particularly in winning over the villagers to the Allied side. When the Chindits were withdrawn from action they brought many new recruits for the Burma Rifles back with them. Once again the 2nd Battalion gained many decorations, including ten M.C.s. In the far north considerable bodies of Kachin levies were also hitting out from the base at Fort Hertz, and Chin guerrillas formed part of the forces in the Fort White area.

The school of jungle war in which the Chindits and the levies won their spurs was a cruel, bitter school. The troops fought with only light weapons, rifles, tommy-guns, and grenades, without the support of artillery or armour; their rations were meagre, dropped from the sky, procured from villages or even picked out of the jungle. Ancillary services there were none: if men were wounded they kept going—or dropped. It was warfare at its worst, but it forged a Burma Army which peace-time training or even more conventional campaigning would never have produced.

The Burma R.N.V.R., although only a tiny force, saw much service during the years 1942–5; a flotilla equipped with motor launches operated off the creeks and islands of Arakan, frequently making landings in enemy-held territory. The flotilla participated in the maritime assault which led to the unopposed reoccupation of Rangoon.

Meanwhile, 'on the other side of the hill', the Burma National Army was providing a different sort of training school for the army of the future. By 1944 the BNA was composed of 6 battalions of infantry, 2 of anti-aircraft personnel, and 1 of sappers and miners. An officers' training school was established at Mingaladon, and recruit training centres were opened at Mingaladon, Pyinmana, Mandalay, and Maymyo. Organization, training, equipment, and uniform were all on the standard Japanese model. There were Japanese instructors, and the Japanese High Command believed that the BNA was firmly under its control. But the young Thakin battalion commanders were successful in maintaining the separate character of the force. There can be little doubt that the BNA soon came to hate their Japanese masters because of their attitude of tyrannical superiority. Recruits and cadets were slapped and insulted, the BNA had to salute all Japanese personnel, but no courtesies were paid to BNA officers in return. The BNA was at first almost entirely Burmese throughout its ranks, but later a Karen battalion is said to have been added. The moving spirit was San Po Thin, who established contact with Aung San, who was genuinely anxious to make a settlement with the Karens. He agreed to the appointment of Major Kya Doe, an ex-Sandhurst regular officer then living in poor circumstances; and San Po Thin, virtually by a trick, succeeded in persuading Kya Doe to join the BNA. He was appointed Colonel in charge of organization and training.[1] The BNA took part in one or two skirmishes against the Fourteenth Army, but it was mainly employed on internal security duties until its defection to the British side in March 1945. The BNA has appeared in these pages in a generally unfavourable light, but there can be no doubt that many of its officers were genuinely idealistic patriots and many of its privates were simple peasant lads attracted by the glamour that enlistment offered.

After the liberation of Rangoon, under the terms of the agreement concluded between Admiral Mountbatten and Aung San, personnel of the BNA were to be given the opportunity of enlisting in the post-war regular army. The nucleus for this new army was the 2nd Burma Rifles, which had been re-formed in March 1945 as a conventional infantry battalion. Its composition was one-third Karen, one-third Kachin, and one-third Chin, and among its officers 8 Karens, 3 Chins, and 1 Kachin held the King's Commission.

When the formation of new infantry battalions was planned, one radical departure was made: regiments were organized not on the old basis of 'class companies' but as 'class battalions'. Demands for this innovation came from two opposite quarters: Aung San and the AFPFL, and the Karen leaders. In his negotiations with Mountbatten Aung San had fought for the incorporation of the former BNA battalions into the new army as organized units; this had been strongly resisted on the British side and, in theory, the principle of individual recruitment was upheld. But Aung San went on to demand that Burmese should not be mingled in formations with the other races, but should be formed into purely Burmese battalions. This would have the desired effect of keeping the former *yebaws* of the BNA together as they would form an overwhelming majority in the Burmese units. On the Karen side, with memories of BIA atrocities in Myaungmya and Papun still

---

[1] See Morrison, *Grandfather Longlegs*, pp. 197–200. This work contains much material on the pre-war Burma Rifles and on its war-time services.

vivid, there was the strongest repugnance to Karens serving alongside the 'murderers of their kinsfolk'. On 11 July 1945 Aung San presented a definite four-point demand that the army should be organized on a 'class battalion' basis, and on 15 July Admiral Mountbatten signified his assent.

Three new regiments were thereafter created, the Karen Rifles, the Kachin Rifles, and the Chin Rifles. These were formed entirely (except for a handful of British officers) from within the respective racial groups. Five battalions of the Burma Rifles became Burmese throughout; these were, originally, the 1st, 3rd, 4th, 5th, and 6th battalions, which were formed almost exclusively from former BNA troops, most (but by no means all) of their Burmese officers being former *yebaws*.[1] Despite the new arrangements, some battalions, including the staunch old 2nd, were still 'mixed' units with the hill peoples of Burma and also Gurkhas within their ranks. Apart from Gurkhas (numbers of whom are domiciled in Myitkyina and the Shan States), the recruitment of Indians almost entirely ceased.[2] The Frontier Force and Military Police were once again amalgamated in one force (known after 1948 as Union Military Police). Some military police battalions were formed out of the former levies of hill peoples and the Karen guerrillas of Force 136, but the greatest number were drawn from Burmese political adherents of the AFPFL, some being PVOs, some Socialist supporters.

The Burma Navy was also developed. Within a few months of the liberation of Rangoon the navy had been expanded to five times its war-time strength: its vessels now included thirty motor launches and, by the end of 1945, it had taken over all the tasks performed by the Royal Navy in Rangoon and the other ports.[3] A beginning was also made with the creation of a Burma Air Force Volunteer Reserve, for which a nucleus existed in a number of young Burmans who had served with the R.A.F. The regular Burma Air Force came into being in December 1947.

During Aung San's struggle for national independence in 1946 and later, close liaison was maintained with those battalions of the army and military police containing former members of the BNA and PVO. The officers were identified closely with

---

[1] At a meeting in Kandy on 6 September 1945 with Aung San, Admiral Mountbatten promised 200 commissions to PBF officers. This promise was honoured 'in spite of the fact that the recruitment of other ranks had not been proportionate' (*Report of Supreme Allied Commander*, p. 205, n. 1).

[2] Burma-domiciled Indians are, in fact, enlisted in the Service Corps, Signals, Medical Corps, &c. on an individual basis.

[3] *Burma's Navy*, 1946.

the political struggle, and these battalions came to see themselves as the real power behind the politicians. When the AFPFL took over the Government in October 1946 the BNA element in the army became even more openly identified with Aung San and his Cabinet. Aung San, although no longer formally connected with the army, was always referred to as *Bogyoke*, General.[1] The 3rd Burma Rifles was known as the 'Bodyguard Battalion' and was permanently stationed at Mingaladon. All this flattering association with the central direction of affairs came to an end with the assassination of Aung San. His successor, U Nu, was a civilian through and through;[2] the army commanders were now regarded as the professional servants of the State, no more as comrades in leadership of the nation. Because independence was now assured, there was no need for politicians to smile upon the soldiers who might provide the means to challenge British authority. Aung San's death caused a gap in the whole national life, but nowhere so much as in the Burmese battalions of the army and the PVO who now experienced a tremendous loss of direction, as well as the consciousness that their prestige had undergone a sudden eclipse.

With the attainment of independence the services of the few remaining British officers were abruptly terminated. This was in marked contrast to the situation in Pakistan and India: both these countries retained large numbers of British officers in their service. In India they were mainly employed as advisers, in training establishments or in technical services (signals, engineers, &c.); but in Pakistan, in addition, many British officers were retained in the fighting formations. Both India and Pakistan appointed British Generals to command their armies. In the navies and air forces the proportion of British officers was even higher. Within a decade almost all these British officers had departed, but their temporary retention smoothed over the first difficult years of transition and helped the two new armies to build upon the old foundations new standards and traditions no whit inferior to the old. Burma, with only a tithe of the martial experience of India and Pakistan to call upon, dispensed with every single British army officer. This drastic step did not, in the event, break the new army: much of the credit must go to the young Burman

---

[1] Admiral Mountbatten was always punctilious in according Aung San the rank of Major-General, although this was purely a Japanese-awarded rank.

[2] In his charming autobiography, *Burma under the Japanese* (London, Macmillan, 1954), U Nu pokes fun at himself as a potential guerrilla fighter (p. 106): 'Everyone was well aware that [in handling a gun] I should be worse than useless, because I would be just a hindrance.'

officers who rose to the tremendous demands of the situation, but credit should also be given to the British Military Mission which was set up, under the Bo Let Ya–Freeman agreement.[1]

The British Military Mission was small in numbers; its members were drawn from the three fighting services, but the army was predominant; there were some 35 officers and some 35 other ranks. Staff officers assisted in the setting up of an army headquarters, with departments for planning, operations, supply, &c. Instructors assisted at the Officers' Training School, Maymyo, and at different training establishments, such as the Armoured Fighting Vehicles Centre, Meiktila. And advisers assisted with the drafting of scales of equipment and the procurement of weapons and other military requirements from the United Kingdom and other Commonwealth countries. The members of the mission were all British service officers. The model for the Burma Army was therefore, for the first time, the British Army and not the Indian Army.

Any hope of steady development of the new army was over-turned by the onset of civil war. During the summer of 1948 three of the former BNA battalions of the army[2] mutinied, together with certain ancillary units: the rising was largely due to the dissatisfaction of the commanders and their officers with the routine of peace-time soldiering and a desire for supreme political power. That the 4th Burma Rifles was not affected by mutiny was probably due to its associations with Bo Ne Win, former commanding officer of the 4th Battalion, who in 1948 was a Brigadier, later becoming Commander-in-Chief.

The army mutinies, together with the Communist rising, led to the forming of *ad hoc* irregular forces. The levies were first raised in 1947 at the time of the Red Flag risings, many being little better than gangs of toughs. In August 1948 more organized units were raised: the Union Auxiliary Force, with Tin Tut as Brigadier and Inspector-General of the Force. Soon after, in September 1948, 52 companies of Territorials, *sitwundans*, were raised for local service in the districts; they absorbed the personnel of the levies. There followed the dreadful clashes between Burmese and Karens, often provoked by the irresponsibility of the undisciplined irregular forces. Finally, in February 1949, all the regular Karen battalions mutinied; two Kachin battalions were also temporarily disaffected as well as some Gurkhas and other tribal troops. The prevailing consideration was often the personal influence of a commanding officer: several of the Karen colonels were well known in the

[1] See above, p. 32, n. 4.
[2] 1st, 3rd, and 6th Burma Rifles.

army, trusted and liked by other hill peoples as well as by their own folk. They pulled along the rank and file in their own heedless plunge into defiance of the legal government.

As a result of the identification of the Karen regiments with the KNDO rising, all Karen members of the armed services were relieved of their posts and placed upon half-pay. Most were confined in 'rest camps', where they were kept for several years. Eventually they were discharged. In consequence, the army lost most of its experienced officers and n.c.o.s. Only three senior Karen officers remained on the active list, and one of these, Brigadier Kya Doe, saw no more active service. It is no uncommon experience today to meet in Delta villages men who, despite obvious poverty, still preserve a presence of authority; conversation may reveal that they were once at Sandhurst or the university, that they hold the M.C. and can recall some of the hardest-fought battles of the Fourteenth Army. Today they pursue some aimless occupation, whiling away lives that are now meaningless and hopeless.

The early months of 1949, after the defection of the Karen battalions, were the army's most severe test. Some of the best troops and most of the professional leaders were gone: the gaps were hastily filled by new men. Inevitably there was an amateurish atmosphere about many of the new army's operations. For instance, during the long-drawn-out battle before Insein, Karen patrols were able, one night, to enter the positions of the Government forces without the slightest challenge and conducted a bombing raid causing considerable damage for several hours, finally withdrawing with their numbers intact. The explanation was that two neighbouring units had taken up positions which did not link up, so that a hill feature in the centre was completely unguarded. Neither the higher command nor the unit commanders considered it necessary to ensure that the front line was, in fact, continuous. And as the raid developed, each unit was so much concerned for its own protection that no attempt was made to support neighbouring positions.

In this situation the Government cause was greatly assisted by unchallenged command of the air.[1] At independence the Burma Air Force consisted of a few flights of miscellaneous machines, many of them training-planes. The Commanding Officer was Wing-Commander Shi Sho, a former member of 607 Squadron, R.A.F., and a Karen. He quietly withdrew when

---

[1] With one exception: the capture of Maymyo was achieved by Karen rebels who forced two foreign pilots at pistol-point to fly them to Maymyo, where the garrison was caught unawares. Otherwise the KNDO captured a few planes on the ground, but they had no pilots to fly them.

the Karen troubles began in February 1949, being succeeded
by Wing-Commander Selwyn James Khin, a former Battle of
Britain pilot, a Burmese Christian, and a young man of considerable daring and charm, possessing the gift of leadership.
He led his pilots on hundreds of sorties, and on several occasions
the Air Force succeeded in breaking up rebel formations which
appeared to be poised to attack government troops in critical
positions. Wing-Commander Khin was eventually killed on an
operational flight over Kengtung in June 1950. Wing-Commander T. Clift was then appointed in his place. Thus the
first three leaders of the Burma Air Force have been members
of minority communities: a Karen, a Burmese Christian, and
an Anglo-Burman.

The Burma Navy also made its own significant contribution
during the crisis months. Its post-war role was that of coastal
defence, but it was now required to take part in the land war
against the rebels. The navy possessed (and still possesses) a
former Royal Navy frigate, *Mayu*, which now assisted towards
relieving Moulmein, and later Bassein, from the grip of the
KNDO. *Mayu* later operated against the military police
mutineers in Arakan. One Burma Navy vessel, the river-boat
Sabe, manned by a largely Karen crew went over to the
KNDO's, but in general, just as the Government had control
over the air, so there were no ships to oppose those of the
Government upon the inland waterways. The navy operated
Inland Water Transport craft, *Seinda*, *Sab-an*, &c., heavily
armoured and firing oerlikons and other pieces, and almost
its entire effort was directed towards inland action.

Somehow the desperate months from February to April 1949
were endured and the Government was able to rally its
scattered forces. Reinforcements of arms and equipment were
provided by Britain and India. New battalions were formed.
Whereas the Karens had formerly contributed the largest
element in the fighting forces, the Kachins now provided the
main recruiting ground; the Kachin Rifles were expanded
from three to six battalions. Three new battalions of Shan Rifles
were constituted, and later a battalion of Kayah Rifles, enlisting Shans, Red Karens, and other hill folk. The 4th Burma
Regiment was formed as a Gurkha battalion, and other
battalions of the Burma Regiment were composed of the lesser
hill peoples, such as the Lahus. Although the numbers of
regiments on racial lines have greatly increased, the long-term
policy of the Government, it is always emphasized, is to replace
the 'class' regiments by units drawing their recruits from a
medley of all the peoples of the Union. The Government has

resisted proposals in Parliament made by Arakanese M.P.s that an Arakan Battalion should be constituted.

U Nu has spoken of 1951 as the year when the armed forces began to be 'properly organized', and of the following years as the 'development period', when units were changed from being 'stooges, without backbone, at the beck and call of this or that organization' into 'dependable custodians of the Union Constitution'.[1] The fighting strength of the army was also much expanded; in February 1949, the lowpoint, there were about 6 loyal battalions;[2] these had increased to 9 in January 1952, and a year later rapid expansion raised the total to 41 battalions. This expansion was largely achieved by enrolling members of the irregular forces into the regular army. The *sitwundans*, the territorial force, was first raised as a temporary body, with a statutory limitation to its term of life: this life has been extended every year, but the intention remains that its members should be enrolled in the army or disbanded.

One factor that prolongs the existence of the irregular forces is the present need for a large low-grade 'militia' to provide static guards for the system of communications and other government installations which are constantly liable to rebel attack. Another consideration is that a high proportion of the irregulars are former rebels, most of whom have surrendered with their arms: if they were discharged, having no other trade but that of arms, they might well return to banditry and violence. As a result, the *sitwundans* have been retained in every district, along with the 'Peace Guerrillas' (the ABPO private army) and the village organization of *kins*, home guards, as well as large numbers of military police. However, large numbers of auxiliaries have been absorbed into the regular army, and the *sitwundans*, who at one period numbered over 16,000, have been reduced to 8,000 or less. From 1 October 1955 the Government introduced a new security scheme, the *Pyu Saw Hti* town and village defence scheme. This plan was not a success, and it was superseded by the National Solidarity Associations, which took over village defence, among their duties.[3]

provide for stabilizing the army at fifty battalions. One of the principal difficulties in attaining this goal lies in securing

---

[1] At Lawksawk Academy, *Nation*, 15 February 1955 and *BWB*, 22 September 1955 to conference of commanding officers.

[2] It is impossible to give a definite estimate; most units were scattered about the countryside in isolated detachments; whether the detachment mutinied or quietly disintegrated or sat on the fence or remained actively loyal was often decided by the personal lead given by its commander. Many had second thoughts. Probably the true position will never be known.

[3] For details, see p. 61.

sufficient numbers of officers of the right standard to provide leadership for the new troops. The officers hastily commissioned in 1949 and the following years were a motley collection. Some were promoted from the ranks, having displayed daring in fighting the enemy: many of these were rough and unlettered. Others were political appointees, who might or might not make keen soldiers. Many others were patriotic young students who threw up their university careers because their country was in danger. Few of these officers underwent proper courses of training, but in succeeding years they have been sent on courses appropriate to their acquired rank: platoon commanders' courses, company commanders', and senior officers' courses. Almost all this 'refresher' training has been done with the British Army, either at army schools and centres in the United Kingdom or with the British Army of the Rhine, or more rarely at British establishments in Malaya and Hong Kong. An occasional officer has attended the Pakistan Staff College at Quetta, and others have gone to Australia and New Zealand, but none have gone to India for training: perhaps it is desired to make a clean break from all the old links with the Indian Army.

The most promising young candidates for a commission have been sent for training in Britain. After some weeks at a unit for the preliminary preparation of cadets, they proceed to Sandhurst for the regular course of training. Most of them find the going tough in the early months, but the great majority of Burma cadets have passed out of Sandhurst with credit. The cadets who merely undergo the course at the Officers' Training School, Maymyo, do not approach the same standard.

To attract young men of the desired quality the army offers pay which compares very favourably with that of the civil service: a Second Lieutenant receives more than a Sub-Divisional Officer and a Major more than a Deputy Commissioner (in former days the pay of the civil service was considerably higher than that of the army for equivalent ranks and grades).[1] In the higher ranks a Major-General receives more pay than the Chief Secretary, the head of the civil service, but at the same time there is no tendency to over-exalt the senior officers. In Siam there are a dozen full Generals gleaming with gold braid, some of whom have only a nebulous connexion with the army. In Burma the Commander-in-Chief of all the fighting services, Bo Ne Win, is only a Lieutenant-General. The head

---

[1] Pay scale (figures in brackets are basic pay, other figures include allowances): 2nd Lieut. (K250) K395, Captain (K525–600) K631–806, Lieut.-Colonel (K1,100–1,200) K1,231–1,338, Brigadier (K1,400) K1,550, Major-General (K1,800) K1,975 (rates in force in 1949). Some rates of pay in the civil service are cited on p. 154, n. 3.

of the Air Force is an Air Commodore and that of the Navy a Commodore. The officers who command districts hold the rank of Brigadier (Burma is divided into two districts, equivalent to divisions). Brigades are actually commanded by Colonels or Lieutenant-Colonels, and battalion commanders are almost all Majors. There is a clear intention on the part of the civil Government to prevent the senior commanders from acquiring too high rank, to ensure that their circumstances remain modest like those of most middle-class Burmans. There is also something very admirable in Burma's decision to resist the attraction of making an easy impression of military might by parading quantities of Generals and Colonels before the eyes of the world.

Promotion was, of course, very rapid in the early days of independence. In 1949 most battalion commanders were young men of thirty.[1] Although promotion has not, perhaps, been so meteoric in subsequent years, the rapid expansion of the army has served to keep pace with the numbers of new officers. In 1960 many senior officers were still young: both Brigadier Aung Gyi and Colonel Maung Maung were in their early forties. Most battalion commanders were between 30 and 40,[2] and most company commanders are officers with six years' service or often less. The rigorous testing of almost continuous service in the arduous school of jungle and guerrilla warfare has provided an effective process for the selection and discarding of battalion commanders, and those that have survived are all men of quality, stamped as fit leaders. The junior officers appear to be more uncertain. Some, especially the Sandhurst-trained officers, impress the observer as forceful leaders, keen and professionally well qualified. Others act as though overwhelmed by their new responsibilities. They go through the drill which they have learned at the training school with a sort of flat competence, but a real crisis might find them floundering, unable to lead or even to think.

To a striking extent, the officer corps has developed a homogeneous, professional character which is quite remarkable

[1] Dept. of Information, *Burma's Freedom, the Second Anniversary*, carried obituaries of two such officers. Lieut.-Colonel Hrang Thio was born in 1919. He enlisted as a rifleman in 1939, fought throughout the War (Burma Gallantry Medal) and received a King's Commission in 1944. Promoted Major 1945. After training in Britain, promoted Lieut.-Colonel in December 1947, appointed Commanding Officer 1st Chin Rifles, killed in action August 1949. Lieut.-Colonel Bo Kyin was born in 1916, enlisted as rifleman in 1938, Jemadar (G.C.O.) 1939, Burma Gallantry Medal 1942; left behind in Burma. Led a resistance group, and 1945 rejoined the army, commissioned as 2nd Lieut., promoted Captain, 3rd Burma Rifles; March 1949 promoted Lieut.-Colonel in command of North Burma Sub-District. Killed in action August 1949.

[2] It is said that the most senior battalion commander enlisted in the ranks in 1937.

in view of the heterogeneous origins from which they have emerged. As examples of the unity which is being welded out of diversity, one might compare the careers of some senior officers.

Brigadier Louis Lazum Tang is a Christian Kachin who enlisted as a rifleman and served for about fifteen years in the ranks before being awarded his Commission. During the war years he fought with the Chindits, winning the M.B.E. When brought before the Frontier Areas Inquiry Committee in 1947, he asseverated 'I am not a politician and I do not intend to be one either.' He later made good that declaration. In 1949, as a Lieutenant-Colonel, he first raised the 3rd Kachins; he recaptured Lashio from the PVO, was promoted Brigadier, and given the task of retaking Maymyo. Later he was responsible for frustrating Naw Seng's plans to rouse the Bhamo Kachins to the rebel side. He has now retired.

Brigadier Douglas Blake is an Anglo-Indian. During the war he was granted an emergency commission and fought with the Fourteenth Army. He stayed on with the new Burma Army, and first came into prominence when, as a Colonel, he directed the attacks which finally cleared the KNDO out of Insein. Promoted Brigadier, he was in charge of the first large-scale operation against the KMT in March 1953, when the three brigades under his command drove the KMT out of the heart of the Shan State. Later he directed operations in Thaton against the KNDO. With no influential friends to recommend him, a member of a community that is not highly regarded under the present régime, he has made his way to the top solely by virtue of his soldierly qualities.

Among the senior officers who first saw service in the BNA and PBF, two have particularly shaped the concept of the army as the guardian of the nation: Brigadier Aung Gyi, the deputy Chief of Staff, and Colonel Maung Maung, Director of Military Training. The former led the negotiations in Bangkok in 1953 for the withdrawal of the KMT from Kentung (see p. 347). Both men are supposed to have played a major part in arranging for General Ne Win's assumption of power in October 1958. Both have taken the lead in the measures to build up national self-discipline, such as the formation of the National Solidarity Associations. Aung Gyi was entrusted with another diplomatic operation as the leader of the delegation to negotiate with the Chinese in 1960 (see p. 378). Men like these have evolved a concept of the army as outside and even perhaps above politics:

Out of this diverse material, the new professional class of officers has emerged. No special code (such as that of the old type of British officer with his peculiar shibboleths) has as yet emerged in Burma, but the officers' corps has come to regard itself as a 'band of brothers' and, perhaps more than any other group in Burma, has subscribed to the Union idea, has forsaken particularism for a loyalty to the country at large.

It might not be unfair to the new generation of Burma Army officers to suggest that their relations with their men are much more like those found in European armies—of a formal, parade-ground nature—instead of that old easy, familiar relationship which was one of the features of strength of the old Indian Army and the old Burma Rifles. Most of the young officers of today come from urban, middle-class families, and many are graduates of the university. They have acquired a certain attitude to life which separates them from the bucolic lads in the ranks. The old officer would probably spend a day free from duties out shooting with the men of his company; the new officer spends the day on a visit to a cinema in the nearest town, in company with his brother officers. These comments are much less apposite to the units composed of the hill peoples, where the indigenous officers (even though they also may be university graduates) are much closer to their men. Many of these units are commanded by Anglo-Burmans who keep up the old semi-paternal tradition. Some of these Anglo-Burman commanding officers bear names that were well known in the army and the administration during the hundred years of Burma's connexion with Britain.

The men in the ranks are not so very different from other peasant soldiers: simple, easy-going, obeying orders like the ox, but liable to childish fears and obstinacies; giving their devotion to a leader who wins their confidence, and only superficially affected by abstract concepts of loyalty. But while many of the present-day soldiers are lads of this type, there are others who have been caught up for a while in the clangor of extremist nationalism; perhaps before joining the army they have been hangers-on in the *claque* of some political organization; they may have been 'underground' with the rebels. This introduction to the outside world may have given them the idea that soldiering is a life of boozing, wenching, and swaggering. With such men as these the quality of leadership and discipline enforced by their officers is of decisive importance. Where discipline is lacking, service personnel have all too often behaved like boors and bullies, particularly in their behaviour towards the civil population. Numerous examples of military offensiveness to civilians have been reported in the Press; perhaps the most serious was when some air force personnel decided to beat up the Rangoon Zoo, to avenge some alleged slight. Arriving in service trucks, 200 B.A.F. men proceeded to attack the Zoo Superintendent and the keepers until their rage at last abated.[1] In July 1952 the Commander-in-Chief published a general order on the subject of indiscipline. He stated that he 'had received numerous complaints of soldiers taking revenge on civilians'. He observed that 'it is disgraceful that they should use their weapons against the civilian population'.[2] But his words were not entirely sufficient. In 1955 U Nu still found it necessary to deplore those 'who swagger with revolvers dangling on their belts or with rifles in their hands, dizzy with newly-acquired power and arrogant in dealing with people'.[3]

One of the weaknesses of the present-day army is a total lack of experienced n.c.o.s: any young, educated n.c.o. who shows promise is promptly recommended for a commission. For a time after independence the Burma Army kept on the old Indian Army ranks of Jemadar and Subadar; but later the British practice was adopted, and platoons are now commanded by subalterns. The old G.C.O.s have disappeared, and with them a valuable steadying influence. It may be said that a man who was worth promotion to Jemadar is worth promotion to Second Lieutenant, so that the loss is more apparent than real: but the requirement that a candidate for a commission must have passed matriculation may rule out many stalwart old soldiers.

The new army is continually improving standards of discipline and of loyalty to regiment and nation. On parade, on ceremonial occasions, the turn-out and bearing of the new army is most impressive, and in the 1954 offensive against the KMT, 'Bayinnaung', the army may be said to have proved itself as an integrated fighting force: for the first time large-scale operations were carried out as by an army and not by an assorted number of battalions. Co-operation was achieved between units, different arms of the service, and between the army and the air force. Some at least of the credit for this success is due to the British Military Mission and to the training given in British establishments to Burma service personnel.

How far is the Burma Army of today modelled upon the British Army? The casual observer might well be astonished that the army of the independent republic of Burma, completely dissociated from the Commonwealth, has retained

[1] *Nation*, 23 October 1951.
[2] ibid., 5 July 1952.
[3] U Nu's address to the commanding officers, *BWB*, 22 September 1955.

all the appearances of a British force. Troops continue to be dressed in uniform which is identical with British tropical kit and for operational duties wear jungle battle-dress which is, in fact, British issue. Officers wear British peaked caps or berets, and other ranks usually wear Gurkha-style broad-brimmed hats. The badges of rank of n.c.o.s and even the distinctive badges of several arms of the service are British: for instance, the Burma Artillery badge displays a gun, with the motto 'Ubique', as does the Royal Artillery. Those who are entitled to British decorations and campaign stars continue to wear them alongside the new republican medals. Perhaps more important than these surface similarities are the facts that the Burma Army is armed and supplied very largely with British weapons and equipment, its organization and methods are on the British model, and British staff exercises, reports, and appreciations are regularly received and utilized.

The Burma Navy and Air Force would appear to be even more closely patterned on British lines. The Burma Navy still flies the White Ensign, although the Star of Burma is now quartered with St. George's Cross. Burman cadets undergo the regular course at Dartmouth, and petty officers may also be sent to Britain for training. The B.A.F. is even more closely linked with the R.A.F. Not only flying officers but also almost all those in the ranks, after a brief period of basic instruction, are dispatched to the United Kingdom or to Australia for their main training. B.A.F. pilots fly with R.A.F. squadrons, and all machines used in Burma from Spitfires to Vampires are British.

All this may seem to indicate that the policy of the Burma Government is to preserve a close association between the armed forces of the new state and those of the former guardian Power, on the same basis that Pakistan, India, and Ceylon have chosen to establish with Britain. But such a deduction would be altogether too sweeping. In conformity with its policy of strict neutrality and disengagement from either Power bloc, the Nu Government began at an early date to look with some misgiving at the Military Mission and the identification with British defence arrangements which it seemed to reflect. On the whole, the relations of the Mission with the Burma Government were cordial, and in several cases individual relations between members of the Mission and their Burman 'opposite numbers' were more than cordial. But there were complaints: arms ordered on the Burma Government's behalf by the Mission during the Korean War period were often very slow in arriving, owing to priority demands elsewhere. The Mission was expensive, its members enjoyed diplomatic status—and it was undeniably British. On 4 January 1954, at the request of the Burma Government, it was brought to an end.

Efforts were made to ensure that when foreign military advice was required it should be sought from the 'uncommitted' countries, and especially from Burma's closest ideological friends, Israel and Yugoslavia. As early as June 1952 a 'Study and Observation Mission', composed of representatives of the three fighting services with Kyaw Nyein as Leader and Brigadier Kyaw Zaw as Deputy Leader, toured Europe to collect data on defence matters. The mission spent some time in Yugoslavia, and in December 1952 a Yugoslav Military Mission, led by Lieutenant-General Ljubo Vukovic, came to Burma. Following these exchanges, a mountain battery of the Burma Artillery was equipped with Yugoslav 76 mm. cannon. The association of the two countries became yet closer after the visit of Marshal Tito to Burma in January 1955, when it was agreed that Yugoslavia would equip one brigade of the Burma Army with weapons. In June 1954 a military mission led by Colonel Aung Gyi and Commodore Than Pe visited Israel to study that country's scheme of national service with a view to its introduction into Burma. The *Pyu Saw Hti* defence scheme would appear to have borrowed some features from the defence of collective settlements in Israel. A number of Burman service officers have also gone there for training, and Israel has sold some reconditioned Spitfires. These developments have not made any significant difference to Burma's general military policy; large numbers of service personnel continue to be trained in Britain, and when the first Burmese girls were selected to inaugurate the Burma Air Force (Women's Service) it was to Britain that they were sent, in May 1955, to study at the W.R.A.F. Officers' Cadet Training Unit.

Eventually, however, Burma's associations with Britain in service matters will almost inevitably be balanced by new connexions with the Communist bloc if Burma is to retain a genuinely non-partisan position in world affairs. In September 1955 a military mission which included all the highest-ranking officers of the armed services, led by Lieutenant-General Ne Win, visited China. The mission spent two months inside that country, visiting units of the Chinese army, armament factories, and training establishments. The purpose of the mission was to study the possibility of introducing Chinese weapons and equipment into the Burma services, and to establish friendly relations with Chinese military leaders. 'Friendship between Burma and China would be cemented by a closer link between the armed forces of the two countries', Bo Ne Win announced upon his arrival in China.[1]

But the overriding aim of Burma's leaders is to stand clear of both the Power groups, and partly with this in mind a new Defence Services Academy has been built at Lawksawk in the Southern Shan States. This institution received its first intake of cadets in June 1955. Candidates are to be between 16 and 18 years old, and will have to pass a stiff entrance examination; 100 cadets will be taken every year. They will spend four years at the academy, receiving a dual education, part military, part academic, and opportunities will be afforded for taking university degrees. The chief aim of the academy will be to develop a 'high standard of moral character and personal discipline, and a sincere sense of responsibility'.[2] Cadets will go from the academy into all three fighting services. The sending of cadets to Sandhurst and Dartmouth will, in all probability, cease.

One unstated aim of the new academy is to make a break from the mass methods and political diversions which have bogged down educational advance in other institutions in Burma today. Carefully selected youths will be given a better education than is available elsewhere, far away from any town and from politics. For one of the tasks for the army of tomorrow which U Nu and other leaders often emphasize is the part which the army must play in promoting citizenship and social responsibility, and in giving a lead in matters of education and health. Every year the Prime Minister calls together all Commanding Officers and addresses them on political and social themes. He continually lays stress upon the obligation of the army to behave as the servant and guide of the nation. So far it cannot be said that the army has made full use of its opportunities. Too many units distributed in detachments on garrison duty have been content—officers and men—to lounge away the time, listless and indolent. But there have been instances where unit commanders have utilized periods of inactivity to educate their troops, and then have set the soldiers to inculcate their lessons among the folk with whom they are quartered.

The role of the army in the nation, as the events of the years 1958–60 have emphasized, is that of preserving internal peace and order rather than of acting as a defensive force against external attack. Indeed, an oft-repeated theme of U Nu and other AFPFL leaders is their belief in the friendly intentions of Burma's neighbours. The disposition of the armed forces, as

[1] *BWB*, 6 October 1955.
[2] The academy was later transferred to Maymyo.

it was early in 1959, appears to be in accordance with such a belief. It is entirely adapted to the needs of internal security, and appears to have little relevance to the possibility of external attack. There is, for instance, no central strategic reserve, such as the army of Siam possesses.

DISPOSITION OF INFANTRY BRIGADES, 1959

1st Brigade:	Shwebo, Monywa, Sagaing Districts
2nd Brigade:	Toungoo and Pegu Districts
3rd Brigade:	Karen State
4th Brigade:	Southern Shan State
5th Brigade:	Moulmein, Mergui, Tavoy Districts
6th Brigade:	Northern Shan State
7th Brigade:	Kachin State, Katha District
8th Brigade:	Bassein, Myaungmya, Henzada Districts
9th Brigade:	Eastern Shan State
10th Brigade:	Central Burma
11th Brigade:	Mandalay, and North-Central Burma
12th Brigade:	Maubin, Pyapon, Hanthawaddy Districts
13th Brigade:	Insein, Tharrawaddy, Prome Districts

All brigades were deployed against the insurgents in 1959, 8 and 9 Brigades being especially heavily engaged. Only 6 and 11 Brigades can be regarded as providing a strategic reserve.

The army is almost entirely an infantry force: the brigade formations are all styled 'Light Infantry Brigades', and there are practically no supporting arms. There are 3 field batteries, and 1 mountain battery of artillery only; there is 1 armoured regiment, for whose use 23 Comet tanks have been delivered. All this does not add up to an army designed for modern warfare. In reserve, there are about 15–20 territorial battalions (which number will be reduced as personnel are absorbed into the regular army) and about 20 battalions of military police. Both of these forces are equipped to fight local guerrillas only.

The other two services are so small that they form no sort of deterrent to attack. The air force has a few modern jet fighters but no bombers. It has two Bristol freighters, but no other aircraft to undertake airborne activities. And yet in the Shan and Kachin States airborne operations offer almost the only means of rapid deployment. The navy also is limited to flotillas of light craft (*Mayu* has reached its full term of usefulness), but Burma can well discount the probability of invasion from the sea. Presumably the possibility of invasion by land is also discounted: nevertheless, within the last ten years the forces of both Burma's eastern neighbours, China (1946) and Siam (1942–5), have been quartered upon the soil of Burma, and without her assent. Burma's military leaders may be right in deciding that the circumstances that brought these uninvited guests to her territory will never recur: an appeal to history would give a dusty answer, but the course of Asian history may have undergone a fundamental change during the decade of 1945–55.

Meanwhile, the entire capacity of the armed forces is concentrated upon preserving the régime which their own leaders have created. Despite disappointments—indeed, obvious failures —both in economic development and in the restoration of internal security, the forces have demonstrated complete loyalty to General Ne Win. The removal of Brigadier Aung Gyi, formerly Deputy Chief of Staff, and of numerous other high and middle ranking officers has caused no obvious strain. Ne Win continues to exercise supreme command as Chief of the Defence Staff. The Vice-Chief of Staff for the Army in succession to Aung Gyi is Brigadier San Yu. With the somewhat embittered departure of 'Tommy' Clift from leadership of the Air Force, Brigadier Thaung Dan became Vice-Chief of Staff (Air), while Commodore Thaung Tin is Vice-Chief for the Navy. The services appear to have faith in the Burmese Way to Socialism, whatever doubts have arisen elsewhere. This may be one of the causes for their isolation from the civil population, despite constant efforts, through working parties labouring alongside the people, to demonstrate that army and nation are indivisible.

Will a Nasser ever appear to make a Neguib of General Ne Win? Although the unexpected is always just round the corner in South-East Asia, there is no sign that the General will go until he decides the time has come to depart. It is thought that Brigadier Thaung Dan would be his most likely successor at the head of the services.

XII

FOREIGN RELATIONS

SURROUNDED on the west, the north, and the east by countries which are stronger than herself, Burma is, in the words of U Nu, 'hemmed in like a tender gourd among the cactus'.[1] It is impossible to regard foreign affairs as something remote or academic: blunders in foreign policy could have direct repercussions at home. In particular, Burma is vulnerable to the technique of subversion by an unfriendly Power amongst those of her communities not yet completely reconciled to the Union. The efforts which have been made since independence to maintain an independent foreign policy in this precarious situation have been partly based upon a traditional policy of withdrawal and isolation, and partly upon a new concept—as yet not formulated in any detail—towards all-round international goodwill. This new approach has not yet been understood or appreciated in many outside countries. Burma, under the influence of U Nu, is attempting to achieve relationships of understanding and goodwill not only with countries that have the same international outlook as herself (such as India), but also with other nations (such as Siam) who have taken up positions in world politics that are radically different or even antagonistic. Realizing that Burma counts for nothing as a unit in the world's capital of destructive force, U Nu is attempting to make his country an influence in an entirely new sphere of international relations in which there is a total emphasis on the good qualities of the nations of the world: on all the influences that transcend international disagreement and emnity. This aspect of Burma's foreign policy is identified very largely with the personal philosophy of U Nu. Another aspect is the promotion of international Socialism and the encouragement of anti-colonial movements, and this is identified almost entirely with Ba Swe and Kyaw Nyein. Burma cannot be said to have evolved a 'foreign office' foreign policy: a corps of professional diplomats is being built up, but for many years foreign policy will be based more upon personalities than upon system and organization (although not perhaps to the same extent as internal government policy).

Burma's traditional attitude to the outside world was defined

---

[1] *From Peace to Stability*, p. 102. Nu has employed this simile frequently, cf. *Nation*, 24 December 1954.

above as isolationist; this was, of course, only another outcome
of the geography of the country; Burma's mountain bastions
presented formidable obstacles to overland invaders, and the
great invasions that changed the face of Asia were approaching
their furthermost limits when they finally reached Burma. The
conquests of the Mongols and the Manchus in China and Central Asia; the Turki, Mongol, and Moghul invasions of India;
all these waves of domination rolled towards South East Asia, but
spent their force before penetrating Burma's jungles and hills.

Most of the external contacts and quarrels of the Burmese
were with their near neighbours, the Tais and Mons to the
east, Kachins to the north, Arakanese and Manipuris to the
west. Although all these neighbours enjoyed periods of successful aggression against Burma, on balance the Burmese more
than held their own. Contacts with the Great Powers beyond
were very limited. The armies of China appeared in Burma
in the thirteenth and seventeenth centuries but left no lasting
impression upon the country. The might of India's rulers was
never felt in Burma: through two centuries the fleets of Arakan
terrorized riverine Bengal, and only once, in 1665–6, did the
Governor of Bengal make effective retaliation—without the
faintest reverberation in Burma proper. All these events are
half-forgotten by modern Burmans, but everybody knows that
under the Konbaung kings in the eighteenth and early nineteenth centuries the armies of Burma conquered Arakan,
Manipur, and Assam to the west, and utterly vanquished Siam
to the east, adding vast new provinces to the Burmese Empire.
Most memorable of all, when China again invaded north Burma
from 1765 to 1768, her professional armies were utterly out-
fought, and the Chinese Viceroy was forced to sue for peace.
Burma from behind her mountain barriers could defy the
Emperor of the World. This was the grandiose tradition of
victory which the Burmese carried into the nineteenth century;
and so, when their forces invaded Bengal in 1824, they were
dumbfounded to have the tables turned upon them by the despised Kalas under the direction of those petty traders, the British.

Among the later Konbaung kings only Mindon Min conducted his relations with the British on a basis of realism, all
the others attempted to act in accordance with past grandeurs,
the court at Ava was the centre of the world, all outside was
unimportant; but Mindon maintained amicable realistic relations with the British throughout a quarter of a century. The
Government of India treated Mindon somewhat ungraciously,
as yet another Indian princeling. The principal aim of Mindon's
policy was to ensure recognition as an independent sovereign,

and to this end he attempted to establish direct relations with Queen Victoria, as well as making diplomatic contacts with the courts of Europe and the President of the United States. His successor, Thibaw Min, attempted to play a more ambitious role, and he ventured on the dangerous game of calling in the French to redress the balance against the British. No more disastrous gambit could have been attempted (nor would have been attempted if the King and his advisers had possessed any first-hand knowledge of the outside world). The Government of India and the British Government were inordinately sensitive to France's evident desire to build up a rival Indo-Chinese Empire: the threat of a French satellite upon the borders of the British-Indian Empire was the principal reason for the annexation of Upper Burma.[1]

From the 1880's to the 1940's Burma cannot be said to have played any independent part in international affairs. In the great political system of South Asia which the Foreign and Political Department at Simla wished to create, Burma represented an outer bastion, not dissimilar to Afghanistan. Simla was not interested in any further eastward expansionist activities, and would have preferred to set a limit to British responsibilities along the line of the Salween River, beyond which there would be a kind of neutral zone between the British and French spheres of activity (comparable to Persia as between India and Russia). When French activity along the Mekong ruled out the idea of a series of 'buffer states', the British asserted the rights inherited from the Burmese kings up to the River Mekong—but not beyond, although the suzerainty of Kengtung could have been exploited to establish footholds on the far side of the Mekong. In the absence of a 'forward policy' Burma's foreign relations were limited largely to the creation of a satisfactory frontier with Siam and China. The boundary with Siam was settled to the general agreement of both parties before the end of the nineteenth century, apart from a minor adjustment in Siam's favour made in 1940. The boundary with China was also settled, to a large extent, by co-operative delimitation by the end of the nineteenth century. But the whole question of sovereignty was clouded by the 'multiple loyalties' which many Kachin and Shan chiefs had acknowledged, professing allegiance of a sort to the rulers of Burma and Siam, or to Burma and China, or even to all three. In the first years after the annexation of Upper Burma the

---

[1] cf. the verdict of J. L. Christian: 'The evidence is that [British] expansion in Burma was due to fortuitous causes rather than to deliberate design. Had Theebaw's government not become involved in French intrigue, it is unlikely that annexation would have occurred' (*Burma and the Japanese Invader*, p. 263).

British agreed to a continuance of the decennial ceremonial
'tribute' from Burma to China of a gift of gold flowers. The
British also waived any claims to Kenghung, a state beyond the
Mekong owing a shadowy allegiance to Kengtung and to
Burma; but when China retroceded part of Kenghung to
French Indo-China, in direct contravention of undertakings
to Britain, the decennial 'tribute' was discontinued.[1] The
opportunity was also taken to readjust the more uncertain
and unsatisfactory sections of the frontier and to negotiate the
perpetual lease of a small hill area, the 'Namwan Assigned
Tract', from China, to facilitate communications between
Bhamo and Namkhan.[2] Two stretches of territory remained
thereafter undemarcated: in the extreme north the so-called
'triangle' between rivers Nmai Kha and Mali Kha remained in
dispute, while a strip 200 miles in length in the Wa country
was also claimed by both sides: in both cases the disputed
areas were reported to contain valuable mineral deposits.
However, it cannot be said that these remote regions of track-
less jungle and mountain posed any substantial international
problem: to both Chinese and Burmans it was an unknown
land in which neither nation had the slightest desire to settle.

The advent of the Nationalist régime in China led to a
heightening of Chinese national feeling with regard to her
southern neighbours. Two representatives from the Chinese
community in Burma were elected to the National Assembly
of China, and the Chinese Consulate-General in Rangoon was
a centre of Nationalist activity. However, the great majority
of Chinese residents in Burma appeared to be well content to
regard their hospitable foster-land as home, and the Burmese
continued to regard the immigrant Chinese as cousins rather
than as foreigners. China's war with Japan represented itself
to the more articulate Burmans in two aspects. There was some
admiration for China's struggle against the invader among the
younger politicians, and Thakin Nu led a goodwill mission to
Chungking in 1939. But there were also politicians who viewed
with the utmost misgiving the building up of the Burma Road,
insisting somewhat churlishly on the exaction of customs duties
upon war material destined for China, and enforcing a 1 per
cent. transit tax.[3] When in 1942 the KMT troops entered

---

[1] Space does not permit any discussion of the exact significance of this 'tribute'—
the Burmese records refer to these missions by the names of *let-saung pannā*, meaning
'gifts', 'letters' or *let-saung let-net* which nowadays means 'weapons'.

[2] An annual rent of Rs.1,000 was paid by the Government of Burma to China for
this lease.

[3] These levies were actually paid by the British taxpayer: when the extension of
the railway from Lashio into China commenced, the cost was also borne directly
by Britain.

Burma, as the allies of the (British) Burma Army, they were much detested for their harsh treatment of the civil population. During the Japanese occupation, when underground movements were organized, the Chinese played little or no part, in contrast to their dominant role in Malaya and Siam. Although Chiang Kai-shek insisted on withdrawing his troops from the North Burma theatre at the most critical phase of the 1945 offensive, this was not the last occasion on which Chinese troops were seen on Burma's soil. In February 1946 a Chinese column reappeared in Myitkyina District and rejected all protests at their unwarranted presence, until a formidable British land and air force was mobilized to dislodge them.

During the Ba Maw régime the members of his Government received certain opportunities to make contacts with the other national leaders of East Asia,[1] but no articulate foreign policy emerged.

When the AFPFL came into office, Thakin Lun Baw became Executive Councillor for Foreign Affairs, but the driving force, as in all things, was Aung San. No coherent foreign policy was evolved, but great emphasis was given to the establishment of anti-colonial solidarity in South East Asia. In 1947 both the other major freedom movements in South East Asia were invited to send representatives to Rangoon. The Viet Minh set up an agency headed by Dr. Tran Van Luan; Indonesia's representative was Marjornami. Within the first year of independence Burma established diplomatic relations with seven other Powers,[2] but the only intimate relations were with the two peoples with whom Burma had been closely associated for almost a century: India and Britain. Relations with Nationalist China were cordial (China was one of the Powers to sponsor Burma's admission to the United Nations in April 1948) despite the emphatic claim made by China in November 1947 to 77,000 square miles of Burma's territory, all that lies to the north of Myitkyina.[3] During the first two years of independence the Government of Burma can hardly be said to have had time to formulate a foreign policy. U Nu has related how he had to resist the lunatic fringe in his Cabinet in the early days who pressed him to follow up independence by declaring war on Britain and the United States:

[1] The Foreign Minister, Thakin Nu, recorded later that the Foreign Office was nicknamed the 'Telegraph Office' because all they did was to send off complimentary telegrams when foreign statesmen had birthdays (Nu, *Burma under the Japanese*, p. 85).

[2] The United Kingdom, the United States, India, Pakistan, China, Siam, and France.

[3] *New Times of Burma*, 27 November 1947.

in reply U Nu unrolled a world map and invited his colleagues to study it closely. After a few minutes the would-be world-shakers asked whether a token declaration of war would not be possible.[1] The spirit of the old Konbaung times when Burma was believed by her rulers to be the greatest Power in the world was still not quenched.

Kyaw Nyein was Foreign Minister until his resignation in April 1949; he was succeeded by Dr. E Maung in the 'emergency' Cabinet, and he handed over charge to Sao Hkun Hkio in December 1949. However, no slight is implied to these three able leaders in suggesting that the principal architect of Burma's foreign policy has been the Prime Minister, U Nu. On the eve of independence U Nu proclaimed

> To prevent the destruction of our liberties . . . we need good allies. In a world where the battle is to the strong, our country cannot stand alone. . . . Further, it would be no happy state for us to hang on the skirts of a powerful ally. We must be in a position to take a leading part, a decisive part, in any war in which we may be engaged. We must seek good allies, but we must also strive to be strong ourselves.[2]

However, U Nu did not go on to suggest whither Burma should look for allies, probably because the AFPFL and the country were acutely divided upon the issue. The Socialists would wish to go to Soviet Russia, but this would have alarmed all the conservative elements in the country. The Karens, and to a lesser extent the Shans and Kachins, would have preferred to conclude an alliance with Britain: but this would have been repugnant to the Socialists as a 'sell-out' to the 'Imperialists'. And so nothing more was heard of the desirability of allies; and yet, in September 1949, U Nu did go on record in the following terms:

> Among the three powers, the British, the Americans and the Russians, the British are closest to us for a variety of reasons. To be candid, there are a number of things which the British advise us to do, but these assignments do not include such works as setting fire to the Union. . . . Our relations with the British are thus absolutely straightforward, and our relations with other countries must be equally straightforward.[3]

Already U Nu was formulating the principles which were to determine the course Burma would adopt during the following years. To a mass rally on 11 December 1949 he declared:

---

[1] *From Peace to Stability*, p. 45.
[2] *Towards Peace and Democracy*, p. 33.
[3] *From Peace to Stability*, p. 22.

In regard to our foreign policy, we are convinced that the course we have adopted is the best in the circumstances of our country and we are therefore pursuing it steadfastly no matter how strongly it is criticized. Our circumstances demand that we follow an independent course and not ally ourselves with any power bloc. Any other course can only lead the Union to ruin. . . . The only political programme which we should pursue is the one which we genuinely believe to be the most suitable for our Union, whatever course the British, the Americans, the Russians and the Chinese Communists might follow. . . . Be friendly with all foreign countries. Our tiny nation cannot have the effrontery to quarrel with any power. If any country comes with an offer of a mutually beneficial enterprise, welcome it by all means . . . but . . . in laying down political programmes, do not forget to ensure that it is fully suited to the requirements of the Union.[1]

During these first two years of independence there were other signs pointing to future lines of development of Burma's foreign policy. During the struggle of the Republic of Indonesia against Dutch authority Burma, in company with other Asian states and following the leadership of India, gave considerable moral support to Indonesia. The republic was given *de facto* recognition by Burma in November 1948, and a representative, Thakin Tha Kin, was sent to establish relations with the Indonesian Government. A ban was placed upon the use of Mingaladon Airport by Dutch planes in December 1948, at the time of the second Dutch 'police action', being withdrawn in July 1949, after the conclusion of a truce between the contestants. Following the Hague Agreement of December 1949, on 27 December Burma recognized the Republic of Indonesia as *de jure* the sovereign Power of the archipelago. Perhaps the most notable portent was Burma's reaction to the Communist victory in China. After the fall of Nanking to the Communists in April 1949 the Burmese Ambassador, U Myint Thein, stayed on in the erstwhile capital, until his recall to Rangoon in October 1949. On 18 December Burma recognized the new order, being the first state outside the Communist bloc so to do.[2] This although Burma's domestic Communists were then engaged in all-out war against the Government.

During 1950 Burma's foreign policy appeared to be entering into a new phase. When in July the Security Council condemned the aggression of North Korea against her neighbour, Burma voted in favour of the motion. In Parliament U Nu made a

[1] ibid., pp. 51–53.
[2] Sardar Panikkar states that the Burma Government specially requested India to delay recognition so that Burma could be first in the field (*In Two Chinas* (London, 1955), p. 68).

vigorous defence of this step. He compared the circumstances of South Korea with those of Burma: Burma was also a small nation with inadequate defences, and he declared that

> it won't do to simply stare at this state of affairs and tremble. If only we are in right earnest to maintain our independent status, we must do something to defend our hearths and homes against aggression. . . . When we joined the United Nations . . . what was foremost in our thoughts was the expectation of United Nations assistance when our country is subjected to aggression by a stronger power. We have pinned our faith to the United Nations Organization on that score.
>
> With this advantage in view, we felt a reciprocal obligation to contribute our mite to the United Nations when that great organization tackles any aggression in any place at any time. . . . So far as I can see, it will never do for us to try to be too clever and sit on the fence. If we are foolish enough to try that sort of trick, we ourselves will find ourselves face to face with aggression some day.

U Nu went on to express the doubts which had previously assailed him with regard to the capabilities of the United Nations: would the failings of the League of Nations be repeated? He concluded

> Korea has dispelled these doubts . . . as soon as aggression started in South Korea, the United Nations went to its assistance. This has set up a noble precedent. Henceforth, if aggression occurs elsewhere, there too the United Nations must step in. . . . This is the great hope, the only hope for small member nations like us.[1]

Despite U Nu's careful declarations of his country's dissociation from both Power blocs, the alignment of Burma with the 'free' nations of the world on the issue of Korea did seem to suggest to some observers that Burma had come to regard Communist aggression as the vital threat to world peace, just as it was a major threat to internal security. Yet Burma's next stand in the United Nations represented an apparent volte-face: on 30 January 1951, when the United States introduced a motion in the Assembly branding China as aggressor for her intervention in Korea, Burma voted along with the Communist bloc against the motion. Burma and India were the only two non-Communist Powers to oppose the American motion.[2] This apparent contradiction was in fact a logical continuation of Burma's individual policy of refusing to commit herself to either Power bloc: believing that General MacArthur's incursion into North Korea had blurred the

---

[1] *From Peace to Stability*, pp. 98–101. The whole speech merits study as offering an excellent review of the principles of Burma's foreign policy.

[2] The voting was 44 in favour, with 9 abstentions and 7 against the motion.

original issue of aggression, Burma and India were not prepared to condemn China for intervening across the Manchurian border.

The reception which this stand met in the United Nations may have done something to make U Nu and his Government less than enthusiastic for the United Nations as a truly representative international organization above the struggle between the two Power blocs. However, 1951 also saw Burma's acceptance of American aid upon a sizeable scale; Burma was, by conviction, strictly neutral, but the pull of close practical associations with Britain and the United States moulded Burma's attitude more in concert with the 'Western' world. All the time Burma's leaders steadily resisted any involvement with military or political alignments. On almost every public occasion U Nu was at pains to indicate that the acceptance of foreign aid was strictly conditional on there being 'no strings'. The occasion of the 1952 Pyidawtha Conference gave him an opportunity to restate at length the Union's policy of friendship towards all but involvement with none. The case of Korea now served not as an encouragement to active participation in the United Nations, but as a warning of the fate of small nations involved in the duel between the Great Powers and, added U Nu,

Judging from the situation of our Union, our position is not so different from that of Korea. We are within an arm's reach from Soviet Russia and Red China as well as from Britain and the United States sphere of influence. Consequently, whether we turn our guns in the direction of Red China and Soviet Russia or in the direction of the Anglo-Americans, we shall fare the same fate as Korea.[1]

There can be no doubt that the lesson which the Korean War presents to Asian nations such as Burma is very different from the conclusions which seem so evident to Powers more remote from possible aggression, such as the United States. The former see only that South Korea's freedom has been paid for by the physical destruction of the country's economy, the uprooting and ruin of the lives of millions, and the division of one people into two warring groups. From Korea Burma drew the lesson that almost any fate is preferable for a small nation to that of becoming a battlefield for the world's great conflict.

In 1952 the problem which, more than any other, has influenced Burma's foreign policy during the first period of

[1] *Towards a Welfare State*, p. 31.

independence built up towards a crisis, that problem being the Kuomintang invasion of Burma's eastern borderlands. This invasion appeared likely to ignite all the most combustible elements in the frontier situation. Burma, so anxious to be on good terms with Communist China, might nevertheless be accused of harbouring its enemies, the KMT, who behaved in the most opportunist and unprincipled fashion, raiding into China and withdrawing into Burma. What better excuse could Communist China wish for if desiring to intervene in Burma than this almost legitimate *casus belli*. The KMT were concentrated in eastern Kengtung, the Wa States, and Bhamo District: all areas that had been the subject of vague Chinese claims in the past. Would the new Chinese Communist Government let slip such a chance to seize these coveted areas? In such a dangerous situation, to the Burmese leaders, any Power that regarded their difficulties with the KMT with sympathy was assuredly a friend; any Power which exacerbated these difficulties, even unintentionally, was unfriendly. During 1952 many in Burma came to believe that there must be American backing for the KMT. Several approaches were made to the American Embassy in Burma, with a view to moving the State Department to put pressure upon Formosa to withdraw these forces from Burma: but nothing came of these approaches. Few were so naïve as to say that the American Government was encouraging the KMT, but many argued that if America wished to put a stop to this adventure, it could be done by exerting pressure upon Chiang Kai-shek: perhaps by withholding aid, without which his régime must collapse. In coming to these conclusions Burmans were simplifying the situation; merely to take one factor, they were under-estimating the compulsion which Chiang felt to demonstrate his intransigence towards the Americans to whom he owed so much. However, it is also true that there were irresponsible Americans, individuals who encouraged the KMT adventurers in Burma.[1] Indignation in Rangoon rose steadily, culminating in the discovery of the bodies of three white men alleged to be Americans among the KMT dead, together with the seizure of arms and equipment stamped with current United States Army markings, in the big spring battles of 1953. On 17 March 1953 the Burma Government suddenly notified the United States Government of their decision to terminate American aid. No formal explanation of this dramatic decision

[1] A correspondent of the *New York Herald Tribune*, Homer Bigart, quoted by the Madras *Hindu* of 26 March 1953, produced a long dispatch on American activities in Siam, the shuttling 'back and forth on mysterious missions between Bangkok and Liu's [the KMT] airstrip north of Kengtung', the 'smuggling of supplies', &c.

was ever issued, but the Burmese public has remained convinced that it arose out of the Burma Government's conviction that it was absurd to accept American aid while American aid was also being utilized to support and encourage Burma's enemies.

The next step was to present a complaint to the United Nations. On 25 March Sao Hkun Hkio dispatched an account of KMT activities to the Secretary-General, which ended with the notification of a draft resolution which Burma proposed to submit to the vote of the Assembly. This proposed 'to condemn the Kuomintang Government of Formosa for the said acts of aggression, and to take all necessary steps to ensure immediate cessation of the acts of aggression by the Kuomintang Government of Formosa against the Union of Burma.' Reactions from the KMT side were mixed; spokesmen in Formosa mostly maintained a bland denial that the forces in Burma were under the orders of Chiang Kai-shek; but the Nationalist chargé d'affaires at Bangkok stated positively that the troops were operating under the orders of Formosa—but that they were in undemarcated territory.[1] The Asian-Arab bloc in the United Nations was almost solid in its support of Burma's case; only Siam and the Philippines differed from the majority. Commonwealth countries also signified their support for Burma, but the United States attempted to play the unpopular role of 'honest broker' between the two countries, and this was the attitude adopted by the Pan-American group. When the bluntly-worded Burmese resolution was brought before the Assembly, Mexico, as spokesman for the American bloc, put forward a counter-resolution in much more vague and general terms. This did not even identify the forces in Kengtung with the KMT: there was a reference to 'the presence of hostile activities and depredation of foreign forces in the territory of the Union of Burma', and that was all. The resolution went on to recommend that 'the negotiations now in progress through the good offices of certain member states should be pursued in order to put an end to this serious situation'. This watered-down resolution was adopted by fifty-nine votes, with Nationalist China abstaining. Burma did not press for a vote upon her own directly-worded formula.

Although Burma accepted the compromise resolution, and entered into weary months of negotiation at Bangkok with the elusive representatives of Formosa, this feeble response to a situation of intense urgency was taken as final evidence that the United Nations could not be relied upon as a defence

[1] *The Times*, 29 March 1953.

against aggression. Many in Burma (as well as in India and other neutral Asian lands) noted the marked contrast with which aggression was received by the United Nations in the case of Korea and of Burma. The inference was drawn that members of the United Nations could only be persuaded to take action on aggression by a Communist Power. When the aggression was committed by a professed antagonist of Communism, it was met by casuistry, was indeed almost condoned.

Throughout this period and the following years the attitude of Communist China was patient and sympathetic. At no stage did Red China utilize the KMT situation to bring pressure to bear upon Burma, and this forbearance was naturally received with gratitude by the Government and thinking public of Burma.

One other international event of some note in 1953 was the convening of an Asian Socialist Conference at Rangoon in January. This conference, the first of its kind, was attended by representatives from ten countries in Asia and the Middle East.[1] In addition there were 'fraternal observers' from Europe, including Attlee from Britain and Milovan Djilas from Yugoslavia. As the only country where a Socialist Government was actually in office, Burma enjoyed a certain pre-eminence among the Asian nations. U Ba Swe was elected Chairman of the conference: U Nu played no part in the proceedings. It was decided that further conferences should be held biennially, but in order to establish some continuity a bureau—a kind of supervisory committee—was set up, to meet every six months. A small permanent staff was also organized, with headquarters in Rangoon. As a result of the first meeting of the bureau (at Hyderabad in July 1953) an Anti-Colonial Bureau was constituted, largely to effect contacts with anti-colonial movements in Africa. The first meeting of the Anti-Colonial Bureau was held at Kalaw (Southern Shan States) in May 1954.[2] The principal result of the Kalaw Conference (which was also under the chairmanship of Ba Swe) was a decision to designate an international anniversary, the Dependent Peoples' Freedom Day, every 30 October. This anniversary has since been celebrated with considerable publicity in Burma under the auspices of the Socialist Party leaders. Kyaw Nyein presided over the first anniversary in 1954 and Ba Swe over the second:

---

[1] Burma, Egypt, India, Indonesia, Israel, Japan, Lebanon, Malaya, Nepal, and Pakistan.

[2] At first this meeting was planned to take place at Bandung, but the Government of Indonesia refused its sanction. Indonesia feared that if entry visas were granted to the Israeli delegates this would give offence to the Arab and perhaps other Muslim states. It may also be that the Government did not wish the Partai Sosialis of Indonesia to derive kudos from sponsoring such a gathering.

on neither occasion did U Nu take part in the rallies. In all these Asian Socialist meetings Burma's Socialist leaders are clearly the moving spirits. In November 1954 another meeting of Asian Socialists took place at Tokyo; once again Ba Swe was elected Chairman, and he now called upon the Bureau, the executive committee, to endorse the 'Five Principles' of co-existence. He also urged Asian Socialists to increase their study of trade unionism, and to this end a Trade Union Seminar was held at Rangoon in May 1955 under the auspices of the TUC(B). This was inaugurated by Ba Swe with M. A. Raschid in the chair.

Developments toward pan-Asian Socialist solidarity were eclipsed by the wider movement towards an Afro-Asian under-standing. This may be said to have begun with the Asian Relations Conference convened at New Delhi in March 1947 by Pandit Nehru, who suggested the creation of a permanent organization of Asian peoples with headquarters and a secre-tariat in India. This proposal was received with little enthusiasm by the leaders of South East Asia, being regarded as a bid for Indian leadership, and came to nothing. The subsequent con-ference convened at New Delhi in January 1949 in support of Indonesia, while important in its effects upon Dutch policy, did not result in any further Asian co-operation. For several years the new Asian countries were immersed in their own problems, but a measure of joint consultation was provided by the Colombo Plan, inaugurated in 1950. The founder-members were India, Pakistan, Ceylon, and Malaya, with those of the 'white' Commonwealth countries which were prepared to render assistance under the Plan. This group has been gradually enlarged by the adherence of most of the countries of South and East Asia: Burma joined the Plan in March 1952. A permanent secretariat was established at Colombo, and frequent meetings for consultation took place between the participating countries. 'Colombo' acquired some-thing of the connotation of 'Geneva' as an international con-ference centre. In April–May 1954 a meeting took place between the Prime Ministers of India, Pakistan, Ceylon, Burma, and Indonesia at Colombo, and although there was no link whatsoever between this conference and the economic co-operation organization, the meeting was known as the Colombo Conference and the participants have since been collectively called the 'Colombo Powers'. Perhaps the most significant aspect of this new association is that the thread which unites these nations is not neutralism, anti-colonialism, state socialism, or parliamentary government—although all these themes play their part in the association: the common bond is simply that they are Asians. Just as the nations of Western Europe or of the Middle East may be said to possess a common denominator which transcends all sorts of minor and major differences, so a definite Asian, or rather South Asian, outlook has come into focus. This conception must take into account such divisions as the Indo-Pakistan conflict over Kashmir, which indeed flared up at Colombo and was only smothered by the efforts of U Nu—but such divergences have emerged also in Western Europe or the Middle East in the process of evolving a conscious, common outlook. The conference was able to agree upon a number of fundamental issues, as, for instance, in calling for the admission of Communist China into the United Nations. The next meeting of the Colombo Powers occurred on 28 and 29 December 1954 at Bogor in Java, very largely upon the initiative of the Government of Indonesia. This conference considered one major item only: the convening of an Asian-African Conference in Indonesia in April 1955.

The conference at Bandung has been hailed as the beginning of a new era in Asia: it may also appear that it coincides with a new phase in Burma's foreign affairs. It might not be unjust to suggest that up to 1954 Burma had built up relations with foreign countries more or less on empirical lines. The doctrinaire convictions of the Socialist leaders would have identified Burma more with the Soviet bloc, whereas practical considerations led to close relations with Britain and to an increasing extent with the United States. From 1955 conscious efforts can be detected towards adhering to a deliberate foreign policy. It may be that practical considerations, notably economic requirements, will dictate Burma's foreign relations for all time, or it may be that Burma will evolve her own unique place in world politics. Whatever the future, the period from 1948 to 1954 was a formative phase in which Burma was concerned more with adjusting her relations with individual countries than with practising an all-round foreign policy. In working out Burma's relations with other lands one becomes aware, time and again, of a certain ambivalence, of lines of force attracting and repelling: doubtless some ambivalence is to be detected in the relations of most countries—as for instance, between Britain and the United States—but the contrasts in the case of Burma seem to have a peculiar intensity.

Although Burma has no formal links with the Commonwealth it may be useful to consider, *seriatim*, relations with this group, beginning with the two countries with the oldest established connexions, Britain and India.

It cannot be said that Burma and Britain built up any very solid relationship during the hundred years in which their destinies were yoked together. Only a handful of Burmans studied or worked in Britain before the First World War, and even between 1920 and 1940 only a few hundred Burmans were able to see Britain at first-hand. There was no development in Burma to compare with the cultural fusion which took place in Indian thought—the emergence of a dualistic Indo-British mind. Some Burmans, especially in the services and in the colleges, did identify themselves, ardently or reluctantly, with British legal and political principles, but their number was minute. On the British side the number of Englishmen brought to Burma was very few compared to those absorbed by India. It was an axiom of the old British House of Commons that no one was interested in India: nevertheless a succession of officials, and a few missionaries and merchants, did establish a definite British-Indian voice and viewpoint in English public life, as well as a tradition of Indian service and a large English literature of India. The size of the British community in Burma was so small and the period of British rule so brief that no comparable Burma connexion ever developed. To the average Englishman, Burma conjured up one poem and perhaps a short story by Kipling—Kipling, who spent three days in Burma. It is probably true, as Burmese nationalists assert, that the predominant British interests in Burma were the half-dozen great business houses, and theirs was the voice that was listened to at Whitehall and Westminster.[1] And so when Burma became independent, there were no powerful bonds to hold the two nations together—only the inheritance of British institutions, and a moderate-sized British commercial stake in the country.

The attitude of the new Burma Government to Britain included two main elements, a respect for British ideals and a suspicion of British imperialism. The two elements are so intertwined that it is not unusual to find them both included in the same political speech. Friendliness towards Britain is most marked, as would be expected, in those most influenced by British traditions: the higher civil service, the leaders of the Bar, responsible journalists, college teachers, and pre-war army men. Dislike of Britain is voiced loudest by politicians, among whom this attitude has become a habit. The KNDO revolt

[1] It is only fair to add that there is but one case on record where the Burma Government was moved to actively consider the interests of a British firm. The interest of the Burma Corporation in the Lufang mines was upheld in 1934-5, in the face of Chinese opposition, by the dispatch of a column of troops. There is nothing to show that in this the Burma Government exceeded its lawful obligations.

was used as ammunition by those who feared British imperialism:
it was taken for granted that the British must be behind the
Karens.[1] Without directly accusing the British Government,
AFPFL leaders nevertheless are wont to talk darkly of the
'imperialists' who are never precisely identified.[2] There are
exceptions to this attitude, however: U Nu, while uncompromisingly critical of British colonialism as seen in Kenya,
for instance, makes no secret of his admiration for the British
people and their political traditions.[3] And there are other
politicians who, while reluctant to make public their debt to
Britain, are not ungenerous in private conversation. And
everywhere, among every class of society, there is a strange
nostalgia for 'the British time'. Looking back over the weary
years of civil war and the Japanese occupation, the old days
have acquired the quality of a golden age among all who are
forty or over. The listener is tempted to smile when a prominent
former collaborator with the Japanese assures him that 'Things
were so much better in the British time.'

However delusively agreeable such sentiments may be to a
British listener, they have little bearing upon the future; in
Burma perhaps more than in most countries it is accepted that
Britain's days as a world leader are over, while at the same
time economic and political ties are withering fast away. This
does not mean that Britain and Burma are any the worse
friends; relations have probably become more cordial as the
years have passed, but the Burmese attitude is that of the boy
who has left school and become a man towards his old schoolmaster; as the memory of the dislike of school discipline fades,
so the former pupil grows to appreciate his debt of learning to

[1] It was the custom of some KNDO bands in the early days, after sacking a
government police station or treasury, to run up the Union Jack over the smoulder-
ing ruin: this certainly gave some colour to these beliefs.

[2] Kyaw Nyein at the 'Martyrs' Day' Rally, 1955, said: 'The Imperialists began
to bring these newly-independent countries [Burma, &c.] under their fold. They
began to incite the minority groups to . . rise in rebellion. . . . The KNDO's under
the leadership of Saw Ba U Gyi were made use of to achieve the ends of the
Imperialists.'

[3] It would be easy to compile an anthology in praise of England from the Prime
Minister's speeches. To quote only two examples: 'English discipline and system are
the cynosure of the whole world. The perseverance and tenacity of purpose of the
British nation are such that they can "take it" in any adverse circumstances. The
British zeal and perseverance deserve to shine as an example to the entire world.
And in the sphere of administration the British have set an example to the world
for honesty and integrity' (*Towards a Welfare State*, p. 30). Or 'We should emulate
the excellent example set by political parties in the United Kingdom. . . . The
defeated party simply goes on presenting its programme to the people with a view
to avenging its defeat at the next General Election. . . . If we want our Union to be
stable like the United Kingdom, our political parties should emulate the political
parties of that country in the observation of set principles' (*BWB*, 29 September
1955).

his old teacher. Burma shook off the atmosphere of school very rapidly: those tenuous ties which still linked the two countries after the coming of independence were all dissolved within five or six years. The backing of Burma's finances by a Currency Board in London, the sale of Burma's rice through the British Ministry of Food, the Ottawa Tariffs Agreement, the British Military Mission—all had been terminated by the end of 1953. There remains only the remnant of former economic interests, and a sort of intellectual connexion in the continued training of young Burmans at British universities, service establishments, and other institutions. Affection or respect for England lives mainly in fading memories of a Deputy Commissioner who taught his people to abhor the *shiko*, the obeisance of humiliation, or of the scholar who revealed to his students the glories of their ancient past, or of the Forest Officer who led two or three jungle villages out of a fearful world of malignant demons, starvation, and poverty.

In this writer's view the eclipse of the British tradition in Burma must be accepted gracefully. In a smaller way, a new tradition of co-operation with the Commonwealth may be created out of the Colombo Plan and other training schemes: but it must be accepted that the British influence will be but one of many—and not by any means the leading influence in Burma. Also, if U Nu's retirement proves to be permanent, his open-minded attitude might not be echoed by successors whose dominant outlook would be not a generous recognition of Britain's ideals but a dogmatic hostility to Britain as a still active colonial Power, with strong criticism of the situation in Malaya, Kenya, and elsewhere. Meanwhile, the official attitude of the Nu Government to British colonialism has been tempered by the memory of the satisfactory manner in which colonialism was wound up in Burma. Like most of the newly enfranchised countries, Burma is very alert to use the Assembly and the Trusteeship Committee of the United Nations to bring pressure to bear upon colonial Powers: but references to Britain have been markedly restrained and frequently complimentary. A particularly graceful expression of this understanding attitude was contained in a speech by Burma's representative, U Thant, delivered in October 1952. Of the British representative's speech U Thant commented

He spoke with pride—and quite a legitimate one at that—that the country he represented had given freedom to nearly a dozen countries which are represented in this General Assembly. My country happens to be one of them, and I want to take this opportunity of expressing our heartfelt thanks to the United Kingdom for their far-sight and magnanimity in granting us independence—real, genuine independence—without bloodshed, without resentment and without ill-feeling.[1]

Burma has made very little of the continuance of colonial rule in Malaya, largely because of this publicly expressed acceptance of Britain's good faith. This understanding has been assisted by the direct, informal, personal contacts built up with Burma's leaders by Malcolm MacDonald as Commissioner-General in South East Asia. In the present personalized condition of foreign affairs in Burma, such face to face contacts are worth much more than careful cordiality on paper.

Elements of ambivalence exert their pull upon the relationship between Burma and India. On the one hand Burmese leaders look to India with admiration as the hope of present-day Asia: on the other hand Burmans are not without disquiet at the economic thraldom which India partly represents. There is a general acknowledgment of Burma's obligation to her great neighbour for inspiration in the struggle for freedom. Speaking on the second anniversary of Indian independence U Nu declared: 'Though I have met the Mahatma [Gandhi] only once,[2] I have always regarded him as my *guru* [spiritual master].' He continued, 'I cannot adequately describe the great personal qualities of Pandit Nehru. He has deservedly earned the respect and admiration of the whole world.'[3] During the succeeding years Nu and Nehru have built up a close understanding and friendship. The two statesmen are strikingly dissimilar in personality but almost as one in their international viewpoint. This has led some critics to assert that Burma's foreign policy is merely a duplication of India's upon a smaller scale.[4] Yet there are points of difference: to name perhaps the two most significant, India has the Commonwealth link which, in the field of diplomacy, offers possibilities of consultation and discussion closed to Burma, and gives India a surer touch in her diplomatic moves; on the other hand Burma has no King Charles's Head comparable to Kashmir and Goa to add an obsessional streak to her international outlook. Whereas Burma's leaders have visited most of the leading countries only on rare occasions, their visits to India are a commonplace;

---

[1] *Burma*, April 1953, p. 49. One month later James Barrington of Burma made a telling comparison between the attitude to self-government in colonial territories of France and Britain (ibid., p. 38).
[2] At Delhi in December 1947.
[3] *From Peace to Stability*, pp. 1–2.
[4] It has been stated that before the crucial United Nations resolution upon Chinese aggression in Korea, Burma's spokesman had instructions to cast his vote according to India's decision (*Nation*, 3 February 1951).

similarly Pandit Nehru has come to Rangoon many times: and so the interchanges between the two neighbours are not attended by the publicity and ballyhoo which has surrounded so many diplomatic visits in the new Asia. U Nu summed up his own attitude to India in an address to M.P.s in September 1955, saying

The governments of India and of Burma have affectionate regard for each other. . . . In Burma's fight for independence, the Burmese leaders and people drew inspiration from Indian leaders and people. . . . Our Union is eight years old. During this period, India has never asked for help from Burma. If I remember aright, Burma has asked for substantial help from India on three different occasions. . . . The reason why we can always approach India for help in our time of need is because there is firm Indo-Burmese friendship.[1]

None the less, as U Nu with his customary frankness admitted in the same speech, there is a reverse side to the relationship of the two countries. The insecure position of Indians in Burma has been touched upon in a previous chapter.[2] Few of the Indians domiciled in Burma surrender all links with their ancestral land, and in particular, the Chettyar community in Madras forms a powerful group in its home province, and has campaigned in the Indian Press and Parliament for a satisfactory settlement of claims arising from land nationalization in Burma. In response to their representations their case was taken up by the Indian Government, and in June 1950 a delegation from India conducted talks with the Burma Government; a second Indian delegation came to Burma in December 1953. As a result of these discussions amending legislation was introduced into the Union Parliament to make compensation for expropriation more equitable. However, until compensation is actually paid, this issue will serve as an international irritant. A second undercurrent of ill-feeling was revealed during the trade talks on rice purchases held during the opening months of 1954. On the Burmese side it was held that India was using the difficulties created by the accumulation of enormous unsold stocks to force down prices unfairly; on the Indian side there was annoyance that Burma, with (at that time) huge overseas balances, should be standing out for a figure much above the prevailing world price, while regarding India's suggestions of a more realistic rate as the avarice of the *bania*. The final agreement, which gave Burma a high price, but deducted a proportion in payment of Burma's separation debt, was a suitable compromise, but ill-feeling remained, and was not improved by attempts to include inferior rice among the

[1] *BWB*, 29 September 1955.　　　　[2] See above, p. 188.

shipments to India.[1] The efforts of Burma to exclude foreigners from the import-export trade have affected Indian merchants perhaps more intensely than other foreigners. Indians attempting to enter or leave Burma have also been treated with what U Nu has temperately called 'lack of courtesy'.[2] Under the leadership of U Nu and Pandit Nehru such differences have been no more than pinpricks; but, once again, a change of government and the accession of more chauvinist leaders could lead to delicate matters being handled less delicately.

In July 1951 Burma and India concluded a Treaty of Friendship.[3] This commences with a declaration that 'the two states recognize and respect the independence and rights of each other', and that 'everlasting peace and unalterable friendship' shall exist between them; no specific provisions were incorporated into the treaty. At the end of March 1953 Pandit Nehru and U Nu conducted a brief joint tour of the Burma-India border in the Kohima-Khamti area. Naga tribes bestride the political frontier, and those on the Indian side have put forward demands for a separate state; these have been backed by a display of force. It would therefore appear to be in the interest of both the Powers to co-ordinate their tribal policies. This 1953 tour coincided with the KMT crisis, and when Nehru attended a Press conference at Khamti, Burmese reporters pressed the Indian Premier hard for some assurance of military support for Burma. Nehru completely evaded giving any direct answer to this very pertinent question.[4] However, it must be assumed that India could not contemplate the occupation of Burma by a third Power without taking steps to oppose such an occupation.

Burma's relations with Pakistan, also a neighbour with a contiguous frontier, have the appearance of being less intimate than with India. This is superficially surprising; Burma has many Muslims in high positions, including two Cabinet Ministers, while Hindus have virtually no place in public life; also, Burma and Pakistan might be expected to have a common bond in that both are 'succession states' from the old Indian Empire and might wish to reinsure against any possibility of reincorporation.[5] But these factors have not operated: for a

---

[1] See above, p. 264.
[2] *BWB*, 29 September 1955.
[3] The full text is given in *Burma*, October 1951, pp. 51–52.
[4] *BWB*, 8 April 1953.
[5] Cf. the view expressed by a former Pakistan Cabinet Minister, 'Ceylon and Burma are looked upon as allies, being potentially in the same position as Pakistan is in relation to the great neighbour India, which is suspected of nursing a growing imperialism against her neighbours' (I. H. Qureshi, *The Pakistani Way of Life*, London, 1956, p. 68).

period indeed relations between the two countries were clouded. Before independence there was a movement for the adherence of two townships in Akyab District, Buthidaung and Maungdaw, to Pakistan;[1] when this was brushed aside by the Constituent Assembly of Burma there followed the *Mujahid* terrorist campaign, which was to some extent Islamic in purpose—although Muslims were often among its victims. It was alleged that, when pressed, the *Mujahid* leader Cassim would withdraw across the frontier where he was supported with arms and money by East Pakistan landlords. This unpleasant situation was largely resolved when Cassim was finally arrested and lodged in a Pakistan jail in June 1954. Another small source of tension was the existence of a Burmese (Arakanese) Buddhist community some 16,000 strong at Barisal in East Pakistan, originally founded in 1794 by refugees from persecution by forces of the Ava Government in Arakan; another 80,000 Burmans (mainly Arakanese) are scattered about the Chittagong Hill Tracts and Cox's Bazaar. There have been reports of ill-treatment by Islamic zealots, and one or two Buddhist monks have been expelled.[2] Finally, the Burma-Pakistan boundary, the Naaf River, a winding creek with half-submerged islands and shifting channels, presents endless possibilities of petty frontier disputes: at the end of 1953 an attempt was made to survey the river's course and determine an agreed frontier line.

However, none of these points of disagreement amount to anything at all inflammatory. In June 1952 a Treaty of Friendship was signed between the two countries in terms almost identical with those of the treaty with India.[3] In subsequent years Pakistan's policy of active alignment with the West, membership of SEATO and the Baghdad Pact, and acceptance of American military aid has naturally precluded any extensive international co-operation with Burma. But, in conformity with U Nu's policy of friendship with those of different minds, Pakistan's westward course has not affected mutual relations.

As the home of *Theravada* Buddhism, Ceylon is a land much revered by Burmese Buddhists. Contacts between the two countries, according to historical evidence, go back to the eleventh century A.D. at least. The Buddhist revival of today has led to a considerable exchange of travellers, most bent on

[1] In Buthidaung town about 60 per cent. of the population are classified according to the current census as Pakistanis; in Maungdaw town about 45 per cent. are Pakistanis (see Census, Release No. 3, 1953).
[2] *Nation*, 16 May 1949.
[3] Text in *Burma*, October 1952, pp. 52–53.

religious missions or pilgrimages. In addition Ceylon has been one of Burma's best customers for rice, and as only small quantities of Ceylon's products are shipped in return, these transactions provide Burma with much-needed sterling. But the association of the two countries has not become as close as might be expected; both are small nations overshadowed by a mighty continent and mutual associations might have been expected to develop. This has not happened, and observation might suggest that much more than a few hundred miles of open sea separates the two countries. The Ceylonese are essentially cosmopolitan and outward-looking, modest in their national ambitions, content to retain many links with Britain after independence, and perhaps the most enterprising interpreters of the Commonwealth idea in Asia. The Burmese are inward-looking, nourish a high national pride and intend to keep aloof from any international undertakings. And so one may expect to see the two countries remain friendly but not intimate in years to come.

The only other Commonwealth country to have established direct diplomatic relations with Burma is Australia: legations were first set up in 1952. Previously, except for some Australian mining engineers working in Burma, contacts had been negligible, but Australia's growing awareness of 'the Near North' has led to a rapid increase in the traffic between the two countries. An Australian trade mission visited Burma in November 1954, and during 1955 there was a sizeable expansion of Colombo Plan aid from Australia, who was in fact the largest contributor among the Commonwealth countries. In addition the Australian Foreign Minister, Richard Casey, by frequent visits to Rangoon has, somewhat like Malcolm MacDonald, developed a happy acquaintanceship, frank and unemotional, with Burmese leaders and senior officials.

Another group with obvious affinities towards Burma are the nations of South East Asia.

Burma has been mixed up with Siam more, perhaps, than with any other country. Many a time have Burmese armies marched upon Siam, and the ancient rivalry between the two countries may be likened somewhat to that of England and France; similarly, Burma has drawn heavily upon Siamese culture, and in the Shan States this may be accounted a major influence. With long historical connexions, 1,000 miles of common frontier, and a common religion, no two countries could be more closely related. Within the first few years after 1948 the two countries have run the entire gamut of diplomatic relations, from suspicion and hostility to cordial friendship.

There were no special developments until the KMT troops in Kengtung began to cause trouble. Opinion in Rangoon then became coloured by the knowledge that these KMT forces were receiving supplies and reinforcements through Siam. Early in 1953 the Thai Government closed the frontier with Burma; the principal route affected was the road from Chiengmai into Kengtung via Tachilek; in normal times this was Kengtung's principal trade channel, and the effect of closure was to create shortages and high prices in the Eastern Shan States. When, in October 1953, the KMT were persuaded to agree to evacuate their troops, Siam and the United States supervised the operation. Some friction with Burma occurred when the Thai Government refused to permit a Burmese observation team to leave Bangkok to witness the working of the airlift to Formosa for themselves. Finally, Burma lost all faith in the KMT intention to honour their agreement, and resumed military operations. In the course of air attacks on KMT positions the B.A.F. inadvertently bombed Thai villages in November and December 1953. In a public speech on 9 February 1954 the Thai Premier, Pibul Songgram, accused Burma of 'general unfriendliness'. After further frontier infringements by aircraft, anti-aircraft units of the Thai Army were moved up to the Kengtung border with orders to open fire upon any Burmese plane violating the frontier.[1] Fortunately this tense situation was not permitted to deteriorate any further towards actual conflict: Burma apologized for the unfortunate mistakes of her planes and proffered compensation, which was settled at K1,20,000 (Bhat 4,10,000 in Siamese currency). During the following months both governments worked to improve relations; there was an exchange of missions at different levels, including visits by Burma's Minister for Home Affairs, Bo Khin Maung Gale, and by Siam's Police General, Phao Sriyanond. At the end of 1954 the Thai Government reopened the road into Kengtung. On his way to the Bogor Conference in the last days of 1954 U Nu stopped at Bangkok, and in his own disarming fashion he apologized to the people of Siam for 'past misdeeds' by Burma, such as the destruction of the old capital, Ayuthia. He went on to attribute the recent improvement in Thai-Burmese relations to the 'magnanimous attitude and friendly policy' of the Thai Government.[2] This charming speech was very well received in Siam, and when U Nu next visited Bangkok, in July 1955, Pibul Songgram returned the money paid over by Burma in compensation for

[1] *Nation*, 11 March and 11 April 1954.
[2] *BWB*, 5 January 1955.

the bombing incidents, averring that this was intended as a 'sincere manifestation' of friendship. U Nu reciprocated by handing the cheque to the Burmese Ambassador for use in performing works of merit in Siam. In October 1955 the Burma Government waived all rights to compensation in respect of the Thai occupation of Kengtung and Mongpan in 1942–5.[1] These gestures form a pleasing demonstration, if only on a small scale, of international amenities in a world in which threats and abuse have come to form the small change of diplomatic intercourse.

In Siam this growing friendship towards Burma has coincided with a full-blooded acceptance of SEATO and committal to American military plans in East Asia; this apparently non-complementary policy might indicate that Siam wishes to have a friend at court if it were ever decided that SEATO should be discarded for peaceful co-existence, or it may simply mean that Siam wishes to be certain that one flank is secure in case the other is attacked. In either event, Burma's friendship is not unimportant to Siam.

With the other countries of South East Asia Burma's foreign policy is not actively concerned, except in the context of anti-colonialism. From Indonesia have come the Vice-President, Prime Ministers, and other leading politicians on goodwill visits, and Burma's first Treaty of Friendship was concluded with Indonesia in March 1951. Trade has also expanded between the two countries, somewhat one-sidedly, as Indonesia cannot offer Burma any much-needed product in return for rice.

Burma's attitude to Cambodia and Laos was for some years equivocal: there was some doubt whether their Governments were genuinely representative of their peoples, but by 1954 these doubts had been settled and in August Burma gave formal recognition to both states. During November 1954 the then King of Cambodia, Norodom Sihanouk, paid a state visit to Burma; his attractive personality made a distinct impression upon all who met him. Sharing the same religion and similar cultural traditions, relations between the two lands, which were entirely closed during the colonial period, may develop into a modest intimacy. Burma's principal contacts with Laos have concerned the KMT problem: the two countries have a common frontier for some 160 miles along the Mekong, and as a result of operations in January and March 1955 KMT troops sought refuge in the Laotian borderland. Conferences were held in

---

[1] A considerable amount of property was dismantled and taken away during these three years by the Thai occupation forces.

Kengtung and in Vientiane in May 1955 between representatives of the two countries to co-ordinate action against the
KMT. The Philippines have not so far appeared over Burma's
horizon, and the two states have not established diplomatic
relations. Towards Viet Nam Burma's attitude has remained
non-committed. There was no contact with the Bao Dai
régime, but neither was formal recognition accorded to the
Viet Minh, although a semi-official representative was established at Rangoon from 1947 onwards. *En route* to China late
in 1954, U Nu spent a day at Hanoi in conversation with Ho
Chi Minh. A joint communiqué stated that the two countries
would conduct their relations on the basis of the Five Principles
of Co-existence, and expressed the hope that relations between
the two countries would be strengthened.[1] In November 1956,
U Nu visited South Viet Nam at the invitation of President
Ngo-Dinh-Diem, accompanied by Justice U Thein. Subsequently a Consul General representing South Viet Nam was
appointed at Rangoon, while later a Consul General for North
Viet Nam was also received.

Two other countries fall into a special kind of category as
far as Burma is concerned: Israel and Yugoslavia. In pursuing
a policy of neutralism Burma has a close partner in India, but
seems to feel a need to identify herself with other small states
like herself, and not only with one of the world leaders. And
so Burma has developed a strange sympathy with Israel and
Yugoslavia, two other nations who are somewhat 'out on a
limb'. Actually Burma does have interests which are shared
with these two nations, more especially with Israel. As a former
British mandate Israel has a certain basic identity with Burma;
although this aspect is not stressed at all, the common carry-
over of much from the British period in the procedure and
techniques of administration, educational methods, and service
organization, makes it easy for persons from the two countries
to establish common ground. The people of Israel come from
different countries, but find their unity in a common religious
heritage. They are building up a modern state out of negligible
resources, under a government that is a coalition in which the
prevailing ideology is Socialist in the British, welfare, empirical
sense; and in the *kibbutz* they have developed a form of social
service which is non-compulsory but also places strong emphasis
upon the community. All this is attractive to AFPFL politicians
of the school of U Nu. Israel, on her side, amid the arid desert
of Arab hatred, is emotionally concerned to find friends. U Nu

[1] *BWB*, 8 December 1954.

was the first foreign Prime Minister to tour the country, and his visit was welcome visible evidence that there are foreign countries taking a friendly interest in Israel's endeavours. However, at a Press conference for Israeli newsmen U Nu went out of his way to recall that Burma is 'friendly both with your country and the Arab states'.[1] Burma must not appear particularist in international goodwill.

The image of Yugoslavia has been fixed upon the minds of the people of Burma with considerably more elaborate propaganda: there is the definite desire on the part of some leaders to transform Burma into the Yugoslavia of Asia. This is the declared programme of Ba Swe and Kyaw Nyein. Certainly the two countries have many affinities: both have federal constitutions and include within their boundaries diverse races and religions, both are situated precariously on the very edge of the Communist world empire, both are endeavouring to take revolutionary strides from a medieval, agricultural society towards a modern industrialized order; and both are committed whole-heartedly to a policy of neutralism which they hope to galvanize into something dynamic, a positive force among the nations. Many in Burma would wish to carry the comparison farther: a curtain of legend has already descended over much that happened in the struggle for independence, and many now would compare the AFPFL resistance record to the long, bitter guerrilla war of the Partisans in Yugoslavia against a ruthless German Army. In making such a comparison *The Burman* (6 January 1955) declared 'Marshal Tito has often been referred to as the Aung San of Yugoslavia, and in turn *Bogyoke* [Aung San] has been called the Tito of Burma.' Building up this analogy between the two nations, there are those who wish to see Burma's political, social, and economic system fashioned according to the Communist, or Marxist, model developed in Yugoslavia. This Burma-Yugoslav *entente* may be said to have had its origins about 1952: the first Yugoslav Ambassador presented his credentials in February 1951. However, a myth has gained currency that during the crisis months of 1949, when the Burma Army was without arms or ammunition, the situation was saved, when no other country was willing to help, by Yugoslavia's sending arms to Burma from her own scanty resources. Many Burmans feel that this timely help put their country under a debt of gratitude to Yugoslavia. This myth has never received any support from any public pronouncement by any Burmese leader, but it is firmly believed by many responsible Burmans. The basis of this tale

[1] *BWB*, 16 June 1955.

would seem to be that U Nu made an appeal for arms to Nehru, who sanctioned the diversion of a shipment of British arms from India to Burma: but there is no glamour in British or Indian help. Marshal Tito has himself announced that the 'struggle . . . in the course of World War II . . . forged links of close friendship and of brotherhood between the peoples of our two countries. The links that were thus established have naturally been strengthened in the post-war periods.'[1] One may compare this potpourri of fact and fancy with the statement made by U Nu at the same time to *Borba*, the Yugoslav official newspaper, that 'our political and economic patterns are not the same'.[2] Just how different the easy-going, democratic, very human government and administration of Burma is from the authoritarian régime of Yugoslavia, based upon the mass mind and never-relaxed security services, was brought home to Burmans by the visit of Marshal Tito to Burma in January 1955—and in particular to those Burman reporters who covered the tour. Not that the visit was anything but a success: the Marshal impressed all who met him not only as a leader of force and fire but also as a very human being. But all the time the visit provided *aperçus* of the Communist mind, culminating in a Press conference at which the Yugoslav Foreign Minister treated all efforts by Burmese and foreign reporters to probe for the motives behind his official news hand-out as attacks, to be answered by counter-attacks. This, the first view of the mechanism of a totalitarian state at first-hand, left many Burmese intellectuals pondering.

Co-operation between the two countries on an official level has developed further: more and more Yugoslav technicians and engineers are coming to Burma, and Yugoslavia is importing unwonted quantities of rice. In June 1955 U Nu paid a return visit to Yugoslavia and received a spectacular welcome as 'Our Friend'. Both U Nu and Tito laid great emphasis upon 'active co-existence'. In a public speech U Nu remarked that

> Yugoslavia and Burma have provided the world with a concrete demonstration of the possibilities of co-existence between those who subscribe to different political and economic systems. . . . The common policy adopted by countries like Yugoslavia and Burma encouraging mutual negotiation and agreement has considerably enlarged the area of peace.[3]

Burma's relations with Japan are in a class apart. The Japanese occupation was a considerable shock to Burmans of

[1] *BWB*, 12 January 1955.
[2] ibid.
[3] ibid., 16 and 23 June 1955.

every degree; it was doubly indignifying to be insulted and humiliated by those who had advertised themselves as 'fellow Asiatics'. The general reaction has been voiced by U Nu:

I have been a puppet myself during the Japanese régime as a puppet minister and I know what it means to be a puppet . . . when one has to bow to the command of the Japanese masters and shout 'Tenno Heika Banzai' [Long live the Japanese Emperor] at their bidding. . . . How we detested those days when every second person you met was a Japanese agent and when arrests and subsequent disappearances were the order of the day.[1]

It is possible that there are some Burmans who still, secretly, retain something of their former admiration for this master race that penetrated the secret of success and victory. Some Ministers have spoken in complimentary terms about the Japanese in Burma,[2] and when Japanese goods were once again exported there was no discrimination against them in Burma; rather they were bought in larger quantities than ever before: between 1949 and 1953 the value of imports from Japan was doubled.

Burma refused to attend the general conference convened at San Francisco in 1951 for the signing of a peace treaty with Japan. In 1953 discussions began between Burma and Japan towards a reparations settlement and the conclusion of a peace treaty. At first there was a wide divergence of views: Japan offered compensation of $100 million, while Burma put in a claim for $400 million—but both sides had motives for desiring agreement. Burma, without any foreign aid programme, was having to finance all development from internal resources; Japan greatly desired to gain an entry into South East Asia; if agreement were reached with one nation, it might serve as an inducement to others to follow. In August 1954, after preliminary meetings at Rangoon, Kyaw Nyein as Acting Foreign Minister proceeded to Tokyo to conduct negotiations. After one week both sides were reported to be standing by their original offers and deadlock seemed to have ensued. However, the Burmese delegation did not leave Tokyo, as at one time they threatened, and one month later, after fifteen main meetings, a draft agreement was reached on a compromise basis, giving Burma $200 million in goods and services,

---

[1] *From Peace to Stability*, pp. 156–7.

[2] U Win said that the Japanese in Burma 'were very nice people' (*Nation*, 10 October 1952) and Kyaw Nyein declared that the Japanese occupation 'was greatly helpful' to Burma in obtaining freedom from the British (ibid., 8 September 1954), but both these speeches were delivered in Tokyo.

together with a Japanese loan of $50 million, spread over a period of ten years. This agreement was formally signed at Rangoon on 5 November 1954, together with a Treaty of Peace: the latter included a clause whereby Japan promised to re-examine Burma's claims whenever a final settlement of the compensation claims of the other countries of South East Asia was attained.

After this settlement normal diplomatic relations were established, and the leaders of the two countries voiced their desire for future friendship and co-operation. The first Burmese reactions were cautious: there was apprehension that the reparations agreement might be exploited to bring Burma once again within a Japanese-dominated 'economic empire': hence the insistence that 'joint ventures' between the two countries must be on a basis of 60 per cent. Burmese and 40 per cent. Japanese investment.[1] Burma will have to conduct her political and economic relations *vis-à-vis* Japan with wary foresight if an unwelcome reliance upon Japanese favour is to be avoided.

The most testing aspect of Burma's foreign policy has been the manner in which the world giants have been approached: 1955 served to place overwhelming emphasis upon Burma's relations with China and Russia, but in previous years there were more visible signs of interchanges between Burma and the United States.

In a previous chapter attention was drawn to the brevity of American intervention in South East Asia:[2] this is true, notwithstanding that American missionaries were established in Burma before Britain had annexed a yard of Burmese soil. For nearly a century and a half the American Baptist Mission has been working in Burma, and apart from the benefits rendered by efforts in the fields of education, agricultural improvement and medicine, the mission has played a major part in the political and cultural development of modern Burma by the operation of its printing-press from which, ever since the 1820's, has poured a flow of works in Burmese and other indigenous languages. But despite this important missionary connexion, there has never grown up a Burma equivalent of 'the China Lobby' to exert pressure upon the formulation

---

[1] This means that Burma will have to find a capital sum of $75 million for the projected joint ventures. Where will this sum come from? An arrangement was negotiated by Kyaw Nyein whereby the money will be partly found by loans from the Japan Export-Import Bank, these loans to be set against Burma's reparations. In short, Burma will not have an unencumbered majority holding in the proposed joint Burmese-Japanese enterprises (see *BWB*, 27 October and 17 November 1954).
[2] See above, pp. 109–10.

of foreign policy upon Capitol Hill, although the origin of the power of the China Lobby is often said to be 'the dime put by the American child into the missionary box'. The explanation as to why American missionary endeavours in Burma led to no comparable pressure group is to be found partly in the size of the work: the numbers of American missionaries in Burma were never more than 200, while there were something like 2,000 American Protestant China missionaries, including the staffs of American universities established in China. But, more important, it would be fair to suggest that the average American missionary after a few years' service in Burma came to regard the British 'colonial' Government as an ally and not as an enemy of the missionary effort. There would even appear to be a distinct correlation between the expansion of American missionary activities and the expansion of British administration.[1] And so American missionary writing and thought came to accept, broadly, the bona fides of the British administration in Burma right down to independence, and did not develop any political line of its own, although in many other fields of thought the American missionaries made substantial contributions to knowledge of Burma, and certain American institutions—notably Bucknell University, Lewisburg, Pennsylvania —built up a Burma connexion. After independence the American Baptist Mission wisely decided that, in the interest of the Burma Baptist community, it was essential to dissociate the mission completely both from internal politics and from American foreign policy.[2]

As a result, American policy towards Burma began in 1948 from first principles: not one American in a hundred could have stated accurately Burma's location on the world map.[3] The United States began with one massive advantage: whereas Britain symbolized to the peoples of Asia the forces of 'colonialism' and 'exploitation', America symbolized freedom and leadership in the struggle of colonial peoples. To those in Burma who were perhaps confused by the decision of all the other peoples in Southern Asia newly enfranchised by the

[1] This conclusion was formed after reading a historical thesis by the Revd. Addison J. Eastman, but that writer does not necessarily himself subscribe to such a view.

[2] There was the case of the American missionary Seagrave, famed as the author of *Burma Surgeon* and head of the Namkhan Hospital, who was tried in the Union courts for alleged associations with Naw Seng, being finally completely cleared: he, however, had previously severed all connexions with the American Baptist Mission. Dr. Russell Andrus, the economist, acted for a time as Secretary at the American Embassy, but this was not followed by other such appointments.

[3] In 1942 a prominent American public figure called upon to make a broadcast about the Far East remarked to an adviser 'But Burma is an island isn't it?' (see P. W. Thayer, ed., *Southeast Asia in the Coming World* (Baltimore, 1953), p. 268).

British—India, Pakistan, and Ceylon—to remain in the Commonwealth, there was assurance in the American record of a complete break with Britain and the greatness that ensued.[1]

The first American approach to Burma consisted in reciprocating the sentiments of 1776, but when, during 1948 and 1949, Burma appeared to be heading towards anarchy, American policy planners virtually wrote off the Burma Government as a spent force.[2] After the Nationalist régime in China had ignominiously broken down, while the Burma Government refused to collapse, American opinion swung to the opposite extreme, viewing the survival of the Nu Government as a triumph of democracy over Communism. In 1951 and 1952 came the high-water mark of intercourse between the two countries. Even at this period there were many in Burma who viewed American aid with suspicion: that the head of the KTA group was *Colonel* Homer B. Pettit did not go without comment, and the expansion of Mingaladon Airport was interpreted by some as preparations to provide a base for the United States Air Force (although the scheme for reconstruction at Mingaladon was planned before the agreement for American aid had been signed). Many would hold that it is out of place to give currency to such wild rumours in any serious review of foreign affairs, but that is to ignore the substratum of emotionalism which is the basis of international relations in Asia today. For the image which America suggested to the Eastern mind was changing in the early 1950's: from being the symbol of freedom, America was becoming associated with a fancied imperialist counter-attack.[3] All these emotional doubts boiled up in 1952 in infuriated exasperation as the KMT crisis intensified, apparently with the tacit acceptance of the United States, since from 1951 onwards the Burma Government had made repeated requests for American influence to be asserted, without effect. The nadir of ill-feeling was reached

[1] A handbook entitled *Burma* issued by the Ministry of Information in 1954 states in the introduction that Burma is 'The first country to gain independence from the British ever since the United States first achieved that distinction in 1776.' The presuppositions underlying that statement deserve some thought.

[2] cf. Philip Jessup, President Truman's roving ambassador: Burma is 'well-nigh hopeless' (*Daily Telegraph*, 25 March 1950).

[3] A summary of the indictment is contained in U Nu's speech at Rangoon University Convocation, 2 December 1953: 'In North Africa the United States is supporting the colonial Imperial systems which are most loathsome to the Africans. In Spain also the Americans support the Fascist-Franco régime. In Indo-China they are helping and encouraging the French colonial rulers who are not acceptable any more to all the Indo-Chinese. If you look at China also, you will find that the extreme reactionary Chiang Kai-shek group, which had been ousted from China because the Chinese masses could not stomach them any more, have to be picked on by the Americans to give them support and assistance.'

with the termination of American aid (March 1953); as the
KMT situation remained explosive, U Nu addressed a personal
letter to President Eisenhower in October 1953, but without
result. When, in November 1953, Vice-President Nixon paid
a brief visit to Burma, he was received by popular demonstrations of anti-American hostility. The Vice-President, reporting
on his visit, stated 'I am convinced that it is vital to find a
solution as speedily as possible to the KMT problem . . . it is
the major point of irritation between the United States and
Burma.'[1] But no immediate solution materialized, and relations
between the two countries remained lukewarm.[2] During 1954
the United States became increasingly preoccupied with the
need to check the Communist advance, and in South East Asia
there was a concentration upon Siam as the Power most likely
to offer opposition to Communism, and upon Indo-China as
the actual scene of battle. Burma faded right out of State
Department calculations—in July 1954 the American Ambassador to Burma went on leave, and then handed in his resignation.
No move was made to find a replacement, and no new Ambassador was appointed for ten months. On the Burmese side mistrust
of American policy simmered on; the Manila Treaty (September
1954) and the organization of SEATO for military defence
only added to Burmese hostility. On the occasion of Dependent
Peoples' Day Ba Swe stated that 'The United States is reviving
colonialism by impressing small nations into its defence and
economic systems. This endangers world peace and must be
opposed as an evil contributing to the downfall of nations.'[3]
Towards the end of 1954 a leading Burmese business man,
Henzada U Mya, was deprived of his American agencies, it was
alleged at State Department instigation, for exporting rubber
to China in defiance of strong protests by the American
Embassy.[4] U Nu's visit to China in December 1954 was not
popular in America, and his somewhat naïve suggestions for
solving the conflict between America and Red China were
received with irritation by the State Department. U Nu
suggested that if the United States withdrew its forces from the
Formosa straits 'then the possibility of peacefully liberating
Taiwan would arise'.[5] U Nu tried to allay American suspicion of
this visit by announcing that he would be delighted to visit the

[1] *New York Times*, 27 November 1953.
[2] It should be mentioned that relations between Americans in Burma and
Burmans in the United States with their temporary hosts have remained cordial
throughout these periods of national misunderstanding. Probably Burmans find
Americans, as individuals, more agreeable than any other Westerners.
[3] *Nation*, 31 October 1954.
[4] ibid., 2 December 1954.
[5] ibid., 24 December 1954.

United States: this suggestion was received in silence at Washington. Burmese hints that America should purchase Burma's rice surplus for distribution to needy countries as an alternative to direct aid also met with no response. In February 1955 John Foster Dulles called at Rangoon, immediately after the Bangkok Conference of the SEATO Powers: he had a ninety minutes' talk with U Nu and his colleagues, and although there was absolutely no approach towards mutual appreciation of the other's policies, at least these statesmen had an opportunity of judging the other's sincerity.

One may hope to see relations between the two countries conducted in future less on a basis of emotionalism and preoccupation with external world issues. It is something of a weakness that there are practically no American business men working in Burma to provide a touch of salty realism (possibly Britain is represented in Burma by too much business realism).[1] As none of the many temporarily-resident Americans have actually to earn their keep, they have no incentive to discover actualities in Burma, or to identify themselves honestly with the country's fortunes. The outlook of many Americans is coloured by an unreal idealism, while at the same time everything is viewed through American spectacles.[2]

One absurd item is the small-scale rivalry between representatives of Britain and the United States for the privilege of being 'top Power' in independent Burma: rivalry became obsolete when China emerged as 'top Power', but it made little sense at any time. It behoves Britain to accept the new situation: that American funds and resources are now so much greater as incvitably to take first place in any programme of assistance or advice in such fields as education, economics, engineering, or the social sciences. But it might be recognized in the United States that Britain has still an immense fund of knowledge and experience of Burma. American studies of Burma, although now proceeding on an increasing scale, lack any kind of depth: knowledge or materials concerning Burmese history or culture before about 1950 are almost non-existent, while in British libraries there is a wealth of *Birmanica*; printed documents, manuscripts, copies of inscriptions; and there are scholars with specialized knowledge. Americans can, if they wish, deepen their understanding of the new Burma by drawing upon this fund of experience and knowledge.

If the symbolism of America has loomed large in the mind of newly-independent Burma, an even more portentous, if more

---

[1] There are said to be only two American business men operating in Burma.
[2] But this observation becomes less true with every year that passes.

distant, role has been played by Soviet Russia. In their student days almost all the future AFPFL leaders regarded Russia as the light of the world. This admiration persisted among many until after independence, and was not conclusively shaken by the propaganda encouragement given to the Communist rebellions on their doorstep by the Soviet Press and radio, together with vilification of the AFPFL Government as 'imperialist running-dogs'. Not until February 1951 did the first Burmese Ambassador take up his duties at Moscow; in the following May a Soviet Ambassador arrived in Rangoon. Initially the contacts following these exchanges were few. On 'Martyrs' Day', July 1952, in reply to criticisms that Burma was committing herself to the American camp by the acceptance of American economic aid, U Nu made a public declaration that his Government would be very happy to entertain any offer of aid from Russia or China: no response to this invitation was ever announced.[1]

Not until 1954 did Burmese leaders begin to make personal contacts with Russia; from that year a steady stream of missions, official or semi-official, went by invitation to the Soviet Union.[2] These new contacts did not indicate any radical change in policy: perhaps more remarkable was the forthright pronouncement by Kyaw Nyein, formerly an ardent admirer of Russia, condemning Soviet colonialism to the members of the Asian Socialist Anti-Colonial Bureau: 'The Soviet form of imperialism, he believed, was even more dangerous [than Western colonialism] because it is more ruthless, more systematic and more blatantly justified in the name of world Communist revolution.'[3] This critical attitude is in marked contrast to the adulation of all that is Russian constantly voiced by the 'parliamentary' Communists, the BWPP.

But despite ideological detachment, Burma was drawn towards more actual contacts with Russia by the trade negotiations initiated early in 1955, and resulting in a large-scale agreement in July. Burma's relations with Russia, no less than with Britain and America, may be expected to be modified by practical considerations as much as by political inclination.

Whatever room for manœuvre Burma has in formulating policy towards Great Powers such as Britain, Japan, Russia, or the United States, there can be no question of vacillation towards China. Under any circumstances Burma has first to

---

[1] *Nation*, 21 July 1952.

[2] In 1954 there was an agricultural mission headed by Thakin Kyaw Tun, Minister for Agriculture, and a trade mission led by Thakin Tin, Minister for Land Nationalization. There had been a cultural mission to the USSR in 1952.

[3] *BWB*, 26 May 1954.

consider this gigantic and enigmatic neighbour, whose presence overshadows all the northern borderlands. Probably the Union Foreign Office devotes more of its attention to Chinese affairs than to all other countries together.

An outsider cannot hope to guess at the principles which govern China's long-term plans towards Burma; but one may deduce that, as with much Communist planning, a dual policy exists, providing for the establishment of a position of influence through friendly means, with more forceful methods available in readiness should the first approach not give satisfaction. Throughout its brief history the Communist Government has behaved 'correctly' towards Burma, and has consistently soothed Burma's anxieties on the subject of the KMT intruders by offering assurances that, so long as 'adequate steps' are taken against the KMT, this issue will not be permitted to cause trouble between the two countries.[1] A second matter that causes concern in Rangoon is the question of delimiting the frontier. Communist China appears to have continued the traditional imperial policy of slow, silent attrition. All the time there are stories of boundary stones shifted into Burmese territory, of the seizure of border tribes—people who stray too near the Chinese frontier guards, and of Chinese troops 'flag-marching' where the frontier has not been finally settled, as in the Wa States. Concerning all these problems the Burma Government maintains a cautious reticence in public pronouncements: it has admitted, however, that China has now refused to accept the annual 'rent' for the Namwan Assigned Tract, and is negotiating over its future status with Burma.[2] There is also the question of Kokang State, a tiny principality north of the Wa States, ceded to British Burma under the Peking Convention of 1897. Out of a total population of 49,000, 40,000 are Chinese; the remainder are hill tribes, mainly Palaungs. The people of Kokang are often treated as aliens by the Burmese authorities, although they are said to wish to exercise their rights as citizens of the Union (the young Sawbwa of Kokang is a member of the Chamber of Nationalities).[3] Minor adjustments in the frontier will undoubtedly be made within a general circle of agreement.[4]

The infiltration of Chinese into Burma presents a more

[1] cf. Panikkar, In Two Chinas, p. 169.
[2] U Nu in Nation, 1 March 1955.
[3] Nation, 6 December 1954 and 18 June 1955.
[4] During the Kuomintang régime maps were printed under official Chinese auspices showing much of northern Burma as Chinese territory. Circulation of these maps appears to have continued since the Communist revolution, but inquiries by representatives of the Burma Government have called forth denials that these maps have any significance or any official countenance. (See also p. 378 n. 1.)

serious problem: Chinese overland immigration has substantially increased since the Second World War but received
little attention until the KMT question became serious; the
Burma Government then took steps to watch the border, closing
all entry routes between the Shweli and Salween Rivers (i.e. the
frontier east of Bhamo). Frontier officials have been unable to
prevent illegal entry, and a steady stream of immigration
continues. Many are refugees from Communist oppression;
others, possibly, are Communist agents. In every possible way
the Chinese Government ensures that its nationals in Burma
are kept in touch with the homeland. Every variety of Chinese
overseas organization—Chambers of Commerce and other
trade associations, trade unions, schools, temples, even
Christian churches—all have their quota of Communist
rapporteurs. So long as Burma and China remain on friendly
terms this creates no difficulty: but the Chinese in Burma do
represent a potential fifth column, growing ever larger and
more powerful.

The Kachin State is an area where China might, under
different circumstances, desire to exercise influence. The
strength of the Kachin population in Burma has never been
accurately computed, but it must be between 300,000 and
400,000: Kachins living over the border in Yunnan are said to
number 100,000.[1] There have been reports of propaganda
advocating a united Kachin State—which might include also
the Kachins living across in Assam. No serious attempt has
been made to launch a popular campaign towards this end: it
remains a weapon that could be unsheathed whenever desirable.
Meanwhile, links have been created between the Kachins of
China and Burma. Naw Seng represents the military side of
the organization in Yunnan, and Duwa Marang Lashan is the
political chief. They have contacts, as for instance with the
BWPP, whose leader in Bhamo District is Duwa Gawlu Brang.
In the somewhat confused state of Kachin politics, with all
sorts of personal rivalries simmering, an irredentist movement
might find some willing adherents. But it is problematical
whether the occasion for such a movement will ever arise.

Even more obscure is the relationship between the Burma
Communists and the Chinese. There is evidence that in 1950
Than Tun planned the 'Aung Zeya' operation to overrun
north Burma, with some expectation of help from China. The
Korean War ruled out any possibility of Chinese assistance—if,
indeed, it was ever promised—but Than Tun maintained

[1] According to Li Cheng-tchoang. See J. Siguret, *Territoires et Populations des
Confins du Yunnan* (Peking, 1937), p. 123.

contacts with China and dispatched delegations in 1951, 1952 (twice), and 1953; this last mission was led by Thakin Than Myaing and Bo Zeya (formerly one of the 'Thirty Comrades' and a battalion commander in the post-war army). They were specifically charged to secure Chinese aid, but early in 1955 Than Myaing returned without even promises of future aid; Bo Zeya returned equally empty-handed a few months later.[1] When U Nu was at Peking the Chinese Government professed their ignorance of these two guests: this seems highly improbable, but it may be that their standing is so petty that the Central Government never troubled themselves about them, dismissing them as local guerrillas such as the local Yunnan administration could handle. It appears that China has given up all interest in the Burma Communists; in view of their puerile record over the last ten years, they offer no prospect of ever succeeding, and to support them might embroil the Chinese Government in their misadventures. Peking appears to regard the constitutional Communists, the BWPP, as worthy of encouragement and assistance. But up to the mid-1950's they represented only a tool of potential future value. Chinese policy has concentrated on turning the Nu Government's neutrality policy to good account.

Up to 1954 the principal influence in Burma's foreign policy was undoubtedly the understanding with India; thereafter, judging purely from external evidence, China appears to have held the key. The first real contact between the leaders of the two countries was in June 1954, when Chou En-lai took the trouble to halt at Rangoon on his return to China after the first fruitless sessions of the Geneva Conference. The Five Principles of Co-existence had just been enunciated at New Delhi, and they were adopted by the Nu Government with equal enthusiasm. A joint communiqué reaffirming the Five Principles was issued stating, among other things, that 'peaceful co-existence of countries with different social systems would be ensured, and the threat and fear of aggression and interference in internal affairs would give place to a sense of security and mutual confidence'. The communiqué went on, 'The people of each nation should have the right to choose their own State system and way of life without interference from other nations. Revolution cannot be exported.'[2]

Next came U Nu's visit to China in December 1954. The main theme of his speeches was the long historic friendship between their two countries, and Burma's desire to see friendship grow throughout the world. It seems undoubted that the

[1] *Nation*, 7 June and 13 September 1955.   [2] *BWB*, 7 July 1954.

transparent good nature of the Burmese Prime Minister made its mark upon all who met him in China as in other countries. Speaking at a farewell banquet U Nu gave solemn assurances that the Government of Burma would 'under no circumstances be stooges of any power . . . we will never turn false . . . we want peace more than any other thing'. U Nu went on to voice the fear oppressing mankind of another war, and the immense benefits that would follow a relaxation of tension between China and America. Nu then propounded his belief in the essential goodness of all men: 'As a people the Americans are very generous and brave. In the sphere of scientific knowledge the Americans have developed to such an extent that they can make this world a happy and prosperous place to live in.' He then reiterated his regard for China and announced that, in order that Burma should not seem to lean to one side or the other, his Government 'far from accepting one-sided aid that may cause apprehension in the minds of either of these two countries will not even entertain thoughts of accepting such aid'. U Nu concluded: 'As a friend of both, we want these two countries to be on the friendliest of terms. . . . I will exert my utmost to bring about an understanding between the People's Republic of China and the United States of America.'[1] Such a declaration in a land where everything American is almost automatically suspect showed considerable courage and stature. The communiqué issued at the end of the visit reaffirmed the previous declarations of mutual regard for sovereignty, and foreshadowed a development of trade relations in the opening of new consulates and of land and air communications between Burma and China. To the Burma Government these clear public declarations by the China Government of their accept- ance of Burma's independent sovereign status formed the real core of the agreement.

On U Nu's return to Rangoon the editor of the *Nation* shrewdly observed that the visit to Peking had strengthened the Prime Minister's self-confidence, had given him a new concept of world affairs, and helped to put him among the leaders of world opinion.[2] From this time an additional impetus was given to Burma's foreign affairs, in particular by U Nu's new interest in world travel.

The next occasion on which Burma played an international role was at the Bandung Conference—the Afro-Asian Conference of April 1955. The preliminary announcement issued from Bogor seemed to indicate that the aim of the meeting was to bring together representatives of nations who had previously

[1] *BWB*, 15 December 1954.   [2] *Nation*, 21 December 1954.

never met in order that they might get to know one another. The actual working out of the Conference was different: many nations seized the occasion to advocate individual policies, to raise grievances (Kashmir, Formosa, &c.), or to launch attacks upon colonialism, Zionism and, most of all, Communism. Pandit Nehru, the leading advocate of goodwill and under-standing, was put out by these exchanges more than was Chou En-lai. U Nu's role was confined largely to pouring oil on troubled waters, but he found occasion to give at least one imaginative exposé of his own concept of co-existence. Commending the Five Principles to the Political Committee of the conference, he observed:

There are some who say that only knaves or fools would place all their faith in these five principles, and that some kind of guarantee or deterrent is necessary to ensure their observation by all parties. In other words, they work on the assumption that the other party is not to be trusted. As we all know, mistrust begets mistrust, and suspicion begets suspicion. It may have been permissible in the days of con-ventional weapons for nations to live in a perpetual atmosphere of suspicion and mistrust. But in the nuclear age, such a concept is obsolete. We cannot afford to live in mistrust of our neighbours. We have to learn to live with them in mutual trust and confidence, and where this happy state has not existed in the past, someone has to break the ice. For trust also begets trust, and confidence begets con-fidence. The extremely close and cordial relations which Burma today enjoys with Thailand after years of misunderstanding and suspicion, indicates what can be achieved by the application of this policy.[1]

Next came U Nu's visits to Israel, Yugoslavia, Britain, the United States, and Japan. In America U Nu faced up to the blaze of publicity—the Press, radio, and television—in his usual relaxed, amiable manner, and created exactly the impression of friendly, unassuming goodwill that was most beneficial. In addressing Congress U Nu reminded the Senators that the foreign policy which Burma was now following—'to avoid big Power alliances'—was exactly the policy pursued by the United States in its first hundred years, and that both nations had been criticized and misunderstood on the same score. As in China he had praised America, so now he tried to explain the aims and activities of Communist China to the United States. It cannot be said that U Nu's words were heeded, but his personality was certainly not soon forgotten. He, in turn, learnt a lot from his visit: he was impressed by the average American's

[1] Ministry of Information, *Resurgence: Premier U Nu at Bandung* (Rangoon, 1955), pp. 7–8.

love of liberty and his desire for peace. Perhaps the most valuable impression that he retained was this: that America, despite the aberrations of a few, is no land of warmongers, it has a vital stake in preserving world peace.

Finally, in October, the Prime Minister set out on his third tour within twelve months. His itinerary included India, Afghanistan, Russia, Finland, Sweden, Denmark, and Poland: most of these visits were of very brief duration, but fourteen days were spent in the USSR. His tour included a brief visit to Tashkent, Samarkand, and Kazakhstan, and U Nu appears to have been very impressed by this glimpse of Soviet Asia. And so, at a dinner given for the ambassadors at Moscow of all the Bandung Conference nations, U Nu concluded his speech with a toast to 'the participation of the Soviet Union in future Afro-Asian Conferences'.[1] This spontaneous gesture took everybody completely by surprise. (The proposal was later quietly withdrawn.)

The joint communiqué issued at the end of the visit, although not introducing any specifically new element into Burma's policies, did nevertheless represent an unreserved Burmese endorsement of all the principal features of Russia's attitude to world issues. On the Far East, and more particularly as regards disarmament and the use of nuclear weapons, Burma was made to echo the Russian point of view. Almost certainly, U Nu did not realize the full significance of this apparent alignment with the Communist world.[2]

A considerably greater propaganda impact was made by the return visit of Marshal Bulganin and Mr. Khrushchev to Burma. The virulent glee with which Khrushchev castigated the colonial record of the British in Asia made big headlines in the world Press, and was undoubtedly very agreeable to some Burmese political leaders; but more thoughtful Burmans found this farrago distasteful, especially when Khrushchev began to point out faults in the construction of the Great Cave of the Sixth Buddhist Council. The vast crowds who were turned out in their thousands and asked to cheer these strange white men who were so voluble may have extracted some entertainment value from the speeches, translated laboriously into Burmese. By the end of the visit the crowds were beginning to feel that the enthusiasm was rather overdone.[3] The communiqué at the end of the visit reiterated the Soviet viewpoint on disarmament and went on to condemn the creation of Power

---

[1] *The Times*, 2 November 1955.

[2] The joint statement is reproduced in *BWB*, 10 November 1955.

[3] cf. *Nation*, 15 December 1955: 'Having had to generate so much artificial warmth, we are somewhat short of breath.'

blocs and to commend 'non-participation in such blocs'. Certain issues in Asia—the unification of Korea, a settlement in Indo-China, and the return of Formosa to Communist China—were mentioned as demanding immediate attention. At the same time it was announced that Russia would construct and equip a technological institute in Rangoon. This Russian 'gift' would be reciprocated by a Burmese 'gift' of an appropriate quantity of rice.

The exact significance of this propaganda *feu de paille* may not become clear for some time. Was this a mere foray, an exploratory raid, or was it the opening move in a planned long-term campaign? If the visit of the two leaders is followed up by the creation of Soviet economic and technical services in Burma, the existing links with the West may be weakened. Past experience, however, shows that the provision of economic and technical aid does not automatically create gratitude in the recipient; a Russian aid programme on Soviet lines could produce unexpected results. But in any case it is as yet far from certain that Russia will think it worth while to invest large sums in Burma when more promising fields lie closer to hand—as in the Middle East. If Russian activities end with the technological institute, it is worth recalling that the Burmah Oil Company endowed Rangoon University with an Engineering College twenty-five years ago, without any marked manifestations of appreciation by Burmese politicians ensuing. The immediate internal effects of the Russian visit were to give a fillip to the flagging fortunes of the Burma Communists, who promptly launched a propaganda drive for a coalition Government with the AFPFL.

At the end of 1955 the Russians might consider that they had dominated the year's diplomatic events for Burma, but a careful observer might conclude that the real significance of the year was the steady growth in Chinese contacts with Burma. During the year three major Chinese delegations visited the country: a large and very effective cultural mission (led by Vice-Minister Cheng Chen-to) in February, an agricultural mission in March, and an official Chinese Buddhist delegation in April and May. There were also visits by Chou En-lai and Chen Yi, the Deputy Prime Minister (before Bandung), and by the President of the Peace Committee of the Republic, Kuo Mo-jo. In one month, September 1955, three major Burmese missions set off for China: a cultural mission of seventy led by U Win; a military mission of senior officers led by Lieutenant-General Ne Win; and a Buddhist delegation headed by Chief Justice Thein Maung, whose mission was to bring back to Burma a sacred tooth relic of the Buddha. Dominating all else was the unresolved problem of border demarcation.

In November 1956 U Nu (then out of office) went to Peking for discussions with Chou En-lai; three main areas were in dispute. Not far from the 'high conical peak', the northern terminus of the demarcated frontier, three village tracts were claimed by China: Hpimaw, Gawlum, and Kangfang. They were indisputably Kachin settlements, but the Chinese had traded and collected taxes there. The Namwan Assigned Tract, a recognized historical appendage of China, was the second area and the third was the Wa border, where the agreement between the British and Chinese Governments concluded in 1941 was not finally ratified. U Nu was successful in getting negotiations on to an amicable basis, but no agreement was reached: the Kachin State leaders were most unwilling to cede Kachin terri-tory to China. In June 1957 Justice Myint Thein led another mission to Peking. Broad agreement was reached in regard to the three villages: the Chinese scaled down their initial demand for 150 square miles of territory towards the Burmese offer of 56 square miles, and also agreed to recognize the MacMahon Line as the northern boundary. But they still pressed their claim to the Namwan tract. A visit by Ba Swe and Kyaw Nyein to Peking in December 1957 brought agreement no nearer. In June 1959, as a compromise, General Ne Win suggested that China might consider exchanging the Namwan tract for a strip of territory inhabited by the Panhung and Panlap (Wa) tribes. The proposal was well timed: China seized upon the opportunity to demonstrate that the Five Principles still held good.

An agreement was signed by Ne Win and Chou En-lai on 28 January 1960. China recognized the 'traditional customary line' (i.e. the MacMahon Line) in the north, tacitly dropping the vast cartographical claims of the past. The three villages were 'returned' to China. The Namwan tract was 'turned over' to Burma, and the Panhung–Panlao area 'turned over' to China; otherwise, the agreement of 1941 concerning the Wa border was accepted. The agreement was followed by a treaty of friendship between the two countries, signed in Rangoon.[1]

This settlement was rightly regarded by the Burmese as a considerable feat. However, it may constitute a cloak for more dubious Chinese activities: the embrace of the Elder Brother has become almost suffocating.

[1] A full account of the negotiations was given by U Nu in his speech to Parlia-ment, 28 April 1960 (*BWB*, 5 May 1960). See also the author's 'Burma's North-east Borderland Problems', *Pacific Affairs*, December 1956.

XIII

'OUR TRUE HISTORY LIES AHEAD'

'WE shall waste no energies in lamentations or bitterness over the past. Our heritage is proud and strong, but our true history lies ahead. And there is much to be done.' These words occur in the introduction to *Pyidawtha, the New Burma* (p. 10), and they are typical of all that is best and bravest in this new nation; but they also serve to illustrate the problems facing whosoever attempts to form even a tentative assessment within the first decade after Burma's independence. Clearly, no sort of dogmatic conclusions can be based upon the little that has so far been achieved in Burma, especially when the best part of the energies of the Government and the government services have been expended in the long-drawn-out task of defeating the internal rebellions and the KMT invasion. On the other hand no service is done to Burma by automatically recounting the ambitious plans for land reform, industrialization, and social welfare which have been given so much publicity, and accepting these without any critical analysis as the evidence of the progress of the new Burma. The commentator has to set present achievements and failures alongside future plans and projects and, placing these in the balance, guess to the best of his ability what is preponderant among these uncertain elements. U Nu has declared that 'with the whole country enjoying peace, and all of us without exception exerting our utmost for rehabilitation, it will take about twenty years to make the Five Pillars [of national independence] sufficiently strong'.[1] If, under the most favourable circumstances, independent Burma will not begin to take shape for twenty years, how can one arrive at even a finite portrayal of the Union of Burma after only one troublous decade?

However, in the present-day world of South East Asia, where the unexpected is always just about to happen, postponement of the task of forming an assessment will not necessarily make it any easier to come to a final conclusion: the situation after another ten years is likely to be as fluid as it is today. But an 'interim report', however incomplete, seems worth while: and as U Nu has said in another context, 'someone has to break the ice'. At the time of writing Burma appears to be poised upon the brink of great changes, but as yet there

[1] *Address by U Nu at Rangoon University*, 22 December 1951.

has been no really fundamental transformation.[1] This survey
gives an account of Burma's condition after the termination
of British rule but before the effective implementation of the
plans of the independent Burma Government. No more is
attempted than to indicate the framework of society existing
before and after the transfer of power, the direction in which
the national leaders appear to be driving the social machine
at the outset of their journey, and the potentialities of present-
day Burma and its leaders for attaining the desired destination.
In short, it is hoped by making a rough survey of the ground
to provide future students with a starting-point and with some
data to assist them in more conclusive inquiries.

An admirer of the British Empire might hesitate before commending Burma as an illustration of the virtues of British rule.
It is true that the country was endowed with all those institutions in which Britain has made her own especial contribution
to the arts of government: a parliament, open courts of justice
where a man is innocent unless he is proved guilty, a professional, non-political civil service, a system of local government,
a free Press, and a university established in the liberal tradition.
Yet one might be reluctant to claim that all or any of these
institutions were successfully transplanted in Burmese soil. In
part the reason may have lain in the Burmese capacity to absorb
outside influences and give them a distinctive native character.
But a greater reason was the historical accident that Burma was
annexed by the British Government of India, and was treated
almost throughout the entire duration of the British connexion
as a remote, backward, difficult, Indian province. Instead of
Burma's political and administrative problems being examined
on their own merits, they were disposed of in the backwash of
Indian political and administrative reforms. Similar effects
followed in the economic sphere: British rule led to the opening
up of the Delta rice granary, the building of communications,
and the utilization of new mineral wealth. But although
Burmans shared in the prosperity which followed this expansion
of production, they remained essentially a nation of petty rice
farmers; they made no entry into the modern world of commercial enterprise. Many would lay the responsibility for this,
first upon English *laissez-faire* economics, and secondly on the
Indian entanglement once again; Indian merchants, mechanics,
and middlemen developed Burma's new economy, not Burmans.
This economic argument is powerful, but not conclusive:

---

[1] One of the strongest impressions said to have been formed by Marshal Tito
during his 1955 visit was the extent to which Burma still continued upon the lines
laid down by the British.

Malaya was freed at an early stage from Indian political supervision, but this did not serve to assist the expansion of Malayan economic enterprise; Indonesia's economy was developed under government direction, but the indigenous share in commercial economic activities was less strong than in Burma.

Whatever the underlying reasons, Burmese society remained static, wrapped in its own concepts and customs, and the great mass of the people were taken unaware, as it were, by independence. The political leaders were themselves children of this society and, despite education at the university, their horizon was limited. Their political goal was simple: immediate independence: and their methods were equally elemental. To attain independence they launched an all-out assault to paralyse the British administration. They were successful: government was brought very near to anarchy; but 'they have sown the wind and they shall reap the whirlwind'. When British rule came to an end, the belief in a government of law and order, so laboriously hammered out, had given way to political boss rule, in which violence was the pathway to power. This conclusion cannot be said to have reflected credit on either Burmans or British, despite expressions of mutual satisfaction. Britain failed to afford enough young Burmans first-hand experience in the working of British institutions and ideas and ultimately failed to create any vision of loyalites wider and higher than a narrow, truculent, national pride. And so, as independence was attained, the case for remaining within the Commonwealth went by default. In a major sense the story of Britain's rule in Burma is one of failure. One can only hope that British statesmen will realize that the case of Burma offers many lessons to all who genuinely hold a belief in the idea of a new multi-racial Commonwealth. But something was transmitted to the new Burma: the administrative tradition and a slender foundation of representative government. These ideas had at once to face the challenge of political gangsterdom.

Amid the assaults that followed, it is almost impossible to overstate the part played by U Nu's steadfast grip upon the reins of government, supported throughout by lieutenants such as U Tin, the Finance Minister, and Bo Ne Win. Credit is also due to the Socialists who, at a critical moment on resigning from the Cabinet, set a precedent by not launching a rebellion, being content to await a parliamentary come-back. The AFPFL coalition will be able, in the years to come, to display its record in the first years of independence with some pride. Maintaining a united front, the AFPFL rallied the country under the shock of the Cabinet assassinations and led it into independence and through the testing years of civil war. If the Government had rested upon unstable alliances of party leaders pursuing their own ambitions, as was the case in pre-war Burmese politics (and as has largely been the case in independent Indonesia), Burma could not possibly have survived the assaults of 1948 and 1949. Burma might well, as in the historic past, have broken up into half a dozen little chiefdoms, some Communist, some communal. The credit for the survival of the Union devolves largely upon the AFPFL and upon U Nu.

During the first eight years of independence the Ministers and other responsible leaders have had to learn their duties while they actually discharged these same duties. It has not been surprising that some decisions have been misconceived: U Nu, with characteristic self-depreciation, has described his own efforts up to 1954 as 'muddling through'.[1] At first the leaders of Burma wanted to change the face of their country overnight, to revolutionize the political, economic, and social system by total state planning and direction.[2] They formulated ambitious plans with no clear conception of how to transform their visions into reality. But as the experience of the Ministers has grown their management has become more sure and steady. The difficulties experienced following the drop in world rice prices, although infinitely frustrating to men in a hurry to fulfil far-reaching programmes, may be beneficial in the long run, by compelling Ministers to reconsider their planning in more realistic terms, with the elimination of non-essentials and some sort of list of priorities to distinguish between primary and secondary needs. Several conclusions are suggested by the experiences of the first few years. The Burmese leaders have to learn much more about the problem of reconciling the particular and the general, in the co-ordination of the activities of different departments and services. They have to learn that in a democratic country, relying upon voluntary implementation by the people of proposals by the Government, planning must be related to capabilities and customs and to the willingness of the mass of the people to support the new schemes. Only under a totalitarian régime can a government discount popular feeling; in a democracy, enthusiasm and propaganda are not enough; people have to be educated towards understanding their own stake in the new national ventures. The Pyidawtha schemes, and the voluntary service in connexion with the Sixth Buddhist Council, have shown the strength and weakness of

[1] Nu to ABPO Conference, *Nation*, 20 June 1954.

[2] In this vein, U Nu addressed a gathering of American business men: 'We have been in a hurry and we are in a hurry. We have waited for a long time and we feel we must accomplish a great deal in a short time' (*BWB*, 21 July 1955).

present attitudes towards state undertakings. For these and other reasons planning ought to be more flexible and empirical: the Government ought not to undertake blind commitments in accordance with the plans of foreign technical experts who will not themselves be responsible for putting their proposals into practice. Burma's leaders allowed themselves to become hypnotized by the prognostications of the KTA experts: long after the programme of investment postulated in their report had been abandoned, the leaders were still looking forward to attaining the goal set out in the KTA programme.[1] If planning is to have any practical value, and is not merely to be regarded as a delightful exercise of the imagination, then it must grow out of the actual resources of Burma and its people and not be modelled upon some abstract idea of what is desirable.

As Burma moves into the second decade of independence, it is entering a period when the social system will be subject to even greater stresses. During the first few years Burma was able to coast along under the momentum acquired during the British period. Despite the disruption of the Japanese occupation and the civil war, much that is essential continued to go on as before. Public works engineers, office superintendents, engine drivers, inspectors of police, directors of hospitals, many of the people in posts of responsibility like these have continued to perform their duties according to rules and precepts learned long ago. But this momentum will not continue indefinitely: Burma deliberately discarded all British personnel after independence, and the new men have received training that, in many cases, has been disorganized and rudimentary. What will happen when the elders start to go?

The situation was diagnosed with considerable insight by the editor of the *Nation* when he commented that the younger generation in Burma 'have lived all their lives in an atmosphere of destruction and violence, of patchwork and make-do, and in a world whose physical area . . . has shrunk to a narrow strip of fairly accessible country' so that men and women are rapidly forgetting the standards of former days.[2] There is

---

[1] In the speech quoted above (*BWB*, 21 July 1955), U Nu talked about developments 'geared to 1960': but the decision had already been accepted that the KTA targets could not be achieved before 1968 at earliest.

[2] *Nation*, 20 May 1953. A vivid example of this decline is contained in a description of New Zealand written by a senior but still young Burmese official: 'We travelled hundreds of miles by car during the day and sometimes during the night with no armed escort whatsoever. On the election day . . . our drivers stopped to cast their votes. . . . I expected to see lots of guards and policemen near the polling booths, but not a single uniform was in evidence' (*Burma*, April 1955, p. 85). The conditions which so surprised him were a commonplace in the Burma of a generation ago.

always the possibility that if at any time the leadership of U Nu and his experienced associates and advisers were removed, the condition of the country might deteriorate to a state where the discontented would express their resentment in yet another challenge at arms to legitimate authority. U Nu has on several public occasions dwelt upon

> The evil [Burmese] tradition of wresting power by force. Burmese history is full of instances where a king is overthrown by a contender by force, and who in turn is similarly ousted by a still more forceful rival. Except for the glorious periods of Anawrata, Bayinnaung and Alaungpaya, Burma has been a battlefield for warring states, each cutting one another's throat.[1]

The threat of the violent overthrow of the State had been largely overcome by the middle 1950's: but, in the light of Burma's history, the cycle of violence may come round again. However, it is possible to envisage two solid guarantees against any renewal of contests by force: the growth of a responsible parliamentary opposition, and the development of a genuine Union spirit transcending communal divisions.

Up to 1956 there had been no sign of any effective constitutional opposition emerging; nor, despite the doubtless genuine reiteration by AFPFL leaders of their belief in parliamentary methods, was there any indication that the AFPFL wished to have to face an effective challenge at the polls. Their attitude to potential rivals was hardly encouraging. U Ba Pe and his associates languished in jail while their trial for conspiracy dragged on'interminably.[2] Dr. Ba Maw was said to be living under the shadow of possible government action, even Dr. E Maung with his moderate and minute Justice Party was served with notice that action would be taken if criticism of AFPFL methods went too far.[3] The only parliamentary opposition remains the BWPP caucus, whose sole purpose is to bring about a Communist revolution, and the Arakan group of M.P.s with their regional limitations. Neither group can possibly form even the germ of a future alternative government. The AFPFL leaders talk of twenty, forty, or fifty years of AFPFL government: they may have reason for prophesying thus, but it seems unlikely that any political party can remain alert, responsive to public feeling, and free from corruption during such a protracted term of uninterrupted office. Opposition is bound to develop among the younger generation, a

[1] *Towards Peace and Democracy*, p. 145; cf. Nu to commanding officers, *BWB*, 22 September 1955.

[2] Ba Pe and others were arrested on 4 December 1954 on a charge of treason: after four years the charges were abandoned.

[3] *The Times*, 31 December 1955.

generation which will take the struggle for independence for granted; indeed such opposition has already been signally indicated by the Communist victories in the student unions. Unless this opposition can find constructive, parliamentary opportunities for putting its case, and can look forward to some hope of defeating the AFPFL Government at the polls, it will renounce constitutional methods for violence.

The 1956 General Election did not bring about any radical change in the pattern of Burmese politics.[1] The AFPFL leaders were sufficiently shaken by their losses to release U Nu from the premiership for the purpose of purging the League of 'pernicious elements', but the parrot-cry of 'fifty years of AFPFL rule' continued to be uttered, and many ministers appeared to be unaware of the need for reform in party and government. The emergence of a more coherent and confident opposition gave grounds for hope that a genuine party system might, in time, develop. Associated with the opposition were several moderates and progressives, whose position was determined by their dislike of the AFPFL. But the dominant element was the BWPP, whose avowed goal was and is a Marxist revolution. The Government Front Bench was also reinforced by men whose ideas turned in a similar direction. Altogether, the 1956 election provided a reminder that for important elements in Burma's political life, 'democracy' is equated with a 'People's Democracy'. The future for parliamentary and party government continued to be far from secure.

The other necessity for Burma if it is to withstand attack, either internal or external, is the bringing together of the different races of the country. It cannot be said that this process has advanced very far, despite the staging of demonstrations of unity on such occasions as Union Day. Whichever of the constituent states that one examines, there are signs of disunity. Kachins and Chins are certainly the two races most in harmony with Burma proper, but there are dissensions in Kachin politics and dissatisfaction among Chin army pensioners and others. Amongst the Shans many of the former feudal leaders dislike and suspect the AFPFL Government, and a few even talk about secession when the necessary ten-year period is completed. The Arakanese remain discontented, believing that their area is ignored in the development programmes and that their enterprising, intelligent sons have insufficient scope in the service of the new Burma. But, above all, the Karens remain unhappy and aloof, brooding over past wrongs and fearful of future subservience to the Burmese. The central

[1] This paragraph was written in June 1956.

Government can claim that it has done a great deal to cater for these minority races, but much more than strict justice requires to be. done, if there is to be confidence between the Burmese and the other peoples. Traces of former overlordship and feelings of racial superiority must be completely abolished.[1] In particular, there is room for a more generous policy towards the Karens: the present truncated Karen State of mountain and jungle could be extended so as to form a genuine, viable, regional unit, more suited to the dignity of the second-largest community in the Union. Instead of the village Pa-an, it might be endowed with a suitable headquarters town in Moulmein, and its boundaries enlarged to include most or all of Amherst, Thaton, and Toungoo Districts. It is true that large areas of mixed Karen and Burmese population would be included within such a Karen State, but both the Kachin and Shan States already include within their boundaries substantial percentages of peoples of other races. An expanded Karen State would still leave over half of the Karen community outside its territory in the Delta districts, but such a move would provide unmistakable evidence that the central Government intended to give the Karens their full share in the national life. U Nu has said 'Mistrust begets mistrust . . . trust also begets trust, and confidence begets confidence.' The relations between the Burmese and the other indigenous races will only become completely satisfactory when this excellent maxim is fully put into practice.

The first decade of independence was a severe trial for the new country, but thenceforward a period of relative stability appeared to be dawning. The years 1956–60 seemed to afford a demonstration that all the main elements in the nation— parliament, the political parties, the army, the electorate—had decided to accept and work the democratic system. Two years later, all was changed. Burma swung violently on to a new course. The new régime claimed to be revolutionary, and it certainly made a complete break with the recent past. But no new dynamic was unleashed, and in many respects the military appeared to be withdrawing into the remote past of the old dynasty, when the outside world was ignored.

A balance sheet of the successes and failures of the Nu era would show more on the credit than the debit side: but only

[1] The feeling of many of the hill peoples was expressed in a statement issued by the Council of Nationalities, an organization representing opposition elements from all the hill peoples, following Kyaw Nyein's speech on Dependent Peoples' Freedom Day, 1954. The Council drew attention to Burma's own dependent peoples: 'the states are, in fact, colonies of Burma proper and the "governments" which rule them are only puppet organizations', and much more to this effect (*Nation*, 6 November 1954).

if weight is given to the traditional Burmese values of tolerance, compassion, and meritorious acts, and these are rated higher than concrete achievement. Inheriting the leadership of a country never wholly unified throughout history and recently shattered by war and rebellion, U Nu achieved much in the direction of reconstruction and reconciliation. For ten years he held together a coalition whose members were pulling in different directions, he allayed many of the suspicions of the minority peoples and induced them to co-operate, and he promoted an atmosphere of amity in all Burma's dealings with foreign countries. To a generation of Burmese intellectuals who had accepted without critical inquiry the doctrines of Marx, he presented a philosophy which brought Socialism, Liberalism, and Buddhism into something like a synthesis.

On the debit side, Nu did not comprehend that law and order must be restored in Burma before economic and social policy could be implemented. Having almost achieved the impossible in rescuing the country from fragmentation and collapse in 1948–9, he relaxed too soon the drive for pacification in order to pursue the phantom of 'instant' Utopia. Too readily, he leant a gullible ear to the plausible assurances of his foreign experts. He imagined that Burma could at one stride become a modern industrialized community, without undergoing any of the bitter experiences of the older industrial nations. While on the political plane, which he so profoundly understood, he was able to project an assuring image of democracy, on the economic plane he was out of his depth and only succeeded in showing that a Welfare State was beyond the capacity of the democratic régime. So was the way left open for the military to assert that they could do better.

When he first assumed power in 1958, there is some cause to suppose that Ne Win was a reluctant dictator, ready to return to his real job of running the army. Even in 1962, he may have required some persuasion from his lieutenants—Aung Gyi, Maung Maung, and Tin Pe—before he took the decision to overthrow civil government. Then, the evidence shows that Ne Win increasingly took over the making of the crucial decisions. The options were narrowed down. Early assurances that there would be no wholesale nationalization were followed by the absorption of all economic activity, down to the operations of the stallholders in the market place. At first, the political parties in opposition to U Nu were given some encouragement; especially the 'stable' AFPFL and the near-Communist National United Front. Then, in March 1964, all political parties were dissolved, leaving only the Burma

Socialist Programme Party as a label to identify the Government's supporters.

Gradually, those coadjutors who might incline towards parliamentary democracy were displaced. Brigadier Maung Maung went as ambassador to Israel, and Brigadier Aung Shwe was sent to Canberra. Then in February 1963, Brigadier Aung Gyi, popularly regarded as the *éminence grise* behind the General, was removed and exiled to the far north. The only dominant personality to remain in power was Brigadier Tin Pe, the most committed Marxist among the leadership. He took over responsibility for implementing economic policy from Aung Gyi. Time and again, foreign observers anticipated that Tin Pe's economic miscalculations must bring about his demission: but every new shuffle of the cards of power saw Tin Pe confirmed in the direction of economic policy. A less controversial figure who has also stayed secure in a key position is Colonel Kyaw Soe, Minister for Home Affairs.

General Ne Win is no 'charismatic leader'. He dislikes public appearances, and spends long periods away from Burma, ostensibly for medical purposes. Despite his own enjoyment of the turf and the golf-course, he has prohibited horse-racing and other Western amusements in Burma.

If the element of personal glory or personal popularity has no attraction to Ne Win, why does he retain power? It does appear that he wishes to create a new social order. The anniversary of the coup, 2 March, is celebrated as Peasants' Day, and is the occasion for declarations of policy. Peasants' Day 1966 saw the General issue a promise that what he called 'true democracy' would emerge to transfer power to the people. The Chief Justice, Dr. Maung Maung is supposed to be drafting a constitution to implement this promise; but its form has not been disclosed. There is talk of setting up local peasants' councils—perhaps the counterpart of the Basic Democracies in Pakistan—but no blueprint has appeared.

Burma in 1966 is a hermit land. They have come to terms with Communist China: terms which entail a strict policy of non-alignment and non-involvement. They see with dread what happens to a country like Vietnam which allows the West to take over. They seek to exclude the outside world so that they may find their own destiny. It is a sad sequel to the vision of international co-operation which was glimpsed by U Nu who was at last released from confinement in October 1966, though still under political interdiction. While the storm blows in South-East Asia, Burma closes the door and hopes that one day the sun will shine.

* Denotes persons imprisoned by the military government in 1962.
(All persons are listed under their first personal name, ignoring styles such as 'Bo', 'Thakin', 'Sao', &c.)

AUNG PA, Karen, b. 1919, Henzada District. Educ. Rangoon University, B.A. 1941. Schoolmaster, Joined Karen Youth Organization, 1946: General Secretary, 1948. M.P. 1947. Vice-President, Union Karen League from 1949. Minister for Karen State, 1953–5; Minister of Health, 1955–6.

AUNG SAN, Burmese, b. 1916, Magwe District. Educ. Rangoon University, Secretary, Students' Union, B.A. 1938. General Secretary, *Dobama Asi-ayon*, 1939–40. In Tokyo, 1940–1. Commander, BIA, 1942; Minister for Defence under Ba Maw, 1943–5. President, AFPFL, 1945–7; Deputy Chairman of Governor's Council from October 1946. Negotiated agreement in London with British Government, January 1947. Assassinated, July 1947.

AUNG THAN (1), Burmese, brother of Aung San. Educ. Rangoon University. Entered government service (assistant *myook*). M.P. 1947. Left AFPFL in October 1949. Unsuccessfully contested Lanmadaw constituency, 1951. Head of 'Democratic Rights Protection Committee'. Member of Rangoon Corporation, 1954.

AUNG THAN (2), see SETKYA, Bo.

AUNG ZAN WAI, Arakanese, pre-war M.P. and member of *Sinyetha* Party. M.P. 1947, Minister for Social Service, 1948; Minister for Minorities, 1948–51.

BA CHOE, (*Deedok*, pen-name), Burmese, b. 1893. Deputy inspector of schools, resigned, 1921. Journalist, founder of Fabian League. Member of Goodwill Mission to China, 1939. Member of Privy Council under Japanese; member Governor's Council, 1946–7; assassinated, July 1947.

BA GYAN, Burmese, schoolmaster. President, East Asiatic Youth League, 1942. M.P. 1947; Minister for Judicial Affairs, 1948. Now practising law.

BA KHAING, Karen, b. Henzada District. Organized Karen Youth Organization; M.P. 1947; member Governor's Council; assassinated, July 1947.

BA MAUNG CHAIN, Mrs., Karen, b. 1905, Bassein. Daughter of Sir San C. Po. Educ. Rangoon University. Senior Mistress American Baptist Mission High School, Bassein; wife of head of the Public Works Department; first Minister for Karen State, 1952–3; President of YWCA (Burma); Chairman of United Nations Association (Burma).

BA MAW, Burmese (said to be partly Armenian), b. 1897 in Christian family. Educ. Cambridge and Bordeaux (PH.D.). Schoolmaster and barrister. First prominent as defender of *Galon* rebels; Minister, 1934. Attended coronation of George VI as first Premier of Burma. Formed *Sinyetha* Party; Prime Minister 1936–9. Interned, 1940, for anti-war propaganda. Head of Japanese-sponsored Government (*Ahnashin*) 1942; Head of State (*Adipati*), 1943–5. Interned in Japan, 1946; returned to re-form *Mahabama* Party; interned, 1947.

BA PE, Burmese, b. 1885. Editor of the *Sun*, member of legislature from 1923; three times visited London upon political missions; Minister, 1930–2, 1934–6, 1939–40; Member of Governor's Council, 1946; dismissed upon unproven charge of corruption. Arrested, November 1954, for alleged conspiracy to overthrow the Government in 1949. Released, October 1958.

BA SAING, Mahn, Karen, b. 1906, Henzada. Educ. Rangoon University. Minister for Karen Affairs, 1948–52.

* BA SAW, Arakanese, M.P. 1947. Appointed Deputy Commissioner, Akyab, 1948: removed, 1950. Minister for Minorities, 1952; Minister for Relief and Resettlement, 1952–4; Minister for Social Welfare from 1954. Minister for Religious Affairs, Social Welfare and Mass Education, 1956.

BA SEIN, Thakin, Burmese (also known as 'Gandhi Sein'), b. 1910. Educ. Rangoon University, President of Students' Union, 1930–1; founded *Dobama Asi-ayon*; visited India, 1939, close contact with Hindu Mahasabha. Caught attempting to go to Japan, 1940; interned. Under Japanese appointed Burmese Ambassador to Manchukuo. Interned, released, and appointed to Governor's Council, 1945. Accompanied Aung San on mission to London, 1947; refused to sign agreement. Interned, 1947, founded Burma Democratic Party.

BA SWE, Thakin, Burmese, b. 1915, Tavoy District. Educ. Rangoon University, Secretary of All-Burma Students' Union 1938–9. Chief of Civil Defence in Japanese *Keibotai*, 1942–5. President of Socialist Party, 1945, but gave way to Thakin Mya. Special Commissioner, 1949. M.P. for Taikkyi, 1952; entered Cabinet as Defence Minister; Deputy Prime Minister; President of the TUC(B); President of the Socialist Party. Prime Minister, 1956–7.

BA TIN, Thakin, see GHOSAL, H. N.

BA U, Sir, Burmese, b. 1887, son of U Po Hla, Deputy Commissioner (a close friend of Sir San C. Po). Educ. American Baptist Mission High School, Bassein, Rangoon College, Cambridge University, B.A. 1912. Called to the English Bar, 1913. District and Sessions Judge, 1921; Judge of the High Court, 1930; Judge of the Supreme Court under the Japanese; Chief Justice of the Union, 1948; Chairman of the Regional Autonomy Commission, 1948–9, and of the Parliamentary Elections (Supervision) Commission, 1951. President of the Union, 1952–7. Now known as Dr. Ba U. Author of *My Burma*.

BA U GYI, Saw, Karen, son of a rich landlord. Called to the English Bar; did not practise, lived idle life. Was related by marriage to Sir San C. Po. Associated with Aung San in latter's efforts to work with the Karens, 1944–5. When Sir San C. Po felt unable to continue as Karen leader, and his own sons declined to enter politics, Ba U Gyi succeeded to the leadership on family grounds. Member of Governor's Council, 1946; resigned; formed Karen National Union. Joined revolt in February 1949; killed, Kawkaraik, August 1950.

BA WIN (1), Burmese, b. 1891. Superintendent of Excise, pre-war M.P. and Mayor of Rangoon. Minister for Home Affairs in Ba Maw's Government, 1942–5; now in business.

BA WIN (2), Burmese, brother of Aung San; member of Governor's Council; assassinated, July 1947.

BA ZAN, Mahn, Karen, first commander of KNDO. Said to be member of Kawthulay Government, turned Communist.

CHAN HTOON, Burmese, Constitutional Adviser before independence; Attorney-General, 1948; Judge of the Supreme Court, 1954; Honorary Secretary of Union Buddha Sasana Council.

CHIT HLAING, Burmese, b. 1879; called to the English Bar. President of GCBA; delegate to Round Table Conference 1931; President, Legislative Council, 1932 and Speaker, House of Representatives, 1937; Privy Councillor under Japanese. 1951, formed Union of Burma League; d. 1952.

* CHIT MAUNG, Thakin (1), Burmese, M.P. 1947, ABPO leader, joined BWPP, October 1949.

* CHIT MAUNG, Thakin (2), Burmese, Minister for Housing from November 1954; Minister for Public Works from September 1955, Minister for Information, June 1956; Socialist.

* E MAUNG, Dr., Burmese, b. 1898, Monywa. Educ. Rangoon University and Cambridge University, B.A., LL.B. 1921. Secretary, Buddhist Law Codification Committee, 1924–30; Advocate-General, 1945; Prosecutor for U.K. at International Military Tribunal, Tokyo, 1946; took part in drafting Anglo-Burmese Treaty and the Constitution, 1947; Foreign Minister, 1949; Acting Chief Justice of the Union, December 1949–June 1950; Vice-Chancellor of Rangoon University, 1949–52; supervised reconstruction of Shwemawdaw Pagoda, Pegu. Resigned from Supreme Court and formed Justice Party, 1954.

GHOSHAL, H. N., Indian, born in Bengal but brought up in Burma. Known as Thakin Ba Tin. Member of Communist Party of India. Went underground with Than Tun and remains high in Communist counsels.

* HKUN HKIO, Sao, Shan, b. 1912. Educ. Framlingham College, Suffolk, and Cambridge University, B.A. 1937. Succeeded his father as Sawbwa of Mongmit, 1937; M.P. 1947; succeeded Sawbwa of Mongpawn (his brother-in-law) as Counsellor for the Frontier Areas after the latter's assassination; Minister for the Shan State, 1948; undertook several foreign missions, 1947–9; took over Foreign Affairs portfolio in addition to Shan State, December 1949. Deputy Premier, June 1956.

HLA BU, Burmese, Professor. Educ. British universities; Principal of Judson College, 1937–42; leader of Burma Baptists; member of Peace Protection Committee, 1949.

HLA MAUNG (1), Abdul Hamid, Arakanese, member of I.C.S.; Secretary for Finance and Revenue and (jointly) Secretary for National Planning. Later Secretary to the Economic and Social Board. Ambassador to Yugoslavia, 1955.

HLA MAUNG (2), one of the 'Thirty Comrades', Ambassador in China and in Siam.

HLA MAUNG (3), Thakin, see ZEYA, Bo.

HLA PE (1), Taungthu, b. Thaton, pre-war M.P. and Deputy Speaker. Minister for Forests in the Ba Maw Government, 1943–5. Associate of Aung San till 1947; joined KNU. In revolt in Southern Shan States, leader of Taugthus or Pa-os.

HLA PE (2), see LET YA, Bo.

HLA TUN, Dr., Karen, leader of UKO, Socialist. Minister for the Karen State, 1955.

* HMU AUNG, Bo, Burmese, one of the 'Thirty Comrades'. PVO chief; President of 'Yellow' (pro-Government) PVO; Minister, 1948–February 1949 (resigned); Special Commissioner, 1949. Resigned from AFPFL, July 1950, when PVO disbanded. M.P. 1952, refused Cabinet office; elected Deputy Speaker, House of Representatives. Became Speaker, December 1953, on death of U Mya. Trustee of Shwe Dagon Pagoda.

HTIN AUNG, Dr., Burmese, son of U Pein, Deputy Commissioner and brother of Tin Tut. Educ. Rangoon University and Trinity College, Dublin, PH.D. 1936. Sometime Professor of English, Geography, and Anthropology at Rangoon University. Administrator of the University, 1946–9, Rector, 1949–58. Author of *Burmese Drama* and editor of *Burmese Folk Tales*.

HTOON AUNG GYAW, Sir, Arakanese, b. 1897. Educ. Calcutta and Cambridge Universities. Finance Minister, 1937–40; Adviser to the Burma Government in Exile, 1942–5; Finance Member of Governor's Council, 1945–6.

HUNTER, THAHMWE, Saw, Karen, pre-war Deputy Inspector of Schools; war-time guerrilla fighter, leader of KNU, successor to Ba U Gyi as head of Kawthulay Government. Later known as Saw Hunter Kawkasa ('ruler').

KHIN KYI, Daw, Burmese, daughter of a Christian pastor; nurse. Wife of Aung San, succeeded him as M.P. for Lanmadaw, resigned 1948. Chairman of Social Planning Commission, established in 1953. Chairman of Council of Social Service.

* KHIN MAUNG GALE, Bo. Burmese, b. 1912, Toungoo, son of a government servant. Educ. Rangoon University, B.A. 1937. Schoolmaster, officer in BIA, founder-member of Socialist Party. Member Frontier Areas Inquiry Committee. Minister of Forests and Agriculture, 1950. Minister for Home Affairs, 1952–6. Minister for Finance and Revenue, 1956. Vice-President of ABPO

*KHIN MAUNG LAT, Abdul Latif, Indo-Burmese, Muslim, b. 1913, Myaungmya. Educ. Rangoon University, B.A. 1939, B.L. 1941. Worked in East Asiatic Youth League and Indian Independence League under the Japanese; General Secretary of Burma Muslim Congress on its formation in 1945; M.P. 1947, served on Constitution Committee. 1950, became Minister for Judicial Affairs; also for a time held portfolio for Social Services, later Health (till 1955).

KODAW HMAING, Thakin, Burmese, b. 1876, monk, journalist, author of the *New Glass Palace Chronicle* (1922). Co-founder of *Dobama Asi-ayon*. After 1945 retired from active politics: Burma's G. B. Shaw. President, China-Burma Friendship Society; awarded Stalin Peace Prize, December 1954.

KO KO GYI, Burmese, Socialist, Minister for Commerce and Supply; in 1949 arrest for embezzlement ordered, but absconded. Reported to be with rebel PVOs.

KYAW MIN, Arakanese. Educ. Britain, member of I.C.S., became Financial Commissioner. Resigned, took up business and law. Director of the *Nation*. 1950, contested Akyab seat against AFPFL and secured overwhelming majority. After 1951 election organized Arakanese group, IAPG.

KYAW MYINT (1), Burmese, son of U Pein, Deputy Commissioner and brother of TinTut. Educ. Rangoon College and Cambridge University. Judge, 1947—member of Constitution Committee; Supreme Court Judge.

KYAW MYINT (2), Burmese, educ. Rangoon University, Vice-President of Students' Union. Founder-member of Socialist Party; M.P. 1947; Minister for Industry and Mines, 1948–9 (resigned with Socialists); returned to Cabinet, 1950; Minister for Industry, Mines, Commerce, and Supply. Transferred to Ministry for Democratization of Local Administration. Dismissed, 1953; sent to prison, July 1954. Released, November, returned to Parliament as independent M.P.

*KYAW NYEIN, Burmese, b. 1915, Pyinmana. Educ. Rangoon University, B.A. 1937, B.L. 1941. Member of Supreme Council, Burma Revolutionary Party. Cabinet Secretary, and later Nu's deputy as Vice-Minister of Foreign Affairs in Ba Maw's Government. Succeeded Than Tun as Secretary-General of AFPFL, October 1946. Accompanied Aung San on London mission, January 1947. Minister for Home and Judicial Affairs, February, 1947; Deputy Premier and Foreign Minister, November 1948; resigned from Cabinet, April 1949; returned, 1951, as Minister for Co-operatives. After 1951 election refused Cabinet office to concentrate on work as Secretary-General of AFPFL. Took over from Kyaw Myint as Minister for Industry, 1953. Acting Foreign Minister, 1954. Deputy Premier, June 1956.

* KYAW TUN (or DUN), Thakin, Burmese; from 1952 Minister for Agriculture and Forests; Secretary-General of ABPO.

KYIN, Burmese, member of I.C.S.; Secretary for Finance and Revenue; Ambassador at New Delhi, London, Moscow.

* LAW YONE, Sino-Burman, Catholic. Pre-war assistant *myook*; war-time associate of Aung San; temporary editor of *New Times of Burma*, 1947; founder and editor of the *Nation*.

LET YA, Bo, Burmese, originally Thakin Hla Pe, one of the 'Thirty Comrades'. Battalion commander in BIA; Deputy Prime Minister after Aung San's death; Governor's Counsellor for Defence: negotiated Defence Agreement with U.K. Resigned, 1948. Thereafter in business: entered into 'Joint Venture' with Japanese fishery company.

LUN BAW, Thakin, Burmese, b. 1898. Schoolmaster and lawyer. M.P. 1936; member of *Komin Kochin Ahphwe*; interned, 1941; Minister of Public Works Recovery in Ba Maw's Government, 1943–5; Governor's Counsellor for Foreign Affairs, 1947; Chairman Public Service Commission from 1947.

LWIN, Thakin, Burmese, b. 1915. Educ. Rangoon University. Secretary, Oilfield Workers' Association, 1938–41; interned, 1940. M.P. 1947; President, TUC(B), 1948; Minister for Labour and Public Works, August 1948–January 1949; withdrew from AFPFL, October 1949; formed BWPP and Burma TUC.

* MIN GAUNG, Bo, Burmese, b. 1920. One of the 'Thirty Comrades'. Adjutant and Personal Assistant to Aung San, 1942–5; General Secretary of PVO, 1945; District Superintendent of Police, 1946; M.P. 1947; Minister for Public Works from 1950; later Minister for Highways and Rehabilitation; Minister of Supplies, 1955. Minister for Transport and Communications, 1956.

MIN MAUNG, 'General', Karen, regular army officer. Battalion commander, 1949, mutinied; military head of Kawthulay Government.

MYA, (Henzada), Burmese. Pre-war, wealthy rice- and oil-mill owner. Member of *Myochit* Party; M.P. 1936; Minister of Commerce and Industry under Ba Maw, 1943–5; M.P. 1947; Minister for National Planning, Commerce, and Industry, 1947–8. Leading industrialist and capitalist; Chairman, Burmese Chamber of Commerce.

MYA, (Pyawbwe), Burmese, b. 1896. Journalist, proprietor of *Burmese Review*; Headmaster of National High School, Pyawbwe;. M.P. 1936, *Sinyetha* Party; Minister under the Japanese; Minister of Transport, 1946–8; Speaker of House of Representatives, 1948–53, when d.

MYA, Thakin, Burmese, b. Tharrawaddy. M.P. 1936–40, organized Workers' and Peasants' Party; interned, 1940; executive without portfolio, 1942, under Japanese; Deputy Prime Minister, 1943–5; President Socialist Party and President ABPO; Minister for Home and Judicial Affairs and later Finance and Revenue; assassinated, July 1947.

MYA SEIN, Daw, Burman, daughter of U May Oung, Member of the Executive Council for Home Affairs, 1924–6. Educ. Rangoon and Oxford Universities, B.LITT. Delegate to League of Nations, Geneva, 1931; Member of Burma Delegation to

London Round Table Conference, 1932; member of Rangoon Corporation; member of Goodwill Mission to China, 1939; escaped to China, 1942: Ministry of Information Lecturer, 1942–5. Lecturer at Rangoon University; President of National Council of Women in Burma. Nu Lecturer at American Universities, 1955–6; author of *The Administration of Burma*.

*MYINT THEIN, Justice, Burmese, son of U Pein, Deputy Commissioner and brother of Tin Tut. Educ. Rangoon College and Cambridge University, called to English Bar, 1925; Barrister, Assistant Public Prosecutor, 1930; Sessions Judge, 1945; Constitutional Adviser for Frontier Areas, 1947; member Constitution Committee. Ambassador to Nationalist China, 1948–9, and to Communist China, 1950–1. Judge of Supreme Court, 1952; Chairman of State Reforms Delegation to India, December 1952; Burma's representative at U.N. 1953.

NAW SENG, Kachin, Burma Rifleman and war-time Chindit, post-war Captain and Adjutant of 1 Kachins; February 1949, persuaded his battalion to mutiny, assumed military command of KNDO forces in central Burma as 'Brigadier'. After campaign in Shan States, August–September 1949, driven into China. Now battalion commander in service of China.

NE WIN, Lieut.-General, originally Thakin Shu Maung, Burmese, b. 1910, Prome. Educ. Rangoon University, left without degree, 1930. Employee in Post Office; member of *Dobama*; one of the 'Thirty Comrades', Commander of BNA, 1943–5, Japanese Colonel; Commander of PBF, 1945. Taken into post-war army as Major, 2nd in Command of 4th Burma Rifles, then C.O.; M.P. 1947; Brigadier 1948; succeeded Smith-Dun as Commander-in-Chief, Major-General, February 1949. From April 1949 to August 1950, Minister for Defence and Home Affairs. Prime Minister October 1958–April 1960.

*NU, Thakin, Burmese, b. 1907, Wakema, Myaungmya District. Educ. Rangoon University, B.A. 1929; worked as Superintendent of National High School, Pantanaw, then returned to University to read law. Elected President of Students' Union, 1935; became Treasurer of *Dobama*, 1937; member of Goodwill Mission to China, 1939; interned, 1940. Foreign Minister under Ba Maw, 1943–5; Vice-President of AFPFL, 1945–7; President of Constituent Assembly, 1947; Prime Minister, July 1947. Negotiated Treaty with Britain, October 1947. Dropped title of 'Thakin', 1952. Author of *Burma Under the Japanese*, *The People Win Through*, &c. Took over Religious Affairs and National Planning Ministries in addition to duties as Prime Minister, Relinquished premiership, 1956–7. Resumed office, but resigned, October 1958. Prime Minister, Feb. 1960–Feb. 1962.

OHN, Burmese. Educ. Rangoon University and Britain. Minister for Commerce and Supply, 1948–9; thereafter, Ambassador in London and in Moscow (1951–6).

PAW TUN, Sir, Arakanese, b. 1883. Headmaster, Methodist High School and Government High School, Rangoon, 1904–8; district official, 1912–25; Barrister; M.P. from 1925; Mayor of Rangoon; Minister for Home Affairs, 1937; Prime Minister, January–June 1942; Adviser to Governor of Burma, Simla, 1942–5; Member for Home Affairs of Governor's Council, 1945–6; d. 1955.

PE THA, Saw, Karen. Judicial Minister, 1940–2; murdered by Thakins, Myaungmya, June 1942.

PO KUN, Bo, Burmese. One of the 'Thirty Comrades', leader of PVO after Aung San's death; Minister for Public Works and Rehabilitation, 1947–8. Went underground, July 1948; leader of 'White' (rebel) PVOs.

*RASCHID, M. A., Indian Muslim, b. 1912. Educ. Rangoon University, B.A., B.L.; General Secretary of Students' Union, and first President of All-Burma Students' Union. President of Shop Assistants' Welfare Society; post-war Chairman of Court of Industrial Arbitration; Minister for Housing and Labour, 1952; Minister for Trade Development, 1954; Minister for Mines, 1956; Vice-President of TUC(B).

RIVERS, A., see THAN AUNG.

SAM HTUN, Sao, Shan, Sawbwa of Mongpawn. Leading negotiator at Panglong, February 1947; member, Frontier Areas Inquiry Committee; Governor's Counsellor for the Frontier Areas; assassinated, July 1947.

SAN CROMBIE PO, Sir, Karen. Worked his way through college in United States; medical doctor; member of pre-Reforms Legislative Council; member of Burma delegation to Montagu-Chelmsford Committee; member of Whyte Committee; member of Senate, 1937–42; author of Burma and the Karens; d. 1946.

SAN PO THIN, Saw, Karen. Son of a rich landowner, travelled around United States in a circus with Dr. Po Min and his white elephant. Later worked as a handicrafts teacher, sent to Britain to learn toy-making. Joined Burma Army Service Corps, 1940; from 1944, associate of Aung San. Member, Governor's Council; President of Karen Youth Organization, 1947; Minister for Education, 1947–8; appointed Brigadier and Special Commissioner, Bassein, beginning of 1949; arrested on suspicion of attempting to form a private army in May. Released, he joined Ba Sein's Democratic Party, January 1951. Arrested while electioneering, April 1951. Released, he attempted to join forces with the KNDO, who repulsed all overtures. Now reported to be living near Siam border as KMT agent.

SANKEY, Saw, Karen. Captain with Force 136, member of Frontier Areas Inquiry Committee, leader of KNU. Late 1948 plotted to seize Rangoon, went underground with KNDO.

SAW, U, Burmese, b. 1900, Tharrawaddy. Pleader; M.P. (intermittently)from 1928; took title Galon after defence of the rebels of 1931; visited Japan, May 1935; owner and editor of the Sun;

formed *Myochit* Party and *Galon Tat* (private army) 1938; jailed for sedition by Ba Maw, 1938; Minister, 1939; Prime Minister, 1940–2; visited Britain and United States, end of 1941; made contact with Japanese Ambassador, Lisbon, so interned in Uganda, 1942–5. Re-formed *Myochit*, 1946; wounded by alleged hireling of Aung San; accompanied Aung San to London, January 1947; repudiated agreement. Arrested, July 1947, for murder of Cabinet Ministers; sentenced December; hanged, May 1948.

SEIN DA, Arakanese, monk, Red Flag Communist, leader of revolt in Arakan. Surrendered, January 1958.

SEIN HMAN, Bo, Burmese. One of the 'Thirty Comrades', PVO leader. Minister without portfolio, 1948; Special Commissioner, Insein District, 1949. Went underground.

SETKYA, Bo, Burmese, originally Thakin Aung Than, student leader. One of the 'Thirty Comrades'; Vice Minister for National Defence under Japanese; Secretary to Aung San in London, January 1947; entered business, proprietor of three factories, President of Port Workers' Union, Treasurer of TUC(B); M.P. 1951; Socialist contact-man.

SHEIN HTANG, Chin, b. 1895. Ranger in Forest Service; 1916–19, served with 1/70th Burma Rifles; returned to Forest Service; retired, 1950, as Extra Assistant Conservator. Minister for Chin Affairs, 1952–4; Minister for Relief and Resettlement from 1954.

SHU MAUNG, Thakin, see NE WIN, Bo.

* SHWE THAIK, Sao, Shan, b. 1896, served in Burma Rifles during First World War and till 1923. Became Sawbwa of Yawnghwe in 1929; served again in Burma Army, 1940–2; played prominent part at Panglong Conference, February 1947; became President of the Supreme Council of United Hill Peoples; followed Nu as President of Constituent Assembly. First President of the Union, 1948–52; Speaker of the Chamber of Nationalities from 1952. Died in military custody, November 1962.

SINWA NAWNG, Kachin. Second son of Duwa of Sima, Myitkyina District (but comes from Kamaing, near Jade Mines?). Educ. Buddhist monastery, Mogaung. Worked with Japanese irregular forces during war. Associate of Aung San; member of Frontier Areas Inquiry Committee, and Deputy Counsellor for Frontier Areas, 1947; Minister for Kachin State, 1948–53; formed People's Economic and Cultural Development Organization. 1955, returned to Cabinet as Minister for National Solidarity. Ambassador to China, 1964.

SOE, Thakin, Burmese, employee of Burmah Oil Company, Communist Thakin, interned 1940. Organized guerrillas, Pyapon District, 1943–5; denounced Than Tun and led Red Flag Communists into rebellion, March 1946. Still underground.

THA DIN, Saw, Karen, member of Karen Goodwill Mission to Britain, 1946. Leader of KNU, interned in 1949; released and disappeared.

THA GYAW, 'Bonbauk' (Bombthrower), Arakanese, Red Flag Communist leader.

THA KIN, Thakin, Burmese. Representative of Burma in Indonesia, 1948; Minister of Commerce and Co-operation, 1952-4; rejoined Cabinet, October 1955.

THAN AUNG (A. Rivers), Anglo-Burman, Catholic, b. 1902, Myaungmya, son of Police Inspector. Master at St. Paul's High School, Pleader. M.P. 1947. Minister for Relief and Resettlement, April 1950; Minister for Education, September 1950. President Anglo-Burmese Association.

THAN TUN, Thakin, Burmese, b. 1915, Pyinmana, village schoolmaster. *Dobama* delegate to 1940 session of Indian National Congress. Executive, and later Minister for Agriculture under Japanese, 1942-5; General Secretary of AFPFL, 1945-6; Leader of White Flag Communists; commenced rebellion, 1948.

THANT, Burmese, a colleague of U Nu when both were teachers at Pantanaw National High School; Secretary for Information, 1948-54; Burma's representative at U.N., 1952; Secretary to the Prime Minister, 1954; Secretary to the Economic and Social Board, 1955. *Eminence grise.*

THEIN MAUNG, Justice, Burmese, b. 1890, son of a *myothugyi* (hereditary circle headman). B.A. Calcutta, 1910; B.A. and LL.B. Cambridge, 1912. Visited London, 1919-20 and 1933-4 for constitutional talks; member of Rangoon Corporation, 1922: Mayor, 1931; Minister for Education, 1936; Advocate-General, 1938-41; Minister of Justice under Japanese, 1943-5; Chief Judge of the High Court, 1948-52; Chief Justice of the Union, 1952. Trustee of the Shwe Dagon Pagoda; Vice-Chairman of Union Buddha Sasana Council.

THEIN PE, Thakin, Burmese. Educ. Rangoon University, student leader. Walked out to India in disgust with Japanese, 1942; employed on radio propaganda, 1942-5; maintained contacts with Thakins; joined Communist group in AFPFL, 1945; Cabinet Minister for fortnight, 1946; thereafter journalist and 'leftist' politician. Member of Rangoon University Council. Author of *What Happened in Burma, Tet-pongyi*, &c.

* TIN, Burmese, b. 1897, Henzada District. On staff of *New Light of Burma*, 1920-47, becoming manager and proprietor; Privy Councillor under Japanese; Honorary Treasurer of AFPFL from 1945; Minister for Finance and Revenue, 1948-56.

* TIN, Thakin, Burmese, b. 1903, Pyawbwe, son of Deputy Superintendent of Police. Third-grade Pleader, member of *Dobama* and People's Revolutionary Party; President of ABPO, 1941; officer in BIA, 1942; Political Secretary to Ba Maw Government; President of ABPO from 1946; Minister for Agriculture, 1947-9 (resigned with Socialists); Minister for Land Nationalization, from 1952; took on additional portfolio of Democratization of Local Administration, 1953. Deputy Premier, June 1956.

TIN TUT, Burmese, son of U Pein, Deputy Commissioner. Educ. Dulwich College and Cambridge University. Entered I.C.S.

(said to be senior Burmese member); Vice-Chancellor of Rangoon University, 1940; Adviser for Reconstruction to Burma Government in Exile, 1942–5; resigned from I.C.S., 1946; became Member for Finance and Revenue in Governor's Council. Minister for Foreign Affairs, 1948; August, resigned from Cabinet to become Inspector General of Auxiliary Forces (Brigadier); on leaving office of *New Times of Burma* (which he owned and edited), assassinated, December 1948.

TUN BYU, Justice, Burmese, b. 1895. Educ. Cambridge University, B.A. 1916; called to English Bar. Government Law Officer from 1926; Advocate-General under Japanese, 1942–5; Advocate-General, 1947–8; High Court Judge, then (1950) Chief Justice of High Court.

TUN OK, Thakin, Burmese, b. 1906. Educ. Rangoon and Colombo. Member of *Dobama* Party, went to Japan, 1940; trained as administrator and installed as Chief Administrator of Rangoon, 1942; Executive for Forests, 1942–3. As associate of Ba Sein, fell from favour, Ambassador to China. Minister for National Planning, 1946; thereafter, in opposition.

*TUN PE, b. 1900, Meiktila District. Editor of *Bama Khit*, when Japanese official paper. Post-war editor of *Hanthawaddy*. Minister for Information, 1948–52; Minister for Union Culture, 1952–3; resigned, expelled from AFPFL; founded and edited *Htoon Daily*; author of *Sun Over Burma*.

TUN SHEIN, *see* YAN NAING, Bo.

TUN WIN, Sino-Burman, b. 1917, Tavoy. Educ. Rangoon University, Treasurer of Students' Union, Schoolmaster. Officer in BIA; M.P. 1947; editor of *Mandaing* (AFPFL paper), 1951–2; Minister of Information, 1952–6. Minister for Commodities, Distribution and Co-operatives, 1956.

U THWIN, Sir, Burmese, wealthy rice-mill owner and landlord. Trustee of Shwe Dagon Pagoda; President of Privy Council under Japanese; Chairman of Peace Mission, 1948–9.

VAMTHU MAUNG, Chin, b. 1900, Kanpetlet. Served in 1/70th Burma Rifles, 1917–25, reaching rank of Subadar; Headmaster of National School; Minister for Chin Affairs, 1948–52.

VUM KO HAU, Chin, served as officer in Chin Levies. Leader of Chins at Panglong Conference; Deputy Counsellor for Frontier Areas, 1947. Left politics to become Deputy Secretary at Foreign Office. Minister to France and Netherlands, 1955.

*WIN, Indo-Burmese, b. 1905, Insein District. Educ. Rangoon University. Schoolmaster from 1930. Welfare officer during Japanese period; President TUC(B), 1946; member of Governor's Council, 1946 (Industry and Labour); High Commissioner, later Ambassador for Burma at New Delhi; Minister for Education, 1948–9 (resigned with Socialists); Minister for Defence, Home and Religious Affairs, 1950; Minister for Religious Affairs and National Planning, 1952; additional portfolio of Union Culture, 1953; appointed Ambassador at Washington, November 1955.

*WIN MAUNG, Mahn, Karen, b. 1916, Bassein District. Educ. Rangoon University. Clerk in Burmah Oil Company and government office. Enlisted in army, 1940, commissioned 1942. Made way to India, 1944; trained by Force 136 and parachuted into Toungoo area March 1945. Joined AFPFL, became Vice-President of Karen Youth Organization, and then President of the UKL, 1949; Minister for Industry and Labour, July 1947; Minister for Transport and Communications, 1948–56. President of the Union, 1957.

WUNNAH, Sao, Karen (Shan mother), b. Loikaw, son of Sawbwa of Kantarawaddy. Fought with Karen guerrillas under Force 136, 1945; Minister for Karenni State from 1948.

YAN NAING, Bo, Burmese, formerly known as Thanmani Tun Shein, b. 1918. Educ. Rangoon University, Secretary of Students' Union. Attended 1940 session of Indian National Congress; one of the 'Thirty Comrades'; battalion commander in BIA, then Chief of Operations Department, A.D.C. to Ba Maw, whose daughter he married. Interned, 1948–50; Chairman of opposition Municipal Affairs Council, 1955. After 1962 coup, escaped to Thailand to organize resistance.

ZA HRE LIAN, Chin, Christian, b. 1923. Educ. Mandalay College. Enlisted in Burma Rifles, commissioned, served 1942–5; appointed to Burma Civil Service, Deputy Commissioner, Kanpetlet; M.P. for Falam, 1951; unanimously elected by Chin M.P.s as Minister, but vetoed by U Nu. Appointed Minister for Chin Affairs, October 1954.

ZAU LAWN, Duwa, Kachin, Christian, b. 1910, Bhamo District, where his family are hereditary leaders. Headmaster of American Baptist Mission School, Bhamo, for nine years. Organized and led units of the Kachin Levies, 1942–5; member of Supreme Council of United Hill Peoples, 1947; M.P. 1947; organized Kachin National Congress; 1951, KNC gained largest number of seats in Kachin State; Minister for Kachin State, 1953–6.

ZAU RIP, Duwa, Kachin, supporter of Sinwa Nawng. M.P. from 1947; Finance Minister in Kachin State, 1952–3.

ZEYA, Bo, Burmese, formerly Thakin Hla Maung. Educ. Rangoon University, President of Students' Union, 1940–1. Shot in leg in Mandalay riots, 1939; one of the 'Thirty Comrades', Chief of General Staff of BIA; joined AFPFL, 1945, supporter of Than Tun. O.C. 3rd Burma Rifles in post-war regular army; induced his battalion to mutiny, 1948, joined Than Tun, made 'Commander in Chief' of Communist forces; mission to China, 1953–5.

NOTE ON PRINTED SOURCES

THE following book-list is not presented as a full-scale bibliography but is designed to indicate the chief sources on contemporary events available in print to the Western reader. This study of Burma is concerned, largely, with the processes of change and development taking place during the early years of independence, but there remains a broad area of social life and custom, of economic activity, and even of administrative practice which, despite recent upheavals, continues to be much the same as it was twenty, fifty, or even a hundred years ago. For an introduction to Burmese ways of life and thought, the reader will do best to turn to the classic studies of Burma written during the last hundred years. Full bibliographies will be found in J. L. Christian's *Modern Burma* and D. G. E. Hall's *History of South-East Asia* (London, 1955), but for convenience a brief selection of those works most frequently consulted in the preparation of this book are included under the heading 'Background and General'.

Among works dealing with Burma since independence, by far the largest number are publications of the Burma Government, many of which, naturally, present the government point of view. There are a number of economic surveys, containing statistical and other material in detail; but as most of these surveys employ different bases and methods of classification, their comparative value is limited. These classes of material are given under the heading 'Official Publications since Independence'.

I. BACKGROUND AND GENERAL

Andrus, J. R. *Burmese Economic Life*. Stanford University, 1947.

Anstey, Vera. *The Economic Development of India*. London, 1929.

Christian, J. L. *Modern Burma*. Berkeley, Univ. of California, 1942.

—— *Burma and the Japanese Invader*. Bombay, 1945. (A reprint of *Modern Burma*, with additional chapters.)

—— *Burma*. London and Bombay, 1945.

Crosthwaite, Sir C. *The Pacification of Burma*. London, 1912.

Donnison, F. S. V. *Public Administration in Burma*. London, 1953.

Furnivall, J. S. *An Introduction to the Political Economy of Burma*. Rangoon, 1931.

—— *Colonial Policy and Practice*. London, 1948.

Hall, D. G. E. *Burma*. 2nd ed. London, 1956.

Harvey, G. E. *History of Burma*. London, 1925.

Hla Pe. *Konmara Pya Ƶat*. Vol. i. London, 1952. (The Introduction provides an account of Burmese literature in the nineteenth century.)

Htin Aung. *Burmese Drama*. London, 1937.

Knappen-Tippetts-Abbett Engineering Company, in association with Pierce Management Inc. and Robert R. Nathan Associates, Inc. *Comprehensive Report on Economic and Engineering Survey of Burma for*

Ministry of National Planning. Rangoon, 1953 (mimeo). Vol. i: *Introduction, Economics, Agriculture, Irrigation.* Vol. ii: *Transport and Communications.* Vol. iii: *Minerals.*

Morrison, Ian. *Grandfather Longlegs; the Life and Gallant Death of Major H. P. Seagrim.* London, 1947.

Mountbatten, Admiral Lord L. *Report to the Combined Chiefs of Staff by the Supreme Allied Commander, South-East Asia, 1943–45.* London, 1951.

Mya Sein. *The Administration of Burma.* Rangoon, 1938.

Nisbet, John. *Burma Under British Rule—and Before.* 2 vols. London, 1901.

Nu, Thakin. *Burma Under the Japanese.* London, 1954.

Parker, E. H. *Burma, with Special Reference to her Relations with China.* Rangoon, 1893.

San C. Po, Sir. *Burma and the Karens.* London, 1928.

Tinker, Hugh. *The Foundations of Local Self-Government in India, Pakistan and Burma.* London, 1954.

Tun Wai. *Burma's Currency and Credit.* Calcutta, 1953.

Yule, Sir Henry. *A Narrative of the Mission . . . to the Court of Ava in 1855.* London, 1858.

II. OFFICIAL PUBLICATIONS BEFORE INDEPENDENCE

Binns, B. O. *Agricultural Economy in Burma.* Simla, 1943.

Burma: Statement of Policy by His Majesty's Government, May 1945. Cmd. 6635.

Burma During the Japanese Occupation. 2 vols. Simla, 1943–4.

Burma Handbook. Simla, 1944.

The Constitution of the Union of Burma. Rangoon, 1947.

Frontier Areas Committee of Enquiry, 1947. *Report Presented to H.M. Government in the United Kingdom and the Government of Burma.* Rangoon, 1947.

Memoranda Submitted to the [Indian] Statutory Commission. Rangoon, 1930.

III. OFFICIAL PUBLICATIONS SINCE INDEPENDENCE[1]

MINISTRY OF INFORMATION

Burma's Fight for Freedom. 1948.

Burma's Freedom, the First Anniversary. 1949.

Burma's Freedom, the Second Anniversary. 1950.

In October 1950 the Information Department began publication of a quarterly review, *Burma.* Every year the January issue (beginning with *Burma, the Third Anniversary,* Jan. 1951) contains accounts of government activities during the previous year, corresponding somewhat to the pre-war *Administration Reports.*

Burma and the Insurrections. 1949.

The Pyidawtha Conference, 1952; Resolutions and Speeches. 1952.

[1] All published in Rangoon.

The Burmese Revolution, text of speech by U Ba Swe. 1952.

Collected Speeches by U Nu:
  Towards Peace and Democracy. 1949.
  From Peace to Stability. 1951.
  Towards a Welfare State. 1952.
  Forward with the People. 1955.
  Resurgence: Premier U Nu at Bandung. 1955.
Burma Weekly Bulletin (from April 1952).

MINISTRY OF EDUCATION

Education in Burma; Before Independence and After Independence. 1953.
The Education Plan for the Welfare State and the Teacher. 1954.
Report on Public Instruction in Burma for the Year 1946–47. 1954.

MINISTRY OF NATIONAL PLANNING

Economic Survey of Burma, 1951. 1951. (Thereafter published annually.)
The National Income of Burma. 1951. (Thereafter published annually.)
Our Goal and Our Interim Programme. 1953.
The New Burma; a Report from the Government to the People of Burma.
  Mimeo. 1954.
*Pyidawtha, the New Burma; a Report from the Government to the People
  of Burma.* 1954. (An amended and expanded version of the
  mimeographed publication.)

MINISTRY OF HOME AFFAIRS

Final Report of the Administration Reorganisation Committee. Rangoon,
  1951.
Report of a Survey of Public Administration in Burma. 1954. (Confidential.)

MINISTRY OF AGRICULTURE AND FORESTS

The Land Nationalization Act, 1948. 1948. (Contains introductory
  speeches of U Nu and Thakin Tin.)

MINISTRY OF LAND NATIONALIZATION

The Seventh Annual Conference of the All-Burma Peasants' Organization.
  1954. (Speech by Thakin Tin introducing revised land nationalization programme.)

UNION BANK OF BURMA

Quarterly Bulletin and *Monthly Review.*

CENTRAL STATISTICAL AND ECONOMICS DEPT.

Quarterly Bulletin of Statistics.

IV. PUBLICATIONS OF INTERNATIONAL
ORGANIZATIONS

International Bank for Reconstruction and Development, Dept. for
  Operations in Asia and Middle East. *The Economy of Burma.* 1953
  (mimeo.).
United Nations Technical Assistance Agency. *Report of the United
  Nations on Public Administration in Burma,* by F. J. Tickner. 1954
  (mimeo.).

INDEX

Note: All Asians are indexed under their first names except those generally known by surnames, as Nehru, Pandit Jawaharlal.

Reprinted lithographically by Jarrold and Sons Ltd, Norwich